CITIZEN MARX

Citizen Marx

REPUBLICANISM AND THE FORMATION OF KARL MARX'S SOCIAL AND POLITICAL THOUGHT

BRUNO LEIPOLD

PRINCETON UNIVERSITY PRESS
PRINCETON & OXFORD

Published by Princeton University Press
41 William Street, Princeton, New Jersey 08540
99 Banbury Road, Oxford OX2 6JX

press.princeton.edu

All Rights Reserved

Library of Congress Cataloging-in-Publication Data

Names: Leipold, Bruno, author.
Title: Citizen Marx : Republicanism and the formation of Karl Marx's
   social and political thought / Bruno Leipold.
Description: Princeton : Princeton University Press, [2024] | Includes
   bibliographical references and index.
Identifiers: LCCN 2024005090 (print) | LCCN 2024005091 (ebook) |
   ISBN 9780691205236 (hardback) | ISBN 9780691261867 (ebook)
Subjects: LCSH: Marx, Karl, 1818–1883. | Republicanism. | Communism. |
   Philosophy, Marxist. | BISAC: POLITICAL SCIENCE / History & Theory |
   SOCIAL SCIENCE / Sociology / Social Theory
Classification: LCC HX39.5 .L43 2024 (print) | LCC HX39.5 (ebook) |
   DDC 335.4—dc23/eng/20240607
LC record available at https://lccn.loc.gov/2024005090
LC ebook record available at https://lccn.loc.gov/2024005091

British Library Cataloging-in-Publication Data is available

Editorial: Matt Rohal and Alena Chekanov
Production Editorial: Natalie Baan
Jacket Design: Karl Spurzem
Production: Erin Suydam
Publicity: William Pagdatoon
Copyeditor: Anne Cherry

Jacket image: *Huldigung der Freiheit. Zur Erinnerung an die Reichstagswahl 1893*,
Walter Heubach. Originally published in the magazine *Der Wahre Jacob*, Nr. 183,
29.7.1893.

This book has been composed in Arno

Printed in the United States of America

10 9 8 7 6 5 4 3

For my grandparents,
&
Brigitte Leipold, *Tante und Genossin.*

CONTENTS

ILLUSTRATIONS

FOR NON-ENGLISH PRIMARY sources I have tried to cite both the original and an English translation. As I have made my own translations, they do not necessarily correspond to the cited English text. I have kept original spelling in citations and titles of works. For Marx and Engels's works, I cite both the *Marx Engels Gesamtausgabe* (*MEGA*) and the *Marx Engels Collected Works* (*MECW*). For the diminishing number of texts not yet published in the *MEGA*, I revert to the older standard German edition, the *Marx Engels Werke* (*MEW*). I have separated references to the original text (e.g., *MEGA* or *MEW*) and the translation (e.g., *MECW*) by a forward slash. Parts of the *MEGA* are freely available at https://megadigital.bbaw.de; the entire *MECW* can be accessed at https://lwbooks.co.uk/marx-engels-collected-works/read-and-search-online, and digital copies of the *MEW* can be freely borrowed from archive.org.

For volume 1 of Marx's *Das Kapital* (*Capital*), I cite the final German version Marx brought to publication, the 1872–73 second edition (*MEGA* II.6), noting when it differs significantly from the 1867 first German edition (*MEGA* II.5), the 1872–75 French translation supervised by Marx (*MEGA* II.7) or the 1883 third (*MEGA* II.8) and 1890 fourth (*MEGA* II.10) German editions produced by Engels. For the text once known as Marx and Engels's *Die deutsche Ideologie* (*The German Ideology*), I cite the individual manuscripts from which that work was editorially constructed. This reflects the recent consensus (embodied in the *MEGA* I.5 edition) that these unpublished 1845–47 writings were intended as articles for a quarterly journal project rather than a single coherent book.

I have tried to keep as much reference information in the footnotes as possible, so that readers are not forced to flip back and forth between the text and a bibliography. For a few frequently cited texts, I use the following abbreviations:

BdK. Bund der Kommunisten: Dokumente und Materialien. 3 volumes. Berlin: Dietz Verlag, 1970–84.

Briefwechsel und Tagebuchblätter. Arnold Ruge, *Briefwechsel und Tagebuchblätter aus den Jahren 1825–1880.* Edited by Paul Nerrlich. 2 volumes. Berlin: Weidmannsche Buchhandlung, 1886.

English Republic. The English Republic. Edited by William James Linton, 4 volumes. London: J. Watson, volumes 1–2, 1851–53, and Brantwood: Linton, volumes 3–4, 1854–55.

MECW. References are to Karl Marx and Friedrich Engels, *Collected Works*, 50 volumes. London: Lawrence and Wishart; Moscow: Progress Publishers; New York: International Publishers, 1975–2005.

MEGA. References are to (section and volu me of) Karl Marx and Friedrich Engels, *Gesamtausgabe*. 70 volumes completed to date. Berlin: Dietz Verlag, 1975–98; Akademie Verlag, 1998–. The *MEGA* is divided into Section I: Works, Articles and Drafts; Section II: *Capital* and Preliminary Works; Section III: Letters to and from Marx and Engels; and Section IV: Excerpts, Notes and Marginalia.

MEGA digital. References are to the relevant entry in the megadigital.bbaw.de database. The outstanding volumes from Section III (letters from January 1866 onward) and Section IV are (sadly) published solely in this online database rather than as printed volumes.

MEGA$^\circ$. References are to (section and volume of) Karl Marx and Friedrich Engels, *Historische-kritische Gesamtausgabe: Werke, Schriften, Briefe*. 12 volumes (of projected 42) completed. Frankfurt am Main: Marx-Engels Archiv, 1927; Berlin: Marx-Engels-Verlag, 1929–32; Moscow: Marx-Engels-Verlag, 1935.

MEW. References are to Karl Marx and Friedrich Engels, *Werke*, 39 volumes plus "Ergänzungsbände." Berlin: Dietz Verlag, 1957–.

Philosophie des Rechts. References are to G. W. F. Hegel, *Grundlinien der Philosophie des Rechts*, edited by Eva Moldenhauer and Karl Markus Michel, Frankfurt am Main: Suhrkamp, 1970; and *Elements of the Philosophy of Right*, edited and introduced by Allen W. Wood, translated by H. B. Nisbet, Cambridge: Cambridge University Press, 1991. References are to sections (§); an "A" indicates Hegel's "Remarks (*Anmerkungen*)" and a "Z" indicates editorial "Additions (*Zusätzen*)."

Redaktionsbriefwechsel. References are to *Der Redaktionsbriefwechsel der Hallischen, Deutschen und Deutsch-Französischen Jahrbücher (1837–1844)*. Edited by Martin Hundt. 2 volumes. Berlin: Akademie Verlag, 2010.

Werke und Briefe. References are to Arnold Ruge, *Werke und Briefe*. Edited by Hans-Martin Sass. 12 of 13 volumes published. Amsterdam and Aalen: Scientia Verlag, 1988–.

Material has been reproduced with permission from the following publications:

Bruno Leipold, "Marx's Social Republic: Radical Republicanism and the Political Institutions of Socialism," in *Radical Republicanism: Recovering the Tradition's Popular Heritage*, eds. Bruno Leipold, Karma Nabulsi, and Stuart White (Oxford: Oxford University Press, 2020), 172–193.

Bruno Leipold, "Chains and Invisible Threads: Liberty and Domination in Marx's Account of Wage-Slavery," in *Rethinking Liberty before Liberalism*, ed. Hannah Dawson and Annelien de Dijn (Cambridge: Cambridge University Press, 2022), 194–214.

I HAVE BEEN THINKING and writing about Marx and republicanism for a long time—much longer than I ever anticipated I would. Again and again, I thought I was finished, only to find another letter, a further Marx critique, yet more republican contemporaries, that had to be included. Republicanism, as I learned and hope to convince the reader, touched upon and influenced so many aspects of Marx that it was difficult to know when or where to end. As deadlines sailed by, I was kept going by the conviction that trying to come to grips with Marx and republicanism said something important about his thought and political life: that republican freedom suffused Marx's critique of the social domination of capitalism and that he believed that this domination could only be overcome through democratic republican political institutions. Rarely is it adequately appreciated that by making the latter integral to the goal of collective ownership, Marx distinguished his republican communism from the antipolitical socialism and anticommunist republicanism of his day. By placing Marx's thought in the context of these competitors, I hope this book provides a clearer sense of his commitment to politics, democracy, and freedom. Those commitments are unsurprisingly denied in the many caricatures of Marx's ideas but are also frequently obscured by commentators on Marx who should know better. Though this is a historical study, I have been drawn to Marx and republicanism because I believe that his republican commitments are still central to the political and social struggles of our day.

It is hard to know when a book is ready and, contrary to Mark Twain, had I taken more time I would probably have simply written a longer one. But I believe it is comprehensive enough that I am now happy, and more than a little relieved, to lay it before the reader. Bringing it to completion gives me an opportunity to thank the very many people who helped me along the way. I want to begin by expressing my deep gratitude to David Leopold. When as a student I first opened his book on the young Marx, I had only intended to check a few pages, but I soon realized that it would be impossible not to read it all. It opened my eyes to the possibility that through careful analytic and contextual study, Marx's sometimes opaque writings could be clarified and understood as political interventions in the debates of his times. One of the foremost academic privileges that I have enjoyed was being subsequently supervised by David for the doctoral thesis that eventually became this book. Since then, whenever I have been too quick to assume influence or have overstated some claim, I am fondly reminded of him peering over his glasses and suggesting that it might be a bit more complicated than that. While I have an increasingly forlorn hope that our colleagues and students might one day be able tell our names apart, their confusion always leaves me feeling a little flattered.

This project has had to pass through many academic hoops and I'm grateful to those who've helped the book make it to publication. Two reviewers, who subsequently identified themselves as William Clare Roberts and Terrell Carver, provided incredibly generous comments on the manuscript. Their insightful reading helped sharpen the book's contribution, and I felt very privileged to be supported by scholars whose political and contextual approach to Marx I so admire. Lea Ypi and Jonathan Wolff provided similar support at an earlier stage in the project, and their advice was instrumental in the transition from thesis to book. John Filling supervised the very earliest incarnation of this project; his powerful lectures first spurred my interest in Marx, and he deserves the credit (or blame!) for starting me on the path that led to this book. Matt Rohal has been a model editor, deftly shepherding the book from proposal to proofs, while providing unfailingly helpful advice from the smallest publication questions to the bigger picture of the book's central arguments. I am furthermore very grateful to the excellent team at Princeton University Press, Natalie Baan, Elizabeth Blazejewski, Alena Chekanov, Anne Cherry, Susan Clark, Jess Massabrook, Terri O'Prey, William Pagdatoon, Karl Spurzem, Steve Stillman, and Erin Suydam, for their hard work in bringing the book to publication.

Academic work would be a very lonely world without the friendship and advice of the colleagues and comrades who populate it. Pascale Siegrist is owed special thanks for patiently (or mostly patiently) allowing me to repeatedly interrupt her work in our various shared offices over the years and answering what must amount to several thousand historical questions. With her encyclopaedic knowledge and linguistic gifts, she has generously helped a self-taught historian become a little less amateurish. Mirjam Müller has been an endless source of support and guidance ever since we started on our academic careers. Her socialist-feminist criticisms reminded me when to discuss Marx's own emancipatory limitations. Jan Kandiyali read most of the book and provided annoyingly insightful comments, forcing several rewrites; I am very grateful to him for this and for our conversations at LSE and beyond. Stuart White and Karma Nabulsi, my fellow radical republicans, showed me that republicanism was not just a theory but a political movement of republicans who lived and died for their ideals. Anne Phillips was an outstanding mentor at LSE and went above and beyond to offer counsel and support. Samuel

Hayat helped organize a short but productive stay at Sciences Po, Paris. James Muldoon has never stopped encouraging me to think and write (faster!) about republican socialism. Udit Bhatia has been a continual guide on democracy and democratic theory. Max Krahé offered much-appreciated insight on questions of capitalism and political economy. Without Avram (Avi) Alpert's sage advice to write a good enough, not perfect, book, I might never have been able to send off the manuscript.

Several institutions have assisted me with research materials, including the Bibliothèque nationale de France, the Boston Public Library, the British Library, the Geheimes Staatsarchiv Preußischer Kulturbesitz, the Internationaal Instituut voor Sociale Geschiedenis, the Universitätsbibliothek Basel, the Russian State Archive of Socio-Political History, and the Beinecke Library at Yale University; I am especially grateful to Julie Herrada for her help with a visit to the Karl Heinzen Papers at the University of Michigan Library. A fellowship at The New Institute provided an ideal institutional home to complete the book, and I am very thankful to its wonderful fellows and staff: Christiane Müller and Britta Neumann helped track down several obscure sources; Tom Bodensteiner, Ina Krug, and Jannic Welte created an incomparably congenial environment. I have been awed by the generosity of scholars willing to answer questions about their specialties, and I am indebted in this regard to Frederick C. Beiser, Elias Buchetmann, Patrick Carey, Jürgen Herres, Stephen Houlgate, Philip Schofield, and Diana Siclovan. I would also like to express a special thanks to the LSE students who attended my course on *The Idea of Freedom* and whose probing questions helped me to think more carefully about the nature of freedom.

The friendship, at times virtual and socially distanced, of Yas Alttahir, Johannes Gerling, Leona Leipold, Marion Lieutaud, James Muldoon, and Mirjam Müller carried me through lockdowns and the more joyful times since. My sister Lele, Zelda co-adventurer, has been an irreplaceable source of love and support and has done her best to keep me alive both in and outside of Hyrule. Similarly, friends in and beyond political theory have ensured that my various academic stops from Frankfurt to Florence, London to Hamburg, have felt like home; my heartfelt thanks to Signy Gutnick Allen, Paul Apostolidis, David Axelsen, Anthea Behm, Gabrielle Bieser, Christine Braun, Julia Costet, Puneet Dhaliwal, Richard James Elliott, Akwugo Emejulu, Roop Gill, Alice Gustson, Ariane Haase, Frederic Hanusch, Vincent Harting, Ronan Kaczynski, Hwa Young Kim, Jens van 't Kloster, Johannes Kniess, Shiru Lim, Xufan (Nadia) Ma, Sabrina Martin, Tobias Müller, Marius Ostrowski, Liban Parker, Tom Parr, Tomás Quesada-Alpízar, Minna Salami, Kai Spiekermann, Tania Shew, Andreas Sorger, Lukas Slothuus, Rahel Süß, Stephanie Wanga, Felix Westerén, and Tim Wihl. My siblings, Tara, Maya, Nikhil, Brendan and Sean Jackson; and my parents, Steve Jackson, Rosalind Reeve and Gerd Leipold, have provided the unconditional love that has sustained me when I needed it most. Additional thanks to my father for his help deciphering some of the more difficult nineteenth-century German handwriting. Marion Lieutaud first won my heart with her Marx comics and kept it with her fierce loyalty, intellect, and courage. She has had a first-row seat for all the tribulations of writing and her belief that I could, would, and should finish gave me the strength to do so. Her conviction that academic work should have an emancipatory purpose beyond the comforting confines of the university continues to inspire me.

In the first draft of these acknowledgments, I had dedicated the book solely to my German and Irish and English grandparents, Emma and Leo Leipold and Rosemary and Gordon Bull. They played an outsized role in our upbringing and created for us two homes away from home. Their untiring willingness to listen to my precocious enthusiasms might have prepared me badly for academic peer review, but without it I might never have developed the confidence to do any of this. I miss them hugely.

While reviewing the final edits to the manuscript my aunt Brigitte Leipold passed away. She showed me that socialism was not only an ideal to work and fight for, but a way to live one's life and treat one another. She brought joy to every room she entered, effortlessly reciting everything from Brecht to Bombadil and the Bandiera Rossa. She experienced firsthand a system that had betrayed most of its socialist ideals yet managed to never lose hope *dass der Mensch eines Tages fliegen wird.*

CITIZEN MARX

Introduction

Cit[izen] Engels said . . . Before our ideas could be carried into practice, we must have the Republic . . . the republic gave a fair field for the working classes to agitate.

Cit[izen] Marx was convinced that no Republican movement could become serious without becoming social. The wire pullers of the present move[ment] of course intended no such thing.

—*MINUTES OF THE GENERAL COUNCIL OF
THE INTERNATIONAL WORKING-MEN'S ASSOCIATION (IWMA)*[1]

IN NOVEMBER 1850 the Chartist newspaper *The Red Republican* published the first English translation of the *Manifest der Kommunistischen Partei* under the modified title "German Communism: Manifesto of the German Communist Party." Using the standard form of address among nineteenth-century radicals, the editor named "Citizens *Charles Marx* and *Frederic Engels*" for the first time as the authors of the revolutionary document that had appeared on the eve of the revolutions that swept across Europe two years earlier.[2] The translation was carried out by Helen Macfarlane, a Scottish feminist and socialist republican, who had authored several of her own articles in *The Red Republican* under the male pseudonym Howard Morton and was acquainted with Marx and Engels through the radical exile community in London. Her translation was subsequently supplanted in English-language discussions by the

---

1. "Meeting of the General Council March 28, 1871," *MEGA* I.22: 526 / *MECW* 22: 587.

2. "German Communism: Manifesto of the German Communist Party," *The Red Republican*, no. 21 (9 November 1850): 161. "Citizen" originated in the French Revolution as an egalitarian replacement for aristocratic titles. It was only toward the end of the century that it was superseded by "Comrade"; see Jonathan Sperber, *Karl Marx: A Nineteenth-Century Life* (New York: Liveright Publishing, 2013), 535.

now-standard 1888 edition carried out by Samuel Moore and supervised by Engels. Yet Macfarlane's translation retains much of value for modern readers, not least because of her attempt to render a new social and political vocabulary into English. "Proletarians" was used interchangeably with "wage-slaves," the "lumpenproletariat" became the "Mob," and the "petty bourgeoisie" was referred to by the appealing coinage "shopocrats." The achievements of the Macfarlane translation have, however, been unfortunately overshadowed by its peculiar rendition of the manifesto's striking opening line, "Ein Gespenst geht um in Europa—das Gespenst des Kommunismus." While the 1888 translation rendered it "A spectre is haunting Europe—the spectre of Communism," Macfarlane's version read, "A frightful hobgoblin stalks throughout Europe. We are haunted by a ghost, the ghost of Communism."

Marx and Engels's choice of *The Red Republican* for the translation of their manifesto was a natural one, not only because of their deep respect for the Chartist movement but because the paper embodied an emerging fusion of socialist criticism with the political demands of republicanism. As Helen Macfarlane and editor George Julian Harney made clear in the paper's opening pages, social and political reform were inextricable. Macfarlane defended what she called "the new—and yet old—religion of Socialist-democracy," which insisted "that political reform must *precede* all attempts to improve the condition of the people," and she chided the antipolitical socialist movements of British Owenists and French Saint-Simonians whose abstention from politics meant that "they have never yet been able to put their Social Theories *into practice*."[3] Harney, for his part, argued that democratic political institutions would always be under threat from the "aggressions of the propertied classes . . . who will conspire to subvert popular Suffrage, the moment an attempt may be made to make the ballot-box an instrument for the protection of the poor." Thus "representative institutions, universal sufferage [*sic*], freedom of the press, trial by jury . . . are all utterly valueless, unless associated with such social changes" that would enable the "actual sovereignty of society." Harney consequently concluded that "Political freedom is incompatible with social slavery."[4]

3. Howard Morton [Helen Macfarlane], "Chartism in 1850," *The Red Republican*, no. 1 (22 June 1850): 2–3. On Macfarlane, see David Black, *Helen Macfarlane: A Feminist, Revolutionary Journalist, and Philosopher in Mid-Nineteenth Century England* (Lanham: Lexington Books, 2004); David Leopold, "Macfarlane, Helen," in *Oxford Dictionary of National Biography*, online ed. (Oxford University Press, 2018), https://doi.org/10.1093/odnb/9780198614128.013.100743.

4. L'Ami du Peuple [George Julian Harney], "The Charter and Something More!," *The Red Republican*, no. 1 (22 June 1850): 1–2. On Harney, see Albert Schoyen, *The Chartist Challenge: A Portrait of George Julian Harney* (London: Heinemann, 1958).

The title of the *Red Republican* encapsulated this bold new fused social and political program. Harney mused that adding "this new-fangled 'Red'" to the already dangerous "Republican," would mean that a jury, "on being informed of the title of your publication, would at once convict you" and "[e]ven the Liberals would say 'hanging is too good for such a fellow.'"[5] The title did indeed prove too bold. Booksellers refused to stock the paper, and Harney was worried enough about official prosecution that he eventually changed the name to the less directly confrontational *Friend of the People* (inspired by Jean-Paul Marat's French revolutionary paper, *L'ami du peuple*). When the final issue of *The Red Republican* appeared on 30 November 1850, its closing article happened to be the final section of the "Manifesto of the German Communist Party," so that the paper's last words read, "Let the Proletarians of all countries unite!" (a slightly less captivating, but more accurate, version than the better-known translation: "WORKING MEN OF ALL COUNTRIES, UNITE!").[6] But this was not the only appeal to the working class made in the final issue of the *Red Republican*. Serialized alongside the "Manifesto" was a set of articles, entitled "Republican Principles," which just a few pages before Marx and Engels's more famous appeal had concluded with the call "WORKING-MEN! I appeal to you . . . [to] join me to begin the foundation of our English Republic!"[7]

The author of "Republican Principles" was William James Linton, a Chartist and artisan engraver, who had become known in London's radical circles through his friendship and political association with Giuseppe Mazzini, at the time Europe's most prominent republican. It was Linton who designed and engraved the dramatic masthead of *The Red Republican*, which depicted the republican symbols of the liberty cap, the spear, and the fasces, sitting on top of the revolutionary motto "EQUALITY, LIBERTY, FRATERNITY" (see figure 1). Linton's intellectual contribution to *The Red Republican* was intended as an extended explication of the principles articulated in the manifesto of the European Central Democratic Committee, an organization set up by Mazzini to coordinate the activities of the European republicans exiled in London after the failed revolutions.[8] In the introduction to "Republican Principles," Linton

---

5. [George Julian Harney], "Our Name and Principles," *The Red Republican*, no. 1 (22 June 1850): 4.

6. Marx and Engels, "Manifesto of the German Communist Party," *The Red Republican*, no. 24 (30 November 1850): 190. The original German reads, "*Proletarier aller Länder, vereinigt euch!*"

7. W. J. Linton, "Republican Principles," *The Red Republican*, no. 24 (30 November 1850): 187.

8. "Aux Peuples! Organisation de le démocratie," *Le Proscrit: Journal de la république universelle*, no. 2 (August 1850): 3-13 / "To the Peoples, Organization of Democracy," *The Red*

EQUALITY, LIBERTY, FRATERNITY.

EDITED BY G. JULIAN HARNEY.

No. 21.—Vol. I.]   SATURDAY, NOVEMBER 9, 1850.   [Price One Penny.

German Communism.

MANIFESTO OF THE GERMAN COMMUNIST PARTY.

(Published in February, 1848.)

The following Manifesto, which has since been adopted by all fractions of German Communists, was drawn up in the German language, in January 1848, by Citizens *Charles Marx* and *Frederic Engels*. It was immediately printed in London, in the German language, and published a few days before the outbreak of the Revolution of February. The turmoil consequent upon that great event made it impossible to carry out, at that time, the intention of translating it into all the languages of civilized Europe. There exist two different French versions of it in manuscript, but under the present oppressive laws of France, the publication of either of them has been found impracticable. The English reader will be enabled, by the following excellent translation of this important document, to judge of the plans and principles of the most advanced party of the German Revolutionists.

It must not be forgotten, that the whole of this Manifesto was written and printed before the Revolution of February.

A frightful hobgoblin stalks throughout Europe. We are haunted by a ghost, the ghost of Communism. All the Powers of the Past have joined in a holy crusade to lay this ghost to rest,—the Pope and the Czar, Metternich and Guizot, French Radicals and German police agents. Where is the opposition which has not been accused of Communism by its enemies in Power? And where the opposition that has not hurled this blighting accusation at the heads of the more advanced oppositionists, as well as at those of its official enemies?

Two things appear on considering these facts. I. The ruling Powers of Europe acknowledge Communism to be also a Power. II. It is time for the Communists to lay before the world an account of their aims and tendencies, and to oppose these silly fables about the bugbear of Communism, by a manifesto of the Communist Party.

CHAPTER I.

BOURGEOIS AND PROLETARIANS.

Hitherto the history of Society has been the history of the battles between the classes composing it. Freemen and Slaves, Patricians and Plebeians, Nobles and Serfs, Members of Guilds and journeymen,—in a word, the oppressors and the oppressed, have always stood in direct opposition to each other. The battle between them has sometimes been open, sometimes concealed, but always continuous. A never-ceasing battle, which has invariably ended, either in a revolutionary alteration of the social system, or in the common destruction of the hostile classes.

In the earlier historical epochs we find almost everywhere a minute division of Society into classes or ranks, a variety of grades in social position. In ancient Rome we find Patricians, Knights, Plebeians, Slaves; in mediæval Europe, Feudal Lords, Vassals, Burghers, Journeymen, Serfs; and in each of these classes there were again grades and distinctions. Modern Bourgeois Society, proceeded from the ruins of the feudal system, but the Bourgeois régime has not abolished the antagonism of classes.

New classes, new conditions of oppression, new forms and modes of carrying on the struggle, have been substituted for the old ones. The characteristic of our Epoch, the Era of the Middle-class, is that the struggle between the various Social Classes, has been reduced to its simplest form. Society incessantly tends to be divided into two great camps, into two great hostile armies, the Bourgeoisie and the Proletariat.

The burgesses of the early Communes sprang from the Serfs of the Middle Ages, and from this Municipal class were developed the primitive elements of the modern Bourgeoisie. The discovery of the New World, the circumnavigation of Africa, gave the Middleclass—then coming into being—new fields of action. The colonization of America, the opening up of the East Indian and Chinese Markets, the Colonial Trade, the increase of commodities generally and of the means of exchange, gave an impetus, hitherto unknown, to Commerce, Shipping, and Manufactures; and aided the rapid evolution of the revolutionary element in the old decaying, feudal form of Society. The old feudal way of managing the industrial interest by means of guilds and monopolies was not found sufficient for the increased demand caused by the opening up of these new markets. It was replaced by the manufacturing system. Guilds vanished before the industrial Middle-class, and the division of labour between the different corporations was succeeded by the division of labour between the workmen of one and the same great workshop.

But the demand always increased, new markets came into play. The manufacturing system, in its turn, was found to be inadequate. At this point industrial Production was revolutionised by machinery and steam. The modern industrial system was developed in all its gigantic proportions; instead of the industrial Middle-class we find industrial millionaires, chiefs of whole industrial armies, the modern Bourgeois, or Middle-class Capitalists. The discovery of America was the first step towards the formation of a colossal market, embracing the whole world; whereby an immense developement was given to Commerce, and to the means of communication by sea and land. This again reacted upon the industrial system, and the developement of the Bourgeoisie, the increase of their Capital, the superseding of all classes handed down to modern times from the Middle Ages, kept pace with the developement of Production, Trade, and Steam communication.

We find, therefore, that the modern Bourgeoisie are themselves the result of a long process of developement, of a series of revolutions in the modes of Production and Exchange. Each of the degrees of industrial evolution, passed through by the modern Middle-class, was accompanied by a corresponding

addressed himself to "the countrymen of Milton and Cromwell" and declared that through his articles he hoped to "establish the basis of a really republican party, by rendering republican principles plain and easy of comprehension." Marx and Engels had similarly opened their "Manifesto" with the declaration that "It is time for the Communists to lay before the world an account of their aims and tendencies, and to oppose these silly fables about the bugbear of Communism, by a manifesto of the Communist Party."[9]

Linton's "Republican Principles" and Marx and Engels's "Manifesto of the German Communist Party" thus provided a literally side-by-side attempt to set out the principles of republicanism and communism. Reading their two manifestos together showcases several key differences between the two traditions. Linton opened with an explication of the meaning of the trinity of "Equality—Liberty—Humanity" (a term he thought was more inclusive than "Fraternity") that formed the "battle-cry of the Republican"; Marx and Engels's began with a portrayal of the rise of the bourgeoisie and their unrelenting "need of an ever-increasing market for their produce, [which] drives the Bourgeoisie over the whole globe."[10] Where "Republican Principles" condemned any political system in which "a caste rules . . . [with] tyrants on one side, and slaves upon the other," the "Manifesto of the German Communist Party" railed against the "modern slavery of Labour under Capital" in which proletarians were subject to a "despotism" where they were "not only the slaves of the whole middle-class (as a body) . . . they are daily and hourly slaves . . . of each individual manufacturing Bourgeois."[11] While Linton argued that emancipation would only be achieved through "the regular association of all classes, the organized association of the people," Marx and Engels identified the new class of proletarians as "the only truly revolutionary Class amongst the present enemies of the Bourgeoisie."[12] Finally, where "Republican Principles" defended a system of "free Nations" united in a "universal FEDERATION OF REPUBLICS," the "Manifesto of the German Communist Party" declared that "[t]he Proletarian has no Fatherland" and predicted the "obliteration" of "National divisions and antagonisms."[13]

Yet these seemingly stark differences can distract us from some of the manifestos' commonalities. As much as Marx and Engels were focused on the social

Republican, no. 12 (7 September 1850): 94–95. For the ECDC, see Christine Lattek, *Revolutionary Refugees: German Socialism in Britain, 1840–1860* (London: Routledge, 2006), 88–94.

9. Linton, "Republican Principles," 110; Marx and Engels, "Manifesto," 161.

10. Linton, "Republican Principles," 110–11; Marx and Engels, "Manifesto," 162.

11. Linton, "Republican Principles," 172; Marx and Engels, "Manifesto," 171.

12. Linton, "Republican Principles," 125; Marx and Engels, "Manifesto," 171.

13. Linton, "Republican Principles," 187; Marx and Engels, "Manifesto," 182.

dependency of workers, they also believed that workers were "the slaves . . . of the Bourgeois political regime" and defended a strategy where "the first step in the proletarian revolution, will be the conquest of Democracy," criticizing forms of socialism that "oppose all political movements in the Proletariat." Linton, for his part, did not restrict himself to political criticism, but also condemned the domination of the "wages slave" and the "factory slave," and insisted that it was the "business of Government" to end their dependency.[14] Their respective social programs were also not as far apart as we might assume. Linton defended three core social policies in "Republican Principles": free access to the land through nationalization, free state education, and the provision of free credit. The "Manifesto of the German Communist Party" included a ten-point list of demands that similarly called for the "[t]he national appropriation of the land," "[c]entralisation of credit in the hands of the State," and "[t]he public and gratuitous education of all children."[15]

Where these social programs did come apart was the defining issue of private property. Linton opposed the communist demand for the abolition of private property, as "we do not believe that 'the institution' of private property is inevitably a nuisance. Our complaint is . . . not that the few have, but the many have not." Marx and Engels, on the other hand, insisted that it was not simply a question of abolishing private property as such but specifically the *"abolition of Bourgeois property,"* private property based on the exploitation of wage-labor, and in this specified sense they were unapologetic that "the Communists might resume their whole Theory in that single expression—*The abolition of private property.*"[16] Linton and his fellow republicans believed that people had a right to the private property they had worked to create, but also that it was the state's duty to be "the Nation's Banker, to furnish each individual with the material means—the capital—for work." Providing free credit and free land would mean that workers could acquire the means to work independently and break free from the "mischievous middle-men called capitalists." For Marx and Engels, such schemes were a desperate attempt to save "the property of the small shopkeeper, small tradesman, [and] small peasant" which the "progress of industrial development is daily destroying." They insisted that trying to restore an economy of independent artisans and peasants was hopeless in the face of the productive and competitive advantages of large-scale capitalist industry. Such attempts were "even reactionary, for they attempt to turn backwards the chariot wheels of History." Rather than try to restore individual

14. Linton, "Republican Principles," 156; Marx and Engels, "Manifesto," 171, 183, 190.
15. Linton, "Republican Principles," 156, 164; Marx and Engels, "Manifesto," 183.
16. Linton, "Republican Principles," 147; Marx and Engels, "Manifesto," 181.

property, communism would build on the achievements of capitalism and its "mass of productive power" by collectivizing the "instruments of production in the hands of the State."[17] They believed that only collective ownership of the means of production (which Marx would later think could be carried out through worker cooperatives rather than simply state ownership)[18] could adequately address the social dependency of the proletariat and destroy the power of capital. Republicanism and Marx and Engels's communism were thus divided as to whether the private property of small-scale independent producers should be universalized, or capitalist private property abolished and replaced by common ownership.

Over the course of the nineteenth century, these competing social and political visions repeatedly came into conflict, but also opened opportunities for mutual engagement, political alliances, and intellectual fusion. The publication of the "Manifesto of the German Communist Party" and "Republican Principles" in *The Red Republican* was just one example of the broader struggle of republicans and communists to define the goals of the radical movement and secure the support of the working class. As we will see, it was also just one of many instances of how republicanism was central to the formation of Marx's social and political thought.

Marx and Republicanism

In 1913, Lenin provided one of the most enduring portraits of Marx's intellectual formation, depicting him as having inherited and synthetized three national traditions: "German philosophy, English political economy and French socialism."[19] This triadic account is memorable but problematic. As David

17. Linton, "Republican Principles," 156; Marx and Engels, "Manifesto," 171, 182–83. Of course, Marx and Engels were not directly responding to Linton's articles (which postdate their original publication). But, as is shown in chapters 4 and 5, these arguments were directed at republican interlocutors like Karl Heinzen.

18. Marx, "Address of the International Working Men's Association (Inaugural Address)," *MEGA* I.20: 10 / *MECW* 20: 11; *Das Kapital*, vol. 1, *MEGA* II.6: 328n / *MECW* 35: 336n; *Das Kapital*, vol. 3, *MEGA* II.15: 431 / *MECW* 37: 438.

19. Vladimir Lenin, "The Three Sources and Three Component Parts of Marxism," in *Lenin Collected Works*, vol. 19 (Moscow: Progress Publishers, 1963), 23–24. For a defense, see G. A. Cohen, "The Three Sources and Component Parts of Marxism," in *Marxism, Mysticism and Modern Theory*, ed. Suke Wolton (London: Macmillan, 1996), 1–6. Such triadic accounts have their origin in Moses Hess's *Die europäische Triarchie* (Leipzig: Otto Wigand, 1841). For Marx and Engels's use of this triadic image (though with French socialism interestingly replaced by French "politics," which better captures socialism's republican heritage), see Engels, "Progress of Social

Leopold argues, apart from demoting the influence of Belgium, where Marx spent an oft-forgotten exile from 1845–48, it simplifies the contribution of any of these countries to a single discipline, suggesting, for instance, that the English (more accurately British, and particularly Scottish) influence on Marx only extended to political economy rather than, say, Britain's own tradition of socialism.[20] From the perspective of this book, the triadic account also falls short because if we want to understand the influences on Marx's thought we have to understand the formative role played by European republicanism.[21]

The complex influence of republicanism on Marx's thought, however, resists easy reduction to wholesale adoption or rejection (encapsulated by the contrasting points raised by Citizen Engels and Citizen Marx about republicanism in the meeting of the IWMA cited in this chapter's epigraph). Influence should be understood as not only the causal tracing of an affinity, when Marx's ideas can be shown to have been inherited from republicanism, but also negative influence, when Marx formed his ideas in opposition to republicanism.[22] Marx both incorporated republican commitments into his communism to critique antipolitical socialisms and positioned this republican communism to supplant anticommunist republicanism. Republicanism thus formed a body of ideas and political movement out of which and against which Marx shaped and defined his own communism.

Complicating the picture further is that Marx's relationship to republicanism changed over the course of his life. The overarching argument of this book, and what gives it its organizing structure, is that his relationship proceeds in three principal periods.[23] To give an initial snapshot: first, Marx began his political career in 1842 as a republican committed to overcoming the arbitrary power of despotic regimes through a democratic republic in which the people held active popular sovereignty through public administration by citizens and

---

Reform on the Continent," *MEGA* I.3: 495 / *MECW* 3: 392–93; Marx, "Kritische Randglossen zu dem Artikel: "Der König von Preußen und die Socialreform: Von einem Preußen," *MEGA* I.2: 459 / *MECW* 3: 202; Marx, *Entwurf über Friedrich List, MEGA* I.4: 579 / *MECW* 4: 281.

20. David Leopold, "Karl Marx and 'English Socialism,'" *Nineteenth-Century Prose* 49, no. 1 (2022): 6–7, 20–21.

21. That is not to say that republicanism is only a European phenomenon (as is often suggested in orientalist and Western-centric accounts of the tradition), only that it is the form of republicanism that most influenced Marx.

22. For this general distinction (and for the idea of affinity without causally traceable influence), see Leopold, "Karl Marx and 'English Socialism,'" 11–12.

23. These correspond to the three parts of the book, whose titles are loosely based on Marx's classification of republics into "democratic," "bourgeois," and "social" in *Der achtzehnte Brumaire, MEGA* I.11: 103–4, 174–75 / *MECW* 11: 109–10, 181–82.

the control of representatives through binding mandates, a position from which, over the course of 1843–44, he progressively transitioned to communism (chapters 1–3). Second, from this new communist standpoint, in the years leading up to the 1848 Revolutions and its aftermath, Marx both criticized republicanism and also incorporated the republican opposition to arbitrary power into his social critique of capitalism and the commitment to a democratic republic into his politics, though his more radical ideas of a polity with far-reaching political participation receded into the background (chapters 4–6). Third, spurred by the Paris Commune of 1871, those ideas eventually reemerged later in Marx's life, when he came to see extensive popular control and participation in legislation and public administration as essential to the realization of communism (chapter 7). Marx thus came to a fuller synthesis of his early republicanism and his later communism.

Chapter 1 opens with an account of Marx's early republican journalism. In Marx's first definitive statement of his politics, in early 1842, he criticized not just Prussia's absolute monarchy but the liberal goal of a reformed constitutional monarchy, while expressing his frustration at the difficulty of realizing a modern "Res publica" in Germany.[24] Strict official censorship meant that in his public journalism Marx avoided frontal attacks on the Prussian regime and instead concentrated on particular instances of its arbitrary power. He criticized Prussia's feudal estate assemblies for their exclusion of the people and consequent failure to represent the common good and attacked press censorship for making journalists and editors dependent on the character of individual censors. Underlying these criticisms lay a commitment to a republican conception of freedom as the absence of arbitrary power, where freedom is secured by laws made collectively by the citizenry. Marx argued that there was a fundamental opposition between "arbitrariness and freedom," so that a citizen was only free when ruled by law, warning that "I do not at all believe that persons can be a guarantee against laws; on the contrary, I believe that laws must be a guarantee against persons."[25] But Marx also insisted that freedom required not only the rule of law, but for that law to be collectively made by the people, so that "law is the conscious expression of the popular will, in that it originates with it and is created by it."[26] Censorship made it difficult to elaborate that democratic, and dangerous, idea in anything more than isolated glimpses, with Marx only hinting at the necessity of "transforming the

---

24. Marx to Arnold Ruge, 5 March 1842, *MEGA* III.1: 22 / *MECW* 1: 382–83.

25. Marx, "Debatten über Preßfreiheit," *MEGA* I.1: 153 / *MECW* 1: 165; "Debatten über das Holzdiebstahlgesetz," *MEGA* I.1: 217 / *MECW* 1: 243.

26. Marx, "Der Ehescheidungsgesetzenentwurf," *MEGA* I.1: 289 / *MECW* 1: 309.

mysterious, priestly nature of the state into a clear-cut entity of the ordinary people, accessible to all and belonging to all, making the state the flesh and blood of its citizens."[27]

When Prussia banned his newspaper, Marx was freed to turn to a foundational critique of Hegel's defense of constitutional monarchy, as is recounted in chapter 2. In his critique, Marx defended popular sovereignty against Hegel's embrace of monarchical sovereignty, attacked the central role Hegel had attributed to the elite bureaucracy at the expense of popular participation in politics and administration, and criticized Hegel's views on representation and instead defended popular delegacy. Marx condemned Hegel's supposedly constitutional monarch for being "the *hallowed, sanctified embodiment* of arbitrariness" and whose monopolization of sovereignty meant that "all others are excluded from this sovereignty, from personality and from political consciousness."[28] Hegel's bureaucracy, that was supposed to be a neutral arbiter of the general interest, in fact "protect[ed] the *imaginary* generality of [its] ... particular interest," was insulated from effective "guarantee[s] against the arbitrariness of the bureaucracy," and excluded the people from public administration which should in fact "belong ... to the whole people."[29] Against Hegel's defense of a legislature elected on a narrow franchise and without binding mandates, Marx argued for "the *extension* and greatest possible *generalization* of *election*, both of *active* and *passive* suffrage" and insisted that without binding instructions the "deputies of civil society form a society which is not linked with those who commission them."[30] In place of Hegel's constitutional monarchy, Marx defended a "true democracy" in which "the constitution is ... the self-determination of the people ... the people's *own* work ... [and] the free product of man."[31] Alongside this democratic vision, Marx expressed his republican skepticism of the emerging theories of socialism and communism. He attacked "actually existing communism" for its single-minded pursuit of the "[a]bolition of private property" and failure to see the necessity of "partisan participation in politics." "The critic," Marx insisted, "not only can but must engage in these political questions (which according to the views of the cross socialists are beneath their dignity)."[32]

27. Marx, "Replik auf den Angriff eines 'gemäßigten' Blattes," *MEGA* I.1: 333 / *MECW* 1: 318.

28. Marx, *Zur Kritik der Hegelschen Rechtsphilosophie*, *MEGA* I.2: 27, 38 / *MECW* 3: 26, 36.

29. Ibid., 50, 56, 58 / 46, 53–54.

30. Ibid., 130, 133 / 120, 123.

31. Ibid., 31–32 / 29–30.

32. Marx to Arnold Ruge, September 1843, "Ein Briefwechsel von 1843," *MEGA* I.2: 487–88 / *MECW* 3: 143–44.

Nevertheless, within a few short months of writing these lines Marx had overcome his opposition to the abolition of private property and made his own transition to communism, which forms the subject of chapter 3. While that transition involved a political distancing from republicanism it was not a transition to "actually existing communism," but the fashioning of a new form of communism that integrated much of his prior republicanism. His shift from republicanism was driven by a growing disillusionment with the ability of political emancipation, through a democratic republic, to establish truly human emancipation, and by a realization that the proletariat, through its dispossession from property, was uniquely positioned to do so. The former was driven by an assessment that the American and French Revolutions had created republics in which the (laudable) establishment of freedom in the political sphere had been paired with a transference of unfreedom into the social sphere. Marx consequently concluded "that the state can be a *free state* without man being a *free man.*"[33] That critiqued and amended an old republican argument that it is "only possible to be free in a free state."[34] Freedom, Marx insisted, required not just a free state but a *free society*. But as much as Marx may have sometimes wished to condemn republicanism as such with this argument, it was only an indictment of a kind of bourgeois (or liberal) republicanism that had little popular appeal. The republicanism that galvanized broad working-class support across the nineteenth century recognized the social dimensions of freedom long before Marx. Of almost greater consequence for Marx's transition away from republicanism was in fact his identification with the proletarian working class as the agent of future social and political revolution, rather than with the independent artisan worker idealized by republicans.

As is argued in chapter 4, Marx's criticism of the emancipatory limits of the republic eventually hardened into an assessment that the modern republic, as was briefly established in France after the 1848 Revolution, was in fact a "*bourgeois republic* . . . the state whose admitted object it is to perpetuate the rule of capital, the slavery of labor."[35] Marx condemned the bourgeois republic as a regime in which the bourgeoisie held political power, the economy was structured in its class interests, and even its constitution was designed to uphold this political and economic rule. But this criticism did not lead Marx to dismiss the republic as an unworthy political goal. He insisted that the bourgeois republic was "the terrain for the fight for its [the proletariat's] revolutionary

33. Marx, "Zur Judenfrage," *MEGA* I.2: 147 / *MECW* 3: 152.

34. Quentin Skinner, *Liberty before Liberalism* (Cambridge: Cambridge University Press, 1998), 60.

35. Marx, *Die Klassenkämpfe in Frankreich*, *MEGA* I.10: 139 / *MECW* 10: 69.

emancipation," even though it was "by no means this emancipation itself."[36] That position is easily taken for granted but represented a break with the sharply antithetical attitudes to politics and democratic republican institutions that dominated early socialism (chapter 4 consequently devotes extensive space to these antipolitical socialists and Marx and Engels's response to them). While Charles Fourier and Robert Owen hoped to bypass politics through the peaceful spread of communitarian experiments supported by the benevolence of the rich and powerful, Henri Saint-Simon dreamed up technocratic schemes in which popular rule was supplanted by an administration of industrialists and scientific and technical experts. Those attitudes continued to inform the next generation of socialists and communists, who advocated for workers to abstain from politics and focus on raising consciousness through peaceful propaganda and education. In a common complaint, these socialists asked, "Will the republic pay our debts? Will it redeem our pawned goods? Will it clothe and feed us?," and as supposedly "no political institutions are capable of abolishing" these social problems, they urged workers to "not at any time take part in *political revolutions*."[37] They confidently insisted that " 'today's republicans' and their 'notions of "electoral reform", "democracy", "revolution", "Cahiers" are outdated and discounted.' "[38]

When Marx (and especially Engels) initially and independently converted to communism, they briefly shared some sympathy for these antipolitical ideas.[39] But, in part through their growing collaboration, they soon embraced the label of "Democratic Communists," in which the "democratic reconstruction of the Constitution" was taken to be an essential element whereby the working class would be able to come to political power and be in a position to bring about communism.[40] That in essence would remain their central political commitment throughout their lives. Marx and Engels were convinced that civic freedoms and universal (manhood) suffrage were essential tools to expand working-class power and challenge capitalist rule. Marx was confident that "universal suffrage" put the working class and its allies in "possession of the political power" and

36. Ibid., 125 / 54.

37. Herman Semmig, *Sächsische Zustände: Nebst Randglossen und Leuchtkugeln* (Hamburg: C. F. Vogel, 1846), 9, 63.

38. Karl Grün, "Politik und Sozialismus," *Rheinische Jahrbücher für gesellschaftlichen Reform*, vol. 1, ed. Hermann Püttmann (Darmstadt: C. W. Leske, 1845), 136. *Cahiers* were the documents of complaints and instructions carried by representatives to the 1789 Estates General.

39. This moment is documented in chapter 3. In Marx's case it is brief and textually thin, making it difficult to come to very clear or firm conclusions about his political (or antipolitical) views at the time, especially if we compare it with the more fulsome embrace by Engels (whose independent relationship to republicanism deserves its own study).

40. Marx and Engels, "Address of the German Democratic Communists of Brussels to Mr. Feargus O'Connor," *MEW* 4: 24-26 / *MECW* 6: 58–60.

"forces the political rule of the bourgeoisie into democratic conditions, which at every moment help the hostile classes to victory and jeopardize the very foundations of bourgeois society."[41] This position led to a lifelong opposition to forms of socialism that denied the necessity of democratic institutions and political struggle. In the *Manifest der Kommunistischen Partei* they repeatedly condemned antipolitical forms of socialism, which Marx and Engels attacked for opposing republican movements campaigning for political reform and for playing into the hands of reactionary forces by "hurling the traditional anathemas . . . against representative government" (a charge that, as we will see, had in fact already been made by republicans against socialism and which Marx and Engels adopted and redirected).[42] In the IWMA, Marx and Engels continued to associate themselves with the idea that "The social emancipation of the workmen is inseparable from their political emancipation."[43] As Marx put it in a retrospective detailing the history of antipolitics in socialism, one of the most persistent errors that had dogged socialists was "preaching indifference in matters of politics."[44] Marx thus incorporated into his communism the same insistence on the need for politics that the early republican Marx had once criticized "actually existing communism" for ignoring. The communism that he and Engels forged and defended in the years before and after the 1848 Revolutions was consequently in an important sense a "republican communism."[45]

While Marx and Engels thus incorporated republican political commitments into their communism, their communism was still distinguished from republicanism by their differing social visions and account of the appropriate response to capitalism, as is charted in chapter 5.[46] At the time in which Marx

41. Marx, *Die Klassenkämpfe in Frankreich*, MEGA I.10: 148 / MECW 10: 79. Here as elsewhere Marx (like most of his contemporaries) refers to manhood suffrage as universal suffrage. In order to capture both their language and its exclusions, I refer to universal (manhood) suffrage throughout the book.

42. Marx and Engels, *Manifest der Kommunistischen Partei*, MEW 4: 487, 490, 492 / MECW 6: 511, 515, 517.

43. Marx and Engels, "Resolutions of the Conference of Delegates of the International Working Men's Association, assembled at London from 17th to 23rd September 1871," MEGA I.22: 342 / MECW 22: 426.

44. Marx, "L'indifferenza in materia politica," MEGA I.24: 109 / MECW 23: 397. A neglected essay (published in 1873 in the Italian journal *Almanacco Repubblicano*) that deserves wider notice.

45. Engels cites the use of this label in "Das Fest der Nationen in London (Zur Feier der Errichtung der französischen Republik, 22. Sept. 1792)," MEGA I.4: 705 / MECW 6: 13.

46. Marx rarely used the term "capitalism" (though not never, as it has sometimes been claimed). I use it in this book as a shorthand for Marx's more common terminology, including "capitalist mode of production" and "capitalist society."

and Engels formulated their communism, capitalist social relations were far from dominant, with proletarians—whose dispossession from the means of production meant having to work for wages for a capitalist employer—still a minority of the European working classes. Outside of Britain and a few strips of large-scale steam-powered industrial development on the continent, the overwhelming majority of workers were still artisans who were highly skilled, owned their own tools, and labored by themselves or in small workshops.[47] While Marx and Engels seized on the proletarian pockets as the harbingers of the future, republicans celebrated artisans' independence and freedom and tried to stem the growing proletarianization of the working class (and the decline of the even larger population of free peasant proprietors). Republicans consequently argued for an expansive set of social measures, from free credit to land reform, that they believed would reaffirm that independence. They thereby developed a distinct nonsocialist alternative to the unfreedom of capitalism. Marx and Engels's response to this republican social alternative focused not on its relative moral strengths, but on its historical and economic possibilities. While they agreed with parts of the republican social program, they rejected the idea that it was possible to universalize independence through an economy of small property holders, arguing that it was being steadily and irreversibly destroyed by the advance of capitalist industry. In Marx's initial responses to republicanism, he repeatedly dismissed the republican social ideal as a petty bourgeois fantasy. In his mature writings he provided a more sympathetic portrait of the lost independence of artisans and peasants, even as he continued to insist that the competitive pressures of capitalist industry made that world irretrievable.

Though Marx thus rejected the republican social ideal, his own social writings made extensive use of republican ideas to attack the unfreedom and domination of capitalism, as is discussed at the end of chapter 3 on his early economic writings and in chapter 6, which focuses on his later writings, especially *Das Kapital*. The same arguments he had raised as a young republican against the arbitrary power of monarchs and Prussian officials were brought to bear on the despots inside the factory. Being forced to work for a capitalist employer made workers "unfree" since they labored "in the service, under the domination, the coercion, and the yoke of another man."[48] The capitalist

---

47. Jonathan Sperber, *The European Revolutions, 1848–1851*, 2nd ed. (Cambridge: Cambridge University Press, 2005), 12–20; William H. Sewell Jr., "Artisans, Factory Workers, and the Formation of the French Working Class, 1789–1848," in *Working-Class Formation: Nineteenth-Century Patterns in Western Europe and the United States*, ed. Ira Katznelson and Aristide R. Zolberg (Princeton: Princeton University Press, 1986), 45–70.

48. Marx, *Ökonomisch-philosophische Manuskripte*, MEGA I.2: 372 / MECW 3: 278–79.

despot faced few if any checks or controls on their arbitrary power in the work-place, and so "capital formulates its autocracy over its workers, like a private legislator and as an emanation of its own will."[49] Marx insisted that the proletar-ian's wage-slavery (as he and all his radical contemporaries called it) did not end with their personal domination by their individual capitalist employer. While they enjoyed the formal freedom to sell their labor power, their dispossession from the means of production meant that though they did not have to work for any particular capitalist, they did have to work for *a* capitalist. They were thus also structurally dominated by the capitalist class. That had the ideological ad-vantage of obscuring their unfreedom: "The Roman slave was held by chains; the wage-laborer is bound to his owner by invisible threads. The appearance of independence is maintained by a constant change in the person of the indi-vidual employer."[50] Marx held that the maintenance and expansion of these forms of the capitalist's domination were critical to the operation of capitalism because of how they facilitated the exploitation of workers. But he was also keen to stress that the exploitative drive of capitalism involved a form of impersonal domination that subjected all of society, workers and capitalists, to the rule of market imperatives. Marx argued that "the immanent laws of the capitalist mode of production, which through competition dominate the individual cap-italist as external coercive laws, force him to continuously expand his capital in order to keep it."[51] That incessant competitive drive prevented society from freely deciding how to make use of the immense gains of productivity. Freedom, for Marx, would consequently necessitate not only overcoming the domination of the capitalist and the capitalist class, but the domination of the market.

Marx's conversion to communism thus involved a complex mixture of incorporation and rejection of republican social and political commitments. While he opposed the republican social ideal of independent property hold-ers, his own social critique of capitalism continued to be deeply suffused with a republican vocabulary. Politically, his critique of the emancipatory limits of a republic was matched by an equally strong commitment to its necessity for achieving socialism and his fervent opposition to antipolitical socialisms that denied it. But as critical as Marx's political incorporation of republicanism was to the formation of his communism, it was thinner than it might have been. While Marx integrated the importance of political struggle and a demo-cratic republic into his communism, his early republican ideas emphasizing the need for far-reaching popular control and participation largely receded

49. Marx, *Das Kapital*, vol. 1, *MEGA* II.6: 411 / *MECW* 35: 427.
50. Ibid., 529–30 / 573.
51. Ibid., 543 / 588.

from view. His comments on representation suggest that the institution of universal (manhood) suffrage, without further controls on representatives, would be sufficient to eventually bring the working class to power. His views on bureaucracy remained as stridently critical as in his early republican account, but they were unaccompanied by his vision of a polity wherein that bureaucracy would be replaced by popular public administration. Marx thought that the institution of democracy was critical to communism, but he did not go significantly beyond the restricted conception of what was entailed by "democracy" in a bourgeois republic. He thought at this time that it would be sufficient to come to power within the bourgeois republic and utilize its political structures for social ends, rather than communism requiring the transformation of those political structures themselves.

As is shown chapter 7, that position was shaken in March 1871, when the Parisian working class took control of their city and demanded a *social* republic. The radical democratic experiment of the Paris Commune forced Marx to reconsider the political institutions necessary for socialism. He now realized that the "working class cannot simply lay hold of the ready-made State machinery, and wield it for its own purposes."[52] He recognized that the political form of bourgeois society, the bourgeois republic, was an insufficient political form for bringing about communism: "The political instrument of their [the working-class's] enslavement cannot serve as the political instrument of their emancipation."[53] That meant that in place of a bourgeoise republic what was needed was "a 'Social Republic,' that is, a Republic which . . . guarantees . . . social transformation by the Communal organisation."[54] That social republic would radically democratize representation and public administration through the tight control of its delegates and the deprofessionalization of the bureaucracy so that it was carried out by the citizens themselves. Legislative control and the election of public officials (with the power to recall) would transform the state's bureaucrats from "a trained caste . . . [and] haughteous masters of the people into its always removable servants."[55] Binding instructions, representative recall, and frequent elections would similarly ensure that "[i]nstead of deciding once in three or six years which member of the ruling class was to misrepresent the people in Parliament, universal suffrage was to serve the people."[56] The resultant transformation of the state through popular control

---

52. Marx, *The Civil War in France*, MEGA I.22: 137 / *MECW* 22: 328.
53. Marx, *The Civil War in France* (*Second Draft*), MEGA I.22: 100 / *MECW* 22: 533.
54. Marx, *The Civil War in France* (*First Draft*), MEGA I.22: 64 / *MECW* 22: 497.
55. Ibid., 57 / 488.
56. Marx, *The Civil War in France*, MEGA I.22: 141 / *MECW* 22: 333.

and participation would provide "the Republic with the basis of really democratic institutions" and be an important component of realizing freedom, as "freedom consists in transforming the state from an organ superimposed upon society into one completely subordinate to it."[57] Thus the political institutions that had once inspired the young republican reemerged as central components of the polity that Marx thought was necessary for the realization of social emancipation. Republicanism thereby formed an integral element of his communism.

The potential influence of republicanism on Marx's thought has not gone unnoticed. In studies of republicanism, affinities to Marx have been noted in passing in the foundational works that unearthed the buried history of the tradition and established it as the thriving field of study that exists today.[58] Most of the work examining his relationship to republicanism has concentrated on his early thought where an impressive literature has charted the importance of republicanism to his critique of Hegel and the broader Young Hegelian movement (though much less attention has been paid to his republican journalism).[59] Far fewer studies have gone beyond this early period and investigated aspects of republicanism's influence on Marx's later communism.[60] There have, however, been no accounts that comprehensively examine

57. Marx, *The Civil War in France*, *MEGA* I.22: 142 / *MECW* 22: 334; "Kritik des Gothaer Programms," *MEGA* I.25: 21 / *MECW* 24: 94.

58. J. G. A. Pocock, *The Machiavellian Moment: Florentine Political Thought and the Atlantic Republican Tradition* (Princeton: Princeton University Press, 1975), 461, 505; Philip Pettit, *Republicanism: A Theory of Freedom and Government* (Oxford: Oxford University Press, 1997), 141; Skinner, *Liberty before Liberalism*, xn3. See also Quentin Skinner, "Liberty before Liberalism and All That," 3:*AM Magazine*, 18 February 2013, http://www.3ammagazine.com/3am/liberty -before-liberalism-all-that/.

59. For instance, Miguel Abensour, *Democracy against the State: Marx and the Machiavellian Moment*, trans. Max Blechman and Martin Breaugh (Cambridge: Polity, 2011); Warren Breckman, *Marx, the Young Hegelians, and the Origins of Radical Social Theory: Dethroning the Self* (Cambridge: Cambridge University Press, 1999), chapter 7; David Leopold, *The Young Karl Marx: German Philosophy, Modern Politics, and Human Flourishing* (Cambridge: Cambridge University Press, 2007), chapter 4; Gareth Stedman Jones, 'Introduction," in *The Communist Manifesto* (London: Penguin, 2002), chapter 8.

60. For republicanism and parts of Marx's political thought, see Jeffrey C. Isaac, "The Lion's Skin of Politics: Marx on Republicanism," *Polity* 23, no. 3 (1990): 461–88; Alan Gilbert, *Marx's Politics: Communists and Citizens* (Oxford: Martin Robertson, 1981); and Norman Arthur Fischer, *Marxist Ethics within Western Political Theory: A Dialogue with Republicanism, Communitarianism, and Liberalism* (New York: Palgrave Macmillan, 2015). For the influence on his social thought, see William Clare Roberts, *Marx's Inferno: The Political Theory of Capital* (Princeton: Princeton University Press, 2017); and Michael J. Thompson, "The Radical

the enduring influence of republicanism on Marx's social and political thought across his writings.

Given the enormous quantities of ink that have been and continue to be devoted to Marx, that absence is more than surprising.[61] Part of the explanation has to lie in the continued invisibility of republicanism as a living political movement in the nineteenth century. The histories that have so powerfully revived the tradition have rarely ventured into the long century after 1776 and 1789. In Alex Gourevitch's corrective study of nineteenth-century American labor republicans, he observes that the "prevailing historical scholarship" gives "the strong impression that nothing conceptually meaningful happened in the republican tradition after the American Revolution."[62] Melvin L. Rogers, in his rehabilitation of nineteenth-century African American republicans, similarly notes how their exclusion has helped sustain the "troublesome interpretative claim . . . that by the nineteenth century, republicanism was in retreat or already eclipsed."[63] The consequence of this interpretive assumption has been that when republicanism is considered in relation to Marx's thought, it has often been reduced simply to support for a nonmonarchical political regime or as a dead political language from the Classical or Renaissance world. Republicanism's status as an active ideological and political competitor is rarely properly appreciated.[64] That means that republicanism has often not been given its due, even in studies that have otherwise provided an enviably careful and comprehensive reconstruction of Marx's thought.[65]

My hope is that by considering Marx in the light of republicanism, we might be able to move further past a number of interpretative commonplaces

---

Republican Structure of Marx's Critique of Capitalist Society," *Critique: Journal of Socialist Theory* 47, no. 3 (2019): 391–409.

61. Of the 115 combined entries in two recent compendiums on Marx, not a single one is dedicated to republicanism. See Jeff Diamanti, Andrew Pendakis, and Imre Szeman, eds., *The Bloomsbury Companion to Marx* (London: Bloomsbury, 2019); and Matt Vidal et al., eds., *The Oxford Handbook of Karl Marx* (Oxford: Oxford University Press, 2019).

62. Alex Gourevitch, *From Slavery to the Cooperative Commonwealth: Labor and Republican Liberty in the Nineteenth Century* (Cambridge: Cambridge University Press, 2015), 9.

63. Melvin L. Rogers, *The Darkened Light of Faith: Race, Democracy, and Freedom in African American Political Thought* (Princeton: Princeton University Press, 2023), 102.

64. Roberts's contextual study of Marx's *Das Kapital* is a laudable exception; see *Marx's Inferno*, 1–9.

65. I am here thinking particularly of the still unsurpassed works by Richard N. Hunt, *The Political Ideas of Marx and Engels*, 2 vols. (Pittsburgh: University of Pittsburgh Press, 1974, 1984) and Hal Draper, *Karl Marx's Theory of Revolution*, 5 vols. (New York: Monthly Review Press, 1977–2005).

that, despite the efforts of these more careful interpreters, continue to dog assessments of Marx's thought, particularly the idea that he was not committed to politics, democracy, or freedom. Marx has often filled a convenient position in narratives that criticize the decline of politics in socialist or more broadly modern political thought. Hannah Arendt provided an influential portrait of Marx when she condemned him for his supposed "repugnance to the public realm," his "obsession with the social question and his unwillingness to pay serious attention to the questions of state and government."[66] Sheldon Wolin similarly presented Marx as part of a century of thought that "was nearly unanimous in its contempt for politics."[67] More recently, Axel Honneth has squeezed Marx into a single monolithic socialist tradition that "simply ignored the entire sphere of political deliberation," failed to appreciate the value of "democratic popular rule," and was thus left with an "inadequate understanding of politics."[68] The irony of many of these judgments is that they would function better as a description of the antipolitical forms of socialism that Marx tried to displace. A study of Marx and republicanism helps show that one of Marx's great contributions was to place politics (and especially democratic politics) at the heart of socialism. I also hope that it reveals Marx to have been more interested in political and constitutional questions than the usual caricature of his work would suggest. I do not, of course, pretend that this study alone could dislodge the Cold War–inflected picture of Marx as a totalitarian antidemocrat. But I do hope that it will be harder to maintain that "Marx was not committed to democracy at all."[69]

Finally, it is still not adequately appreciated that Marx's principal political value was freedom, rather than, say, equality or community. As a young journalist, he keenly observed that "Freedom is so much the essence of man, that even its enemies implement it while combating its reality. . . . No man combats freedom; at most he combats the freedom of others."[70] That commitment to freedom, and antipathy to those who would deny it to others, motivated his social and political thought and activism throughout his life. Where Marx's commitment to freedom is acknowledged, it is usually reduced to an endorsement of

66. Hannah Arendt, *The Human Condition*, 2nd ed. (Chicago: University of Chicago Press, 1998 [1958]), 165; Hannah Arendt, *On Revolution* (London: Penguin, 1990 [1963]), 258.

67. Sheldon Wolin, *Politics and Vision: Continuity and Innovation in Western Political Thought* (Princeton: Princeton University Press, 2016 [1960]), 323.

68. Axel Honneth, *The Idea of Socialism: Towards a Renewal*, trans. Joseph Ganahl (Cambridge: Polity, 2017), 26, 32–33.

69. Allan Megill, *Karl Marx: The Burden of Reason (Why Marx Rejected Politics and the Market)* (Lanham: Rowman & Littlefield, 2002), 117.

70. Marx, "Debatten über Preßfreiheit," *MEGA* I.1: 143 / *MECW* 1: 155.

some conception of positive freedom as self-realization or fulfilment.[71] I do not mean to deny that such conceptions evidently played a role in Marx's thought (Marx, like most people, had more than one conception of freedom). But I do think that the role played by republican freedom has been neglected.[72] A concern expressed across his writings was that people were unfree when they were dominated—subjected to arbitrary power that they did not control—an unfreedom that Marx believed capitalism and its imitation of democracy inflicted upon the immense majority.

In order to bring these contributions and republican commitments to the fore, I have tried to reconstruct what republicanism meant at the time of Marx's political engagement. As was discussed above, this period barely features, if at all, in histories of republicanism, or its existence is even actively denied. Accounts often begin with either the ancient Greek or Roman Republics, then skip over nearly a thousand years to the renaissance Italian city-states, then jump to the English commonwealth of the seventeenth century, and finally conclude with the American Revolution in the late eighteenth century (with lip service sometimes paid to the French Revolution).[73] That narrative timeline already problematically excludes, for instance, the way in which republicanism was appropriated and reshaped in the Haitian Revolution.[74] Moreover, that narrative is frequently accompanied by claims that republicanism disappeared in the nineteenth century, having supposedly "been largely

---

71. For instance, Allen Wood, *Karl Marx*, 2nd ed. (New York: Routledge, 2004), 48–54; Isaiah Berlin, *Two Concepts of Liberty: An Inaugural Lecture Delivered before the University of Oxford on 31 October 1958* (Oxford: Clarendon Press, 1958), 53. But see also Berlin's more inadvertently compelling description of Marxian freedom as not wanting to be "ruled by foreign masters . . . or . . . classes" (ibid., 45).

72. See, however, William Clare Roberts, "Marx's Social Republic: Political Not Metaphysical," *Historical Materialism* 27, no. 2 (2019): 41–58. For a response from the perspective of positive freedom, see Paul Raekstad, *Karl Marx's Realist Critique of Capitalism: Freedom, Alienation, and Socialism* (Cham: Palgrave Macmillan, 2022), 61–62, 130–31.

73. For a typical example, see Pettit, *Republicanism*, 19; and Frank Lovett and Philip Pettit, "Neorepublicanism: A Normative and Institutional Research Program," *Annual Review of Political Science* 12 (2009): 12.

74. For this complex process, see Laurent Dubois, "Our Three Colors: The King, the Republic and the Political Culture of Slave Revolution in Saint-Domingue," *Historical Reflections* 29, no. 1 (2003): 83–102; Laurent Dubois, *Avengers of the New World: The Story of the Haitian Revolution* (Cambridge: Belknap Press, 2004), chs. 7–8; Sudhir Hazareesingh, *Black Spartacus: The Epic Life of Toussaint Louverture* (London: Allen Lane, 2020), 8–12, 39–40, 65–66, 99–100, 123–26, 154–57, 357–58. On republicanism in the French Caribbean more broadly at the time, see Laurent Dubois, "Republican Antiracism and Racism: A Caribbean Genealogy," *French Politics, Culture & Society* 18, no. 3 (2000): 5–17; Laurent Dubois, *A Colony of Citizens: Revolution and Slave Emancipation in the French Caribbean, 1787–1804* (Chapel Hill: University of North Carolina Press, 2004).

overtaken by liberalism."[75] Yet, as Rachel Hammersley writes in her exceptional recent history of republicanism, that narrative is simply "false," and she urges a greater focus on nineteenth-century republicanism, since the tradition was "transformed during this period from a doctrine primarily articulated by political elites to one that appealed to artisans, workers, and, by the 1870s, even women and newly enfranchised former slaves."[76] By examining the republicanism of nineteenth-century Europe in relation to Marx, this book has the subsidiary aim of helping to resurrect its overlooked place in the larger history of the republican tradition.[77]

Republicanism in Nineteenth-Century Europe

In 1831, Félicité de Lamennais, the onetime ultramontane priest turned liberal Catholic, observed that "the word republic . . . by its vague meaning, is marvellously suitable to incite the most opposed passions." Yet he maintained that a general definition of a republic was possible as a regime that "excludes the absolute authority of one person, and places the right of legislation in the whole people, or in a part of the people." Following a categorization going back to Montesquieu, Lamennais labeled the former regime a "democratic republic" and the latter an "aristocratic republic." Under this definition, Lamennais concluded that France's recently established liberal July Monarchy was actually a republic, since, though it had a king, "ultimate authority" rested in the legislature and hence the people who controlled it.[78] Implicit but left

75. Eric MacGilvray, "Republicanism," in *The Encyclopedia of Political Thought*, ed. Michael T. Gibbons, vol. 7 (Oxford: Wiley-Blackwell, 2015), 3235. See also Skinner's claim that during the nineteenth century the republican view of liberty "increasingly slipped from sight," *Liberty before Liberalism*, ix.

76. Rachel Hammersley, *Republicanism: An Introduction* (Cambridge: Polity Press, 2020), 174.

77. My focus is on the European republicanism that Marx most directly encountered. For studies of nineteenth-century republicanism in, for instance, the Americas and the Middle East, see José Antonio Aguilar and Rafael Rojas, eds., *El republicanismo en Hispanoamérica: Ensayos de historia intelectual y política* (Mexico City: Fondo de Cultura Económica, 2002); Gabriel Entin, "Catholic Republicanism: The Creation of the Spanish American Republics during Revolution," *Journal of the History of Ideas* 79, no. 1 (2018): 105–23; Roberto Gargarella, "Elections, Republicanism, and the Demands of Democracy: A View from the Americas," in *Comparative Election Law*, ed. James A. Gardner (Cheltenham: Edward Elgar, 2022), 236–49; Banu Turnaoğlu, *The Formation of Turkish Republicanism* (Princeton: Princeton University Press, 2017), chapter 3.

78. F. de La Mennais, "De la République," *L'Avenir* (9 March 1831), in *Oeuvres complètes*, vol. 10 (Paris: Paul Daubrée et Cailleux, 1836–37), 269–70/"On the Republic," in *Lamennais: A Believer's Revolutionary Politics*, ed. and trans. Richard A. Lebrun, Sylvain Milbach, and Jerry Ryan (Leiden: Brill, 2018), 79–80.

unsaid in Lamennais's argument was that the July Monarchy was consequently an aristocratic republic, as only a tiny part of the people, men who met the requisite property threshold (less than 0.5% of the population), could vote in national elections. Lamennais's intervention was partly directed at more conservative liberals (he pushed for extending the franchise to all men except those who "have a dependent position"),[79] as well as republicans still smarting from their failure to institute a republic in the 1830 Revolution. Lamennais's more encompassing definition of a republic was deliberately meant to run against the increasing conflation of a republic with a democratic regime with universal (manhood) suffrage.[80] While republics—and republicanism—had in previous centuries often been associated with various mixed forms of government (combining monarchy, aristocracy, and democracy), republicanism in nineteenth-century Europe was firmly democratic.[81]

Republicanism and democracy were so tightly associated in the nineteenth century that the labels "republican" and "democrat" were used largely interchangeably. Republicans often preferred to refer to themselves as "democrats," or "radicals," the other popular synonym, which avoided the dangers of a direct attack on royal authority.[82] (One reason perhaps for the continued invisibility

79. Ibid., 277 / 83. The subsequent 19 April 1831 election law lowered (but did not remove) the property franchise (to 200 francs in taxes) for national elections, increasing the existing voting population by 50% to some 160,000 men, at that time 0.5% of the population; see Malcolm Crook, *How the French Learned to Vote: A History of Electoral Practice in France* (Oxford: Oxford University Press, 2021), 29–30, 235.

80. For this change in meaning, see Wolfgang Mager, "Republik," in *Geschichtliche Grundbegriffe: Historisches Lexikon zur politisch-sozialen Sprache in Deutschland*, ed. Otto Brunner, Werner Conze, and Reinhart Koselleck, vol. 5 (Stuttgart: Klett-Cotta, 1984), 618–19.

81. Insofar as the mixed constitution continued to be defended in the nineteenth century it was by liberals; see Uwe Backes, *Liberalismus und Demokratie—Antinomie und Synthese: Zum Wechselverhältnis zweier politischer Strömungen im Vormärz* (Düsseldorf: Droste, 2000), 123–50. For an attempt to distinguish between an "Italian-Atlantic" and a "Franco-German" republicanism, respectively committed to a mixed constitution versus democratic popular sovereignty, see Philip Pettit, "Two Republican Traditions," in *Republican Democracy: Liberty, Law and Politics*, ed. Andreas Niederberger and Philipp Schink (Edinburgh: Edinburgh University Press, 2013), 169–204. That stylized distinction, however, has little purchase in the nineteenth century. For a convincing argument that democracy was more prominent in earlier forms of republicanism than often assumed, see Annelien De Dijn, "Democratic Republicanism in the Early Modern Period," in *Rethinking Liberty before Liberalism*, ed. Hannah Dawson and Annelien De Dijn (Cambridge: Cambridge University Press, 2022), 100–116.

82. Maurice Agulhon, *The Republican Experiment, 1848–1850*, trans. Janet Lloyd (Cambridge: Cambridge University Press, 1983), 14; Stephan Walter, *Demokratisches Denken zwischen Hegel und Marx: Die politische Philosophie Arnold Ruges; Eine Studie zur Geschichte der Demokratie in*

of the tradition in the nineteenth century). Nineteenth-century republicans did tend to be "republicans" in the narrow sense of antimonarchism, but they insisted that it was not a core or even a necessary component of their republicanism. In 1819, Richard Carlile (while imprisoned for publishing the works of Thomas Paine) defended changing the title of his magazine to *The Republican*, because the "etymology and meaning of the word Republican" showed that "it really means nothing more when applied to government, than a government which consults the public interest—the interest of the whole people." While it was true that "in almost all instances where governments have been denominated Republican, monarchy has been practically abolished; yet it does not argue the necessity of abolishing monarchy to establish a Republican government." What mattered to Carlile was being ruled by a parliament "possessing a Democratic ascendancy, renewed every year," and the extension of "the suffrage of representation to every man." A "real Republican government" would then be free to decide whether it wanted to keep "the present system of hereditary monarchy."[83]

Republicans' commitment to democracy flowed from one of their most central values: popular sovereignty. The 1843 opening editorial of *La Réforme*, which would become one of France's two main republican newspapers, addressed itself to "all friends of progress and liberty" and declared that "Our goal is to demand and pursue, until satisfaction, the full and genuine implementation of the principle of the Sovereignty of the People."[84] The opening 1848 editorial of the English Chartist journal *The Republican* (subtitled *A Magazine Advocating the Sovereignty of the People*) similarly argued that "the foundation of all Liberty" rested on the principle "That the voice of the People is the only legitimate source of supreme authority: in a word, we desire to see acknowledged everywhere, the Sovereignty of the People."[85] A few months later, the election platform of German republicans for the 1848 Frankfurt National

---

Deutschland (Düsseldorf: Droste, 1995), 51–52; Peter Wende, *Radikalismus im Vormärz: Untersuchungen zur politischen Theorie der frühen deutschen Demokratie* (Wiesbaden: Franz Steiner, 1975), 8. Engels argued that "The English Chartist is politically a republican, though he rarely or never mentions the word . . . and calls himself in preference a democrat"; see *Die Lage der arbeitenden Klasse in England, MEGA* I.4: 441 / *MECW* 4: 518.

83. R[ichard] Carlile, "To the Readers of the Republican," *The Republican*, vol. 1 (London, 1819): ix. For the history of the association of a "republic" with only nonmonarchical regimes, see James Hankins, "Exclusivist Republicanism and the Non-Monarchical Republic," *Political Theory* 38, no. 4 (2010): 452–82.

84. "La Réforme," *La Réforme*, no. 1 (29 July 1843): 1. The other being *Le National*, the organ of bourgeois republicanism; see Agulhon, *The Republican Experiment*, 17.

85. [C. G. Harding], "Introductory," *The Republican: A Magazine Advocating the Sovereignty of the People* (London: J. Watson, 1848), 1.

Assembly promised to "*establish freedom*" through new institutions "which will preserve sovereignty with the people for all time."[86]

"Universal suffrage" was republicanism's core institutional demand for the realization of popular sovereignty. For most republicans, universal suffrage actually meant "manhood suffrage," the expansion of the franchise to all adult men through the removal of property and educational qualifications.[87] Republicans rarely included women in this ideal of expanded political suffrage. As Whitney Walton has shown, that was also true of some of the most prominent French republican women, such as George Sand and Marie d'Agoult. While they challenged patriarchal ideals of republican motherhood, where women's only political role was to rear male citizens in the home, and though they advocated radical reforms to marriage, divorce, education, and employment to promote women's social and civil equality, they stopped short of endorsing women's political enfranchisement.[88] Yet a few republicans did take the "universal" in universal suffrage seriously and defended women's inclusion in the franchise. Amalie Struve, after being imprisoned and forced to flee into exile for her role in trying to bring about a German democratic republic in the 1848 Revolutions, subsequently chastised her fellow republicans for "excluding women from universal suffrage," demanding "on what grounds can man, who has put liberty, equality and fraternity on his banner, make women more unfree than the most unfree subject of some prince?"[89]

86. [Arnold Ruge], *Motivirtes Manifest der Radical-democratischen Partei in der constituir: Nationalversammlung zu Frankfurt am Main* ([1848]), 2 [n.p.].

87. A perspective missing in Pierre Rosanvallon, "The Republic of Universal Suffrage," in *The Invention of the Modern Republic*, ed. Biancamaria Fontana (Cambridge: Cambridge University Press, 1994), 192–205. See, in contrast, Siân Reynolds, "Marianne's Citizens? Women, the Republic and Universal Suffrage in France," in *Women, State and Revolution: Essays on Power and Gender in Europe since 1789*, ed. Siân Reynolds (Amherst: University of Massachusetts Press, 1987), 102–22.

88. Whitney Walton, *Eve's Proud Descendants: Four Women Writers and Republican Politics in Nineteenth-Century France* (Stanford: Stanford University Press, 2000), chapters 5–7, esp. pp. 227–33.

89. Amalie Struve, "Die Stellung der Frauen im Leben," *Deutscher Zuschauer*, no. 25 (31 December 1851): 198–99, reproduced in *Frauenrechte sind Menschenrechte! Schriften der Lehrerin, Revolutionärin und Literarin Amalie Struve*, ed. Monica Marcello-Müller (Herbolzheim: Centaurus Verlag, 2002), 68–69. See further Marion Freund, "Amalie Struve (1824–1862): Revolutionärin und Schriftstellerin—ihr doppelter Kampf um Freiheits- und Frauenrechte," in *Akteure eines Umbruchs: Männer und Frauen der Revolution von 1848/49*, vol. 2 (Berlin: Fides, 2007), 689–732. Amalie Struve's feminist republicanism can be contrasted with Emma Herwegh's contemporaneous republicanism that was largely uninterested in women's emancipation; see Marion Freund, "Emma Herwegh (1817–1904): Ein Leben für die Freiheit 'als das Einzige, was des Kampfes wert ist,'" in *Akteure eines Umbruchs*, 3: 278–79.

Few republicans, however, believed that extension of the franchise (whether male or female) was sufficient for real democracy and popular sovereignty. Their reading of Rousseau (who continued to be nineteenth-century republicans' principal intellectual influence) left them suspicious of representatives. They consequently understood representation as a kind of delegation, where representatives (or delegates) were to be closely watched and controlled by the citizens who elected them. Concretely that might involve annual elections (as with Carlile and the Chartists who followed him), binding instructions for delegates (known as an imperative mandate), and/or the power to recall delegates. An 1845 manifesto of the republicans associated with *La Réforme*, for instance, maintained that "Those who govern, in a well-constituted democracy, are only the mandatories of the people, they therefore must be responsible and revocable."[90]

Some further believed (again drawing on an understanding of Rousseau, as well as the unrealized 1793 Jacobin constitution) that such delegates would need to be paired with institutions realizing "the direct sovereignty of the people," in which citizens gathered in primary assemblies would play a role in the formation and/or ratification of laws.[91] The necessity for democracy and civic participation was also, for some republicans, not limited to legislation but extended to public administration. Johann Georg Wirth proposed making "all public officials elected *by all and from all the citizens* of the state, directly accountable to the people and dismissible by the same," with the result that the functions of professional state officials would be "passed to citizens, who perform this service alternating in turns."[92] The 1847 Offenburger program, which helped seal the divide between German republicans and liberals ahead of the impending revolution, demanded, alongside a call for democratic representation, "a popular state administration," in which "The over-government of officials is replaced by the self-administration of the people.'[93] Few republicans

90. "Aux démocrates," *La Réforme* (15 July 1845): 1.

91. Julius Fröbel, *Grundzüge zu einer RepublikanischenVerfassung für Deutschland* (Mannheim: Heinrich Hoff, 1848), 7–8; [Alexandre] Ledru-Rollin, *Plus de président, plus de représantants* (Paris: Bureau de la Voix du Proscrit, 1851); [W. J. Linton], "Direct Sovereignty of the People," *The English Republic* (1851), 1: 233–42. See further Anne-Sophie Chombost, "Socialist Visions of Direct Democracy: The Mid-Century Crisis of Popular Sovereignty and the Constitutional Legacy of the Jacobins," in *The 1848 Revolutions and European Political Thought*, ed. Douglas Moggach and Gareth Stedman Jones (Cambridge: Cambridge University Press, 2018), 94–119.

92. J. G. A. Wirth, *Die Rechte des deutschen Volkes: Eine Vertheidigungsrede vor den Assisen zu Landau* (Nancy, 1833), 47, 57–58.

93. "Die Forderungen des Volkes" (1848), Article 12, reproduced in *Menschenrechte und Geschichte: Die 13 Offenburger Forderungen des Volkes von 1847*, eds. Sylvia Schraut, et al. (Stuttgart: Landeszentrale für politische Bildung Baden-Württemberg, 2015), 12–13 / "Offenburg Programme

of the nineteenth century would thus have been satisfied with what passes for "democracy" today.

Next to popular sovereignty and democracy, core concepts of nineteenth-century republicanism were the trinity of values inherited from the French Revolution: *liberty, equality,* and *fraternity*. In republican thought this cluster of concepts was closely interwoven and justified in terms of each other, as is particularly clear from the above cited 1845 manifesto in *La Réforme,* which argued that "A democratic government is one which has the sovereignty of the people as its principle, universal suffrage as its origin and as its goal the realization of the formula: liberty, equality, fraternity."[94] Liberty has long been rightly recognized as a core concept of republicanism, but nineteenth-century republicanism was also distinguished by its inclusion of equality and fraternity.[95] Equality, for instance, meant that liberty had to be universalized and not the exclusive privilege of small set of citizens, a feature that nineteenth-century European republicans believed blighted not only the monarchies they opposed but aristocratic and slave-based republics. As Linton argued, in Athens "[t]here was liberty, but not *equality,*" and in the American republic, "Freedom is not universal; equality does not exist."[96] Equality was understood to ground not only civic and political rights for all (including the extension of suffrage),[97] but to include the requisite material equality to avoid dependency (without thereby, they argued, going over to "the equal condition of all men—as dreamed of by some of the Socialists").[98]

---

of South-West German Democrats, 10 September 1847," in John Breuilly, *Austria, Prussia and the Making of Germany 1806–1871,* 2nd ed. (Abingdon: Routledge, 2011), Document 29, pp. 138–39.

94. "Aux démocrates," *La Réforme* (15 July 1845): 1. For the general importance of understanding ideologies in terms of the organization of concepts, see Michael Freeden, *Ideologies and Political Theory: A Conceptual Approach* (Oxford: Clarendon Press, 1996), 85–87.

95. Sudhir Hazareesingh, *Intellectual Founders of the Republic: Five Studies in Nineteenth-Century French Republican Political Thought* (Oxford: Oxford University Press, 2001), 19–20. See also Sudhir Hazareesingh, *Political Traditions in Modern France* (Oxford: Oxford University Press, 1994), 80.

96. [W. J. Linton], "Democracy and Republicanism," *The English Republic* (1854), 4: 65; see also "Liberty and Equality," *The English Republic* (1854), 3: 121–32. For the emergence of equality in modern republican thought and its complex inclusion (and exclusion) in American republicanism, see Gourevitch, *From Slavery to the Cooperative Commonwealth,* chapter 1.

97. See, for instance, the linking of equality to universal suffrage in Bronterre O'Brien's editorial note in *Buonarroti's History of Babeuf's Conspiracy for Equality* (London: H. Heatherington, 1836), 214n.

98. Linton, "Republican Principles," 110; see also [W. J. Linton], "A Republican Catechism," *The English Republic* (1851), 1: 145–49.

Now attached to an ideal of equality, liberty continued to be a core concept of republicanism in the nineteenth century. As was suggested in the republican defenses of popular sovereignty cited above, republicans understood freedom to be essentially connected with democracy. In an 1834 essay, "De l'absolutisme et de la liberté," Félicité de Lamennais (by now alienated from both the Catholic Church and the liberal July Monarchy and on his way to being probably the most widely read and translated republican of the 1830s and 1840s)[99] gave the following definition: "Personal liberty, or the right to live and act freely, implies the absence of any will, of any power which would impose arbitrary limits on this same liberty, that is to say, it implies the cooperation of each member of society in the law that governs society."[100] Freedom for Lamennais was thus the absence of arbitrary power, where that meant not being subjected to the will of another and instead having democratic control over the laws to which one was subject. This was a view of freedom that Lamennais repeatedly defended. A few months later, in his *Paroles d'un croyant* (*Words of a Believer*), which Christopher Clark aptly describes as "a global literary sensation,"[101] Lamennais rejected the liberal pretensions to freedom of the July Monarchy, demanding of his readers, "Are you the one who has chosen those who govern you, who command you to do this and not to do that . . . ? And if it is not you, how are you free?"[102]

The unearthing of the distinctiveness (and critical potential) of this republican conception of liberty has been one of the central contributions of the modern revival of republicanism.[103] Republican liberty differs from a number of influential alternative conceptions of freedom. It can be contrasted with so-called positive views of freedom, where freedom consists in mastering one's internal irrational desires. It is also crucially distinguished from *freedom as*

99. For Lamennais's three-part political journey, see Sylvain Milbach, "Introduction," in *Lamennais: A Believer's Revolutionary Politics*, 2–12.

100. F. de la Mennais, "De l'absolutisme et de la liberté: Dialoghetti," *Reveu des deux mondes*, vol. 3 (1 August 1834): 302. See the translations, *Absolutismus und Freiheit: Dialoghetti* (Bern: J. J. Burgdorfer, 1834); *Dell'assolutismo e della libertà: Dialoghetti* (Italia: 1834), n.p.; "Del absolutismo y de la libertad," in *Palabras de un creyente* (Paris: Rosa, 1834), 277–335; "Absolutism and Liberty," [trans. Orestes Brownson], *The Boston Reformer*, vol. 3, no. 71 (13 September 1836): 1; and *El absolutismo y la Libertad* (Barcelona: F. Sanchez, 1843).

101. Christopher Clark, *Revolutionary Spring: Fighting for a New World, 1848–1849* (London: Penguin, 2023), 132.

102. Lamennais, *Paroles d'un croyant* (Paris: Eugène Renduel, 1834), 104–5 / *Words of a Believer* (New York: Charles de Behr, 1834), 96; and *Lamennais: A Believer's Revolutionary Politics*, 150.

103. Thanks especially to the foundational work by Phillip Pettit and Quentin Skinner, in, for instance, Pettit, *Republicanism* and Skinner, *Liberty before Liberalism*. Its continued importance to nineteenth-century republicanism has so far, however, been insufficiently realized.

noninterference (often referred to as negative freedom), under which someone is considered free insofar as they are not interfered with. Republican freedom as the absence of arbitrary power (or as it is also known, *freedom as nondomination*) requires more than this. Under republican liberty, you are unfree even when no one actually interferes with you, if a master retains the arbitrary capacity to interfere with you (arbitrary in the sense that that they can interfere according to their own pleasure rather than according to rules that you control). It is thus domination and not interference that compromises liberty for republicans. Domination matters for republicans, because of how arbitrary power forces those subject to it to contort themselves and their character in order to please or placate their dominator. That remains a concern even when a particular master is well disposed and rarely if ever interferes with those they dominate. For republicans, the servant, slave, or subject of a benevolent master is as unfree as someone who lives under a cruel or despotic one. What matters is not the character, the good or bad will, of the dominator but that they are, regardless of their individual disposition, in a position of domination over someone. Arbitrary power thus cannot be addressed through better or kinder masters and rulers, but has to be rendered nonarbitrary through rules that are controlled by those subjected to that power.

The importance of that insight had long been recognized in the republican tradition and continued to be defended in the nineteenth century—often by reference to those older examples. As Linton argued in his 1854 essay on "Slavery and Freedom":

> Hear what that truest freeman and noble servant of his country even unto death,—hear what Algernon Sidney said of Slavery: "The weight of chains, number of stripes, hardness of labour, and other effects of a master's cruelty, may make one servitude more miserable than another; but he is a slave who serves the best and gentlest man in the world, as well as he who serves the worst, if he *must* obey his commands and depend upon his will."[104]

Algernon Sidney's classic seventeenth-century depiction of the nature of freedom and slavery was one of the most influential statements of the

---

104. [W. J. Linton], "Slavery and Freedom," *The English Republic* (1854), 3: 90 (see also, however, Linton's attempt to combine this with a positive conception of liberty [ibid., 83]). Linton's citation slightly alters the final line, which in the original reads ". . . and he does serve him if he must obey his commands and depend upon his will": Algernon Sidney, *Discourses Concerning Government*, ed. Thomas G. West (Indianapolis: Liberty Classics, [1698]1990), ch. III.21. Linton used the same extract from Sidney as the epigraph to "Republican Measures," *The English Republic* (1851), 1: 121 and as a standalone definition of "Slavery" in *The National: A Library for the People*, ed. W. J. Linton (London: J. Watson, 1839), 214. See also the discussion in Stuart White, "The Republican Critique of Capitalism," *Critical Review of International Social and Political Philosophy* 14, no. 5 (2011): 566.

republican complaint against arbitrary power.[105] Sidney also provided one of the quintessential definitions of republican freedom, arguing that "liberty solely consists in an independency upon the will of another, and by the name of slave we understand a man, who can neither dispose of his person nor goods, but enjoys all at the will of his master," and he insisted that this required a person to be "governed only by laws of their own making."[106] For Sidney, this idea grounded a critique of absolute monarchy for making the people slaves of an arbitrary ruler, but where "the people" was understood as an independent, propertied male elite.[107] When Linton employed Sidney's definition, a hundred fifty years later, it served not only a more democratic political purpose (Linton argued that the "[w]orking men of England, *for* whom but not *by* whom the laws are made . . . are slaves"), but also as an indictment of the social dependency of women, as marriage forced them to "surrender the natural right of sovereignty and stoop to be the property and possession of their lords," and of workers, as the "arbitrary threats of hunger" meant that they were "under the power of another class of men who dispose of them as they think fit."[108] As Alex Gourevitch has shown, American labor republicans continued to use Sidney—against Sidney's own elitist intentions—to make this social critique into the late nineteenth century.[109]

Much of Linton's argument was reliant on that made by Lamennais in his hugely popular 1839 pamphlet *De l'esclavage Moderne* (*On Modern Slavery*), which Linton translated into English.[110] Lamennais made the established

105. For the use of Sidney in contemporary republican theory, see Pettit, *Republicanism*, 34; Philip Pettit, *Just Freedom: A Moral Compass for a Complex World* (New York: W. W. Norton, 2014), 28; and Frank Lovett, *A General Theory of Domination and Justice* (Oxford: Oxford University Press, 2010), 153.

106. Sidney, *Discourses Concerning Government*, I.5.

107. For Sidney's complex democratic and anti-democratic themes, see Tom Ashby, "Democracy in Algernon Sidney's *Discourses Concerning Government*," in *Republicanism and Democracy: Close Friends?*, ed. Skadi Siiri Krause and Dirk Jörke (Cham: Springer, 2023), 81–111.

108. Linton, "Slavery and Freedom," 90–91. Despite Linton's reference here to the political exclusion of "working men," he defended women's suffrage; see W. J. Linton, "Universal Suffrage: The Principle of the People's Charter," in *The Republican: A Magazine Advocating the Sovereignty of the People* (London: J. Watson, 1848), 165–68.

109. Gourevitch, *From Slavery to the Cooperative Commonwealth*, 14–16, 103.

110. *De l'esclavage moderne* went through five editions in France within a year, as well as editions printed in Belgium and Switzerland. Translations swiftly followed into English, *Modern Slavery*, trans. William James Linton (London: J. Watson, 1840); German, *Die moderne Sklaverei*, trans. J. Eckenstein (Weissenburg: n.p., 1840); three separate Spanish editions, e.g., *La esclavitud moderna*, trans. Adriano (Barcelona: Mata y de Rodalles, 1840); Portuguese, *A escravidão moderna*, trans. João Maria Nogueira (Lisbon: Imprensa Nacional 1845); and later into Italian, *Della schiavitù moderna* (Milan: Robecchi Levino, 1862), and Dutch, *De slavernij van heden* (The

republican point that the French people were "politically enslaved" since they lived "under the domination . . . [of] their lords and masters who pay 200 francs in taxes, [who] alone are invested with the right to participate in the making of laws, disposing of them, their persons, their freedom, and their goods, according to their own caprices."[111] But what made Lamennais's pamphlet so explosive was the social extension he made to this argument. In one of the earliest definitions of "proletarians" as "those who, possessing nothing, live uniquely by their labor," Lamennais argued that their reliance on wages to survive made proletarians "dependent on the capitalist, irresistibly his subject, for in the purse of one is the life of the other." This dependency meant that between "the capitalist and the proletarian, therefore, almost the same actual relations exist as between the master and the slave in ancient societies." Though proletarians enjoyed the freedom to sell their labor, which Lamennais considered "an immense advantage over the ancient slave," the proletarian's dependency on a capitalist meant that "this freedom is only fictitious."[112] (Nowhere in Lamennais's discussion of the "modern slavery" of wage-labor does he acknowledge that "ancient" chattel slavery was still very much in existence, including in France's colonies).[113]

For Lamennais the answer to the proletarian's political and social slavery was unequivocal: it required the extension of both the franchise and property to all, as "liberty depends on two linked, inseparable conditions, property and participation in government." At the same time, Lamennais insisted that the socialist and communist alternative of abolishing private property through state-ownership would not result not in "universal liberty" but in the "universal

---

Hague: Liebers, 1885). Spanish translations were also printed in Chile, *De la esclavitud moderna*, trans. Francisco Bilbao (Santiago de Chile: Imprenta Liberal, 1843), and Uruguay, *De la esclavitud moderna*, trans. D. M. Paler (Montevideo: Imprenta del 18 de Julio, 1847). For the influence of Lamennais's pamphlet in Chile, see James A. Wood, *The Society of Equality: Popular Republicanism and Democracy in Santiago de Chile, 1818–1851* (Albuquerque: University of New Mexico Press, 2011), 136, 159–67.

111. F. Lamennais, *De l'esclavage moderne* (Paris: Pagnerre, 1839), 60–61 / *Modern Slavery*, 16.

112. Ibid., 30–36 / 9–10. See also the translation in *Lamennais: A Believer's Revolutionary Politics*, 279–98, and the discussion in Michael Löwy, "Peuple réveille-toi! Lamennais, critique de l'esclavage capitaliste," in *De l'esclavage moderne*, by Félicité Robert de Lamennais (Paris: Passager clandestin, 2009), 11–22.

113. For the often purely metaphorical role of chattel slavery in republican discussions of liberty, rather than the actual experience or writings of the enslaved, see Alan Coffee, "A Radical Revolution in Thought: Frederick Douglass on the Slave's Perspective on Republican Freedom," in *Radical Republicanism: Recovering the Tradition's Popular Heritage*, ed. Bruno Leipold, Karma Nabulsi, and Stuart White (Oxford: Oxford University Press, 2020), 47–64.

slavery" of a dominating state power.[114] The republican conception of freedom thus grounded the republican's defense of political democracy and their (non-socialist) alternative to capitalism.

The republican conception of freedom also implied a special understanding of the relationship of liberty to law. Under a freedom as noninterference view, coercive laws by definition limit freedom (even if they might increase the overall amount of liberty). But if liberty means the absence of arbitrary interference, then interference that is not arbitrary does not undermine freedom. That implies the possibility that being subjected to a law might not necessarily make one unfree but in fact constitute one's freedom.[115] As Lamennais argued, "far from destroying or altering primitive liberty, the law is merely the exercise of this liberty." But critical to this argument, for Lamennais and republicans generally, was that it was only law of a particular kind that did not infringe liberty, that is, when "the general will . . . the will of the people . . . constitutes the law." In clear debt to Rousseau, Lamennais argued that it was possible to maintain our individual liberty in society through the creation of a "collective sovereignty of all or the sovereignty of the people," in which the laws which govern the people are "rules which they impose on themselves."[116] With that democratic condition in place, and only then, does the law not undermine freedom. As Karl Heinzen argued, "Law is only law when it is the rightful expression of those who are subjected to it. Law is the general guideline of the expressed will of free citizens, who voluntarily obey it."[117] Freedom as the absence of arbitrary power, as it was understood by republicans, meant not simply being subject to the rule of law but that the law had to be democratically controlled by the people.[118]

114. F. Lamennais, *Du passé et de l'avenir du peuple* (Paris: Pagnerre, 1841), 140–41, 152–53 / *Words of a Believer and the Past and Future of the People*, trans. L. E. Martineau (London: Chapman and Hall, 1891), 188, 193–94. For Lamennais's account that freedom required not just the franchise but also that representatives were tightly controlled, see *De l'esclavage modern*, 88–92 / 23–24.

115. For the theoretical argument behind this idea, see Pettit, *Republicanism*, 65–66; Philip Pettit, "Law and Liberty," in *Legal Republicanism: National and International Perspectives*, ed. Samantha Besson and José Luis Martí (Oxford: Oxford University Press, 2009), 39–59.

116. F. Lamennais, *Le livre du peuple* (Paris: H. Delloye & V. Lecou, 1838), 73–74 / *The Book of the People*, trans. J. H. Lorymer (London: H. Heatherington, 1838), 32–33.

117. K. Heinzen, *Eine Mahnung an die teutschen Liberalen* (Herisan: Literarischen Institutes, 1846), 36–37.

118. Thus, in addition to republican freedom differing from freedom as noninterference, it also differs from a narrower conception of arbitrary power, where that means simply being subject to consistent rules, even if one has no hand in the making of those rules. For this reason, Pettit has subsequently clarified that republican freedom is better understood as an opposition

Republicans' inclusion of democracy in their conception of freedom marked a clear divide with liberals. Arnold Ruge argued that "liberalism . . . [was] completely mistaken about the concept of freedom," which required that the "laws of free beings had to be their own product."[119] While liberals and republicans overlapped in some regards, including an opposition to arbitrary feudal institutions and the introduction of civic freedoms, democracy was the Rubicon that liberals were unwilling to cross.[120] Nineteenth-century liberals believed in the importance of representative government, but rejected extending the suffrage to all, maintaining that political participation should be limited to the capable through property and educational qualifications on the vote.[121] As one influential 1840 encyclopedia entry on liberalism put it, the "true essence of freedom" did not require "unmediated rule of the people," and insisted that the "reasonable liberal does not at all demand that affairs of state are decided by unmediated universal suffrage," as this would be "destructive, constantly leading back to the original state of civil society."[122]

The importance of democracy to delineating these political formations can also be seen in the three main competing political regimes of nineteenth-century Europe: absolute monarchy, constitutional monarchy, and a democratic republic (see figure 2).[123] (This tripartite classification, as we will see, plays an

---

to "uncontrolled interference" rather than the potentially misleading "arbitrary interference"; see *On the People's Terms: A Republican Theory and Model of Democracy* (Cambridge: Cambridge University Press, 2012), 58. For an account of the centrality of this aspect to republican (or democratic) freedom to which I am indebted, see Annelien De Dijn, *Freedom: An Unruly History* (Cambridge: Harvard University Press, 2020).

119. Arnold Ruge, "Vorwort: Eine Selbstkritik des Liberalismus," *Deutsche Jahrbücher*, no. 1 (2 January 1843): 4; "A Self-Critique of Liberalism," *The Young Hegelians: An Anthology*, ed. Lawrence S. Stepelevich (Amherst: Humanity, 1983), 245. As I argue in chapter 1, liberals in this period (at least in Germany) were more likely to defend a nondemocratic version of freedom as nondomination, rather than necessarily freedom as noninterference.

120. Jeremy Jennings, "Early Nineteenth-century Liberalism," in *The Oxford Handbook of the History of Political Philosophy*, ed. George Klosko (Oxford: Oxford University Press, 2011), 331; Wolfgang J. Mommsen, "German Liberalism in the Nineteenth Century," in *The Cambridge History of Nineteenth-Century Political Thought*, ed. Gareth Stedman Jones and Gregory Claeys (Cambridge: Cambridge University Press, 2011), 416–17.

121. Alan S. Kahan, *Liberalism in Nineteenth-Century Europe: The Political Culture of Limited Suffrage* (Basingstoke: Palgrave Macmillan, 2003).

122. [Paul von] Pfizer, "Liberal, Liberalismus," in *Staats-Lexikon oder Encylopädie der Staatswissenschaften*, ed. Carl von Rotteck and Carl Theodor Welcker, vol. 9 (Altona: Johann Friedrich Hammerich, 1840), 719.

123. David Blackbourn, *The Fontana History of Germany 1780–1918: The Long Nineteenth Century* (London: Fontana Press, 1997), 130–34; Clark, *Revolutionary Spring*, 109–29; Sperber, *The European Revolutions, 1848–1851*, 56–57.

Die Zeitungs-Politiker.

Der Radicale.   Der Liberale.   Der Conservative.
Republikaner.   *Constitutioneller.*   *Absolut Monarchist.*

FIGURE 2. Unknown artist, *Die Zeitungs-Politiker* (*The Newspaper Politicians*) (1850). Courtesy of Herzog August Bibliothek Wolfenbüttel: Graph. C: 215. The illustration depicts the three main political factions at the time: "The Radical/ Republican," "The Liberal/Constitutionalist," and "The Conservative/Absolute Monarchist." Compare this with a contemporaneous view from Britain, which appeared in the *Morning Chronicle* (July 1851): "It is seen that, within 40 years, the *Royalists* have fallen before the *Liberals*—the *Liberals* before the *Republicans*,— and now the *Republicans* tremble before the *Socialists*." This newspaper extract was appended as an epigraph to an English translation of one of Marx's articles on the June Days uprising; see Dr. Marx, "June 29, 1848," *Notes to the People*, no. 16 (16 August 1851), 312.

underappreciated role in Marx's constitutional thought.) Before the transformations brought about by the 1848 Revolutions, conservatives could look to the absolute monarchies in Prussia, Austria, and Russia; liberals took inspiration from the constitutional regimes in Britain, France, and various southern German states, while republicans were left with the memory of the First French Republic and the ambiguous example of the American Republic.[124] At

124. The nineteenth-century Latin American and Caribbean republics played less of a role in the European republican imagination (though the question would deserve greater study). For an interesting account of the influence in the 1820s of the Haitian republic on British

the two extremes, absolute monarchy meant individual rule by the sovereign unconstrained by a constitution or an effective legislature, while a democratic republic implied not simply the removal of the monarch but a constitution that enshrined equal civic rights and democratic popular sovereignty. Constitutional monarchy, on the other hand, was considered (by its supporters and detractors) to be a compromise or halfway house, in which the monarch's power was checked by a constitution, civic rights were introduced but heavily circumscribed, and popular rule was avoided through a property franchise on elections to a lower house and the balancing power of an (often unelected) upper house of notables.[125] (Constitutional monarchy in the nineteenth century thus differed from its usual contemporary connotation of a representative democracy that happens to have a hereditary monarch as the ceremonial head of state.) Republicans and liberals could thus form a limited alliance when it came to opposing absolute monarchy, but they disagreed on the regime that should replace it. Understanding the liberal antipathy to democracy in the nineteenth century is critical to understanding republicanism as a distinct political movement and not simply subsuming it under the liberal umbrella—an interpretive commonplace that has contributed to the erasure of nineteenth-century republicanism.

Republicanism in nineteenth-century Europe was thus centrally a political movement dedicated to the introduction of democracy and popular sovereignty. That meant not only a franchise free from property qualifications but extensive participation and popular control in representative government and public administration. Underlying and uniting those institutional aims was a distinctive conception of liberty, understood as the absence of arbitrary power or domination, where citizens had to collectively control the laws to which they were subject. That conception of liberty was not limited to the political sphere but also grounded republicans' social objection to the dependency of capitalist wage-labor. For the more radical and popular republicans, this arbitrary power had to be overcome by measures that universalized small-scale property ownership and secured the independence of self-employed artisans and peasants.[126]

---

republicans like Richard Carlile, see James Forde, *The Early Haitian State and the Question of Political Legitimacy: American and British Representations of Haiti, 1804–1824* (Cham: Palgrave Macmillan, 2020), 147–49, 173–82.

125. For a sense of these restrictions on civic rights, including press freedom and freedom of association, see Pamela Pilbeam, *The Constitutional Monarchy in France, 1814–1848* (Harlow: Longman, 2000), 55–56, 60–65.

126. I provide some discussion of the liberal or bourgeois strains of republicanism in chapters 4 and 5 but focus less on them as they were not as distinct from liberalism and represented less of a competing threat to working class support for Marx's communism. For discussion of

Marx in (and beyond) the Nineteenth Century

This book is written in the spirit that there is much to be gained from studying Marx's thought in its historical context. That means that the book devotes significant attention to reconstructing the social and political thought of Marx's contemporaries, through a close reading of their articles, speeches, and works, in order to bring to light the kind of political intervention Marx was trying to make with his work. While I do not think that this is the only way one can fruitfully engage with Marx's work, I do think it is a curiously underutilized approach (especially when compared with treatments of other canonized figures).[127] It is an especially important approach for the central question of this book, because it allows for the recovery of both republicans and antipolitical socialists as living competitors to Marx's communism. The vitality and the nature of their thought is easily occluded if one restricts oneself solely to Marx's own writings. Marx was never the most generous guide to the views he attempted to displace; nor did he, understandably, always explicitly signpost the views he was criticizing.

Reading the work of republicans is also critical to avoid simply transposing into the nineteenth century a conception of republicanism that has been shaped by twenty-first-century academic requirements or a reading of republicanism formed only by the Renaissance or Classical worlds.[128] Nineteenth-century republicanism is more interesting, varied, and surprising than such a transposition would allow for. I have thus tried to reconstruct republicanism as they saw it (without thereby limiting myself to their own assessment of their ideas). That has involved a study of the works of leading republican figures (such as Mazzini or Lamennais), as well as the manifestos, newspapers, and journals that built the wider movement and are critical to the reconstruction of any tradition of thought. Interspersed in the book are several in-depth intellectual and biographical portraits of republicans, including Karl Heinzen, William James Linton, and Arnold Ruge, whom I have chosen not only for their proximity to Marx (in the

moderate and radical republicanism, see Samuel Hayat, *Quand la République était révolutionnaire: Citoyenneté et représentation en 1848* (Paris: Seuil 2014); for a lively portrait of Marie d'Agoult's moderate republicanism, see Jonathan Beecher, *Writers and Revolution: Intellectuals and the French Revolution of 1848* (Cambridge: Cambridge University Press, 2021), chapter 4.

127. For a recent example of a noncontextual but highly stimulating reading of Marx, see Jan Kandiyali, "The Importance of Others: Marx on Unalienated Production," *Ethics* 130 (2020): 555–87. For a defense of contextualist approaches to Marx, see Terrell Carver, "Marx and the Politics of Sarcasm," *Socialism and Democracy* 24, no. 3 (2010): 102–18.

128. For the importance of this point in a different republican context, see Leigh Jenco, "What Is 'Republican' about Republican Chinese Thought (1895–1949)?," in *Republicanism in Northeast Asia*, ed. Jun-Hyeok Kwak and Leigh Jenco (Abingdon: Routledge, 2015), 85–108.

case of Heinzen and Ruge) or attempt to spell out a comprehensive republican political philosophy (as with Linton), but also to give a sense of how republicanism and the struggle for its ideals shaped the lives of its adherents.[129]

Given the value of studying Marx in his historical context, it is a shame that two of the most prominent recent biographies of Marx have given the impression that contextualizing Marx in the nineteenth century entails consigning him to it. Jonathan Sperber's and Gareth Stedman Jones's widely noted biographies have genuine merits, but they are motivated by that unfortunate assumption, having seemingly forgotten "that to historicize a subject is not to bury it."[130] In Stedman Jones's account, context often overshadows the focus on clarifying Marx's actual ideas and serves to suggest their seeming irrelevance to the modern world.[131] In Sperber's account this is explicit; he maintains that a contextual approach reveals Marx to be a "figure of a past historical epoch, one increasingly distant from our own . . . what Marx meant by 'capitalism' was not the contemporary version of it," and he claims that attempts to make his ideas relevant through contemporary ideas and theories are "singularly useless pastimes."[132] I share neither of these convictions. I think that concepts drawn from contemporary analytic political theory, for instance, can not only provide for productive modern reinterpretations of Marx but also, when applied carefully, help illuminate historical context by clarifying the nature of different political positions.[133] I have found the contemporary theoretical literature on freedom and domination especially helpful in this regard. I am, moreover, not convinced that the problems of the nineteenth century are as distant as Sperber assumes. Much has, of course, changed, but it is also "easy to be seduced by historical distance."[134]

129. For a sense of the risks and sacrifices made by republicans for their ideals, see, for instance, the revolutionary memoirs of [Emma Herwegh], *Zur Geschichte der deutschen demokratischen Legion aus Paris: Von einer Hochverräterin* (Grünberg: W. Levyson 1849); and Amalie Struve, *Erinnerungen aus den badischen Freiheitskämpfen* (Hamburg: Hoffmann & Campe, 1850).

130. Peter Ghosh, "Constructing Marx in the History of Ideas," *Global Intellectual History* 2, no. 2 (2017): 150. See similarly the criticism in David Harvey, *Marx, Capital and the Madness of Economic Reason* (London: Profile Books, 2017), xiii; Sven-Eric Liedman, *A World to Win: The Life and Works of Karl Marx* (London: Verso Books, 2018), x–xii.

131. See, for instance, Gareth Stedman Jones, *Karl Marx: Greatness and Illusion* (London: Allen Lane, 2016), 135, 202–3, 234–35, 271, 429–30, 537–38. For critique, see David Leopold, "More Greatness than Illusion: Stedman Jones on Marx," *European Journal of Political Theory* 18, no. 1 (2019): 128–37.

132. Sperber, *Karl Marx*, xiii–xviii.

133. For a particularly successful combination of analytic and contextual methods, see Leopold, *Young Karl Marx*.

134. Gourevitch, *From Slavery to the Cooperative Commonwealth*, 174.

Tenacious struggle has in some places managed to ameliorate aspects of the social domination of capitalism that Marx critiqued. But it has neither disappeared nor have its essential contours been overcome.[135] If I thought that Marx had nothing to say about this, I would not have written this book.

To that end, I am attracted to a conception of contextualism that sees its task as the unearthing of the past in order to reevaluate present assumptions and refocus our future politics. In an appealing account of the contribution that intellectual history can make, Quentin Skinner depicts the historian of political thought as a "kind of archaeologist, bringing buried intellectual treasure back to the surface, dusting it down and enabling us to reconsider what we think of it."[136] Such an intellectual archaeology allows us to see that our current assumptions were not the only possibilities but rather one set among several possible paths that were not taken.[137] Deciding whether and how that intellectual treasure should inspire us to strike out on a new path is a further and necessary task. But by showing us the alternatives that existed behind us, the history of political thought can challenge us to see that they could also lie ahead. In the closing pages of the book, I suggest two such resources that might be drawn from the study of Marx and republicanism: first, reclaiming the idea that freedom lies at the heart of a social critique of capitalist domination and, second, that popular democratic institutions are essential to overcoming that domination. While I offer these possibilities, and aim to develop them in future work, I also hope that by placing Marx in his unfamiliar historical context, I can provide readers with an opportunity to draw out their own resources.

135. See for instance, Alex Gourevitch, "Bernie Sanders Was Right to Talk about Wage Slavery. We Should Talk About It, Too," *Jacobin*, 24 January 2020, https://jacobin.com/2020/01/wage-slavery-bernie-sanders-labor.

136. Skinner, *Liberty before Liberalism*, 112.

137. Ibid., 116–17.

PART I

The Democratic Republic

1

A German *Res Publica*

> Attitudes were changing, almost unconsciously, in accordance with the
> changing times. The compass needle swinging over its dial has its equivalent
> in men's souls. Everyone was preparing for a forward step. Royalists were
> becoming liberal, liberals were becoming democrats.
>
> —VICTOR HUGO ON PARIS IN 1830[1]

> I am by the necessity of my nature a republican, and perhaps already in
> this moment a citizen of a republic. I can no longer live in states, without
> wilfully damning myself to continued hypocrisy, where even censorship
> has stopped being true [to itself], proved by the daily confiscation of already
> censored books.
>
> —GEORG HERWEGH TO KING FREDERICK
> WILLIAM IV, 6 DECEMBER 1842[2]

MARX'S EARLIEST writing on republicanism (that we know of) was an essay
he wrote in 1835 as a seventeen-year-old for the Latin component of his *Abitur*,
the exam that qualifies German secondary school graduates for university. He
approached the exam question, concerning what had been the happiest period

---

1. Victor Hugo, *Les Misérables*, trans. Norman Denny (Penguin, 2012 [1862]), 555.

2. Reproduced in *Studien zur Rheinischen Zeitung und zu ihrer Forderung nach Handelsfreiheit und Grundrechten im Deutschen Bund*, ed. Götz Langkau and Hans Pelger (Trier: Karl-Marx-Haus, 2003), 226. Herwegh's letter followed an audience with the king to discuss the censorship of his poetry and writings. The letter's unauthorized publication in the *Leipziger Allgemeine Zeitung* led to Herwegh's swift expulsion from Prussia.

in Roman history, by contrasting the Republic with the rule of Augustus. Marx praised the Republic as a time of simple morals and the striving for greatness and the common good by public officials and the citizenry—achievements that he argued were marred, however, by the neglect of rhetoric and learning and the recurrent struggle between patricians and plebeians. In contrast, Augustus's reign was marked by an artistic and literary flourishing and an end to social strife, though Marx cautioned that these successes came at the cost of "all freedom, even all appearance of freedom," since law was now exclusively made by the sovereign and the principal magistracies were concentrated "in the hands of one man." Yet, because of Augustus's mild and benevolent rule, Marx observed that the Roman people did not believe that they had been deprived of their freedom, to the extent that they could "doubt who is the sovereign and whether they themselves rule or are ruled over." Rather than straightforwardly declare for one period or the other, Marx insisted that each regime was the most suitable for the particular historical conditions it faced. While the Republic had in its time stimulated its citizens to strive for greatness, Marx concluded that the expansion of the empire and the disappearance of virtue and morals among the people meant that by the time of Augustus it had become the case that "a ruler is more capable than a free republic of giving freedom to the people."[3]

Predictably, some commentators have been unable to resist the temptation to seize on this essay as an early expression of Marx's supposed lifelong commitment to "dictatorship."[4] But the teenaged Marx's nuanced and qualified defense of Augustus's absolutism was more likely a reflection of the need to meet the expectations of his conservative Latin teacher,[5] who was an exception in the otherwise enlightened and liberal education that Marx received at the Trier *Gymnasium*. The school embodied the more advanced political attitudes and conditions in Marx's native Rhineland, which, despite being ruled from afar by the reactionary and absolutist Prussia, had experienced some of the liberating aspects of the French Revolution while being annexed to France from 1797 to 1814. That included Jewish emancipation, allowing Marx's father to briefly study and practice law, before that opportunity was snatched from him by the conservative turn in Prussian politics, which forced him to convert

3. Marx, "An principatus Augusti merito inter feliciores reipublicae aetates numeretor?," *MEGA* I.1: 466–69 / *MECW* 1: 639–42.

4. Robert Payne, *Marx* (New York: Simon and Schuster, 1968), 38.

5. The political positions in the essay match those of Marx's fellow students and likely reproduced the material taught in class. See *MEGA* I.1: 1207; and Michael Heinrich, *Karl Marx und die Geburt der modernen Gesellschaft*, vol. 1 (Stuttgart: Schmetterling Verlag, 2018), 114–16.

to Protestantism and largely suppress his enlightenment liberal leanings.[6] With little direct evidence, it is this liberal upbringing and education in the midst of an authoritarian regime that provides the most likely rough guide to the very young Marx's political views.

When Marx took his first steps into the public realm as a journalist in early 1842, we begin to get a clearer sense of his own emerging republican politics. Marx had turned to journalism after an academic career had been closed to him by the Prussian crackdown on Young Hegelian thought. He started to write for the newly founded Cologne newspaper, the *Rheinische Zeitung*, and was swiftly appointed its editor-in-chief. Privately, he expressed his frustration with Prussian despotism and even a reformed liberal constitutional monarchy, while committing himself to the cause of a German "res publica."[7] But Marx was opposed to calling openly for this radical demand (as some fellow Young Hegelians insisted on doing), which he argued would only provoke the Prussian government into harsher censorship and hamper efforts to build a broad oppositional coalition with liberals. His journalism and editorial strategy consequently avoided explicit overarching constitutional criticism of Prussia and concentrated on attacking particular institutions of arbitrary power, such as press censorship and feudal estate assemblies, which formed an overlapping target for *Vormärz* liberals and republicans. His own republican sympathies came to the fore through the more forthright and popular arguments he advanced for reform than many liberals were willing to offer, as well as a few scattered hints of a more radical constitutional position. In spite of Marx's best attempts to thereby stay within the boundaries of officially tolerated criticism, the popularity of the paper's informed critical coverage posed too much of a threat to the Prussian government, and it ordered the paper to cease publication by the end of March 1843. Marx's first foray into journalism thus lasted for just over a year. Elucidating the nature of its republicanism forms the subject of this chapter.

I begin with the political and intellectual context of Marx's early journalism, focusing on the radicalization of his fellow Left Hegelians in response to the growing authoritarianism of the Prussian state in the early 1840s. I then turn to this journalism, first setting out Marx's defense of the freedom of the press and the rule of law against arbitrary power. Second, I explore Marx's underlying conception of republican freedom, where people are free when they are not subjected to arbitrary power, a freedom understood as being ruled by laws

6. On the influence of Heinrich Marx and the Rhenish context on (Karl) Marx, see ibid., 1:41–79, 88–96; and Jonathan Sperber, *Karl Marx: A Nineteenth-Century Life* (New York: Liveright Publishing, 2013), chapter 1.

7. Marx to Arnold Ruge, 5 March 1842, *MEGA* III.1: 22 / *MECW* 1: 382–83.

that are the collective product of the people. Finally, I examine Marx's criticisms of feudal representative assemblies and his suggestive account of a more expansive and popular form of representation closely tied to the common good of the people. Throughout, I show how these republican positions both overlapped with and subtly went beyond those offered by Marx's contemporary liberals, in contrast to interpretations that have seen his journalism as simply an expression of liberalism.[8]

Left Hegelianism and Prussian Authoritarianism in *Vormärz* Germany

Frederick William IV's accession to the Prussian throne in June 1840 was met by widespread hopes that he would usher in a new era of liberalizing reform and finally realize the promise made by his father in 1815 to issue a constitution. Various other German states had succumbed to popular pressure and become constitutional monarchies in the two *Verfassungswellen* (constitutional waves) that followed the creation of the German Confederation (e.g., Baden, Bavaria, and Württemberg in 1818–19) and the outbreak of the July Revolution in France (e.g. Saxony, Hesse-Kassel, Brunswick, and Hanover in 1831–33).[9] But Prussia under Frederick William III stubbornly resisted any reform efforts beyond the consolidation of its bureaucratic apparatus. In 1840 it remained a semifeudal, absolutist state, where sovereignty and authority rested with the king, executive power was exercised by his appointed ministers and a powerful hierarchical bureaucracy, political and civic rights were severely curtailed or nonexistent, the press was tightly monitored and censored, and political participation was restricted to consultative *Landtage* organized along and elected by social estates. In this suffocating political atmosphere, it is not surprising that many hoped a new king would mean that a breath of fresh air was finally about to blow across Prussia. The Young Hegelian Edgard Bauer reported from Berlin to his

8. See, for instance, Werner Blumenberg, *Karl Marx: An Illustrated Biography*, trans. Douglas Scott (London: Verso, 2000 [1962]), chapter 4; Jon Elster, *An Introduction to Karl Marx* (Cambridge: Cambridge University Press, 1986), 6; Rolf Hosfeld, *Karl Marx: An Intellectual Biography*, trans. Bernard Heise (New York: Berghahn, 2013), 13–20; Norman Levine, *Marx's Discourse with Hegel* (Basingstoke: Palgrave Macmillan, 2012), 142–79; Peter Singer, *Marx: A Very Short Introduction* (Oxford: Oxford University Press, 2000), 24–25; Paul Thomas, *Karl Marx* (London: Reaktion, 2012), 41–44.

9. See Dieter Grimm, *Deutsche Verfassungsgeschichte 1776–1866: Vom Beginn des modernen Verfassungsstaats bis zur Auflösung des Deutschen Bundes* (Frankfurt am Main: Suhrkamp, 1988), chapter 5.

better-known brother, Bruno, that "Most cherish the greatest expectations of the new government, the King will hold himself above the parties."[10]

A few early moves by Frederick William IV—pardoning political convicts, rehabilitating dismissed professors, relaxing press censorship—seemed to confirm these hopes. However, it quickly emerged that these were not the product of a modernizing liberal impulse but confused expressions of the king's romantic and patriarchal conception of his rule (confirming Arnold Ruge's more sober prediction that the impending accession of the crown prince and his coterie of "gentlemen romantics" actually meant that the "reaction [was] flowering").[11] The new king soon rebuffed petitions for constitutional reform and set about building his vision of a Christian state that could withstand the revolutionary pressures of the age.[12] There was little space in this state for what the king had condemned as the "dragon-seed of Hegelian pantheism."[13] Having previously enjoyed a measure of toleration, the Young Hegelians began to feel the consequences of official state hostility. The new education and religious affairs minister, Friedrich Eichhorn, opened an investigation into Bruno Bauer's religious unorthodoxy in August 1841 that culminated in his dismissal from the University of Bonn in March 1842. The closing of academic careers to Young Hegelians (a move of particular consequence for the aspiring young Marx) was accompanied by a crackdown on their journalistic and literary output. In the spring of 1841 Prussia demanded that Ruge submit his *Hallische Jahrbücher*, which had emerged as the primary organ of Left Hegelianism, to its stricter censorship rather than that of the more liberal Saxon government (the journal had up to that point been edited in Prussian Halle but was published in Saxon Leipzig).[14] Ruge responded by shifting the journal's editorial office across the border to Dresden and changing the name to the *Deutsche Jahrbücher* in July 1841, a ploy that temporarily succeeded until the Saxon government (under sustained Prussian diplomatic pressure) banned the journal in January 1843.

10. Edgar Bauer to Bruno Bauer, 13 June 1840, *Briefwechsel zwischen Bruno Bauer und Edgar Bauer während der Jahre 1839–1842 aus Bonn und Berlin* (Charlottenburg: Verlag von Egbert Bauer, 1844), 86.

11. Ruge to Adolph Stahr, 5 May 1840, *Briefwechsel und Tagebuchblätter*, 1: 205.

12. David E. Barclay, *Frederick William IV and the Prussian Monarchy, 1840–1861* (Oxford: Clarendon Press, 1995), chapters 3–4; James J. Sheehan, *German History: 1770–1866* (Oxford: Clarendon Press, 1989), 621–25.

13. Frederick William (IV) to Christian Karl Josias von Bunsen, 21 March 1840, *Geheimes Staatsarchiv Preußischer Kulturbesitz*, BPH, Rep. 50 J. 244a. Bl. 34ᵛ.

14. Matthew Bunn, "'Censorship Is Official Critique': Contesting the Limits of Scholarship in the Censorship of the Hallische Jahrbücher," *Central European History* 47, no. 2 (2014): 375–401.

These authoritarian actions accelerated the already ongoing radicalization of a section of the Young Hegelians, drawing them further to the left of the political spectrum.[15] While some of them had already begun at the close of the previous decade to express open frustration at the lack of political reform in Prussia,[16] these critiques of absolutism remained broadly within the bounds of the liberal constitutionalism set out by Hegel. Hegel had maintained that "the state (which in this case means constitutional monarchy) . . . must be regarded as a great architectonic edifice, a hieroglyph of reason which becomes manifest in actuality" and dismissed the "*republic* or more specifically democracy" as requiring "no further discussion . . . in face of the developed Idea [of the state]."[17] Hegel's colleague, friend, and editor of the first posthumous edition of Hegel's *Philosophie des Rechts* (*Philosophy of Right*), Eduard Gans, showed greater openness to republican institutions than did Hegel.[18] But Gans (who taught Marx criminal and Prussian law in Berlin) still characterized his own political beliefs, at least in public, as adhering to a "representative monarchy" that would be a "true Aristotelian . . . middle" between "medieval regressions" and "anarchist conditions."[19] Were it not for his untimely death in 1839, Gans

---

15. This process is discussed in extensive detail in Ingrid Pepperle, *Junghegelianische Geschichtsphilosophie und Kunsttheorie* (Berlin: Akademie, 1978), 49–88, esp. 78–81. See also David McLellan, *The Young Hegelians and Karl Marx* (London: Macmillan, 1969), 22–31; and John Edward Toews, *Hegelianism: The Path toward Dialectical Humanism, 1805–1841* (Cambridge: Cambridge University Press, 1980), 356–69. For the importance of differentiating between Left Hegelianism and the broader Young Hegelian movement, see Lars Lambrecht, "Wer waren die Junghegelianer?," in *"Umstürzende Gedanken":Radikale Theorie im Vorfeld der 1848er Revolution*, ed. Lars Lambrecht (Frankfurt: Peter Lang, 2013), 175–90.

16. [Arnold Ruge], "Karl Streckfuß und das Preußenthum," *Hallische Jahrbücher*, no. 262 (1 November 1839): 2100–2102; [Karl Friedrich] Koeppen, "Über Schubarths Unvereinbarkeit der Hegelschen Lehre mit dem Preußischen Staate," *Telegraph für Deutschland*, no. 58 (April 1839): 458.

17. Hegel, *Philosophie des Rechts*, §279, §279Z.

18. For comparison of Hegels's and Gans's constitutional thought, see Hans-Christian Lucas, "Bemerkungen zur Historisierung und Liberalisierung von Hegels Rechts- und Staatsbegriff durch Eduard Gans," in *Eduard Gans (1797–1839): Politischer Professor zwischen Restauration und Vormärz*, ed. Reinhard Blänkner, Gerhard Göhler, and Norbert Waszek (Leipzig: Leipziger Universitätsverlag, 2002), 124–29; Wolfgang Schild, "Erbmonarch oder Wahlpräsident: Eine Differenz zwischen Hegel und den Hegelschülern Gans und Michelet," in *Philosophie der Republik*, ed. Pirmin Stekeler-Weithofer and Benno Zabel (Tübingen: Mohr Siebeck, 2018), 208–15.

19. Gans's 1835 summary of his politics was intended for an encyclopaedia entry, but was only published after his death in [Moritz Kind], "Ueber Eduard Gans," *Hallische Jahrbücher*, no. 113 (11 May 1840): 903; see, further, Norbert Waszek, "War Eduard Gans (1797–1839) der erste Links— oder Junghegelianer?," in *Die linken Hegelianer: Studien zum Verhältnis von Religion und Politik im Vormärz*, ed. Michael Quante and Amir Mohseni (Paderborn: Wilhelm Fink, 2015), 33–34.

would have witnessed, and may even have participated in, the Left Hegelians' outright abandonment of this moderate position.

As the authoritarian direction of the new Prussian regime crystallized, Left Hegelians lost what remaining faith they had in the idea that it was amenable to liberal reform, and they consequently turned to more radical answers. Similar to the radicalization process outlined by Victor Hugo in Paris ahead of the 1830 Revolution, over the course of 1841–42 the leading figures of the movement, Arnold Ruge, Bruno Bauer, and Ludwig Feuerbach, came to the conclusion that a constitutional monarchy was an insufficient and unstable compromise that was surpassed, in constitutional design and historical development, by a republic.[20] As one moderate Hegelian lamented, in less than two years the *Hallische* and *Deutsche Jahrbücher* had "left the theory of constitutional monarchy and gone over to *republicanism*."[21]

The programmatic summation of this radical transition was provided by Ruge in his "Eine Selbstkritik des Liberalismus" ("A Self-Criticism of Liberalism"), which opened the *Deutsche Jahrbücher*'s first issue of 1843. With the journal's prohibition imminent, Ruge launched an all-out assault on liberalism's (and by extension his own former) principles and preferred constitutional setup, in what effectively amounted, in the words of one contemporary observer, to openly "calling for the German republic."[22] Ruge argued that the German constitutional states celebrated by liberals were in fact doubly unfree. Externally, they were subjected to the wills of the large states in the German Confederation, Prussia, and Austria, so that all their constitutional guarantees and civil rights existed only insofar as they were "*tolerated*" by these powers, which meant that their "freedom is therefore a freedom that exists in fantasy, because it is *gifted*." Domestically, the states' constitutions and laws were, similarly, "*gifted*" by their sovereign and hence the rights they conferred on their subjects were only a "self-limitation" on his power rather than being the outcome of the "general and sovereign people's spirit." Liberals, Ruge charged, might thus be formally committed to freedom but

20. Bruno Bauer, *Die gute Sache der Freiheit und meine eigene Angelegenheit* (Zürich und Winterthur: Verlag des literarischen Comptoirs 1842), 119; Ludwig Feuerbach, *Grundsätze der Philosophie: Notwendigkeit einer Veränderung* (c. late 1841), in *Entwürfe zu einer Neuen Philosophie*, ed. Walter Jaeschke and Werner Schuffenhauer (Hamburg: Felix Meiner, 1996), 133; Arnold Ruge to Karl Rosenkranz, April 1842, *Briefwechsel und Tagebuchblätter*, 1: 271–72. Notably, David Friedrich Strauß, arguably the founding figure of Young Hegelianism, never made the transition to republicanism and broke with the Left Hegelians over their radicalization. He would go on to be a strident liberal critic of the republic during the 1848 Revolutions; see Frederick C. Beiser, *David Friedrich Strauß, Father of Unbelief: An Intellectual Biography* (Oxford: Oxford University Press, 2020), 14–15, 180–212.

21. Karl Rosenkranz to Arnold Ruge, 8 April 1842, *Redaktionsbriefwechsel*, 1027.

22. Hermann Ewerbeck to Wilhelm Weitling, 31 January 1843, *BdK*, 1: 157.

were actually "completely mistaken about the concept of freedom," which in fact demanded that the "laws of free beings had to be their own product."[23] Instead of liberalism's apolitical superficiality, where "political life existed only as sham and shadow," what was needed was widespread participation in public life, an armed populace, and mass popular education, so that the "educated and organized people rules itself." Ruge forcefully concluded with the rallying call for "*the dissolution of liberalism into democratism.*"[24]

The process by which the Left Hegelians differentiated themselves from the liberal opposition was part of a larger development of a distinct radical movement in *Vormärz* Germany, culminating in separate democratic and liberal factions in the Frankfurt Parliament of 1848.[25] Ruge acted as a bridge figure between Left Hegelians and the wider German republican movement, of whom some of the most prominent were Robert Blum, Friedrich Hecker, Julius Fröbel, Gustav (von) Struve, and Johann Georg Wirth.[26] The contributions of women to *Vormärz* republicanism has tended to be overlooked, but it is being slowly recognized with a recent focus on figures such as Mathilde Franziska Anneke, Louise Aston, Louise Ditmar, Emma Herwegh, Henriette Obermüller-Veneday, Louise Otto-Peters, and Amalie (von) Struve.[27] Left Hegelians shared the wider republican movement's political commitment to popular sovereignty and a republic, but their republicanism was also marked by an ethical ideal of citizens acting for the common good and realizing their universal nature over particular private concerns, a strand particularly exemplified in the writings of Bruno Bauer.[28] This Hegelian ethical legacy preceded

23. Arnold Ruge, "Vorwort. Eine Selbstkritik des Liberalismus," *Deutsche Jahrbücher*, no. 1 (2 January 1843): 4/"A Self-Critique of Liberalism," *The Young Hegelians: An Anthology*, ed. Lawrence S. Stepelevich (Amherst: Humanity, 1983), 244-45.

24. Ibid., 11-12/257-59.

25. Wolfgang J. Mommsen, "German Liberalism in the Nineteenth Century," in *The Cambridge History of Nineteenth-Century Political Thought*, ed. Gareth Stedman Jones and Gregory Claeys (Cambridge: Cambridge University Press, 2011), 416-21.

26. Hartwig Brandt, "Republikanismus in Vormärz: Eine Skizze," in *175 Jahre Wartburgfest 18. Oktober 1817–18. Oktober 1992*, ed. Klaus Malettke (Heidelberg: Carl Winter, 1992), 121-52; Peter Wende, *Radikalismus im Vormärz: Untersuchungen zur politischen Theorie der frühen deutschen Demokratie* (Wiesbaden: Franz Steiner Verlag, 1975), 31–47.

27. See the respective entries in Frank-Walter Steinmeier, ed., *Wegbereiter der deutschen Demokratie: 30 mutige Frauen und Männer* (Munich: C. H. Beck, 2021); and in the invaluable collection Helmut Bleiber, Walter Schidt, Susanne Schölz, & Rudolph Zewell, eds., *Akteure eines Umbruchs: Männer und Frauen der Revolution von 1848/49*, 6 vols (Berlin: Fides, 2003–2020).

28. Warren Breckman, "Arnold Ruge and the Machiavellian Moment," in *Die linken Hegelianer: Studien zum Verhältnis von Religion und Politik im Vormärz*, ed. Michael Quante and Amir Mohseni (Paderborn: Wilhelm Fink, 2015), 127; Gareth Stedman Jones, "The Young Hegelians, Marx and Engels," in *The Cambridge History of Nineteenth-Century Political Thought*, ed. Gareth

the Left Hegelians' political endorsement of a republic. At the beginning of 1841, when Ruge was still distancing himself from the "abstractions of republicanism," he simultaneously insisted on the importance of public spiritedness and maintained that the "state is not a *res privata*, but a *res publica*."[29] The subsequent Left Hegelian abandonment of constitutional monarchy reflected a growing belief that only a republican state with extensive political participation would realize their ethical principles.

The Left Hegelians' rejection of constitutional monarchy was key to their break with contemporary liberalism. As Dieter Langewische writes in his seminal study, German liberals were committed to replacing absolutism with *"constitutional monarchy*, not the republic. This was *the* central difference between liberals and democrats, who had since the [18]30s and increasingly in the pre-revolutionary decade differentiated themselves from each other."[30] The Left Hegelian critique characterized constitutional monarchy as an unstable and undesirable compromise between an absolute monarchy and a republic. In an article in *Deutsche Jahrbücher* in February 1842, Edgar Bauer argued that "constitutionalism is everywhere nothing but the transition to republicanism . . . [E]ither monarchy or republic. What lies between, is precisely only an in-between thing (*Mittelding*), hermaphroditic (*zwitterhaft*) and wavering, which is good for nothing more than preparing the transition from the former to the latter."[31]

Bauer's portrayal of constitutional monarchy as an objectionable hybrid (*Zwitter* carries a pejorative connotation of hermaphroditism, offensively so from a modern perspective) was a standard one in Left Hegelian circles.[32] For example, Moses Hess condemned liberal constitutional thought as a "hybrid

---

Stedman Jones and Gregory Claeys (Cambridge: Cambridge University Press, 2011), 565. For Bauer's republicanism, see Douglas Moggach, "Introduction: Hegelianism, Republicanism, and Modernity"; "Republican Rigorism and the Emancipation of Bruno Bauer," in *The New Hegelians: Politics and Philosophy in the Hegelian School*, ed. Douglas Moggach (Cambridge: Cambridge University Press, 2006), 1–23, 114–35; and Douglas Moggach, *The Philosophy and Politics of Bruno Bauer* (Cambridge: Cambridge University Press, 2003).

29. Ruge, "Vorwort," *Hallische Jahrbücher*, no. 1 (1 January 1841): 3.

30. Dieter Langewiesche, *Liberalismus in Deutschland* (Frankfurt am Main: Suhrkamp, 1988), 21.

31. Edgar Bauer, "[Review:] *Vom Geist: Schwert und Handschlag für Franz Baader* . . . von Moritz Carriere," *Deutsche Jahrbücher*, no. 37, (14 February 1842): 148. For Edgar Bauer's republicanism, see Charles Barbour, "'The True Practice Is Theory': Edgar Bauer, Republicanism, and the Young Hegelians," *International Critical Thought* 12, no. 4 (2022): 640–60. See also Erik Gamby, *Edgar Bauer: Junghegelianer, Publizist und Polizeiagent* (Trier: Karl-Marx-Haus, 1985).

32. Gustav Mayer, "Die Anfänge des politischen Radikalismus im vormärzlichen Preußen," *Zeitschrift für Politik* 6 (1913): 60, 67.

theory (*Zwittertheorie*)," while Karl Nauwerck presented liberal reformists as a "a kind of hermaphrodite (*Zwitter*)," which necessarily ends with the "transformation of reformists into radicals."[33] Left Hegelians were thereby echoing arguments made by an earlier generation of German republicans at the 1832 Hambach Festival (a key moment in the history of *Vormärz* Germany). One of its central participants, Johann Georg Wirth, had proclaimed that "Every constitutional monarchy, as an unnatural and artificial hybrid (*Zwitterding*), carries within itself the germ of its own destruction and dissolves itself into a free state (*Freistaat*)."[34]

We find strikingly similar language in Marx's first definitive statement of his own political views.[35] In a letter from March 1842, Marx offered Ruge a prospective article for the *Deutsche Jahrbücher* that would critique Hegel's constitutional thought, where "the core [point] is the struggle against *constitutional monarchy* as a through and through self-contradictory and self-abolishing hybrid (*Zwitterdings*). Res publica is not even translatable into German."[36] With this, Marx was clearly declaring his intellectual allegiance to the Left Hegelian

33. [Moses Hess], "Das Rätsel des 19. Jahrhundert, *Rheinische Zeitung*, no. 109 (19 April 1842); K.[arl] Nauwerck, "Conservatismus und Radicalismus," *Deutsche Jahrbücher*, no. 197 (19 August 1842): 788. See also [Moses Hess], "Socialismus und Communismus," in *Einundzwanig Bogen aus der Schweiz*, ed. Georg Herwegh, vol. 1 (Zurich & Winterthur: Literarischen Comptoirs), 87 / "Socialism and Communism," in *The Holy History of Mankind and Other Writing*, ed. and trans. Shlomo Avineri (Cambridge: Cambridge University Press, 2004), 111.

34. Johann Georg Wirth, *Die politische Reform Deutschlands* (Strasburg, 1832), 32. See also the description of constitutional monarchy as a "*Zwitterding*" and an "unnatural thing (*Unding*)" in the defense speeches of Wirth's associate Philipp Jakob Siebenpfeiffer, in *Zwei gerichtliche Vertheidigungsreden von Siebenpfeiffer* (Bern: Literarisches Comptoir, 1834), 10, and *Der Unpartheiische: Ein Encyclopadisches Zeitblatt für Deutschland*, no. 122 (20 August 1833): 486. See further, Wolfgang Mager, "Republik," in *Geschichtliche Grundbegriffe: Historisches Lexikon Zur Politisch-Sozialen Sprache in Deutschland*, ed. Otto Brunner, Werner Conze, and Reinhart Koselleck, vol. 5 (Stuttgart: Klett-Cotta, 1984), 627–29.

35. Marx's doctoral dissertation (completed in March 1841) contains a brief elliptical critique of the "liberal party" but also maintains that it "achieves real progress," see *Differenz der demokritischen und epikureischen Naturphilosophie*, MEGA I.1: 69 / MECW 1: 86. See further Heinrich, *Karl Marx*, 1:352–59. For differing assessments of whether the indirect evidence of Marx's early politics should lead us to describing him as a liberal monarchist before he became a republican, see Richard N. Hunt, *The Political Ideas of Marx and Engels*, vol. 1 (Pittsburgh: University of Pittsburgh Press, 1974), 26–27; Warren Breckman, *Marx, the Young Hegelians, and the Origins of Radical Social Theory: Dethroning the Self* (Cambridge: Cambridge University Press, 1999), 272–73.

36. Marx to Arnold Ruge, 5 March 1842, MEGA III.1: 22 / MECW 1: 382–83. The following year, Marx excerpted Chateaubriand's conservative condemnation of France's 1830 constitutional monarchy as "an amphibious political form with the head of a king and the tail of a

project, spearheaded by Ruge, of critiquing their inherited Hegelian commitment to constitutional monarchy.[37] But his more ambiguous stance on translating the Latin "Res publica" (literally "public thing," but can variously mean "state," "political community," "public life," or "republic") contrasts with the more full-throated declarations for the republic made in Bauer's and Wirth's comparable statements. His likely meaning was to convey to Ruge his frustration with the political backwardness of German politics and philosophy, especially as represented by Hegel, and the inability to envision or realize a more radical polity. Richard Hunt also plausibly suggests that Marx had been making a literal complaint that "censorship prevent[ed] the translation of *res publica* into *Republik*."[38] (Ruge had indeed been forced to remove a positive reference to the "republic" by the censor just two months before Marx's letter.)[39] Marx was thus indicating his intellectual dissatisfaction with the liberal goal of constitutional monarchy and consequent support for a republic, while also showing an awareness of the present political limits of openly calling for or acting on that commitment.

---

people," see François-René de Chateaubriand, *De la restauration et de la monarchie élective* (Paris: Normant Fils, 1831), 27; Marx, "Exzerpte aus Chateaubriand," *MEGA* IV.2: 153.

37. See, however, the idiosyncratic reading that Marx actually thought that it was the struggle *against* constitutional monarchy, and not constitutional monarchy *itself*, that was contradictory, and so the passage in fact "disavow[s] any republican intentions on Marx's part," in Levine, *Marx's Discourse with Hegel*, 146. That relies on an unlikely grammatical reading of the passage (as is clearer in the original German wording) and ignoring the context and purpose of the letter. Marx was pitching an article to Ruge, whose personal and editorial shift to republicanism had by then become apparent. For his part, Ruge had taken Marx to already be a republican in September 1841 (when Ruge was still hesitant about his own position), describing Marx as being committed to the "philosophical republic" and the "montagne" (the radicals of the French Revolution); see Arnold Ruge to Adolf Stahr, 8 September 1841, *Redaktionsbriefwechsel*, 826 (see also the report on Marx's politics as a "confused revolutionary," in Georg Jung to Arnold Ruge, 18 October 1841, *MEGA*[⊕], I.1, Halbband 2: 261–62). Ruge's later correspondence treats Marx as a collaborator who shares the same political position; see Arnold Ruge to Robert Prutz, 8 January 1842, *Briefwechsel und Tagebuchblätter*, 1: 259, *Redaktionsbriefwechsel*, 931; and Arnold Ruge to Marx, 25 February 1842, *MEGA* III.1: 370, *Redaktionsbriefwechsel*, 979–80. In Marx's own subsequent correspondence with Ruge, he poked fun at the inaction and hypocrisy of Saxon liberal parliamentarians in the face of state censorship; see Marx to Arnold Ruge, 9 July 1842, *MEGA* III.1: 30 / *MECW* 1: 391.

38. Hunt, *Political Ideas of Marx and Engels*, 1:31.

39. Arnold Ruge to Robert Prutz, 8 January 1842, *Briefwechsel und Tagebuchblätter*, 1: 259. Ruge attributed the growing censorship of the *Deutsche Jahrbücher* to the government's reaction to its theological radicalism and its "political republicanism," Arnold Ruge to Jakob Veneday, 22 April 1842, *Redaktionsbriefwechsel*, 1038.

This recognition would lead to a significant difference with some Left Hegelians when Marx embarked on his journalistic and editorial career with the *Rheinische Zeitung*. The newspaper had begun publishing on 1 January 1842, and had been founded by a group of liberal Rhenish financiers and industrialists hoping to take advantage of Prussia's seeming liberalization. But under its chaotic first editors it published a series of radical theological and political provocations. Edgar Bauer was, for instance, allowed to restate his arguments from the *Deutsche Jahrbücher* in a bombastic and widely circulated broadside against liberal half-measures and the "hybrid creature (*Zwittergeschöpf*)" of constitutional monarchy.[40] Marx thought this was wholly irresponsible. In a letter to one of the newspaper's owners, he warned that though Bauer's arguments had a place in scientific journals (like the *Deutsche Jahrbücher*), printing them in popular newspapers would only serve to alienate liberal allies and lead to sharpened censorship and possible suppression of the newspaper. Marx cautioned that this was exactly the fate that had befallen Wirth's *Deutsche Tribune* ten years before. He instead insisted that the proper role of the *Rheinische Zeitung* was to work with those committed to "winning freedom step by step, within the constitutional framework" and to leave "general theoretical arguments about the state political system," such as his promised article "against Hegel's theory of constitutional monarchy," to journals where they were less likely to incite the government.[41]

When Marx was appointed editor in mid-October 1842, he swiftly put into practice this more disciplined editorial strategy of stridently pressing for liberal reforms while reining in overtly radical commentary.[42] He closed the newspaper's pages to contributions from *Die Freien* (The Free), a loose grouping of Left Hegelians in Berlin marked by their ultraradical propagandizing and with which Edgar Bauer, for instance, was associated.[43] Marx further

40. [Edgar Bauer], "Das Juste milieu," *Rheinische Zeitung*, no. 156 (5 June 1842), Beiblatt.

41. Marx to Dagobert Oppenheim, ca. mid-August–late September 1842, *MEGA* III.1: 31–32 / *MECW* 1: 392–93.

42. As Michael Evans rightly stresses, this more disciplined strategy is obscured by the frequent suggestion that Marx's editorial takeover led to the radicalization of the paper; see *Marx and the Rheinische Zeitung* (Manchester: Department of Government, University of Manchester, 1995), 17.

43. Key figures normally associated with the *Freien* include Eduard Meyen, Ludwig Buhl, Max Stirner, and the Bauer brothers. See Olaf Briese, "Vormärzlicher Anarchismus: Das Beispiel der Berliner Junghegelianer und 'Freien,'" in *Findbuch archivalischer Quellen zum frühen Anarchismus: Beiträge zur Erschließung von Akten aus Berliner Archiven über die 'Freien' (1837–1853)*, ed. Wolfgang Eckhardt (Bodenburg: Verlag Edition AV, 2021), 19; Ernst Schulte-Holtey, "Die Freien [Berlin]," in *Handbuch literarischkultureller Vereine, Gruppen und Bünde 1825–1933*,

publicly sided with Ruge and Georg Herwegh in their falling out with the *Freien*, sparked in part by Herwegh's sensational audience with the Prussian king.[44] (They in turn responded by accusing Marx—to his irritation—of failing to confront the government and the censor, branding him guilty of "conservatism").[45] As part of his editorial strategy, Marx presented the *Rheinische Zeitung* to Prussian government officials as a critical but loyal paper of "German liberalism," whose only aim was to strengthen Prussia's position.[46] With this more defined and disciplined political positioning, combined with its popular exposés of the social and political conditions in the Rhineland, subscriptions soon soared to nearly four times their previous level.[47]

In Marx's own articles, as we will see in the coming sections, he focused on demands around which liberals and radicals could form a common front, the rule of law, freedom of the press and modern representative assemblies.[48] In a strategy common to *Vormärz* radicalism,[49] Marx was careful to present himself as an internal critic of liberalism, committed to defending "true liberalism" against "half-hearted liberalism."[50] His arguments were pitched at pushing the edges of liberalism in a more popular direction. That provided hints and flashes of a more radical polity with extensive popular participation. He described his political ideal, for instance, as "transforming the mysterious, priestly nature of the state into a clear-cut entity of the ordinary people (*Laienwesen*), accessible to all and belonging to all, making the state the flesh and blood of its citizens."[51] But he avoided explicitly naming what such a state would be. The most direct

---

ed. Wulf Wülfing, Karin Bruns, and Rolf Parr (Stuttgart & Weimar: J. B. Metzler, 1998), 108. For an argument that Edgar and Bruno Bauer were sympathetic to but independent of the *Freien*, see Wolfgang Bunzel and Lars Lambrecht, "Group Formation and Divisions in the Young Hegelian School," in *Politics, Religion, and Art: Hegelian Debates*, ed. Douglas Moggach (Evanston: Northwestern University Press, 2011), 35–36.

44. Marx, "Herweghs und Ruges Verhältnis zu den Freien," *MEGA* I.1: 371-2 / *MECW* 1: 287. See further Wolfgang Eßbach, *Die Junghegelianer: Soziologie einer Intellektuellengruppe* (Wilhelm Fink, 1988), 214–26. For Ruge's criticism of the *Freien's* "ultra-opinions (*Ultrameinung*)," see Arnold Ruge to Robert Prutz, 18 November 1842, *Redaktionsbriefwechsel*, 1157.

45. Marx to Arnold Ruge, 30 November 1842, *MEGA* III.1: 38–39 / *MECW* 1: 394–95.

46. Marx to Justus Wilhelm Eduard von Scheper, ca. 12–17 November 1842, *MEGA*, III.1: 34.

47. Inge Taubert, "Karl Marx und die 'Rheinische Zeitung für Politik, Handel und Gewerbe,'" in *Rheinische Zeitung für Politik, Handel und Gewerbe: Unveränderter Neudruck* (Leipzig: Zentralantiquariat der Deutschen Demokratischen Republik, 1974), 17.

48. Wende, *Radikalismus im Vormärz*, 49.

49. Ibid.

50. Marx, "Debatten über Preßfreiheit," *MEGA* I: 1: 168 / *MECW* 1: 180; "Die 'liberale Opposition' in Hannover," *MEGA* I: 1: 250 / *MECW* 1: 265.

51. Marx, "Replik auf den Angriff eines 'gemäßigten' Blattes," *MEGA* I.1: 333 / *MECW* 1: 318.

constitutional criticism that Marx allowed himself was in an editorial footnote on the liberal opposition in Hanover. He here observed that "true liberalism" would demand neither a return to the Hanoverian absolutist state of 1819 or the recently retracted 1833 liberal constitution, but a "completely new state form corresponding to a deeper, more thoroughly matured and *freer* popular consciousness."[52] Readers of the *Rheinische Zeitung* could reasonably infer that if absolutist and liberal constitutional states were ruled out, Marx thought Hanover should become a democratic republic.[53] But making such a demand explicit or about Prussia itself would have been anathema to Marx's political strategy.[54] In 1842, Marx was therefore a convinced republican, but one who believed that the prevailing political conditions made it impossible to call immediately and openly for a republic and instead necessitated working with and within the broader liberal oppositional movement.[55]

Despite Marx's laborious attempts to navigate the limits of officially tolerated opposition, by early 1843 the Prussian government had had enough. The *Rheinische Zeitung*'s stinging critical investigations of Rhenish conditions and its rapidly growing circulation posed even more of threat to the regime than the "empty radicalism of the Freien."[56] When the Russian government angrily complained about an anti-Czarist article (penned by Marx), the Prussian government required little convincing, and in January 1843 it ordered publication to cease before 1 April 1843.[57] Marx tried to defend the newspaper against the official charge that the newspaper was committed to "undermining the monarchical principle," claiming that the *Rheinische Zeitung* was not in favor of a *"particular state form,"* only an *"ethical and rational political community (Gemeinwesen)"* that could be realized in *"every* state form."[58] Such a nuanced defense of its politics was unlikely to sway a government that had come to the firm conclusion that, in the words of one senior Prussian official, "Dr. Marx"

---

52. Marx, "Die 'liberale Opposition' in Hannover," *MEGA* I.1: 250/ *MECW* 1: 265.

53. Marx himself provided this trifold division of possible constitutions in his contemporaneous "Der leitende Artikel," *MEGA* I.1: 187-88/ *MECW* 1: 200.

54. Hunt, *Political Ideas of Marx and Engels*, 1:42.

55. It is therefore not quite accurate to say that at this point Marx had "arrived at openly declared republicanism"; see Breckman, *Marx, the Young Hegelians, and the Origins of Radical Social Theory*, 273.

56. Evans, *Marx and the Rheinische Zeitung*, 17–18.

57. See [Marx], [Die russische Note über die preußische Presse], *Rheinische Zeitung*, no. 3 (4 January 1843): 1. This article has only relatively recently been attributed to Marx; see Langkau and Pelger, *Studien zur Rheinischen Zeitung*, which reproduces the article and the relevant diplomatic correspondence.

58. Marx, *Randglossen zu den Anklagen des Ministerialrescripts, MEGA* I.1: 351/ *MECW* 1: 363.

held "ultra-democratic convictions" that were in "complete contradiction with the principle of the Prussian state."[59]

Freedom of the Press and the Rule of Law

Marx's first ever article to appear in print was, appropriately enough, a defense of the free press.[60] Freedom of the press was also the subject of the article that would have been Marx's first publication, but which, ironically enough, Ruge thought wouldn't get past the *Deutsche Jahrbücher*'s censor. It had to wait another year to see the light of day in a collection Ruge published in the less restrictive Switzerland.[61] This first brush with censorship was typical of the constraints, and the corresponding editorial rigmarole, imposed by the repressive Carlsbad Decrees of 1819. These mandated the prepublication censorship of all publications under twenty printer's sheets (i.e., 320 pages) across the German states and longer publications subjected to possible postpublication censorship.[62] Marx bitterly complained that being subject to this censorship regime meant that the censor of the *Rheinische Zeitung* "every day, mercilessly shreds the paper, so that it often can barely appear."[63] By targeting this regime in his articles Marx was taking on what was widely seen as *the* defining political issue of the day.[64] His intervention was spurred by a set of debates on press freedom in the Rhenish *Landtag* in the summer of 1841 and a Prussian ministerial

59. See the marginal note of Regierungsrat Ernst Wilhelm Bitter to the 18 March 1843 report of the *Rheinische Zeitung*'s censor, Wilhelm von Saint Paul, in Joseph Hansen, ed., *Rheinische Briefe und Akten zur Geschichte der politischen Bewegung 1830–1850*, vol. 1. (Essen: G. D. Baedeker, 1919), 490n2.

60. See Marx, "Debatten über Preßfreiheit," which appeared in May 1842 in the *Rhenisiche Zeitung*.

61. It finally appeared as "Bemerkungen über die neueste preußische Censurinstruction," *Anekdota über die neuesten deutschen Philosophie und Publicistik*, ed. Arnold Ruge, vol. 1 (Zürich and Winterthur: Literarischen Comptoirs, 1843), 56–88.

62. Up until the autumn of 1842, Prussia went beyond the Carlsbad requirements and subjected *all* publications, regardless of length, to prepublication censorship. See further Bärbel Holtz, "Zensur und Zensoren im preußischen Vormärz," in *Zensur im Vormärz: Pressefreiheit und Informationskontrolle in Europa*, ed. Gabriele B. Clemens (Tübingen: Jan Thorbecke Verlag, 2013), 105–19. Marx later commented that trying to circumvent censorship through longer publications was pointless, as "books of more than twenty printed sheets are not books for the people," Marx to Arnold Ruge, 13 March 1843, *MEGA* III.1: 44 / *MECW* 1: 398.

63. Marx to Arnold Ruge, 30 November 1842, *MEGA* III.1: 37 / *MECW* 1: 393.

64. See, for instance, [Heinrich Karl] Jaup, "Preßfreiheit," *Staats-Lexikon oder Encyclopädie der Staatswissenschaften*, ed. Carl von Rotteck and Carl Welcker, vol. 13 (Altona: Hammerich, 1842), 331.

instruction from 24 December 1841 that directed censors to take a more lenient approach to the existing censorship laws. While some Prussian liberals welcomed the ministerial instruction as a "pleasant Christmas present" that demonstrated the "liberal and broad-minded (*freisinnige*) intentions of the government,"[65] Marx insisted that the instruction was actually a "*pseudo-liberal*" gesture that tried to shift attention from the institution of censorship to the actions of individual censors.[66]

Marx argued that a close reading of the ministerial instruction showed that, in reality, the directive entrenched the paternalism and arbitrariness of the existing censorship regime. He documented how, again and again, the ministerial instruction avoided clearly defined, objective legal standards in favor of subjective personal judgment and disposition, with the result that "*all objective standards are abandoned*" and thus the instruction "introduces arbitrariness in the place of law."[67] This included the vague definitions of defamation and pernicious political tendencies and even the seemingly benign direction to censors to allow for "serious and modest investigations of the truth." Marx argued that these vague definitions made journalists "dependent on the *temperament* of the censor" who decided how to interpret those ambiguous terms.[68] Similarly, Marx noted that the supposedly positive instruction to censors that they should allow for the discussion of internal political matters in fact stipulated only that the "censor *can* [allow this], but he does not have to, there is no necessity."[69]

Marx concluded that the instruction thus continued to place censors in a position of arbitrary power over the editors and writers they monitored, a system he describes as one where the censor "is accuser, defender and judge in a *single person*" and "*unaccountable*" to the public.[70] Marx claimed that this "unification" of power in one person "contradicts all the laws of psychology" and reflected the "arrogant imaginary idea that the police state has of its officials," where induction into its service is supposedly sufficient to "convert a weak mortal . . . into a saint."[71] Marx charged the state with thereby distrusting the ability of citizens to freely and responsibly express their opinions, while, in the same breath, arrogantly demanding that citizens should place "unlimited trust

65. Julius Eduard Hitzig, "Einige Worte über die Bedeutung des Ministerial-Circulars vom 24. December v. J. in Bezug auf die Handhabung der Censur," *Berlinische Nachrichten von Staats-und gelehrten Sachen*, no. 24 (29 January 1842): 3.

66. Marx, "Bermerkungen über die neueste preußische Censurinstruction," *MEGA* I.1: 98 / *MECW* 1: 110.

67. Ibid., 109, 117 / 122, 129.

68. Ibid., 101, 107, 110 / 113, 119–20, 123.

69. Ibid., 103 / 115.

70. Ibid., 118 / 130

71. Ibid., 110, 118 / 122, 130.

in the estate of officials" to "act quite impersonally, without animosity, passion, narrow-mindedness or human weakness."[72] The consequence was that "the official is raised above the laws of psychology, while the general public remains under them."[73] For Marx, censorship thus placed an unreasonable faith in an individual's ability to fairly exercise their unconstrained power over others, when the experience of human psychology shows that such power has to be accountable and limited by objective legal norms. Marx believed that the unsurprising result of handing arbitrary power to the censor was to create a servile press, eager to please the censor and the authorities, a press characterized by "its hypocrisy, its lack of character, its eunuch's language, its dog-like tail-wagging."[74]

Marx's criticism of the arbitrariness of censorship was a standard complaint in liberal arguments for a free press.[75] A further common liberal defense of a free press—and one we do not find in Marx's writings—was that it was a necessary accompaniment to representative government and replacement for direct democracy. As one of the most prominent *Vörmarz* liberals, Carl Theodor Welcker, argued, since the "*daily, unmediated democratic* assemblies . . . of all citizens" that existed in ancient states had become impossible in large modern states, a free press provided all citizens with the ability to participate politically by giving them the opportunity to read reports of the legislature's activities and respond through public debate. Welcker thought this was a superior form of participation to "*unmediated democratic* cogoverning (*Mitregieren*)," since it presented citizens with a "more mature discussion" than that of "democratic popular speakers" in a direct assembly.[76] This kind of liberal argument for a free press saw it as a vital component in sustaining what they thought was the right kind of "*public opinion* . . . grounded in the moral judgment of the better and more intelligent" citizens on which representative government relied and where the press "enlightened the people about its own interests."[77]

Marx certainly shared the idea that an important justification of the free press was that it allowed citizens to be kept abreast of and to debate political matters. He described the press as a "speaking ribbon that connects the

---

72. Ibid., 110 / 122.

73. Ibid., 118 / 130.

74. Marx, "Debatten über Preßfreiheit," *MEGA* I.1: 146 / *MECW* 1: 158.

75. See, for instance, Jaup, "Preßfreiheit," 342. For the administrative background to this arbitrariness, see Holtz, "Zensur und Zensoren im preußischen Vormärz," 113–15.

76. C[arl] Th[eodor] Welcker, *Die vollkommene und ganze Preßfreiheit* (Freiburg: Universitäts Buchhandlung der Grebrüder Groos, 1830), 7–10. See further, Roland Gehrke, "Reflexionen zum Stellenwert der Pressefreiheit im politischen Denken von Karl Theodor Welcker," in *Karl von Rotteck und Karl Theodor Welcker: Liberale Professoren, Politiker und Publizisten,* ed. Hans-Peter Becht and Ewald Grothe (Baden-Baden: Nomos, 2018), 109–24.

77. Jaup, "Preßfreiheit," 341.

individual with the state" and as "the spirit of the state, which can be spread to every cottage, cheaper than coal gas."[78] But he never argued that a free press acts as a substitute for democracy and was unlikely to have been sympathetic to the idea. For one, his defense of the free press exhibits much greater sympathy for ancient democracies and their faith in the capacity of all citizens to exercise political judgment. Marx wrote that states "like ancient Athens" which trusted in the "people's common sense (*Volksvernunft*)" were states of "independence and self-reliance."[79] He also noted that while the Athenian democratic leader Pericles could rightly boast of "knowing the needs of the state," Prussian legislators laughably considered themselves to be the "hereditary leaseholders of political intelligence."[80] Marx further characterized Pericles's time as the period of "Greece's greatest internal flourishing."[81]

These comments do not necessarily imply that Marx favored simply reviving ancient direct democracy (his subsequent comments, explored later in the chapter, show an awareness of the need for some form of representation). But they do suggest skepticism toward the idea that political wisdom was the preserve of elites, whether political, administrative, or cultural. In this vein, Marx also argued that not only is a "cobbler" and a "day-laborer" just as, or even more, knowledgeable than a "lawyer" or a "theologian" about their particular professional spheres and the issues that affect them, but they should all, as citizens, have the right to "write about the most general, about the state."[82] Marx's conception of the free press also differs from the liberal account, in that he presented the press not as an external body that educates and enlightens the people, but as something that is part of and belongs to the people, describing it as the "embodiment of a people's faith in itself . . . the ruthless confession of a people to itself . . . [and] the spiritual mirror in which a people can see itself."[83] That reflected Marx's

---

78. Marx, "Debatten über Preßfreiheit," *MEGA* I.1: 153 / *MECW* 1: 165.

79. Ibid., 126 / 137.

80. Ibid., 169 / 181.

81. Marx, "Der leitende Artikel in Nr. 179 der 'Kölnischen Zeitung,'" *MEGA* I.1: 177 / *MECW* 1: 189.

82. Marx, "Debatten über Preßfreiheit," *MEGA* I.1: 164 / *MECW* 1: 176. Marx's argument has a certain similarity, perhaps deliberate, to the Platonic dialogue between Socrates and Protagoras over whether the "carpenter, smith or cobbler, merchant or ship-owner" possess sufficient wisdom and judgment beyond their technical expertise to discuss general "matter[s] of state policy"; see Plato, *Protagoras*, trans. C. C. W. Taylor (Oxford: Clarendon Press, 1991), 319a. It may also be an allusion to Hegel's sentiment that "just as one need not be a shoemaker to know whether one's shoes fit, so is there no need to belong to a specific profession in order to know about matters of universal interest," Hegel, *Philosophie des Rechts*, §215Z.

83. Marx, "Debatten über Preßfreiheit," *MEGA* I.1: 153 / *MECW* 1: 165.

diverging conception of the relationship between citizens, society, and the state, where citizens are not "educated from above" but instead the "state ... [is] an association of free human beings who educate one another."[84]

We have seen how a key component of Marx's critique of press censorship was that it unjustifiably exposed writers to arbitrary power. That is a complaint that Marx made again and again in his early journalism. In a subsequent article on a draft law on wood theft, he criticized how it would put poor peasants at an even greater mercy of the private power of forest owners and wardens. Marx specifically picked out the proposal to remove forest wardens' life appointment (wardens were semi-public officials, privately employed by forest owners but with certain state guarantees and duties, such as determining the value of stolen wood). Marx argued that removing their security of employment would make it even harder for the forest warden to "behave impartially toward the accused when he is the unconditional servant of ... [the forest owners'] arbitrary power."[85] Similarly to his analysis of the state's attitude toward its censors and bureaucrats, Marx condemned the "romantic conception of the forest owners" that their own "personal excellence" would be a sufficient guarantee for them to fairly exercise their power over those accused of wood theft. In fact, Marx added, what the forest owners really want is to have the "freedom to deal with the infringer of forest regulations as [they] see fit ... [and] at [their] discretion" so that they had *"plein pouvoir"* (full power) over them.[86] The general principle at stake here was the importance of an empire of laws in limiting the arbitrary power of men, with Marx telling the readers of the *Rheinische Zeitung* that "I do not at all believe that persons can be a guarantee against laws; on the contrary, I believe that laws must be a guarantee against persons."[87] Marx ended his discussion with a spirited endorsement of the rule of law, insisting that "no one, not even the most excellent legislator, can be allowed to put himself above the law he has made."[88]

84. Marx, "Der leitende Artikel in Nr. 179 der 'Kölnischen Zeitung,'" *MEGA* I.1: 181/ *MECW* 1: 193.

85. Marx, "Debatten über das Holzdiebstahlgesetz," *MEGA* I.1: 217 / *MECW* 1: 242.

86. Ibid, 217–19 / 243–44.

87. Ibid. 217–18 / 243. For the republican idea of an "empire of laws, and not of men" (as James Harrington influentially put it), see Philip Pettit, *Republicanism: A Theory of Freedom and Government* (Oxford: Oxford University Press, 1997), 39; Quentin Skinner, *Liberty before Liberalism* (Cambridge: Cambridge University Press, 1998), 75.

88.. Marx, "Debatten über das Holzdiebstahlgesetz," *MEGA* I.1: 217-18 / *MECW* 1: 243. For a legal analysis of the text, see Jörg Arnold, "Karl Marx und das Holzdiebstahlgesetz," in *Menschengerechtes Strafrecht: Festschrift für Albin Eser zum 70. Geburtstag* (Munich: C. H. Beck, 2005), 25–48.

Republican Freedom, Arbitrary Power,
and Democratic Self-Rule

Freedom was the central moral and political value that Marx appealed to in his early journalism. He maintained that the desire for freedom has a preeminent position in human nature. Opponents of a free press were led to the absurd conclusion that "freedom is not part of man's essence" when "freedom [is] after all the species-being (*Gattungswesen*) of all spiritual existence."[89] Because of freedom's importance to our nature, Marx argued that "freedom can never cease to be of value to mankind and "unfreedom is the real mortal danger for mankind."[90] In a Kantian turn of phrase, Marx criticized the "feudal . . . romantic . . . gentlemen" who opposed freedom of the press because they "regard freedom not as the natural gift of the universal sunlight of reason, but as the supernatural gift of a specially favorable constellation of the stars," and so believed freedom to be "merely an *individual property* of certain persons and social estates."[91] Such opponents of a free press thus did not, according to Marx, oppose freedom of the press as such; they simply opposed giving freedom of the press to the population at large rather than to a restricted segment of society. Marx expanded on this idea to make one of the most insightful points of his early journalism: that freedom is universally valued *by* all but not always valued universally *for* all. As he put it,

> Freedom is so much the essence of man, that even its enemies implement it while combating its reality; they want to appropriate for themselves as a most precious ornament what they have rejected as an ornament of human nature.
>
> No man combats freedom; at most he combats the freedom of others. Hence every kind of freedom has always existed, only at one time as a special privilege, at another as a universal right.[92]

Marx thus accorded freedom a central position in his political and historical analysis—but what did he mean by freedom? Marx interestingly clarified his understanding of freedom in the course of responding to an argument made by an aristocratic deputy in the Rhennish *Landtag*. Maximilian von Loe had argued against a proposed press law because it might have equally arbitrary outcomes to the existing censorship.[93] In response, Marx provided an impassioned

89. Marx, "Debatten über Preßfreiheit," *MEGA* I.1: 146 / *MECW* 1: 158.

90. Ibid., 152 / 164.

91. Ibid., 139 / 151.

92. Ibid., 143 / 155.

93. *Sitzungs-Protokolle des sechsten Rheinischen Provinzial-Landtags* (Coblenz: 1841), 113-15. For identification of the *Landtag* speakers in the anonymized transcripts, see *MEGA* I.1: 999–1001.

defense of the rule of law as constitutive of freedom and nonarbitrary rule. He argued that though censorship is formally enshrined in law it is not a "*real* law," because its essential nature is to subject writers to the arbitrary power of an individual (the censor), whereas a press law brings the operation of the press into the proper sphere of legal regulation and thus, Marx claimed, under "the rule of freedom itself."[94] Marx consequently dismissed the deputy's argument, insisting that "censorship and press law are as different as arbitrariness and freedom."[95] Freedom is therefore, by Marx's account, the opposite or absence of arbitrary power.

This conception of freedom entails a particular connection to law, that Marx elaborates in a celebratory passage on the law:

> Laws are not repressive measures against freedom, any more than the law of gravity is a repressive measure against motion . . . Laws are rather the positive, clear, universal norms in which freedom has acquired an impersonal, theoretical existence independent of the arbitrariness of the individual. A statute-book is a people's bible of freedom.[96]

Marx's claim that laws do not restrict a person's freedom might have an initially counter-intuitive aspect to it, especially to modern eyes. It stands in stark opposition to the view, particularly associated with Jeremy Bentham, that "[e]very law is an evil, for every law is an infraction of liberty."[97] That is

94. Marx, "Debatten über Preßfreiheit," *MEGA* I.1: 149–50 / *MECW* 1: 162–63.

95. Ibid., 153 / 165. Ruge was especially impressed with aspect of Marx's argument, praising it in his own discussion of press freedom; see "Die Presse und die Freiheit," *Anekdota über die neuesten deutschen Philosophie und Publicistik*, vol. 1 (Zurich and Winterthur: Literarischen Comptoirs, 1843), 110–11.

96. Marx, "Debatten über Preßfreiheit," *MEGA* I.1: 150/ *MECW* 1: 162. Interpreting Marx as defending freedom as the absence of arbitrary power in this passage contrasts with the suggestion that Marx here endorses a "*positive* concept of freedom" that links law to freedom because it is "realisation of the essence of a human being"; see Alexandros Chrysis, *"True Democracy" as a Prelude to Communism: The Marx of Democracy* (Cham: Palgrave Macmillan, 2018), 77. That argument, however, confuses why Marx thinks freedom is important with what he thinks freedom itself consists in.

97. The familiar quote comes not directly from Bentham but from the immensely popular French edition produced by his collaborator Étienne Dumont; see Jérémie Bentham, *Traités de législation civile et pénale* (Paris: Bossange, Masson et Besson, 1802), 79. For a similar passage in Bentham's manuscripts, see *Of the Limits of the Penal Branch of Jurisprudence*, ed. Philip Schofield (Oxford: Clarendon Press, 2010), 76, as well as *Rights, Representation, and Reform: Nonsense upon Stilts and Other Writings on the French Revolution*, ed. Philip Schofield, Catherine Pease-Watkin, and Cyprian Blamires (Oxford: Clarendon Press, 2002), 334. Whether Marx was familiar with this aspect of Bentham's thought is speculative (Marx's earliest explicit mention of

arguably, today, the more widely accepted view of law's relationship to freedom.[98] But, as we saw in the introduction, that view of the law in fact depends upon a particular conception of freedom. That is freedom understood as the simple absence of interference, an understanding of freedom that Bentham played a significant historical role in propagating.[99] Under freedom as noninterference, all laws (or at least coercive laws) inherently involve some reduction in freedom. It thus creates a justificatory hurdle to any legal and state intervention. By contrast, under the republican conception of freedom that Marx advances, laws do not inherently inhibit a person's freedom. If laws are nonarbitrary then the interference that they sanction is not arbitrary interference, and they thus do not constrain someone's freedom.[100]

Why did Marx think that law has a nonarbitrary character? He provided something of an answer when he considered Maximilian von Loe's position that arbitrariness was unavoidable in "imperfect . . . human institutions" as arbitrariness simply meant "acting according to one's individual views," and so "arbitrariness is . . . as inseparable from a press law as censorship."[101] For Marx, this amounted to an argument that since law must be administered by "imperfect . . . human" judges acting according to their own views, one may as well "submit yourself to the goodwill" of a censor. Marx replied that there was a categorical "difference between a judge and a censor," because while a censor is subordinated to other bureaucrats, a judge "has no superiors but the law," which means that a judge applies a "general" law "as *he understands* it after conscious examination . . . to a particular case," while a censor decides particular cases in line with how the law is "*officially interpreted* for him" and whether the

---

Bentham is not until 1845). The influence of Bentham's legal thought in *Vormärz* Germany was modest but more extensive than sometimes assumed; see Steffen Luik, *Die Rezeption Jeremy Benthams in der Deutschen Rechtswissenschaft* (Köln: Böhlau, 2003), 94–172.

98. Isaiah Berlin, for instance, credits Bentham's words with providing a central statement of modern negative liberty; see Isaiah Berlin, *Two Concepts of Liberty: An Inaugural Lecture Delivered before the University of Oxford on 31 October 1958* (Oxford: Clarendon Press, 1958), 8n2, 33.

99. Pettit, *Republicanism*, 35–50; Philip Pettit, "Law and Liberty," in *Legal Republicanism: National and International Perspectives*, ed. Samantha Besson and José Luis Martí (Oxford: Oxford University Press, 2009), 39–59; Yiftah Elazar, "Liberty as a Caricature: Bentham's Antidote to Republicanism," *Journal of the History of Ideas* 76, no. 3 (2015): 417–39.

100. Marx's view is thus, in this regard, closer to Pettit's, rather than Skinner's, conception of republican liberty, since the latter believes liberty is undermined by both domination and interference; see Philip Pettit, "Keeping Republican Freedom Simple: On a Difference with Quentin Skinner," *Political Theory* 30, no. 3 (2002): 339–56; and Skinner, *Liberty before Liberalism*, 83n54.

101. *Sitzungs-Protokolle*, 114.

case aligns with the "opinion of the censor and his superiors." Moreover, Marx noted that the "dependent censor is himself a government organ," whereas an "independent judge belongs neither to me nor to the government." Marx also favorably contrasted the "open act" of subjecting oneself to the judgment of a court with a censorship regime that keeps its decision-making "hidden" and "shuns the light of day."[102] Marx's comments thus suggest that the law, and the surrounding legal system, is nonarbitrary, because its rules and procedures are characterized by generality, neutrality, transparency, and independence from the government.[103]

In addition to these formal and procedural characteristics, several suggestive remarks from Marx indicate a thicker, democratic conception of what makes law nonarbitrary.[104] Following his above-cited description of law as the "positive, clear, universal norms in which freedom has acquired an impersonal, theoretical existence," Marx went on to argue that,

> Laws . . . cannot prevent a man's actions, for they are indeed the inner laws of life of his action itself, the conscious mirror reflections of his life. The law thus steps back in the face of man's life as a life of freedom, and only when his actual behavior has shown that he has ceased to obey the natural law of freedom does law in the form of state law force him to be free . . . [105]

Here the same point that law does not constrain one's freedom is supported by a seemingly different argumentation from that explored above: Marx suggests that law does not constrain one's freedom because it in some way corresponds to one's own life. But that idea, again somewhat counterintuitive, is not given further explanation or defense by Marx in the text.

One possibility is that he has in mind something like the Hegelian idea that the laws do not inhibit freedom as one comes to recognize that they reflect the requirements of reason and the institutional conditions for one's own

---

102. Marx, "Debatten über Preßfreiheit," *MEGA* I.1: 153–54 / *MECW* 1: 165–66.

103. Ibid. Marx acknowledges that it may not be possible for "all *arbitrariness* [to be] *absolutely* excluded" and that judges can err, but insists that this is the consequence of the "unreliability of an individual intellect" rather than the "unreliability of an individual character."

104. For discussion of procedural and more substantial accounts of arbitrary power, see Samuel Arnold and John R. Harris, "What Is Arbitrary Power?," *Journal of Political Power* 10, no. 1 (2017): 55–70. For a defense of a procedural, nondemocratic view of arbitrary power, see Frank Lovett, *A General Theory of Domination and Justice* (Oxford: Oxford University Press, 2010), 111–17. For critique, see Orlando Lazar, "A Republic of Rules: Procedural Arbitrariness and Total Institutions," *Critical Review of International Social and Political Philosophy* 22, no. 6 (2019): 681–702.

105. Marx, "Debatten über Preßfreiheit," *MEGA* I.1: 151 / *MECW* 1: 162.

self-realization.[106] While that may be part of Marx's meaning, it would not make sense of the essay's extensive engagement with the idea of arbitrary power nor explain Marx's specific use in the above paragraph of the phrase that law "force[s] him to be free." The latter is a fairly transparent reference to Rousseau's notorious claim that "whoever refuses to obey the general will . . . shall be forced to be free."[107] (Marx copied out this passage in his notes on Rousseau the following year.[108]) Rousseau justified that claim through the hugely influential argument that law does not undermine one's freedom when one has had an equal part in the shaping of it, when law is therefore self-imposed or self-made law: "obedience to the law one has prescribed to oneself is freedom."[109] Obeying self-made law has this freedom-preserving character, for Rousseau, partly because it is the "condition which . . . guarantees him against all personal dependence."[110]

Marx's nod to Rousseau's "forced to be free" suggests he was trying to convey to his readers the idea that if laws were to preserve freedom, they had to not only satisfy the formal procedural criteria he had outlined but be democratically made by the people. Spelling out that idea more explicitly in the article would, however, have risked an intervention by the *Rheinische Zeitung*'s censor. That dangerous Rousseauian idea is also buried in an aside in a subsequent article on divorce law, where Marx argued that we avoid "making arbitrariness the law" when "law is the conscious expression of the popular will (*Volkswillens*), in that it originates with it and is created by it."[111] Marx thus

106. As is argued in Andrew Chitty, "The Basis of the State in the Marx of 1842," in *The New Hegelians: Politics and Philosophy in the Hegelian School*, ed. Douglas Moggach (Cambridge: Cambridge University Press, 2006), 231. On Hegel, law, and freedom, see Dudley Knowles, *Hegel and the "Philosophy of Right"* (London: Routledge, 2002), 236–38; Alan Patten, *Hegel's Idea of Freedom* (Oxford: Oxford University Press, 1999), 190–91; Allen W. Wood, *Hegel's Ethical Thought* (Cambridge University Press: Cambridge, 1990), 40–41, 50–51.

107. Jean-Jacques Rousseau, *Du contrat social*, in *Oeuvres complètes*, vol. 3 (Paris: Gallimard, 1964), bk. I, ch. 7 / *The Social Contract*, in *The Social Contract and Other Later Political Writings*, ed. Victor Gourevitch (Cambridge: Cambridge University Press, 1997), bk. I, ch. 7. In part because of such statements, Pettit was originally keen to distance Rousseau from his understanding of republican freedom; see Pettit, *Republicanism*, 19, 30, though also see the partial corrective in Philip Pettit, "Two Republican Traditions," in *Republican Democracy: Liberty, Law and Politics*, ed. Andreas Niederberger and Philipp Schink (Edinburgh: Edinburgh University Press, 2013), 176–77. See further Annelien De Dijn, "Rousseau and Republicanism," *Political Theory* 46, no. 1 (2018): 59–80.

108. Marx, "Exzerpte aus Rousseau," *MEGA* IV.2: 92.

109. Rousseau, *Du contrat social*, bk. I. ch. 8.

110. Ibid., bk. I. ch. 7. On this point, see Frederick Neuhouser, 'Freedom, Dependence, and the General Will," *The Philosophical Review* 102, no. 3 (1993): 369–73.

111. Marx, "Der Ehescheidungsgesetzenentwurf," *MEGA* I.1: 288–89 / *MECW* 1: 308–9.

held that law upholds our freedom as the absence of arbitrary power when it is collectively made by the people, and we are therefore ruled not by a foreign (and hence arbitrary) will, but by our own.[112] That means that, for Marx, the rule of law is not by itself sufficient for upholding our freedom as the absence of arbitrary power; it has to also be law made by the popular will.

This combined view distinguishes Marx's conception of freedom from the liberal view defended by Karl von Rotteck in his influential entry on "Freiheit" in the *Staats-Lexikon* (the political encyclopedia he co-edited, often described as "the Bible" of *Vormärz* liberalism).[113] On the one hand, von Rotteck argued that freedom meant being "independent of any alien will or alien power" and that "*law (Recht) is nothing else than the rational ordering . . . of external freedom.*"[114] He was even willing to draw on the Rousseauian idea that when one enters a "*social contract . . .* [and] *submits to a general will*," obeying this authority "does not conflict with legal freedom."[115] Rotteck's view thereby departed from the strict freedom as noninterference view of law, as defended by Bentham. But Rotteck also rejected any democratic interpretation of his view of freedom where "political freedom is assigned to the people as a whole" since "*unlimited democracies* mostly transform into wild despotism. Political Freedom or the power of the collective easily devours or suppresses all particular rights of the individual."[116] Only state authority circumscribed to a limited sphere and hemmed in by the protection of the rights of the individual, including "freedom of *thought* and *conscience*, freedom of *speech* and the *press*, freedom of *occupation* and *trade*," would preserve freedom.[117]

---

112. While this Rousseauian view might be thought to diverge from Pettit's conception of freedom, it is, in fact, not far from Pettit's claim that the law does not infringe freedom as nondomination when "the people collectively control the formation of law"; see Pettit, "Law and Liberty," 53. The more relevant distinction seems to be what institutions are required to realize the idea of nonarbitrary power as democratic collective control, with Marx and Rousseau willing to countenance more popular institutions than Pettit. See further Robin Celikates, "Freedom as Non-arbitrariness or as Democratic Self-rule? A Critique of Contemporary Republicanism," in *To Be Unfree: Republicanism and Unfreedom in History, Literature, and Philosophy*, ed. Christian Dahl and Andersen Nexø Tue (Bielefeld: Transcript, 2014), 44–48.

113. Mommsen, "German Liberalism in the Nineteenth Century," 413. For the importance of Rottek's definition, see Annelien De Dijn, *Freedom: An Unruly History* (Cambridge: Harvard University Press, 2020), 260–63.

114. [Carl von] Rotteck, "Freiheit," *Staats-Lexikon oder Encylopädie der Staatswissenschaften*, ed. Carl von Rotteck and Carl Welcker, vol. 6 (Altona: Hammerich, 1838), 61, 66.

115. Ibid., 68–69.

116. Ibid., 70–71.

117. Ibid., 69.

Marx's own discussion of the law and freedom clearly shows a similar concern for the protection of rights such as the freedom of the press and the guarantee of an independent judiciary. But he departed from liberals like Rotteck by also tying law and freedom to the collective will of the people. Marx's view matches that of Ruge, who, as discussed above, had argued that liberals were "completely mistaken about the concept of freedom" because the "laws of free beings had to be their own product."[118] (Ruge also praised Rousseau's *Du contrat social* as the "gospel of freedom."[119]) The dividing line between liberals and republicans (at least in this historical instance) was thus not necessarily between liberals supporting freedom as the absence of interference and republicans supporting freedom as the absence of arbitrary power (as in some historiography of freedom).[120] The divide instead manifested itself in different understandings of what nonarbitrary power consists of, with liberals equating it with the rule of law and the protection of individual rights, while republicans insisted that these had to be supplemented by democracy.

Feudal, Liberal, and Radical Representation

Vormärz Prussia had no national representative body, and representation was limited to *Provinziallandtage* (provincial assemblies). These were purely consultative bodies, without the ability to advance legislation, convened at irregular intervals by the king and elected according to estates (*Stände*) and a franchise that excluded women, Jews, and those below the requisite property requirements. The Rhenish *Provinziallandtag*, for instance, which in the summer of 1841 held only its sixth session since 1826, was made up of four or five princes and twenty-five deputies apiece from the noble, urban, and rural estates, so that estates consisting, respectively, of 470, 490,000, and 1,680,000 people were assigned the same number of representatives, and the various franchise restrictions reduced the voting population to less than 100,000 (about 4.5% of the total population).[121] This form of feudal estate representation was anathema to liberals and radicals alike who wanted it replaced with a modern, national representative assembly, though liberals had no objection to the continuation of a property-based franchise and envisioned representatives holding a relatively

---

118. Ruge, "Selbstkritik des Liberalismus," 4/244-45.

119. Arnold Ruge to Adolf Stahr, 7 November 1841, *Briefwechsel und Tagebuchblätter*, 1: 247; *Redaktionsbriefwechsel*, 864

120. Pettit, *Republicanism*, chapter 1; Skinner, *Liberty before Liberalism*.

121. These are the figures for 1828; see Joachim Stephan, *Der Rheinische Provinziallandtag 1826–1840: Eine Studie zur Repräsentation im frühen Vormärz* (Köln: Rheinland-Verlag, 1991), 100–101.

free mandate, whereas radicals wanted such assemblies to be tightly controlled by citizens, elected by universal manhood suffrage, and supplemented by other participatory mechanisms.[122] Marx's criticism of the Rhenish *Provinziallandtag* exhibits both an unequivocal rejection of estate representation and a more veiled critique of the liberal model of representation.

Marx's central charge against estate representation was that it prioritized the particular interests of the estate representatives over not only the particular interests of those excluded from the assembly but also the general interests of the people as a whole. Due to their "specific composition," the *Provinzialland-tage* were "nothing but an association of particular interests which have the privilege to assert their *particular limits* against the state" and "must treat all general interests and even particular interests different from itself as things extraneous and alien."[123] Nothing demonstrated this more clearly for Marx than the *Provinziallandtag*'s debates on wood theft. The assembly's deputies systematically sided with the interests of the forest owner over "the poor, politically and socially propertyless many" who relied on their customary rights to the forest for survival.[124] This was an unsurprising outcome when the assembly included the "law-giving forest owner" who "confused . . . his two roles, that of legislator and that of forest owner," and whose attitude toward the state was that it was "an instrument of the forest owner and his interest" and simply "his business manager."[125] Marx thought this a grave failing of the assembly deputies who had a duty to represent not only particular interests but the general interests of the Rhine province, and "in case of conflict there should not be a moment's delay in sacrificing the representation of particular interest to representation of the interests of the province."[126] (The debates on the wood theft law in the *Provinziallandtag* might be thought a good example of why Marx thought law had to be democratically made in order to be non-arbitrary, since the expected result of excluding the mass of citizens meant that their interests were not taken into account in the formation of law.)

To this charge sheet Marx added that the assembly had refused to publish its proceedings in full. He argued that the assembly would not "be under its

122. Uwe Backes, *Liberalismus und Demokratie—Antinomie und Synthese: Zum Wechselver-hältnis zweier politischer Strömungen im Vormärz* (Düsseldorf: Droste, 2000), 369–74.

123. Marx, "Über die ständischen Ausschüsse in Preußen," *MEGA* I.1: 284-85 / *MECW* 1: 305.

124. Marx, "Debatten über das Holzdiebstahlgesetz," *MEGA* I.1: 204 / *MECW* 1: 230.

125. Ibid. 219, 225–56 / 245, 251–52. An interesting foreshadowing of Marx and Engels's more famous description that the "executive of the modern State is but a committee for managing the common affairs of the whole bourgeoisie"; see *Manifest der Kommunistischen Partei, MEW* 4: 464 / *MECW* 6: 486.

126. Marx, "Debatten über das Holzdiebstahlgesetz," *MEGA* I.1: 235 / *MECW* 1: 262.

[the province's] control" until the publishing of their debates was "no longer left to the arbitrariness of its [the assembly's] wisdom but has become a legal necessity."[127] Citizens had a right to know what their representatives said and debated in the assembly and exert public pressure on them—it could not simply be up to the discretion of the deputies to decide what the public should hear.[128] An assembly, Marx claimed, "flourishes only under the great protection of the *public spirit*, just as living things flourish only in the *open air*."[129] Ensuring this kind of public control and scrutiny was critical, because "A representation which is divorced from the consciousness of those whom it represents is no representation."[130]

Liberals would have been amenable to some of these arguments, including that representatives should represent the general interests of the nation and that the assembly should be a site of public political discussion, as well as the rejection of estate representation. They would, however, have been less sympathetic to Marx's idea that representation is not real representation when representatives are not forced to represent the "consciousness of those whom [they] represent," given their support for the Burkean idea that representatives should be independent from their constituents. They may also have objected to Marx's complete opposition to estates, since at least some liberals were willing to strategically countenance various compromise solutions.[131]

Where Marx stood on the crucial liberal-radical dividing line of manhood suffrage and property qualifications is hard to definitely establish on the basis of his early journalism. It has been argued that Marx was rejecting "equal voting rights"[132] when he argued that "[w]e demand not that in the representation of the people that actually existing differences should be ignored," only that they should be based on the "actual differences" and not the outdated estate categories.[133] While that could indicate support for some limits on extending the franchise based on differences in property, Marx's subsequent discussion suggests he was in fact referring to differing geographic interests. Indirect evidence for Marx's opposition to property qualifications might be found in his critical remarks on the influence of the particular interests of estates over the state, which he at points also extends to the influence of private property more

127. Marx, "Debatten über Preßfreiheit," *MEGA* I.1: 134 / *MECW* 1: 145.

128. Ibid., 134 / 146.

129. Ibid., 139 / 151.

130. Ibid., 136 / 148.

131. Backes, *Liberalismus und Demokratie*, 358, 369.

132. Heinz Boberach, *Wahlrechtsfragen im Vormärz: Die Wahlrechtsanschauung im Rheinland 1815–1849 und die Entstehung des Dreiklassenwahlrechts* (Düsseldorf: Druste, 1959), 78.

133. Marx, "Über die ständischen Auschüsse in Preußen," *MEGA* I.1: 276 / *MECW* 1: 296.

broadly, saying that it results in "the complete degradation of the state."[134] That could suggest an opposition to suffrage limits based on property since such limits would bias the state in favor of the particular interests of the propertied. More definitive evidence is provided by a set of international comparisons that Marx makes. Marx first favorably contrasted the "French and English deputies [who] are elected . . . as *representatives of the people*" with the system in Prussia, where the deputies are only *"representatives of landownership."*[135] Marx thereby indicated a preference for the liberal systems of representation in France and Britain over the system in Prussia. But when Marx then compared the residual feudal property requirements in Prussia with the more modern British and French property qualifications, he added as an aside that those "systems, by the way, we by no means agree with."[136] At the time of Marx's article, property qualifications limited the national voting population to about 2–3% of adult men in France and 15–20% in Britain.[137] By distancing himself from these models, Marx seems to have been signaling his support for a more extensive franchise. Expressing himself more openly, however, would have been anathema to his strategy of not unnecessarily opening a breach with the wider liberal movement.

Having rejected Prussian estate representation and (subtly) criticized the limits of the liberal models in France and Britain, Marx did not provide much detail on his most preferred system of representation. But some interesting clues are provided in a cryptic ensuing passage:

> In general, to be represented is something passive; only what is material, spiritless, dependent, imperiled, requires representation; but no element of the state is allowed to be material, spiritless, dependent, imperiled. Representation must not be conceived as the representation of something that is not the people itself, but only as its *self-representation* (*Selbstvertretung*), as a state action that is not its sole, exceptional state action, [and] is distinguished from other expressions of its state life merely by the universality of its content. Representation must not be regarded as a concession to defenseless weakness, to impotence, but rather as the self-reliant vitality of the supreme force.[138]

134. Marx, "Debatten über das Holzdiebstahlgesetz," *MEGA* I.1: 215/ *MECW* 1: 241.

135. Marx, "Über die ständischen Auschüsse in Preußen," *MEGA* I.1: 282/ *MECW* 1: 302–3.

136. Ibid. England's (or more accurately Britain's) system of representation, particularly as described by Montesquieu, was an important model for German liberals; see Backes, *Liberalismus und Demokratie*, 332–33.

137. Alan S. Kahan, *Liberalism in Nineteenth-Century Europe: The Political Culture of Limited Suffrage* (Basingstoke: Palgrave Macmillan, 2003), 37.

138. Marx, "Über die ständischen Ausschüsse in Preußen," *MEGA* I.1: 285 / *MECW* 1: 306.

While some have been eager to interpret the passage as a demonstration of Marx's supposed "larger objection to representation," that is a misleading simplification.[139] Marx is certainly objecting to forms of representation that leave citizens as "passive" observers of the political process, and he claims that this is true of most forms of representation. But he is also defending a kind of representation where representation is the *self-representation* of the people and in which representation is not the people's "sole, exceptional" form of involvement in political life (what this participation might involve remains unelaborated). Self-representation, Marx argues, does not see representation as a necessity because of the people's "weakness" or "impotence," but as part of a political system where the people form the "supreme force" in the state. Marx's radical view thus combines a critique of liberal representation where it completely displaces the people's political participation with an acknowledgment that representation should still play some (if unspecified) role in what he calls a "true state."[140]

Coda

Marx's early journalism was defined by the tortuous task of continuously pushing for progressive political reform without provoking the Prussian government into outright suppression of the *Rheinische Zeitung* through overt radicalism. Within those parameters, he defended a free press and the rule of law, and condemned the arbitrary power of censors, forest owners, and feudal legislators, while only covertly hinting at more radical ideas on representation and the expansive political role he wanted citizens to play in the state. Underlying Marx's critiques of arbitrary power was his central commitment to freedom. His republican conception of freedom (which has not been sufficiently appreciated) required not only the rule of law, but that laws be democratically made by the people. That view subtly distinguished him from the nondemocratic view of liberty defended by contemporary liberals. Yet Marx still insisted on the need for a broad front with liberals in order to more effectively challenge Prussian absolutism, and he consequently opposed the ultraradical provocations of the Left Hegelian *Freien*. Balancing such conflicting pressures, while doing his utmost to push against the limits of political and social transformation, was, as we will see, a recurrent feature of Marx's political life.

139. Gareth Stedman Jones, *Karl Marx: Greatness and Illusion* (London: Allen Lane, 2016), 112.
140. Marx, "Über die ständischen Ausschüsse in Preußen," *MEGA* I.1: 285/ *MECW* 1: 306.

2

True Democracy

MARX'S REPUBLICAN CRITIQUE
OF THE MODERN STATE, 1843

The development of the state to constitutional monarchy is the achievement
of the modern world.

—GEORG WILHELM FRIEDRICH HEGEL[1]

Is not the feudal state overcome through its consequence, the absolute
monarchy; this itself not overcome by its consequence the revolution and
the restoration and constitutional monarchy; this itself through their
consequence, the republic?

—BRUNO BAUER[2]

"ONE DAY," soon after the 1830 July Revolution "Hegel was a guest at the
crown prince's table. 'It is a scandal,' said the royal host, 'that Professor [Edu-
ard] Gans is making republicans out of all of our students. His lectures on your
philosophy of right, Professor, are always attended by hundreds and it is well
known that he gives your account a completely liberal, even republican coloring. Why don't you yourself give the lectures?'"[3] Stung by the crown prince's
criticism, Hegel replied (at least in Arnold Ruge's secondhand telling) that
he was not aware of Gans's transgressions and promised to restart the lecture
course. Whether or not that was in fact the motivating cause, Hegel did take

1. Hegel, *Philosphie des Rechts*, §273A.
2. Bruno Bauer, *Die gute Sache der Freiheit und meine eigene Angelegenheiten* (Zurich & Winterthur: Literarischen Comptoirs, 1842), 119.
3. Arnold Ruge, *Aus früherer Zeit*, vol. 4 (Berlin: Franz Duncker, 1867), 431.

up lecturing again on the philosophy of right in the autumn of 1831—a task that he had been happy to delegate to Gans since 1827. However, Gans and Hegel were now in direct competition, both lecturing on the same topic in the same term. The students' clear preference for Gans's lecture led to a bout of jealousy on the part of the aging Hegel, to the loyal Gans's considerable mortification. The old friends were able to reconcile two days later—but only on Hegel's deathbed. Hegel had become suddenly ill (attributed, but potentially mistakenly, to cholera) and he died on 14 November 1831, having delivered only the first of his proposed political philosophy lectures.[4]

The future Frederick William IV's accusation that Gans was turning his students (which later included Marx) into republicans was certainly an exaggerated fear.[5] But Gans did provide a more forthright defense of liberal constitutionalism in his lectures than Hegel's characteristically cautious approach (despite his undoubted commitment to a constitutional monarchy). Gans also signaled to his students a degree of openness to the future possibility of some republican institutions (compared to Hegel's outright dismissal).[6] The crown prince was therefore not entirely wrong to worry that Gans was giving Hegel's political philosophy a "completely liberal, even republican coloring."[7] But, as the crown prince's reaction shows, too open an advocacy of liberal and especially radical ideas was a hazardous endeavour in *Vormärz* Prussia, forcing writers into much more coded and careful statements of their ideas.

4. Terry Pinkard, *Hegel: A Biography* (Cambridge: Cambridge University Press, 2000), 655–59; Johann Braun, *Judentum, Jurisprudenz und Philosophie: Bilder aus dem leben des Juristen Eduard Gans* (Baden-Baden: Nomos, 1997), 85–86, 185–87.

5. Marx studied criminal law with Gans in 1836–37 and Prussian law in 1838, but he did not formally attend Gans's philosophy of right lectures (titled Natural Law and Universal Legal History). See Michael Heinrich, *Karl Marx und die Geburt der modernen Gesellschaft*, vol. 1 (Stuttgart: Schmetterling Verlag, 2018), 193–94. Whether Marx may have informally attended or indirectly known of their contents is speculative. For the (quite limited) evidence of Gans's influence on Marx, see Norbert Waszek, *Eduard Gans (1797–1839): Hegelianer—Jude—Europäer: Texte und Dokumente* (Frankfurt am Main: Peter Lang, 1991), 37–41.

6. Gans argued, in contrast to Hegel, that both a king and a president could conceivably be head of state, and he speculated that America's republican practice might one day arrive in Europe. Gans also endorsed a more inclusive set of representative institutions than Hegel, but at the same time argued in favor of British-style property qualifications on voting. His openness to aspects of "republicanism" thus did not extend to democracy. See Eduard Gans, *Naturrecht und Universalrechtsgeschichte: Vorlesungen nach G. W. F. Hegel*, ed. Johann Braun (Tübingen: Mohr Siebeck, 2005), 213–14, 228–29. Gans can thus be seen as a bridge figure between the more cautious (or conservative) liberalism of Hegel and the radicalism of the Left Hegelians.

7. As is argued by Johann Braun, "Einleitung," in Gans, *Naturrecht und Universalrechtsgeschichte*, xxi–xxv.

It was this necessity that had grated so deeply on Marx during his editorial career at the *Rheinische Zeitung*. He told Ruge that he was tired of fighting "for freedom" with "pinpricks rather than clubs" and the unedifying "bowing and scraping" that censorship necessitated. He quipped that by banning the *Rheinische Zeitung* the "government has given me back my freedom."[8] Marx used this newfound freedom to engage in an assault on both Prussian absolutism and Hegel's constitutional monarchism. Marx retreated to the Rhenish spa town of Kreuznach, where he married his longtime fiancée, Jenny von Westphalen. In Kreuznach he planned his future editorial collaboration with Ruge (who visited Marx in July), eventually settling on Paris as their base of operations to publish the *Deutsche-Französische Jahrbücher* and moving there in October 1843.[9] The intervening four or five months spent in Kreuznach were some of the most intellectually formative of Marx's life. He extracted a copious set of notes from an enormous reading list; contributed to a programmatic set of letters that were edited by Ruge and printed in the *Deutsche-Französische Jahrbücher*; and finally found the time for his long-planned critique of Hegel's account of the modern state.

In his letters, Marx condemned the despotic treatment of subjects and the exclusion of the mass of citizens from political participation that resulted from the arbitrary rule of absolute monarchs. In his critique of Hegel, Marx rejected his constitutional model of monarchy, which Marx argued only fractionally extended participation to the king's ministers, his bureaucrats, and the propertied elite. Marx expressed a preference for a republic over a constitutional monarchy, but also criticized the American model of a republic, where the people were still estranged from the political sphere and consigned to particularism of civil society. Marx thereby provided a republican critique of the three main competing models of the modern state.

But in perhaps the *Kritik's* most surprising and unique move, Marx did not end his constitutional critique with these three models, as, for instance, in the typical analysis of Bruno Bauer, where the republic appears as the final transcendent constitutional form that supersedes constitutional and absolute monarchy. Instead, Marx added and endorsed a fourth constitutional category,

---

8. Marx to Arnold Ruge, 25 January 1843, *MEGA* III.1: 43 / *MECW* 1: 397. Marx similarly said that it had become "impossible for me to write under Prussian censorship or to live in the Prussian atmosphere," Marx to Arnold Ruge, 13 March 1843, *MEGA* III.1: 45 / *MECW* 1: 400.

9. Helmut Elsner, "Karl Marx in Kreuznach 1842 / 43: Daten-Personen-Kreuznacher Exzerpte," in *Studien zu Marx' erstem Paris-Aufenthalt und zur Entstehung der* Deutschen Ideologie (Trier: Karl-Marx-Haus, 1990), 117–18.

a "true democracy (*wahren Demokratie*)."[10] In this as yet unrealized constitutional form, Marx argued that the people would hold active sovereign power through the popular public administration of general interests (rather than by professional civil servants) and the tight control over representatives through binding instructions. The people's alienation from general interests in the modern state would be overcome and they would act for the common good in their daily lives. In this democracy "the constitution is . . . established as the people's *own* work . . . as a free product of man" and would realize the desire "of *all* to be real (active) *members of the state* . . . to give themselves a *political being*."[11] "Democracy," Marx consequently insisted, "is the solved riddle of all constitutions."[12]

I begin the chapter with a more detailed account of Marx's intellectual activities during his time in Kreuznach and the account of the modern state he developed there. I then analyze Marx's critique of each of the three modern state forms, absolutist, constitutional, and republican, followed by an outline of Marx's account of a future democratic regime that is supposed to supersede the modern state. I criticize interpretations that see Marx's endorsement of a democracy and his critique of the particularism of the modern republic as evidence of Marx's having transitioned to a democratic position that is distinct from republicanism or of his having already transitioned from republicanism to communism. I end with an outline of Marx's early republican criticism of existing communisms.

Kreuznach and the Study of the Modern State

Over a lightning two-month period, from July through August 1843, Marx made his way through twenty-three books that were themselves frequently multivolume works, filling five notebooks with excerpts.[13] These *Kreuznacher Hefte* (*Kreuznach Notebooks*), as they are often called, consisted, on the one hand, of histories and contemporary observational accounts of various modern and historical states, with a particular emphasis on France and the French

10. Marx, *Kritik*, *MEGA* I.2: 32 / *MECW* 3: 30. Though I have used "true democracy" as the title of this chapter, Marx uses the term only once in the *Kritik*, and it is not clear that he invests much weight in the term, as compared to his use of "democracy" simpliciter.

11. Ibid., 31, 128 / 29, 118.

12. Ibid., 31 / 29.

13. I follow the dating of the *Kreuznacher Hefte* given by the editors in *MEGA* IV.2: 609. But it has sometimes been argued that they were in fact composed over a longer period, from May 1842 to August 1843; see Hans-Peter Jaeck, "Marx' 'Kreuznacher Exzerpte,'" *Jahrbuch für Geschichte*, 1982, 73–110.

Revolution, as well as America, England, Germany, Sweden, and the Venetian Republic. On the other, Marx read three classic works of constitutional and political theory: Machiavelli's *Discorsi sopra la prima deca di Tito Livio* (*Discourses on the First Decade of Titus Livius*) (1531), Montesquieu's *De l'esprit des lois* (*The Spirit of the Laws*) (1748) and Rousseau's *Du contrat social* (*The Social Contract*) (1762). All three authors had made appearances in Marx's journalism, suggesting that Marx already possessed at least a passing knowledge of their thought and that his Kreuznach reading was meant to deepen or refresh this understanding.[14] In his journalism, he had credited Machiavelli, Montesquieu, and Rousseau as being among those (alongside Campanella, Hobbes, Spinoza, Grotius, Fichte, and Hegel) who "began to regard the state through human eyes and to deduce its natural laws from reason and experience, and not from theology."[15]

Of the three, Marx's most extensive notes are on Montesquieu, with a particular focus on the first eleven books of *De l'esprit des lois*, often considered to be the sections of most interest, including the discussions of the principles of different governmental forms and the separation of powers (though Marx's notes also include a sprinkling of extracts from the final twenty books). Marx's extracts from *Du contrat social* are from the first three books of the text, covering Rousseau's central ideas on sovereignty, general will, and representation, and break off at the neglected final fourth book (and so Marx's notes do not cover, for instance, the sections on Roman political institutions and civic religion). Marx's Machiavelli notes are the shortest of the trio, essentially covering only the first third of the *Discorsi*. Marx read Machiavelli in a German translation, extracting some of the key ideas around the antagonistic relations between the nobles and the people in a republic.

While critical attention has naturally been drawn to these three classic works, the most consequential of Marx's readings that summer might actually have been a now almost completely forgotten travelogue, *Men and Manners of America* (1833), by the Scottish army officer Thomas Hamilton. As I argue below, Hamilton's account of America played a decisive role in Marx's account of a modern republic. The *Kreuznacher Hefte* primarily takes the form of copied out direct quotes with only a very sparse number of comments, making it difficult to discern Marx's opinions of his readings aside from his general

---

14. Marx, "Debatten über Preßfreiheit," *MEGA* I.1: 149 / *MECW* 1: 161; "Debatten über das Holzdiebstahlsgesetz," *MEGA* I.1: 202/ *MECW* 1: 227.

15. Marx, "Der leitende Artikel," *MEGA* I.1: 188-89 / *MECW* 1: 201. Montesquieu is not initially listed with the others, but a subsequent positive mention in the next paragraph suggests Marx also thought this applied to him.

interest in the topic.[16] His overall intentions in engaging in this enormous reading are not entirely clear, but it seems likely that it was undertaken with the aim of supporting Marx's primary intellectual pursuit at the time—his critique of Hegel's constitutional monarchy.

From roughly March to September 1843 (though the exact date is unknown), Marx finally managed to set down this long-planned critique, producing a hundred-page untitled manuscript, now usually known as *Zur Kritik der Hegelschen Rechtsphilosophie* (*Contribution to a Critique of Hegel's Philosophy of Right*) (hereafter *Kritik*).[17] Marx's *Kritik* takes the form of a paragraph-by-paragraph commentary on the final part of Hegel's *Grundlinien der Philosophe des Rechts* (*Elements of the Philosophy of Right*) (1820), which deals with the state and its internal constitutional makeup.[18] This section of Hegel's great work is often considered to be the least interesting and least convincing part of the book, even by otherwise sympathetic Hegel scholars, with one summarizing it as "a very turgid project" justifying a "ramshackle constitutional structure."[19] Marx's choice to focus on this section, rather than what, for instance, Hegel had to say about property or civil society, is sometimes seen as

16. A less restrained interpretative approach to these extracts is, in contrast, taken in Norman Arthur Fischer, *Marxist Ethics within Western Political Theory: A Dialogue with Republicanism, Communitarianism, and Liberalism* (New York: Palgrave Macmillan, 2015), 23–40.

17. Charles Barbour has recently challenged the traditional dating of the *Kritik*. He argues that while the surviving *Kritik* manuscript certainly postdates March 1843, the first half of it was likely copied by Marx from an earlier nonextant version he had begun in early 1842. Barbour argues that Marx then likely turned to the research embodied in the *Kreuznacher Hefte* in order to write the second half of the *Kritik* manuscript. Barbour maintains (rightly, in my view) that because of the positions defended in the first half of the *Kritik*, this dating would support reading Marx's 1842 journalism in a republican, rather than liberal, light. See Charles Barbour, "The Kreuznach Myth: Marx, Feuerbach and the 'Critique of Hegel's Philosophy of Law,'" *History of Political Thought* 44, no. 2 (2023): 390–414.

18. Marx's comments cover a slightly reduced number of paragraphs (§261–§313) from Hegel's subsection on the internal constitution. The first sheet of the original manuscript is missing, and it is probable that this contained Marx's comments on §257–60. The loss is regrettable not least because it would have covered Hegel's critique in §258A of Rousseau's social contract. Marx broke off the manuscript at §313 and did not comment on the remaining paragraphs in the subsection or the closing subsections on the relations between states (§330–40) and world history (§341–60).

19. Dudley Knowles, *Hegel and the* Philosophy of Right (London: Routledge, 2002), 326–27. For a convincing defense of focusing on exactly these institutional specifics of Hegel, see Elias Buchetmann, *Hegel and the Representative Constitution* (Cambridge: Cambridge University Press, 2023), 3, 18–19.

an inexplicable "oddity."[20] But Marx seems to have been drawn to it precisely because it provided him with a relatively detailed portrayal and philosophical justification of the lineaments of a modern constitutional monarchy.[21]

Marx's working approach in the *Kritik* was to laboriously copy out Hegel's paragraphs and subject them to individual lengthy critique. He claimed that Hegel would thereby be "translated into prose" and plain "German."[22] But the result is a text that is often less approachable than the hardly reader-friendly original. Marx never published the *Kritik* (it only finally appeared in 1927), and its clunky paragraph format suggests that Marx intended it as a self-clarificatory groundwork for an eventual public critique of Hegel's political philosophy,[23] a project that Marx continued to pursue for at least another year.[24] Despite being one of Marx's most extensive pieces of writing from the period (and certainly his most extensive discussion of politics), the *Kritik* has traditionally received less attention that Marx's other early writings (especially compared to the *Ökonomisch-Philosophische Manuskripte* from 1844). That relative neglect has begun to be remedied in more recent accounts of the young Marx's thought, which have also (in contrast to earlier interpretations) tended to stress the democratic and republican dimensions of the *Kritik*.[25]

20. Andrew Vincent, *Theories of the State* (Oxford: Basil Blackwell, 1987), 156.

21. Marx's interest in that subject at the time might also be gleaned from his notes on Montesquieu, where he copied out Montesquieu's well-known judgment that Britain was "a nation where the republic hides under the form of monarchy" and added (in a rare supplement of his own words) that this was a "constitutional monarchy." See Montesquieu, *De l'esprit des lois*, in *Oeuvres complètes*, vol. 2 (Paris: Gallimard, 1951), bk. V, ch. 19 / *The Spirit of the Laws*, ed. Anne M. Cohler, Basia Carolyn Miller and Harold Samuel Stone (Cambridge: Cambridge University Press, 1989), bk. V, ch. 19; Marx, "Exzerpte aus Montesquieu," *MEGA* IV.2: 109.

22. Marx, *Kritik, MEGA* I.2: 7, 17 / *MECW* 3: 7, 16.

23. Twenty years later, Arnold Ruge used a similar but more polished format for his critique of the same section of Hegel in his *Aus früherer Zeit*, 4: 381–419. Ruge makes many of the same republican criticisms of Hegel as Marx, and his text might be thought of as an approximation of what Marx's *Kritik* would have looked like had he brought it to publication.

24. This should not be confused with Marx's "Kritik der Hegelschen Rechtsphilosophie: Einleitung" (1844), published in the *Deutsch-Französische Jahrbücher* (dealt with in chapter 3). Though Marx intended his longer critique of Hegel to form the continuation of that article had the *Deutsch-Französische Jahrbücher* not been discontinued, see *MEGA* I.2: 581. For the first published version of the *Kritik*, see *MEGA*⑩, I.1, Halbband 1: 403–553.

25. Miguel Abensour, *Democracy Against the State: Marx and the Machiavellian Moment*, trans. Max Blechman and Martin Breaugh (Cambridge: Polity, 2011); Étienne Balibar and Gérard Raulet, eds., *Marx démocrate: Le Manuscrit de 1843* (Paris: Presses universitaires de France, 2001); Alexandros Chrysis, *"True Democracy" as a Prelude to Communism: The Marx of Democracy* (Cham: Palgrave Macmillan, 2018), chapters 3–4; David Leopold, *The Young Karl Marx:*

While the *Kritik* has the inherent interpretive drawbacks of an unpublished text not meant for public consumption (though also the advantage of not being subject to censorship), we do have one public source of Marx's political views at the time, namely Marx's contributions to "Ein Briefwechsel von 1843" ("A Letter-Exchange from 1843"). This text formed part of the *Deutsch-Französische Jahrbücher*'s opening programmatic statement (alongside Ruge's introductory "Plan") and consisted of eight edited letters between Ruge, on the one hand, and Mikhail Bakunin, Ludwig Feuerbach, and Marx, on the other. Three letters from Marx were included in this exchange, dated March, May, and September 1843, which provide some insight into Marx's political views at the time. That includes his suggestive statement on the need for "Human beings, that is thinking beings, free men, republicans."[26]

Interpretive difficulties arise, however, because none of original letters have survived, and we know that Ruge heavily edited the exchange by inserting phrases and rearranging and combining letters so that they formed a coherent conversation.[27] The exact contents of the "Marx" letters thus cannot be straightforwardly attributed to Marx.[28] We therefore should not put too much weight on individual statements in the letters, such as the above "free men, republicans," which may well have been inserted by Ruge. At the same time, it would be a mistake simply to dismiss the contents of the letters as exclusively corresponding to Ruge's views.[29] For one, Ruge himself noted that the final September letter was authentically Marx's.[30] Moreover, even if the language of parts of the letters seems to originate with Ruge, many of the

---

German Philosophy, Modern Politics, and Human Flourishing (Cambridge: Cambridge University Press, 2007), 254, 260.

26. Marx to Ruge, May 1843, "Briefwechsel von 1843," *MEGA* I.2: 475 / *MECW* 3: 134.

27. Ruge characterized his editing process as "writing several letters on the basis of originals from Bacun[in], Feuerb[ach], Marx and myself," Ruge to Julius Fröbel, 19 December 1843, *Redaktionsbriefwechsel*, 1331. We do not know enough about the editing process to know if Marx was in a position to oversee the final contents of the letters. For some description, see Ruge to Catharina Sophia Ruge, 28 March 1844, *Briefwechsel und Tagebuchblätter*, 341.

28. Engels later claimed that "Marx told me more than once that his part of it had been tinkered with by Ruge who had inserted all manner of nonsense," Engels to Wilhelm Liebknecht, 18 December 1890, *MEW* 37: 527; *MECW* 49: 93–94.

29. As in Allan Megill, *Karl Marx: The Burden of Reason (Why Marx Rejected Politics and the Market)* (Lanham: Rowman & Littlefield, 2002), 99–100.

30. Ruge wrote that all the letters in fact had "*one* author," with the exception of Feuerbach's and Marx's September letter; see Ruge to Jakob Veneday, 7 March 1844, *Redaktionsbriefwechsel*, 1339. Ruge also left out Marx's September letter when he later reprinted all the other contributions to the "Briefwechsel von 1843" in his *Sämmtliche Werke*, 2nd ed., vol. 9 (Mannheim: J. P. Grohe, 1848), 113–42.

substantive positions defended by Marx in the letters overlap with those in his other contemporary writings.[31] We should therefore treat the letters (even those from March and May) as being potentially indicative of Marx's views (if not necessarily his own language) and check whether they align with his contemporaneous views for further support.

The combined thematic focus of the *Kritik*, "Ein Briefwechsel von 1843," and the excerpts in the *Kreuznacher Hefte* can be summarized as an investigation into the "emergence, character and the (future) replacement of the modern state."[32] The most important finding that Marx derived from this investigation was that the central differentiating characteristic of modern states was that they were what Marx called "abstract" or "political states," by which he meant states wherein the political sphere and civil society had become split apart.[33] Marx argued that no such division could be found in previous historical state forms. In medieval states a person's political position and privileges were directly tied to their socio-economic status. Their socio-economic status as serfs, merchants, or lords, for instance, determined their political rights.[34] There was thus no separation between the two spheres, since "the *estates of civil society* as such and the *estates in the political senses* were identical."[35] Marx argued that a similar unity existed in ancient states, where a slave's socio-economic position meant that they had their "political existence destroyed."[36] But ancient unity also had more positive sides, and Marx judged the ancient Greek city-states to have had a unified character because the widespread political participation of its citizens meant that "the *res publica* is the real private affair of the citizens."[37] Ancient and medieval states were thus characterized by the absence of the political/civil society distinction that marks modern states. Marx identified the French Revolution as the key historical moment in the emergence of the modern state, since it "completed the transformation of the *political* into *social* estates" so that "*social* differences . . . are without significance in political life. The separation of political life and civil society was thereby completed."[38]

31. Inge Taubert, "Ein Briefwechsel von 1843. In: Deutsch-Französische Jahrbücher. Zur Authentizität des Textes," *Beiträge zur Marx-Engels-Forschung* 1 (1977): 29–45.

32. I take this apt summary from Leopold, who uses it describe Marx's early political thought as a whole; see Leopold, *Young Karl Marx*, 11.

33. Lucio Colletti, "Introduction," in *Early Writings*, by Karl Marx (London: Penguin, 1975), 33–34; Leopold, *Young Karl Marx*, 66–67.

34. Marx, *Kritik*, MEGA I.2: 33 / MECW 3: 32.

35. Ibid., 78 / 72.

36. Ibid., 120 / 110.

37. Ibid., 34 / 32.

38. Ibid., 89 / 80.

Marx associated the separation of civil and political spheres in modern abstract states with the emergence of a distinct set of interests and characteristics. Civil society was the realm of particular interests and was marked by *"private egoism," "individualism,"* and *"atomism."*[39] In contrast, the political sphere was supposed to be the realm of general or universal interests (*allgemeine Interessen*), which corresponds to humanity's "species-content (*Gattungsinhalt*)." But Marx argued that because the modern state only provided a limited and narrow form of political engagement, "the *true actuality* of *universal interests is merely formal.*"[40] Marx furthermore repeatedly characterized the political sphere in the modern state as remote from the everyday life of the citizen, calling it a "distant state . . . which does not touch him or his independent reality," and depicting political life in the modern state as *"life in the airy regions"*; and he contrasted the "heaven of its [the state's] generality" with the *"earthly existence* of its [civil society's] existence."[41] The modern state is thus characterized by citizens spending their daily lives in civil society pursuing particular and egoistic interests, with only very limited opportunities for acting on general matters in a remote political sphere. That feature of modern states corresponds to a further sense of what Marx means by "abstract" or "political" states—that in modern states the people are detached or alienated from the state. Whereas in ancient states there was a "substantial unity between people and state," the "otherworldly nature of the . . . [modern] political state" is the "affirmation of their estrangement."[42]

Marx credited Hegel with being the "only" philosopher to have recognized the cleavage between the political sphere and civil society as the defining characteristic of the modern state.[43] Hegel had argued that this cleavage gave the modern state a complexity that premodern states lacked, making previous staples of constitutional analysis outdated. He insisted that the "old classification of constitutions into *monarchy, aristocracy,* and *democracy* presupposes a *still undivided and substantial unity.*" Thus, while this classification was "true and correct" for the ancient world, where states lack *"depth* and *concrete rationality,"* it did not apply to modern states that did exhibit those characteristics.[44] Marx concurred with Hegel that the ancient tripartite division of constitutions was unsuitable to the modern world. As Marx put it, in "unmediated monarchy, democracy and aristocracy there is as yet no political constitution as

39. Ibid., 45, 88, 90 / 42, 79, 81.

40. Ibid., 33, 68 / 31, 63.

41. Ibid., 32–33, 87-88 / 31, 77–78.

42. Ibid. 32–33 / 31.

43. Ibid., 78 / 72.

44. Hegel, *Philosophie des Rechts,* §273A.

distinct from the actual, material state or the other content of the life of the people."[45] But where Marx parted ways with Hegel is that he believed that the split between the state and civil society was a partly regrettable feature of the modern world, which would be transcended in a future democracy that (as we will see) both draws from and supersedes the ancient model of "unmediated . . . democracy."

(Prussian) Absolute Monarchy

Absolute monarchy receives short shrift in the *Kritik*—unsurprising given the text's primary focus on Hegel's constitutional model and, perhaps, because Marx did not think it merited serious theoretical consideration. Marx's only explicit mention of absolutism is to note that while the French Revolution confirmed the division between civil society and the political sphere, this process had already been under way "in the *absolute monarchy*" that preceded it.[46] But the fight against absolutism and the corresponding frustration with the political backwardness of Germany is the central theme of all the letters, including Marx's, in "Ein Briefwechsel von 1843." That theme is aptly summarized by the call, in Bakunin's letter, for a "German 1789."[47]

In Marx's first letter, dated soon after the Prussian censorship of the *Rheinische Zeitung*, he reported to Ruge that the regime's "glorious mantle of liberalism" had been exposed for the sham it was and now its "disgusting despotism in all its nakedness is disclosed to the eyes of the whole world."[48] Marx ominously predicted that the Prussian Hohenzollern's "comedy of despotism" would end the same way that it had for the "Stuarts and the Bourbons."[49] In his reply, Ruge (affecting a political stance that he did not share in order to heighten the exchange's conversational nature) expressed greater skepticism about Germany's readiness for revolution, but maintained that he still hoped for a revolution because it would mean the "transformation of all hearts and the raising of hands in the name of the honor of free men, for the free state, that belongs to no lord, but to the public spirit (*öffentliche Wesen*), which only belongs to itself."[50] Bakunin, in turn, gently chided Ruge for giving up on the Germans

---

45. Marx, *Kritik*, *MEGA* I.2: 33 / *MECW* 3: 32.

46. Ibid., 89 / 79. The inclusion of absolute monarchies within the category of modern states is also implied by Marx's aside about "modern, including constitutional, monarchies"; see ibid., 65 / 60.

47. Bakunin to Ruge, May 1843, "Ein Briefwechsel von 1843," *MEGA* I.2: 480.

48. Marx to Ruge, March 1843, "Ein Briefwechsel von 1843," *MEGA* I.2: 471 / *MECW* 3: 133.

49. Ibid., 471-72 / 134.

50. Ruge to Marx, March 1843, "Ein Briefwechsel von 1843," *MEGA* I.2: 473.

too easily, even if he accepted that a political revolution was not imminent. Bakunin wrote his letter on the Île de St.-Pierre in Switzerland, where Rousseau had spent an idyllic six weeks in 1765 while seeking refuge from the political persecution following the 1762 publication of *Du contrat social* and *Émile*.[51] Bakunin reported to Ruge that "my belief in the victory of humanity over priests and tyrants, is the same belief that the great exile [Rousseau] poured into millions of hearts."[52] After comparing the Germans to the ancient Greeks, Bakunin ended his letter from "Rousseau's Island" with an orientalist call for Germans to once more fight for the "downfall of the Persians."[53]

Marx's withering assessment of Prussian despotism in "Ein Briefwechsel von 1843" suggests four criticisms of absolute monarchs: their attitude toward and treatment of their subjects, their effect on wider society, their monopolization of political life, and the arbitrary nature of their rule. Though we cannot rule out that parts of these criticisms may stem from Ruge, the contents of the arguments are not out of character with Marx's other writings at the time.[54] Marx first argued that despots viewed their own subjects with contempt and treat them accordingly. Marx recalled an infamous episode from the Battle of Berezina, part of Napoleon's disastrous retreat from Russia, where the emperor's alleged response to the sight of his own soldiers drowning in the river was to joke, "*Voyez ces crapauds!*" ("Look at those toads!").[55] Marx maintained that the episode was symptomatic of the attitude and behavior of all despots, whether a world-historical figure like Napoleon or the "wholly ordinary" king

---

51. On his stay, see Maurice Cranston, *The Solitary Self: Jean-Jacques Rousseau in Exile and Adversity* (Chicago: University of Chicago Press, 1999), 133–40.

52. Bakunin to Ruge, May 1843, "Ein Briefwechsel von 1843," *MEGA* I.2: 480–81.

53. Ibid., 482. For Bakunin's stay on the island, see E. H. Carr, *Michael Bakunin* (London: Macmillan, 1975), 17–18. For the recurrent use of the Orient as republicanism's despotic "other," see Patricia Springborg, *Western Republicanism and the Oriental Prince* (Oxford: Polity Press, 1992).

54. These criticisms are also not drawn from the two sections of Marx's letters that the *MEGA* editors conclude are especially likely to spring from Ruge; see *MEGA* I.2: 943, 945.

55. Marx to Ruge, May 1843, "Ein Briefwechsel von 1843," *MEGA* I.2: 476 / *MECW* 3: 138. Though Marx cautions that the story is probably fictional (it was a staple of German anti-Napoleonic propaganda), there does seem to be some contemporary basis for it; see Joseph de Maistre to M. le Comte de Front, 17 (29) December 1812, *Oeuvres complètes de J. de Maistre*, vol. 12 (Lyon: Vitte et Perrussell, 1886), 337; *Joseph de Maistre et Blacas: Leur correspondance inédite et l'histoire de leur amitié*, ed. Ernest Daudet (Paris: Plon, 1908), 214. It is also not the only instance of Napoleon expressing such views about his soldiers; he once told Metternich that "a man such as I am does not give a fuck about the lives of a million men," cited in Wolfram Siemann, *Metternich: Strategist and Visionary*, trans. Daniel Steuer (Cambridge: Belknap Press, 2019), 351.

of Prussia. A "despot always sees people as degraded. They drown before his eyes and for his sake in the mud of ordinary life" as "the sole idea of despotism is contempt for man, the dehumanized man."[56] Marx concluded that "for despotism brutality is a necessity and humanity an impossibility."[57]

Marx further argued that despotic rule corrupted all members of society, both in their character and in relations with each other. In a vivid image, Marx said that the Prussian king was "lord of the world, of course, only because he fills it with his society as maggots do a corpse."[58] The king maintained a society of masters and servants, where the former know that the "world belongs to them" and the latter have learned that they are "the property of their masters" and that their "function is to be obedient, devoted and attentive" to their masters." This "philistine world" was a result of the "[c]enturies of barbarism [that] engendered and shaped it" and it was only the "French Revolution which once more restored human beings."[59] Marx claimed that a king could never turn "his subjects into free, real human beings" because the "monarch is always only the king of the philistines."[60]

Marx also charged absolute monarchs with hoarding political power and denying their people their human nature as political beings. Marx remarked that in Prussia the "only political person" was the king, while his subjects, who are in fact "political animals," were reduced to just a "breed of slaves or horses."[61] That Aristotelian thought is subsequently made explicit, when Marx quips in response to Aristotle's claim that "man is by nature a political animal (*zoon politikon*)" that German society was so depoliticized that "the German Aristotle who wished to derive his Politics from our conditions, would write at the top of it: 'Man is a social, but wholly apolitical, animal.'"[62]

Finally, Marx attacked the arbitrary nature of absolute monarchy. Rule by an absolute monarch meant being "guided exclusively by his whims" so that

56. Marx to Ruge, May 1843, "Ein Briefwechsel von 1843," *MEGA* I.2: 477 / *MECW* 3: 138.

57. Ibid., 479 / 141.

58. Ibid., 475 / 134.

59. Ibid., 476 / 137.

60. Ibid., 478 / 139.

61. Ibid., 476, 477 / 137, 139.

62. Ibid. See Aristotle, *Politics*, in *The Politics and the Constitution of Athens*, ed. Stephen Everson (Cambridge: Cambridge University Press, 1996), bk. I, ch. 2, 1253a3–4 and bk. III, ch. 6, 1278b19. Marx may have intended to allude to the well-known description of Hegel as the "German *Aristotle*" by his student K. F. Bachmann in his "System der Wissenschaft, von G. W. Fr. Hegel," *Heidelbergische Jahrbücher der Literatur*, Abt. 1, Heft 4 (1810), 146. If so, Marx's critique of a depoliticized German society and its citizens can also be read as a pointed dig at Hegel's political philosophy.

"his personality determines the system" and "[w]hat he does . . . what he thinks . . . that is what in Prussia the state thinks or does." The unsurprising result of this uncontrolled power was a series of "ridiculous and embarrassing situations" and "fickle, headless and contemptible" decisions, which would not end as "long as whim retains its place." Marx lamented that little more could be expected of a ruler in a country where the "people have never known any other law but the arbitrary will of its kings."[63]

Marx claimed that these criticisms were true not only of absolute monarchy but could be expected to characterize any monarchical system. He made this point through a discussion of Montesquieu's division of constitutions in *De l'esprit des lois,* parts of which Marx had also extracted during his reading of the text that summer.[64] Montesquieu distinguished between three main types of government: (1) republican, (2) monarchical, and (3) despotic.[65] Montesquieu argued that in both monarchical and despotic government sovereignty rested in one person, but these were differentiated from each other by the fact that monarchies were ruled in accordance with law, while despotisms were ruled by personal will. Montesquieu further divided republican forms of government into (a) democratic and (b) aristocratic types, depending on whether the people as a whole or only part of the people held sovereign power.[66] Montesquieu maintained that each of these forms of government has an associated "principle," the underlying human passion which drives that form of government. For despotic governments it was *fear*; for monarchical governments *honor*; for aristocratic ones, *moderation*; and for democratic ones, *virtue*[67] (see figure 3).

In response, Marx objected to Montesquieu's attempt to differentiate between monarchy and despotism. He argued that these were really "names for a *single* concept," or at best slightly varying instantiations of the same underlying principle. Marx insisted that Montesquieu was wrong to claim that the principle of monarchy is honor, when it was actually "the despised, the despicable, *the dehumanized man*." Wherever the "monarchical principle has a majority behind it, human beings constitute the minority," and where it is not even questioned, "there are no human beings at all."[68] The implication would

63. Marx to Ruge, May 1843, "Ein Briefwechsel von 1843," *MEGA* I.2: 477 / *MECW* 3: 138–39.

64. Marx, "Exzerpte aus Montesquieu," *MEGA* IV.2: 106–7.

65. Montesquieu, *De l'esprit des lois,* bk. II, ch. 1.

66. Ibid., bk. II, ch. 2.

67. Ibid., bk. III, chs. 1–8. Hegel discusses Montesquieu's three regime types and their underlying principles in *Philosophie des Rechts* §273A, which suggests the possibility that Marx may have turned to Montesquieu while addressing that section of Hegel in the *Kritik.*

68. Marx to Ruge, May 1843, "Ein Briefwechsel von 1843," *MEGA* I.2: 477 / *MECW* 3: 138.

Sovereignty

people   *one*

(1) Republican   Rule

whole people   *part of the people*   *laws*   *personal will*

(a) Democratic   (b) Aristocratic   **(2) Monarchical**   **(3) Despotic**
(Virtue)   (Moderation)   (Honor)   (Fear)

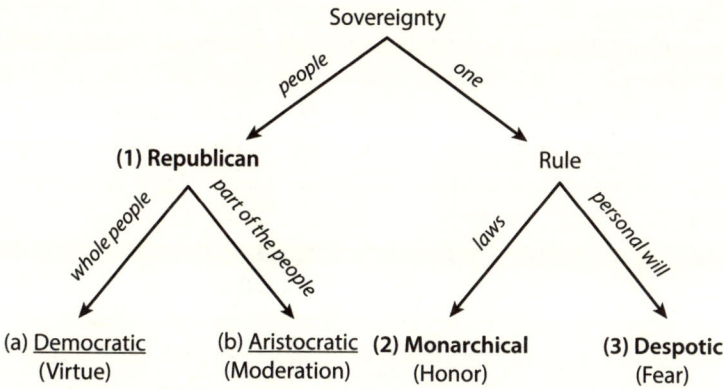

FIGURE 3. Montesquieu's constitutional typology. Governmental types are in
bold, subtypes are underlined, and associated principles are in parentheses.

seem to be that attempts to constitutionalize an absolute monarchy would still
leave a regime that was fundamentally opposed to the rule of the people. Marx
thus provided a republican critique of absolute monarchy for its arbitrary and
politically exclusive nature, while expressing skepticism that a constitutional
monarchy would do much better. That thought was properly developed by
Marx in his republican critique of Hegel's model of constitutional monarchy,
to which I now turn.

(Hegel's) Constitutional Monarchy

It might once have been considered controversial to examine Hegel under the
rubric of constitutional monarchy. A long interpretative tradition has condemned him as an "apologist for Prussian absolutism."[69] That understanding
was influential for parts of the twentieth century, driven by the slapdash scholarship of Karl Popper, but also has its predecessors in the some of the early
Vormärz liberal reaction to Hegel, including influential critical entries in Rotteck and Welcker's *Staats-Lexikon.*[70] Despite the longevity of this interpretive

69. Karl Popper, *The Open Society and Its Enemies: New One-Volume Edition* (Princeton:
Princeton University Press, 2013[1945]), 249.

70. Karl Hermann Sheidler, "Hegel'sche Philosophie und Schule," *Staats-Lexikon,* ed. Carl
von Rotteck and Carl Welcker, vol. 7 (Altona: Hammerich, 1839), 607–46; and "Hegel
(Neuhegelianer)," *Staats-Lexikon,* ed. Carl von Rotteck and Carl Welcker, 2nd ed., vol. 6 (Altona: Hammerich 1847), 629–64. See further Charles Barbour, "A Liberal before Liberalism:
Karl Hermann Scheidler and the New Hegelians," *Modern Intellectual History* 18, no. 3 (2021):
658–80.

tradition, there is little to say for it and it is dismissed by nearly all modern scholars of Hegel.[71] Quite simply, the political institutions that Hegel defends in the *Philosophie des Rechts* do not correspond to the Prussia of 1820.[72] Hegel endorses a constitutional monarch, equality before the law, freedom of the press, trial by jury, Jewish emancipation, a national legislative assembly, and a civil service appointed solely on merit (rather than noble birth).

That is not to say that Hegel did not provide ammunition to his critics through the somewhat accommodationist gloss in the preface to his work or that Prussia had no influence over his thought. But it is more accurate to say that Hegel's rational state "resemble[s] Prussia not as it ever was, but Prussia as it was to have become" if Stein and Hardenberg's liberal reform movement had not been defeated in 1819.[73] More recent scholarship has also emphasized the diversity of German constitutional influences on Hegel's thought, including that of his native Württemberg and the various German states he worked in before moving to Prussia in 1818 for the final thirteen years of his life.[74] While Hegel was certainly no radical, he was opposed to reactionary absolutism and was committed to moderation and liberal reforms. In the apt summation of the French liberal Victor Cousin: "He was profoundly liberal without being the least republican."[75]

71. See, for instance, Shlomo Avineri, *Hegel's Theory of the Modern State* (Cambridge: Cambridge University Press, 1972), 115–17; Michael O. Hardimon, *Hegel's Social Philosophy: The Project of Reconciliation* (Cambridge: Cambridge University Press, 1994), 24–37; Stephen Houlgate, "Introduction," in *Outlines of the Philosophy of Right*, by G. W. F Hegel, trans. T. M. Knox (Oxford: Oxford University Press, 2008), vii–viii; T. M. Knox, "Hegel and Prussianism," *Philosophy* 15, no. 57 (1940): 51–63.

72. The following account is heavily indebted to the succinct discussion in Leopold, *Young Karl Marx*, 57–61.

73. Allen W. Wood, "Editor's Introduction," in *Elements of the Philosophy of Right*, by G. W. F. Hegel, trans. H. B. Nisbet (Cambridge: Cambridge University Press, 1991), x. For some important differences, however, between Hegel and the reform movement, see Daniel Lee, "The Legacy of Medieval Constitutionalism in the *Philosophy of Right*: Hegel and the Prussian Reform Movement," *History of Political Thought* 29, no. 4 (2008): 628–29.

74. Elias Buchetmann, "Hegel's Intervention in Württemberg's Constitutional Conflict," *History of European Ideas* 46, no. 2 (2020): 157–74; Buchetmann, *Hegel and the Representative Constitution*, 38–39.

75. Victor Cousin, "Souvenirs d'Allemagne: Bataille de Lützen.—M. Fries.—M. Sulpice Boisserée.—M. Creuzer.—H. Hegel.," *Revue des deux mondes*, vol. 64, no. 3 (August 1866): 616. I do not aim to take a stand on the debate about whether Hegel was a liberal (as against, say, being a communitarian)—I only maintain that his institutional prescriptions largely match those of nineteenth-century liberalism.

While the "Prussian interpretation" of Hegel has been nearly universally discredited, it lives a curious afterlife in the still quite widespread assumption that Marx subscribed to it. Versions of the claim can be found, perhaps excusably, in various general studies on Marx or the modern state,[76] as well as in Hegel scholarship keen to shield Hegel from the Prussian misreading.[77] But, remarkably, the claim even makes its way into scholarship focused on Marx's *Kritik*.[78] Convincing textual evidence is rarely supplied for these claims, if it is supplied at all.[79] There is in fact no reason to think that Marx changed his mind about the nature of Hegel's state from his 1842 judgment that it was a "*constitutional monarchy*" and as such a "through and through self-contradictory and self-abolishing hybrid."[80] Indeed, in the *Kritik* Marx explicitly judges Hegel to have "deduced not a patriarchal, but a *modern constitutional* king."[81]

This does not mean that Marx thought Hegel's ideas had *no* affinity with the Prussian state.[82] As discussed below, Marx makes a particular connection between Hegel's civil service and the Prussian bureaucracy. But, insofar as

76. Sidney Hook, *From Hegel to Marx: Studies in the Intellectual Development of Karl Marx* (New York: Reynal & Hitchcock, 1936), 19–20; Duncan Kelly, "Karl Marx and Historical Sociology," in *Handbook of Historical Sociology*, ed. Gerard Deranty, Engin F. Isin, and Margaret R. Somers (London: Sage, 2003), 16; Michael Rosen, "Karl Marx," in *Routledge Encyclopaedia of Philosophy*, ed. Edward Craig, vol. 4 (London: Routledge, 1998), 118; Martin Shaw, *Theory of the Global State: Globality as Unfinished Revolution* (Cambridge: Cambridge University Press, 2000), 35; Vincent, *Theories of the State*, 156–57.

77. Thom Brooks, "No Rubber Stamp: Hegel's Constitutional Monarch," *History of Political Thought* 28, no. 1 (2007): 92n4; Andrew Buchwalter, *Dialectics, Politics, and the Contemporary Value of Hegel's Practical Philosophy* (New York: Routledge, 2012), 41; Karl-Heinz Ilting, "Hegels Begriff des Staates und die Kritik des jungen Marx," *Rivista di filosofia* 7–8–9 (1977): 144; Bernard Yack, "The Rationality of Hegel's Concept of Monarchy," *The American Political Science Review* 74, no. 3 (1980): 709.

78. Lloyd D. Easton and Kurt H. Guddat, "Introduction," in *Writings of the Young Marx on Philosophy and Society*, by Karl Marx (Indianapolis: Hacket, 1997 [1976]), 12; M. W. Jackson, "Marx's 'Critique of Hegel's *Philosophy of Right*,'" *History of European Ideas* 12, no. 6 (1990): 800, 808; Joseph O'Malley, "Editor's Introduction," in *Critique of Hegel's "Philosophy of Right,"* by Karl Marx, trans. Annette Jollin and Joseph O'Malley (Cambridge: Cambridge University Press, 1970), li.

79. One commentator simply cites the one passage where Marx mentions absolute monarchy in the *Kritik*, seemingly unaware that Marx is referring to neither Hegel nor Prussia. See Thom Brooks, *Hegel's Political Philosophy: A Systematic Reading of the Philosophy of Right* (Edinburgh: Edinburgh University Press, 2007), 162n2.

80. Marx to Arnold Ruge, 5 March 1842, *MEGA* III.1: 22 / *MECW* 1: 382–83.

81. Marx, *Kritik*, *MEGA* I.2: 104 / *MECW* 3: 94.

82. Leopold, *The Young Karl Marx*, 61.

Marx can be said to criticise Hegel for philosophically reproducing and justifying the status quo, it is not primarily the *Prussian* status quo that Marx has in mind but that of the two model constitutional states of Europe: Britain and especially France. These states play as prominent a role in the *Kritik* as Prussia does, and it is these states that Marx has in mind when he accuses Hegel of "converting all the attributes of the constitutional monarch in today's Europe into the absolute self-determinations of the *will*."[83] There is thus as little basis for attributing a Prussian absolutist reading of Hegel to Marx as there is to Hegel himself. Indeed, many years after the *Kritik*, when Engels wrote to Marx to condemn recent attempts to paint Hegel "as the discoverer (!) and glorifier (!!) of the royal Prussian *idea of the state* (!!!)," Marx readily replied that anyone who wished to "repeat the old Rotteck-Welcker muck" about Hegel would do better to "keep his mouth shut."[84]

Having hopefully cleared the ground of misconceptions about Hegel (and Marx's view of Hegel), we can now turn to the substance of Hegel's state (and Marx's critique thereof). Hegel presents his rational state as composed of three elements: (1) the *monarchical* or *princely* power (2) the *executive* power, and (3) the *legislative* power (figure 4 is an attempt to depict the institutional details of these three elements).[85] Hegel considered this a superior tripartite conceptualization of the modern constitutional state to Montesquieu's separation of executive, judicial, and legislative powers, which Hegel believed set up the powers in competition with each other rather than as elements of an organic whole.[86] Since Marx's *Kritik* closely follows Hegel's own sequence of presentation, his critique of Hegel's state can be profitably divided

---

83. Marx, *Kritik*, MEGA I.2: 26 /MECW 3: 25. France was only a partially constitutional monarchy when Hegel published the *Philosophie des Rechts* in 1820. Marx treats France's subsequent 1830 July Monarchy as a truer instantiation of the *"principle* of constitutional monarchy" than that which "Hegel [had] tried to develop" and Britain as a constitutional monarchy contemporaneous to Hegel whose *"empirical* political existence Hegel has in mind." See Marx, *Kritik*, MEGA I.2: 122–23 / MECW 3: 113.

84. Engels to Marx, 8 May 1870, and Marx to Engels, 10 May 1870, *MEW* 32: 501, 503; *MECW* 43: 509, 511.

85. This presentation is indebted to the version in Kenneth Westphal, "The Basic Context and Structure of Hegel's *Philosophy of Right*," in *The Cambridge Companion to Hegel*, ed. Frederick C. Beiser (Cambridge: Cambridge University Press, 1993), 269. For the complicated and counterintuitive positioning of the judiciary and public authority, see Hardimon, *Hegel's Social Philosophy*, 206–9.

86. Hegel, *Philosophie des Rechts*, §273, §272A, §273A. For further discussion of these elements and their evolution from Hegel's earlier lectures, see Ludwig Siep, "Hegels Theorie der Gewaltenteilung," in *Hegels Rechtsphilosophie im Zusammenhang der europaischen Verfassungs-*

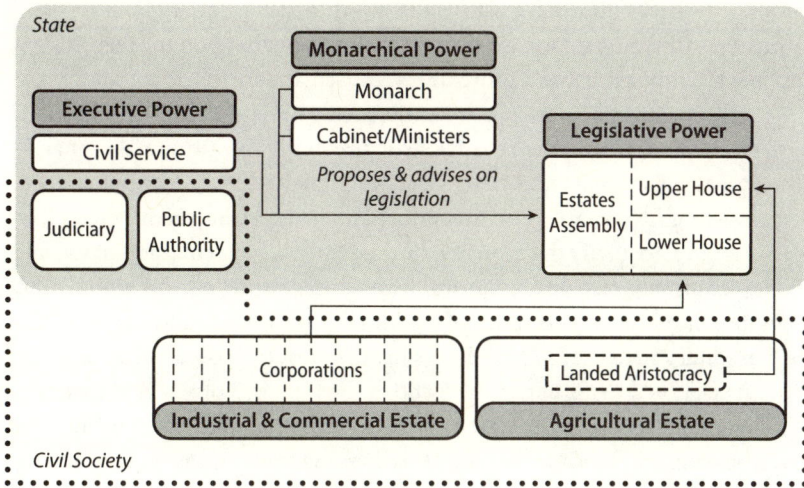

FIGURE 4. Hegel's constitutional structure

into his objections to each of the three elements, and the following discussion is structured accordingly. Underlying Marx's republican critique of all three elements is that Hegel had removed the people from effective political power and participation and that therefore his "constitutional monarchy is compatible only with the *people en miniature*."[87]

Hegel's monarchical or princely power (*fürstliche Gewalt*) is made of the monarch and his ministers. The king (Hegel prefers a male monarch) has a seemingly circumscribed role in the constitutional structure. The monarch cannot "act arbitrarily" because he is bound by the advice of his ministers who submit laws and decisions to him for approval, and Hegel assures us that the king "often has nothing more to do than to sign his name," is simply "someone to say 'yes' and to dot the 'i,'" and therefore the "particular character of [the throne's] occupant is of no significance."[88] On the other hand, Hegel reserved to the monarch the right to pardon criminals and, importantly, the right to appoint and dismiss ministers. He also insisted that the monarch must be hereditary (rather than elected) and that the state's sovereignty rests in him in alone, making him

---

geschichte, ed. Hans-Christian Lucas and Otto Pöggeler (Stuttgart: Frommann-Holzboog, 1986), 400–404.

87. Marx, *Kritik, MEGA* I.2: 93 / *MECW* 3: 84.

88. Hegel, *Philosophie des Rechts*, §279A, §280Z, §283. See §166Z for Hegel's suggestion that women are unsuitable to lead the state. See further Brooks, "No Rubber Stamp: Hegel's Constitutional Monarch," 104–5.

the final, decisive figure in legislative and constitutional matters.[89] Hegel's king is thus a constitutional monarch but one who, depending on the features one chooses to emphasize, has a more or less muscular constitutional role.[90]

Hegel's constitutional monarch has been judged "[p]erhaps the greatest internal weakness" within the broader structure of his constitutional monarchy and "[v]irtually no one today finds Hegel's arguments for . . . [the monarch] to be compelling."[91] Marx was no exception, and he especially hammered Hegel for his attempt to justify the monarch through the Hegelian method of speculative logic: turning ordinary, empirical features of existing constitutional monarchs into the necessary demands of the Idea.[92] Hegel, for instance, insisted that the hereditary nature of monarch was justified not by base considerations of avoiding factional strife, but by the fact that the monarch provides the element of individuality in the state and the "natural *birth*" of an individual is "inherent to its very concept."[93] Marx dismissed this dizzying argument as proving nothing beyond the platitude that the monarch has to be born. He thus retorted, "That man becomes a monarch by birth can no more be made into a metaphysical truth than the immaculate conception of the mother Mary."[94] Hegel further embarrassed himself, according to Marx, with his insistence that the monarch should have an "unrestricted choice" of their ministers, to which Marx replied, "[i]n the same way the 'unrestricted choice' of the monarch's *valet* can be derived from the absolute Idea."[95] Marx had no more sympathy for Hegel's defense of the monarch's right to pardon. In a reappearance of his familiar objection to arbitrary power, Marx argued that this power amounted to a "prerogative of *mercy*" and "[m]ercy is the highest expression of *haphazard arbitrariness* (*zufälligen Willkühr*)."[96] Thus, for all of Hegel's constitutional niceties, Marx maintained that arbitrariness remained "the essential attribute of the monarch," so that "one individual is the *hallowed, sanctified embodiment* of arbitrariness

89. Hegel, *Philosophie des Rechts*, §279, §282–283, §300.

90. Knowles helpfully distinguishes between a "hard" and "soft" reading of the monarch's power. See *Hegel and the* Philosophy of Right, 329–30; as well as Brooks, "No Rubber Stamp: Hegel's Constitutional Monarch."

91. Respectively, Westphal, "The Basic Context and Structure of Hegel's *Philosophy of Right*," 262; Hardimon, *Hegel's Social Philosophy*, 215.

92. Marx, *Kritik*, *MEGA* I.2: 26 / *MECW* 3: 25. Ruge had made the same complaint in his "Die Hegelsche Rechtsphilosophie und die Politik unsrer Zeit," *Deutsche Jahrbücher*, no. 191 (12 August 1842): 763.

93. Hegel, *Philosophie des Rechts*, §280, §281A.

94. Marx, *Kritik*, *MEGA* I.2: 34 / *MECW* 3: 33.

95. Ibid., 38 / 36.

96. Ibid., 37 / 35.

(*Willkühr*)," with the result that "The constitution of the constitutional monarch is *irresponsibility* (*Unverantwortlichkeit*)."[97]

In addition to Marx's objections to the individual arbitrary powers that Hegel assigned to the monarch, Marx also rejected Hegel's attempt to assign him sovereignty. Hegel had argued that sovereignty must rest in in "*one* individual, the *monarch*," justified by the need for a single individual to have the final, decisive say.[98] Hegel was willing to grant a limited legitimacy to the idea of *Volkssouveränität* if that was understood as either external national independence or the idea that internal sovereignty rested with the state as a whole.[99] "But," Hegel continued,

> the usual sense in which the term popular sovereignty (*Volkssouveränität*) has begun to be used in recent times is to denote *the opposite of that sovereignty which exists in the monarch*. In this oppositional sense, popular sovereignty is one of those confused thoughts which are based on a *garbled* notion of the *people*. *Without* its monarch . . . *the* people is a formless mass.[100]

Marx was wholly unimpressed by this argumentation. He replied that the only thoughts that were "confused" or "*garbled*" were "exclusively Hegel's."[101] Even if sovereignty must reside in a single individual, Hegel had not shown that this individual must be a monarch.[102] To the two limited uses that Hegel allowed to *Volkssouveränität*, Marx first responded that if a monarch enjoyed external sovereignty in his own right there would be no need to refer to the people (the *Volk* in *Volkssouveränität*), thus implying that the monarch in fact only enjoyed sovereignty because he was the representative of the people. Second, Marx

---

97. Ibid., 37–39 / 35–37.

98. Hegel, *Philosophie des Rechts*, §278–79.

99. Since *Volk* can mean both "nation" and "people," the German *Volkssouveränität* lacks the linguistic differentiation available in English and French between national sovereignty (*souveraineté nationale*) and popular sovereignty (*souveraineté populaire*). See Duncan Kelly, "Popular Sovereignty as State Theory in the Nineteenth Century," in *Popular Sovereignty in Historical Perspective*, ed. Richard Bourke and Quentin Skinner (Cambridge: Cambridge University Press, 2016), 273–74.

100. Hegel, *Philosophie des Rechts*, §279A.

101. Marx, *Kritik*, MEGA I.2: 29 / MECW 3: 28.

102. Ibid., 27 / 25. Gans had made a similar point in his lectures, since "though in republics some activity is carried out by assemblies, only one individual makes the crucial decision" and so there is "no difference between a monarch and a president." Gans consequently subtly renamed Hegel's monarchical/princely power (*fürstliche Gewalt*) the state power (*Staatsgewalt*), and argued it could be either republican or monarchical; see Gans, *Naturrecht und Universalrechtsgeschichte*, 213–14.

thought it typical of Hegel to be prepared to grant sovereignty to an "abstract" thing like the state, while denying it to a "concrete . . . living" thing like the people.[103] Marx further disputed the suggestion (though it is unclear if this is Hegel's reasoning) that popular sovereignty is confused because it posits the people's sovereignty against the monarch's sovereignty, when in fact sovereignty, by definition, can have only one ultimate power. Marx argued that Hegel has dodged the central political debate because insisting that the sovereignty of the people is the opposite of the monarch's sovereignty does not mean that they are two opposed aspects of one sovereign, but that they are "two *entirely contradictory concepts of sovereignty.*" The choice then is over which of these is the correct idea of sovereignty. As Marx put it (switching to English to emphasize the allusion to Hamlet), "Sovereignty of the monarch or sovereignty of the people, that is the question."[104]

Within that question, Marx sided definitively against the "illusion" of monarchical sovereignty, which he thought had the consequence that "all others [apart from the monarch] are excluded from this sovereignty, from personality and from political consciousness."[105] Marx's concomitant endorsement of popular sovereignty interpreted the idea in a particularly active form, where popular authority and involvement were not limited to a singular founding moment but were a continuous feature of the political system.[106] He argued that in a democracy "not merely *implicitly* and in essence but existing in reality, the constitution is constantly brought back to its actual basis, the *actual human being*, the actual *people*, and established as the *people's* own work. The constitution appears as what it is, the free product of man."[107] This active popular sovereignty included, for Marx, a people's continuous right to renew or replace their constitution: "Has the people the right to give itself a new constitution? The answer must be an unqualified 'Yes,' because once it has ceased to be an actual expression of the will of the people the constitution has become a practical illusion."[108] In summary, Marx rejected the arbitrary power that Hegel granted to his supposedly constitutional monarch as well as Hegel's attempt to assign sovereignty to the monarch. Instead, Marx endorsed an active conception of popular sovereignty, where the people play an ongoing role in the running of their polity.

103. Marx, *Kritik*, *MEGA* I.2: 27 / *MECW* 3: 25.

104. Ibid., 29–30 / 28.

105. Ibid., 27 / 26.

106. For the idea of active popular sovereignty, see Stuart White, "Rousseau and the Meaning of Popular Sovereignty," in *Ideas That Matter: Democracy, Justice, Rights*, ed. Debra Satz and Annabelle Lever (Oxford: Oxford University Press, 2019), 67–88.

107. Marx, *Kritik*, *MEGA* I.2: 31 / *MECW* 3: 29.

108. Ibid., 61 / 57.

The core of Hegel's second constitutional element, the executive power (*Regierungsgewalt*), is the professional civil service.[109] The civil service is the "universal estate (*allgemeine Stand*)" tasked with providing a universal perspective in contrast with the particularism of civil society.[110] It implements and enforces the decisions of the monarchical power and advises on legislation. The impartiality and integrity of civil servants is guaranteed, according to Hegel, by their independent salary, training, and professional ethic, as well as their supervision from above by the king and more senior bureaucrats and from below by the civil society corporations.[111] While aspects of Hegel's civil service are clearly inspired by Prussian practice, he also insisted that all positions must be filled on the basis of merit rather than noble birth (as was the case in Prussia), so that "every citizen [has] the possibility of joining the universal estate."[112] Commentators normally judge the executive to be the "real seat of power" in Hegel's constitution so that neither "the prince nor . . . the people, but . . . an educated class of professional civil servants" are the real driving force in the state.[113]

For Marx, Hegel's civil service was in fact a "*bureaucracy*," an unaccountable and elite body which served its own interest and excluded the people from public administration.[114] Marx argued that Hegel's confidence in the civil service's ability to act in the general interest was severely misguided. Individual civil servants were instead motivated by the "*hunt for higher posts, the making of a career*" so that "the state objective turns into his private objective" and, on the collective level, "department objectives [are transformed] into objectives of the state." Rather than being the universal estate of Hegel's imagining, the bureaucracy was thus in fact a "*particular, closed* society within the state" that "protect[s] the *imaginary* generality of [its] . . . particular interest" and consequently the bureaucracy takes the state in its "possession, its *private property*."[115] The end result is that the supposed "*matters of general concern*" decided upon by the bureaucracy fail to match the "actual concerns of the people."[116]

---

109. Hegel, *Philosophie des Rechts*, §287. The executive also includes what Hegel calls the *Polizei* (usually translated as the public authority) and, somewhat unusually, the judiciary, both of which Hegel introduces earlier in *Philosophie des Rechts*. It is not immediately apparent how the civil service differs from the public authority (*Polizei*) discussed in §231–49, which regulates and administers the needs of civil society. It is possible that the civil service is a superior body dealing with more general matters.

110. Ibid., §205, §291, §303.

111. Ibid., §294–294A, §295, §296.

112. Ibid., §291.

113. Respectively, Hardimon, *Hegel's Social Philosophy*, 215; Wood, "Editor's Introduction," xxiv.

114. Marx, *Kritik*, MEGA I.2: 48 / MECW 3: 44.

115. Ibid., 50–51 / 46–47.

116. Ibid., 66 / 62.

The bureaucracy's delusional belief in its defense of the general interest was, Marx argued, accompanied by a haughty and insular attitude that views political consciousness among the people as a threat to its authority. For Marx, "The general spirit of the bureaucracy is the *secret*, the mystery, preserved within itself by the hierarchy and against the outside world by being a closed corporation. Avowed political spirit, as also political mindedness, therefore appear to the bureaucracy as *treason* against its mystery."[117] Marx was furthermore unimpressed by the accountability mechanisms Hegel had put in place against abuses of power. He argued that relying on supervision by superiors forgets not only that a bureaucratic hierarchy protects its own but that superiors are in fact the "*chief*" abusers.[118] Moreover, relying on a civil servant's education fails to take into account how easily this is overruled by the everyday experience of the job that provides the civil servant with his "bread." Similar to his earlier journalistic attacks on the unconstrained power of censors and forest owners, Marx concluded that it is not enough to rely on the "man within the official" to stop official abuse. Hegel had consequently not provided sufficient "guarantee against the arbitrariness of 'executive civil servants.'"[119]

While Marx ridiculed Hegel for "literally" lifting part of his description of the civil servant's responsibilities from "the Prussian Civil Code," Marx did recognize that Hegel's account was a mixture of the civil service's current reality and what Hegel thought it should become.[120] Yet for Marx Hegel's reforms did not go nearly far enough. He compared Hegel's specification that every citizen has the opportunity to be a civil servant to the idea that "[e]very Catholic has the opportunity to become a priest." That is, it is an opportunity that inherently only a minority can take advantage of and one that does not stop the church from confronting the ordinary Catholic as an "otherworldly power."[121] Marx further argued that by making citizens move to "*another* sphere" in order to engage in general matters, Hegel has tacitly shown that citizens of his state have no such ability in their "*own* sphere."[122] The vast majority of Hegel's citizens were thus excluded from engaging in general matters in their everyday existence. Marx found this to be intolerable situation and one that would be remedied in his preferred state: "In the true state (*wahren Staat*) it is not a question of the opportunity of every citizen to devote himself to the universal

117. Ibid., 51 / 47.

118. Ibid., 56 / 52.

119. Ibid., 57 / 53.

120. Ibid., 48–49 / 44–45.

121. Ibid., 54 / 50. This is not the only anti-Catholic comparison Marx makes with the bureaucracy, also referring to the latter as "state-Jesuits, state-theologians"; ibid. 50 / 46.

122. Ibid., 54 / 50.

as one particular estate, but the capacity of the universal estate (*allgemeinen Standes*) to be really universal—that is, to be the estate of every citizen."[123] Marx here provided a suggestive account of an alternative to the public administration of general concerns, one where all citizens—and not just the select elite in Hegel's civil service—have the actual capacity to participate. Marx tied the importance of having this actual capacity to the realization of a central part of one's nature. Responding to Hegel's insistence on the need for examinations to enter the civil service, Marx argued that no one should be subjected to an exam to qualify as a "good citizen" because having the "necessary 'political knowledge' is a condition without which a person in the state lives outside the state, cut off from himself, from the air."[124] Restricting citizenship to an exam is, Marx continued, "nothing but a Masonic rite, the legal recognition of a knowledge of citizenship as a privilege."[125] Marx thus considered participation in public administration, and the knowledge one gains through it, to be essential, intrinsic aspects of our being (without it one is "cut off from . . . the air") and thus something all must have real access to. In summary, Marx rejected Hegel's attempt to make the civil service the exclusive and privileged administrator of general interests and instead envisaged a state where the "executive power . . . belongs . . . to the whole people."[126]

The third element of Hegel's constitution, the legislative power (*gesetzgebende Gewalt*), contains the final institutional piece of his state structure: a bicameral Estates Assembly made up of an Upper and a Lower House. These correspond to the two estates in Hegel's account of civil society: (1) the agricultural estate and (2) the industrial and commercial estate. The Upper House is reserved for the landed aristocracy, who Hegel argued were "*entitled* to such a career by *birth*, without the contingency of an election," because their inalienable, inherited property insulated them from the fluctuations of commerce and industry as well as guaranteed their independence from both the executive and the people.[127] Hegel's Lower House is made up of deputies from the second estate, who are not elected by individuals organized in geographic constituencies (as in modern constitutional practice), but by the memberships of corporations.[128] Hegel insisted that this was necessary to guard against individualism and social atomism and to ensure that the deputies were tied to

123. Ibid.

124. Ibid., 55 / 51.

125. Ibid.

126. Ibid., 58 / 54.

127. Hegel, *Philosophie des Rechts*, §305–7.

128. Ibid. §308–11. Corporations are, in Hegel's thought, essentially guild-like trade associations for each significant area of the economy.

the concrete interests of all the major branches of civil society.[129] Hegel speci-fied that the deputies must be propertied and have previously held positions of authority in the state or in corporations. They must also be free from bind-ing instructions, since being "commissioned or mandated agents" would limit their ability to form an assembly that freely deliberates on matters of universal concern—matters that the deputies have a "better understanding of" than those "who elect them . . . themselves possess."[130] Finally, Hegel limited the power of the Estates Assembly by giving the executive a role in overseeing and advising on legislation and the monarchical power the right to propose and make the final decision on legislation.[131]

The consequence of Hegel's legislative scheme is a severe curtailment of political participation by the masses. Aside from the exclusion of all women and children (Hegel says this is "obvious"), his rational state denies the right to vote to small farmers and peasants, as well as day laborers and the unem-ployed, since they are not members of corporations.[132] Citizens lucky enough to be corporation members are still denied the right to stand for elections if they lack sufficient property or prior state experience. This institutional exclu-sion of the mass of citizens is by design—the deliberate outcome of Hegel's very low estimation of the people's political capacities. The people, he claimed, is "elemental, irrational, barbarous, and terrifying" and does not "*know best* what is in their own best interest" as this requires "profound cognition and insight, and this is the very thing which 'the people' lack."[133] Thus, while Hegel can be seen to have a certain "*philosophical affinity*" with elements of

---

129. Ibid., §308, §311A.

130. Ibid. §309, §310–310A. While Gans diverged from Hegel's corporation model of repre-sentation by defending a more modern, individual form of representation (as found in Britain), Gans endorsed Hegel's opposition to instructions, arguing that deputies must defend the gen-eral interest and not the particular interests of constituencies, and so the deputy "must be a free man to act for the [general] interests of his voters"; see Gans, *Naturrecht und Universalrechtsge-schicht,* 229.

131. Ibid., §300. The power to propose legislation is not clearly assigned in the *Philosophie des Rechts,* but is explicitly given to the monarchical power in the 1817–18 lectures that preceded the text; see Hegel, *Vorlesungen über die Philosophie des Rechts: Nachschriften zu den Kollegien 1817/18, 1818/19 und 1819/20,* in Hegel, *Gesammelte Werke,* vol. 26.1 (Hamburg: Felix Meiner, 2014), 192 / *Lectures on Natural Right and Political Science: The First Philosophy of Right,* trans. J. Michael Stewart and Peter C. Hodgson (Berkeley: University of California Press, 1995), 275.

132. Hegel, *Philosophie des Rechts,* §301A. See Knowles, *Hegel and the* Philosophy of Right, 360. For Hegel's political exclusion of women, see Buchetmann, *Hegel and the Representative Constitution,* 180–85.

133. Hegel, *Philosophie des Rechts,* §301A, §303A.

republicanism, such as an emphasis on the common good, the fact that he is "considerably less enthusiastic about *active* political participation for ordinary citizens" is perhaps the aspect that most distances him from the tradition.[134]

Given its stringent limits on popular participation, it is no surprise to find that Marx was as little enamored of Hegel's legislature as he is of the other two elements of Hegel's constitution. But here the nature of Marx's criticism undergoes an important shift. While he took Hegel to have successfully (if objectionably) outlined a modern constitutional state for the first two elements, Marx charged Hegel with having abandoned this ambition with the legislature. By giving the landed aristocracy the hereditary right to sit in the Upper House and making the Lower House a body of corporations, Marx argued that Hegel had failed to realize the core principle of modern states: the separation between state and civil society. Thereby, Marx insisted, "Hegel has completely sunk back to the medieval standpoint and has entirely given up his 'abstraction of the political state.'"[135]

Marx's contrasted Hegel's Upper House with the Chamber of Peers (*Chambre des pairs*), France's second chamber established after the Restoration. Marx noted that the French chamber represented an "advance" in history because its members were appointed rather than being hereditary office holders. It thus severed the automatic link between the peers' aristocratic status in civil society and their political rights. Marx argued that the Chamber of Peers was thus a truer instantiation of the "*principle* of constitutional monarchy" that "Hegel tried to develop" than Hegel's own legislative institutions and should be seen as the "*real* creation of the constitutional monarchy." Marx further chastised Hegel with having learned the wrong lesson from British constitutional history. Marx insisted that the lesson was not that the hereditary House of Lords should be emulated but that we should recognize the "progress" realized through the growth of relative power of the House of Commons.[136] A hereditary Upper House was, for Marx, an affront to political equality. It made "*participation in the legislature . . . an innate* human right" for the landed aristocracy, the same aristocrats who have "mocked . . . *innate human rights*" and now hypocritically demand the "right of a particular race of men to be entrusted with the highest dignity of the

134. Alan Patten, *Hegel's Idea of Freedom* (Oxford: Oxford University Press, 1999), 39.

135. Marx, *Kritik, MEGA* I.2: 123 / *MECW* 3: 114. While Marx points to real inconsistencies in Hegel's account, Hegel was not simply offering a return to the old estate-based representation, but a middle ground between it and the competing theories of national representation. See Buchetmann, "Hegel's Intervention in Württemberg's Constitutional Conflict"; Lee, "Legacy of Medieval Constitutionalism in the *Philosophy of Right*," 624.

136. Marx, *Kritik, MEGA* I.2: 122–23 / *MECW* 3: 113.

legislature."[137] Marx attacked Hegel for opposing elections to the Upper House for being supposedly "contingent" when Hegel was happy to assign political power on the basis of the "physical accident of birth." In fact, Marx maintains, elections are the "conscious product of civil confidence."[138]

Finally, Marx objected to Hegel's argument that the landed aristocracy's property guarantees their independence. Marx argued that the implication of this is that "political independence does not flow *ex proprio sinu* [from its own bosom] of the political state" but from the "incidental" ownership of private property. Instead, Marx seems to imply, independence should be the "gift of the political state to its members" and the state's "animating spirit."[139] Moreover, Marx thought that by allocating the aristocracy's landed property a central place in the constitution, Hegel has inverted the proper relationship between state and private property: "Hegel makes citizenship, political existence and political conviction attributes of private property, instead of making private property an attribute of citizenship." Rather than making private property subordinated to the state's regulation, Hegel has created a state where "at the highest summits therefore the state appears as private property."[140]

Turning to the Lower House, Marx chided Hegel for designing a chamber whose ideal composition would be deputies with prior experience of state administration and thus in essence a "chamber of civil service *pensioners.*"[141] Marx further criticized Hegel's Lower House for containing a central contradiction: Hegel wanted the assembly to both deliberate on matters of universal concern and have deputies linked to the interests of the corporations of civil society. The predictable result would be that deputies "commissioned as representatives (*Repräsentanten*) of *universal* concerns . . . actually represent [the] particular concerns" of their corporation. Hegel also undermined his own aims by ruling out instructions for deputies, which results in the "deputies of civil society form[ing] a society which is not linked with those who commission them." Deputies without instructions, Marx insists, means that "Formally they are commissioned, but once they are *actually* commissioned they are *no*

---

137. Ibid., 114 / 105. It is noteworthy that Marx's criticism of Hegel concerns Hegel's *denial* of political rights to all and not the view normally imputed to Marx that he thought all rights were "illusory," as suggested in Dean Moyar, "Hegelian Conscience as Reflective Equilibrium and the Organic Justification of *Sittlichkeit,*" in *Hegel's Elements of the Philosophy of Right: A Critical Guide,* ed. David James (Cambridge: Cambridge University Press, 2017), 94.

138. Marx, *Kritik, MEGA* I.2: 114 / *MECW* 3: 105.

139. Ibid., 116 / 107.

140. Ibid., 120 / 111.

141. Ibid., 134 / 124.

longer mandatories. They are supposed to be *deputies* (*Abgeordnete*), and they are *not*."[142]

Marx also criticized Hegel for his rejection of a democratic franchise for the Lower House. Hegel had argued that the "idea that *all* individuals ought to participate in deliberations and decisions on the universal concerns of the state . . . seeks to implant in the organism of the state a *democratic* element *devoid of rational form*."[143] In response, Marx first defended the legitimacy of the desire to take part directly in the legislature. That desire reflected a genuine need "of *all* to be real (active) *members of the state* . . . to give themselves a *political being* . . . to demonstrate and give effect to their being as something *political*."[144] A "member of the state" who is denied the chance to properly participate in the decisions and deliberations of their state "would be an *animal*."[145] Political participation was thus, Marx again implies, an important aspect of our human nature.

But, as Patricia Springborg has rightly noted, Marx thought that this need and desire for participation did not have to be realized through direct participation in the legislature.[146] In fact, Marx argued that Hegel had wrongly interpreted the aims of the democratic struggles in France and Britain in this regard. The "real point of the dispute" in these countries was "not whether civil society shall exercise the legislative power through representatives or by all individually" but in fact over "the *extension* and greatest possible *generalization* of *election*, both of *active* and *passive* suffrage" (i.e., the right to vote and stand in election).[147] The goal of modern democratic struggle was thus, on Marx's account, not direct participation but the extension of the right to vote and stand for office. Marx in fact thought that there were good reasons to fight for democratic representation rather than direct participation. He argued that making use of representatives in legislative matters was justified both by the large numbers of citizens in modern states ("the best reason that can be advanced against the direct participation of all") and the need for a certain division of labor between citizens (otherwise the "individual would have to do everything at once; whereas society both lets him act for others and others for him").[148] Marx thus thought that direct participation in the legislature was not necessary,

142. Ibid., 132–33 / 122–23.

143. Hegel, *Philosophie des Rechts*, §308A.

144. Marx, *Kritik*, MEGA I.2: 128 / MECW 3: 118.

145. Ibid., 127 / 118.

146. Patricia Springborg, "Karl Marx on Democracy, Participation, Voting and Equality," *Political Theory* 12, no. 4 (1984): 537–56.

147. Marx, *Kritik*, MEGA I.2: 130 / MECW 3: 120.

148. Ibid., 126, 127 / 116, 118.

and the demand for political inclusion could (at least partially) be realized through having the right to stand for office and electing representatives with an extended democratic franchise. Whether Marx thought this extended franchise should also include women is unclear from the text. As he does not take the opportunity to comment on Hegel's political exclusion of women, his silence suggests he has no disagreement with Hegel on this front.

Marx's openness to representation should not, however, be misunderstood as an endorsement of the kind of representation that we are familiar with today, where representatives are not formally constrained by the wishes of their constituents.[149] As we saw above, Marx criticized Hegel for ruling out the practice of citizens instructing their deputies. Marx would thus seem to have a form of representation in mind where citizens exercise control over their representatives by giving them binding instructions on how they should act in the legislature. This would help avoid a problem Marx identified with Hegel's system where political participation (for those who are granted it) is reduced to only taking part in elections, making the people's *"political* act, a *single and temporary* one" and reducing participation to just "a *sensational* act . . . a moment of *ecstasy*."[150] This was the same complaint Marx had made in his journalism that representation is unacceptable where this is construed as the people's "sole, exceptional state action" that they engage in.[151]

Marx's language bears a certain resemblance to what is undoubtably the most famous critique of representation, and Marx had recently been reminded of it in his Kreuznach readings. In *Du contrat social*, Rousseau argued that "Sovereignty cannot be represented. . . . The English people thinks it is free; it is greatly mistaken, it is free only during the election of Members of Parliament; as soon as they are elected, it is enslaved, it is nothing."[152] This enormously influential statement on representation unsurprisingly produced the lasting impression that Rousseau thought liberty was only realizable through direct democracy in small states where representation was unnecessary. But in his later *Considérations sur le gouvernement de Pologne* (*Considerations on the Government of Poland*) (1772) Rousseau nuanced this view. Here he argued that

149. For the definitive account of the centrality of this aspect to modern representative states, see Bernard Manin, *The Principles of Representative Government* (Cambridge: Cambridge University Press, 1997), 163–67.

150. Ibid., 121 / 112.

151. Marx, 'Über die ständischen Ausschüsse in Preußen," *MEGA* I.1: 285 / *MECW* 1: 306.

152. Rousseau, *Du contrat social*, in *Oeuvres complètes*, vol. 3 (Paris: Gallimard, 1964), bk. III, ch. 15 / *The Social Contract*, in *The Social Contract and Other Later Political Writings*, ed. Victor Gourevitch (Cambridge: Cambridge University Press, 1997), bk. III. ch. 15. Marx excerpted the first part of the passage in "Exzerpte aus Rousseau," *MEGA* IV.2: 100–1.

liberty was in fact possible in large modern states if legislators were subjected to frequent elections and forced to "adhere exactly to their instructions."[153] Marx thus defended, in the course of his critique of Hegel, a very similar view of representation to the one taken by Rousseau[154]—namely, that where the size of states makes representation necessary this must be a form of representation where deputies are tightly controlled by the people through fixed instructions (often referred to as representatives having an *mandat impératif*, or imperative mandate).[155]

In addition to Marx's rejection of Hegel's account of representation, Marx also argued that the stark dichotomy Hegel has set up between representation and direct participation was one still stuck in the separation between state and civil society. That is, it "presupposes the separation of real life from the life of the state."[156] In a democracy that division no longer exists so that all citizens' ability to act on universal matters is "realized in their living reality" and not only "through *deputies*."[157] Marx provided nearly no concrete detail on what this more extensive account of participation would involve, except to gesture toward the vision of popular public administration he described in contrast to Hegel's bureaucracy. He goes so far as to argue that the "*executive power* should be the goal of popular desire, much more than the legislative power, the *metaphysical* state function."[158] Political participation for the common good is thus,

153. Rousseau, *Considérations sur le gouvernment de Pologne*, in *Oeuvres complètes*, 3: 979 / *Considerations on the Government of Poland* in *The Social Contract and Other Later Political Writings*, 201.

154. It is not clear whether this similarity is intentional or incidental. Marx shows subsequent awareness of Rousseau's *Considérations* in a (dismissive) comment in his 1847 "Die moralisierende Kritik," *MEW* 4: 353 / *MECW* 6: 334. Marx's view on representation in the *Kritik* is closer to Rousseau's considered position than, for instance, Edgar Bauer. Bauer cited Rousseau's famous critique of representation in support of a complete rejection of any form of representation in "Das Juste-Milieu," *Rheinische Zeitung*, no. 233 (21 August 1842), Beiblatt.

155. Marx's 1843 extracts include several references to the imperative mandate, particularly its contested status in the constitutional debates of the French Revolution; see Marx, "Exzerpte aus Wachsmuth," *MEGA* IV.2: 172, 174, and "Exzerpte aus Ranke," *MEGA* IV.2: 186. For this history, see Michael P. Fitzsimmons, *The Remaking of France: The National Assembly and the Constitution of 1791* (Cambridge: Cambridge University Press, 1994), 46–50, and Rachel Hammersley, *French Revolutionaries and English Republicans: The Cordeliers Club, 1790–1794* (Woodbridge: Boydell Press, 2005), chapter 1, and pp. 142–44.

156. Marx, *Kritik*, *MEGA* I.2: 125 / *MECW* 3: 115.

157. Ibid., 129 / 119.

158. Ibid., 129 / 119. Marx also argues that is even more important that the executive power is in the hands of the "whole people" than the legislative power; ibid., 58 / 54. At the same time, Marx claims that the legislature has been responsible for the "great, organic, general

on Marx's account, realized not only through the election and instruction of delegates to the legislature but through the everyday administration of public affairs by citizens.

That fragmentary democratic republican vision stands in stark contrast to the state envisaged by Hegel, where political participation and acting for the common good is severely restricted to a tiny minority, consisting of the monarch, professional bureaucrats, hereditary aristocrats, and propertied corporation representatives. In the *Kritik*, Marx thus provided a comprehensive republican critique of Hegel's constitutional monarchy and the way in which its monarchical, executive, and legislative elements exercised arbitrary power and excluded the people.

The (Modern) Republic

Marx's critical attitude to absolute and constitutional monarchy is something we would expect to find in any republican text of the time. One of the most surprising and original features of the *Kritik* was that Marx did not then simply outline a democratic republic as the third kind of constitution and defend it against the first two. This tripartite account of constitutions was entirely standard in constitutional analysis at the time and one that Marx had in fact used the year before in his journalism, where he had argued that "Christians live in states with different political constitutions, some in a republic, others in an absolute monarchy, and others still in a constitutional monarchy."[159] Rather than simply reproduce these three options in the *Kritik*, Marx instead introduced a fourth constitutional category, "democracy," and distinguished this from a "republic." He argued:

> In democracy the *abstract* state has ceased to be the dominant element. The struggle between monarchy and republic is itself a struggle within the abstract state. The *political* republic is democracy within the abstract state

revolutions," such as the French Revolution, because it is the "representative of the people, the will of the species." The executive in comparison has been responsible for the "small revolutions, the retrograde revolutions, the reactions," because it is the "representative of the particular will, of subjective arbitrariness"; ibid., 61 / 57. These seemingly contradictory views on the legislature and the executive might be explained by Marx's differing assessment of their role in current and historical constitutional struggles compared to their ideal role in a future society.

159. Marx, "Der leitende Artikel," *MEGA* I.1: 187–88 / *MECW* 1: 200. The same tripartite division of constitutions still appears thirty years later in Marx, *Le Capital*, vol. 1, *MEGA* II.7: 671 / *MECW* 35: 742 (passage added in French edition and integrated in 3rd German edition; see *Das Kapital*, vol. 1, *MEGA* II.8: 705).

form. The abstract state form of democracy is therefore the republic; but it here ceases to be the *merely political* constitution.[160]

Marx thus defined a democracy as a state in which the modern divide between the political sphere and civil society has been overcome, while he categorized the republic as falling within the category of modern abstract/political states that also includes absolutist and constitutional monarchical states. (He similarly argued that "[i]n monarchy . . . and in the republic . . . political man" is divided from "unpolitical man, private man").[161] At the same time, the above passage also indicates that Marx thought that of the modern abstract/political states, the republic was the regime closest to a democracy ("The *political* republic is democracy within the abstract state form").[162] Marx thus expressed a preference for a republic over both constitutional and absolutist monarchy, while also considering democracy to be the most preferable constitutional type of all.

It is important to recognize how unique this distinction between a republic and a democracy is for the time in which Marx wrote the *Kritik*. Ruge treated them as essentially inseparable (if not completely synonymous), arguing that the "constitution of the state is, if it is a real one, always a republic, and the republic is never a real one, when it is not a democracy" and, similarly, after summarizing the aims of his journal, claimed, "This is the *republic*, this is the *democracy* of the [Deutsche] Jahrbucher."[163] That conflation is also evident in other parts of the political spectrum. Ernst von Bülow-Cummerow's 1842 treatise on the Prussian constitution (which Marx had repeatedly critiqued in his journalism) tried to argue that there were only two kinds of constitution: monarchy and "a republic (a pure democratic constitution)."[164] Even in Marx's own

160. Marx, *Kritik*, *MEGA* I.2: 32 / *MECW* 3: 31.

161. Ibid., 31 / 30.

162. Marx elsewhere says that a "*constitutional monarch*" is "the idea of the constitutional state in its sharpest abstraction"; ibid., 119 / 109.

163. Arnold Ruge to Karl Rosenkranz, mid-April 1842, *Briefwechsel und Tagebuchblätter*, 271–72; [Arnold Ruge], "Rechtfertigung der Deutschen Jahrbücher gegen die Motive zu ihrer Unterdrückung," *Revue des Auslandes*, vol. 2, no. 4 (Leipzig: Otto Wigand, April 1843): 20; *Redaktionsbriefwechsel*, 1197. For the interchangeability of republic and democracy in Left Hegelian writing, see, for instance, Karl Nauwerck, "[Review:] *Rede zur Feier des Aller. Geburtsfestes . . . ,*" *Deutsche Jahrbücher*, no. 6 (7 January 1843): 24; and, more generally in the *Vormärz*, see Wolfgang Mager, "Republik," in *Geschichtliche Grundbegriffe: Historisches Lexikon Zur Politisch-Sozialen Sprache in Deutschland*, ed. Otto Brunner, Werner Conze, and Reinhart Koselleck, vol. 5 (Stuttgart: Klett-Cotta, 1984), 618–19.

164. [Ernst von] Bülow-Cummerow, *Preußen, seiner Verfassung, seine Verwaltung, sein Verhältnis zu Deutschland* (Berlin: Veit und Comp., 1842), 40. For Marx's criticism of Bülow-Cummerow, see "Der Kommunismus und die Augsburger 'Allgemeine Zeitung,'" *MEGA* I.1: 238 / *MECW* 1:

public writing contemporaneous to the *Kritik,* he made no obvious differentiation between democracy and republic, treating both regimes as the goal of
those who want an "organization of free human beings."[165]

Marx's desire to distance his democracy from a republic in the *Kritik* is
therefore both curious and requires explanation. Part of the explanation may
lie in the differentiation in the original passage in Hegel which Marx was commenting on. Here Hegel had said that he refers to "a *republic* or more specifically democracy" because the term "republic covers many other empirical
mixtures (*Vermischungen*)."[166] Hegel thus seemed to separate a republic from
a democracy, in order to distinguish his criticism of a democratic republican
regime from the older possible understanding of a republic as a mixed constitution made up of monarchical, aristocratic, and democratic elements.[167]
Marx might consequently have been employing the same distinction in order
to differentiate his understanding of democracy from a republic understood
as a mixed constitution. This may have formed a part of Marx's intention (especially when considered in light of some of Marx's indirect references to Aristotle's idea of the mixed constitution, discussed below). But the primary clue
to Marx's meaning comes from the sole example of a modern republic that
he names in the *Kritik:* the American republic. In the *Kritik,* Marx makes the
surprising claim that "Property, etc., in short, the entire content of the law and
of the state is, with few modifications, the same in North America as in Prussia.
The *republic* there is thus a mere state *form,* as is the monarchy here. The content of the state lies outside these constitutions."[168]

The simple equation Marx seems to make here between the American and
Prussian states has been the subject of harsh criticism. Gareth Stedman Jones
damns Marx's judgment that the differences between the two states are supposedly "secondary and inessential" as the final nail in a "rigid and impoverished"

216; "Replik auf die Denunziation eines 'benachbarten' Blattes," *MEGA* I.1: 336 / *MECW* 1: 321;
Randglossen zu den Anklagen des Ministerialreskripts, MEGA I.1: 353/ *MECW* 1: 365; and Karl
Marx to Arnold Rüge, 20 March 1842, *MEGA* III.1: 24 / *MECW* 1: 384–85.

165. Marx to Ruge, May 1843, "Ein Briefwechsel von 1843," *MEGA* I.2: 478 / *MECW* 3:
139–40.

166. Hegel, *Philosophie des Rechts,* §279.

167. Hegel subsequently suggests that the three elements of his constitutional monarchy
could be understood as a mixed constitution where the "monarch is *one; several* participate in
the executive power, and the *many* at large participate in the legislative power." But ultimately
he argues that this is a "superficial" and misleading understanding because while the "democratic and aristocratic elements . . . do occur in *monarchy* . . . they have lost their democratic and
aristocratic character"; ibid., §273A.

168. Marx, *Kritik, MEGA* I.2: 32 / *MECW* 3: 31.

analysis of the modern state.[169] Certainly, Marx's comparison is such a provocative exaggeration—and in seeming contradiction with much of Marx's own criticisms of Prussia—one wonders whether Marx would have expressed himself more carefully had the text been brought to publication. But, rather than dismiss it out of hand, we should first try to understand how and why Marx came to this judgment.

The most likely source for Marx's opinion on the American republic was his contemporaneous reading of Thomas Hamilton's two-volume *Men and Manners in America* (1833).[170] Hamilton's travelogue, published two years before the first volume of Tocqueville's *De la démocratie en Amérique* (*Democracy in America*), was part of a burgeoning literature in the 1830s of Europeans traveling to America for insights into the rise of democracy in their own country.[171] Hamilton's contribution to this literature was dismissed by John Stuart Mill for displaying all the "incompetency and presumption of the travelling Tory."[172] While his observations were certainly less theoretically accomplished than Tocqueville, Hamilton still had a keen eye for describing the political, social, legal, and cultural institutions and conventions of the young republic and its citizens. He observed a relatively wide cross-section of American society, from New York workers to Louisiana slaves, and was given access

169. Gareth Stedman Jones, *Karl Marx: Greatness and Illusion* (London: Allen Lane, 2016), 135.

170. Since we cannot date the *Kritik* or the *Kreuznacher Hefte* with complete confidence, we cannot completely rule out the possibility that Marx had not read Hamilton when he made his remark about America in the *Kritik*. We know that Marx must have read Hamilton before he wrote "Zur Judenfrage" (ca. mid-October to mid-December 1843), as he cites Hamilton several times in that article. It is thus possible that Marx read Hamilton after writing the *Kritik* (ca. mid-March to end of September 1843) and before writing "Zur Judenfrage." If that was the case, the provenance of his judgment on the American republic in the *Kritik* would, however, remain something of a mystery. In "Zur Judenfrage," Marx mentions two other authors on America, Tocqueville and his traveling companion Gustave de Beaumont, and he quotes the latter's *Marie, ou l'esclavage aux etats unis* (Paris, 1835) several times. But, similarly to Hamilton, we do not know when Marx studied these authors (or even if he properly read Tocqueville), and there are no surviving Marx extracts for either Tocqueville or Beaumont.

171. For the British discussion, see Elizabeth J. Deis and Lowell T. Frye, "British Travelers and the 'Condition-of-America Question'": Defining America in the 1830s," in *Nineteenth-Century British Travelers in the New World*, ed. Christine DeVine (Farnham: Ashgate, 2013), 121–50; on Hamilton, see 135–37, 140–42.

172. John Stuart Mill, "State of Society in America" (1836), in *Collected Works of John Stuart Mill*, vol. 18 (Toronto: University of Toronto Press, 1977), 97. While Hamilton's work has been largely forgotten, there have been at least two reissues, in 1968 (New York: Russell & Russell) and in 2009 (Cambridge: Cambridge University Press).

to past, present, and future presidents (respectively, James Monroe, Andrew Jackson, and Martin van Buren). As a Tory opponent of the 1832 Reform Act, Hamilton was resolutely opposed to America's experiment in democracy and extended suffrage (at least for white men),[173] especially as a model to be emulated by Britain (his explicit motivation for publishing the book). But he also perceptively analyzed the racial discrimination he witnessed in the North (he argued that "grinding and humiliating ... universal and unconquerable prejudice" meant that a supposedly *"free"* Black man was in fact *"a masterless slave"*), as well as being outraged by the institution of chattel slavery, which he presciently predicted could only be overthrown by a "great and terrible convulsion".[174]

Marx read Hamilton in a (rather loose) German translation from 1834 and extracted an extensive set of notes, which focused particularly on America's nascent labor movement, materialistic culture and constitutional structures. Despite Marx's repeated citations of Hamilton in his subsequent article "Zur Judenfrage" ("On the Jewish Question"), the significance of Hamilton on Marx's political evolution has, with a few important exceptions, been underappreciated.[175] As has recently been argued, Hamilton was Marx's earliest introduction to a working-class movement—the American "Workies"—operating within conditions of a relatively broad suffrage that extended to waged workers.[176]

But the most immediate effect of reading Hamilton on Marx was the unedifying picture it painted of America's social structure and culture, in spite of its republican political institutions. Reflecting on America's self-conception as the "land of freedom and equality," Hamilton argued that this may be true when understood as there being no legally privileged estate, but "in any wider acceptation it is mere nonsense. There is quite as much practical equality in Liverpool as New York. The magnates of the Exchange do not strut

---

173. At the time of Hamilton's visit, free Black men could vote in a few (mostly northern) states, though the trend was for the removal of property qualifications to be accompanied by growing racial exclusion from the suffrage. See Donald Ratcliffe, "The Right to Vote and the Rise of Democracy, 1787–1828," *Journal of the Early American Republic* 33, no. 2 (2013): 246–47.

174. Hamilton, *Men and Manners in America*, 2 vols. (Edinburgh: William Blackwood, 1833), 1: iv, 90–100, 2: 228.

175. Lewis S. Feuer, "The North American Origin of Marx's Socialism," *The Western Political Quarterly* 16, no. 1 (1963): 53–67; August H. Nimtz Jr., *Marx, Tocqueville, and Race in America: The "Absolute Democracy" or "Defiled Republic"* (Lanham: Lexington, 2003), 9-13; Maximilien Rubel, "Notes on Marx's Conception of Democracy," *New Politics* (Winter 1962): 83–85.

176. See the excellent analysis in Sean F. Monahan, "The American Workingmen's Parties, Universal Suffrage, and Marx's Democratic Communism," *Modern Intellectual History* 18, no. 2 (2021): 379–402.

less proudly in the latter city than in the former."[177] Marx extracted this comparison between America and Hamilton's monarchical home state, and there is a noticeable affinity to Marx's own comparison of America to his monarchical Prussia. Marx was also particularly taken by Hamilton's horror at the materialism and money-grubbing nature of American society. In a long passage, extracted by Marx and approvingly reproduced in full in Marx's "Zur Judenfrage," Hamilton presented the "pious and politically free" New Englander, in the following terms: "*Mammon* is their idol, they worship him not only with their lips but with all the energies of their body and soul. The earth is in their eyes nothing else but a stock market and they are convinced that as mortals in the here below they have no other purpose than becoming richer than their neighbors."[178]

In other words, Marx found in Hamilton's description of America the same egotistical behaviour in the sphere of civil society and disregard of the pursuit of universal matters that repelled him in the monarchies of Europe. Thus, what Marx meant when he said that Prussia and America are all "mere state *form*[*s*] . . . the content of the state lies outside of the constitution" is that in both states the particularistic ethos of civil society dominated over the political sphere and the limited availability the latter provides for acting for "the truly universal." Marx recognized that, of course, the degree of political exclusion and alienation from universal matters varied between these states. (He noted that "*Monarchy* is the perfect expression of this estrangement. The *republic* is the negation of this estrangement within its own sphere.") But, in Marx's eyes, the American republic fundamentally remained a state where the political sphere still had an "otherworldly nature" and the citizens are consigned to the "*earthly existence*" of private and egoistic pursuits in civil society.[179]

Thus, by differentiating a republic from a democracy, Marx was trying to distance his vision of a democratic state from what he had recently read about the most prominent example of a modern republic (at a moment when the American republic was increasingly being described as a democracy).[180] That

177. Hamilton, *Men and Manners*, 1: 109; Marx, "Exzerpte aus Hamilton," *MEGA* IV.2: 267.

178. Here (and where indicated below) I retranslate the subtly differing German version that Marx encountered. See Hamilton, *Die Menschen und die Sitten in den vereinigten Staaten von Nordamerika*, trans. L. Hout (Mannheim: Heinrich Hoff, 1834), 1: 109 (compare with Hamilton, *Men and Manners*, 1: 213 and similar descriptions in 1: 115). The description of New Englanders as "pious and politically free" is Marx's own addition; see "Exzerpte aus Hamilton," *MEGA* IV.2: 267; "Zur Judenfrage," *MEGA* I.2: 165 / *MECW* 3: 170–71.

179. Marx, *Kritik*, *MEGA* I.2: 33 / *MECW* 3: 31.

180. As is seen in Hamilton, for instance, *Men and Manners*, vol. 1: 19, 49, 215, 217, 287, 298–99, vol. 2: 4, 57. See also Bülow-Cummerow, *Preußen, seiner Verfassung*, 41.

undoubtably involved a degree of flattening the differences between republican America and monarchical Prussia. But it also reflected a more realistic and informed opinion of America than some of Marx's Hegelian republican contemporaries. A year before the *Kritik*, Bruno Bauer fancifully described America as "the true form of the modern republic, the true rebirth, i.e., the higher reproduction of the Greek state form."[181]

Given Marx's preference for a democracy over a republic, one might naturally wonder whether he should in fact be thought of in this period as a democrat rather than a republican.[182] One could do so if one were to give a stipulative definition of one ranged against the other. But that would make little contextual sense in 1843, since the terms *democrat* and *republican* were used virtually interchangeably and there was certainly no differentiable political faction of democrats as against republicans. Perhaps more importantly, aside from his unusual differentiation between democracy and republic,[183] there is little in Marx's substantial criticism of the republic and his contrasting account of a democracy that his fellow contemporary republicans would have disagreed with.

Take, for instance, Johann Georg Wirth's celebrated marathon seven- to eight-hour defense speech at his trial for attempted overthrow of the government for his part in the Hambach Festival, delivered a decade before Marx's *Kritik*.[184] In his speech, which contributed to his sensational acquittal by the jury, Wirth provided an unapologetic defense of a democratic republic. But he also warned that the "transformation of an absolute monarchy into a limited

---

181. [Bruno Bauer], "[Review:] *Deutschlands Beruf in der Gegenwart und Zukunft* von Theodor Rohmer," *Rheinische Zeitung*, no. 158 (7 June 1842), Beiblatt. Even the more sober Ruge thought that "[t]he Greeks, these through and through political people . . . were as free as the North Americans"; see "Die Hegelsche Rechtsphilosophie und die Politik unsrer Zeit," *Deutsche Jahrbücher*, no. 189 (10 August 1842), 756. In general, however, German republicans tended to look more to the French republican example and left the American republic to the admiration of German liberals; see Charlotte A. Lerg, *Amerika als Argument: Die deutsche Amerika-Forschung im Vormärz und ihre politische Deutung in der Revolution von 1848 / 49* (Bielefeld: Transcript, 2011), 197–98, 213.

182. As is suggested by Chrysis's thesis that Marx's *Kritik* represents an intermediary democratic stage between Marx's republican journalism and his subsequent communism; see Chrysis, *"True Democracy" as a Prelude to Communism*, 101, 103–4, 213.

183. It is worth noting that Marx qualifies his criticisms of the republic as a critique of the *"political* republic," *Kritik*, *MEGA* I.2 32 / *MECW* 3: 31, suggesting that his concern is with abstract forms of the republic, not republics per se.

184. See further Elisabeth Hüls, *Johann Georg August Wirth (1798–1848): Ein politisches Leben im Vormärz* (Düsseldorf: Droste, 2004), 326–42.

or constitutional one, yes even the transformation of both into the pure democratic governmental form, the republic" would not be a true reorganization of the state if reform only touched the "*outer* form" of the state and not its "*inner*" organization.[185] If reform was restricted only to the political sphere and did not penetrate society then such states would be only "*formal states (Formstaaten)*" where "everyone always only thinks of providing for himself, and unconcerned for the universal only pushes *himself* above others"—a fate that Wirth predicted threatened the American republic.[186] Alongside a range of social measures, Wirth insisted that the internal political organization of the "republican state form" and the "resolute implementation of the principle of popular sovereignty" had to involve public administration by the people, where the functions of professional state officials would be "passed to citizens, who perform this service alternating in turns"—a vision realized by making "all public officials elected *by all and from all the citizens* of the state, directly accountable to the people and dismissible by the same."[187]

Wirth thus rejected an egoistic, purely formal republic unconcerned for the social sphere (like the American republic) and contrasted it with a republic where all citizens would be actively engaged in public administration for the common good. The core elements of Marx's democracy and his critique of a superficial republic were thus hardly unique to the *Kritik* but a central feature of one of the more prominent statements of *Vörmarz* republicanism. It would consequently be misleading to think of the *Kritik* as a democratic critique of republicanism. Rather the *Kritik* is more usefully thought of as containing a republican critique of a certain form of the modern republic.[188]

A (Future) Democracy

Having set out how and why Marx distinguished a modern republic from a democracy, we can turn to Marx's conception of the latter. While critiquing Hegel's constitutional monarchy was the near exclusive preoccupation of the *Kritik*, the text also contains a fragmentary positive account of this democratic regime. Angered by Hegel's dismissal of a "*republic* or more specifically democracy" as requiring "no further discussion . . . in face of the developed Idea [of

---

185. J. G. A. Wirth, *Die Rechte des deutschen Volkes: Eine Vertheidigungsrede vor den Assisen zu Landau* (Nancy, 1833), 24.

186. Ibid., 31–32, 36.

187. Ibid., 47, 57–58.

188. Jeffrey C. Isaac's interpretation that "Marx's critique [in the *Kritik*] of political republicanism itself bears the traces of republicanism" is thus closer to the mark; see "The Lion's Skin of Politics: Marx on Republicanism," *Polity* 23, no. 3 (1990): 472.

the state],"[189] Marx launched into a furious set of rather obscure and chiastic contrasts in defense of democracy:

> Democracy is the truth of monarchy; monarchy is not the truth of democracy. Monarchy is necessarily democracy inconsistent with itself; the monarchical element is not an inconsistency in democracy. Monarchy cannot be understood in its own terms; democracy can . . . Democracy is the genus constitution. Monarchy is one species, and a poor one at that. Democracy is content and form. Monarchy is supposed to be only a form, but it falsifies the content. . . . In monarchy we have the people of the constitution, in democracy the constitution of the people. Democracy is the solved *riddle* of all constitutions.[190]

While the meaning of some of these contrasts is not immediately apparent, the central difference between the two state forms that Marx is trying to propose is relatively easy to discern. He thought that monarchies were abstract/political states where the state and civil society were differentiated from each other, while a democracy is a state where that alienating division has been overcome. "In monarchy," Marx explained, "political man has his particular mode of being alongside unpolitical man, the private man"; and as one of the "*abstract* state forms," civil society in a monarchy exists as "*particular* mode . . . of existence alongside the *political* state." "In democracy," by comparison, "the *formal* principle is at the same time the *material* principle," i.e., acting for universal interests is not restricted to only a limited and formal realization in the political sphere but extends across all of the state and civil society, and so democracy "is the true unity of universal and particular."[191] This difference between monarchy and democracy is relatively straightforward to grasp in the abstract (if the reader will excuse the pun). But what it means concretely in terms of alternative institutions and social structures remains initially opaque. We have already seen that Marx was unimpressed by the modern American republic as a model for democracy. By comparison, he was much more enthusiastic about the historical model of the ancient Greek city-states and especially democratic Athens.

Given Marx's previous praise of Athens in his journalism and the generally high regard for the classical Greek world in Left Hegelian thought, it is no surprise to find that the *Kritik* contains a positive appraisal of several aspects of the ancient city-states. Marx believed that the Greek city-states did not display the alienating distinction between state and civil society of modern

189. Hegel, *Philosophie des Rechts*, §279.
190. Marx, *Kritik*, MEGA I.2: 30-31 / MECW 3: 29.
191. Ibid., 31 / 30.

abstract states, arguing that "in Greece, the *res publica* is the real private affair of the citizens, their real content," so that there was a "substantial unity between people and state."[192] Marx also archly praised the example set by "Greek and Roman statesmen," whose achievements he notes were carried out without ever having to pass Hegel's civil service examinations.[193] Indeed, insofar as Marx's critique of Hegel's elite bureaucracy is inspired by an alternative model of public administration, it would seem to be the example set by Athens. Democratic Athens dispensed with a professional bureaucracy, instead filling nearly all public offices through lottery and limiting them to one-year, usually nonrepeatable terms. Consequently, one estimate concludes that in addition to the celebrated Assembly that was open to the entire citizenry (at its height some 40,000 citizens, with some 6,000 in regular attendance), over the course of a decade a quarter to a third of the total Athenian citizenry would have served in the Council of Five Hundred, thousands more would have taken part in citizen juries, and at any one time hundreds of citizens would have filled the huge range of lottery-selected public offices.[194] Richard Hunt thus plausibly argues that, with its mass, rotating involvement of citizens in nearly all administrative posts rather than a permanent, professional bureaucracy, "no other political structure in the Western tradition so closely resembles Marx's ideal as Periclean Athens."[195]

In addition to Marx's positive remarks on ancient Greece, his defense of democracy involves an oblique criticism of one of democratic Athens's greatest internal critics: Aristotle.[196] That is revealed if we delve further into one of the initially obscure comparisons Marx makes between democracy and monarchy. Marx claims that "Democracy is the genus constitution (*Verfassungsgattung*). Monarchy is one species, and a poor one at that" and that "Democracy stands to the other constitutions as the genus stands to its species; except that here the genus itself appears as an existent, and therefore as one *particular* species."[197] From the text alone it is not clear what point Marx was trying to make by unusually describing democracy as both a particular species of

192. Marx, *Kritik, MEGA* I.2: 34 / *MECW* 3: 32.

193. Ibid., 55 / 51.

194. M. I. Finley, *Politics in the Ancient World* (Cambridge: Cambridge University Press, 1983), 71–74.

195. Richard N. Hunt, *The Political Ideas of Marx and Engels*, vol. 1 (Pittsburgh: University of Pittsburgh Press, 1974), 83–84.

196. For the importance of understanding Aristotle and other key classical thinkers as antidemocratic opposition within Athens, see Josiah Ober, *Political Dissent in Democratic Athens: Intellectual Critics of Popular Rule* (Princeton: Princeton University Press, 1998).

197. Marx, *Kritik, MEGA* I.2: 30-31 / *MECW* 3: 29–30.

constitution and the genus constitution. But it is explicable as soon as we understand it as a response to Aristotle's hugely influential classification of constitutions in book 3 of the *Politics*.

Aristotle here classified constitutions based on two criteria: who ruled (the one, the few, or the many) and to what end they ruled (for the common good or the particular good of the ruler or ruling class). This produced a sixfold classification, with three "correct" constitutions that rule for the common good and three corresponding "deviant" constitutions that rule in the sectional interest (see figure 5). Aristotle called the constitution ruled by the one for the common good *kingship* and its deviant partner *tyranny*. A constitution ruled by the few for the common good was an *aristocracy*, while rule by the few for their own interest was an *oligarchy*. For the constitutions ruled by the many, Aristotle labeled the deviant constitution *democracy*. So far, so expectedly elitist. But when Aristotle came to the final constitution—rule by the many for the common good—he did something odd, he called this constitution by the same term, *politeia* (πολιτεία, "constitution"), that he had been using for discussing constitutions as such.[198] Aristotle thus used the same term to describe constitutions in general and a particular example of a constitution. This presents what can be called "a "genus-species" ambiguity, where the same word is used to mean now a genus and now one of the species of that genus.[199] To avoid this ambiguity some translations of Aristotle's *Politics* distinguish the species from the genus by calling the species of correct constitution ruled by the many a *polity*. But this conceals that Aristotle intentionally used the same word for both genus and species.[200]

Aristotle's general purpose in conflating genus and species across his works was to highlight what was "the most fully developed species within the genus," and thus by using the genus term for the species of *politeia*, Aristotle seems to have been signaling that it was the constitution most developed in advancing the good associated with living in a political community.[201] Aristotle subsequently

198. Aristotle, *Politics*, bk. III, ch.7, 1279a–b. By comparison, in Plato's very similar classification that influenced Aristotle, democracy is used as the term for *both* the law-abiding and law-breaking constitutions ruled by the many; see Plato, *Statesman*, ed. Julia Annas and trans. Robin Waterfield (Cambridge: Cambridge University Press, 1995), 291d–292a, 302b–e. For an insightful critical discussion, see Mogens Herman Hansen, "Aristotle's Alternative to the Sixfold Model of Constitutions," in *Aristotle et Athènes*, ed. Marcel Piérart (Paris: Boccard, 1993), 91–101.

199. Richard Robinson, *Aristotle Politics Books III and IV* (Oxford: Oxford University Press, 1995), 23.

200. Ibid., 24.

201. Kevin M. Cherry, "The Problem of Polity: Political Participation and Aristotle's Best Regime," *The Journal of Politics* 71, no. 04 (2009): 1407, 1411–13.

	Correct	Deviant
One	Kingship	Tyranny
Few	Aristocracy	Oligarchy
Many	Politeia ("constitution")	Democracy

FIGURE 5. Aristotle's constitutional typology

defined the *politeia* as a mixture of oligarchy and democracy that avoided the pitfalls of those two deviant constitutions.[202] It also seems to be the same regime that Aristotle later calls the "middle constitution," which he maintains is the best realizable constitution because of the stability it achieves by concentrating power in the middle citizens (Aristotle regards kingship and aristocracy as, in some regards, the best constitutions, but too prone to devolving into tyranny and oligarchy, the worst forms of constitutions).[203] As the best constitution, the "middle constitution" provides the standard by which the other constitutions, including the various types of democracies and oligarchies, are to be ranked in accordance with their distance from it.[204]

Returning from Aristotle's *Politics* to Marx's *Kritik*, we can see that Marx was effectively reversing Aristotle's classification. By describing democracy as both the genus and a species of constitution, Marx was making democracy rather than Aristotle's *politeia* the genus constitution. By implication it is democracy, and not a *politeia*, that is the correct constitution where the many rules for the common good. Making democracy the genus served the same purpose for Marx as for Aristotle: to designate the most fully developed or

---

202. Aristotle, *Politics*, bk. IV, chs. 8–9, 1293b–1294b.

203. Ibid. bk. IV, ch. 11, 1295a–1296b. For the reasons why the "middle constitution" should be treated as the same constitutional form as the "constitution (*politeia*)," see Robinson, *Aristotle Politics Books III and IV*, 100–101. For an opposing view, see Curtis Johnson, "Aristotle's Polity: Mixed or Middle Constitution?," *History of Political Thought* 9, no. 2 (1988): 197–99.

204. Aristotle, *Politics*, bk. IV, ch. 11, 1296b1–7.

best form of constitution that is the standard against which all other constitutions should be measured.[205] Marx argued that "all forms of state have democracy *for* their truth and that they are therefore untrue insofar as they are not democracy."[206] Given the evident similarity between Marx's and Aristotle's discussion, as well as Marx's well-established familiarity with and respect for Aristotle's thought, it seems quite likely that Marx's description of democracy as the genus constitution was a deliberate response to Aristotle.[207] Though we should not overburden the point given the indirect nature of the evidence, this gives some grounds for thinking that Marx subtly intended his democracy to be contrasted with Aristotle's *politeia*, where *politiea* is understood as a mixed constitution that tempers the rule of the many through the rule of the few. That interpretation would also be supported by the long tradition of equating Aristotle's *politeia* with a "republic" and Marx's critique of that constitution.[208]

Marx's implied criticism of Aristotle on democracy provides further support to the idea that Marx's understanding of democracy takes some inspiration from Athens and the Greek city-states. We have already examined Marx's expressed admiration for the ancient city-states for their unity of public and private life and the extensive participation of citizens in public affairs. It also clear that Marx envisaged his democracy as reviving certain aspects of the ancient world. As he wrote to Ruge in May 1843: "The self-confidence of the human being, freedom, has first of all to be aroused again in the hearts of these [German] people. Only this feeling, which vanished from the world with the Greeks . . . can again transform society into a community of human beings united for their highest aims, into a democratic state."[209]

205. For a further use of genus and species categories in Marx's writing, see "Debatten über Preßfreiheit," *MEGA* I.1: 161 / *MECW* 1: 173.

206. Marx, *Kritik*, *MEGA* I.2 32 / *MECW* 3: 30.

207. This link between Marx and Aristotle goes unnoticed in Norman Levine, *Marx's Resurrection of Aristotle* (Cham: Palgrave Macmillan, 2021); and even in David J. Depew, "The Polis Transfigured: Aristotle's *Politics* and Marx's *Critique of Hegel's "Philosophy of Right"* in *Marx and Aristotle: Nineteenth-Century German Social Theory and Classical Antiquity*, ed. George E. McCarthy (Savage, MA: Rowman & Littlefield, 1992), 37–73. Though see the interesting remarks on the similarity between Marx's social thought and Aristotle's justification of the mixed constitution in G. E. M. de Ste. Croix, *The Class Struggle in the Ancient Greek World: From the Archaic Age to the Arab Conquests* (London: Duckworth, 1981), 74–76.

208. For instance, in Gans's lectures he lists Aristotle's three correct constitutions as "monarchy . . . aristocracy . . . [and] politeia or republic"; see Gans, *Naturrecht und Universalrechtsgeschichte: Vorlesungen nach G.W.F. Hegel*, ed. Johann Braun (Tübingen: Mohr Siebeck 2005), 21; Eduard Gans, *Naturrecht und Universalrechtsgeschichte*, ed. Manfried Reidel (Stuttgart: Klett-Cotta, 1981), 36.

209. Marx to Ruge, May 1843, "Ein Briefwechsel von 1843," *MEGA* I.2: 475–76 / *MECW* 3: 137.

But despite these positive appraisals, it is just as crucial to recognize that Marx's democracy was not a simple return to the ancient world. Two features in particular distinguish Marx's account of democracy from the previous ancient example of what he calls "unmediated . . . democracy (*unmittelbaren . . . Demokratie*)."[210] These suggest that Marx thought his preferred regime had not been fully realized in any historical or existing examples of states. The first difference with Athenian democracy is evident in Marx's denial of the feasibility and necessity of citizens directly participating in the legislature. We saw how in his critique of Hegel Marx argued that the size of modern states and the legitimacy of a degree of division of labor justify a certain form of representation or delegation in the legislative assembly. Marx's democracy thus contains a clear institutional difference to ancient democratic Athens and its celebrated Assembly (*ekklēsia*), where all citizens had the opportunity to directly participate in law-making.[211] It is thus misleading to describe Marx as advocating "direct democracy," given the term's association with the Athenian direct participation in the legislature.[212] At the same time, Marx does not make the well-established argumentative move, whereby accepting that large modern populations make direct democracy infeasible is then paired with an insistence that the only feasible alternative is representative democracy, understood as a system where representatives are not formally constrained by their constituents once elected. As we saw in his critique of Hegel, Marx advocated, under the possible influence of Rousseau, for legislative deputies to be constrained by the formal instructions given to them by constituents. Marx thus supported neither direct participation in the legislature nor unconstrained representation, but a system whereby deputies are instructed by the people and bound to those instructions. Marx's democracy therefore presents a third way between Athenian direct democracy and modern representative democracy—a system for which there is no settled name in the literature, but which David Leopold helpfully labels "popular delegacy."[213]

(Given that Marx's democracy includes a form of representation, his distinction between republic and democracy does not track James Madison's famous definition that the "difference between a Democracy and a Republic"

<hr>

210. Marx, *Kritik*, MEGA I.2: 33 / *MECW* 3: 32.

211. For the ways in which Athens's directly democratic Assembly actually made extensive use of supplemental lottery-based institutions, see Manin, *Principles of Representative Government*, chapter 1.

212. As is done in Depew, "The Polis Transfigured," 61; and Z. A. Pelczynski, "Nation, Civil Society, State: Hegelian Sources of the Marxian Non-Theory of Nationality," in *The State and Civil Society: Studies in Hegel's Political Philosophy*, ed. Z. A. Pelczynski (Cambridge: Cambridge University Press, 1984), 268.

213. Leopold, *Young Karl Marx*, 254.

is that in a democracy the people "assemble and administer the Government in person" whereas in a republic "the scheme of representation takes place."[214] As we saw in the above section, Marx's differentiation between the two regimes is not based on whether representation takes place, but on the differing relationships between the state and civil society.)

The second feature that distinguishes Marx's democracy from ancient democracy is that he values some of the individual rights and freedoms associated with modern states, and at several points he suggests that there was an improper unity between state and civil society achieved in ancient and medieval states. Throughout the *Kritik* Marx expresses opposition to any person's political status being privileged or restricted by their status in civil society. That includes the landed aristocracy who had "mocked . . . *innate human rights*" but demanded the "*innate* human right" to sit in the legislature for themselves or, most starkly, the practice of ancient slavery, which had the consequence that slaves' "political existence was destroyed."[215] Furthermore, Marx's praise of the way in which the ancient Greeks treated "the *res publica* as the real private affair" is tempered by the less flattering description that in Greece "the private individual is a slave" and that "Among the Greeks civil society was the *slave* of political society."[216] These (metaphorical) comparisons to slavery suggest that while Marx thinks that the relationship between state and civil society in ancient states was superior to that of modern abstract states, ancient states had not achieved a fully admirable unity either. Marx's language suggests that he agrees with Hegel's analysis that ancient states had not given sufficient weight to the individuality of civil society, that civil society had been too fully subordinated to political society. Marx's rejection of a false kind of unity is even more evident in his account of medieval states. Marx says that these exhibited a unity between political and civil society spheres but a unity that was based on "*unfree* man." They were thus what Marx twice calls the "*democracy of unfreedom*," because they achieved a kind of unity (hence "*democracy*") but an unenviable one because it did not include the freedoms associated with the modern state (hence "*unfreedom*").[217] Marx also stressed that as objectionable as the social divisions in modern civil society are, they are still "an advance in history" over the political divisions in the medieval

---

214. James Madison, "The Federalist No. 10," in *The Federalist, with Letters of "Brutus,"* ed. Terence Ball (Cambridge: Cambridge University Press, 2003), 43–44.

215. Marx, *Kritik*, MEGA I.2: 114, 120 / *MECW* 3: 105, 110.

216. Ibid., 34, 79 / 32, 73. For Arnold Ruge's similar critique that Plato and Aristotle gave insufficient space to civil society, see *Aus früherer Zeit*, IV: 83–84.

217. Marx, *Kritik*, MEGA 1.2: 33 / *MECW* 3: 32.

system of estates; and he similarly maintained that a "representative constitution is a great advance" over an estate constitution.[218]

According to Marx, then, both ancient and (especially) medieval states failed to achieve the right kind of unity between their civil society and political spheres, because of their failure to provide sufficient space for individuality in civil society and the freedom and rights of modern states to all citizens. Only a future democracy, on Marx's account, achieves the right kind of unity. There are thus traces of a certain Hegelian dialectical structure in Marx's view—that ancient and medieval states exhibited an *undifferentiated unity* between their political and civil society spheres, modern states exhibit a *differentiated disunity*, and a future democracy will contain a *differentiated unity*.[219] That is also suggested by what seems to be a three-part contrast by Marx: "In the states of antiquity the political state makes up the content of the state to the *exclusion* of the other spheres; the modern state is a *compromise* between the political and the unpolitical state. In democracy the abstract state has ceased to be the *dominant* factor."[220]

This suggestive account of a historical progression of constitutional forms culminating in a future democracy that both returns to and supersedes earlier states is fragmentary to say the least. But Marx's assorted comments on the various constitutional forms across history lend themselves to a typological reconstruction. Marx mentions the following constitutional forms: for the ancient and medieval world, *monarchy, aristocracy,* and *democracy*;[221] for the modern world, *absolute monarchy, constitutional monarchy,* and *republic*; and, finally, the future *democracy*. A constitutional typology for these various regimes is attempted in figure 6, which assembles Marx's account into a more coherent structure than is in fact found in the *Kritik*, with the aim that this might aid in the understanding of the text and potentially correspond to what Marx might have argued in a more polished published work (without thereby claiming that it definitely corresponds to what Marx might have produced).

218. Ibid., 85, 89 / 75, 79.

219. For this dialectical structure in Hegel's thought and applied to Marx's views on labor, see G. A. Cohen, "Marx's Dialectic of Labor," *Philosophy & Public Affairs* 3, no. 3 (1974): 235–61.

220. Marx, *Kritik,* MEGA I.2: 32 / MECW 3: 31, emphasis added. However, it is not entirely clear if Marx intends the comment on democracy as a contrast to both ancient and modern states.

221. Recall that Marx says that in premodern "unmediated monarchy, democracy and aristocracy there is as yet no political constitution as distinct from the actual, material state"; ibid., 33 / 32. Marx gives less attention to different medieval political forms but does refer to the medieval "*democracy of unfreedom*" and the "feudal monarchy"; ibid., 63, 119 / 59, 109.

Concrete ← ——————————————————— → Abstract

Free

Democracy
(Future)

Republic
(Modern)

Constitutional Monarchy
(Modern)

Monarchy, Aristocracy,
Democracy
(Ancient & Medieval)

Absolute Monarchy
(Modern)

Unfree

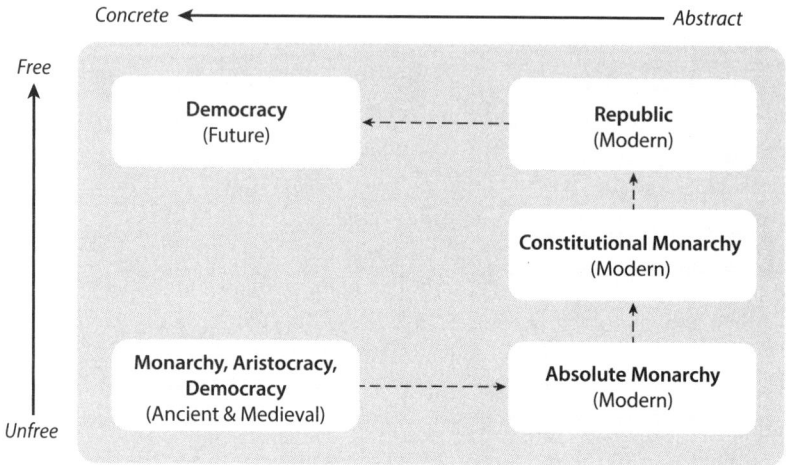

FIGURE 6. Reconstruction of Marx's constitutional typology and historical progression.

The reconstruction tracks Marx's explicit distinction between abstract (modern) states and nonabstract (ancient, medieval, and future) states. Following Marx's own language elsewhere in the *Kritik*, we can label these nonabstract states as concrete states.[222] Figure 6 also includes a second comparative dimension, between freer and less free states, that tries to capture Marx's various comments on how ancient and medieval states exhibit a defective unity because of their failure to provide freedoms to all citizens (most obviously his description of the medieval world as the "*democracy of unfreedom*"). That dimension also tracks the order of preference Marx holds for the modern state forms, with constitutional monarchy an advance over absolute monarchy and a republic an advance over both. The mirrored positioning of a (future) democracy and a (modern) republic reflects Marx's characterization of the republic as "democracy within the abstract state form." Finally, the two categorical dimensions (abstract and concrete; free and unfree) combine to produce a constitutional typology that also reflects the historical progression suggested by Marx's account, whereby the future democracy both restores the concrete nature of the premodern world and supersedes it by maintaining the freedoms of the modern world.[223]

222. Marx says that "The state is an abstraction. The people alone is what is concrete," and "The political state is the *mirror of truth* for the various elements of the *concrete state*"; ibid., 29, 117 / 28, 107.

223. As such, the reconstruction of Marx's account also reflects a Hegelian picture of history and constitutional change as a progressive dialectical process, one common to Left Hegelian

A Republican Critique of Communism

Marx's *Kritik* provided a republican critique of the modern state, primarily in the form of Hegel's constitutional monarchy but also as a republic in the American model. That critique exists on a continuum with the arguments that subsequently led him to communism the following year, as is explored in chapter 3. But a widespread interpretation holds that the *Kritik* already represents Marx's conversion to communism. Shlomo Avineri provocatively argues that,

> The *Critique* contains ample material to show that Marx envisages in 1843 a society based on the abolition of private property and on the disappearance of the state. Briefly, the *Communist Manifesto* is immanent in the *Critique of Hegel's Philosophy of Right* . . . [It is thus] impossible to construe his *Critique* as a radical democratic or republican tract.[224]

Avineri's position has been influential in subsequent commentary on the *Kritik*.[225] But, despite the popularity of this interpretation, there is in fact remarkably little textual evidence for the underlying set of claims (that Marx believes in the abolition of the state and private property), which supposedly justifies seeing the *Kritik* as Marx's abandonment of republicanism for communism.

---

thought. Bruno Bauer's depiction, cited in the epigraph, of each state form being "overcome by its consequence" so that there is a progression from the feudal state to absolute monarchy, then to constitutional monarchy and finally to a republic, is a typical example; see Bauer, *Die gute Sache der Freiheit*, 119. This Hegelian *progressive* view of history might be interestingly contrasted with an older republican view that sees history as a *cyclical* process, as in Polybius's influential application of Aristotle's constitutional schema, whereby each correct constitution necessarily transforms into its deviant counterpart, which is then in turn replaced by the next correct constitution that then also eventually decays, leading to a continuous cycle of constitutions (a cycle only temporarily arrested by a mixed constitution). On the role of this Polybian idea in republican thought, see J. G. A. Pocock, *The Machiavellian Moment: Florentine Political Thought and the Atlantic Republican Tradition* (Princeton: Princeton University Press, 1975), 76–80.

224. Shlomo Avineri, *The Social and Political Thought of Karl Marx* (Cambridge: Cambridge University Press, 1968), 34, 38.

225. Avineri's position is endorsed by both Hunt, *Political Ideas of Marx and Engels*, 1:50, and Warren Breckman, *Marx, the Young Hegelians, and the Origins of Radical Social Theory: Dethroning the Self* (Cambridge: Cambridge University Press, 1999), 283–84. Similar views can also be found in Colletti and McLellan, who argue respectively that "the conclusion of Marx's argument in the *Critique*: [is] the suppression of politics and the extinction of the state" and that "republicanism is not adequate to this new form of society, which involves the disappearance of the state." See Colletti, "Introduction" to Marx, *Early Writings*, 44; and David McLellan, *Marx before Marxism* (London: Macmillan, 1970), 115.

Avineri cannot point to any direct statement in the *Kritik* of Marx's supposed belief in the abolition of private property (since none can be found in the text). Avineri instead supplies a circuitous argument based on Marx's belief that the people should take the place of Hegel's bureaucracy as the "universal class." He argues that since "a class cannot be truly universal unless it is everybody's class, or—to put it otherwise—unless class differences disappear," and since "class is based on property, and property is by nature differential," then Marx's supposed belief in the end of class is also a belief in the "disappearance of property."[226] Each of these argumentative steps is itself questionable and unsupported by textual evidence. It remains unclear why we should understand Marx's remarks that the "universal estate" (a better translation than "class" in this case) should be the "estate of every citizen" as a belief in the abolition of class and property, when his meaning is quite plainly that every citizen should share in the public administration of universal interests rather than those tasks being reserved to Hegel's bureaucracy.[227] There is nothing to suggest that Marx thought this popular administration required that property distinctions between citizens be abolished (especially if Athens is taken to be the reference model, where popular self-administration coexisted with property and class distinctions). Insofar as Marx criticized private property in the *Kritik*, we have already seen that this was in fact directed at private property having an improper relation to the political sphere, particularly through Hegel's defense of giving the aristocracy legislative power because of their landed property ownership. Marx's position in the *Kritik* is not that private property should be abolished, but that it should be suitably constrained and subordinated to the political sphere.

A slightly stronger claim could be made for Marx's supposed belief in the end of the state, with two remarks in the *Kritik* lending themselves to this interpretation. First, having argued that "in democracy the state" becomes "truly general," Marx then continues: "The latest French [writers] have understood this to mean that in true democracy (*wahren Demokratie*) the *political state disappears* (*untergehe*). This is correct insofar as the political state qua political state, as constitution, no longer passes for the whole."[228] Second, Marx argues that "*Electoral reform* within the *abstract political state* is therefore the demand (*Forderung*) for its *dissolution* (*Auflösung*), but also for the *dissolution of civil society*."[229]

Understandably, these remarks have given the impression that Marx believes in the end of the state. But David Leopold has convincingly shown that

226. Avineri, *Social and Political Thought of Karl Marx*, 37.

227. Marx, *Kritik*, MEGA I.2: 54 / MECW 3: 50.

228. Ibid., 32 / 30.

229. Ibid., 131 / 121.

a careful reading overturns that initial impression.[230] In both remarks, Marx in fact only discusses the abstract, political state and not the state as such (even specifying that he means the "political state qua political state"). That implies that Marx believes that it is only those objectionable features of modern abstract states that disappear (that is, their divide between political and civil society spheres, and the distance between the state and the people), and not that all the features that we associate with states disappear (such as binding decisions on issues of common concern in a given territory). Both remarks also display a degree of distancing on Marx's part from the claims in question; in the first, Marx says he is discussing the claims made by the "latest French" writers, and in the second, the "demand (*Forderung*)" for electoral reform rather than electoral reform itself. The latter suggests that Marx means that the demand for electoral reform in the modern state reveals a desire for political participation that the modern state cannot satisfy, but which a future democratic state would. In addition, at various points of the *Kritik*, Marx seems happy to describe this future political association as a state, calling it a "true state (*wahren Staat*)" and a "rational state (*vernünftigen Staat*)."[231] Leopold therefore concludes that Marx's position is "not that the state as such ceases to exist, but only that the political community no longer takes an "abstract" form."[232] The abstraction of the modern state is accordingly overcome through what Leopold aptly calls Marx's three "quasi-institutional threads" (extensive political participation for the common good, public administration by the people, and popular delegacy rather than representative democracy), drawn from the "civic republican tradition," which "function to bridge the gap between individuals and the political community."[233] Thus the overcoming of the modern split between state and civil society, which Marx envisages will occur in a future democracy, occurs through changes in the political constitution and not through social reform to property.[234]

A careful sifting of the evidence shows that Marx did not advocate for the end of the state and private property in the *Kritik*. But one final piece of textual

230. Leopold, *Young Karl Marx*, 254–62. See also Richard Nordahl, "Marx and Utopia: A Critique of the 'Orthodox' View," *Canadian Journal of Political Science* 20, no. 4 (1987): 763–65.

231. Marx, *Kritik*, MEGA I.2: 54–55 / MECW 3: 50–51.

232. Leopold, *Young Karl Marx*, 260.

233. Ibid.

234. Ruge subsequently outlined a very similar idea, arguing that "the abolition of the split between state life (*Staatsleben*) and human life is the politicization of all people—everyone forms the polis"; see *Zwei Jahre in Paris: Studien und Erinnerungen*, vol. 2 (Leipzig: Wilhelm Jurany, 1846), 63.

evidence from the text might suggest a conversion to communism.[235] Marx argues that the "atomism" of modern civil society can be traced to "the community, the communist being (*das Gemeinwesen, das communistische Wesen*), in which the individual resides, is civil society separated from the state."[236] But this reference to communism hardly signals a wholesale ideological conversion. Marx is using "communist" in the thin sense of our communal and other-regarding nature, a feature of our human nature that he thinks is inadequately realized in modern states. Such uses of "communism" can be found also in Feuerbach's writings and those of other republican figures at the time.[237] In the same summer as the *Kritik*, Julius Fröbel argued that while republicans were "decidedly *opposed*" to the communist "*abolition of property*," they were in one "sense . . . decidedly *communistic*" because they believed that a "*spirit of community*" should imbue all of society and were opposed to the "*egoism* that poisons public life."[238]

The *Kritik* therefore does not mark Marx's supposed conversion to communism.[239] That is even more obvious if we examine Marx's explicit public criticisms of communism and socialism at the same time as the *Kritik*. These appear in his September letter in the "Briefwechsel von 1843," written in Kreuznach a few weeks before his move to Paris (the letter for which we also happen to have the most confidence of Marx's authorship). Marx here expressed a degree of sympathy with communism as a "particular manifestation . . . of the humanistic principle" and even admits that there may be "some imaginary and possible communism" to which his critique may not apply. But Marx calls the "actually existing communism" of "[Étienne] Cabet, [Théodore]

235. As pointed to in Avineri, *Social and Political Thought of Karl Marx*, 34.

236. Marx, *Kritik*, 88 / 79.

237. Leopold, *Young Karl Marx*, 215. Bakunin (at this point not yet an anarchist or communist) argued that while he rejected the communist label, he did believe in a "*true communism*," understood as a "*community* of free people"; see his "Der Kommunismus," *Schweizerischer Republikaner*, no. 44 (2 June 1843): 204–5, and no. 45 (6 June 1843): 212.

238. [Julius Fröbel], "Programm des Republikaners," *Schweizerischer Republikaner*, no. 47 (13 June 1843): 222. Marx wrote to Fröbel a few months later complaining of the "pseudo-republicans" in the Swiss government who were hindering Fröbel's work on the *Deutsch-Französische Jahrbücher*; see Marx to Julius Fröbel, 21 November 1843, *MEGA* III.1: 62 / *MECW* 3: 353.

239. Added to this, a year after the original *Kritik* Marx claimed he was reworking it into a "new examination" of the topic. Marx to Feuerbach, 11 August 1844, *MEGA* III.1: 63 / *MECW* 3: 354. According to Ruge, at least, Marx's new critique would this time "communistically criticize Hegel's natural law." Arnold Ruge to Max Duncker, 29 August 1844, *Studien zur Marxs Paris Aufenthalt*, 211.

Dézamy [and Wilhelm] Weitling" a "dogmatic abstraction" and argues that it is the task of critics, like Ruge and himself, to clarify its dogmatic propositions to its proponents.[240]

Marx directed an array of criticisms against these "actually existing" communists.[241] He first rejected their complete opposition to private property, which he thought was a "one-sided realization of the socialist principal," when in fact—in a provocative twist—"[a]bolition of private property and communism are not at all identical."[242] Marx continued that this one-sided emphasis was evident also in communism's crude materialism, which focuses only on the "one side . . . the *reality*" of man's existence at the expense of his "other side . . . [his] theoretical existence" (a set of criticisms that could have been directed at Dézamy's strict egalitarian distribution of property).[243] Next, Marx attacked the communist tendency toward utopian system-building rather than engaging in immanent critique of existing society. He singled out *Voyage en Icarie* (1840), Cabet's detailed literary depiction of a fictional communist society, as a mistaken attempt to confront people with a "ready-made system" rather than work from their existing concerns.[244] The critic, Marx insists, "does not dogmatically anticipate the world, but finds the new world through criticism of the old one."[245]

Finally, and most extensively, Marx criticized existing communists for their indifference to politics. Marx insisted that while communists had dismissed discussion of state forms and political institutions for their supposed social irrelevance, these political questions were, in fact, intimately related to social ones. "The political state," Marx claims, "expresses within its form *sub specie reipublicae* [as a particular form of state] all social struggles, needs and truths."[246]

---

240. Marx to Ruge, September 1843, "Ein Briefwechsel von 1843," *MEGA* I.2: 487 / *MECW* 3: 142-43. Ruge evinces a similar attitude to socialists and communists in his contemporaneous preface to Louis Blanc, *Geschichte der zehn Jahre von 1830 bis 1840*, trans. Gottlob Fink (Zürich und Winterthur: Verlag des literarischen Comptoirs, 1843), v–vi.

241. In contrast to these communists, Marx says he is more positive about the "socialist teachings" of Charles Fourier and Pierre-Joseph Proudhon. But we should resist the impulse to see this as a differentiation between socialism and communism, because Marx's subsequent usage in the letter equates the two.

242. Marx to Ruge, September 1843, "Ein Briefwechsel von 1843," *MEGA* I.2 487 / *MECW* 3: 143.

243. See Théodore Dézamy, *Code de la communauté* (Paris, 1842), 264–65.

244. Marx to Ruge, September 1843, "Ein Briefwechsel von 1843," *MEGA* I.2: 487 / *MECW* 3: 143.

245. Ibid., 486 / 142.

246. Ibid., 488 / 143.

He gave the example of the political struggle between a system of estates and a modern representative system (the question he had himself addressed in his journalism). Marx maintained that these contrasting systems must be the object of critique because they "only express in a *political* way the difference between the rule of man and the rule of private property." Thus even "the most specialized political question" cannot be beyond the target of the critic. Moreover, Marx argued that engaging in these questions is how a broad political coalition could be formed, since by taking up the interests that already moved the wider population, such as the fight between estate and representative systems, one could build a "large party." Marx concluded that there was a necessity for "partisan participation in politics" and that "The critic not only can but must engage in these political questions (which according to the views of the crass socialists are beneath their dignity)."[247]

Marx's strident view on the necessity of engaging with political questions can be contrasted (and was possibly directed against) the position taken by Weitling. While Weitling rejected the old estate system of inherited political privilege, he had little time for the demand for representation.[248] The "boring, donkey-like, quarrelsome debates of the many-headed constitutional and republican hydra" were just "chaff thrown into the eyes of peoples so that they do not see who eats their grain."[249] "What is the point," Weitling asked, "of us having the right to throw a name in the election pot, when after the election we see that the rich are in the right and we in the wrong."[250] Weitling also had little trust in the ability of democratic elections and what "republicans . . . call rule by the people (*Volksherrschaft*)" to promote talent to office, given the inability of the "prejudiced stupid masses" to recognize said talent.[251] He instead hoped to escape politics through what he called the "rule of knowledge (*Herrschaft des Wissens*)": a complex system of concentric bodies of scientists, inventors, and production experts, culminating in a so-called "*Trio* or Three-Men Council" made up of the greatest "geniuses in *medicine, physics* and *engineering*."[252]

---

247. Ibid., 488 / 144.

248. Wilhelm Weitling, *Garantien der Harmonie und Freiheit* (Vivis: Verlag des Verfassers 1842), 129.

249. Ibid., 132, 135–36.

250. Ibid., 225.

251. Ibid., 130–31, 141; "Die Regierungsform unsers Prinzips," *Die Junge Generation*, no. 6 (June 1842): 84.

252. Weitling, *Garantien*, 129, 136. Waltraud Seidel-Höppner has, however, recently stressed the democratic side of Weitling's technocratic system, since he believed that the necessary scientific expertise should be universalized through education; see her *Wilhelm Weitling (1808–1871): Eine Politische Biographie* (Frankfurt am Main: Peter Lang, 2014), 393–94, 400–401.

Given Marx's democratic republican sympathies, it is no surprise that he was repelled by this technocratic and antipolitical vision. While he thought that existing communisms had grasped at something important, they had done so in a deeply misguided way. In September 1843, his attitude to communism was that of a critical but sympathetic observer—unconvinced yet clearly agitated by the challenge it posed to existing radical political ideas, an attitude common to republican commentary on communism at the time.[253] Marx's explicit plan for his move to Paris was to "help the dogmatists to clarify their propositions to themselves" and bring the communists to a more reasonable position.[254] It is then easy to see a certain irony in that Marx's planned confrontation with communism in Paris actually ended with his conversion to communism. A story could thus be told that Marx's gaze into the communist "abyss" ended with the abyss gazing into him.

But that would be too simple a narrative. If we study Marx's criticisms of existing communism—its opposition to private property, its utopianism, its antipolitics—it is clear that Marx did not so much convert to communism as fashion a new form of it. His skepticism of utopianism and his commitment to politics would come to be central distinguishing features of his communism. Even on the all-important question of private property, where Marx did change his mind, he continued to criticize communisms that crudely equalized or leveled all forms of property and did not specifically focus on abolishing capitalist private property (i.e., that produced by wage-labor).[255] As we will see in the coming chapters, Marx thus built a new form of communism out of his republican criticisms of existing communism.

Coda

The young republican Marx's study of the modern state resulted in a critique of the three main competing models of his era, from absolute and constitutional monarchy to a republic, as well as his suggestive development and defense of an alternative future democracy. Only by placing his critique in its context

253. See especially the above-cited articles by Fröbel and Bakunin in the *Schweizerischer Republikaner* in the summer of 1843. Marx had also displayed a similar attitude the year before, when he had defended the *Rheinische Zeitung* against the charge of spreading communism; see Marx, "Der Kommunismus und die Augsburger 'Allgemeine Zeitung,'" *MEGA* I.1: 240 / *MECW* 1: 220.

254. Marx to Ruge, September 1843, "Ein Briefwechsel von 1843," *MEGA* I.2: 487 / *MECW* 3: 142.

255. Marx, *Ökonomisch-philosophische Manuskripte*, *MEGA* I.2: 386–89 / *MECW* 3: 293–97; Marx and Engels, *Manifest der Kommunistischen Partei*, *MEW* 4: 475 / *MECW* 6: 498; Marx, "Kritik des Gothaer Programms," *MEGA* I.25: 11–16 / *MECW* 24: 83–88.

were we able to properly appreciate what was typical and what distinctive in this account. While his separation of a republic from a democracy went against the grain of the contemporary equation of the two, his reasons for doing so did not distinguish him from his fellow republicans; the same goes for some of the passing remarks that have led interpreters to implausibly pronounce Marx's conversion to communism. A careful study of Marx's texts in their political context shows that in 1843 he held to a characteristically republican vision in which the distance between the political sphere and civil society was overcome through citizens' widespread political participation in the governing and administration of their democracy. His concern at the time was not with bridging this divide through the abolition of private property. As with many of his fellow republicans, he opposed this communist demand, along with the communist rejection of politics, while being sympathetic to the communist critique of the egoism of modern civil society. Through his criticisms of the unaccountability of constitutional monarchs and their bureaucracies, Marx also continued to express his opposition to arbitrary power that had so marked his republican journalism. That abiding concern would soon, as we will see in the following chapter, be transferred from these political institutions to his engagement with arbitrary power in capitalist society.

3

Soldiers of Socialism

MARX'S TRANSITION TO COMMUNISM, 1843–45

The circumstance of [economic measures] . . . having emanated from the privy council of an arbitrary monarch, or the representative assembly of a free state . . . cannot affect the immutable principles by which the economist is to form his opinion upon them.

—JOHN RAMSAY MCCULLOCH. EXTRACTED BY MARX IN 1844.[1]

Without a tear in their grim eyes,
They sit at the loom, the rage of despair in their faces;
We have suffered and hunger'd long enough;
Old Germany, we are weaving a shroud for thee
And weaving it with a triple curse.
We are weaving, weaving!

—FROM HEINRICH HEINE'S "DIE SCHLESISCHEN WEBER" ("THE SILESIAN WEAVERS")[2]

IN NOVEMBER 1843 Friedrich Engels made his first public statement of his new communist convictions.[3] In an article for the Owenist journal *The New Moral World*, he endeavored to provide his English audience with an overview

1. J. R. M'Culloch, *A Discourse on the Rise, Progress, Peculiar Objects, and Importance, of Political Economy* (Edinburg: Archibald Constable, 1824), 74–75; Marx "Exzerpte aus MacCulloch," *MEGA* IV.2: 476. Marx studied an 1825 French translation of MacCulloch and translated parts of the text, including the above, into German.

2. English translation by Engels for *The New Moral World* in December 1844; see Engels, "Rapid Progress of Communism in Germany I," *MEGA* I.4: 508 / *MECW* 4: 232.

3. In Engels's articles for Julius Fröbel's *Schweizerischer Republikaner* a few months earlier he had reported his positive impression of English socialism without necessarily endorsing it; see "Briefe aus London. III," *MEGA* I.3: 463 / *MECW* 3: 389.

of the development of socialism and communism (he used the terms inter-changeably) in France and Germany. Engels argued that German communism had two distinct parties. One was a popular movement of traveling artisan workers who had imbibed new social ideas on their visits to France and whose political and intellectual leader was Wilhelm Weitling. The other was a philo-sophical movement of Young Hegelians who had radicalized Hegel's thought so that they first became "declared Atheists and Republicans" and then, "by developing further and further the consequences of their philosophy, became Communists." By Engels's account, in 1842 only a few Young Hegelians had realized the "insufficiency of political change, and declared . . . that a *Social* revolution based upon common property, was the only state of mankind agreeing with their abstract principles," while the "leaders of the party, such as Dr. Bruno Bauer, Dr. Feuerbach, and Dr. Ruge" remained in the republican camp. "Communism, however, was such a *necessary* consequence of New Hegelian philosophy," Engels continued, that "in the course of this present year [1843], the originators of it had the satisfaction of seeing one republican after the other join their ranks." Engels listed "Dr. Hess . . . Dr. Ruge . . . [and] Dr. Marx" as converts and expressed his hope that the "remainder of the re-publican party will, by-and-by, come over too."[4]

According to Engels, then, Moses Hess, Arnold Ruge and Marx had all supposedly converted from republicanism to communism by November 1843. Engels was writing from Manchester, where he had had moved one year be-fore, and he had only indirect access to these apparent developments. His most likely informant was Hess, who was certainly a communist and had been for a few years.[5] Hess in fact tried to claim credit for having converted Engels from an "Anno I [the first year of the French Republican calendar] revolution-ary" to "the most eager communist," when Engels had visited Hess in the *Rhe-inische Zeitung*'s Cologne editorial office on his way to England in the autumn of 1842.[6] (Engels's first meeting with Marx occurred a few weeks later, when Engels returned to the newspaper's office—a meeting Engels later described as "distinctly chilly."[7]) But a study of Engels's subsequent articles shows that Hess at most whetted Engels's appetite for socialism and Engels in fact

4. Engels, "Progress of Social Reform on the Continent," *MEGA* I.3: 508–9 / *MECW* 3: 405–6.

5. See the editorial discussion in *MEGA* I.3: 702.

6. Moses Hess to Berthold Auerbach, 19 June 1843, *Moses Hess Briefwechsel*, ed. Edmund Silberner ('s-Gravenhage: Mouton, 1959), 103.

7. Engels to Franz Mehring, end of April 1895, *MEW* 39: 473; *MECW* 50: 503. Marx associ-ated Engels with the ultraradicalism of the *Freien* that he was trying to purge from the *Rheinische Zeitung*.

continued to espouse his democratic republican commitments some months after meeting Hess and traveling to England.[8] Assuming Hess was Engels's subsequent informant, a similar case of overoptimism on Hess's part might have been at play in Engels's report of Ruge's and Marx's supposed conversions to communism.[9] While Ruge was sympathetic to its social critique, he never converted to communism, and Marx's conversion still lay several months before him. At the time of Engels's article, Marx had been in Paris for just under a month. He had moved to the city to edit the *Deutsch-Französische Jahrbücher* with Ruge and stayed until his expulsion by the French government (on Prussia's request) at the end of January 1845. It is in this period in Paris that Marx underwent his transition from republicanism to self-identifying communist. This chapter charts that transition.

As we saw in chapter 2, Marx left Germany committed to "true democracy" and critical of communism's apolitical stance and overemphasis on the abolition of private property. His first articles in Paris, which were published in the *Deutsch-Französische Jahrbücher* and are the subject of the opening section of this chapter, demonstrate how swiftly his thought had developed from this position. He no longer thought "democracy" an adequate description of his politics and now aligned himself with the proletariat's goal of abolishing private property to achieve true human emancipation. But he also remained firmly committed to political emancipation, leaving him in an ideological gray zone, unwilling to explicitly commit himself to communism. His scruples did not last long, however, and he soon broke with Ruge over Ruge's failure to go over to communism. I consequently, in the second section, turn to an extensive discussion of Ruge's republican thought as a comparison with that of Marx. The ideological distance that opened up between the two was quickly evident in their differing responses to the Silesian Weavers' Revolt in June 1844—the subject of the third section of this chapter.[10] While Ruge lamented the worker's lack of political goals, Marx celebrated that the revolt had shown

8. David Gregory, "Karl Marx's and Friedrich Engels' Knowledge of French Socialism in 1842–43," *Historical Reflections / Réflexions Historiques* 10, no. 1 (1983): 147. On Engels's early republicanism, see the editorial discussion in *MEGA* I.3: 13–15, 23–24, and Richard N. Hunt, *The Political Ideas of Marx and Engels*, vol. 1 (Pittsburgh: University of Pittsburgh Press, 1974), 93–104.

9. In February 1845, Engels made the similarly hopeful but mistaken claim that "Dr. Feuerbach ... has declared himself a Communist"; see "Rapid Progress of Communism in Germany II," *MEGA* I.4: 540 / *MECW* 4: 235.

10. These played out in the German-Parisian newspaper *Vorwärts!* (*Forward!*), the same paper that published Heine's famous tribute to the weavers and their triple curse against God, King, and Country), see H. H.[eine], "Die armen Weber," *Vorwärts!*, no. 55 (10 July 1844): 1. Heine subsequently gave the poem its better known title, "Die schlesischen Weber."

that workers were not "soldiers of the republic" but "soldiers of socialism."[11] I show how Marx's defense of the weavers represented a sharp antipolitical turn in his thinking, typical of early communism. That stance, however, did not last long and was less pronounced than the explicit antidemocratic position evident in the transition to communism in figures like the early Engels. Yet Marx's initial partial repudiation of some of his republican political inheritance did not stop him from continuing to deploy republican ideas in his first study of political economy, undertaken in the spring and summer of 1844. I thus close the chapter with a fourth and final section, showing how Marx's early critique of political economy condemned the domination to which both capitalism and the capitalist subjected the worker, leaving them alienated and unfree.

Human and Political Emancipation

Paris offered Marx and Ruge a relative haven of press freedom for their joint journalistic venture after the parallel suppression of their respective *Rheinische Zeitung* and the *Deutsche Jahrbücher* in January 1843. Paris also provided them an almost unparalleled intellectual atmosphere at the forefront of political and social developments. Marx excitedly predicted that it was the "new capital of the new world."[12] Their *Deutsch-Französische Jahrbücher* (which might be seen as the next stage in the geographic expansion of Ruge's *Hallische* and then *Deutsche Jahrbücher*) was supposed to be more than just a German journal published in France and, rather, the means to further a true "Franco-German scientific alliance."[13] Marx and Ruge tried to include French contributors from across the spectrum of progressive thought, from Alphonse de Lamartine and Félicité de Lamennais to Louis Blanc and Étienne Cabet. But the language barrier and the French incomprehension and aversion to their Hegelian atheism meant that the journal was forced to go ahead with exclusively German contributions. The moderate republican Marie d'Agoult, for instance, declared herself "too French" to understand the project of the "jeune école hégélienne," with its "taste for abstraction, [and] the insane stubborness of the absolute."[14]

---

11. Marx, "Kritische Randglossen," *MEGA* I.2: 461 / *MECW* 3: 204.

12. Marx to Ruge, September 1843, "Ein Briefwechsel von 1843," *MEGA* I.2: 486 / *MECW* 3: 142.

13. Marx to Ludwig Feuerbach, 3 October 1843, *MEGA* III.1: 58/*MECW* 3: 349. For this plan, see Beatrix Mesmer-Strupp, *Arnold Ruges Plan einer Alliance intellectuelle zwischen Deutschen und Franzosen* (Bern: W. Dürrenmatt, 1963), chapters 3–4.

14. Daniel Stern [Marie d'Agoult], "George Herwegh et les hégéliens politiques," *La Presse* (17 November 1843): 1; Marie d'Agoult to Georg Herwegh, between 25 and 27 February 1844, *Au Printemps des dieux: Correspondance inedite de la Comtesse Marie d'Agoult et du poète Georges*

The first (and as it would transpire final) double issue of the journal appeared in February 1844 and was opened by Ruge's "Plan" and the edited letters in "Ein Briefwechsel von 1843" that were discussed in chapter 2. In the journal's introduction, Ruge called for a "German *Contrat social*" and the "unification of the German and French people under the same humanistic principle."[15] This vague humanism papered over significant ideological differences among the contributors. This stretched from the oppositional liberalism of Johann Jacoby to Ruge's republicanism and the outright communism of Moses Hess and Friedrich Engels, the latter of which sent two articles from Manchester, including his important "Umrisse zu einer Kritik der Nationalökonomie" ("Outlines of a Critique of Political Economy"). Marx himself contributed two articles to the journal, which were the product of his rapidly evolving thought since arriving in Paris: "Zur Judenfrage" and "Zur Kritik der Hegel'schen Rechts-philosophie: Einleitung" ("Critique of Hegel's Philosophy of Right: Introduction"), hereafter "Kritik: Einleitung."[16] Both articles are misleadingly titled. "Zur Judenfrage" is not primarily about the question of Jewish emancipation, and the introduction to a critique of Hegel mentions Hegel only once (though presumably the subsequent full critique that Marx never wrote would have more extensively engaged with Hegel).[17] The common theme of the articles was in fact the distinction between political and what Marx called human emancipation, and what agent could bring about the latter.

Marx's "Zur Judenfrage" was ostensibly a response to Bruno Bauer's 1843 *Die Judenfrage* (*The Jewish Question*) and his follow-up article, "Die Fähigkeit des heutigen Juden und Christen, frei zu werden" ("The Capacity of Present-Day Jews and Christians to Become Free"), where Bauer argued against Jewish emancipation. In his dull and offensive tirade, Bauer maintained that in order for Jews to be fully incorporated as citizens they would have to give up their particular identity as Jews. Political emancipation in the modern state, Bauer

Herwegh, 1843–1867, ed. Marcel Herwegh (Paris: Gallimard, 1929), 42. See further Jonathan Beecher, *Writers and Revolution: Intellectuals and the French Revolution of 1848* (Cambridge: Cambridge University Press, 2021), 135–36.

15. Arnold Ruge, "Plan der Deutsch-Französischen Jahrbücher," in *Deutsch-Französische Jahrbücher*, ed. Arnold Ruge and Karl Marx (Paris: Bureau der Jahrbücher, 1844), 6, 12.

16. While "Zur Judenfrage" is sometimes thought to have been written in Kreuznach, I follow the *MEGA* editors' reasoning that both it and "Kritik: Einleitung" date from mid-October to mid-December 1843; see *MEGA*, I.2: 650–51.

17. The "Kritik: Einleitung" was not an introduction to the *Kritik* from 1843 but an introduction to a new critique of Hegel that was supposed to appear in future issues of the *Deutsch-Französische Jahrbücher*.

claimed, required the renunciation of all religion.[18] Marx roundly rejected Bauer's view, arguing that the modern state was in fact perfectly compatible with citizens maintaining their religious—including Jewish—faith.[19] Marx argued that Bauer's study was flawed because he had only examined Jewish emancipation in relation to Christian absolutist states (Prussia) and liberal constitutional states (France and the southern German states) and ignored the American republic, "where the political state exists in its complete development."[20] Drawing on his reading of the studies of Gustave de Beaumont, Alexis de Tocqueville, and Thomas Hamilton, Marx argued that had Bauer examined the American case, he would have seen that in the most politically advanced country, where there was no state religion and no religious requirement for political rights, "religion not only *exists*, but displays a *fresh and vigorous vitality*."[21] The experience of the American republic showed that a state could emancipate itself from religion without the people themselves being free of religion. Consequently, the real problem—and the actual focus of "Zur Judenfrage"—was that *political* emancipation in the modern state did not result in *human* emancipation.

Marx turned this insight into a broader social critique of property and civil society in the modern state. Returning to a point he had raised against Hegel's account of his rational state, Marx argued that a defining and laudable feature of the modern state was the removal of property qualifications from the right to vote and stand for office. He argued that Hamilton was "from the political standpoint completely right" to have observed that this development in many American states meant that "*The masses have won a victory over the property owners and*

18. Douglas Moggach, *The Philosophy and Politics of Bruno Bauer* (Cambridge: Cambridge University Press, 2003), 145–49. Bauer further endorsed the anti-Semitic position that Judaism was an especially particularistic religion in comparison to the supposedly more universalistic Christianity; see David Leopold, "The Hegelian Antisemitism of Bruno Bauer," *History of European Ideas* 25, no. 4 (1999): 182, 185.

19. For the importance of this political difference between Marx and Bauer, the wider context of Jewish emancipation at the time, and the question of Marx's own supposed anti-Semitism, see David Leopold, *The Young Karl Marx: German Philosophy, Modern Politics, and Human Flourishing* (Cambridge: Cambridge University Press, 2007), chapter 2.

20. Marx, "Zur Judenfrage," *MEGA* I.2: 145 / *MECW* 3: 150; see also Marx and Engels, *Die Heilige Familie*, *MEGA* I.4: 116-18 / *MECW* 4: 114–16. This is indeed an odd oversight in Bauer's work, given his republican commitments and his own account of the political limitations of the French *juste-milieu* regime; see Bruno Bauer, *Die Judenfrage* (Braunschweig: Friedrich Otto, 1843), 72 / *The Jewish Problem*, trans. Helen Lederer (Ohio: Hebrew Union College—Jewish Institute of Religion, 1958), 75–76.

21. Marx, "Zur Judenfrage," *MEGA* I.2: 146 / *MECW* 3: 151.

financial wealth."[22] But, Marx continued, the "political annulment of private property" in the modern state did not mean that private property is "abolished (*aufgehoben*)"—in fact the modern state "presupposes" that it is not.[23] When the modern state abolishes distinctions based on "*birth, social rank, education, occupation*" it does so only insofar as these are no longer restrictions on "every member of the people's *equal* participation in popular sovereignty," but the modern state allows such distinctions to exist "*outside* of the state sphere, in *civil society.*"[24] Property thus ceases to be a basis for political inequality but continues to be a basis of social distinction. Marx argued that this was the natural outcome of the modern state's definitional split between political sphere and civil society, which meant that the modern state did not truly free people from obstacles to their freedom, it only relegated those obstacles to civil society. He observed that in the modern state "man was not freed from religion, he received religious freedom. He was not freed from property, he received freedom to own property. He was not freed from the egoism of business, he received freedom to engage in business."[25] This, Marx argued, was the central emancipatory failure of the modern state: "The limits of political emancipation are evident at once from the fact that the *state* can free itself from a restriction without man being *really* free from this restriction, that the state can be a *free state* (*Freistaat*) without man being *a free man.*"[26]

This critique is undoubtably of central importance to understanding Marx's changing relationship to republicanism. Marx is explicitly attacking the idea that the *Freistaat* (a synonym for republic) was sufficient for emancipation. It amounts to a stern amendment to the old republican view—articulated by the early modern humanists—that it is "only possible to be free in a free state."[27] That view was grounded in the republican idea of freedom, that a person cannot be free in an absolutist state since their ruler can interfere with their lives at will. To be free requires a state where political power is properly constrained by law and (more or less extensive) popular participation in government. Marx's critique was that this was not sufficient for a person to be free if they remained unfree in civil society. In order to be free, a person has to live not only in a free *state* but in a free *society*.

---

22. Ibid., 148 / 153; Hamilton, *Die Menschen und die Sitten in den vereinigten Staaten von Nordamerika*, trans. L. Hout, vol. 1 (Mannheim: Heinrich Hoff, 1834), 146 (the phrase does not appear in the English original).

23. Marx, "Zur Judenfrage," *MEGA* 1.2: 148 / *MECW* 3: 153.

24. Ibid.

25. Ibid., 161 / 167.

26. Ibid., 147 / 152.

27. Quentin Skinner, *Liberty before Liberalism* (Cambridge: Cambridge University Press, 1998), 60.

But, while this is undoubtably a central part of why Marx transitioned from republicanism to socialism, it is too quick to say that "Zur Judenfrage" thus constitutes, as Richard Hunt argues, "Marx's open announcement of his conversion, his definitive repudiation of his former republican views, of mere 'political emancipation.'"[28] Marx's essay is certainly a critique of a kind of republicanism (and indeed liberalism) that is entirely restricted to the political realm and allows unfreedom and inequality to flourish in civil society. But such a purely "political" republicanism was restricted to a minor part of the wider republican movement.[29] The mainstream of republicanism at the time was thoroughly aware of the social dimensions of freedom and the limits of merely political emancipation.[30] Georg Wirth had already argued in 1833 that "not even the purest popular sovereignty and the most expansive democratic republic" would by itself be enough to end the dependency of the emerging class of wage-laborers; and Julius Fröbel (the *Deutsch-Französische Jahrbücher*'s publisher) had the summer before Marx's critique stressed that republicans had to address the *"economic obstacles* to the development of democracy."[31] Few republicans thought the struggle ended with political reform. As Bronterre O'Brien put it, "[w]here or when did we pretend that these [political reforms] were *sufficient*. Never; nowhere"; they were instead the "means to an end" of the people's comprehensive emancipation.[32] What actually distinguished republicans from socialists and communists was not that republicans were solely committed to political emancipation but that they had a different conception of what social measures should accompany political emancipation. Republicans thought social dependency should be addressed through measures that reaffirmed the independence of artisan workers and peasant farmers, such as free education and free state credit, and progressive income and inheritance taxes, while remaining "resolutely *against abolition (Abschaffung) of property*" called for by socialists and communists.[33]

28. Hunt, *Political Ideas of Marx and Engels*, 1: 68.

29. See the discussion of the bourgeois republicans in chapters 4 and 5.

30. For a useful reminder that earlier republicans were also not solely concerned with political freedom, see Annelien de Dijn, "Republicanism and Egalitarianism: A Historical Perspective," unpublished manuscript.

31. J. G. A. Wirth, *Die Rechte des deutschen Volkes: Eine Vertheidigungsrede vor den Assisen zu Landau* (Nancy, 1833), 35; [Julius Fröbel], "Programm des Republikaners," *Schweizerischer Republikaner*, no. 47 (13 June 1843): 222.

32. Bronterre O'Brien, "Reply to Mr. Owen," *The Poor Man's Guardian*, no. 198 (21 March 1835): 468.

33. Fröbel, "Program des Republikaners," *Schweizerischer Republikaner*, no. 47 (13 June 1843): 222, and no. 48 (16 June 1843): 229; see also Wirth, *Die Rechte des deutschen Volkes*, 36–38, 66,

Marx's critique of the limits of political emancipation is thus not enough to justify concluding that he had converted from republicanism to socialism; we have to analyse what social alternative he thought was necessary for human emancipation. Certainly, Marx's criticism that political emancipation had neither "freed [man] from property" nor led to it being "abolished (*aufgehoben*)" suggests a changed attitude from his earlier critique of this socialist demand.[34] (Though we should remind ourselves that *Aufhebung* might also be translated by the more open-ended term "supersession.") Further evidence of his more critical standing toward a republican political economy can be found in his skepticism that the "abolition (*Aufhebung*) of private property" could be achieved through the Jacobin's revolutionary measures of "maximum [price controls], ... confiscation [of traitors' property], ...[and] progressive taxation," which he argued ultimately ended with the "reestablishment ... of private property."[35]

But the most important development in Marx's thinking in this regard is found not in "Zur Judenfrage" but in the "Kritik: Einleitung." There, in one of the essay's two most memorable features, Marx for the first time identified the proletariat as the agent of revolution.[36] Marx argued that successful revolutions bring together a theory or philosophy with a class of people with an interest in its realization.[37] In the French Revolution, the bourgeoisie managed to present its particular class interest as the general interest of society, when it had in fact only emancipated those who "possess money and education." The impending German revolution, which Marx maintained cannot be a "partial, *solely* political revolution" but must be a "*radical* revolution," requires a class that would truly carry out a "*universal, human* emancipation."[38] That class, Marx declared, was the proletariat whose emancipation would mean the

---

and O'Brien, "Reply to Mr. Owen," no. 199 (28 March 1835): 473–74. In Moses Hess's categorization of the 1844 French political landscape, he argued that liberals were only interested in "reforms in favor of political freedom" while democrats "strive for social equality." He then subdivided democrats into "pure democrats, i.e. socialists ... or communists" who wanted to abolish private property and "anticommunist democrats" who wanted to maintain it and only "organize labor," Moses Hess, "Briefe aus Paris," *Deutsch-Französische Jahrbücher*, 116, 119.

34. Marx, "Zur Judenfrage," *MEGA* I.2: 148, 161 / *MECW* 3: 153, 167.

35. Ibid., 151 / 156. Marx does not, at this point, insist on the need to differentiate the question of abolishing private property by distinguishing particular forms of private property (e.g., bourgeois or petty bourgeois private property).

36. The other is Marx's much-cited and much-misunderstood remark on religion and opium in "Kritik: Einleitung," 171 / 175. See G. A. Cohen, *If You're an Egalitarian, How Come You're So Rich?* (Cambridge: Harvard University Press, 2000), 79–81.

37. Marx, "Kritik: Einleitung," *MEGA* I.2: 177–78 / *MECW* 3: 182–83.

38. Ibid., 179 / 184.

"dissolution of all estates" rather than the raising of a particular class to rule over others. He claimed that the proletariat's special position as a propertyless class in a society based on private property ("a class of civil society that is not a class of civil society") gives it a unique role in the overthrow of society and the emancipation of all from private property.[39] The abolition of private property is thus the universalization of the proletariat's own class position:

> When the proletariat proclaims the *dissolution of the hitherto existing world order* it merely states the *secret of its own existence,* for it *is* the dissolution of that world order. When the proletariat demands the *negation of private property*, it merely raises to the rank of a *principle of society* what society has made *its* principle . . . [40]

This breakthrough was so important to Marx's transition from republicanism to communism not because he now thought the working class would lead the revolution, but because of *which* working class he turned to. Republicanism had traditionally drawn its strength from the working class, but from a predominantly artisan working class, where individual or small groups of artisans produced using their own tools in their own workshops. Marx had instead identified the proletarian working class, who were driven by their lack of property to sell their labor to capitalist employers in large-scale industry, as the revolutionary social actor that would bring about human emancipation. Marx was thereby shifting to a different social basis of support for radical politics. This would lead to a lifelong struggle with both republicanism and artisan forms of socialism, but in the "Kritik: Einleitung" Marx remained wholly unaware of the collision course this had set him upon.[41]

Marx's "discovery" (as it is often referred to) of the proletariat in Paris might easily be taken for granted as the natural outcome of being exposed to the capital's supposedly more advanced industrial conditions compared with those in the German states.[42] But the Parisian working class (like that of much of Europe outside of Britain and a few strips of industrial development on the Continent) was in fact still overwhelmingly made up of artisans. An 1848 survey found that in half of all Paris's workshops the owner worked alone

39. Ibid., 181 / 186.

40. Ibid., 182/187.

41. His first inkling of this conflict comes a few months later when he praises the French and English proletariat as well as the "theoretical contributions of German artisans (*Handwerker*)" but complains that the "German artisan is still too much of an artisan"; Marx to Feuerbach, 11 August, *MEGA* III.1: 63–64 / *MECW* 3: 355.

42. As in Hal Draper, *Karl Marx's Theory of Revolution*, vol. 1 (New York: Monthly Review Press, 1977), 136–38.

or with just one employee, and only one in ten workshops employed more than ten workers.[43] There was thus hardly much of an existing proletariat in Paris for Marx to discover. Marx's seizing on the proletariat was a combination of an abstract theoretical breakthrough about the social preconditions of human emancipation and his readings of empirical reports on the pace of industrial and social developments in Britain and America that he would have found in Engels and Hamilton. Engels had reported in the *Deutsch-Französische Jahrbücher* of the transformative power of industrial steam-powered industry and its result in the "division of humanity into capitalists and workers, a division that every day becomes ever more acute and . . . is *bound* to deepen" (though it is not clear if Marx had read Engels before writing the "Kritik: Einleitung").[44] In Marx's encounter with Hamilton he had read that "In *New York*, civil society has already actually divided into two parts: the working people and those who can live comfortably, without having to earn their living through manual labour."[45] Hamilton had further predicted that the "great majority of the people will be without property of any kind," in line with America's "destined" path to being a "great manufacturing nation."[46] Such predictions from afar (rather than reflecting the actual conditions in his immediate Parisian or prior German context) impressed Marx enough to pin his expectations on an emergent social class that still barely existed, and all the resultant political struggles with artisan radicalism that this entailed.

Marx's critique of private property and discovery of the proletariat were certainly significant milestones in his transition from republicanism to communism. They give strong grounds for thinking that, at least in terms of substantive positions, he had transitioned to communism. But we should be careful about simply describing his articles in the *Deutsch-Französische Jahrbücher*

43. Mark Traugott, *Armies of the Poor: Determinants of Working-Class Participation in the Parisian Insurrection of June 1848* (Princeton: Princeton University Press, 1985), 5–10; on this study, see Joan W. Scott, "Statistical Representations of Work: The Chamber of Commerce's *Statistique de l'Industrie à Paris, 1847–48*," in *Work in France: Representations, Meaning, Organization, and Practice*, ed. Steven Laurence Kaplan and Cynthia J. Koepp (Ithica: Cornell University Press, 1986), 335–63.

44. Engels, "Umrisse zu einer Kritik der Nationalökonomie," *MEGA* I.3: 479, 481 / *MECW* 3: 428, 430. Marx received Engels's article in November 1843, but in badly damaged form (due to police interference).

45. Hamilton, *Die Menschen und die Sitten*, 1: 151 (compare with Hamilton, *Men and Manners*, 1: 299); Marx, "Exzerpte aus Hamilton," *MEGA* IV.2: 271.

46. Hamilton, *Men and Manners*, 1: 305–6. See further Sean F. Monahan, "The American Workingmen's Parties, Universal Suffrage, and Marx's Democratic Communism," *Modern Intellectual History* 18, no. 2 (2021): 391–95.

as "planting the banner of communism."[47] Nowhere in either essay does he identify himself with (or even mention) socialism or communism. Given that other contributors (Engels and Hess) were willing to do so we should take seriously Marx's decision not to. Part of the explanation probably lies in Marx's own political confusion or uncertainty of how to position himself. As Michael Löwy aptly puts it, this was "a phase of ideological loss of bearings" for Marx.[48] It is likely that in spite of his more critical attitude toward private property he still held to many of the other criticisms of existing socialisms and communisms that he had raised in "Ein Briefwechsel von 1843" (which, despite predating "Zur Judenfrage" and the "Kritik: Einleitung," was published at the same time in the *Deutsch-Französische Jahrbücher*). The concern Marx raised in the letter exchange about maintaining a broad political coalition may have led him to prefer the more ecumenical goal of "human emancipation" to outright communism. Indeed, while the socialist implications of "Zur Judenfrage" were evident to some contemporary readers,[49] they were certainly not obvious to everyone. Max Stirner thought the essay an example of radical Feuerbachian thought rather than socialism or communism; and Ruge saw no difficulty in positively identifying himself with Marx's closing call that human emancipation would only come about when "man reabsorbs in himself the abstract citizen, and . . . has become a *species-being* in his everyday life."[50] In a period of ideological upheaval and formation like the 1840s, it is not surprising that observers would attach divergent interpretations to contested concepts like human emancipation or the *Aufhebung* of private property.[51]

47. Joachim Höppner, "Einleitung," *Deutsch-Französische Jahrbücher* (Leipzig: Philipp Reclam, 1973), 29. At the same time, it goes too far in the other direction to claim that Marx was still a "German Jacobin for whom the proletariat existed primarily as the instrument of revolution"; George Lichtheim, *Marxism: An Historical and Critical Study* (London: Routledge and Kegan Paul, 1961), 38n1. Not least because Marx was consistently critical of the Jacobins in not only "Zur Judenfrage," *MEGA* I.2: 151, 157 / *MECW* 3: 156, 162, but even in his republican early writings; see "Bemerkungen über die neueste preußische Censurinstruction," *MEGA* I.1: 107 / *MECW* 1: 119.

48. Michael Löwy, *The Theory of Revolution in the Young Marx* (Chicago: Haymarket Books, 2005), 40.

49. Karl Grün, *Bausteine: Zusammengetragen und mit einem Sendschreiben an seine Osnabrücker Freunde begleitet* (Darmstadt: C. W. Leske, 1844), xxviii.

50. David Leopold, "The Non-Essentialist Perfectionism of Max Stirner," in *Perfektionismus der Autonomie*, ed. Douglas Moggach, Nadine Mooren, and Michael Quante (Leiden: Wilhelm Fink, 2019), 273. Arnold Ruge, "Offene Antwort an Herrn Heinrich Bornstein," *Vorwärts!* no. 54 (6 July 1844), 3; Marx, "Zur Judenfrage," *MEGA* I.2: 162-63 / *MECW* 3: 168.

51. Irene Fanto, *Karl Marx und sein demokratischer Gegner Arnold Ruge* (Vienna: PhD dissertation, 1937), 92.

Marx's reluctance to identify with socialism and communism also likely stemmed from his continued objection to their indifferent attitude to politics. Throughout "Zur Judenfrage," Marx was at pains to emphasize that though political emancipation was insufficient for human emancipation, it was necessary for it. He insisted that political emancipation was still a "big step forward" and, though it might not be "the final form of human emancipation," it was the "final form of human emancipation *within* the hitherto existing world order."[52] In the middle of his characterization of political emancipation as emancipation through a "*detour* (*Umweg*), through an *intermediary*," he stressed that it was, however, also "a *necessary intermediary*."[53] He furthermore praised the political achievements of the French Revolution, which Marx said turned "state affairs into affairs of the people" and made the state into a "matter of *general* concern." That praise was tempered by Marx's realization that "Throwing off the political yoke meant at the same time throwing off the bonds which restrained the egoistic spirit of civil society." But that should not overshadow the fact that Marx thought the French Revolution's "unleashing of the political spirit" was a positive and necessary development.[54]

Indeed, Marx went beyond this defense of political emancipation to criticize the way in which the political rights that secure political participation were undermined by the egoism of civil society. That becomes clear when we delve into Marx's much misunderstood critique of rights in "Zur Judenfrage." The most persistent myth about "Zur Judenfrage" is that Marx dismissed the value of human rights as such.[55] Marx in fact only criticized a *subset* of rights. As Jeremy Waldron acutely notes, Marx "took very seriously" the distinction implied in the title of the *Déclaration des droits de l'homme et du citoyen* (*Declaration of the Rights of Man and the Citizen*) (1789).[56] Marx consequently argued that human rights were divided into the *droits de l'homme* (rights of man) and the *droits du citoyen*

---

52. Marx, "Zur Judenfrage," *MEGA* I.2: 150 / *MECW* 3: 155.

53. Ibid., 147 / 152.

54. Ibid., 160–61 / 166. Jan Kandiyali has raised with me the possibility that Marx may have thought political emancipation to be a necessary step in order to reach human emancipation but not a necessary component of human emancipation itself (and hence it might not form a part of a humanly emancipated society). While I think that reading cannot be ruled out, I do not think there is positive evidence in favor of it either.

55. For critique of this myth, see Leopold, *Young Karl Marx*, 150–63; Igor Shoikhedbrod, *Revisiting Marx's Critique of Liberalism: Rethinking Justice, Legality and Rights* (Cham: Palgrave Macmillan, 2019), 58–67.

56. Jeremy Waldron, *"Nonsense upon Stilts": Bentham, Burke and Marx on the Rights of Man* (London: Methuen, 1987), 129.

(rights of the citizen).[57] In order to substantiate this distinction Marx engaged in a detailed study of the 1789 Declaration, its 1793 and 1795 successors, and the corresponding French constitutions of 1791, 1793, and 1795, as well as the Pennsylvanian and New Hampshire state constitutions. (It is insufficiently recognized how much of "Zur Judenfrage" is based on close constitutional analysis). He justified this selection with the claim that the American and French revolutionaries were the "*discoverers*" of human rights.[58] On the basis of these documents, Marx defined the rights of man as the "rights of egoistic man, of man separated from the other men and from the community," giving religious freedom and especially the right to private property as prime examples.[59] The rights of the citizen, on the other hand, Marx defined as "*political* rights, rights that can only be exercised in a community with others," whose "content is *participation* in the *community*, and specifically in the *political* community (*politischen Gemeinwesen*), in the *life of the state*."[60] Marx does not give specific examples of the rights of the citizen, but he was probably referring to articles like III and VI of the 1789 Declaration, which enshrined the people's right to participation in sovereignty and in the formation of the general will. Marx's critique of rights was explicitly restricted to the rights of man and does not extend to the rights of the citizen. The failure to recognize the force of this distinction leads to the erroneous interpretation that Marx's "degradation of liberal rights to freedom" included a rejection of the political "right to self-determination."[61]

Marx's distinction between the rights of man and the rights of the citizen corresponds to his earlier distinction between the modern state's foundational split between civil society and the political sphere. That distinction had been a conceptual centerpiece of Marx's *Kritik* and continued to shape his thinking in "Zur Judenfrage." As in the *Kritik*, Marx argued in "Zur Judenfrage" that in the political sphere of the modern state people had a formal but limited ability to act for general interests and realize their essence as a "*communal being*," while in civil society they were forced to follow their egoistic private interests.[62] Similarly, Marx argued that the rights of the citizen enshrined the people's ability to act in common with each other for general interests in the

---

57. Marx, "Zur Judenfrage," *MEGA* I.2: 156 / *MECW*: 160-1 (in the text Marx refers to the 1789 Declaration in its incarnation as the preamble to the 1791 Constitution).

58. Ibid.

59. Ibid., 157/162

60. Ibid., 156 / 160–61.

61. Axel Honneth, *The Idea of Socialism: Towards a Renewal*, trans. Joseph Ganahl (Cambridge: Polity, 2017), 35.

62. Marx, "Zur Judenfrage," *MEGA* I.2: 149 / *MECW* 3: 154.

political sphere, while the rights of man protected the "individual withdrawn into himself into the confines of his private interests and private caprice" in civil society.[63]

Moreover, Marx's criticism that the sphere of civil society dominated the political sphere is paralleled by his criticism that in the modern state the rights of man are prioritized over the rights of citizen. As evidence, Marx pointed to Article II of the 1789 Declaration, which stated that "[t]he *aim* of all *political association* is the *preservation* of the natural and imprescriptible rights of man." Marx emphasized that this justification was repeated even in the supposedly more radical 1793 Jacobin Declaration.[64] Marx objected to the idea that the justification of the rights of the citizen lay in the role they played in protecting the egoistic rights of man. The French revolutionaries had thereby,

> reduce[d] citizenship, and the *political community*, to a mere *means* for maintaining these so-called rights of man, that thereby the *citoyen* is declared to be the servant of egoistic *homme*, that the sphere in which man acts as a communal being is degraded to a level below the sphere in which he acts as a partial being, and that, finally, it is not man as *citoyen*, but man as *bourgeois* who is considered to be the *essential* and *true* man.[65]

The rights guaranteeing participation in communal affairs cannot, according to Marx, be treated as a "mere *means*" for pursuing self-interest in civil society, but have (by implication) their own inherent value.

For Marx, the degradation of the rights of the citizen below the rights of man was emblematic for how despite the French revolutionaries' talk of political freedom they had in fact enshrined bourgeois liberty. As evidence he turned again to the 1789 and 1793 Declarations, summarizing their nearly identical definition of "liberté" in Articles IV and VI, respectively, as "freedom is the right to do and perform everything which does not harm others."[66] Marx condemned this conception of freedom, claiming that it is the "freedom of man as an isolated monad withdrawn into himself" where each person is assigned

63. Ibid., 158–59 / 164.

64. Ibid.

65. Ibid. Marx made a similar complaint about the denigration of press freedom by relating it to freedom of trade in "Debatten über Preßfreiheit," *MEGA* I.1: 157, 159–63 / *MECW* 1: 169, 171–75.

66. Marx, "Zur Judenfrage," *MEGA* I.2: 157 / *MECW* 3: 162. Annelien de Dijn argues that despite the explicit definition given to liberty in the 1789 Declaration, if it is taken together with Articles III and VI, the document actually defends a conception of freedom as democratic self-government and not simply freedom from government interference; see *Freedom: An Unruly History* (Cambridge: Harvard University Press, 2020), 222–25.

a sphere to "move *without harming* others," with the law keeping people apart like a "stake marking the boundary between two fields."[67] Marx was thus critiquing what we would now call negative liberty or liberty as noninterference and its association with a private sphere that cannot be interfered with.[68] In contrast, Marx suggested that a conception of freedom should see each person's relation to other people as the *"realization"* rather than a *"barrier* to his freedom."[69] The only alternative conception of freedom mentioned in "Zur Judenfrage" that meets this criterion is the "category of *political freedom,"* which Marx argued corresponded to the rights of the citizen that guarantee *"participation . . . in the political* community."[70] Marx thus continues, as in his earlier journalism, to defend a broader conception of freedom requiring democratic political participation from the narrower conception of freedom as noninterference.

Marx's political position in "Zur Judenfrage" and "Kritik: Einleitung," that the proletariat would bring about human emancipation through the abolition of private property, while still emphasizing the necessity and value of political emancipation, left him in a relatively ideologically lonely position, and it is not surprising that he felt unwilling to identify with either republicanism or existing socialism and communism.[71] A clear indication of this ideological unmooring can be seen in his changed use of "democracy." In the *Kritik* he had identified democracy as the future polity that would supersede the republic (itself, he argued, the most advanced form of the modern state compared to constitutional and absolutist monarchies) by overcoming the modern state's alienating divide between the political sphere and civil society. In "Zur Judenfrage," Marx continued to use the same tripartite categorization of the modern state and to treat the republic as its most developed form. But, in a significant yet uncommented-on departure, he now treated "democracy" and "republic"

67. Marx, "Zur Judenfrage," *MEGA* I.2: 157 / *MECW* 3: 162.

68. Isaiah Berlin, *Two Concepts of Liberty: An Inaugural Lecture Delivered before the University of Oxford on 31 October 1958* (Oxford: Clarendon Press, 1958), 7–9.

69. Marx, "Zur Judenfrage," *MEGA* I.2: 158 / *MECW* 3: 163.

70. Ibid., 156 / 161. Marx may have thought that further conceptions of freedom met this desideratum, but none are referred to in the text.

71. The uniqueness of Marx's position is demonstrated by how easily he was misunderstood by contemporary communists. An anonymous contributor to *Vorwärts!* (perhaps Heinrich Bürgers or Hermann Ewerbeck) defended Marx against the accusation that he had dismissed all human rights in "Zur Judenfrage." It argued that Marx had only criticized the bourgeois rights of man and not social rights (such as "the right to existence to work, etc.") while at the same time arguing that *"social* rights are the *only human rights"* since "political rights will not fill your or my stomach"; see [Anon], "Eine Antwort," *Vorwärts!,* no. 53 (3 July 1844): 2. That attempted defense failed to realize that Marx had defended political rights and not even mentioned social rights.

synonymously. He wrote that the "*democratic* state . . . relegates religion to a place among the other elements in civil society," creates a "dualism . . . between the life of civil society and political life," and so in "political democracy . . . man is not yet a *real* species-being."[72] "Democracy" in "Zur Judenfrage" thus becomes identical with what Marx preferred to call "republic" in the *Kritik* and ceases to be his preferred term for an alternative that would overcome the modern state's alienating dualism. That leaves Marx with no satisfactory alternative vocabulary or label to describe his politics.

That ideological hesitancy ended very soon after the publication of the *Deutsch-Französische Jahrbücher* in February 1844. Julius Fröbel informed Marx and Ruge that the financial difficulties of his Swiss publishing house, which had financed the first double issue, made it impossible to support further issues. The search for alternative publishers proved fruitless. The definitive end of the journal came when Marx fell out with Ruge at the end of March. In Ruge's telling, the two had spent an evening together in Marx's apartment when Ruge began complaining of Georg Herwegh's libertine lifestyle. Marx demurred, but the next morning (26 March 1844) he wrote to Ruge to defend Herwegh and break off relations.[73] Marx's decision to sit down and write a formal letter is noteworthy since the two lived in the same house (one wonders how the letter was delivered) and suggests that this was a considered political act that went beyond their immediate personal disagreement.[74] In the letter, Marx seems to have not only defended Herwegh but explained that his and Ruge's political differences made further collaboration impossible. As Ruge subsequently reported, Marx had said "he could no longer work together with me, since I was only a politician, whereas he was a communist."[75]

Ruge was completely bewildered by Marx's behavior. He could not understand how "[f]rom September 1843 to March 1844 he [Marx] had progressed to the 'crass socialism'" that Marx had himself criticized in his final letter of the "Briefwechsel von 1843."[76] Ruge thought it "impossible" that Marx found

---

72. Marx, "Zur Judenfrage," *MEGA* I.2: 151, 154 / *MECW* 3: 156, 159. The qualifier "political" democracy might suggest that "social" democracy could lead to a reconciliation between spheres, but it is not a term that Marx turns to here.

73. Arnold Ruge to Catharina Sophia Ruge, 19 May 1844, *Briefwechsel und Tagebuchblätter*, I: 350–51; *Redaktionsbriefwechsel*, 1360–61.

74. Mesmer-Strupp, *Arnold Ruges Plan einer Alliance intellectuelle*, 132. See also Engels to Marx, 19 November 1844, *MEGA* III.1: 250 / *MECW* 38: 9–10.

75. Arnold Ruge, *Zwei Jahre in Paris: Studien und Erinnerungen*, vol. 1 (Leipzig: Wilhelm Jurany, 1846), 140. Marx also seems to have complained that Ruge failed to use his own resources to finance the continuation of the journal.

76. Ibid.

the "sad activities [of German communists] politically important."[77] "An unpolitical communism," Ruge declared, was a "stillborn product," and he predicted (prophetically for Marx's future intellectual development) that *"If communism is to achieve something, it has to appear in association with a **political** movement."*[78] Ruge tried to keep relations civil, expecting Marx's anger to pass, and even wished him well in working out his newfound principles. But once Marx publicly and aggressively criticized Ruge's position on the Silesian Weavers' Revolt, Ruge became equally uncompromising.[79] He denounced Marx in anti-Semitic terms and tried to block future publications of Marx's work.[80] As with many relationship breakups, mutual friends, such as Bakunin, were caught in the crossfire, a situation made more awkward by the fact that for several months Marx and Ruge continued to be neighbors.[81]

What caused Marx to finally take the step of self-identifying as a communist and so emphatically break with Ruge's republican politics? The answer must necessarily be speculative since the crucial letter to Ruge from 26 March has not survived (nor have any other letters from Marx in the period).[82] It is possible that Marx realized that the combination of his various positional shifts—his disillusionment with the American and French Republics, his

77. Arnold Ruge to Karl Moritz Fleischer, 9 July 1844, *Briefwechsel und Tagebuchblätter*, I: 359.

78. Ibid.

79. See the change in tone in the letters flanking Marx's article, Ruge to Hermann Köchly, 25 July and 12 August 1844, in Arnold Ruge, *Werke und Briefe*, 12: 486–88.

80. Ruge to Catharina Sophia Ruge, 6 October 1844; Ruge to Julius Fröbel, November and 6 December 1844, *Briefwechsel und Tagebuchblätter*, I: 367, 379–81.

81. Ruge to Hermann Köchly, 15 October 1844, *Werke und Briefe*, 12: 490–91. Marx and Ruge's enmity was relatively long-standing. But much later Ruge did read *Das Kapital* and described it in glowing terms as an *"epoch-making work"* that showed "broad erudition and a brilliant dialectical talent"; Arnold Ruge to H. Steinthal, 25 January 1869, *MEW* 32: 696 / *MECW* 43: 542. Marx consequently ironically claimed that Ruge had finally been "converted to *communism*"; Marx to Engels, 27 January 1870, *MEW* 32: 432 / *MECW* 43: 417.

82. The letter's existence (but not its contents) is also attested to in Moses Hess, "Dottore Graziano's Werke: *Zwei Jahre in Paris, Studien und Erinnerungen* von A. Ruge," *Deutsche-Brüsseler Zeitung*, no. 62 (5 August 1847): 2, an article written in collaboration with Marx; see *MEGA* I.5: 1737–39. It is possible that Karl Heinzen was citing this letter when he wrote that Ruge and Marx fell out when Marx "discovered that communism was the 'most advanced standpoint'"; see Karl Heinzen, *Erlebtes: Zweiter Theil; Nach Meiner Exilierung*, vol. 4 of *Gesammelte Schriften* (Boston: Selbstverlag, 1874), 432. Speculatively, Ruge may have shown Heinzen the letter or summarized its contents for him. Heinzen showed some familiarity with the breach at the time; see K. H[einzen] "[Review:] *Zwei Jahre in Paris* . . . von Arnold Ruge," in *Die Opposition*, ed. K. Heinzen (Mannheim: Heinrich Hoff, 1846), 329.

critique of private property, his embrace of the proletariat—could no longer be plausibly contained under the banner of republicanism and democracy and amounted to an encompassing ideological and political conversion to communism. It is possible that this made him more sympathetic to the antipolitical stance of existing communists that he had previously opposed, which is suggested by the strongly antipolitical position he subsequently took in his public critique of Ruge. More generally his conversion is likely to have been facilitated by his meetings in Paris with prominent socialists and social critics (including Louis Blanc, Victor Considerant, Pierre Leroux, and probably George Sand, Flora Tristan, and Étienne Cabet),[83] which would have given him a more realistic picture of socialism than was possible from Germany (though none of these figure claimed credit for converting Marx in the way Hess did for Engels). We further know that at some point in Marx's stay in Paris he attended meetings of French and German workers and came into contact with various underground communist worker associations, including the Bund der Gerechten (League of the Just), which under Marx and Engels's influence later become the Bund der Kommunisten (Communist League). By his own account, these worker meetings had a striking impact on him.[84] But what evidence there is suggests that these meetings likely took place later in the year, after his conversion.[85] A final likely contributor to Marx's conversion was his first exposure to the importance of political economy through his reading of Engels's contribution to the *Deutsch-Französische Jahrbücher*. Though Marx's own study of political economy lay before him, Engels's article likely further impressed upon him the centrality of social issues and the necessity of a transformative break with his existing political position.

Some combination of these factors led Marx to communism and convinced him that he needed to make a decisive split with Ruge. Their personal falling-out was one casualty in the broader political breach that appeared between republicanism and communism in the 1840s. To get a better sense of what

---

83. Jacques Grandjonc, "Zu Marx' Aufenthalt in Paris: 12. Oktober 1843–1. Februar 1845," in *Studien zu Marx' erstem Paris-Aufenthalt und zur Entstehung der Deutschen Ideologie* (Trier: Schriften aus dem Karl-Marx Haus, 1990), 180. Evidence for Marx's meeting with some of these figures is corroborated by a newly discovered letter from Jenny Marx; see Rolf Hecker and Angelika Limmroth, "Ein bisher unveröffentlichter Brief von Jenny Marx aus Paris vom 26. Dezember 1843," *Beiträge zu Marx-Engels Forschung Neue Folge 2020 / 21* (Hamburg: Argument, 2022), 140–42.

84. Marx to Ludwig Feuerbach, 11 August 1844, *MEGA* III.1: 63-64 / *MECW* 3: 355; *Ökonomisch-philosophische Manuskripte, MEGA* I.2: 425 / *MECW* 3: 313.

85. Grandjonc, "Zu Marx' Aufenthalt in Paris," 184ff; Löwy, *The Theory of Revolution in the Young Marx*, 49–51.

Marx was separating himself from, I turn now to an account of Ruge's republican thought and political activism. Ruge's thought provides something of a yardstick for the distance Marx's communism traveled from the republicanism that he left behind. Ruge's political biography further provides us with a glimpse of an alternative path that Marx could have continued on had he not decided to throw in his lot with communism. The generational divide (Ruge was sixteen years Marx's senior) always made it likelier that Marx, as with other younger figures like Engels, would be more receptive to a new ideology. But such an outcome was not preordained, and it is conceivable that under different circumstances Marx could have remained in Ruge's republican camp.[86]

Arnold Ruge's Republicanism

One of the many sayings falsely attributed to Napoleon is that if you want to understand a man you have to know what was happening in the world when he was twenty.[87] Setting aside provenance, few figures had done more to shape the world Arnold Ruge inherited at twenty than Napoleon. Ruge was born in 1802 to a tenant farmer family on the island of Rügen when it was still part of the Kingdom of Sweden, and it was only after Napoleon's defeat and the Vienna Congress that the island was transferred to Prussia.[88] During Ruge's childhood the island was twice occupied by Napoleon's troops, and his school years were heavily influenced by the patriotic *Freiheitskriege* (1813–15) that liberated the German states from French control. While strongly supportive of these wars of liberation—at thirteen Ruge swore an oath that if "the tyrant returned to our free land" he would "stab him to death with my own

86. Other republican Young Hegelians closer in age to Marx, for instance, never made the transition to communism; see Ingrid Pepperle, *Junghegelianische Geschichtsphilosophie und Kunsttheorie* (Berlin: Akademie, 1978), 104–5.

87. See Garson O'Toole, "To Understand a Person You Have to Know What Was Happening in the World When That Person Was Twenty: Napoleon Bonaparte? G. M. Young? Anonymous?," *Quote Investigator* (blog), 7 November 2022, https://quoteinvestigator.com/2022/11/07/age-twenty/.

88. Biographical details are drawn from Helmet Reinalter, *Arnold Ruge (1802–1880): Junghegelianer, politischer Philosoph und bürgerlicher Demokrat* (Würzburg: Königshausen & Neumann, 2020) and Ruge's autobiography, *Aus früherer Zeit*, 4 vols. (Berlin: Franz Duncker, 1862–67). See also Walter Neher, *Arnold Ruge als Politiker und Politischer Schriftsteller* (Heidelberg: Carl Winter, 1933); Wolfgang Ruge, *Arnold Ruge, 1802–1880: Fragmente Eines Lebensbildes*, ed. Friedrich-Martin Balzer (Bonn: Pahl-Rugenstein, 2004). A helpful bibliography of Ruge's writings up to 1849 can be found in Aldo Zanardo, "Arnold Ruge, giovane hegeliano, 1824–1849," *Annali della Fondazione Giangiacomo Feltrinelli* 12 (1970): 201–64.

hand"—Ruge still welcomed the reforming impulse of Napoleon and his troops and understood the wars as a movement for German freedom and independence rather than opposition to the ideals the French Revolution.[89] He and his fellow *Gymnasium* students were thus outraged by what they saw as Prussia and Austria's betrayal of these emancipatory promises through the enactment of the repressive Carlsbad Decrees of 1819.

At university in Halle, Ruge studied philosophy and joined the underground *Jünglingsbund*, one of the many student *Burschenschaften* aiming at the cultural and political renewal of Germany. Within the movement Ruge pushed for a united German republic and against the mystical, romantic tendencies that characterized much of the movement.[90] Betrayed by one of their members to the authorities, Ruge was arrested in January 1824 and sentenced a year later to fifteen years' imprisonment for high treason, later reduced to five years. He put his prison time to good use, embarking on an extensive study of the ancient Greek classics. The model of democratic Athens become a lifelong inspiration to him, providing him with a political model of self-rule, freedom, and an active citizenry.[91] He later wrote that "We owe everything which is still good and human in the world to the Athenian Republic."[92]

Ruge's release came just in time for him to join the excited German reactions to the 1830 July Revolution, with prison clearly having done little to dampen his enthusiasm for radical ideas.[93] What did, however, lead to a degree of moderation was his transformative encounter soon after with Hegel's philosophy.[94] Ruge had hitherto stubbornly resisted Hegel's charms (after his first reading of the *Philosophie des Rechts*, Ruge's commented that it hardly provided an emulative "role model of a new state").[95] But with Hegel's death in 1831 and the wave of reissues of Hegel's work that followed, Ruge was led to a

89. Ruge, *Aus früherer Zeit*, 1: 55–56, 208–10.

90. Reinalter, *Arnold Ruge*, 36.

91. Stephan Walter, *Demokratisches Denken zwischen Hegel und Marx: Die politische Philosophie Arnold Ruges; Eine Studie zur Geschichte der Demokratie in Deutschland* (Düsseldorf: Droste, 1995), 75–77.

92. Ruge, *Aus früherer Zeit*, 3: 161. See also his praise and translation of Pericles's funeral oration, ibid., 3: 144–59.

93. See his defense of popular sovereignty in [Arnold Ruge], "Ueber das Princip der Bewegung in der Politik," *Blätter für literarische Unterhaltung*, no. 143 (23 May 1831): 622. See also Ruge, *Aus früherer Zeit*, 3: 143–44.

94. Warren Breckman, "Arnold Ruge and the Machiavellian Moment," in *Die linken Hegelianer: Studien zum Verhältnis von Religion und Politik im Vormärz*, ed. Michael Quante and Amir Mohseni (Paderborn: Wilhelm Fink, 2015), 133.

95. Ruge, *Aus früherer Zeit* 3: 341; see also 3: 171, 289.

profound reassessment of whom he came to call "the freest German."[96] Making his way through the *Phänomenologie des Geistes* (1807), *Wissenschaft der Logik* (1812–16), and *Enzyklopädie der philosophischen Wissenschaften* (1817), Ruge was enthralled by what he saw as the rebirth of Greek philosophy, now systematized into a powerful all-encompassing whole. "Here lay spread in front of me," he related, "the whole world of nature and spirit *in a single great elaboration* . . . concept was restlessly brought forth from concept and in a sublime work of art, the system of thought, of nature, and spirit, the Idea appeared in its completion."[97]

Ruge's conversion to Hegelianism, consuming as it was, was not uncritical. He immediately recognized that there were elements of Hegel's system where "the great emancipator" had contradicted his own "principle of development and freedom," which necessitated developing Hegel's philosophy beyond his own intentions.[98] To carry out this task, in 1838 Ruge and Theodor Echtermeyer founded the *Hallische Jahrbücher für deutsche Wissenschaft und Kunst* (*Halle Yearbooks for German Science and Art*), which became the primary public organ of the Young Hegelian movement. Ruge's energetic editorial efforts brought to the journal's pages not just the leading intellectual lights of Young Hegelianism, from David Friedrich Strauss to Ludwig Feuerbach and Bruno Bauer, but dozens upon dozens of lesser-known figures who formed the wider intellectual movement.[99] Less philosophically original than the movement's leading figures, Ruge's primary contribution lay in his organizing ability and his development of the political implications of Young Hegelian thought.[100] In his own rather apt self-description, he acted as the "cavalry general of Hegelianism."[101]

In the early years of the *Hallische Jahrbücher*, Ruge genuinely believed it to be a loyal "orthodox Prussian" journal committed to the regime's historical role and potential to develop as a protestant constitutional monarchy.[102] That hope was definitely dispelled with the accession of the conservative Frederick William IV and the regime's subsequent demand, in spring 1841, that the journal be submitted to its censorship, forcing Ruge to decamp to Dresden in neighboring Saxony and rename it the *Deutsche Jahrbücher für Wissenschaft und Kunst*. The journal

96. Ibid., 3: 289.

97. Ibid., 4: 8–9.

98. Ibid., 4: 9–10, 434.

99. Some 140 separate contributors to the journal have been identified in Andre Spies, "Towards a Prosopography of Young Hegelians," *German Studies Review* 19, no. 2 (1996): 321–39.

100. Walter, *Demokratisches Denken zwischen Hegel und Marx*, 16.

101. Arnold Ruge to Agnes Ruge, 27 November 1838, *Briefwechsel und Tagebuchblätter*, 1: 154; *Redaktionsbriefwechsel*, 242.

102. Ruge, *Aus früherer Zeit*, 4: 484, 498.

now took on an increasingly confrontational tone and radical direction. Karl Rosenkranz, a leading moderate Hegelian, onetime contributor to the journal, and friend, lamented to Ruge that the *Jahrbücher* had "left the theory of constitutional monarchy and gone over to *republicanism.*"[103] To which Ruge unapologetically replied that the "constitution of the state is, if it is a real one, always a republic, and the republic is never a real one, when it is not a democracy."[104]

We saw in chapter 1 how Ruge's January 1843 "Eine Selbstkritik des Liberalismus" ("A Self-Criticism of Liberalism") provided the definitive public statement of the radicalization of a part of the Young Hegelian movement (though for Ruge this was actually a reradicalization, since it represented a return to his pre-Hegelian republicanism). In that article, he denounced the liberal understanding of freedom for failing to see that one could not be free while subject to the arbitrary power of a king or foreign power and that the "laws of free beings had to be their own product."[105] This republican understanding of freedom, where one is free from arbitrary power when one is subjected only to the laws of one's own democratic making, was a consistent theme across Ruge's writings.[106] In his early discussions of press freedom, he declared that censorship makes "all free men *dependent on the subjective pleasure of an individual,* which is the essence of slavery."[107] He used the same conception of freedom to puncture the pretensions of the Prussian monarchy, arguing that it "bound *political human beings* or citizens in unfreedom under 'the higher insight and arbitrary will of the king'; a foreign reason and a foreign will are

---

103. Karl Rosenkranz to Arnold Ruge, 8 April 1842, *Redaktionsbriefwechsel,* 1027.

104. Arnold Ruge to Karl Rosenkranz, mid-April 1842, *Briefwechsel und Tagebuchblätter,* 1: 272; *Redaktionsbriefwechsel,* 1033.

105. Arnold Ruge, "Vorwort: Eine Selbstkritik des Liberalismus," *Deutsche Jahrbücher,* no. 1 (2 January 1843): 4 / "A Self-Critique of Liberalism," *The Young Hegelians: An Anthology,* ed. Lawrence S. Stepelevich (Amherst: Humanity, 1983), 244–45.

106. Helmut Reinalter rightly argues that "freedom stands at the centre of Ruge's political thought," but does not make the connection to Ruge's specifically republican understanding of the idea, instead reducing it to just having the same "meaning as Hegel"; Reinalter, *Arnold Ruge,* 102. Ruge, in fact, argued that Hegelian philosophy was limited to "*theoretical* freedom" and had to be superseded by the "*practical* freedom" brought about by the "*social-democratic republic*"; see Arnold Ruge, *Die Loge des Humanismus* (Bremen: Verlag des Herausgebers, 1852), 18–19. Ruge similarly argued that "by freedom we mean real, human, i.e., political freedom, not some metaphysical idle talk"; Ruge, "Plan der Deutsch-Französichen Jahrbücher," 5. His conception of freedom thus owes less to Hegel than to Rousseau, whose *Du contrat social* Ruge called the "gospel of freedom"; see Arnold Ruge to Adolf Stahr, 7 November 1841, *Briefwechsel und Tagebuchblätter,* I; 247; *Redaktionsbriefwechsel,* 864.

107. [Arnold Ruge], *"Die vollkommene und ganze Preßfreiheit . . . von* C. Th. Welcker," *Blätter für literarische Unterhaltung,* no. 103 (13 April 1831): 450.

his [the citizen's] law, his fate."[108] Being freed of such arbitrary power mattered, Ruge argued (in classic republican fashion), because regardless of how well inclined a master might be, someone "who depends on the *good* will of a foreign [power], depends also on his *bad* will."[109] Later in life, Ruge traced the emergence of this conception of freedom to the Greeks and especially the Athenians. He claimed (in just as classic a case of republican orientalism) that in contrast to their supposedly servile Asiatic neighbors, the Athenians "obey only their own laws and their own elected authorities . . . they have no master and no other ruler than themselves, the community of the free. Only someone who is his own master is free; no other form of political and social freedom exists."[110]

The publication of Ruge's "Selbstkritik des Liberalismus" sounded the death knell of the *Deutsche Jahrbücher*, which was suppressed the following day, with the police quite brutally occupying the journal's printers.[111] Ruge responded to the official justification for the suppression with a point-by-point rebuttal of its charges. Of particular interest for understanding his republicanism is his response to the accusation that the *Jahrbücher* had "dismissed all and every monarchical, even constitutional-monarchical, government power" (the same charge that would be made against Marx's *Rheinische Zeitung* a few weeks later). Ruge argued that the Saxon government's charge of antimonarchism showed a failure to comprehend what the *Deutsche Jahrbücher* had meant by the "concept of the free state, the republic." Their confusion resulted from relying on the "old rough trisection" of constitutions into "monarchy, aristocracy, and democracy or republic," based on whether the highest government power was in the "hands of the one, or the few, or—what is of course presented as a chimera—the many."[112] Ruge accepted that under this conception a republic was directly opposed to a monarchy. But he maintained that the old classification confused the comparatively trivial question of whether the highest government office was held by a "hereditary king or a term-limited *elected* president," with the far more important

108. Arnold Ruge, "Der protestantische Absolutismus und seine Entwicklung," *Deutsche Jahrbücher*, no. 129 (29 November 1841): 513.

109. [Arnold Ruge], "Vorwort zur Verständigung der Deutschen und Franzosen," in Louis Blanc, *Geschichte der zehn Jahre von 1830 bis 1840*, trans. Gottlob Fink (Zürich & Winterthur: Verlag des literarischen Comptoirs, 1843), xxiv.

110. Ruge, *Aus früherer Zeit*, 3: 160; for further orientalist comparisons, see 4: 20, 25.

111. Martin Hundt, "Der Junghegelianismus im Spiegel der Briefe," *Redaktionsbriefwechsel*, Apparat, 33.

112. [Arnold Ruge], "Rechtfertigung der Deutschen Jahrbücher gegen die Motive zu ihrer Unterdrückung," *Revue des Auslandes: Monatschrift für Literatur, Staaten- und Völkerkunde*, ed. L. Meyer and Otto Wigand (Leipzig: Otto Wigand, 1843), Zweiter Jahrgang, 2: 19; also reproduced in *Redaktionsbriefwechsel*, 1196.

one of "from whom that [office's] power emanates, how it is transmitted, [and] by what principle it is administered; in short, if the state is its own end or serves as the private property of individual interests."[113] What matters, in effect, according to Ruge, is whether the structure of the state serves the common interest, not who happens to sit as the symbolic figurehead at the top of it. Ruge was thereby partly resurrecting the old understanding of republic as a *res publica*, where it refers to any state ruled for the common good and not exclusively to a regime without a monarch.[114] As he summarized, the political aim of the *Deutsche Jahrbücher* had in fact been: "the free state, the *republic*, i.e., the state as *political community* (*res publica*), as common property and as the living unfolding organism [and] product of all those, that want and know themselves to be state members."[115]

This was the same strategy taken by Marx in his defense of the *Rheinische Zeitung* against the Prussian's government's charge of antimonarchism; Marx claimed that the newspaper had preferred no "*particular state form*" and only aimed at an "*ethical and rational political community*" which might be realized in "*every* state form."[116] Such a strategy had some merit in maneuvering away from direct confrontation with monarchical authority but seems unlikely to satisfy anyone committed to upholding monarchy as the *only* legitimate state form. Indeed, as soon as Ruge provided some flesh to his understanding of republic, the conflict with the structures of the monarchical state—whether Prussian absolutist or Saxon constitutionalist—was obvious. He clarified that the citizens of his *res publica* included the "as yet spiritually uneducated and materially neglected proletarians (*the rabble; der Pöbble*)," who, through universal state education, would gain the ability take part "indirectly as well as directly" in the "highest interest of the state, in law-making, justice and administration." This would prevent the state from being split into "two unequal, abruptly and hostilely opposed to each other, halves of *rulers* and *ruled*"; instead, in a nod to Aristotle, "all are, at the same time, rulers and ruled."[117]

113. Aristotle's sixfold categorization of constitutions avoids this problem by referring to *both* the number of rulers (one, few, many) *and* the interests they serve (common versus sectional); see chapter 2, figure 5.

114. The modern "exclusivist" view originated in the Italian Renaissance, and from then on increasingly displaced the older meaning; see James Hankins, "Exclusivist Republicanism and the Non-Monarchical Republic," *Political Theory* 38, no. 4 (2010): 452–82. See also Wolfgang Mager, "Republik," in *Geschichtliche Grundbegriffe: Historisches Lexikon Zur Politisch-Sozialen Sprache in Deutschland*, ed. Otto Brunner, Werner Conze, and Reinhart Koselleck, vol. 5 (Stuttgart: Klett-Cotta, 1984), 618–20.

115. Ruge, "Rechtfertigung der Deutschen Jahrbücher," 19; *Redaktionsbriefwechsel*, 1196–97.

116. Marx, *Randglossen zu den Anklagen des Ministerialrescripts, MEGA* I.1: 351 / *MECW* 1: 363.

117. Ruge, "Rechtfertigung der Deutschen Jahrbücher," 19–20; *Redaktionsbriefwechsel*, 1197.

Thus, as much as Ruge's understanding of a republic might have revived an older meaning of *res publica* as the common good, it was otherwise thoroughly modern, in that it was democratic through and through. The *"republic ... the democracy"* that Ruge said the *Deutsche Jahrbücher* had advocated was therefore still a fundamental threat to the existing order, even if he was willing to offer the concession that it was conceivable that a king might in some circumstances and countries remain as the "embodied expression of popular sovereignty."[118] Of somewhat greater potential to appeal to liberal skeptics was Ruge's clarification that his conception of a democratic republic did not endorse the excesses of the French Revolution. Once again deploying his republican conception of liberty, he argued that democracy could not mean an unconstrained power of some citizens over others. *"Freedom* is," he argued, "the negation of every subjective arbitrariness, whether the capricious despotism of the absolute king or the bloody brutality of the unrestrained rabble (*Pöbels*)."[119]

With the *Deutsche Jahrbücher* suppressed, Ruge cast about for his next project, settling on turning the journal into its latest (and, it turned out, final) incarnation, the *Deutsch-Französische Jahrbücher*, now edited with Marx in Paris. Ruge was as excited as Marx at the opportunity to move to the "magic cauldron (*Zauberkessel*)" where "world-history boils."[120] He threw himself into the radical intellectual life of the city, meeting with the who's who of 1840s Parisian socialism, from Flora Tristan to Étienne Cabet, to Victor Considerant, Théodore Dézamy, and Louis Blanc. He struck up a particular friendship with the abolitionist Victor Schœlcher, who challenged the parochialism of Ruge's republicanism. Through him, Ruge came to admire the Caribbean "free republics of escaped negroes," as well as the Haitian self-emancipated slaves who understood *"freedom* in its concise and real meaning" and whose revolution and victory over France and Britain had proven, more than any other event, "the "insurmountable power of the sense of freedom."[121] In spite of his break with Marx and the German communists in Paris, Ruge was caught up in the same January 1845 Prussian expulsion request, to which the French government readily acceded, with the king supposedly proclaiming, *"Il faut purifier Paris des philosophes allemands!"*[122] Though Ruge managed to overturn

---

118. Ibid.

119. Ibid., 17; *Redaktionsbriefwechsel*, 1195.

120. Ruge, *Zwei Jahre in Paris*, 1: 4.

121. Ibid., 1: 171, 180, 188.

122. "Paris must be purified of German philosophers!," ibid., 1: 398–99. Despite their enmity, Marx warned Ruge of the impending expulsion order; Marx to Arnold Ruge, 15 January 1845, *MEGA* III.1: 258 / *MECW* 38: 15.

the order, he was done with the city and moved soon after with his family to Zurich.

In Zurich, Ruge collaborated with fellow exile republicans Julius Fröbel and Karl Heinzen, while also editing his collected works and coming to terms with his painful confrontation with communism in Paris.[123] His initial curiosity and sympathy toward French socialism had been soured by his personal dealings with the German communists. Ruge was still willing to grant that communism was correct in its core demand that the proletarian needed to be "spiritually and bodily liberated from poverty," even if that meant that the "privileged have to suffer."[124] He said he was therefore a "communist" insofar as "every republican and radically free person must be, i.e., that he truly wants the actual liberation of all."[125] But he vehemently rejected the idea that the liberation of all could be achieved through communist measures.

Three main criticisms of communism can be discerned from Ruge's writings from the period, each of them closely tied to communism's failure to realize and respect freedom. First, Ruge condemned communism for failing to give sufficient space for individuality and for prioritizing the collective over the individual. He warned that the "sacrifice of the individual [to the community] can never lead to the liberation of the individual."[126] Communists, he claimed, had it exactly in reverse: community mattered not for its own sake but because of "the free, noble person, that it produces."[127] Second, he criticized the communist belief in the abolition of private property; instead, property should be secured for all. A person who desires to make property serve its real purpose as "the basis of freedom," Ruge tells us, "does not abolish property, he realizes it."[128] Third, and most important for Ruge, he criticized the communist rejection of politics and political reform. He recounted his discussion with Moses Hess on their journey together to Paris, where Hess had supposedly claimed (Ruge may have exaggerated his words) that for communists "[r]evolution . . . is a worn-out political instrument" since "we will one fine morning make a pronunciamento" that would peacefully awaken the people

123. See Arnold Ruge, *Gesammelte Schriften*, 10 vols. (Mannheim: J. P. Grohe, 1846–48); *Sämmtliche Werke*, 10 vols., 2nd ed. (Mannheim: J. P. Grohe, 1847–48).

124. Arnold Ruge to Ludwig Feuerbach, 15 May 1844, *Briefwechsel und Tagebuchblätter*, 1: 345–46.

125. Arnold Ruge to Karl Moritz Fleischer, 15 August 1845, *Briefwechsel und Tagebuchblätter*, 1: 398.

126. Ibid.

127. Arnold Ruge, "Der teutsche Kommunismus," *Die Opposition*, ed. Karl Heinzen (Mannheim: Heinrich Hoff, 1846), 103.

128. Ruge, "Drei Briefe über den Communismus," *Gesammelte Schriften* (1847), 9: 402.

to the superiority of the community of goods.[129] According to Ruge, Hess went on to claim that,

> All this talk of freedom and political reform is outdated. With the republic, juries and a free press one will never go beyond the tyranny of the propertied and the slavery of the majority. All reforms, even the most radical political reforms, are powerless against the foundational evils of society and interest nobody anymore. The content of all and every interest is social reform.[130]

Ruge reacted harshly to this abandonment of the political fight. He mocked the communist belief (presumably with Hess in mind) that their "economic religion, the gospel of *earthly happiness,* could be achieved through the narrow path of need and proclamation, without the spaciousness of politics."[131] Communists, he claimed, failed to understand how "*indispensable the political struggle is*" to achieving any social reform.[132] Further, in their laudable quest to "totalize the realm of freedom" to include "positive and economic freedom," they had, however, "broken with political freedom."[133] "Freedom," Ruge concluded, could not be achieved through "the equal division of need and affluence by the state," which would only result in a "police or slave state."[134]

The outbreak of the 1848 Revolution found Ruge back in Saxony, in Leipzig, and over the next year he threw himself energetically into each stage of the revolutionary events. He immediately took advantage of the new freer conditions to found a daily newspaper, *Die Reform,* that would go on to be the main party organ of the Berlin democrats. When elections were called for the Frankfurt National Assembly (see figure 7), political machinations blocked his selection in Leipzig. But he eventually secured election for a seat in Breslau against the liberal constitutional candidate, through the help of his old friend Bakunin.[135]

In his electoral manifesto, Ruge called on the German people "to declare popular sovereignty . . . to be your permanent, unalienable property."[136] His

---

129. Ruge, *Zwei Jahre in Paris,* 1: 34.

130. Ibid., 1: 39.

131. Ruge, "Der teutsche Kommunismus," 120.

132. Ibid., 119.

133. Ibid., 114–15.

134. Arnold Ruge to Ludwig Feuerbach, 15 May 1844, *Briefwechsel und Tagebuchblätter,* 1: 345–46.

135. Arnold Ruge, "Erinnerungen an Michael Bakunin," *Neue Freie Presse,* no. 4345 (29 September 1876): 1; Ruge, "Episoden aus dem Jahre Achtundvierzig," *Briefwechsel und Tagebuchblätter,* 2: 46–49.

136. Arnold Ruge, "Wahl-Manifest der radicalen Reformpartei für Deutschland," *Die Reform,* no. 16 (16 April 1848): 123.

FIGURE 7. Paul Bürde, *Abgeordnete der Nationalversammlung in der Frankfurter Paulskirche* (*Representatives of the Frankfurt National Assembly*) (1848). Courtesy of Wikimedia Commons. Arnold Ruge is depicted seated at front center, reclining behind the desk.

political reform program called for the abolition of all special privileges for aristocrats and the rich (including property suffrage), the separation of state and church, press freedom, free education, jury trials, and the rights of assembly and association. He further called for not only the replacement of the standing army with a popular militia but the "abolition of the standing army of civil servants" and its replacement with a "cheap government consisting of freely elected men of the people." His proposed social reforms were, however, limited to income and inheritance taxes and a vague call for the "easing of the disparity between work and capital" through a Ministry of Work.[137] However, as the revolution progressed, Ruge paid more attention to social issues and they became central to his 1849 *Die Gründung der Demokratie in Deutschland oder der Volksstaat und der social-demokratische Freistaat* (*The Foundation of Democracy in Germany, or*

137. Ibid., 124.

the People's State and the Social-Democratic Free State), perhaps his most systematic work of social and political theory. As is discussed further in chapter 5, Ruge here set out how a democracy had to be a social democracy where "economic and industrial slavery . . . [i.e.] all forms of *service* and *wage-labor* are abolished."[138] Production was to take place in *Societäten* (partnerships) without capitalist employers, which also secured each individual's contribution so that private property was not abolished but provided to all.[139]

Once elected to the Frankfurt National Assembly, Ruge sat with the Far Left Donnersberg Fraktion, for whom he wrote the equivalent of a party program based on his own manifesto. This called for the Assembly to constitute a German federal democratic republic rather than a German constitutional monarchy (the majority position in the Assembly).[140] Ruge's influence in the Assembly was limited, but he made notable interventions supporting Polish and Italian independence against the claims of German nationalist chauvinism. Increasingly disillusioned by the inaction of the National Assembly, he resigned his seat and moved to Berlin where he was convinced the future revolutionary action lay. He took an active role in the extraparliamentary movement, leading several mass demonstrations to pressure the Prussian National Assembly. After the reactionary turn in Prussia and the banning of *Die Reform*, he returned to Saxony and participated in the May 1849 uprising. Forced to flee after its suppression by Prussian troops, he then traveled to what would be the last act of the revolution in Germany, the uprising in Baden and the Palatinate, and was sent as part of its delegation to Paris to (unsuccessfully) seek support from the French Republic. Looking back, Ruge judged the revolution a failure because it had not carried out the necessary foundational political upheaval: "The people stopped short of not just the throne, but the old state machine."[141]

138. Arnold Ruge, *Die Gründung der Demokratie in Deutschland oder der Volksstaat und der social-demokratische Freistaat* (Leipzig: Verlagsbureau, 1849), 5.

139. Ibid., 35–66. For further discussion, see Walter, *Demokratisches Denken zwischen Hegel und Marx*, 257–64. Ruge's text forms the central theoretical part of his subsequent *Unser System: Oder die Weltweissheit und Weltbewegung unserer Zeit; Zum Unterricht für Jedermann*, 3 vols. (Leipzig, 1850), republished in *Werke und Briefe*, 8: 127–314.

140. Arnold Ruge, "Motiviertes Manifest der radikal-demokratischen Partei . . . ," *Werke und Briefe*, 7: 183–88. Marx and Engels judged the program to have correctly grasped the revolutionary role of the Frankfurt Assembly, as well as being an improvement on the program of the other (more moderate) democratic faction, the Deutscher Hof, but also criticized it for not endorsing a unitary republic; see Marx and Engels, "Programme der radikal-demokratischen Partei und der Linken zu Frankfurt," 74–78 / 48–52.

141. Ruge, "Episoden aus dem Jahre Achtundvierzig," *Briefwechsel und Tagebuchblätter*, 2: 24. See also Ruge, *Gründung der demokratie in Deutschland*, 7–8. Marx had a similar analysis, arguing

Like so many other 1848 revolutionaries, Ruge found refuge in England, first in London and then Brighton. In his initial exile years he took an active role in the international democratic movement. In 1850, he was one of the four founding signatories, alongside Giuseppe Mazzini, Alexandre Ledru-Rollin, and Albert Darasz, of the European Central Democratic Committee, which tried to support and revive the revolutionary movement on the continent. But he grew increasingly isolated from active political life during the reactionary 1850s (again, like many other exiles) and concentrated on making a living through lectures, translations, and German lessons.[142] In a surprising final political act, in the 1860s Ruge became an enthusiastic and vocal propagandist of Bismarck's unification of Germany. Despite their principled political differences, Ruge saw Bismarck as a useful vessel for the creation of a united Germany under Prussian leadership, which he thought would inevitably develop into a democratic republic.[143] Though Bismarck rewarded him for his efforts with an honorary pension in 1877, Ruge was considered too radical to be recalled to Prussia for state service or offered an amnesty. He died in Brighton on 31 December 1880.

Arnold Ruge's principal political and intellectual legacies lie in the central organizing role he played in the Young Hegelian movement and his lifelong commitment to the struggle for press freedom and democracy in Germany. In his indispensable study of Ruge's political philosophy, Stephan Walter aptly describes him as a "zoon politikon" who restlessly "pushed for participation, movement and change."[144] Ruge's political thought, unsystematic as it was, carved out an ideological space that cannot be reduced to socialism or liberalism.[145] His democratic republicanism was centered on an idea of freedom, where no person was subjected to the arbitrary will of another, which required a polity where every citizen took an active and equal role in self-government and a society where no one was forced into servitude for another. In Ruge's own words, the "democratic principle is that *conscious self-determination*

---

that the revolution had failed because it had only "reformed the highest political summit, and left the foundations untouched, the old bureaucracy, the old army, the old prosecuting magistrate boards, the old judges"; see "Verteidigungsrede im ersten Presseprozess gegen die 'Neue Rheinische Zeitung,'" *MEGA* I.8: 420 / *MECW* 8: 317.

142. Reinalter, *Arnold Ruge*, 160, 165–66.

143. See Christian Jansen, "Arnold Ruge nach 1849: Ein politischer Gründer aus dem Abseits des Exils," in *Die Junghegelianer: Aufklärung, Literatur, Religionskritik und politisches Denken*, ed. Helmut Reinalter (Frankfurt: Peter Lang, 2010), 181–89.

144. Walter, *Demokratisches Denken zwischen Hegel und Marx*, 70.

145. Ibid., 19; Warren Breckman, *Marx, the Young Hegelians, and the Origins of Radical Social Theory: Dethroning the Self* (Cambridge: Cambridge University Press, 1999), 221–22.

[should] penetrate and move the whole of society," so that "[t]he foundational pillar of the social-democratic free state is *the understanding* that uncovers every (even economic) form of slavery at its source and immediately generates the *will* and *power* to remove it. . . . This cleansing process . . . never ends."[146]

The Silesian Weavers' Revolt and the Critique of Politics

On 3 June 1844, in the Silesian factory village of Peterswaldau, a small group of twenty weavers, angered by the declining prices of the cotton they spun at home and a history of mistreatment by the textile merchants they sold to, protested at the villa of a particularly hated local merchant. The weavers were violently driven off but returned the following morning, the crowd now having swelled to several hundred. A delegation of weavers aimed to peacefully negotiate with the merchant but were pelted from the villa windows, incensing the crowd, who stormed the villa and its attached offices, destroying and stealing records, textile stocks, and furniture. Local notables managed to project some calm, but the following morning the crowd, now around 1,700 people, moved to a local manufacturer, who only managed to avoid the merchant's fate by buying them off with food and money. A smaller offshoot of weavers moved to the neighboring village of Langenbielau, where they completely destroyed a textile factory (but spared other manufacturers deemed to pay fair wages and prices). The weavers were eventually confronted by the in-house workers of one manufacturer and 150 hastily dispatched troops. In the ensuing tumult the troops shot into the crowd, killing 11 and wounding 26 (one of whom subsequently perished). But, rather than fleeing, the weavers turned on the troops, forcing them into disorderly retreat under a hail of paving stones. The destruction and pillaging was not ended until 600 soldiers were sent to occupy the two villages on 6 June.[147]

The four-day revolt, though limited to a small local area, caused a sensation in the press and much soul-searching in Prussian officialdom, which led to the "first broad public discussion about the 'social question' in Germany."[148] Intellectuals of all stripes weighed in on the revolt (often with only limited access to the actual course of events), subjecting it to a swath of competing interpretations, often acting as a foil for their wider political commitments.[149] This was also true of the German exile community in Paris and the pages of *Vorwärts!*,

146. Ruge, *Gründung der demokratie in Deutschland*, 35.
147. For the events of the revolt, see Christina von Hodenberg, *Aufstand der Weber: Die Revolte von 1844 und ihr Aufstieg zum Mythos* (Bonn: Dietz, 1997), 19–47.
148. Ibid., 70.
149. Ibid., 10.

in which Ruge and then Marx offered starkly opposed viewpoints on the revolt. *Vorwärts!* had begun life in January 1844 as a liberal paper, but soon after the Silesian revolt it came under the radical influence of the collaborators behind the *Deutsch-Französische Jahrbücher,* with Karl Ludwig Bernays as editor and a broader editorial collective that included Marx, Engels, Heine, Herwegh, Bakunin, and, at least at first, Ruge. Marx and Ruge's public feud about the meaning of the revolt was part of the process whereby Marx and his communist associates managed to wrestle control of *Vorwärts!* from the republicanism of Ruge, who soon withdrew from the paper.[150]

In "Der König von Preussen und die Socialreform" ("The King of Prussia and Social Reform"), Ruge tried to play down the wider significance of the revolt. Responding to enthusiastic reports in the French press, Ruge argued that the Prussian king and his officials had never been afraid of the weak weavers who were easily defeated with a small number of troops. Ruge directed part of his critical fire at King Frederick William IV, who had publicly identified the lack of Christian charitable sympathy among his subjects and officials as the underlying cause of the revolt. The king was incapable, Ruge charged, with seeing the real cause in the "state and the organization of society." But Ruge was also keen to expose what he saw as the political limitations of the weavers' revolt. He claimed that an uprising based on the "partial distress of the factory districts" had no chance of being perceived by Germans as a "general affair," and thus it was perceived as equivalent to "some local drought or famine." The mistake made by the German poor, indeed all Germans, Ruge explained, was that they saw their struggle only in terms of "their hearth, their factory, their district" rather than as part of a general political struggle. He predicted, however, that once "the political understanding of Germans discovered the root of social distress," events like the weavers' revolt would be understood as the basis for revolution. He concluded that "A social revolution without a political soul (i.e., without the organizing insight from the universal standpoint) is impossible."[151]

Marx immediately seized the opportunity to publicly differentiate his new communist position from Ruge's, through a ruthless attempt to pick apart each of Ruge's claims in a rapidly composed "Kritische Randglossen" ("Critical Marginal Notes"), which, despite the title, was nearly eight times longer than

150. Jacques Grandjonc, *"Vorwârts" 1844: Marx und die deutschen Kommunisten in Paris* (Berlin / Bonn: J. H. W. Dietz, 1974), 23–39, 46–47; Walter Schmidt, "Zur Geschichte des Pariser Vorwärts von 1844," in *Vorwärts! Unveränderter Neudruck* (Leipzig: Zentralantiquariat der Deutschen Demokratischen Republik, 1975), x–xvii.

151. Ein Preuße [Arnold Ruge], "Der König von Preußen und die Socialreform," *Vorwärts!,* no. 60 (27 July 1844): 4.

the original (a recurring habit of Marx's).[152] Marx first disputed Ruge's factual depiction of the weavers' revolt as a local, sectional affair with a limited impact on the king or wider German society. Marx pointed to the weavers' initial victory against the first wave of Prussian troops and the huge coverage in the German liberal press as evidence for the uprising's strength and societal impact.[153] He criticized Ruge for focusing on the king's supposed lack of alarm when the revolt was not directed "against the King of Prussia, but against the bourgeoisie."[154] Marx further claimed that the weavers had hardly limited themselves to just their local concerns with "hearth, factory, district," when their battle song had proclaimed their "opposition to the society of private property, in a striking, sharp, unrestrained and powerful manner." On Marx's account, the weavers were class-conscious proletarians, whose uprising had a "*theoretical* and *conscious* character" that went beyond earlier worker revolts in France or Germany. The weavers, he claimed, were "conscious about the nature of the proletariat" and had shown their advanced understanding by attacking not just the machines of the "*industrial masters*, the visible enemy" but also destroying the "*merchant account books*" of the "*banquier*, the hidden enemy."[155]

Marx may have been right about the significance of the upset the weavers caused first to the soldiers and then in wider German society, and he quite legitimately critiqued Ruge for adopting at times a lecturing "*schoolmaster*" attitude toward the weavers.[156] But modern scholarship on the Silesian uprising is not sympathetic to the rest of Marx's account. There is little evidence that the weavers had any wider social goals concerning the abolition of private property;[157] they were in fact respectful both to figures of authority and to the merchants and factory owners they considered fair. The weavers attacked the merchants not out of advanced class consciousness but because they were semi-independent outworkers reliant on them rather than a modern wage-earning factory proletariat (and those in-house workers who did participate supported their employer). The Silesian Weavers' Revolt is therefore more accurately seen

152. Marx's "Kritische Randglossen zu dem Artikel 'Der König von Preussen und die Socialreform: Von einem Preußen'" ("Critical Marginal Notes on the Article 'The King of Prussia and Social Reform: By a Prussian'") was published in *Vorwärts!* on 7 and 10 August but was dated 31 July—just four days after Ruge's article appeared.

153. Marx, "Kritische Randglossen," *MEGA* I.2: 446, 458 / *MECW* 3: 190, 200.

154. Ibid., 446 / 190.

155. Ibid., 459 / 201.

156. Ibid., 460 / 202.

157. Christina von Hodenberg politely notes that Marx's claim to the contrary on the basis of the weavers' battle song (the "Blutgericht") can only be explained through "ignorance of the text"; *Aufstand der Weber*, 226. The song's twenty-four stanzas are reproduced on 238–40.

as a "typical early industrial labor unrest with a local horizon—spontaneous, without political motivation and mainly aimed at punishing individual, wage-cutting merchants."[158] Ruge was therefore not wrong to point to the limited perspective of the uprising.

Of greater lasting interest is Marx's theoretical criticisms of Ruge concerning the (un)importance of politics to social transformation. Marx intended to give Ruge a lesson in the "*general* relation of *politics* to *social ills*" by showing how the nature of the modern state meant that no form of state (absolutist, constitutional, or republican) was able to solve the social problem of pauperism.[159] Little could be expected, of course, from the king of Prussia, who Marx agreed saw the problem only in terms of charity and administrative tinkering. But Marx argued that even in the more politically advanced constitutionalist Britain the "progressive advance of pauperism" was attributed not to "the inevitable consequence of modern *industry*" but to maladministration of the disciplinary Poor Laws.[160] More damning for Ruge's position, Marx maintained, was that the record was no better for even the most radical period of the French Revolution, the Convention. Despite having had "the *maximum of political energy, political power*, and *political understanding*," Marx argued, its 1794 attempt, for instance, to use the property of suspects (declared enemies of the Republic) to fund welfare payments to the rural poor had been a dismal failure.[161] He concluded that though "England therefore punishes the poor, the King of Prussia admonishes the rich and the Convention beheads the propertied," none of them succeeded in ending poverty.[162]

According to Marx, the common problem to each of these actors was that each "sees the root of *every* evil in the fact that their opponent and not themselves is at the *helm of the state* (*Staatsruder*). Even radical and revolutionary politicians seek the root of evils not in the *nature* of the state, but in a particular *state form*, which they wish to replace with a *different* state form."[163] The problem with the state, Marx argued, was twofold. The first was the state's self-perception. Marx claimed that, contrary to Ruge's hopes, the "*state* will *never* see the source of *social ills* in the *state* and the *organization of society*." It will instead only blame them on failures in its own administration, because "*administration* is the

---

158. Ibid., 46.

159. Marx, "Kritische Randglossen," *MEGA* I.2: 446 / *MECW* 3: 190.

160. Ibid., 453 / 195.

161. Ibid., 455 / 197. For an assessment of the 1794 measure, see Alan Forrest, *The French Revolution and the Poor* (Oxford: Basil Blackwell, 1981), 82–84.

162. Marx, "Kritische Randglossen," *MEGA* I.2: 455 / *MECW* 3: 198.

163. Ibid., 455 / 197.

organizing activity of the state."[164] The second was the structure of the modern state. Returning to one of the central themes of his *Kritik* and "Zur Judenfrage," Marx argued that the modern state's strict division between civil society and the public sphere left the state powerless to intervene in civil society. He claimed that "where civil life and its labor begins there the [state's] power ends" and that the "*slavery of civil society* is the natural foundation on which the *modern* state rests . . . The existence of the state and the existence of slavery are inseparable." Marx tried to argue that if the state were to intervene in civil society (beyond limited administrative measures), that would mean abolishing the independence of civil society, which in turn would entail the state "abolishing itself, since it exists *only* in [the] contradiction" between the two spheres. No such action could be expected from the state, since "*suicide* is against nature."[165]

On the basis of this argument, Marx believed he had shown the flaw in Ruge's expectation that more politically advanced conditions would see an advanced understanding of social problems. Marx even maintained that the more advanced a country was politically, the less likely it was to see the source of social problems from within "the *principle of the state*, that is, in *present organization of society*" (i.e., the division into opposed spheres and the impotence of the public sphere over civil society) and only "think from within the *framework* of politics" (by which he seems to mean the idea that the state's administrative welfare measures could solve poverty). Marx again pointed to the example of the French Revolution, "the *classical* period of political understanding," arguing that its leading figures had failed to grasp the nature of the modern state and only "saw in social defects the source of political evils" so that "*Robespierre* saw in great poverty and great wealth only an obstacle to *pure democracy*."[166]

From this analysis Marx drew a quite drastic set of strategic implications for how the proletariat should carry out its emancipatory struggle. These are worth citing in full:

> The more developed and universal the *political* understanding of a people, the more does the *proletariat*—at any rate at the beginning of the movement— squander its forces in senseless, useless revolts, which are drowned in blood. Because it thinks in the framework of politics, the proletariat sees the cause of all evils in the *will*, and all means of remedy in *violence* and in the overthrow of a *particular form of state*. The proof: the first uprisings of the *French* proletariat. The Lyons workers believed that they were pursuing only political aims, that they were only soldiers of the republic, whereas actually they were soldiers of socialism. Thus their political understanding

164. Ibid., 455–56 / 197–98.
165. Ibid. 456 / 198.
166. Ibid., 457 / 199.

concealed from them the roots of social distress, thus it falsified their insight into their real aim, thus their *political understanding deceived* their *social instinct*.[167]

Marx here references to two failed uprising of Lyon silk weavers (*canuts*) in 1831 and 1834 (*les révoltes des canuts*). He follows the official interpretation of the panicked authorities, who viewed the uprisings as part of a republican insurrectionary conspiracy (in fact republicanism had made few inroads in the Lyon working class at the time, compared with Paris, and the workers were more motivated by prohibitions on association and, like the Silesian weavers, local price disputes).[168] Marx used this questionable understanding of the Lyon revolts to make the case that a political mindset among workers leads to senseless insurrections to establish a republic, based on the mistaken belief that the "overthrow of a *particular form of state*" would address their social oppression. Workers thus needed to move on from seeing themselves as "soldiers of the republic" and become "soldiers of socialism."

Marx's extreme, seemingly unalloyed criticism of politics in the "Kritische Randglossen" has not been given sufficient attention in scholarship on Marx's transition. A few commentators have rightly questioned whether Marx briefly adhered to the antipolitical positions typical of many socialisms and communisms at the time, particularly so-called true socialism.[169] "True socialism" was the name Marx and Engels subsequently gave to a strain of German socialist thought that advocated abstention from political struggle and indifference to democratic republican institutions. Marx and Engels would later heavily criticize true socialism for these reasons in their *Manifest der Kommunistischen Partei* (1848) and in the debates that preceded it (a confrontation that is discussed in detail in chapter 4). If Marx did briefly endorse some true socialist positions, then his later critique of true socialism would in fact be a form of self-criticism that sought to distance himself from his own previous commitments (which might help explain the vehemence of his later attacks).[170] It

167. Ibid., 461 / 204.

168. Pamela M. Pilbeam, *Republicanism in Nineteenth-Century France, 1814–1871* (Basingstoke: MacMillan, 1995), 120–24; William H. Sewell Jr., *Work and Revolution in France: The Language of Labor from the Old Regime to 1848* (Cambridge: Cambridge University Press, 1980), 206–10.

169. Gopal Balakrishnan, "The Abolitionist—I," *New Left Review* 90 (2014): 123–24; Alan Gilbert, *Marx's Politics: Communists and Citizens* (Oxford: Martin Robertson, 1981), 16.

170. David Leopold, "Marx, Engels and Other Socialisms," in *The Cambridge Companion to The Communist Manifesto*, ed. Terrell Carver and James Farr (Cambridge: Cambridge University Press, 2015), 40; Zwi Rosen, *Moses Hess und Karl Marx: Ein Beitrag zur Entstehung der Marxschen Theorie* (Hamburg: Christians, 1983), 116.

would also imply that Marx's initial transition to communism involved abandoning his prior republicanism before then reintegrating its commitment to political struggle and democratic structures. There's little doubt that Marx expresses some strong antipolitical sentiments in the "Kritische Randglossen," which are reminiscent of true socialist ones. But to come to a firmer judgment we need to get a better grip on the precise nature and extent of Marx's antipolitical stance and establish how long he held to that position before subsequently abandoning it.

In order to answer both questions, it is instructive to turn to a comparison with Engels's own "rapid and complex intellectual evolution" at the time.[171] As we saw in the introduction to the chapter, Marx and Engels first met briefly in the autumn of 1842, but their pivotal encounter was Engels's ten-day visit to Marx in Paris from 23 or 24 August to 1 or 2 September 1844 (i.e., two weeks after the publication of the "Kritische Randglossen").[172] Engels later recounted that this meeting was when "our complete agreement in all theoretical fields became evident and our joint work dates from that time."[173] In fact, however, they arrived with and continued to hold for some time significantly different views about socialism and the transition to it. Engels had already converted to socialism some six months to a year before Marx, during his time in Manchester (November 1842–August 1844), and his initial conversion to socialism involved a much starker abandonment of his republican commitment to democracy and revolution. In Gregory Claey's summary, he embraced the "evolutionary and non-violent strategy of the Owenite socialists, with its emphasis upon the formation of model communist communities and the dissemination of propaganda."[174]

When Engels had just arrived in England, he still wrote in admiring terms to his German audience in the *Rheinische Zeitung* of how the "radical-democratic principles of Chartism" were spreading among the working class.[175] But by the summer of 1843, Engels was expressing sympathy with the English Owenists who "laugh at the mere republicans, since the republic would be just as hypocritical, just as theological, just as unjust in its laws as a

171. David Leopold, "'All Tell the Same Tale': The Young Engels and Communal Settlements in America and England," *Marx-Engels-Jahrbuch* (2009), 8.

172. Estimated dates given in Grandjonc, "Zu Marx' Aufenthalt in Paris," 200.

173. Engels, "Zur Geschichte des Bundes der Kommunisten," *MEGA* I.30: 96-7 / *MECW* 26: 318.

174. Gregory Claeys, "The Political Ideas of the Young Engels, 1842–1845: Owenism, Chartism, and the Question of Violent Revolution in the Transition from 'Utopian' to 'Scientific Socialism,'" *History of Political Thought* 6, no. 3 (1985): 456.

175. Engels, "Stellung der politischen Parteien," *MEGA* I.3: 444 / *MECW* 2: 375–76.

monarchy."[176] And by the autumn he had come out explicitly in favor of communism, which by his account was to be sharply differentiated from and indeed opposed to democracy. While communism was "real liberty, and real equality," Engels declared,

> Democracy is, as I take all forms of government to be, a contradiction in itself, an untruth, nothing but hypocrisy (theology, as we Germans call it), at the bottom. Political liberty is sham-liberty, the worst possible slavery; the appearance of liberty, and therefore the reality of servitude. Political equality is the same; therefore democracy, as well as every other form of government, must ultimately break to pieces. . . . [177]

He furthermore praised Proudhon, for

> having proved that every kind of government is alike objectionable, no matter whether it be democracy, aristocracy, or monarchy, that all govern by force; and that, in the best of all possible cases, the force of the majority oppresses the weakness of the minority. . . . What we want is anarchy; the rule of nobody, the responsibility of every one to nobody but himself.[178]

Engels now also rejected violent revolution, criticizing strains of French communism that intended "overthrowing the present government of their country," maintaining that even Étienne Cabet's supposedly peaceful Icarians "would gladly seize upon any opportunity to establish a republic by force."[179]

Not only did Engels reject a revolution in favor of a democratic republic but he explicitly opposed running the future socialist society along democratic principles. Engels favorably contrasted Wilhelm Weitling's technocratic administrative structures (previously discussed at the end of chapter 2) with those of Cabet, who had specified that in his utopian communist society of Icaria the "political organization is that of a democratic REPUBLIC" where the "people are SOVEREIGN" over their laws, representatives and executive officials.[180] Engels enthusiastically noted that the "chief point, in which Weitling was superior to Cabet," was Weitling's belief in "the abolition of all government by force and by majority, and the establishment in its stead of a mere administration," and where the "officers of this administration" are chosen "not by a majority of the community at large, but by those only who have a knowledge of the

176. Engels, "Briefe aus London III," *MEGA* I.3: 463 / *MECW* 3: 389.

177. Engels, "Progress of Social Reform on the Continent," *MEGA* I.3: 496 / *MECW* 3: 393.

178. Ibid., 503–4 / 399.

179. Ibid., 502 / 397.

180. Étienne Cabet, *Voyage en Icarie*, 2nd ed. (Paris: J. Mallet, 1842), 37-39 / *Travels in Icaria*, trans. Leslie J. Roberts (Syracuse: Syracuse University Press, 2003), 32–34.

particular kind of work the future officer has to perform." Engels assured his readers that this apolitical and antidemocratic administration was secured against the corruption of "all personal motives" because "one of the most important features of the plan" was that the "fittest person" would be selected by "some kind of prize essays" that had been properly anonymized.[181]

In his subsequent three-part article series "Die Lage Englands" ("The Condition of England"), which appeared first in the *Deutsch-Französische Jahrbücher* and then from August–October 1844 in *Vorwärts!*, Engels slightly moderated his attitude toward democracy.[182] He continued to deride those who thought that "immorality only adheres to particular state *forms*," whether a "pure monarchy . . . pure aristocracy . . . [or] democracy" rather than realizing that the problem lay in the "state itself" and the "inhumanity of all state forms."[183] However, he now predicted that the democratic elements of Britain's constitution would win out against its aristocratic and monarchical parts and seemed to welcome that development. But he did so primarily because he thought democracy was a "transitional stage" on the way to "real, human freedom."[184] What Chartists, and other democrats, did not understand was that "Social evils cannot be cured by People's Charters."[185] Democracy was "only a transitional stage" because, he claimed, "mere democracy is not capable of curing social ills" and so the "fight of the poor against the rich cannot be fought out on the ground of democracy and/or politics at all." Democracy was therefore the final political stage, "from which a new element will immediately develop that transcends everything of a political nature. This principle is that of socialism."[186]

Comparing Marx's and Engels's initial conversions to communism, it is clear that they shared a commitment to the idea that "politics" in some sense could not solve the social question. They make very similar comments about the limits of changing the form of the state, including to a democratic republic, and both maintain that the answer lies in realizing that the problem is with the state itself and must therefore be transcended. Their reasons for this differ, with

181. Engels, "The 'Times' on German Communism," *MEGA* I.3: 560-61 / *MECW* 3: 413.

182. The second and third articles were likely written in January–March 1844 and were intended for future issues of the *Deutsch-Französische Jahrbücher*. They may have been revised by Engels while he was in Paris in August and participated in editorial meetings of *Vorwärts!*; see *MEGA* I.2: 562; I.3: 1177–78, 1198–99.

183. Engels, "Die Lage Englands III: Die englische Konstitution," *MEGA* I.3: 569–70 / *MECW* 3: 491–92.

184. Engels, "Die Lage Englands I: 'Past and Present' by Thomas Carlyle. London 1843," *MEGA* I.3: 534 / *MECW* 3: 466.

185. Ibid., 517 / 450.

186. Engels, "Die Lage Englands III," *MEGA* I.3: 589 / *MECW* 3: 513.

Engels (drawing on Proudhon and Weitling) seeming to base his objection to different state forms on their common coercive character (without explaining why this would make the state incapable of addressing social issues), whereas Marx bases his argument on the divide between civil society and the political sphere, and the consequent impotence of the latter, which he takes to be true of all forms of the modern state. An even stronger contrast is that while they both favor an end to the state, there's no suggestion in Marx's "Kritische Randglossen" that this means moving beyond democracy, while it is explicit in Engels's writings.[187] Nowhere does Marx display Engels's antimajoritarian sympathies or endorse Weitling's apolitical administrative designs (Marx in fact presents the state's obsession with "administration" as one of its chief ills).[188]

Perhaps the clearest political difference between Marx and Engels at this point, however, is their view of the transition to socialism. While Engels explicitly rejects violent revolution, Marx, in spite of all his antipolitical criticisms, ends his "Kritische Randglossen" with a dramatic volte-face where he endorses the necessity of revolution, and even political revolution, for transitioning to socialism. Reversing Ruge's call for a "social revolution" with a "political soul," Marx argues for a "*political revolution* with a *social* soul," explaining that

> *Revolution* in general—the *overthrow* of the existing authority and the *dissolution* of the old relations—is a political act. But *socialism* cannot be realized without *revolution*. It requires this *political* act, insofar as it requires

187. As I discuss in chapter 7, the end of the state should not be conflated with the end of politics or the end of democracy. The closest Marx comes to suggesting that communism means overcoming democracy is a cryptic categorization of communisms in his unpublished manuscripts. He describes two forms of communism, first, those which are "still political in nature—democratic or despotic," and second, those that believe in the "abolition of the state" but are still "affected" by private property, and argues that they both rightly aim at overcoming human alienation. But he says they are both superseded by a third form of communism: "*communism as positive* abolition of *private property*, as *human self-estrangement*"; see Marx, Ökonomisch-philosophische Manuskripte, MEGA I.2: 388-89 / MECW 3: 294–96. Few clarifying further details are provided.

188. That said, Marx does highly praise Weitling's *Garantien der Harmonie und Freiheit* (1842), where Weitling sets out this scheme, as a "*vehement* and brilliant literary debut of the German workers"; see Marx, "Kritische Randglossen," *MEGA* I.2: 459/ *MECW* 3: 201; see also Ökonomisch-philosophische Manuskripte, MEGA I.2: 325/ MECW 3: 232. That judgment contrasts sharply with his dismissive account of Weitling the year before; see chapter 2. For his part, Weitling was enthusiastic about Marx's article and thought it showed the compatibility of their views; see Wilhelm Weitling to Karl Marx, 18 October 1844, *MEGA*, III.1: 445, though neither this nor Marx's positive comments proves a wholesale commitment to Weitling's views, which seems unlikely given his antiutopianism and dislike of administration.

destruction and *dissolution*. But where its *organizing activity* begins, where its *end in itself*, its *soul*, steps forth, then socialism discards the *political covering*.[189]

Thus, while Marx presents the future of socialism in very similar terms to Engels as being in some quite unspecified sense beyond politics (recall that Engels says that socialism "transcends everything of a political nature"), at this moment they have different views about the importance of a political revolution for bringing about socialism.

Marx's initial transition to communism thus involves a less stark abandonment of his prior republicanism than for Engels, especially in terms of democracy and revolution. At the same time there is little doubt that Marx's initial conversion goes further in an antipolitical direction than his subsequent, considered account of the politics of communism. Whereas Marx later gives an extensive account of why the political structures of a democratic republic (particularly universal suffrage and civic rights) make a political revolution a prerequisite for socialism, he here reduces the necessity of revolution to a vague endorsement of the "*destruction* and *dissolution*" it brings. Moreover, it is unclear how Marx's closing endorsement of revolution in the "Kritische Randglossen" can be reconciled with the essay's earlier critique of the senselessness of republican insurrections or with Marx's questionable claim that the understanding of how to address social problems is even worse in more politically advanced countries like the First French Republic. Indeed, by dismissing any and all state attempts at addressing the social question as mere "*administrative measures*" and declaring that the modern state is powerless over civil society, Marx leaves no role for the state in social transformation. That contrasts sharply with his later emphasis on the importance of taking state power and using it to push a number of social measures (such as free education, progressive taxation, abolition of inheritance, and centralization of credit and the means of transport "in the hands of the state").[190] Marx in fact gives no hint of how socialism is supposed to be achieved without such state action, leaving open the possibility that he harbors some of the true socialist hopes of transitioning to communism through a purely "social" path of raising consciousness and expanding worker associations. But that is speculative, since Marx gives no detail as to what a nonpolitical path to socialism looks like. Furthermore, the text itself might be read as committing the exact same charge that Marx and Engels later make of true socialism, that it engages in social criticism that

---

189. Marx, "Kritische Randglossen," *MEGA* I.2: 463 / *MECW* 3: 206.

190. Marx and Engels, *Manifest der Kommunistischen Partei*, *MEW* 4: 481-82 / *MECW* 6: 505; see also *Forderungen der kommunistischen Parthei in Deutschland*, *MEGA* I.7: 26 / *MECW* 7: 4.

was appropriate for more politically advanced countries like France but was reactionary in politically backward Germany.[191]

In summary, Marx's "Kritische Randglossen" certainly does contain several antipolitical elements in common with the true socialism that he would later deride. The vehemence of Marx's initial antipolitical stance might be partially explained by the not uncommon phenomenon of ultraradicalism in the newly converted. Given the confused and contradictory positions that Marx defends on the relationship of politics to social transformation, it is not entirely surprising that Ruge did not find it necessary to provide a worked-out response, beyond a brief reply objecting to some of Marx's personal criticism.[192]

Having established that Marx did have an antipolitical true socialist phase (though weaker than that of Engels and some other contemporaries), we can now turn to answering the question of when Marx abandoned that position. An immediate problem arises, however, because the period after the "Kritische Randglossen" is a remarkably quiet one by Marx's standards (at least in terms of publication). He spent the autumn of 1844 expanding the few pages Engels had left behind into the two-hundred-page *Die heilige Familie oder Kritik der kritischen Kritik* (*The Holy Family or Critique of Critical Criticism*), an attack on Bruno Bauer and associates that was published in February 1845.[193] After that, Marx published a single article in 1845 and next to nothing in 1846. This was partly because when he was expelled from France and moved to Brussels, the Belgian government forced him to sign a pledge that he would not "publish in Belgium any work on current politics";[194] partly because he was initially collecting material for his contracted, but never completed, two-volume *Kritik der Politik und Nationalökonomie* (*A Critique of Politics and National Economy*);[195] and partly because in autumn 1845 he began working (with Engels and others)

191. Marx and Engels, *Manifest der Kommunistischen Partei*, MEW 4: 488–78 / MECW 6: 511–12.

192. Ein Preusse [Arnold Ruge], "Der 'angebliche Preusse' zu den Randglossen etc. etc.," *Vorwärts!* no. 66 (17 August 1844): 3. This is at least as likely an explanation as the dogmatic suggestion that Ruge "was incapable of dealing with Marx's political and theoretical arguments," in *MEGA*, I.2: 925. See, similarly, Schmidt, "Zur Geschichte des Pariser Vorwärts von 1844," xvii.

193. The book repeats some of his criticisms of Bauer in "Zur Judenfrage" on human and political emancipation and has some interesting critical comments on the politics of the Jacobins; see Marx and Engels, *Die Heilige Familie*, MEGA I.4: 124 / MECW 4: 122, But it says little about socialist politics directly.

194. See *MEGA* I.4: 730 / MECW 4: 675, 677.

195. Zwi Rosen claims without convincing evidence that in this book Marx intended to show that "the democratic republic, in which the bourgeoisie rules, is the suitable political form for social, that is communist, revolution"; Rosen, *Moses Hess und Karl Marx*, 162.

on the assorted manuscripts intended for a quarterly journal project that failed in July 1846, out of which twentieth-century editors misleadingly constructed a "book" on *Die deutsche Ideologie* (*The German Ideology*).[196] In November 1844 Marx did write a tantalising list of political topics to be addressed in a work on the modern state (including "individual freedom and public authority," "popular sovereignty," "the constitutional representative state and the democratic representative state" and "the *separation of powers*").[197] But he revealed, publicly at least, few details of his political views until his published 1847 critiques of true socialism and republicanism (discussed in chapter 4). We do, however, know that at least by July 1846 he and Engels were publicly identifying themselves as "German Democratic Communists" and celebrating the Chartists for their struggle toward the "democratic reconstruction of the Constitution upon the basis of the People's Charter" through which "the working class will become the ruling class of England."[198]

Fortunately, we have something of a proxy for Marx's views between the publication of the "Kritische Randglossen" in August 1844 and his public adherence to democratic communism in July 1846 through the writings of Engels, who continued to publish extensively over this period. Engels cannot, of course, be treated as a definitive guide for Marx's views. Nor should we assume that once they had had their pivotal meeting in Paris their views converged in a simple linear fashion. Crucially, there is no evidence that Marx had anything like the short-lived "communitarian moment" that Engels went through from the end of summer 1844 to spring 1845, when he returned to work in his father's cotton factory in Barmen.[199] In a series of neglected (and quite fascinating) articles and speeches in this period, Engels enthusiastically reported on the apparent success of several small Christian socialist, Fourierist, and Owenist communities in America and England. He celebrated these experiments

196. For this fascinating editorial history, see Terrell Carver, "*The German Ideology* Never Took Place," *History of Political Thought* 31, no. 1 (2010): 107–27; Terrell Carver and Daniel Blank, *A Political History of the Editions of Marx and Engels's "German Ideology Manuscripts"* (New York: Palgrave Macmillan, 2014). For the textual and theoretical implications, see Sarah Johnson, "The Early Life of Marx's 'Mode of Production,'" *Modern Intellectual History* 18, no. 2 (2021): 349–78; Sarah Johnson, "Farewell to *The German Ideology*," *Journal of the History of Ideas* 83, no. 1 (2022): 143–70.

197. Marx, [Plan einer Arbeit über den modernen Staat], *MEGA* IV.3: 11 / *MECW* 4: 666.

198. Marx and Engels, "Address of the German Democratic Communists of Brussels to Mr. Feargus O'Connor," *MEW* 4: 24–26 / *MECW* 6: 58–60.

199. Leopold, "'All Tell the Same Tale': The Young Engels and Communal Settlements in America and England," 8; David Leopold, "'Socialist Turnips': The Young Friedrich Engels and the Feasibility of Communism," *Political Theory* 40, no. 3 (2012): 347–78.

(especially the Owenist ones) as a model for future socialism and, through their continual expansion, as one potential transitional path to it.[200] Marx, by comparison, never had any time for such small-scale experiments, and Engels would subsequently, partially under Marx's influence, abandon these early enthusiasms.

But alongside his communitarianism, Engels was already nuancing his antipolitical criticisms independently of Marx. As well as endorsing a communitarian transition to socialism (which he thought the likely path for England), Engels speculated that the French "will be likely to prepare and implement communism on a national basis," and he spoke favorably of preparing the grounds for communism through the three measures of free education, reorganization of poor relief, and a progressive tax on capital (leading Ruge to praise Engels as the only German communist to direct his demands "from the beginning toward the state").[201] Significantly, Engels also came to a more positive view of Chartism and the inevitability of revolution through the writing of his *Die Lage der arbeitenden Klasse in England* (*The Condition of the Working Class in England*), which he completed just before joining Marx in Brussels in April 1845.[202]

Once in Brussels, it is likely that their political views increasingly converged and developed in tandem (which is not to say that then or afterward the two were in complete agreement). Of particular importance to their reevaluation of democracy seems to have been their joint trip to Manchester and London from July to August 1845.[203] In London they met with several members of the

200. Interestingly, in contrast to Engels's earlier endorsement of Weitling's antimajoritarian schemes, Engels seems to express some preference for communities where they "elect their administration themselves"; see Engels, "Beschreibung der in neuerer Zeit enstandenen und noch bestehenden communistischen Ansiedlungen," *MEGA* I.4: 226, 228–29 / *MECW* 4: 224, 227.

201. Engels, "Elberfelder Reden," *MEGA* I.4: 529–30 / *MECW* 4: 253–54; Ruge, "Der teutsche Kommunismus," 118.

202. Claeys, "The Political Ideas of the Young Engels," 467–71. See Engels, *Die Lage der arbeitenden Klasse in England*, *MEGA* I.4: 440–49, 467–68 / *MECW* 4: 517–27, 547.

203. In Manchester Marx embarked on another substantial reading list, including making extensive extracts from the antipolitical arguments in the Owenist John Francis Bray's *Labour's Wrongs and Labour's Remedy* (Leeds: David Green, 1839); see especially Marx, "Exzerpte aus Bray," *MEGA* IV.5: 28–32, 58–59. We cannot say what Marx made of these arguments at the time, but he would later single out Bray's book as a prime example of the "indifference in political matters" that had blighted so many forms of socialism; see Marx, "L'Indifferenza in materia politica," *MEGA* I.24: 107 / *MECW* 23: 394. For Marx's research trip to Manchester (and his reading of Bray), see Lucia Pradella's and Mathias Bohlender's chapters in Marcel Van der Linden and Gerald Hubmann, eds., *Marx's Capital: An Unfinishable Project?* (Leiden: Brill, 2018),

London branch of the Bund der Gerechten and leading Left Chartists, including Karl Schapper and George Julian Harney, with Marx and Engels perhaps playing some role in introducing them to each other.[204] We know that in London, "Citizen Engels" helped organize a "meeting of the democrats of all Nations" to explore setting up an international fraternal association, with Schapper, Harney, and Marx likely in attendance.[205] After Marx and Engels returned to Brussels, a festival was duly held on 22 September 1845 for the anniversary of the foundation of the First French Republic in 1795 that marked the emergence of the Fraternal Democrats, a loose organization that combined democratic internationalism with strong socialist leanings, where Schapper, Harney, and later Ernest Jones formed their organizational "triumvirate," and with which Marx and Engels continued to collaborate over the ensuing years.[206]

In a glowing report on the Fraternal Democrats' founding festival, Engels defended the importance of internationalism and the French Republic for communists against the indifference of what he called the "German theories on true socialism" (the first time in which the designation appears in his or Marx's writings).[207] Engels presented communism as the natural heir and consequence of the Revolution's democratic movement, which he claimed had, contrary to some socialist portrayals, already gone beyond "solely political organization" and was "from beginning to end a social movement."[208] In the present day, Engels argued that democracy had become completely inextricable from social issues so that a "purely political democracy" was now impossible and in fact *"Democracy nowadays is communism."* He stressed that

---

243-48 and 257-60, as well as David Leopold, "Karl Marx and 'English Socialism,'" *Nineteenth-Century Prose* 49, no. 1 (2022): 23–27.

204. Christine Lattek, *Revolutionary Refugees: German Socialism in Britain, 1840–1860* (London: Routledge, 2006), 34–36.

205. "Democratic Movement," *The Northern Star*, no. 406 (23 August 1845): 8; Bert Andréas et al., eds., *Association Démocratique, ayant pour but l'union et la fraternité de tous les peoples: Eine frühe internationale demokratische Vereinigung in Brüssel, 1847–1848* (Trier: Karl-Marx-Haus 2004), 55–56.

206. For the Fraternal Democrats, see Henry Weisser, *British Working-Class Movements and Europe, 1815–48* (Manchester: Manchester University Press, 1975), chapter 4.

207. Engels, "Das Fest der Nationen in London (Zur Feier der Errichtung der französischen Republik, 22. September 1792)," *MEGA* I.4: 692 / *MECW* 6: 3. A few months earlier, Engels had criticized what he called "true, pure, German, theoretical communism and socialism." He added that "I make no exception here of my own writing," implying that Engels himself recognized an important shift in his thinking in this period. See Engels, "Ein Fragment Fouriers über den Handel," *MEGA* I.4: 593 / *MECW* 4: 614.

208. Engels, "Das Fest der Nationen in London," *MEGA* I.4: 693–94/ *MECW* 6: 5.

concurrent to the change in democracy, the communist movement was today fully committed to democracy ("democracy has become a proletarian principle"), and so proletarian parties legitimately "inscribe the word 'Democracy' on their banners."[209] He observed that the most advanced political parties had rightly realized that they were "not only republicans, but communists" and that the "proletarians of all nations" were now beginning to operate under "the banner of communist democracy."[210] Engels further reported that a speech celebrating the coming "triumph of republican communism" was greeted with loud and protracted cheers.[211]

The article's clear commitment to democracy as an essential element of communism and its explicit targeting of true socialism makes it a crucial marker in Marx and Engels's evolution away from their earlier antipolitical sympathies. By the following year they would be locked in a heated battle with true socialists to establish that the "aims of communism" could be carried out by "no other means than the forcible, democratic revolution."[212] If we take Engels's autumn 1845 article on the French Revolution as the outer limit of when Marx and Engels distanced themselves from their heterogenous true socialist views, then we can estimate Marx's antipolitical phase as running from either March or August 1844 (his personal and then public break with Ruge) to no later than the late summer of 1845. It may thus have lasted anywhere from a few months to over a year, with the textual basis not allowing for much greater specificity.[213] Marx's initial abandonment of some his republican political commitments when he first converted to communism, brief as this period was and less severe than many other communist converts, is an important dimension of intellectual development and brings his subsequent reintegration of those commitments into even sharper relief.

One element, however, that Marx never reintegrated (even during his much later radical democratic enthusiasm for the Paris Commune) was the intrinsic value he placed on political participation in his early republican political writings and even to an extent in "Zur Judenfrage." In those early writings Marx presented political participation as an important component of human flourishing. Subsequent to his conversion to communism, however, his defense of

209. Ibid.

210. Ibid., 695–96 / 6–7.

211. Ibid., 705 / 13.

212. Engels to the Kommunistische Korrespondenz-komitee, 23 October 1846, MEGA III.2: 54 / MECW 38: 82.

213. Balakrishnan's estimate of a period of more than two years lasting until 1847 is thus too extensive; see Balakrishnan, "The Abolitionist—I," 123, and Gopal Balakrishnan, "The Abolitionist—II," New Left Review 91 (2014): 80.

political participation is solely based on its instrumental value in bringing about social transformation. That changed view is already evident in the "Kritische Randglossen," where Marx says that whatever value a political revolution may have is reduced to bringing about the "*end in itself (Selbstzweck)*" of socialism.[214] Marx's denigration of the intrinsic importance of political participation is even more explicit in an easily overlooked aspect of his critique of Ruge: their disagreement about the meaning and value of *Gemeinwesen*, a complex German term that can be variously translated as body politic, community, commonwealth, political community, polity, or *res publica*. To capture Marx and Ruge's disagreement I have left it untranslated in the following discussion. While Ruge claimed that the Silesian weavers' uprising sprang from the "hopeless isolation of people from the *Gemeinwesen*," Marx countered that by this Ruge only "understood the *political Gemeinwesen*, the *body politic (Staatswesen)*."[215] Marx rejected this political interpretation of *Gemeinwesen*, arguing that:

> the *Gemeinwesen* from which the worker is *isolated* is a Gemeinwesen of a completely different reality and scope than the *political* Gemeinwesen. This Gemeinwesen, from which *his own labor* cuts him off, is *life* itself, the physical and mental life, human morality, human activity, human enjoyment, *human* nature. *Human nature* is the *true Gemeinwesen* of man.[216]

Contemporary readers of the "Kritische Randglossen" might have struggled to pin down exactly what Marx was proposing by this alternative understanding of *Gemeinwesen*, from which a worker's "*own labor*" apparently separated them. Marx was in fact bringing to public view a glimpse of the private (and unpublished) economic and philosophical writings on alienated labor that had consumed him over the previous months. Marx had there developed a now celebrated account of how workers under capitalism are alienated from the kinds of communal production that would realize their human nature. Marx was therefore contrasting Ruge's view of alienation from the *Gemeinwesen*, understood as being excluded from political participation, with being excluded from work that fulfills human needs. Marx claimed that being separated from the latter is "incomparably more universal, more intolerable, and more contradictory than isolation from the political *Gemeinwesen*."[217] That marked a significant contrast to his early political writings, as Marx now considered work

---

214. Marx, "Kritische Randglossen," *MEGA* I.2: 463 / *MECW* 3: 206. He similarly contrasts "political aims" with the "real aim" of socialism; ibid., 461 / 204.

215. Ibid, 462 / 204.

216. Ibid.

217. Ibid., 462 / 205.

to be far more important to human flourishing than politics. In place of his earlier Aristotelian complaints of people being denied their nature as *zoon politikon*, as "political animals," Marx now held that "*man* is more infinite than the *citizen*, and *human life* more infinite than *political life*."[218] Marx consequently argued that no matter how "*particular*" a workers' revolt like that of the Silesian weavers might appear to observers like Ruge, their attempt to realize our human need for unalienated work meant that their struggles "contained within themselves a *universal* soul."[219]

I turn now, in the final section of this chapter, to Marx's writings on alienated labor that underpinned this changed judgment. These may have contributed to a more critical attitude toward the classical republican connection between politics and human nature. But they also reveal how Marx continued to deploy the republican concern with arbitrary power, which had informed his early political journalism, in order now to critique social relations of dependency.

Alienation and Domination

Between roughly May and August 1844, Marx began his first studies of the project that would eventually culminate twenty-three years later in the first volume of *Das Kapital*: his critique of political economy. Over those months in 1844, in something of a "manic episode,"[220] comparable to his time in Kreuznach, Marx furiously caught up with the leading works of political economy, including the writings of Adam Smith, David Ricardo, Jean-Baptiste Say, James Mill, and John Ramsay McCulloch. Alongside and in between his notes on these readings, Marx began writing his own substantive critique of political economy. From this mass of writings and extracts that Marx left unpublished, subsequent editors artificially carved out three incomplete manuscripts, presenting and rearranging them as a more or less coherent work now usually known as the *Ökonomisch-philosophische Manuskripte* (*Economic and Philosophic Manuscripts*), or sometimes *Pariser Manuskripte* (*Paris Manuscripts*).[221] The publication of the

218. Ibid.

219. Ibid. See the similar claim in Marx's manuscripts that when it comes to the emancipation of workers it is not only their liberation that is at stake, since "in their emancipation is contained universal human emancipation"; *Ökonomisch-philosophische Manuskripte, MEGA* I.2: 373 / *MECW* 3: 280.

220. Keith Tribe, "Karl Marx's 'Critique of Political Economy': A Critique," in *The Economy of the Word: Language, History, and Economics* (Oxford: Oxford University Press, 2015), 219.

221. Marx's notes on James Mill's *Elements of Political Economy* (1821), for instance, contain several extended substantive digressions that overlap with the first manuscript, and large parts of the manuscripts are repeated citations from his readings. There is also no philological basis

Ökonomisch-philosophische Manuskripte in 1932 led to a long-running intellectual, and even political, dispute over their importance and relationship to Marx's later critique of political economy, particularly in *Das Kapital*.[222] I want to focus here on how the republican moral and political vocabulary of freedom, servitude, dependence, and domination that suffuses all of Marx's critique of political economy is evident from his earliest economic writings. As I discuss in chapter 6, that critique is undoubtably more theoretically sophisticated and empirically grounded in his later works. At the same time, the interesting connection Marx makes between alienation and domination is most prominently found in his early writings.

A theme running across Marx's early economic writings is his antipathy to relations of dependency. In abstract terms, Marx argued that persons are only properly independent when they are free from living at the arbitrary will of others, particularly in relation to the power over a person's means of existence. He wrote that "A *being* only considers himself independent once he stands on his own feet, and he stands on his own feet as soon as he owes *existence* to himself. A man, who lives by the grace of another, regards himself as a dependent being."[223] Marx applied this objection to owing one's means of existence to the pleasure of another to the relationship between poor debtors and rich creditors. He attacked the power of the rich to decide who among the poor was deserving of credit, arguing that "since the arbitrary pleasure and judgment of the rich man over the poor man confirms or denies his *whole* existence, he is completely dependent on this contingency." Marx expressed particular anger that a poor creditor was put in a dependent position where they had to make a "humiliating *plea* for credit from the rich man." This analysis of individual dependency was interestingly extended by Marx to the power that banks have over the state through the loaning of state credit. Marx says that the "exact same" relation of dependency between creditors and debtors is exhibited in the "game of *government bonds,*" where the state has become the "plaything of merchants." He consequently suggestively refers to the "state domination (*Staatsherrschaft*) of the bank" that has resulted from the "concentration of wealth in

---

to differentiate specifically the three manuscripts as a group from the extracts. See Jürgen Rojahn, "Marxismus—Marx—Geschichtswissenschaft: Der Fall der sog. 'Ökonomisch-philosophischen Manuskripte aus dem Jahre 1844,'" *International Review of Social History* 28, no. 1 (1983): 19–20. For Marx's unconventional and often unnoticed division of the first manuscript into three columns and its interpretive importance, see Margaret Fay, "The Influence of Adam Smith on Marx's Theory of Alienation," *Science & Society* 47, no. 2 (1983): 129–51.

222. Michael Maidan, "The *Rezeptionsgeschichte* of the Paris Manuscripts," *History of European Ideas* 12, no. 6 (1990): 767–81.

223. Marx, *Ökonomisch-philosophische Manuskripte*, MEGA I.2: 397 / MECW 3: 304.

these hands," making them the modern "*Areopagus* of the nation" (the Areopagus was classical Athens's aristocratic council).[224] We have here a brief unelaborated return of the same concern with how economic wealth is converted into corrupting political power that Marx displayed in his early journalistic criticisms of the control exercised by forest owners over the provincial legislature.

Elsewhere in the manuscript, Marx makes an explicit comparison between modern economic dependency and earlier forms of political dependency. He describes the system of private property as one of "*fantasy, caprice* and *whim*," in which

> no eunuch flatters his despot more basely or uses more despicable means to stimulate his dulled capacity for pleasure in order to sneak a favor for himself than does the industrial eunuch—the producer—in order to sneak for himself a few pieces of silver, in order to charm the golden birds out of the pockets of his dearly beloved neighbors in Christ.[225]

Marx's biting comparison of an "industrial eunuch" dependent on the market with the eunuch who serves a despot is a reference to the old republican objection to the role of courtiers in an absolute monarchy.[226] A recurrent feature of classical and early modern republican critiques of monarchy was an objection to how a king's arbitrary power placed those around him in a state of dependence, resulting in obsequious and toadying advisers.[227] They complained that the courtiers and "eunuchs employed by kings" could never "hope to speak truth to power if everyone is obliged to cultivate the flattering arts required to appease a ruler on whose favour everyone depends."[228] Marx invoked this old republican complaint, however, to highlight how much worse modern economic dependency was compared to the political dependency of courtiers ("no eunuch flatters his despot more basely . . . than does the industrial

224. Marx, "Exzerpte aus James Mill," *MEGA* IV.2: 451–52 / *MECW* 3: 216.

225. Marx, *Ökonomisch-philosophische Manuskripte*, *MEGA* I.2: 419 / *MECW* 3: 307.

226. I had earlier interpreted this passage to be referring to the dependency of workers on their capitalist employers; see Bruno Leipold, "Chains and Invisible Threads: Liberty and Domination in Marx's Account of Wage-Slavery," in *Rethinking Liberty before Liberalism*, ed. Hannah Dawson and Annelien De Dijn (Cambridge: Cambridge University Press, 2022), 208–9. But William Clare Roberts has convinced me that Marx is in fact discussing market dependence.

227. Daniel J. Kapust, *Flattery and the History of Political Thought: That Glib and Oily Art* (Cambridge: Cambridge University Press, 2018), 18–20.

228. Skinner, *Liberty before Liberalism*, 90, 94. See also Philip Pettit, *Republicanism: A Theory of Freedom and Government* (Oxford: Oxford University Press, 1997), 61.

eunuch"). While his comparison serves mainly to emphasize how much more severe economic dependency is, his pejorative reference to eunuchs repeats the objectionably masculine interpretation given to the ideal of independence in many articulations of the original republican political complaint.[229]

In addition to these scattered remarks on dependency, Marx's 1844 writings provide the beginnings of his account of how the capitalists' domination over workers allows them to set wages and working conditions in their favor. In his discussion of wages in the first manuscript, Marx presents three contrasting factors that advantage capitalists in the struggle over wages: (1) capitalists can live off the rent and interest generated by their capital, while workers have no independent income or means of subsistence; (2) capitalists face few obstacles to combining with other capitalists for mutual support, whereas collective action by workers is often illegal and costly; and (3) capitalists always have the option of transferring their capital to another industry, while the division of labor means workers' skills are more specialized and they cannot easily move from one industry to another.[230] Marx places special emphasis on the final contrast, arguing that the growth in the division of labor makes the worker "more and more dependent on the capitalist" and that it is "precisely the capacity of the capitalist to direct his capital into other channels" that leaves the worker "who is restricted to some particular branch of labor, destitute, or forces him to submit to every demand of this capitalist."[231] The capitalists' structural advantages thus gives them the bargaining power to force workers to accept their demands and wages that amount to what Marx decried as a "cattle-like existence."[232]

Marx presented the relative power of the two sides engaged in this struggle in starkly opposed terms. While the capitalist had the "capacity" to do with their capital as they like, the worker's ability to survive lay beyond their control. Marx argued that it is a matter of "luck" whether the worker can find a capitalist to employ them and adds that the "demand on which the life of the worker depends, depends on the whims of the rich and the capitalists."[233] By this Marx seems to mean both that the consumption patterns that drive demand are particularly affected by the changing fashions of the rich,[234] and that it is the capitalist

229. For further discussion of this aspect of the republican ideal of independence, see Marilyn Friedman, "Pettit's Civic Republicanism and Male Domination," in *Republicanism and Political Theory*, ed. Cécile Laborde and John Maynor (Oxford: Blackwell, 2008), 252–55; and Lena Halldenius, *Mary Wollstonecraft and Feminist Republicanism: Independence, Rights and the Experience of Unfreedom* (London: Pickering & Chatto, 2015), 27–30.

230. Marx, *Ökonomisch-philosophische Manuskripte*, MEGA I.2: 327-28 / MECW 3: 235–36.

231. Ibid., 328, 332 / 236, 240.

232. Ibid., 327 / 235.

233. Ibid.

234. See also ibid., 330, 422 / 238, 310.

who decides how to respond to changing demand and whether to hire any particular worker. As Marx puts it, the social position of being a capitalist means that the capitalist is the "*executive power* (*Regierungsgewalt*) over labor and its products."[235] Marx's early account of the struggle over wages and working conditions thus depicts the struggle as one where capitalists have arbitrary power over workers and use it to push wages as low as possible. Largely absent, though, are the theoretical breakthroughs Marx later makes in terms of linking the capitalists' domination to the exploitation of surplus value.[236]

While the economic analysis in Marx's 1844 manuscripts has received some attention,[237] by far the most commented on aspect of the manuscripts is his more "philosophical" discussion of alienated labor. But, considering the vast literature devoted to the topic, it is surprising how little of it notes the importance of domination in Marx's account of alienation.[238] In the final part of the first manuscript, Marx lays out four ways in which alienation (which at a general level refers to an inappropriate separation or relation between entities)[239] applies to labor: (1) alienation from the product, (2) alienation from the act of production, (3) alienation from species-being, and (4) alienation from other people. Of these Marx, makes an explicit connection to domination with the alienation from the product and the act of production.

Marx outlines three factors that alienate modern workers from the act of production (by which Marx seems to have in mind particularly the daily experience of laboring in a factory). First, it is unfulfilling; Marx argues that at work the worker "does not affirm, but denies himself, does not feel content but unhappy, does not develop freely his physical and mental energy."[240] Second, it is carried out under compulsion; Marx says it is it is "*forced labor*" carried out merely to survive and is thus "shunned like the plague" when not required. Third, it is not under the control of the worker; Marx argues that work is alienating for the worker because "it is not his own, but someone else's, that it does not belong to him, that in it he belongs, not to himself, but to another." Marx compares the fact that the "worker's activity [is] not his self-directed activity" to how religion makes human thoughts and desires seem to originate from an

235. Ibid., 339 / 247. In the original three-column organization of the manuscripts this description appears alongside the above discussion of wages; see *MEGA* I.2: 190–91.

236. Samuel Hollander, *The Economics of Karl Marx: Analysis and Application* (Cambridge: Cambridge University Press, 2008), 191–93.

237. Ibid., chapter 6.

238. For some discussion, see Rainer Forst, "Noumenal Alienation: Rousseau, Kant and Marx on the Dialectics of Self-Determination," *Kantian Review* 22, no. 4 (2017): 539–44; Pablo Gilabert, *Human Dignity and Social Justice* (Oxford: Oxford University Press, 2023), 79–81.

239. Leopold, *Young Karl Marx*, 67–68.

240. Marx, *Ökonomisch-philosophische Manuskripte*, *MEGA* I.2: 367 / *MECW* 3: 274.

external source, so that they operate as an "alien, divine or diabolical activity" on the individual, rather than being something that has originated in themselves.[241] Marx further claims the worker experiences production "as an alien activity not belonging to him . . . [his] begetting as emasculation . . . as activity which is turned against him, independent of him and not belonging to him."[242] (Note how Marx again links independence to masculinity).

Marx thus linked alienated productive activity to work being *unfulfilling*, carried out under *compulsion* and not *belonging* to the worker. The first two aspects of alienation in the act of production, that work is dull and done out of necessity, are frequently commented upon in the literature, but it is noteworthy how much stress Marx also placed on workers' not having control over their work.[243] Marx repeatedly argued that because a worker has to carry out their labor activity for and under the direction of someone else, the act of production is an alienating one for the worker. Dominated work is thus, by Marx's account, alienated work. That suggests that in order to overcome alienation it is not sufficient to remove the compulsion to work, or to make work more fulfilling and creative; the structure of control in the workplace has to change as well. At the same time, it also suggests that nondominated work might still be alienating if it remains unfulfilling.

The connection Marx makes between domination and alienation and the act of production is relatively straightforward. Harder to grasp is the way in which Marx ties domination to alienation from the product. By alienation from the product, Marx broadly meant that rather than workers producing products that they own for their own need, they produce commodities for exchange that are owned by capitalists.[244] Marx repeatedly claimed that this results in the product becoming a hostile and independent power from the worker who produced it. He says, for instance, that alienation from the product means that the product "exists *outside him* [the worker], independently of him and alien to him, and that it becomes an autonomous power that confronts him, that the life that he has conferred on the object confronts him as something hostile and alien."[245] Marx found this last aspect—that it is the worker's own creation that dominates them—a particularly bitter irony.

241. Ibid.

242. Ibid., 368 / 275.

243. The role of domination is, for instance, absent from two of the most sophisticated recent accounts of Marx's ideas on alienated labor; see Jan Kandiyali, "The Importance of Others: Marx on Unalienated Production," *Ethics* 130 (2020): 555–87, and Leopold, *Young Karl Marx*, 229–34.

244. Marx, "Exzerpte aus James Mill," *MEGA* IV.2: 455 / *MECW* 3: 219–20.

245. Marx, *Ökonomisch-philosophische Manuskripte, MEGA* I.2: 365 / *MECW* 3: 272.

Recalling Frankenstein and his monster, Marx portrayed the worker as giving life to a creature that turns on its creator, describing how "our own product has risen up on its hind legs against us."[246] This animalistic metaphor aside, Marx generally depicted the domination of alienated products as one of *domination by things*, saying that the process results in the worker's "*bondage to the object (Knechtschaft unter dem Gegenstand)*" and that he "becomes a servant of his object."[247] Marx claimed that this was a new development under capitalism: "What was once domination of persons over persons, is now the general domination of the *thing* over the *person*, of the product over the producer."[248]

The image Marx conjures of workers being *dominated by objects* that they themselves have brought to life is evocative but not immediately transparent. His meaning is clearly not literal—a worker's products do not actually come to life like Pinocchio or the sorcerer's broom that sprouts arms and legs and does its own cleaning. But Marx clearly attributed importance to this form of domination that goes beyond metaphorical appearance. His discussion, however, lacks an unambiguous single account linking alienation from the product to domination by objects—not surprising in unpublished, rough manuscripts.

Perhaps the most important linkage that Marx seems to outline arises from the central position he at this point (in contrast to his later thought) gives to alienation from the product in the explanatory functioning of the capitalist system overall.[249] Marx says that "all these [negative] consequences" that he has associated with capitalism can be traced to the worker's separation from the product, including that he "falls under the domination of his product, capital."[250] The worker thus produces not just any object, but rather "capital," in the form of the exchangeable commodities that a capitalist sells on the market. This production for exchange is imbued with tremendous importance by Marx. He argues that this feature of capitalism means that workers no longer produce to satisfy their own direct needs (as with previous producing classes) but "alien" needs to which they are a "slave."[251] Marx adds that this also entails workers' now producing products in exchange for money—a shift that he takes

---

246. Marx, "Exzerpte aus James Mill," *MEGA* IV.2: 464 / *MECW* 3: 226. See also 452 / 217.

247. Marx, *Ökonomisch-philosophische Manuskripte*, *MEGA* I.2: 365-66 / *MECW* 3: 272–73.

248. Marx, "Exzerpte aus James Mill," *MEGA* IV.2: 456 / *MECW* 3: 221. Marx's account of the domination of things was likely influenced by his contemporaneous reading of Eugène Buret and his analysis of the "tyranny of things," in *De la misère des classes laborieuses en Angleterre et en France*, vol. 1 (Paris: Paulin, 1840), 82–83. See Marx, *Ökonomisch-philosophische Manuskripte*, *MEGA* I.2: 348-49 / *MECW* 3: 257, and Marx, "Exzerpte aus Buret," *MEGA* IV.2: 551–79.

249. Allen Wood, *Karl Marx*, 2nd ed. (New York: Routledge, 2004), 3–7.

250. Marx, *Ökonomisch-philosophische Manuskripte*, *MEGA* I.2: 356 / *MECW* 3: 272.

251. Marx, "Exzerpte aus James Mill," *MEGA* IV.2: 455 / *MECW* 3: 220.

as being particularly important in setting the stage for domination by objects. He says that the "complete domination of the estranged thing *over* man has become evident in *money*," and that because of this "*alien mediator* . . . man regards his will, his activity and his relation to other men as a power independent of him and them. His slavery, therefore, reaches its peak."[252]

Domination by objects is thus closely associated with workers being subjected to the vagaries of the production of commodities to be exchanged on the market for money. Alienation from the product and domination by objects consequently acts as a shorthand for the rule by uncontrolled market forces—what Marx refers to as how "economic laws blindly rule the world."[253] That connection becomes particularly clear when Marx discusses the way in which capitalist imperatives have transformed previously aristocratic land management, arguing that

> it is essential that in this competition landed property in the form of capital, manifests its domination over both the working class and the proprietors themselves who are ruined or raised by the laws of movement of capital. The medieval proverb *nulle terre sans seigneur* [no land without master] is thereby replaced by the modern proverb, *l'argent n'a pas de maître* [money has no master], wherein is expressed the complete domination of beaten to death matter (*todtgeschlagnen Materie*) over man.[254]

The domination of objects is thus the "laws of movement of capital" whereby all participants are subjected to the market imperative of competition with each other. Marx thereby importantly extends the scope of domination by objects not just to workers but to the capitalists who are also "ruined or raised" by market forces, which themselves have no "*maître*" (master). Marx emphasized this idea at several points, arguing that "over all rules *inhuman* power, which applies also for the capitalist."[255] That implies that while the worker is subjected to the personal domination of the capitalist, both are subjected to the impersonal domination by objects. Marx thus adds to his description of the capitalist having "executive power" over the worker, cited above, the important clarification that "first the capitalist, by means of capital, exercises his executive power over labor, then, however, capital exercises its executive power over the capitalist himself."[256]

---

252. Ibid., 456 / 221.
253. Marx, *Ökonomisch-philosophische Manuskripte*, MEGA I.2: 348 / MECW 3: 256.
254. Ibid., 360 / 267.
255. Ibid., 426 / 314.
256. Ibid., 339 / 247. There is some similarity here to Marx's brief discussion of the alienation experienced by capitalists in *Die heilige Familie*, MEGA I.4: 37 / MECW 4: 36. See further

Marx believed that the domination that arose from alienation made the worker unfree. At the conclusion of his discussion of alienated labor, Marx rhetorically asks why alienation from the product and from productive activity amount to alien activity and being ruled by an alien power. He playfully considers whether the alien power might be "the *gods*," but answers that though temples might have been built under their supposed orders, "they were never the true lords of labor (*Arbeitsherrn*)."[257] He explains that, in fact, for man,

> if the product of his labor, his labor objectified, is for him an *alien,* hostile, powerful object independent of him, then he relates to it such that another man, alien, hostile, powerful and independent of him, is its master. If he relates to his own activity as an unfree activity, then he relates to it as an activity in the service, under the domination, the coercion, and the yoke of another man.[258]

According to Marx, then, workers engage in "unfree activity" because they labor "under the domination" of a capitalist master. They are alienated from their productive activity because they are subjected to the "yoke of another man." Free productive activity would entail working free from the domination of a master.[259] That working for a capitalist makes the worker unfree is an idea repeated in the manuscripts; Marx says that having to work for a capitalist means that workers "carry out slave-labor, completely losing all their freedom."[260]

Whether Marx also believes that alienation from the product undermines everyone's freedom, in that all are subjected to the arbitrary imperatives of the market, is less clear. The above passage might be read to imply as much, but it does not explicitly link freedom to alienation from the product. Marx is more at pains to stress that at the root of alienation from the product lies a capitalist "master" who owns the product that the worker produces. Marx would thus seem to want to stress that as much as alien market forces might seem to be

---

G. A. Cohen, "Bourgeois and Proletarians," *Journal of the History of Ideas* 29, no. 2 (1968): 211–30. I thank Jan Kandiyali for reminding me of this passage.

257. Marx, *Ökonomisch-philosophische Manuskripte, MEGA* I.2: 371 / *MECW* 3: 278.

258. Ibid., 371–72 / 278–79.

259. In addition to the absence of domination, Marx believes that "truly produc[ing] in freedom" would require that workers produce "free from physical need"; ibid., 369 / 276. Freedom as nondomination is thus an important component of Marx's understanding of free labor but does not exhaust it. On the relation of freedom to necessity in Marx, see Jan Kandiyali, "Freedom and Necessity in Marx's Account of Communism," *British Journal for the History of Philosophy* 22, no. 1 (2014): 104–23; David James, "The Compatibility of Freedom and Necessity in Marx's Idea of Communist Society," *European Journal of Philosophy* 25, no. 2 (2017): 270–93.

260. Marx, *Ökonomisch-philosophische Manuskripte, MEGA* I.2: 329 / *MECW* 3: 237.

completely depersonalized—even supernatural—forces, they still rely on real human masters carrying out their domination over others. As he put it, "Not the gods, not nature, but only man himself can be this alien power over man."[261] Domination by objects is consequently for Marx both masterless and reliant on some being masters over others. He concludes that at the heart of the domination resulting from alienation stands the "capitalist, or whatever one chooses to call the lord of labor."[262]

Coda

Marx's first writings in Paris reveal a growing concern with the emancipatory limits of a republic and a newfound belief in the abolition of private property and the revolutionary role of the proletariat. These were central factors in his conversion to communism. But he still held to the importance of political emancipation and political rights, which may explain his hesitancy in publicly aligning himself with communism and its associated antipathy toward politics. When he was finally willing to take that step, his initial transition involved a complex integration and rejection of his prior republicanism. On the one hand, his concern with freedom and arbitrary power in the political realm was transferred over to his social critique of capitalist domination (too often missed in scholarship on his early writings on alienation). But his commitment to politics itself was obscured in his initial radicalization. There was little evidence of his earlier criticisms of the antipolitics of existing communism—to the bafflement of his erstwhile republican collaborator Arnold Ruge (whose extensive contextual study in this chapter served to highlight a possible path Marx could have taken, or better stayed on, had he not converted to communism). Marx's antipolitical period was brief and not as pronounced as for other early socialists (especially Engels), but it is still insufficiently appreciated in accounts of his transition. That even Marx and particularly Engels could be so enthusiastically, if briefly, drawn to antipolitics (in spite of their prior republicanism) speaks to just how powerful a hold it exercised over early socialism. As we will see in chapter 4, their subsequent effort to build a republican communism involved a drawn-out and laborious struggle to win over the emerging socialist movement to the traditional radical commitment to democracy and politics.

261. Ibid., 371 / 278.
262. Ibid. 372 / 279.

PART II

The Bourgeois Republic

4

The Red Flag and the *Tricolor*

REPUBLICAN COMMUNISM AND
THE BOURGEOIS REPUBLIC, 1845–52

The Republic is declared! We shall be happy now! . . . No more kings, do you
understand? The whole world is free! The whole world free!

—FROM *GUSTAVE FLAUBERT'S* L'ÉDUCATION SENTIMENTALE[1]

[T]he cause of the producers . . . this . . . enslaved class . . . must be fought
under the *Red* flag, for that is the symbol of the new Epoch, "the banner of
the Future." The task given us at present, is to rally our brother Proletarians *en
masse* round this flag, by means of a Democratic and Social Propaganda . . .

—HELEN MACFARLANE[2]

ON THE AFTERNOON OF 25 FEBRUARY 1848, a large, angry crowd gathered
in front of Paris's Hôtel de Ville and demanded that the new French Republic,
proclaimed the night before, abandon the red-white-blue *Tricolor* and adopt
the red flag, the newly emergent emblem of social revolution. Facing them was
Alphonse de Lamartine, the poet, historian, and freshly appointed Minister of
Foreign Affairs (see figure 8). He climbed on top of an old broken chair and
delivered a speech that saved the *Tricolor* as the symbol of the Republic: "the
red flag which you offer us was only paraded around the Champ de Mars,
dragged through the blood of the people . . . whereas the tricolour flag has

1. Gustave Flaubert, *Sentimental Education*, ed. Patrick Coleman, trans. Helen Constantine
(Oxford: Oxford University Press, 2016), 271.

2. Howard Morton [Helen Macfarlane], "The Red Flag in 1850," *The Red Republican*, no. 4
(13 July 1850): 27.

FIGURE 8. Henri Félix Philippoteaux, *Alphonse de Lamartine rejetant le drapeau rouge en 1848* (*Alphonse de Lamartine, before the Hôtel de Ville, Paris, rejects the Red Flag*) (ca. 1848). Courtesy of Wikimedia Commons.

been paraded right round the world, with the name, the glory and liberty of the country!"[3]

Lamartine embodied the outpouring of fraternity and cross-class unity that accompanied the foundation of the republic. He sincerely believed that the "republic [would be] a humane and magnanimous emancipation of all the classes, without oppression for any."[4] It was this atmosphere of hope and intense optimism that Flaubert ironically chronicled in his romantic novel of the period, *L'Éducation sentimentale*, where the ecstatic citizens of Paris are portrayed running through the street shouting that the "People have triumphed! The workers and bourgeoisie are embracing."[5]

But that fraternal spirit between classes could not last. Just four months later, the workers of Paris were raising barricades across the city in response to the provisional government's decision to shut down the National Workshops, which had provided a meager but vital lifeline for the poor and unemployed. For four days, in what came to be known as the June Days, the workers fought the new Republic's troops before succumbing to their superior numbers and arms. Precise figures are hard to establish, but it is likely that the spontaneous uprising saw somewhere between 1,500 and 4,000 insurgents killed, with enraged troops carrying out an unknown number of summary executions.[6] In response to this appalling bloodbath, Marx declared that "Only after being dipped in the blood of the *June insurgents* did the tricolor become the flag of the European revolution—the *red flag!*"[7]

For Marx, the experience of the June Days exposed the democratic republic striven for by generations of republicans for what it truly was: a "*bourgeois republic* . . . the state whose admitted object it is to perpetuate the rule of capital, the slavery of labor."[8] Across his writings on the 1848 Revolutions, he condemned the bourgeois republic as a regime in which the bourgeoisie exercised political power, the economy was structured in its class interests, and even its

---

3. Alphonse de Lamartine, *Histoire de la Révolution de 1848*, vol. 1 (Paris: Perrotin, 1849), 395 / *History of the French Revolution of 1848*, trans. Francis A. Durivage and William S. Chase (Boston: Phillips, Sampson & Company, 1854), 214. Lamartine is referring to the infamous massacres in the Champ de Mars in 1791.

4. Ibid., 1: 365 / 198.

5. Flaubert, *Sentimental Education*, 271.

6. On the June Days, see Mark Traugott, *Armies of the Poor: Determinants of Working-Class Participation in the Parisian Insurrection of June 1848* (Princeton: Princeton University Press, 1985); Bruno Leipold, "The Meaning of Class Struggle: Marx and the 1848 June Days," *History of Political Thought* 42, no. 3 (2021): 464–99.

7. Marx, *Die Klassenkämpfe in Frankreich*, MEGA I.10: 140 / *MECW* 10: 70.

8. Ibid., 139 / 69.

constitution was designed to uphold this political and economic rule. But as hostile as Marx's criticism was, the emancipatory limitations of the bourgeois republic did not lead him to reject it as an unworthy or irrelevant political goal. He maintained that the bourgeois republic would not only drive forward the material capitalist preconditions for communism, its defining constitutional innovations—equal civil and political rights and especially manhood suffrage—would provide the proletariat with the ideological and political weapons to eventually defeat the bourgeoisie.[9] The bourgeois republic was thus for the proletariat "the terrain for the fight for its revolutionary emancipation" even though it was "by no means this emancipation itself."[10]

This chapter is dedicated to elucidating Marx's position on the bourgeois republic: that it was an *insufficient but necessary* step for the emancipation of the proletariat. The novelty of this argument is easily missed. Early socialism was dominated by powerful antipolitical sympathies that denied the necessity of political struggle and a democratic republic for the achievement of socialism. Without an understanding of this context, it is impossible to appreciate properly the extent to which Marx's politics departed from this history. This chapter therefore begins with an extensive overview of the antipolitical threads in early socialism. It then turns to Marx and Engels's own contribution to the emergence of republican communism in the 1840s, by focusing on their conflict with the antipolitical strain of German socialism that they labeled "true socialism." Having established these necessary contextual preliminaries, the chapter then sets out Marx's account of the bourgeois republic and its competitors in the 1848 Revolution. This is followed by his criticisms of the political, economic, and constitutional failings of the bourgeois republic. Finally, the chapter shows why Marx still thought the democratic structures of the bourgeois republic were necessary in order to reach communism and discusses how that position both distinguished him from antipolitical socialisms and also revealed a more limited conception of democracy in comparison with his earlier and later thought.

Antipolitics and Republican Socialism

The central political commitment of the *Manifest der Kommunistischen Partei* was its proclamation that "the first step in the revolution by the working class is to raise the proletariat to the position of ruling class, to win the battle of

---

9. Marx argued that the "foundation of the [bourgeois republic's] constitution is . . . *universal suffrage*," ibid., 195/ 130. (Like nearly all of his contemporaries, Marx uncritically describes the French Republic's manhood suffrage as universal.)

10. Ibid., 125 / 54.

democracy."[11] Marx and Engels presented this as an accepted, nearly uncontroversial piece of the communist political program. But it was, like many claims in this and other manifestos, an implicit critique of competing socialist and communist strategies. From Owenists in Britain to true socialists in Germany and Saint-Simonians in France, a range of socialist currents had an ambivalent, even hostile, relationship to politics, democracy, and revolution. In one form or another they rejected the republican inheritance that saw a revolution and democracy as a necessary precondition for the emancipation of the people. As Pamela Pilbeam summarizes, "[p]olitical rights, even the plan to introduce a measure of democracy in the Jacobin constitution of 1793, were regarded as irrelevant" by many early socialists.[12] Marx and Engels were, by contrast, part of an emerging position within socialism that insisted on those traditional republican commitments.

Gregory Claeys, in his study of these conflicting tendencies in Owenite socialism, helpfully summarizes the broader division that had appeared by 1850:

> the spectrum of socialist political thought was bounded on the one hand by various forms of republican and more traditionally democratic socialism. At the other extreme was a more millenarian, anti-political ideal which assumed that most sources of social conflict would vanish once economic justice and a new social order had been introduced, and thought that many of the mechanisms usually associated with "politics" and the coercive state might therefore be dispensed with.[13]

Claeys rightly cautions that these "republican and anti-political" socialisms were not "pure types, and assumptions from each were intermixed . . . in a variety of ways."[14] Indeed, all forms of socialism, nearly by definition, share some antipolitical sympathies, at least insofar as socialism is united by the claim that emancipation cannot be restricted to the political sphere. There is also an argument that even the most antipolitical socialisms are political in the sense that they are committed to politicizing the social realm by making it a legitimate object of public concern and intervention.[15] We should also bear

---

11. Marx and Engels, *Manifest der Kommunistischen Partei, MEW* 4: 481 / *MECW* 6: 504.

12. Pamela Pilbeam, *French Socialists before Marx: Workers, Women and the Social Question in France* (Montreal and Kingston: McGill-Queen's University Press, 2000), 7.

13. Gregory Claeys, *Citizens and Saints: Politics and Anti-Politics in Early British Socialism* (Cambridge: Cambridge University Press, 1989), 2.

14. Ibid.

15. Ibid., 11–12, 165–66.

in mind Claeys's apt remark that "'anti-politics' is as much a theory of politics as any other."[16]

We can gain greater specificity over how a form of socialism can be antipolitical if we think of it as applying to three overlapping temporal aspects of socialist politics.[17] First, "antipolitical" might refer to an outlook on or assessment of *contemporary* society that fails to properly take into account the centrality of struggle over conflicting interests and instead sees the world in terms of harmony and the possibility for reconciliation and persuasion. Second, "antipolitical" can refer to strategies about the *transition* to socialism that reject participation in political struggle and political institutions and/or are indifferent to the nature of these institutions (whether they are, for instance, democratic, constitutionalist, or absolutist). Third, "antipolitical" can refer to a conception of the *future* socialist society that is free from political conflict and without political institutions, especially democratic ones. The second and third antipolitical aspects are particularly tied to being antidemocratic. As we will see, this was frequently the case in the history of socialism, though the overlap is not perfect. Each of the three aspects should be seen as part of a spectrum; while some socialists, for instance, have actively opposed all political participation, others have merely been less enthusiastic or made it less central to their overall strategy. (We could make a further distinction between considered, deeply held *antipolitical* positions and more unreflective *apolitical* ones.) Furthermore, forms of socialism can and have been antipolitical in one of these three senses but not in another. Keeping these three aspects in mind can thus sharpen our assessment of how and to what extent a particular socialism is or is not antipolitical.

We can apply this framework to the thought of those who are often (but problematically) taken to be the founding triumvirate of socialism: Henri Saint-Simon, Robert Owen, and Charles Fourier. That there is a strong antipolitical dimension to their thought is widely recognized. G. D. H. Cole considered the fact that "all three were deeply distrustful of 'politics' and of politicians" to be one of their most important unifying points.[18] But the nature of their antipolitics and how each one differed from the others is not usually given enough attention. All three certainly shared a similar antipolitical outlook in that they displayed "a certain innocence about the nature of power" and denied that there was a serious conflict of interests between rich and poor,

16. Ibid., 14.

17. For a similar tripartite account of antipolitics, to which mine is indebted, see David Leopold, "Karl Marx and 'English Socialism,'" *Nineteenth-Century Prose* 49, no. 1 (2022): 15–16.

18. G. D. H. Cole, *A History of Socialist Thought*, vol. 1 (London: Macmillan, 1953), 3.

workers and capitalists.[19] All three were consequently convinced that the powerful could be made to see the rationality of their schemes for social improvement and consequently appealed for their benevolent support (in ways that may strike us as shockingly naïve).[20] In other respects, however, they drew quite different implications from their antipolitical outlook for their ideas on the transition to socialism and the politics of a future society.

Perhaps their biggest point of differentiation was that while all three might be thought of as "utopian socialists" in that they believed it was necessary to provide detailed plans of the future, only Fourier and Owen were "communitarian socialists" in that they believed that the transition to socialism would come through the establishment and spread of small-scale intentional communities.[21] Fourier and Owen gave precise instructions for the design of these small communities where members would work and live together (in a closed "parallelogram" building in Owen's model and exactly 1,620 people in the case of Fourier's "Phalanx"). Dozens of experimental communities modeled on their ideas were consequently established in Europe and, especially, North America.[22] Through the power of their example such communities were supposed to inspire others until they had peacefully spread socialism across the globe.

This communitarian transition to socialism was deliberately developed in contrast to the republican insistence on political reform. In Owen's case that involved a long-running feud with Chartism whose campaign for universal manhood suffrage he dismissed. He refused to incorporate Chartist demands into any of platforms on which he stood for parliament between 1832 and 1847 and told the Chartists that "[i]t is not Universal Suffrage, Vote by Ballot, and Annual Parliaments that can affect that which is now required for the people

19. David Leopold, "Scientific Socialism: The Case of Robert Owen," in *Scientific Statesmanship, Governance, and the History of Political Philosophy*, ed. Kyriakos N. Demetriou and Antis Loizidis (London and New York: Routledge, 2015), 193. Leopold directs this comment at Owen, but it applies to all three. See also Keith Taylor, *The Political Ideas of the Utopian Socialists* (London: Frank Cass, 1982), 66.

20. Jonathan Beecher, *Charles Fourier: The Visionary and His World* (Berkeley and Los Angeles: University of California Press, 1986), 355–64; A. L. Morton, *The Life and Ideas of Robert Owen* (London: Lawrence & Wishart, 1962), 21, 30.

21. David Leopold, "'Socialist Turnips': The Young Friedrich Engels and the Feasibility of Communism," *Political Theory* 40, no. 3 (2012): 348–49.

22. See Carl J. Guarneri, *The Utopian Alternative: Fourierism in Nineteenth-Century America* (Ithica: Cornell University Press, 1991); Edward Royle, *Robert Owen and the Commencement of the Millennium: The Harmony Community at Queenwood Farm, Hampshire, 1839–1845* (Manchester: Manchester University Press, 1998).

of all countries," instead advising them to address the "ignorance of their rulers and instructors."[23] He had little time for existing forms of government, whether "despotism, limited monarchy, oligarchy, aristocracy, republicanism, or democracy," which he thought were all incapable of producing happiness or the desired character of the people.[24] He expressed repeated opposition to the principle of democratic elections and the existing capacity of the people to rule, going so far as to advise the French in 1830 to stick with hereditary monarchy rather than turn to a republic.[25] Though Owen was not wholly averse to involvement in politics (he advocated changes to laws on working conditions and stood for parliament),[26] his communitarian transition to socialism was essentially an attempt to bypass the political process.

Saint-Simon, by contrast with Owen and Fourier, had no time for small-scale communitarian experiments separated from society and insisted on the need to establish a parliamentary regime (along British lines) as a necessary stage on the transition from feudalism to the future industrial society. His primary contribution to the antipolitical strain in socialism instead comes from his extreme technocratic account of the (lack of) politics in the future society. Saint-Simon had a deep-grained conviction that "politics is *the science of production*" and so decision-making should be passed to those who were most capable of directing production: industrialists and scientific and technical experts.[27] In a favored (and hugely influential) turn of phrase, Saint-Simon argued that "government" would thereby be transformed into "administration," which he thought was his "most important view on politics."[28] Concretely, Saint-Simon's future technocratic administration would be a tricameral parliament with a Chamber of Invention (made up of 200 engineers and 100 artists),

23. Robert Owen, "Mr. Owen's Views: To the Editor of the Guardian," *The Poor Man's Guardian*, 4, no. 197 (14 March 1835): 460–61. Owen, however, reversed course after 1848, when he endorsed universal suffrage and developed a more positive view of Chartism; see Claeys, *Citizens and Saints*, 91–94.

24. Robert Owen, *The Book of the New Moral World* (1836–1844), in *Selected Works of Robert Owen*, ed. Gregory Claeys, vol. 3 (London: Pickering & Chatto, 1993), 371.

25. Claeys, *Citizens and Saints*, 74–77.

26. Leopold, "Karl Marx and 'English Socialism,'" 16.

27. Henri Saint-Simon, "Lettres de Henri Saint-Simon à un Américain" (1817), in Henri Saint-Simon, *Oeuvres complètes* (hereafter *OCSS*), vol. 2 (Paris: Presses Universitaires de France, 2012), 1497–98 / *Selected Writings on Science Industry and Social Organisation* (hereafter *Selected Writings*), trans. and ed. Keith Taylor (London: Croom Helm, 1975), 167–68.

28. Henri Saint-Simon, "De l'organisation sociale: Fragments d'un ouvrage inédit" (1825), *OCSS*, 4: 3084, 3091 / *Selected Writings*, 267, 269; and Henri Saint-Simon, *Du systéme industriel* (1820 / 21), *OCSS*, 3: 2427 (not in *Selected Writings*).

a Chamber of Examination (200 scientists and 100 mathematicians) and a Chamber of Execution (all leading industrialists). Saint-Simon specified that the industrial leaders in the final chamber would be unpaid "since they should all be rich" and was confident that "arbitrary power cannot be exercised by them" as they had the greatest interest in keeping public expenditure low and efficient.[29] This administration was in any case not supposed to do much or any governing, "in the sense of commanding," since the remaining questions to be decided were "eminently positive and answerable . . . the result of scientific demonstrations, absolutely independent of human will" (Saint Simon suggests these would be: how a society could organize production with its existing knowledge; how that knowledge could be spread and increased; and how this could be done with the most efficient use of time and resources).[30] Though the thrust of Saint-Simon's technocratic proposals were directed against the misrule of aristocratic "idlers," they were also an explicit rejection of democratic rule. Saint-Simon thought that "political liberty . . . the right to participate in public affairs irrespective of capacity" because everyone had or could gain the "the kind of capacity . . . required in politics" was one of the many confusions of present-day politics, and in the future "the cultivation of politics will be entrusted exclusively to a special class of scientists who will impose silence on all twaddle."[31]

Saint-Simon's technocratic antipolitical vision of the future society was thus intimately tied to antidemocratic foundations. But we should resist the idea that this automatically extends to Fourier and Owen as well. Fourier certainly shared a similar depoliticized, conflict-free vision of the future society, in which the only administrative institution was an "Areopagus," composed of senior (male and female) members of the Phalanx's diverse work sections, which issued purely advisory, guiding instructions on overall production. But he also incorporate what might be thought of as a degree of democracy, in that he specified that all members of the Phalanx would take part in daily meetings to organize the details of their work and decide upon them by discussion and majority preference.[32] Owen, for his part, certainly had a paternalist and authoritarian

29. Henri Saint-Simon, "Esquisse du nouveau système politique" (1819), *OCSS*, 3: 2136–41 / *Selected Writings*, 202–5.

30. Henri Saint-Simon, "Onzième Lettre. Deuxième extrait de mon ouvrage sur l'organisation sociale" (1820), *OCSS*, 3: 2212 / *Selected Writings*, 209. Note that there is debate over whether this text should be attributed to Auguste Comte; see *OCSS*, 3: 2104.

31. Saint-Simon, *Du systéme industriel*, *OCSS*, 3: 3248 / *Selected Writings*, 229–30.

32. Taylor, *Political Ideas of the Utopian Socialists*, 124–25; *The Utopian Vision of Charles Fourier: Selected Texts on Work, Love, and Passionate Attraction by Charles Fourier*, ed. Jonathan Beecher and Richard Bienvenu (Boston: Beacon Press, 1971), 249–55.

conception of the running of his proposed communities in transitional circumstances, which excluded those he thought incapable of governing. But, as David Leopold has shown, it is not sufficiently appreciated that Owen believed that once everyone's character had been suitably educated, the final political form of the communities would be a kind of gerontocracy, in which every citizen (men and women) would be called on to take part in domestic government from age thirty to forty and in foreign affairs from age forty to sixty.[33] This was perhaps not democracy, but it did involve political equality and participation for all at some point in their lives. Furthermore, while Owen shared Fourier's and Saint-Simon's belief that there would be no need for coercion and little for his government to do, he did think that laws and a government to make authoritative decisions when there was disagreement were a necessary feature of a socialist society.[34]

Thus, while Saint-Simon, Fourier, and Owen might all have shared a relatively similar antipolitical contemporary outlook and conception of the future society, in that political conflict and coercion would largely or wholly disappear, they diverged on the transitional strategies to reach that future society and each developed differing conceptions of what institutions would still be needed in that future society, with markedly different stances on how democratic these should be.

The divergent antipolitical and antidemocratic strains in Saint-Simon's, Fourier's, and Owen's thought were (initially at least) passed on to the movements they inspired. The leading Saint-Simonian journal *Le Globe* argued in 1831 that they were only in favor of popular sovereignty if this was understood as government *for* the people and not government *by* the people, since "the men most capable at directing and coordinating" and not "the most numerous class" should rule.[35] Saint-Simon's technocratic arguments against democracy were also hugely influential across a range of subsequent socialist currents, as we saw in chapter 2 with Wilhelm Weitling's rejection of democratic elections in favor of being ruled by a trio of the leading experts in medicine, physics, and engineering (Saint-Simon's influence is particularly evident in Weitling's summary statement that "*A perfect society has no government, but an administration*").[36] Meanwhile, the heirs of Fourier continued to push their communitarian experiments as an alternative to political struggle and reform. In her 1839 introduction

33. Leopold, "Scientific Socialism: The Case of Robert Owen," 198, 204–6.

34. Ibid., 202.

35. *Le Globe: Journal de la doctrine de Saint-Simon*, no. 104 (14 April 1831): 1.

36. Wilhelm Weitling, *Garantien der Harmonie und Freiheit* (Vivis: Verlag des Verfassers, 1842), 23.

to the first issue of the Fourierist journal *Le nouveau Monde*, Zoé Gatti de Gamond declared, "Long have we searched for the remedy of the people's ailments in political struggle ... we [now] recognize that the evil resides in the very organization of society" and so "The end we pursue is purely social; we set aside all political questions."[37] In her widely read popularizations of Fourier's ideas, she rejected "violent means, bloody revolutions" and contrasted the strategy of the "republican party," with its hopes of introducing a "form of government ... [with] universal suffrage ... [and] the most extensive political liberty," against what she claimed was the only path to liberation: the peaceful diffusion of Fourier's law of attraction through the gradual establishment and spread of phalanxes.[38] She tried to put this into practice, helping to set up an attempted phalanx in the old abbey of Le Cîteaux (near Dijon) in 1841, but the experiment soon collapsed.[39]

The antipolitical strategy of communitarian experiments was given a continued lease of life through Étienne Cabet and his Icarian movement of the 1840s, though his antipolitics was tempered by the fact that he was much more insistent on political involvement and explicitly specified, as was discussed in chapter 3, that the future socialist society should be a democratic republic.[40] The 1840s also saw the emergence of a further antipolitical (or more neutrally apolitical) strategy that emphasized direct association among workers at the expense of political participation, perhaps most famously articulated by Flora Tristan. While Tristan was more favorable to universal suffrage than she is

---

37. [Zoé] Gatti de Gamond, "Introduction," *Le nouveau Monde: Théorie de Charles Fourier,* no. 1 (15 June 1839): 1.

38. [Zoé] Gatti de Gamond, *Fourier et son système* (Paris: L. Desessart, 1838), 11, 16–19 / *Fourier and His System,* trans. C. T. Wood (London: James H. Young, 1842), 25, 27–28; [Zoé] Gatti de Gamond, *Réalisation d'une commune sociétaire, d'après la théorie de Charles Fourier* (Paris: L'auteur, 1840), 148–49 (section not included in English translation; see *The Phalanstery, or Attractive Industry and Moral Harmony,* trans. An English Lady [Sophia Chichester] [London: Whittaker & Co, 1841]). For the interesting ways in which Gatti de Gamond sanitized Fourier's views on sex and the family, see Janet L. Polasky, "Utopia and Domesticity: Zoé Gatti de Gamond," *Proceedings of the Western Society for French History* 11 (1984): 277–79; Pamela Pilbeam, "Fourier and the Fourierists: A Case of Mistaken Identity?," *French History and Civilization* 1 (2005): 190–91.

39. See the detailed study of Thomas Voet, *La Colonie phalanstérienne de Cîteaux, 1841–1846: Les fouriéristes aux champs* (Dijon: Editions universitaires de Dijon, 2001).

40. Christopher H. Johnson, *Utopian Communism in France: Cabet and the Icarians, 1839–1851* (Ithica: Cornell University Press, 1974), chapters 2–3. Cabet's socialist utopia was less democratic than Owen's, however, in that the status of women's political participation was left ambiguous.

sometimes portrayed,[41] it played little role in her influential proposal for a workers' union. She proposed that workers should voluntarily contribute to a mutual fund to establish workers' palaces that would provide education, housing, work and social support. Tristan's plan was primarily directed at workers, but she also hoped for support from the king and the "sympathy of all classes of society," including the bourgeoisie. She presented the workers' union as a peaceful way to *"prevent revolutions,"* counseling that "workers *would find no advantage in overthrowing the government.* Since [17]89 *many governments have been overthrown,* and what have the workers gained from these revolutions?"[42]

As socialist ideas began to reach a broader audience in the 1830s in both France and Britain, republicans first reacted with a degree of sympathy to their social ideas but, unsurprisingly, rejected their abandonment of politics and democracy and what they saw as the only viable path to emancipation. Early republican responses expressed particular incredulity at the antipolitical attitude that deeply opposed interests could be overcome by rational appeals and moral persuasion directed at the powerful. Saint-Simonians were criticized for thinking that peaceful means were sufficient, when "[t]he republican knows that one never converts the *aristocrats* with sermons or writings . . . iron and cannon will be necessary to check their egoism."[43] The Chartist leader Bronterre O'Brien praised Owen's benevolence but rebuffed his criticisms of Chartism's political strategy by ridiculing Owen's faith in convincing the rich that they shared an interest in his social plans. O'Brien observed that "The idea of cajoling a rich man out of his present enjoyments by telling him he will be more happy in a parallelogram, where he will have to work as well as enjoy, appears to us the most complete hallucination that can enter the mind of man."[44] For O'Brien, Owen's antipolitical stance was closely connected to his political indifference to the form of the state. Because "Mr. Owen fancies that the rich have as great an interest . . . as the poor" in realizing his plans, "he infers that the present aristocratic Government is as likely to realize it as any other we could

41. Flora Tristan, *Promenades dans Londres ou l'aristocratie et les prolétaries anglais*, 4th popular ed. (Paris: Raymond Boquet, 1842), 24n1. See further, Susan Grogan, *Flora Tristan: Life Stories* (London: Routledge, 1998), 109–10.

42. Flora Tristan, *Union ouvrière* (Paris: Prévot, 1843), 81–83, 91, 116–19 / *The Workers' Union*, trans. Beverly Livingston (Urbana: University of Illinois Press, 2007), 105–7, 113, 134–37. For Flora Tristan's socialist feminism, see Kevin Duong, "No Social Revolution without Sexual Revolution," *Political Theory* 47, no. 6 (2019): 809–35.

43. Jules Sambuc, *Paralléle du St.-Simonien et du Républicain* (Paris: J.-L Barnel, 1831), 5.

44. Bronterre O'Brien, "Reply to Mr. Owen," *The Poor Man's Guardian*, no. 200 (4 April 1835): 482; see also p. 476.

substitute in its room." But only in "in extreme democracy," O'Brien insisted, "is there the slightest chance" of real social reform.[45]

Republican attitudes to socialism hardened as the prospects of revolution increased from the mid-1840s and socialism continued to gain influence among the working class. Leading republicans, such as Giuseppe Mazzini, feared that the socialist and communist encroachments on working-class support would divide and weaken the party of movement in a future revolution, and they launched an offensive against it.[46] One of the most aggressive of these assaults was made by Karl Heinzen in a series of broadsides in the years leading up to 1848, including a critical exchange with Marx and Engels (discussed in greater detail below and in chapter 5). Heinzen accused communists of having "taken their sublime indifference to 'politics' so far that it is of no consequence to them if they live in a republic or under the rule of the sabre." What they failed to understand was that all of their social ideas would be impossible to achieve outside of a republic, for "the striving to generalize material happiness cannot bypass the effort for political freedom."[47] On Heinzen's account, socialists and communists were abstract idealists who failed to see the necessity of engaging in the gritty world of politics. He satirized them as throwing "politics completely overboard, in order to rise with the communist balloon toward the happiness-raining dream clouds (*glückregnenden Wolken der Träume*)."[48]

After the collapse of the revolution, dismayed republicans repeated these charges, blaming the revolution's failure on the political indifference of socialists and communists and their premature calls for social revolution. According to William James Linton in 1852, socialists and communists were responsible for the "dissension and weakness brought into the popular camp by their continual preaching of the uselessness of mere political reforms, of the insufficiency of Republicanism and the Republic."[49] He too chastised socialists and communists for failing to understand that it was impossible to try "climbing to the 'higher matters of social reform' without the help of the lower steps of political revolution."[50] Those socialists who tell "men to form happy villages, comfortable coöperative corners, wherein they may shut themselves up in

45. Ibid., 481.

46. Joseph Mazzini, "Thoughts upon Democracy in Europe," *The People's Journal*, ed. John Saunders, vol. 3 (London: People's Journal Office, 1847), 219–20.

47. K. Heinzen, "Gegen die Kommunisten," in *Die Opposition*, ed. Karl Heinzen (Mannheim: Heinrich Hoff, 1846), 63.

48. K. Heinzen, *Die Helden des teutschen Kommunismus: Denn Herrn Karl Marx gewidmet* (Bern: Jenni, Sohn, 1848), 1.

49. [W. J. Linton], "Mazzini and His Socialist Opponents," *English Republic* (1852), 2: 123.

50. [W. J. Linton], "Republican Socialism: An Explanation," *English Republic* (1851), 1: 338.

shabby enjoyments and escape the tumult of political action," were, Linton emphatically stated, "not republicans."[51]

These repeated republican critiques of the antipolitical elements of socialism did not go unnoticed. Together with a growing dissatisfaction with antipolitical strategies (especially the disappointing record of communitarian experiments and the evident failure of the rich and powerful to be peacefully converted to the promise of socialism), these republican criticisms helped spur the emergence of a hybrid ideology of "republican socialism."[52] This merger was built, as William H. Sewell Jr. outlines, on two core commitments: first, that "socialism was a necessary completion of the French Revolution," in that its political freedoms were to be supplemented by social emancipation; and second, that "this could not be achieved without a political revolution and the establishment of a democratic and republican form of government."[53] George Sand, for instance, in her article "La politique et le socialisme" (1844), praised the achievements of the French Revolution and its *Declaration of the Rights of Man and of the Citizen* as an "immortal monument of political science," but pointed to its shortcoming in having enshrined the "wishes, interests and beliefs of the bourgeoisie" and being marked by "the total absence of the notion of solidarity." Turning to the present, she criticized both the "guardians of republican principles" for neglecting the latest philosophies of social reform and Fourierist socialists for their "chimerical" hope in "a small separate society." What was needed today was to "demand from politics a social religion, and from socialism a political

---

51. [W. J. Linton], "Are the Socialists Republicans?," *English Republic* (1852), 2: 70. See also W. J. Linton, "The Icarian Communists of France," *The Republican: A Magazine Advocating the Sovereignty of the People* (London: J. Watson, 1848), 45.

52. This development might easily be straightforwardly celebrated as socialism "growing up" by moving on from its naïve communitarian and utopian beginnings. But, as Barbara Taylor persuasively showed, the utopian dreams of the first generation of socialists were tied to a much more encompassing and integrated sense of women's emancipation than the socialists currents that replaced them, which tended to relegate it to a secondary concern; see *Eve and the New Jerusalem: Socialism and Feminism in the Nineteenth Century* (London: Virago, 1983), esp. the introduction and chapter 9. The extent to which the incorporation of republicanism into socialism might have contributed to this development deserves further study.

53. William H. Sewell Jr., "Artisans, Factory Workers, and the Formation of the French Working Class, 1789–1848," in *Working-Class Formation: Nineteenth-Century Patterns in Western Europe and the United States*, ed. Ira Katznelson and Aristide R. Zolberg (Princeton: Princeton University Press, 1986), 65. Engels argued that the social movement of the nineteenth century was "only the second act of the Revolution . . . that began in 1789 in Paris"; Engels, "Das Fest der Nationen in London," *MEGA* I.4: 694 / *MECW* 6: 5.

organization."[54] She would go on to declare that *"Socialism is the goal, the republic is the means."*[55]

It was this fusion with republicanism that allowed socialism to break out of the sectarianism associated with the Saint-Simonian and Fourierist movements and develop into the mass working-class movement that emerged in 1848.[56] Leading figures in the formation of French republican socialism (though, as Sewell rightly notes, it was really a collectively built project) include the more insurrectionary inflection articulated by Louis Blanqui and, especially, the state-orientated republican socialism of Louis Blanc.[57] In his 1840 *Organization du Travail* and its many subsequent editions, Blanc provided not only a slogan that electrified his contemporaries (the "organization of work") but a popular political project in which, in Salih Emre Gerçek's summary, "[t]he 'social question' . . . became a democratic question—a question of establishing democratic participation in work and in the republic."[58] Indeed,

54. George Sand, "La politique et le socialisme," *L'Éclaireur,* no. 10 (16 November 1844): 1–2; no. 11 (23 November 1844): 1; no. 12 (30 November 1844): 1.

55. G.[eorge] S.[and], "Socialisme. III. L'application de l'égalite, c'est la fraternité," *La Cause du peuple,* no. 2 (16 April 1848): 19. For her republican socialism, see Whitney Walton, *Eve's Proud Descendants: Four Women Writers and Republican Politics in Nineteenth-Century France* (Stanford: Stanford University Press, 2000), 136–38.

56. Samuel Hayat, "Working-Class Socialism in 1848 in France," in *The 1848 Revolutions and European Political Thought,* ed. Douglas Moggach and Gareth Stedman Jones (Cambridge: Cambridge University Press, 2018), 120–39. The 1848 Revolution also had a powerful effect on socialists with long-standing antipolitical sympathies, with Victor Considérant and his Fourierist journal *La Démocratie pacifique* converted "overnight" to the republican cause. See David W. Lovell, "Early French Socialism and Politics: The Case of Victor Considérant," *History of Political Thought* 13, no. 2 (1992): 267; see also Jonathan Beecher, *Victor Considerant and the Rise and Fall of French Romantic Socialism* (Berkeley and Los Angeles: University of California Press, 2001), chapters 8–9.

57. Sewell, "Artisans, Factory Workers, and the Formation of the French Working Class," 65. See further Alan B. Spitzer, *The Revolutionary Theories of Louis Auguste Blanqui* (New York: Columbia University Press, 1957), chapters 5–6. Additional figures included Pierre Leroux, who summarized his contribution as providing a "synthesis" in the "formula of the Republic, [of] what Saint-Simon, Jean-Jacques Rousseau and Owen wanted to say," cited in Leo A. Loubère, "The Intellectual Origins of French Jacobin Socialism," *International Review of Social History* 4, no. 3 (1959): 426. For an invaluable localized account of the development of republican socialism, see Ronald Aminzade, *Class, Politics, and Early Industrial Capitalism: A Study of Mid-Nineteenth-Century Toulouse, France* (Albany: State University Press of New York, 1981), 90–94, 130–48.

58. Salih Emre Gerçek, "The 'Social Question' as a Democratic Question: Louis Blanc's Organization of Labor," *Modern Intellectual History* 20, no. 2 (2023): 397.

Blanc's proposed "social workshops" were explicitly founded on a program for democratic political reform (his workshops were supposed to be state-funded, worker-managed industrial enterprises that would eventually outcompete private industry but that the Second Republic instead bastardized into a public work program for the unemployed with its "National Workshops"). Blanc insisted that "without political reform, no social reform is possible; because if the second is the *goal*, the first is the *means*," and entreated socialists to "possess yourself of this [governmental] power if you do not wish to be overwhelmed by it." He chastised Owen, Saint-Simon, and Fourier for not being "practical reformers," singling out Fourier for leaving organization to the "mercy of individual caprice" and failing to engage with the "the idea of POWER."[59]

Parallel to these developments in France, comparable efforts were made in Britain from the early 1840s onward to unify the Owenist and Chartist movements "under the banner of 'Republican Socialism' or 'Charter Socialism,'" a trend that also accelerated dramatically with the 1848 Revolution.[60] One such effort was made by Helen Macfarlane, whom we met in the introduction as the first English translator of the *Manifest der Kommunistischen Partei*. Macfarlane briefly lit up the world of republican socialism with a rush of articles concentrated entirely in a nine-month period in 1850, which appeared in George Julian Harney's Left-Chartist publications *The Democratic Review*, *The Red Republican*, and *The Friend of the People* (all except one under her male pseudonym, Howard Morton).[61] Weaving together Hegel, Jesus (the "Galilean Republican," the "Nazarean proletarian"), and her readings and translation of Marx and Engels, she provided an original and forceful account of the historical unfolding and modern necessity of "the Gospel of Socialist-Democracy."[62] As part of that fused position, she insisted that Chartism had "progressed from the idea of a simple *political reform* to the idea of a *Social Revolution*," while criticizing the

---

59. Louis Blanc, *Organisation du travail* (Paris: Prévot, 1840), 95–96, 105–106 / *Organization of Work*, trans. Marie Paula Dickoré, in *University of Cincinnati Studies*, vol. 7, no. 1 (1911): 46–47, 50.

60. Claeys, *Citizens and Saints*, 235; see further chapters 6–7 in this book.

61. A collection of her articles and translations can be found in David Black, *Helen Macfarlane: Red Republican. The Complete Annotated Writings, Including the First Translation of the Communist Manifesto* (London: Unkant Publishers, 2014). See further Joan Allen, "'The Teacher of Strange Doctrines'": George Julian Harney and the *Democratic Review*, 1849–1850," *Labour History Review* 78, no. 1 (2013): 81–84; David Black, *Helen Macfarlane: A Feminist, Revolutionary Journalist, and Philosopher in Mid-Nineteenth Century England* (Lanham: Lexington Books, 2004).

62. Howard Morton [Helen Macfarlane], "Democratic Organization," *The Red Republican*, no. 9 (17 August 1850): 68; for her Hegelian inflected account of the rise of socialist democracy, see her three-part "Democracy," *The Democratic Review* (April, May, June 1850), vol. 1: 422–25, 449–53; vol 2: 11–20.

Owenist and Saint-Simonian movements for failing to see "that political reform must *precede* all attempts to improve the condition of the people."[63] She called for all social reformers to unite under a common organization committed to universal suffrage (of all men and women),[64] as the foundation for enacting a "programme of Social Reform *upon Red Republican principles*" that ranged from free education to the nationalization of land, banks, railways, and canals.[65] A sense of her encompassing socialist and republican vision of emancipation can be gleaned from the closing lines of the last article she wrote, calling for

> a republic such as the world has never yet seen. "A republic without helots;" without *poor*; without *classes*; without hereditary hewers of wood and drawers of water, without *slaves*, whether chattel or wages slaves . . . A society . . . not only of free *men*, but of free *women*; a society of equally holy, equally blessed gods."[66]

The Antipolitics of "True Socialism"

While Blancists, Blanquists, and Charter Socialists forged varieties of republican socialism in France and Britain, Marx and Engels were at the forefront of a similar struggle in Germany[67] (though, of course, their influence and interest extended beyond any single national context). Having shed their own antipolitical commitments that marked their initial conversions to communism, they

63. Howard Morton [Helen Macfarlane], "Chartism in 1850," *The Red Republican*, no. 1 (22 June 1850): 2–3.

64. For her defense of women's suffrage, see Macfarlane, "Democracy," 423, and "The Red Flag," 26.

65. Macfarlane, "Democratic Organization," 67–68; "Middle-Class Dodges and Proletarian-Gullibility," *The Red Republcian*, no. 7 (3 August 1850), 51; "The Democratic and Social Republic," *The Red Republican*, no. 17 (12 October 1850): 131–32. The influence of Marx and Engels's similar list of demands in the *Manifest* is visible here.

66. Howard Morton [Helen Macfarlane], "Signs of the Times. Red Stockings *versus* Lawn-Sleeves," *The Friend of the People*, no. 3 (28 December 1850): 19. Macfarlane fell out with Harney three days later, at the New Year's celebration of the Fraternal Democrats and (as far as we know) ceased writing afterward. Reporting on the incident to Engels, Marx declared her to have been the only one of Harney's collaborators "who really had any ideas"; Marx to Engels, 23 February 1851, *MEGA* III.4: 47 / *MECW* 38: 295–96. For the few available details of Macfarlane's subsequent life, see David Leopold, "Macfarlane, Helen," in *Oxford Dictionary of National Biography*, online ed. (Oxford University Press, 2018), https://doi.org/10.1093/odnb/9780198614128.013.100743.

67. Jonathan Sperber, *The European Revolutions, 1848–1851*, 2nd ed. (Cambridge: Cambridge University Press, 2005), 85–86.

waged an acrimonious battle (most of it from outside Germany itself) from 1845 to 1848 against the antipolitical and antidemocratic tendencies that dominated early German socialism. Much of this struggle was focused on fighting the influence of these tendencies within the Bund der Kommunisten (Communist League) and its predecessor, the Bund der Gerechten (League of the Just). The Bund der Gerechten had started life in 1836 committed to the insurrectionary tradition of tiny secret societies. In the early 1840s it had fractured and its branches turned to the gamut of antipolitical strategies and ideas circulating at the time. By 1846 many Bund members were unhappy with both positions and were searching for a new statement of their communist principles.[68] That opened the door to collaboration with Marx and Engels and their commitment to popular working-class struggle and democracy as a precondition for socialism. They joined the Bund in early 1847, effectively merging it with the Kommunistischen Korrespondenz-komitee (Communist Correspondence Committee) that they had founded the year before. The League was then reconstituted as the Bund der Kommunisten at its first congress in June 1847. Engels and League representatives hammered out a new draft program for circulation among the branches. In its dated but not uncharming catechistic style, it committed the League to Marx and Engels's democratic political position:

> [Question] 16. How do you think the transition from the present situation to community of property is to be effected?
>
> —. The first, fundamental condition for the introduction of community of property is the political liberation of the proletariat through a democratic constitution.[69]

Over the ensuing months, Engels further sharpened the draft, adding how alliances should be formed with the democratic parties of the various countries in which the league was active and clarifying that the coming revolution would "[i]n the first place . . . inaugurate a *democratic constitution* and thereby, directly or indirectly, the political rule of the proletariat," depending on how advanced the proletariat was in the respective country.[70] At the Bund's second

---

68. Gareth Stedman Jones, "Introduction," in *The Communist Manifesto*, by Karl Marx and Friedrich Engels (London: Penguin, 2002), 45–49; Martin Hundt, *Geschichte des Bundes der Kommunisten, 1836–1852* (Frankfurt am Main: Peter Lang, 1993), chapters 4–6; Richard N. Hunt, *The Political Ideas of Marx and Engels*, vol. 1 (Pittsburgh: University of Pittsburgh Press, 1974), 154–55.

69. Engels, *Entwurf des Kommunistischen Glaubensbekenntnisses*, BdK 1: 474 / MECW 6: 102.

70. Engels, *Grundsätze des Kommunismus*, MEW 4: 372 / MECW 6: 350.

congress, in November–December 1847, Marx and Engels were tasked with producing the final program, on the basis of the collected feedback from the June draft. The resulting *Manifest der Kommunistischen Partei* openly declared that communists would work for the "union and agreement of the democratic parties of all countries."[71] It also declared that "the first step in the revolution by the working class is to raise the proletariat to the position of ruling class, to win the battle of democracy (*die Erkämpfung der Demokratie*)."[72]

The *Manifest*'s endorsement of joint political struggle with democratic forces for the establishment of democracy was paired with a condemnation of the antipolitical commitments of other socialisms. In the third and most neglected section of the *Manifest* on "Socialist and Communist Literature," Marx and Engels surveyed five kinds of socialism, categorized into three types: "1. Reactionary Socialism," "2. Conservative or Bourgeois Socialism," and "3. Critical-Utopian Socialism and Communism."[73] In the third utopian category they identified an initial grouping of Saint-Simon, Fourier, and Owen, followed by their respective movements and that of Cabet. Marx and Engels criticized what they took to be their characteristic antipolitical outlook that denied the depth of conflicting class interests. The utopian socialists were accused of believing themselves to "stand above all class antagonisms" and "appealing to the whole of society without distinction; nay, by preference to the ruling class," because everyone can be persuaded that their utopian plan is "the best possible plan of the best possible state of society."[74] This antipolitical attitude lead the utopian socialists, Marx and Engels argued, to "reject all political, and especially revolutionary action" and instead put their faith in "the force of example" provided by the "small experiments" of Fourier's "isolated phalansteries," Owen's "home-colonies" and Cabet's "small Icarias" (Marx and Engels thereby unhelpfully conflated the communitarianism of some utopian

71. Marx and Engels, *Manifest der Kommunistischen Partei*, MEW 4: 493 / MECW 6: 519.

72. Ibid., 481 / 504. Richard Hunt attributes this somewhat more ambiguous and clumsy formulation in the *Manifest*, compared with Engels's draft, to the need to compromise with the League's impatient artisan members who thought a democratic revolution would directly result in working-class rule. See the excellent discussion in Hunt, *Political Ideas of Marx and Engels*, 1974, 1:137, 176–91. On the importance of interpreting the *Manifest* as an organizational document, see Hal Draper, *Karl Marx's Theory of Revolution*, vol. 2 (New York: Monthly Review Press, 1978), 195–97.

73. Intriguingly Engels's draft also includes a category of "democratic socialists," who are presented as being the closest to the communists. No names are mentioned, but the descriptions suggests figures like Blanc; see Engels, *Grundsätze des Kommunismus*, MEW 4: 378–79 / MECW 6: 355–56.

74. Marx and Engels, *Manifest der Kommunistischen Partei*, MEW 4: 490 / MECW 6: 515.

socialists with the category as a whole).[75] Marx and Engels complained that these antipolitical strategies of transition went hand in hand with "bitter opposition to the political action of the working class," including Owenists and Fourierists "respectively opposing the Chartists and the *réformistes*" (the movement around the republican newspaper *La Réform*).[76] While Marx and Engels extensively critiqued both the antipolitical attitude and strategies of the utopian socialists, they expended next to no critical energy on utopian socialists' antipolitical plans for a future society. Their one comment in this regard is in fact to praise the Saint-Simonian idea of the "conversion of the state into a mere administration of production" as part of the "highly valuable material" that utopian socialists have put forward.[77] That reflects the fact that though Marx and Engels were deeply opposed to most of the antipolitical aspects of existing socialisms they had a more complicated relation to the politics of the future—an issue set we will set aside until its proper examination in chapter 7.

The other form of socialism attacked in the *Manifest* for its antipolitics is what Marx and Engels label "c) German or 'True' Socialism" (which they categorize as one of the three forms of "Reactionary Socialism," along with "a) Feudal Socialism" and "b) Petty Bourgeois Socialism"). This form of socialism has the distinction of not only being subjected to the most extensive and purely negative assessment in the *Manifest*, but probably being the most obscure to contemporary readers. The justification for their inclusion in the *Manifest*, however, was that at the time of writing, according to Marx and Engels, "with very few exceptions, all so-called socialist and communist publications circulating in Germany belong to the domain of this foul and enervating literature."[78] Marx and Engels accused true socialists of being a form of reactionary socialism because they played into the hands of reactionary forces by abstaining from the struggle for political reform in the German states. The root cause of this, in Marx and Engels's eyes, was that true socialists had uncritically transferred French socialist criticism that assumed a more advanced social and political background to the backward conditions in Germany. True socialists had consequently greeted the stirrings of political reform in Germany with "the traditional anathemas against liberalism, against the representative state, against bourgeois competition, bourgeois freedom of the press, bourgeois

75. Ibid., 490–91 / 515–16. See David Leopold, "Marx, Engels and Other Socialisms," in *The Cambridge Companion to The Communist Manifesto*, ed. Terrell Carver and James Farr (Cambridge: Cambridge University Press, 2015), 45.

76. Marx and Engels, *Manifest der Kommunistischen Partei*, MEW 4: 491–92 / MECW 6: 516–17.

77. Ibid., 490–91 / 516.

78. Ibid., 488 / 513.

legislation, bourgeois liberty and equality" and preached "to the masses that they had nothing to gain, and everything to lose, by this bourgeois movement."[79] Such criticisms made sense, Marx and Engels implied, when used to highlight the emancipatory limits of established institutions, but not to oppose their implementation in the first place. In an inflammatory charge, Marx and Engels maintained that through their opposition to these political institutions and abstention from political struggle, the true socialists had served the "German absolute governments" as a "weapon for fighting the German bourgeoisie."[80]

Who were these German true socialists whose antipolitics went supposedly so far as to aid the forces of reaction? Similarly to Marx and Engels's creation of "utopian socialism," "true socialism" (*wahrer Sozialismus*) is best understood not as a single, coherent movement or body of thought that self-identified with that label, but as Marx and Engels's (derogatory) lumping together of a set of early socialist writers that they perceived as sharing the same failings.[81] The label was likely seized upon by Marx and Engels from its passing usage by Karl Grün, the figure they placed at the center of true socialism.[82] Alongside Grün, Marx and Engels positioned a cast of now almost entirely forgotten figures of early German socialism, including Ernst Dronke, Johannes Georg Kuhlmann, Hermann Kriege, Otto Lüning, Rudolph Matthäi, Hermann Püttman, Hermann Semmig, and (more prominently and complicatedly) Moses Hess.[83] While these figures orbited around an overlapping set of publications, including *Das Westphalische Dampfboot*, the *Rheinische Jahrbücher*, and the *Trierschen Zeitung*, there was no overarching true socialist organizational structure. Nonetheless, Marx and Engels saw them as unified by their supposed superficial combination of French socialist ideas with German philosophy, their extravagant literary style, their celebration of love and common humanity over class struggle, and, finally, their abandonment of political struggle. Marx and Engels even criticized true socialists for a characteristic that might have made for potential common ground—their opposition to the system-building of

79. Ibid., 487 / 511.

80. Ibid., 487 / 512.

81. Doris Köster-Bunselmeyer, *Literarischer Sozialismus: Texte und Theorien der deutschen Frühsozialisten, 1843–1848* (Tübingen: Max Niemeyer, 1981), 2; Diana Siclovan, "The Project of 'Vergesellschaftung': German Socialists, 1843–185" (M.Phil. dissertation, University of Cambridge, 2010), 8.

82. [Karl Grün], "Die Bielefelder 'Monatsschrift.' Erstes Heft. Programm der Redakzion," in *Neue Anekdota*, ed. Karl Grün (Darmstadt: C. W. Leske, 1845), 185; see *MEGA* I.5: 1540.

83. Marx and Engels perceived Hess as providing much of the original inspiration for true socialism, but Hess's position also evolved and Hess subsequently cowrote part of their critique of true socialism.

utopian socialism. Rather than praise them for this feature, Marx and Engels thought true socialists had thereby failed to appreciate utopian socialism's critical elements.[84]

In the years before 1848, Marx and Engels expended considerable intellectual and political energy on identifying and discrediting this true socialist tendency, including a large portion of the unpublished material today known as the *Deutsche Ideologie*. Marx and Engels intended to publish a "Critique of True Socialism" as the second volume of what was first supposed to be a quarterly journal and then an independent two-volume work (the first volume was meant to include the more famous material from the *Deutsche Ideologie* manuscripts on the "Critique of Young Hegelianism"). The plan seems to have been to dedicate five chapters to uncovering true socialism's philosophy, economics, poetry and prose, historiography, and prophecies, along with contributions from other critics of true socialism. After the failure of the project, Marx published one of these chapters in the *Westphalishe Dampfboot* in 1847 (the only part of the *Deutsche Ideologie* manuscripts to appear in Marx's and Engels's lifetimes).[85]

Marx's article was directed at dissecting Grün's popular survey of socialisms, *Die sociale Bewegung in Frankreich und Belgien* (*The Social Movement in France and Belgium*), and formed part of Marx and Engels's broader attempt to combat Grün's influence among German socialists. Grün had gained some prominence through his prolific journalism and as an associate and German translator of Proudhon. Marx and Grün in fact shared a notably similar early biographical trajectory: they were just six months apart in age, studied philosophy together at the universities in Bonn and then Berlin, and subsequently immigrated to Paris after censorship blocked their writings in Germany, where they continued to interact.[86] They even seemed to have professed their newfound socialism in the same week in March 1844, with Marx's freshly published articles in the

---

84. Marx and Engels, "Die 'rheinischen Jahrbücher,' oder die Philosophie des Wahren Sozialismus," *MEGA* I.5: 521–22 / *MECW* 5: 461–62. For this antiutopianism, see for instance O[tto]. Lüning, "Politik und Sozialismus," *Dies Buch gehört dem Volke*, ed. Otto Lüning, Zweiter Jahrgang (Bielefeld: A. Helmich, 1845), 26; Karl Grün, *Die sociale Bewegung in Frankreich und Belgien* (Darmstadt: C. W. Leske, 1845), 352; Hermann Semmig, "Communismus, Socialismus, Humanismus," in *Rheinische Jahrbücher für gesellschaftlichen Reform*, ed. Hermann Püttmann, vol. 1 (Darmstadt: C. W. Leske, 1845), 170. It is therefore misleading to present true socialists as "utopian socialists," as in Auguste Cornu, "German Utopianism: 'True' Socialism," *Science & Society* 12, no. 1 (1948): 97–112.

85. For this textual history, see *MEGA* I.5: 727, 756–59.

86. For Grün's account of the trajectory of their relationship, see Karl Grün to Moses Hess, 6 August 1845 and 1 September 1845, *Moses Hess: Briefwechsel*, ed. Edmund Silberner ('s-Gravenhage: Mouton & Co, 1959), 133–34, 138–39.

Deutsch-Französische Jahrbücher playing some role in converting Grün.[87] But these biographical similarities did not translate to political collaboration, and once it became clear that they had very different visions of socialism, Grün instead became the first on the list of Marx's bitter feuds with fellow Karls (later joined by Karl Heinzen and Karl Vogt). The relationship is unlikely to have been helped by the fact that Grün twice beat Marx to the punch, first by publishing a study grounding socialism in Feuerbach's philosophy (while Marx's *Ökonomisch-philosophische Manuskripte* remained unpublished),[88] and then with his survey of socialisms (while Marx and Engels's contemporaneous plans for a library of socialist translations and commentaries never materialized).

Grün's initial socialist writings were marked by a familiar set of antipolitical and antidemocratic themes. Grün dismissed the idea that socialism should be brought about through a "repeat" of the "dreadful [French] Revolution," as it had only been a *"political* revolution" and what was required today was "something else than *political* reform, than the consolidation of empty rights with which one can still die of hunger."[89] (It is possible that it was this denigration of the legacy of the French Revolution that spurred Engels's defense of its relevance for socialists, in his first intervention against "true socialism," discussed in chapter 3.)[90] In Grün's essay "Politik und Sozialismus," he endeavored to expose the limits of Montesquieu's and Rousseau's constitutional thought, since he took them to be the respective founders of "liberalism" and "radicalism"—the two traditions that Grün maintained had dominated the cause of political reform since the French Revolution. An analysis of both showed that "constitutionalism has no sense" and that "even the most radical consequences of popular sovereignty do not guarantee freedom."[91] Grün took aim at a number of Rousseauian shibboleths held dear by his contemporary republicans. He insisted that the social contract sanctified private property and ridiculed the idea that one could be free by obeying the general will, which

87. Karl Grün, *Bausteine: Zusammengetragen und mit einem Sendschreiben an seine Osnabrücker Freunde begleitet* (Darmstadt: C. W. Leske, 1844), xxviii. Grün's preface is dated 31 March, five days after Marx's letter to Ruge breaking off relations. On Grün's conversion, see Manuela Köppe, "Einleitung," in *Ausgewählte Schriften in Zwei Bänden,* by Karl Grün (Berlin: Akademie Verlag, 2005), 100–107.

88. Karl Grün, "Feuerbach und die Socialisten," *Deutsches Bürgerbuch für 1845,* ed. H. Puttmann (Darmstadt: C. W. Leske, 1845), 49–75.

89. Ibid., 50.

90. Engels, "Das Fest der Nationen in London (Zur Feier der Errichtung der französischen Republik, 22. September 1792.)," *MEGA I.4:* 692 / *MECW* 6: 3.

91. Karl Grün, "Politik und Sozialismus," *Rheinische Jahrbücher für gesellschaftlichen Reform,* ed. Hermann Püttmann (Darmstadt: C. W. Leske, 1845), 101–2.

was in reality the "particular will . . . of the bourgeois."[92] Grün also uncritically repeated the liberal and conservative charge that Rousseau had been responsible for Robespierre and the Terror.[93]

Grün's dismissal of Rousseau's legacy was paired with a wider hostility to democratic government. He argued that the mantras of "today's republicans' 'electoral reform,' 'democracy,' 'revolution' . . . are outdated and discounted."[94] In place of democracy, Grün repeated the technocratic enthusiasms of Saint-Simon and Weitling (though without their detailed accompanying plans), envisaging the replacement of politics and government with "a management, an administration of society" that "does nothing but regulate *consumption*." "The socialist," Grün brightly declared, "turns the question of the 'universal estate' [political participation for all classes] into the question of the choice of *organizational talents*." Rule by the talented and knowledgeable was preferable to rule by the people, which meant being ruled by a "raw, unrestrained crowd . . . a swarm of cannibals."[95] Introducing universal suffrage would simply make one a "*slave* of the majority," since the "will of the majority . . . [is] a foreign will."[96]

Given these antimajoritarian views, Grün unsurprisingly took a dim view of socialists committed to democratic political reform. He criticized Louis Blanc's "*republican socialism*" for being stuck in the eighteenth century and wedded to a "republican theory" that could not get past the tired question of the "best *form of the state*."[97] Grün's main angle of attack was to deny that the institution of universal suffrage (which Blanc assumed would ground his social reform plans) would ever come about. Grün was convinced that universal suffrage would never be decreed by a legislature dominated by the bourgeoisie, since "[t]he bourgeois would [thereby] be committing suicide." Blanc furthermore believed, according to Grün at least, in keeping "an independent society next to the state—a completely unsolvable contradiction." Instead, Grün argued, one needed to break down the division between the two so that "there is no state anymore, since man has then taken back the law *in himself*."[98] There is more than a whiff here of some of Marx's early arguments. Marx had similarly made the antipolitical argument that the state would never intervene in civil society because it would not commit "*suicide*" by abolishing its existential "contradiction" between spheres, and he had concluded his "Zur Judenfrage"

92. Ibid., 120–23.
93. Grün, *Die sociale Bewegung*, 284.
94. Grün, "Politik und Sozialismus," 136.
95. Ibid., 140.
96. Grün, *Die sociale Bewegung*, 359.
97. Ibid., 303, 306.
98. Ibid., 310.

with the arresting claim that emancipation means overcoming this distinction and man's "re-absorb[ing] in himself the abstract citizen."[99] Grün was effectively borrowing Marx's earlier categories and arguments, without acknowledgment, to dismiss the feasibility of Blanc's republican socialism. (Grün's habit of plagiarism was one of Marx and Engels's main complaints.)[100]

Grün's foundational criticism that political institutions, whether liberal or democratic, were incapable of enacting socialism had predictable results for his view of political reform efforts. He argued that the people rightly took no interest in enacting a constitution, which he claimed was the exclusive obsession of liberal property owners.[101] He went so far as to suggest that until liberals had proved that they would deal with social problems, then one may as well "leave the absolute princely powers standing!"[102] Surveying Grün's early journalism, James Strassmaier argues that "the principal theme" was the "futility of liberalism constitutionalism."[103] In place of political reform and involvement in political struggle, Grün had only the vaguest account of how the transition to socialism might be brought about, especially when compared to the detailed communitarian transition plans provided by Fourier and Owen or the worker association proposed by Tristan. What little Grün had to say amounted to a hope that socialism would be brought about by raising consciousness through propaganda and education.[104] He insisted that "The *education question* (*Bildungsfrage*) is the actual main question of socialism."[105] This educational process was supposed to take place within self-organized communities rather than the state, since the state—even the republican "free state"—could never create the "true people" that would be the foundation of a new society.[106] Later, Grün added a little more practical

99. Marx, "Kritische Randglossen," *MEGA* I.2: 456-57 / *MECW* 3: 198-99; "Zur Judenfrage," *MEGA* I.2: 162 / *MECW* 3: 168. See "The Silesian Weavers' Revolt and the Critique of Politics" in chapter 3 of this book.

100. For instance, Marx and Engels, "Karl Grün: *Die soziale Bewegung in Frankreich u. Belgien* (Darmstadt 1845) oder: die Geschichtsschreibung des wahren Sozialismus," *MEGA* I.5: 572 / *MECW* 5: 514.

101. Grün, "Politik und Sozialismus," 99–100.

102. Karl Grün, *Ueber Göthe vom menschlichen Standpunkte* (Darmstadt: C. W. Leske, 1846), 106–7.

103. J. Strassmaier, *Karl Grün: The Confrontation with Marx, 1844–1848* (PhD dissertation, Chicago, Loyola University, 1969), 51.

104. Ibid., 33–34.

105. [Karl Grün], "Die Nothwendigkeit einer Gesellschafts-Reform," *Der Sprecher oder Rheinisch-Westphälischer Anzeiger*, no. 47 (12 June 1844): 1.

106. Karl Grün, "Die wahre Schule: Eine Skizze," *Weser-Dampfboot*, ed. O. Lüning and A. Osterwald (December 1844), 374, 379.

detail to these vague sketches by endorsing Proudhon's ideas on the peaceful spread of exchange banks.[107]

Marx and Engels were deeply concerned by the implications of Grün's antipolitical and antidemocratic thought and tried to limit its influence wherever they could. Marx's attempt in the spring of 1846 to win Proudhon for their Kommunistische Korrespondenz-kommittee and cleave him away from Grün backfired spectacularly, with Proudhon rejecting what he saw as Marx's dogmatic sectarianism.[108] Engels seems to have more success when he traveled to Paris a few months later on behalf of the committee with the aim of rooting out "Grünian true socialism" from the city's branch of the League of the Just and German worker associations.[109] Over the course of several heated meetings, Engels claimed to have converted several workers from their Grünian positions through his pithy tripartite summary of the aims of communism:

> 1) to assert the interests of the proletariat against those of the bourgeoisie; 2) to do so by abolishing private property and replacing the same with community of goods; 3) to recognize no means of attaining these aims other than forceful democratic revolution.[110]

With their commitment to "forceful democratic revolution," Marx and Engels staked out a clear divide between themselves and Grün's skepticism of democracy and hopes for peaceful consciousness raising.

Marx and Engels thought Grün's position not simply ineffective but actively dangerous. In 1847, building toward the argument they would make in the *Manifest der Kommunistischen Partei*, they repeatedly warned that the antipolitics of true socialism would only aid the reaction. Engels argued that the true socialist belief "that political progress, like all politics is evil" provided a "protective wall for the morass of the German status quo."[111] Marx similarly targeted German socialists who had "continually blustered against the liberal bourgeoisie . . . which has benefited nobody but the German governments."[112] True socialists failed to see, Marx insisted, that the political institutions supported by liberals and democrats were essential to the eventual emancipation

107. Strassmeier, *Karl Grün*, 173–78.

108. Marx to Pierre-Joseph Proudhon, 5 May 1846; Proudhon to Marx, 17 May 1846, *MEGA* III.2: 8, 205–7 / *MECW* 38: 39–40.

109. Engels to the Kommunistische Korrespondenz-komitee, 23 October 1846, *MEGA* III.2: 53-54 / *MECW* 38: 81–82.

110. Ibid.

111. Engels, *Der Status Quo in Deutschland*, *MEW* 4: 41–42 / *MECW* 6: 76–77.

112. Marx, "Der Kommunismus des 'Rheinischen Beobachters,'" *MEW* 4: 191 / *MECW* 6: 220.

of the proletariat, and so, "trial by jury, equality before the law, the abolition of the corvée system, freedom of the press, freedom of association and true representation" could "count on the strongest support from the proletariat."[113]

It has been argued that this line of criticism of Grün and true socialism was "profoundly unfair" because, when it came down to it, the true socialists did not support the reaction during the 1848 Revolution but joined the battle for German democracy.[114] Grün, for instance, became an active member of his local democratic club and was even elected to the Prussian National Assembly. But using these subsequent actions as a riposte to Marx and Engels is an odd, even anachronistic defense, since Marx and Engels were only taking true socialist figures at their word when they, in the years before 1848, explicitly called for abstention from liberal or democratic reform efforts. We have already examined Grün's early abstentionist statements, and Engels further highlighted Herman Semmig's 1846 book *Sächsische Zustände* (*Saxon Conditions*) as a prime example of how antipolitics resulted in a "reactionary political tendency."[115] Semmig had begun with a typical socialist critique of republicanism by posing the rhetorical questions "Will the republic pay our debts? Will it redeem our pawned goods? Will it clothe and feed us?"[116] He claimed that nothing could be expected from even a democratic republic because the "causes of our social hardships and evils lie deeper than defective state institutions" and thus "no political institutions are capable of abolishing them." For Semmig, the strategic consequence from this analysis was unambiguous: German workers who had "previously allowed themselves to be set in motion by these liberal bourgeois and to be misguided into tumults," should "not support them in their efforts and struggles" but instead "let them fight it out alone" and "above all do not at any time take part in *political revolutions*."[117] Marx and Engels were not misrepresenting Semmig's position in the *Manifest* or making an unreasonable prediction that this would serve the interests of reactionaries trying to uphold the status quo. Insofar as true socialists did not end up carrying through this political abstentionism, that was a deviation from their stated principles. And, as we will see in the next section, antipolitical sympathies were far from eradicated from the German socialist movement and led to

---

113. Ibid., 197 / 228.

114. Jonathan Sperber, *Karl Marx: A Nineteenth-Century Life* (New York: Liveright Publishing, 2013), 213.

115. Engels, "Manuskript über die wahren Sozialisten," *MEGA* 1.5: 619–20 / *MECW* 5: 556–57.

116. Herman Semmig, *Sächsische Zustände: nebst Randglossen und Leuchtkugeln* (Hamburg: C. F. Vogel, 1846), 9.

117. Ibid., 63–64.

demonstrable divisions with democrats that strengthened the hand of reactionary forces.

A more plausible case can be made that Marx and Engels's criticism was unfair to the nuances between true socialist figures as well as to developments in their thinking between 1845 and 1848. Otto Lüning had launched the *Westphälische Dampfboot* in 1845 with the standard slogans about the social ineffectiveness of politics and at best lukewarm support for constitutional reform efforts (already a difference from Semmig's complete abstentionism).[118] Two years later, however, Lüning was programmatically declaring that "socialism had taken an important step forward" by no longer "angrily turning away from political liberals and radical democrats" and being "ready to participate in their efforts as a means to an end."[119] Grün duly reprinted a new "Prospectus" from the *Westphälische Dampfboot*, setting out that the journal was "far removed from that sovereign disregard for political institutions, the transformation of the state to a constitutional and a truly democratic institution, as was previously displayed by a faction of idealist socialists," to which Grün added that he was in agreement with its "essential elements."[120] Indeed, over the course of 1847 Grün increasingly (though not consistently) moderated his anticonstitutionalism and welcomed the developing reform movement in Prussia.[121]

Key figures in Marx and Engels's construction of "true socialism" had thus moved away from their earlier strong antipolitics and, in fact, moved closer to the politics advocated by Marx and Engels. Their criticism in the *Manifest der Kommunistischen Partei* was thus not so much unfair as partially outdated.[122] And yet, antipolitical elements continued to haunt Grün's thinking in 1848. When the revolution broke out in Paris he could not help himself from taking potshots at the regime's newly instituted universal (manhood) suffrage.[123] He also continued to dismiss the social measures proposed by Blanc, as well as the recently released ones by Marx and Engels, as "dictatorial" because they were carried out by the state (ignoring that both parties specified that these measures were to be

118. [Otto Lüning], "Das Westphälische Dampfboot," *Oeffentliche Anzeigen der Graffschaft Ravensberg*, no. 5 (29 January 1845): 39–40; [Otto] L[üning], "Blicke in die Gegenwart," *Das Westphälische Dampfboot* (February and April 1845), 63, 154–55.

119. [Otto] L[üning], "Zum neuen Jahre," *Das Westphälische Dampfboot* (January 1847), 2–3.

120. [Karl Grün], "Aus dem Westphälischen, im Januar," *Trier'sche Zeitung*, no. 35 (4 February 1847): 1. See Strassmaier, *Karl Grün*, 183–84.

121. Strassmaier, *Karl Grün*, 182–85.

122. Ibid., 195, 204.

123. [Karl Grün], "Paris, 7. März," *Trier'sche Zeitung*, no. 72 (12 March 1848).

carried by democratically elected regimes).[124] Antipolitical habits apparently died hard.

Regardless of the true socialists' later moderation of their political abstentionism, the damage had already been done—at least insofar as it had exposed socialists to an effective and popular republican angle of attack. Karl Heinzen had been publicly warning for some time that "communists would throw themselves into the arms of despotism."[125] He provocatively repeated the charge in the *Deutsche-Brüsseler Zeitung* in September 1847, arguing that their "zealous attempt to paralyze the political struggle" meant that they "effectively allied themselves . . . nearly with the reaction."[126] Heinzen's irate outburst, in a newspaper that Marx and Engels were increasingly associated with, provided an ideal opportunity to neutralize this republican argument and at the same time publicize the distinctness of their own conception of communism. Engels replied immediately to Heinzen (followed by Marx a few weeks later) and insisted that communists were in fact fully committed to the struggle for "democracy" because it would lead to the "political rule of the proletariat, [which is] the first precondition of all communist measures." Communists thus "take the field as democrats themselves" and would "fight side by side" with democrats in the coming revolution.[127] The mistake Heinzen had made, Engels admonished, was taking "Herr Grün" and other "true socialists"—who had indeed attempted to "paralyze the political struggle"—as representative of communism as such.[128] Engels thereby deflected Heinzen's criticism of communism as a handmaiden of reactionary absolutism onto Grün and true socialism.

When Marx and Engels subsequently incorporated that criticism into the *Manifest der Kommunistischen Partei*, they had effectively appropriated republican arguments in order to dismiss other forms of socialism.[129] They thereby defanged not only one of the most potent republican criticisms of existing socialisms but sharpened the distinctiveness of their own communism. That

---

124. For Blanc, see [Karl Grün], "Paris, 26. März," *Trier'sche Zeitung*, no. 92 (1 April 1848); for Marx and Engels, see [Karl Grün], "Paris, 1. April," *Trier'sche Zeitung*, no. 97 (6 April 1848), Beilage and [Karl Grün], "Paris, 26. März," *Kölnische Zeitung*, no. 90 (30 March 1848), Beilage, 1.

125. Karl Heinzen, "Kommunistisches," in *Teutsche Revolution: Gesammelte Flugschriften*, ed. Karl Heinzen (Bern: Jenni, Sohn, 1847), 363 (essay dated November 1846).

126. Karl Heinzen, "Polemik: Karl Heinzen und die Kommunisten," *Deutsche-Brüsseler-Zeitung*, no. 77 (26 September 1847): 4. Robert Owen was subject to a similar charge, with working-class radicals suspecting him of being a government agent sent to distract them from their political campaign; see Claeys, *Citizens and Saints*, 63.

127. Engels, "Die Kommunisten und Karl Heinzen," *MEW* 4: 317 / *MECW* 6: 299.

128. Ibid., 318 / 300.

129. Sperber, *Karl Marx*, 213.

combined the socialist critique of capitalism with the republican insistence on politics, resulting in a hybridized republican communism. This distinguished them, and other figures responsible for the emergence of this merger, from the powerful antipolitical legacy that had dominated socialism since its inception. Marx and Engels did not, of course, think that political struggle and participation in parliamentary processes alone would be enough to carry through a transition to socialism.[130] They wanted a combination of social and political struggle, a bringing together, as Marx once presented it, of trade unionism and Chartism.[131] What they were convinced of, however, was that the complete abandonment of the political terrain was doomed to failure. Seeking a transition to socialism purely through *"doctrinaire experiments, exchange banks and workers' associations,"* was, Marx maintained, equivalent to giving up on society's *"grand collective resources"* and seeking *"salvation behind society's back, in private fashion . . . [and] hence necessarily fails."*[132]

The Many Republics of 1848

The outbreak of the revolution found Marx in Brussels, where he had spent the previous three years after his exile from Paris in 1845. In line with his general political strategy, Marx had there been both a vice president of the Association Démocratique (Democratic Association) and chairman of the Brussels branch of the Bund der Kommunisten.[133] As the first shots were being fired on the Parisian barricades, the *Manifest der Kommunistischen Partei* was rolling off the presses in London (where the League was headquartered). Marx's initial reaction to the revolution is likely to have been as excited as that of Engels, who reported to the Chartist press that "At half-past twelve at night, the train arrived, with the glorious news of Thursday's revolution, and the whole mass of people shouted, in one sudden outburst of enthusiasm: *Vive la République!"*[134] Marx did not have long to celebrate, as the Belgian government, worried about the revolution spreading across the border, ordered him to leave the country in twenty-four hours. The change of regime meant he was once again welcome in Paris, and he embraced the opportunity to witness the revolution up front.

---

130. A criticism that might be made of forms of socialism that do not maintain at least some critical attitude to politics. Too little antipolitics might also be a bad thing.

131. Marx, *Misère de la philosophie, MEW* 4: 179–82 / *MECW* 6: 210–12.

132. Marx, *Der achtzehnte Brumaire, MEGA* I.11: 105 / *MECW* 11: 110-11.

133. For the neglected Association, see Bert Andréas, Jacques Grandjonc, and Hans Pelger, eds., *Association Démocratique, ayant pour but l'union et la fraternité de tous les peuples: Eine frühe internationale demokratische Vereinigung in Brüssel, 1847–1848* (Trier: Karl-Marx-Haus, 2004).

134. Engels, "To the Editor of the Northern Star," *MEGA* I.7: 6 / *MECW* 6: 559.

He spent a month there, waiting for the revolution to make its way to the German states. When street protests duly erupted in Vienna and Berlin in the middle of March, he began preparations for his return to Cologne. Before leaving Paris, Marx, Engels, and the leadership of the Bund der Kommunisten released the seventeen-point *Forderungen der Kommunistischen Parthei in Deutschland* (*Demands of the Communist Party of Germany*), headlined with their central aim for the revolution: "1. The whole of Germany shall be declared a single, indivisible republic."[135]

Once they had arrived Cologne, Marx, Engels, and some of their closest associates from the Bund set up the *Neue Rheinische Zeitung* in June 1848. As editor-in-chief, Marx oversaw the paper's development into the leading radical paper in the Rhineland, with a readership that extended across Germany. The paper was an opportunity to put into practice the political strategy that Marx and Engels had honed over the previous years and fought for in the Bund, which mandated that communists first had to fight alongside republicans for the establishment of a republic.[136] The republic would in turn create the material and political conditions for the subsequent communist struggle against capitalism. In effect, that meant that during the revolution communists had to be republicans before they could again be communists. The consequence was that, much as Marx had in 1842 downplayed open republicanism in the *Rheinische Zeitung* in favor of liberalism, the *Neue Rheinische Zeitung* of 1848 aligned itself with democratic republicanism and minimized its connection to communism. It prominently carried the motto "Organ der Demokratie" ("Organ of Democracy") and pressured the newly constituted Frankfurt National Assembly (tasked with writing a constitution for a united Germany) to "loudly and publicly proclaim the sovereignty of the German people" and establish a "German constitution on the basis of popular sovereignty."[137] Social issues, criticisms of capitalists, and coverage of the emerging labor movement were in contrast largely marginalized in the paper.[138] Marx also downplayed his association with the Bund der Kommunisten, allowing it to go mostly dormant in this period (or even, as some accounts suggest, dissolving it), and he instead took a prominent role in Cologne's Demokratische Gesellschaft (Democratic Society).

135. Marx, Schapper, H. Bauer, Engels, Moll, Wolff, *Forderungen der Kommunistischen Parthei in Deutschland*, MEGA I.7: 25 / MECW 7: 3.

136. The definitive account of their political strategy in these years is Hunt, *Political Ideas of Marx and Engels*, vol. 1, chapters 5–7.

137. Engels, "Die Frankfurter Versammlung," MEGA I.7: 32 / MECW 7: 16. Though its support for a republic was implicit in such calls, the lingering danger of explicitly calling for one meant that the *Neue Rheinische Zeitung* did not to do so until later in the revolution.

138. Sperber, *Karl Marx*, 226; Hunt, *Political Ideas of Marx and Engels*, 1: 196–97.

The central tension this strategy faced was the danger that it would end up engendering the hostility of all the political factions and classes it relied on: the progressive bourgeoisie, the democratic republicans, as well as socialists and workers. The idea, for instance, that the bourgeois republic would prepare the ground for the battle against the bourgeoisie, culminating in their destruction and the victory of communism, was not one that was likely to play well with the bourgeoisie themselves. Engels was directly confronted by this problem when he unsuccessfully tried to raise funds for the *Neue Rheinische Zeitung* among the bourgeoisie in his hometown of Barmen. Writing to Marx, he noted that the "fact is, *au fond,* that even these radical bourgeoisie here see in us their future main enemies, and have no intention of putting any weapons in our hands which we would very shortly turn against themselves."[139] Trying to keep the progressive bourgeoisie largely on their side in the struggle against absolutism meant continually playing down the danger of communism and limiting communist agitation. In the same letter Engels noted that if a "single copy" of their *Forderungen* made it into the Barmen bourgeoisie's hands, "everything would be lost for us."[140]

A similar problem emerged in their attempted alliance with democratic republicans. The one exception the *Neue Rheinische Zeitung* made to its general policy of social silence was its prominent defense of the Parisian workers in the June Days. In his editorial, Marx unequivocally condemned the slaughter and boldly stated that it was the "*right of the democratic press* to place laurels on the brows of the martyred workers."[141] That, however, put Marx and the *Neue Rheinische Zeitung* seriously out of step with the rest of the radical opinion. Republicans almost universally condemned the June Days as an illegitimate uprising against a republic elected by universal suffrage.[142] Sensing the danger of isolation, Marx used a subsequent speech to Cologne's Demokratische Gesellschaft to row back some of his earlier support for the workers.[143]

Conversely, the attempt to accommodate the progressive bourgeoisie and focus efforts on a joint political struggle with republicans carried the danger of alienating the support of workers. It also opened up political space for socialists who questioned the value of political agitation. That problem emerged

139. Engels to Marx, 25 April 1848, *MEGA* III.2: 152–53 / *MECW* 38: 172–73.

140. Ibid.

141. Marx, "Die Junirevolution," *MEGA* I.7: 211 / *MECW* 7: 149.

142. Peter McPhee, "The Crisis of Radical Republicanism in the French Revolution of 1848," *Historical Studies* 16, no. 62 (1974): 71–88.

143. See the newspaper reports of the meetings reproduced in *MEGA* I.7: 769 / *MECW* 7: 556. See further Jonathan Sperber, *Rhineland Radicals: The Democratic Movement and the Revolution of 1848–1849* (Princeton: Princeton University Press, 1991), 300–301.

particularly clearly in Marx and Engels's conflict with Andreas Gottschalk, a popular doctor who in April 1848 founded the Cologne Arbeiterverien (Workers' Association), which quickly expanded to several thousand members of the city's working class. Gottschalk's leadership of the Arbeiterverein embodied the contradictory and ambiguous relationship to politics that marked early German socialism, even as it had evolved away from complete political abstentionism. Though Gottschalk loudly advocated for a republic—even a "worker's republic"—he thought this would come about through peaceful education and enlightenment.[144] His leadership saw the Arbeiterverein swing between political passivity and counterproductive participation. In one of his most damaging actions he called for workers of the Arbeiterverein to boycott the May 1848 elections to the Frankfurt National Assembly, contributing to the democrats' defeat by the conservatives and liberals in the city.[145] In Jonathan Sperber's assessment, Gottschalk "acted like an ultra-leftist, spurning any cooperation with the democrats, boycotting parliamentary elections . . . and calling for a workers' republic when the demand for an ordinary republic was enough to send chills down the spines of the bourgeoisie."[146] In this he was, Sperber continues, simply a "true socialist trying to carry out the doctrine" that the path to socialism would come about through peaceful consciousness raising.[147]

Gottschalk's actions seriously threatened Marx's strategy of backing democratic forces, and when Marx eventually managed to gain greater control over the Arbeiterverien (while Gottschalk was in prison), he steered it in this direction. However, that meant "much more demanding political concept than the one Gottschalk had espoused, requiring verbal moderation and political activism rather than verbal militancy and political passivity," a strategy that was significantly less popular and led to a decline in membership of the association.[148] Marx and Engels's revolutionary strategy thus ran into difficulties from all sides. Their experience led them to subsequently reevaluate their strategy, arguing that while the workers should still fight for the republic, they should not expect support from the progressive bourgeoisie but organize themselves independently of the democratic republicans.[149]

---

144. "Comité-Sitzung vom 18. Mai 1848," *Zeitung des Arbeiter-Vereines zu Köln*, no. 6 (28 May 1848): 1–2; "Generalversammlung des Arbeiter-Vereins am 4. Juni," *Zeitung des Arbeiter-Vereines zu Köln*, no. 8 (11 June 1848): 1–2.

145. *Zeitung des Arbeiter-Vereines zu Köln*, no. 1 (23. April 1848), Extra Beilage: 2.

146. Sperber, *Rhineland Radicals*, 227.

147. Ibid.

148. Ibid., 230. See further Igor Shoikhedbrod, "Marx and the Democratic Struggle over the Constitution in 1848–9," *History of Political Thought* 43, no. 2 (2022): 357–81.

149. Hunt, *Political Ideas of Marx and Engels*, 1: 240–43.

The course of the revolution across Europe swung sharply toward reaction in the second half of 1848. In Cologne, the Prussian authorities used an unsuccessful insurrection in the city at the end of September to briefly shut down the *Neue Rheinische Zeitung*, the Cologne Democratic Society, and the Workers' Association. The paper was able to continue to operate until May 1849, when the Prussian authorities finally expelled Marx and issued an arrest warrant for Engels. While Engels joined the fighting in the Baden-Palatinate campaign, Marx made his way once again to Paris, finding the city in a markedly more reactionary mood. In a familiar story, he was soon made unwelcome by the French authorities. He decided, like so many European radicals, that his only option was to head to London. He arrived in August 1849 for what he thought would be a temporary exile but stayed until the end of his life.

In London, Marx and Engels threw themselves back into the revived Bund der Kommunisten (Communist League) and set up a new journal version of the *Neue Rheinische Zeitung*, now subtitled *Politische-ökonomische Revue*. The journal folded after only few issues in November 1850, but it did give Marx the opportunity to reflect seriously on the events of the preceding two years. While nearly all of his political involvement during the Revolution had been in Germany, he focused the bulk of his theoretical reflections on events in France.[150] The product was a three-part series with the deceptively bland title "1848 bis 1849" ("1848 to 1849"), which Engels republished in 1895 under the name by which the text has been known ever since: *Die Klassenkämpfe in Frankreich* (*The Class Struggles in France*).[151] Marx here began to analyze the experience of the Second French Republic, making the case for why it "was in reality and could only ever have been a *bourgeois* republic."[152] When Louis Napoleon, the elected president of France since December 1848, overthrew the Second Republic in his coup d'état on 2 December 1851, Marx was forced to grapple with how the Revolution had ended in a dictatorship rather than the expected bourgeois republic. The result was perhaps his most famous piece of political analysis: *Der achtzehnte Brumaire des Louis Bonaparte* (*The Eighteenth Brumaire of Louis Bonaparte*) (hereafter *Der achtzehnte Brumaire*). Named after the date (in the republican calendar) of the first Napoleon's coup against the First Republic, it appeared in May 1852 as a

150. In something of a division of labor, analysis of German events was left to Engels in his "Die deutsche Reichsverfassungs-Campagne" ("The German Imperial Constitution Campaign, 1850") and his article series "Revolution and Counter-Revolution in Germany" (1851–52) for the *New York Daily Tribune*.

151. Engels added a fourth section taken from their jointly written "Revue. Mai bis Oktober 1850," which also appeared in the *Neue Rheinische Zeitung: Politische-ökonomische Revue*. For this fourth section, I cite the "Revue. Mai bis Oktober 1850," and for the first three sections, I (a little reluctantly) use the more famous title *Die Klassenkämpfe in Frankreich*.

152. Marx, *Die Klassenkämpfe in Frankreich*, MEGA I.10: 136 / MECW 10: 66.

special pamphlet edition of the New York journal *Die Revolution*. Considering its subsequent fame, its contemporary impact was limited, as only a few copies made their way to the Continent and efforts to republish it in Germany or in an English or French translation came to nothing. Marx was, however, able to later republish it in a second (amended) version in 1869.

An overlooked feature of Marx's analysis of French revolutionary events from 1848 to 1851, in both *Die Klassenkämpfe in Frankreich* and *Der achtzehnte Brumaire*, is the sheer number of republics that Marx refers to. Alongside the more familiar class actors that populate Marx's revolutionary stage,[153] he refers to *red* republics, *social* republics, *democratic* republics, *social-democratic* republics, *bourgeois* republics, *tricolor* republics, *pure* republics, *respectable* republics, *constitutional* republics, *parliamentary* republics, and even *Cossack* republics. While the meaning of these qualifiers is sometimes relatively straightforward, Marx's discussion suggests that they can in fact refer to at least three different characteristics of a republic:

(i) its governing class
  – the class (or faction) that holds political power in the republic
(ii) its *economy*
  – the republic's economic structure and institutions, which serve the economic interests of a particular class
(iii) its *constitution*
  – the republic's constitutional (and political) institutions, which help maintain (i) and (ii)

Distinguishing these aspects allows for the possibility that how a republic is distinguished in one of these dimensions might not necessarily correspond to how it is in another. A republic's economic structure, for instance, might be organized such that it benefits a particular class, but that might not correspond to that same class holding political power.[154]

Much of Marx's revolutionary narrative is dominated by the struggle of different classes and factions to ascend to political power and institute their preferred vision of the republic. Marx observed that when the republic triumphed in February 1848, it remained unclear what kind of republic it would

---

153. On the recurrent theatrical metaphors in Marx's account of the 1848 Revolution, see S. S. Prawer, *Karl Marx and World Literature* (Oxford: Clarendon Press, 1976), 167–68, 178–80.

154. Marx, for instance, argued that in Britain, the landed aristocracy *"governs officially,"* while the bourgeoisie *"rules not officially,"* but in all decisive spheres of civil society." See Marx, "Die britische Konstitution - Layard," *MEGA* I.14: 170 / *MECW* 14: 53; see also Marx, "The Crisis in England," *MEGA* I.14: 166-67 / *MECW* 14: 60. In "Die Parteien und Cliquen," *MEGA* I.14: 102 / *MECW* 13: 642, Marx similarly distinguishes between a "governing caste" and a "ruling class."

be and so "Every party construed it in its own way."[155] He argued that the workers thought they had founded a *social republic*, and indeed between February and June 1848 they had been strong enough to force the social concession that the republic would guarantee the right to work through the National Workshops, thus briefly creating a *"republic surrounded by social institutions."*[156] But Marx maintained that the underdevelopment of the proletariat meant that their demand for a *"social republic* [only] appeared as a phrase, as a prophecy" of things to come, and its inevitable destruction in the June Days left it to "haunt the subsequent acts of the drama like a ghost."[157] The next significant conception of the republic, Marx argued, was the *"democratic republic"* of the petty bourgeoisie.[158] He claimed that in line with their class interests, their vision of the republic entailed "democratic-republican institutions" that do not "supersede [the] extremes, capital and wage-labor" but "weaken their antagonism and transform them into harmony."[159] Thus, by Marx's account, the workers fought for a social republic while the petty bourgeoisie wanted a democratic republic, in which they would each have exercised political rule and instituted their favored social and economic institutions. His account thereby splits in two the popular slogan *"la République démocratique et sociale,"* which had united left discourse in France in 1848.[160] Marx's split between social and democratic republics mischaracterizes democratic republicans as uninterested in social issues and has the unfortunate consequence of suggesting that the workers were not interested in the democratic reform (against Marx's own position). Missing from Marx's account of the workers' social republic in 1848 is also any reference to there being constitutional structures that are particularly suited to advancing their political and economic rule; this only emerges in his discussion of the social republic during the Paris Commune (as is discussed in chapter 7).

While the social and the democratic republic each played a brief role in the revolution, Marx set out how they were pushed aside by the real protagonist of

155. Marx, *Der achtzehnte Brumaire, MEGA* I.11: 103–104 / *MECW* 11: 109.

156. Marx, *Die Klassenkämpfe in Frankreich, MEGA* I.10: 125, 136 / *MECW* 10: 55, 66. The phrase is an allusion to Lafayette's celebration of the 1830 July Monarchy, as a "monarchy surrounded by republican institutions."

157. Marx, *Der achtzehnte Brumaire, MEGA* I.11: 104, 174 / *MECW* 11: 109, 181.

158. Ibid., 174 / 181. Note that in some of Marx and Engels's later usage the "democratic republic" is equated with the "bourgeois republic"; see, for instance, Marx, "Kritik der Gothaer Programms," *MEGA* I.25: 22–23 / *MECW* 24: 96; Engels, 'Réponse à l'honorable Giovanni Bovio," *MEGA* I.32: 102 / *MECW* 27: 271; Engels to August Bebel, 18 August 1886, *MEW* 36: 509 / *MECW* 47: 470.

159. Marx, *Der achtzehnte Brumaire, MEGA* I.11: 124 / *MECW* 11: 30.

160. Pamela M. Pilbeam, *Republicanism in Nineteenth-Century France, 1814–1871* (Basingstoke: MacMillan, 1995), 213, 229; Sperber, *The European Revolutions, 1848–1851,* 206–7.

the story: the *bourgeois republic*. It was this republic that, Marx argued, took "possession of the entire stage" for the predominant part of the revolution.[161] In his discussion of the bourgeois republic, Marx primarily refers to the first two aspects of a republic outlined above. He associates it, for instance, both with the bourgeois class holding political power: "[in] a *bourgeois republic* . . . the whole of the bourgeoisie will now rule on behalf of the people," and with the republic being accompanied by capitalist economy: "the political reconsolidation of bourgeois society, [is] in a word, *a bourgeois republic*."[162] In one interesting contemporaneous discussion of the English bourgeoisie, however, Marx moves back and forth between all three aspects of a bourgeois republic:

> What they [the bourgeoisie] demand is the complete and undisguised ascendancy of the Bourgeoisie, the open, official subjection of society at large under the laws of modern, bourgeois production [ii. *bourgeois economy*], and under the rule of those men who are the directors of that production [i. *bourgeois governing class*] . . . their last word is the *Bourgeois Republic*, in which free competition rules supreme in all spheres of life [ii. *bourgeois economy*]; in which there remains altogether that *minimum* only of government which is indispensable for the administration, internally and externally, of the common class interest and business of the Bourgeoisie [iii. *bourgeois constitution*].[163]

In this final sentence, Marx associates the bourgeois republic with the idea that the bourgeoisie tries to design the constitution and political structures of the republic in such a way that it favors its political rule and economic interests. In summary, when Marx describes a republic as a *bourgeois* republic, he means one (or a combination) of the following:

(i) the bourgeoisie holds political power in the republic,[164]
(ii) the republic is accompanied by a capitalist economy,
(iii) the republic's constitution is organized so as to maintain (i) and / or (ii).

---

161. Marx, *Der achtzehnte Brumaire*, MEGA I.11: 174 / *MECW* 11: 182.

162. Ibid., 104 / 110; *Die Klassenkämpfe in Frankreich*, MEGA I.10: 136 / *MECW* 10: 66.

163. Marx, "The Chartists," *MEGA* I.11: 323-24 / *MECW* 11: 333–34. At other points, Marx emphasized that the bourgeoisie can have an interest in or be forced into expanding the republic's administrative apparatus, particularly in relation to its repressive functions. See Marx, *Der achtzehnte Brumaire*, MEGA I.11: 132, 179 / *MECW* 11: 139, 186.

164. That idea itself elides several possibilities. Marx's considered position was not that the bourgeois republic's politicians were themselves *literally capitalists* or even that they acted at the *behest* of the capitalist class (as the above passage, and others like it, might be read to imply), but that they acted on *behalf* of its interests; see Ralph Miliband, "Poulantzas and the Capitalist State," *New Left Review* 1, no. 82 (1973): 85n4.

Marx further argued that a full understanding of the bourgeois republic required analyzing which faction of the bourgeois was in power. He thus subdivided the bourgeois republic into the *pure* republic (or sometimes *tricolor* republic) of the *republican* bourgeoisie and the *parliamentary* republic (or sometimes *constitutional* republic) of the *royalist* bourgeoisie (see figure 9).[165] On Marx's account, the republican bourgeoisie (unlike the royalist bourgeoisie) did not represent an economically distinct part of the bourgeois class but were only a "clique of republican-minded bourgeois, writers, lawyers, officers and officials."[166] He considered them to be a minor faction of the overall bourgeois class, who ruled from the June Days (when they pushed out the left-wing republicans from the provisional government) until Louis Napoleon won the presidential election in December 1848.[167] Within that period they were in charge of writing the Second Republic's constitution. Marx argued that because the bourgeois republicans realized they were steadily losing what little popular support they enjoyed to the "royalists, the Bonapartists, the democrats, the communists," they did their best to rig the republic's constitution in their favor.[168] He argued that they tried to "safeguard their position," first by making the National Assembly (that they controlled) in theory superior to the president (as we'll see below, Marx argued that in this they failed dramatically); and second, when it became clear that they would lose their parliamentary majority, they made future revisions to the constitution dependent on a parliamentary supermajority.[169] Marx further highlighted how the bourgeois republicans tried to shape the Constitution to protect not just their factional position but also the larger bourgeois class's interests. While they could not directly undo the recent victory of universal manhood suffrage, Marx pointed to their restriction of the electorate through a residency requirement and the stringent qualifications they added to the constitutional rights to "personal freedom, press, speech, association, assembly, education and religious freedom," which meant that the bourgeoisie's "enjoyment of them finds itself unhindered by the equal rights of the other classes."[170] Marx's analysis of the pure republic of

---

165. '[T]he parliamentary republic, [is] the republic of the royalist bourgeoisie . . . the pure republic, [is] the republic of the bourgeois-republicans," Marx, *Der achtzehnte Brumaire, MEGA* I.11: 175 / *MECW* 11: 182. See also ibid., 117 / 123, and *Die Klassenkämpfe in Frankreich, MEGA* I.10: 141 / *MECW* 10: 72.

166. Marx, *Der achtzehnte Brumaire, MEGA* I.11: 107 / *MECW* 11: 112–13. See also *Die Klassenkämpfe in Frankreich, MEGA* I.10: 163 / *MECW* 10: 95.

167. Marx, *Der achtzehnte Brumaire, MEGA* I.11: 108 / *MECW* 11: 114.

168. Ibid., 111 / 117.

169. Ibid., 110–12 / 115–117.

170. Ibid., 109 / 115.

French Republics (1848–51)

Social Republic	Democratic Republic	Bourgeois Republic

Proletariat   Petty Bourgeoisie   Bourgeoisie

Pure Republic		Parliamentary Republic

Republican Bourgeoisie   *Royalist Bourgeoisie*

Legitimists   *Orléanists*

Landowning Bourgeoisie   Industrial & Financial Bourgeoisie

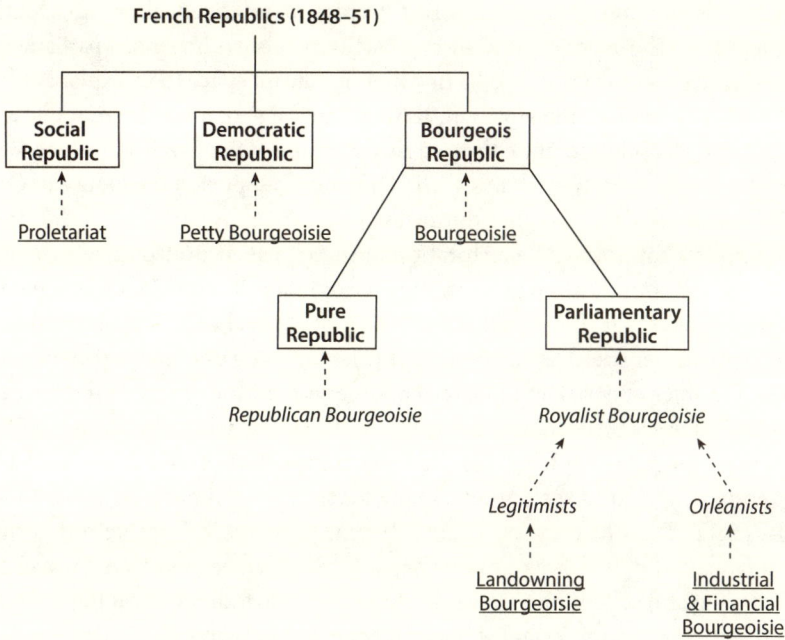

FIGURE 9. Marx's categorization of republics during the 1848 Revolutions. Corresponding ruling classes are underlined, and political factions are in italics.

bourgeois republicans thus makes particular reference to how the constitutional setup of a republic can safeguard the rule of a particular class.[171]

For Marx, the existential problem faced by the bourgeois republicans arose from their unwillingness to ally with the popular classes and the fact that the great majority of their fellow bourgeois class were instinctively and stubbornly royalist, leaving them without their own underlying class basis of support. The republican bourgeoisie were consequently superseded by the royalist bourgeoisie after 1849 May elections, who then "impound[ed] this republic as *its property*," turning it into the parliamentary republic.[172] The curious spectacle of a republic ruled by royalists only lasted until Louis Napoleon's coup at the end of 1851 (Marx joked that the parliamentary republic was thereby finally replaced

171. The pure and parliamentary republics are thus, by Marx's account, primarily differentiated from each other in terms of their respective (i) governing class/faction and to an extent their (iii) constitution, rather than their (ii) economy, since both republics are accompanied by a bourgeois economy.

172. Ibid., 113–14 / 119.

by the *"république cosaque"*).[173] But despite its relatively short life, Marx thought that the experience of the royalist bourgeoisie ruling in the parliamentary republic was crucial, and he devoted significant space to its explanation.

Marx argued that the key to understanding the parliamentary republic lay in its unique ability to unite the two rival factions of the royalist bourgeoisie: the *Legitimists* and the *Orléanists*. The Orléanists supported the House of Orléans, which had ruled France during the July Monarchy of 1830–48, while the Legitimists supported the restoration of the House of Bourbon, which had ruled during the ancien régime and again from 1814 to 1830. Marx was at pains to emphasize that this superficial division over royal claimants actually reflected a deeper social fissure between the landowning bourgeoisie on the one side and the industrial and financial bourgeoisie on the other.[174] The former had its interests protected by the House of Bourbon, while the House of Orléans privileged the interests of the latter. Supporters of each branch subsequently struggled to keep or restore their respective claimant to further their class interests. But they faced the inherent monarchical problem that the "crown could only descend to one head."[175] That left each faction constantly jockeying and scheming to have its particular royal individual on the throne, without ever securely establishing its form of the monarchy.

The bourgeois parliamentary republic provided the perfect solution, Marx maintained, because its depersonalized system of rule allows the two royalist factions to rule together. He observed that "in the bourgeois republic, which bore neither the name *Bourbon* nor the name *Orléans*, but the name *Capital*, they had found the form of state in which they could rule *conjointly*."[176] In the *"nameless realm of the republic"* the two great factions of the bourgeoisie could for the first time work together for their common bourgeois interest, without being distracted by petty dynastic squabbles.[177] Marx emphasized this insight over a dozen times in *Die Klassenkämpfe in Frankreich* and *Der achtzehnte Brumaire*, suggesting that he took it to be one of most crucial historical breakthroughs of the revolution.[178] Marx thought it a significant development that even the more reactionary elements of the bourgeoisie were slowly realizing

173. Ibid., 175 / 182.

174. Ibid., 121–22 / 127–28. Marx argued that the formerly aristocratic landowning class is rightly referred to as bourgeois since "large landed property . . . has been rendered thoroughly bourgeois by the development of modern society."

175. Ibid., 160 / 166.

176. Ibid., 114 / 120.

177. Marx, *Die Klassenkämpfe in Frankreich*, MEGA I.10: 163 / *MECW* 10: 95.

178. See, for instance, ibid., 168, 179–80 / 101, 114; *Der achtzehnte Brumaire*, MEGA I.11: 118, 122, 155, 159–60, 176 / *MECW* 11: 125, 129, 160, 165–66, 183.

that the republic could be bent to their bourgeois interests and be a vehicle for their class rule. He quoted the prophetic words of the Orléanist representative Adolphe Thiers (who would go on to play a foundational and bloody role in the Third Republic) that "We, the royalists, are the true pillars of the constitutional republic," and he noted that Thiers was one of the first to come to the realization that of the available political forms the "republic divides them [the monarchists] least."[179] Maurice Agulhon, perhaps the foremost historian of the French 1848 Revolutions, similarly concluded that the "involuntary experience of the fact that a Republic could be bourgeois" and that the republic "made it possible for rival partisans of monarchy to work together for the aims they shared . . . was surely a discovery that must also be rated as part of this period's historical legacy."[180]

The Insufficiency of the Bourgeois Republic

Marx's verdict on the bourgeois republic, whether pure or parliamentary, was damning. Typical judgments included that the "*bourgeois republic* signifies the unlimited despotism of one class over other classes" and that "the *bourgeois republic* . . . [is] the state whose admitted purpose is to perpetuate the rule of capital, the slavery of labor."[181] The underlying basis for this criticism relates to all three aspects of the bourgeois republic that Marx believed made it bourgeois: that it had a bourgeois governing class, a bourgeois economy, and a bourgeois constitution. These three aspects ensured that the bourgeois republic was insufficient for the emancipation of the proletariat. This section explores each of these aspects in turn.

First, Marx argued that contrary to the democratic expectation that the overthrow of the French July Monarchy by a republic would result in the rule of the people, in fact it resulted in the bourgeois class holding political power: "The *bourgeois monarchy* of Louis Philippe can be followed only by a *bourgeois republic*, i.e., whereas a limited section of the bourgeoisie ruled in the name of the king, the whole of the bourgeoisie will now rule in the name of the people."[182] By holding political power, the bourgeoisie ensured that the state

---

179. Marx, *Die Klassenkämpfe in Frankreich*, *MEGA* I.10: 180 / *MECW* 10: 114; *Der achtzehnte Brumaire*, *MEGA* I.11: 123 / *MECW* 11: 129.

180. Maurice Agulhon, *The Republican Experiment, 1848–1850*, trans. Janet Lloyd (Cambridge: Cambridge University Press, 1983), 191.

181. Marx, *Der achtzehnte Brumaire*, *MEGA* I.11: 105 / *MECW* 11: 111; Marx, *Die Klassenkämpfe in Frankreich*, *MEGA* I.10: 139 / *MECW* 10: 69.

182. Marx, *Der achtzehnte Brumaire*, *MEGA* I.11: 104 / *MECW* 11: 110.

acted in its favor so that the "claims of . . . all the remaining classes of society" are "subjugated to their [the bourgeoisie's] general class interest."[183]

Second, in addition to the bourgeoisie exercising political power, Marx argued that the republic would be bourgeois in that it would maintain (and even cement) the economic structures of bourgeois society.[184] As we saw in chapter 3, this was the central charge made in Marx's 1843 essay "Zur Judenfrage." Marx there argued that the republic would only free people in the political realm and leave them unfree in the social sphere of civil society. This prediction about the social insufficiency of the republic (based on his analysis of the American and First French Republic) was in Marx's eyes confirmed by the experience of the Second French Republic in the 1848 Revolutions. He pointed to the actions of the bourgeois republicans who had allied themselves with radical republicans when they needed to protect the political "*form* of the bourgeois republic" but turned to the royalist bourgeoisie when they wanted to preserve its social "*content*," since "it is the interests of the bourgeoisie, the material conditions of its class rule and class exploitation, that form the content of the bourgeois republic."[185] For Marx, the bourgeois republic was essentially a change in the political scaffolding that didn't touch the underlying social building. He reinforced that criticism via a quip about the First French Republic's short-lived attempt to rationalize the traditional calendar: "The rechristening of the Christian calendar into a republican one, the saintly Bartholomew into the saintly Robespierre, made no more change in the wind and weather than this constitution made or was supposed to make in bourgeois society."[186]

So closely did Marx associate the republic with being simply the political accompaniment of bourgeois society that he often used "republic" and "bourgeois republic" interchangeably. He argued that "the sole legitimate republic, is a republic which is no revolutionary weapon against the bourgeois order . . .

---

183. Ibid., 159 / 165.

184. While Marx tended to contrast "political" institutions or relations with "social" ones, in modern usage we would be more likely to refer to them as "economic." In an attempt at deference to both, I use the terms interchangeably and do the same with bourgeois "society" and bourgeois "economy."

185. Marx, *Die Klassenkämpfe in Frankreich*, MEGA I.10: 142 / MECW 10: 72.

186. Ibid., 146 / 77. The calendar divided the year into twelve months of thirty days each, replaced seven-day weeks with ten-day cycles, decimalized the day into ten hours with 100 decimal minutes and 100 decimal seconds, and began a new chronology so that 22 September 1792 (the founding of the First French Republic) became 1 Vendémiaire Year I. The calendar lasted until 1805 and was briefly revived during the Paris Commune in 1871. For an outline and analysis, see Eviatar Zerubavel, "The French Republican Calendar: A Case Study in the Sociology of Time," *American Sociological Review* 42, no. 6 (1977): 868–77.

in a word, *a bourgeois republic*" and that "the *republic is in general only the revolutionary destructive form of bourgeois society.*"[187] Conflating the republic with the bourgeois republic also served Marx's political purpose of highlighting what he took to be the emancipatory limits of republicanism (at least in its bourgeois form). Achieving the republic would, Marx stressed, not live up to the idealistic hopes of its supporters but instead cement the bourgeois transformation of society.

For Marx, no event captured this bourgeois nature of the republic, in the sense of establishing both the political and the economic rule of the bourgeoisie, more than the June Days. He bitterly commented that it would henceforth be more honest for the republic to replace its motto, "Liberté, Égalité, Fraternité, by the unambiguous words: Infantry, Cavalry, Artillery!"[188] The republic's unwillingness to countenance even the mild social reform of the National Workshops and the brutality with which it put down the resultant uprising were for him decisive evidence that the republic would always side with the interests of the bourgeoisie over the proletariat. He claimed (in terms exaggerated by this recent experience) that "the slightest improvement in its [the proletariat's] position remains a *utopia within* the bourgeois republic."[189] The only positive outcome of the June Days that Marx saw was that the "veil that shrouded the republic was torn asunder," revealing its underlying bourgeois nature and clarifying that the real struggle lay with the "preservation or annihilation of the *bourgeois* order."[190] He claimed that,

> The defeat of the June insurgents, to be sure, had indeed prepared and leveled the ground on which the bourgeois republic could be founded and built up, but it had shown at the same time that in Europe the questions at issue are other than that "of republic or monarchy." It has revealed that the *bourgeois republic* here means the unlimited, complete despotism of one class over other classes.[191]

Marx's deprecating reference to the question "of republic or monarchy" was a rebuke to European, and especially German, republicanism. The opening months of the revolution in Germany had seen an immense public debate over

187. Marx, *Die Klassenkämpfe in Frankreich, MEGA* I.10: 136 / *MECW* 10: 66; *Der achtzehnte Brumaire, MEGA* I.11: 106 / *MECW* 11: 111. Intriguingly, and for not entirely clear reasons, Marx amended *"revolutionary destructive form (revolutionäre Zerstorungsform)"* to *"political upheaval form (politische Umwälzungsform)"* in the 1869 edition of *Der achtzehnte Brumaire.*

188. Marx, *Der achtzehnte Brumaire, MEGA* I.11: 131 / *MECW* 11: 137.

189. Marx, *Die Klassenkämpfe in Frankreich, MEGA* I.10: 139 / *MECW* 10: 69.

190. Ibid., 137 / 67.

191. Marx, *Der achtzehnte Brumaire, MEGA* I.11: 105 / *MECW* 11: 111.

the Frankfurt National Assembly's choice between a republic and a constitutional monarchy. As one newspaper reported, "whether republic [or] whether constitutional monarchy is the better state form, is *discussed everywhere*: all our newspapers are taken up by this fight, all inns and public halls echo a thousandfold this war of words."[192] That debate was also carried out in a pamphlet war between liberals and republicans making their respective cases for a constitutional monarchy and a republic. For both sides, the question of monarchy or republic was the central and burning issue of political life.[193] Republicans declared that "The question: *whether monarchy? whether republic?* has become a vital question (*Lebensfrage*) in our great German fatherland" and that it was the "most important question of the present day."[194] Similarly, Julius Fröbel, the publisher of Marx and Ruge's *Deutsch-Französische Jahrbücher* and prominent republican member of the Frankfurt National Assembly, maintained that "The question: 'whether republic or monarchy?' is firstly a general question of foundational politics."[195] Marx's dismissive attitude to the question "of republic or monarchy" should thus be seen as a deliberate intervention into this debate. Marx was countering the centrality republicans accorded to the question of monarchy or republic by seriously downplaying the emancipatory potential of the republic and insisting that it would actually be a bourgeois republic. His intervention should not be confused with his saying that the question was irrelevant or that one should be indifferent to it (as was the position of antipolitical communists explored later in this chapter), but that it was being eclipsed by what he took to be the far more consequential question of capitalism or communism.

Marx's intervention, however, misrepresented the position of at least the more realist and radical republicans. Fröbel, for one, warned that the "German bourgeoisie" or "money-aristocracy" would try to establish a "capitalist-republic" and so supporters of "the *social republic*" had to "make sure that the huckster- and

---

192. *Augsburger Allgemeine Zeitung*, no. 174 (22 June 1848), cited in Wolfgang Mager, "Republik," in *Geschichtliche Grundbegriffe: Historisches Lexikon Zur Politisch-Sozialen Sprache in Deutschland*, ed. Otto Brunner, Werner Conze, and Reinhart Koselleck, vol. 5 (Stuttgart: Klett-Cotta, 1984), 634.

193. For liberal contributions, see Ludwig von Blum, *Monarchie und Republik: Ein Sendschreiben* (Erfurt: W. Müller'sche Sortiments Buchhandlung, 1848); F. W. Ghillany, *Republik oder Monarchie: Ein Vortrag . . .* (Nürnberg: Bauer und Raspe, 1848); and Carl Heimbach, *Deutsche Monarchie oder Republik?* (Jena: Carl Hochhausen, 1848). Ghillany's is of particular interest for its concise summation of the gamut of liberal objections to republicanism.

194. Respectively, Christian Schilbach, *Volksthümliche Belehrung über das Wesen der Monarchie und Republik* (Oelsnitz: Moritz Wieprecht, 1848), 11, and Julius Wulff, "Deutschland, eine constitutionelle Monarchie oder Republik?," in *!Republik!* (Mannheim: Heinrich Hoff, 1848), 3.

195. Julius Fröbel, *Monarchie oder Republik? Ein Urtheil* (Mannheim: Heinrich Hoff, 1848), 5.

money-changer aristocracy does not come to rule."[196] Fröbel's account of what the constitution of the republic should look like included a range of popular institutions (such as direct participation in primary assemblies) that were intended to maintain real democratic control and that significantly distinguished it from the constitution of the Second French Republic (and indeed that of most modern republics).[197] That was in turn tied to a comprehensive social program of reform (as laid out in chapter 5) that was supposed to flow from a properly democratic constitution. We therefore need to bear in mind that when Marx criticized republicans for failing to see that the republic would be a bourgeois republic, there was an underlying disagreement over what the "republic" entailed. Republicans, for the most part, endorsed a much more democratic constitution than the Constitution of the Republic that Marx took as emblematic of a bourgeois republic. That means that the experience of the Second French Republic and the June Days can provide only partial evidence for Marx's claim that the republic would be bourgeois.

That brings us to the third part of Marx's criticism of the bourgeois republic: his own account of its constitutional limitations. This is perhaps the most neglected aspect of Marx's critique. His account of what makes a republic bourgeois might easily be reduced to a claim about the bourgeoisie forming the governing political class or the republic being accompanied by a bourgeois economy. But Marx also made significant and extensive criticism of how the constitution of the bourgeois republic (and specifically that of the Second Republic) functioned to embed bourgeois rule and constrict popular power. The rest of this section is dedicated to unpacking that criticism and showing how (ironically) it owed much to republican constitutional thought.

Marx's constitutional criticism of the bourgeois republic focused particularly on its concentration of power in the executive at the expense of the legislature. He argued that the fatal flaw in the Second Republic's Constitution was its creation of a powerful president that enabled Louis Napoleon to overthrow the Republic from within. With a directly elected president independent of the legislature, Marx held that the Republic's Constitution simply replaced a "hereditary monarchy" with an "elective monarchy."[198] Returning to the criticism he had made in the *Kritik* of the arbitrary powers Hegel assigned to the monarch, Marx argued that the 1848 Constitution endowed the president

196. Ibid., 4, 10. Marx's and Fröbel's paths crossed during the revolution when they both spoke at the same meeting of the Democratic Club in Vienna on 28 August 1848. See the newspaper reports in *MEGA* I.7: 774.

197. Julius Fröbel, *Grundzüge zu einer Republikanischen Verfassung für Deutschland* (Mannheim: Heinrich Hoff, 1848), 4–6.

198. Marx, *Die Klassenkämpfe in Frankreich*, *MEGA* I.10: 146 / *MECW* 10: 77.

with "all the attributes of royal power," by giving him the right to appoint and dismiss ministers, pardon criminals, dismiss local and municipal councils, and initiate foreign treaties, and by putting him in charge of the armed forces and the state bureaucracy.[199] The Second Republic's Constitution was thus, according to Marx, little more than the "old monarchical machinery . . . with the royalist labels torn off and republican labels stuck on."[200]

A particular danger that Marx detected in a directly elected president was that their power is amplified by the personal nature of their office. He argued that it created a singular figure who towers over the state and appears as a recognizable and identifiable representative of the nation as a whole, in a way that a multimember legislature cannot compete with. He noted that in legislative elections the votes of the nation are "split up among the 750 National Assembly members," but with the presidential election they are "concentrated on one individual." He further claimed that legislators are viewed as only representing "this or that town" and elected out of the "mere necessity" of choosing somebody, in which "neither the cause nor the man is closely examined," whereas for the president "he is the elect of the nation and the act of his election is the trump that the sovereign people plays once every four years."[201] Marx consequently concluded that,

> The elected National Assembly stands in a metaphysical relation to the nation, but the elected president stands in a personal relation to it. The National Assembly, through its individual representatives, well exhibits the manifold aspects of the national spirit, but in the president the national spirit is incarnated. Against the Assembly, he possesses a sort of divine right; he is president by the grace of the people.[202]

Thus, for Marx, the direct election of the president gives him a personal mandate, which resembles a king's royal authority and can be wielded as a weapon against the legislature.

The second feature of the republic's president that Marx found so dangerous was that by putting him in charge of the state bureaucracy and the appointment of its officials, the Constitution had made a massive constituency dependent on him (he estimated France to have some 500,000 public officials as well as their 1,500,000 dependents). Throughout *Der achtzehnte Brumaire*, Marx expressed intense dislike of this bloated executive, in terms strongly

---

199. Marx, *Der achtzehnte Brumaire*, MEGA I.11: 110 / *MECW* 11: 116.
200. Marx, *Die Klassenkämpfe in Frankreich*, MEGA I.10: 146 / *MECW* 10: 77.
201. Marx, *Der achtzehnte Brumaire*, MEGA I.11: 111 / *MECW* 11: 117.
202. Ibid.

reminiscent of his criticisms of the Prussian bureaucracy in the *Kritik*. He condemned the "executive power with its enormous bureaucratic and military organization" as an "appalling parasitic body, which enmeshes the body of French society like a net and chokes all its pores." The state bureaucracy's modus operandi was, Marx claimed, to ignore the actual "*common* interests" of society and instead confront society with what the bureaucracy considers to be the "higher, *general*, interest," and so the administration of common activities and needs is "snatched from the self-activity of society's members and made an object of government activity."[203] In giving the president control of this heaving executive behemoth, as well as the armed forces, Marx argued that "the Constitution assigns actual power" to the president, while the National Assembly is assigned only "moral power."[204] He singled out the Constitution's specification that the president had the power to appoint ministers as a particular failing, with the result that the National Assembly "forfeits all real influence" over the various departments of the state bureaucracy.[205]

Marx thought that by setting up these two rival powers, the president and the National Assembly, the Constitution had created an inevitable destructive conflict between them. He argued that it reproduced the "division of powers" of the Charter of 1830 (the constitution of the July Monarchy), except that now it was "widen[ed] into an intolerable contradiction." The previous "*game of constitutional powers*" in the July Monarchy, where the Chamber of Deputies was repeatedly at odds with the king, now became a much deadlier one played "*va banque*" (staking one's all). That was because the president, by being constitutionally limited to a single four-year term, could only continue his rule past its legal limit by "setting aside the Constitution itself." The Constitution had thereby "challenged its forcible destruction" by giving an ambitious individual, like Louis Napoleon, both the means and the motivation to overthrow the Republic. This was, for Marx, the central weakness of the Constitution. It meant that the Republic was, Marx concludes, "like Achilles, vulnerable in one point, not in the heel, but in the head, or rather in the two heads in which it lost itself—the *legislative Assembly*, on the one hand, the *President*, on the other."[206]

Much of Marx's analysis of the struggle between the legislative and executive powers in the 1848 Constitution, including its vocabulary, was likely drawn from that of Félix Pyat, a journalist, playwright, and radical republican member of the Constituent Assembly (which preceded the National Assembly),

203. Ibid., 178–79 / 185–86.
204. Ibid., 111 / 116.
205. Ibid., 132 / 139.
206. Ibid., 110 / 115–16.

whom Marx had met during his stay in Paris in 1844.[207] During the constituent debates in the Assembly, Pyat took to the rostrum to deliver a vigorous and widely publicized denunciation of the proposed office of the president, arguing that he would be an "elective king" more dangerous than the "hereditary king" he replaced. He predicted that the July Monarchy's "complicated seesaw game" between the Chamber of Deputies and the king would be sharpened into an "inevitable duel" between the two constitutional powers. He instead proposed that "The legislative power must therefore completely dominate the executive power, on pain of the Republic also [like the constitutional monarchy] having two heads, that is to say all the struggles, all the conflicts, all the battles of the constitutional monarchies, with even more risks and perils for liberty."[208] Pyat was, however, immediately followed by Alexis de Tocqueville, one of the drafters of the proposed Constitution, who sprang to the defense of its separation of powers between the legislature and the executive through a president independent of the Assembly (an action Tocqueville later regretted).[209]

Both Pyat and Marx (likely under Pyat's influence) saw the 1848 Constitution as setting up a dangerous structure with "two heads" in conflict with each other, with the executive head dangerously powerful relative to the legislative one, to the extent that that the president resembled what they both described as an "elective" monarch.[210] Moreover, Pyat had given the same warning found in Marx's analysis that the personal nature of the president's office meant that he would be perceived as a better representative of the nation's will. A president, Pyat argued, "would tend to condense, to concentrate, to absorb all powers,

207. See Arnold Ruge to Hermann Köchly, 24 March 1844, *Redaktionsbriefwechsel*, 1347.

208. Félix Pyat, Speech to the National Assembly (5 October 1848), *Compte rendu des séances de l'Assemblée Nationale*, vol. 4 (Paris: Imprimerie de l'Assemblée Nationale, 1850), 651-652.

209. Alexis de Tocqueville, *Souvenirs*, in *Oeuvres complètes*, vol. 12 (Paris: Gallimard, 1964), 189/*Recollections: The French Revolution of 1848 and Its Aftermath*, ed. Olivier Zunz, trans. Arthur Goldhammer (Charlottesville: University of Virginia Press, 2016), 127. For this episode, see Eugene Newton Curtis, *The French Assembly of 1848 and American Constitutional Doctrines* (New York: Columbia University, 1918), 187–88.

210. Marx would likely have been aware of Pyat's speech since it was well publicized in the French radical press including on the front page of *La Réforme*, no. 277 (6 October 1848): 1, whose reporting Marx followed closely. His *Neue Rheinische Zeitung* also carried detailed reports from the Constituent Assembly and would presumably have reported Pyat's speech had it not been temporarily banned at the time (no issues appeared between 27 September and 12 October 1848). A subsequent speech by Pyat, for instance, was praised in the paper as "excellent"; see 'Französische Republik. Nationalversammlung vom 3. November,' *Neue Rheinische Zeitung*, no. 136 (7 November 1848): 4. Much later, Marx would criticize Pyat as an irresponsible provocateur for his call to assassinate Napoleon III in 1868 and moved for the General Council of the International Working Men's Association to censure him.

to represent, to personify, to incarnate the people."[211] Marx's concern with the split-up nature of representation in a multimember assembly in comparison to a single individual president can also be found in Pyat's speech. Pyat predicted that the future president would turn to the legislature and say, "Each of you was elected only by a department, not by France" and "you are in fact only nine hundredths of the people, I by myself am the whole people."[212]

Marx's and Pyat's criticisms of the president and their preference for the legislature place them in a tradition of radical constitutional thought that can be traced back to the Convention period of the French Revolution and the 1793 Jacobin Constitution. In this tradition, which is sometimes called "assembly government" (*gouvernement d'assemblée*), the "legislative assembly, popularly elected, holds undisputed supremacy over all other state organs" and "the executive is strictly subordinated, the servant or agent of the assembly and dismissed at the assembly's discretion."[213] Assembly government differs from regimes with a strict separation of powers—a constitutional doctrine that Marx heavily criticized. His hostility to the doctrine is succinctly expressed in a June 1851 article, "The Constitution of the French Republic, adopted November 5, 1848," for the Chartist journal *Notes to the People*, where Marx provided a detailed assessment of each article of the Constitution (which provided much of the basis for his subsequent constitutional criticisms in *Der achtzehnte Brumaire*). He particularly condemned Article 19, which specified that the "separation of powers is the first principle of a free government." In response, Marx commented, "Here we have the old constitutional folly. The condition of a 'free government' is not the *division*, but the UNITY of power. The machinery of government cannot be too simple. It is always the craft of knaves to make it complicated and mysterious."[214]

Read in isolation this passage can have an alarmingly authoritarian quality, with its seeming endorsement of concentrating power in a single body.[215] But Marx's position was not that there should be no competing or balancing sources of power (he held, for instance, that it was important for "civil society and public opinion to create organs of their own, independent of the

---

211. Pyat, Speech to the National Assembly, 652.

212. Ibid. The 900 refers to the number of deputies in the Constituent Assembly, whereas the 750, referenced by Marx, refers to the number of representatives in the National Assembly.

213. Karl Loewenstein, *Political Power and the Governmental Process* (Chicago: University of Chicago Press, 1957), 81.

214. Marx, "The Constitution of the French Republic adopted November 4, 1848," *MEGA* I.10: 540 / *MECW* 10: 570.

215. This is a general concern with assembly government. Loewenstein condemns it as both "'monolithic' in the extreme" and (revealingly) "arch-democratic, arch-republican"; see *Political Power and the Governmental Process*, 81.

government power").[216] His actual criticism of the separation of powers was that it wrongly concentrated power in the executive at the expense of the legislature. That in turn was grounded in a concern that executive power has a tendency toward independence that escapes the people's control. He argued, for instance, that the "executive power, in contrast to the legislative, expresses the heteronomy of the nation, in contrast to its autonomy."[217] That criticism of the separation of powers was in fact precisely what the doctrine's founding defenders praised about it. Maurice Vile, in his classic study of the separation of powers, writes that the doctrine's founders "assume[d] that the legislature will, or may, be taken over entirely by the democratic element" and that therefore power had to be dispersed to "branches of the government largely or wholly outside the legislature."[218] While the separation of powers is today considered one of the cornerstones of democratic government, its founders explicitly believed that it would serve to limit the democratic influence on the constitution. That is why radical republicans, like Pyat, thought it so essential that the executive should be subordinated to the legislative.[219] Like Marx, Pyat defended what he called the "unity of government," which for Pyat meant that the legislature "appoints" the executive, which has a "simple chairman of the council" rather than an independent and powerful president.[220] Marx's strongly worded criticism of the separation of powers was thus grounded in this radical republican tradition of ensuring that the executive is under the control and supervision of the most democratic branch of government, the legislature.[221]

Marx's critique of the separation of powers in his article is also usefully read in its immediate British context, with his language likely inspired by his interaction with his friend Ernest Jones—and specifically an article Jones had

216. Marx, *Der achtzehnte Brumaire*, MEGA I.11: 132 / MECW 11: 139. This is one of the rare cases, outside of Marx's early writings, where "civil society" is the more appropriate translation of "*bürgerliche Gesellschaft*" than "bourgeois society."

217. Ibid., 178 / 185.

218. M. J. C. Vile, *Constitutionalism and the Separation of Powers* (Oxford: Clarendon Press, 1967), 33.

219. For French radical republican opposition to the office of the President, see Samuel Hayat, "Running in Protest: The Impossible Candidacy of François-Vincent Raispail, December 1848," *Revue Française de Science Politique* 64, no. 5 (2014): 9–11. In the German context, see Arnold Ruge, "Motiviertes Manifest der radikal-demokratischen Partei . . . ," *Briefe und Werke*, 7: 185.

220. Pyat, Speech to the National Assembly, 652.

221. Richard Hunt argues that Marx can be seen as simply deepening a commitment to ministerial responsibility and the "standard European practice of parliamentary rule" in contrast to the kind of extreme separation of powers found in the American Constitution, in Richard N. Hunt, *The Political Ideas of Marx and Engels*, vol. 2 (Pittsburgh: University of Pittsburgh Press, 1984), 144.

written a few weeks before Marx's in the same journal, Jones's *Notes to the People*. Jones was one of the most prominent Chartists in the 1850s and at the forefront of trying to weld a socialist program to the political demands of the Charter (encapsulated by his advice that the "Cap of Liberty" needed "THE BIG LOAF" beside it).[222] Jones and Marx had first met in 1847 in London when they spoke at a meeting organized by the Fraternal Democrats, and they became close once Marx moved to the city, beginning a period of mutual intellectual influence.[223] When Jones launched *Notes to the People* in May 1851, Marx eagerly assisted with the project, helping with some of Jones's articles and contributing his own, including the article on the 1848 French Constitution.[224] Running alongside Marx's article, Jones published his own piece exploring the history of renaissance Florence, including its constitutional structure, and he there made the strikingly similar point to Marx that,

> One mistake, of which the Florentines were guilty, deserves especial notice: they sought safety in a complicated machinery of government, in the famous system of "check and countercheck"; now the fact is government cannot be too simple. If government is *good*, the fewer checks it has in its progress the better; if it is bad, the more complicated its machinery is, the greater is the difficulty in removing or amending it.[225]

Both Jones and Marx thus argue that "government cannot be too simple" and criticize constitutions that make the "machinery of government . . . complicated."[226] Marx's criticism is directed at the separation of powers, while

222. Ernest Jones, "An Address to the People," *The Northern Star*, vol. 13, no. 668 (10 August 1850): 1; see John Saville, *Ernest Jones: Chartist. Selections from the Writings and Speeches of Ernest Jones* (London: Lawrence & Wishart, 1952), 37–43. See further Miles Taylor, *Ernest Jones, Chartism, and the Romance of Politics 1819–1869* (Oxford: Oxford University Press, 2003).

223. For Jones's less-appreciated influence on Marx, see Thierry Drapeau, "'Look at Our Colonial Struggles': Ernest Jones and the Anti-Colonialist Challenge to Marx's Conception of History," *Critical Sociology* 45, no. 7–8 (2019): 1195–1208.

224. For Marx and Engels's contributions to the *Notes to the People* and Jones's subsequent *The People's Paper*, see the discussion in *MEGA* I.10: 705–707 and I.11: 582–92.

225. Ernest Jones, "History of Florence," *Notes to the People*, no. 4 (24 May 1851): 80. Jones's history interestingly hits a number of republican notes; he claimed that *"wherever she [Florence] was free, she was always found constant in the road of virtue"* and that the city's interspersed periods of republican and Medici rule "contrast the greatness of liberty with the effects of servitude"; ibid., 60, 196.

226. The direction of influence is difficult to establish. While Marx would have seen Jones's article before writing his article (the relevant section appeared three weeks before Marx's), it also possible that they arrived at the similar language and analysis together through their frequent personal interactions. For the relevant correspondence, see Ernest Jones to Marx, 23 May and 30 May 1851, *MEGA* III.4: 382, 390.

Jones's is directed at the closely associated, though distinct, system of checks and balances (Marx seems not to have distinguished between these doctrines).[227] For both, the preference for "simple" government springs from their opposition to "complicated" constitutional designs deliberately set up to thwart the democratic will. Their view can be contrasted with the contemporaneous judgment of Alexis de Tocqueville. Drawing on the American experience of the Senate checking the lower house, he unsuccessfully argued for a bicameral legislature in the 1848 French Constitution because he preferred a "somewhat complicated system of checks and balances" to a "simpler theory, bestowing undivided power on a homogenous authority . . . [with] no barriers to its actions."[228]

The rhetorical contrast between "simple" and "complicated" government and the underlying conflicting doctrines has a long history in constitutional thought.[229] A similar divide can be found during the American constitutional debates, with Anti-Federalists advocating a simple constitution that could be easily understood by everyone against the Federalists' complex system of checks and balances, which the Anti-Federalists suspected would limit democratic accountability.[230] Indeed, the Federalists specifically designed these checks and balances with the aim of delaying and cooling the expression of the popular will through the legislature.[231] They believed that the "greatest danger" to representative government was that the "legislature will acquire the

227. The "pure doctrine" of the separation of powers holds that government should be split into three branches, legislative, executive, and judicial, with each branch having a single corresponding function and a complete separation of persons between branches. The theory of checks and balances adds to this that each branch should also have a limited power to intervene in the other branch's functions. See Vile, *Constitutionalism and the Separation of Powers*, 13, 18.

228. Tocqueville, *Souvenirs*, 184–85/*Recollections*, 123; and see Aurelian Craiutu and Jeremy Jennings, "The Third *Democracy*: Tocqueville's Views of America after 1840," in *Tocqueville on America after 1840: Letters and Other Writings* (Cambridge: Cambridge University Press, 2009), 23–25.

229. In the 1793 French constitutional debates, for instance, Condorcet defended legislative supremacy over the executive and critiqued the "complicated machines" of regimes with a separation of powers and bicameral legislatures; see his "Plan de constitution, présenté à la convention nationale . . . ," in *Oeuvres complètes*, vol. 18 (Paris: Heinrichs, 1804), 185 / "A Survey of the Principles underlying the Draft Constitution," in *Condorcet: Foundations of Social Choice and Political Theory*, ed. and trans. Iain McLean and Fiona Hewitt (Aldershot: Edward Elgar, 1994), 199.

230. Herbert J. Storing, *What the Anti-Federalists Were For: The Political Thought of the Opponents of the Constitution* (Chicago: University of Chicago Press, 1981), 53–63.

231. Bernard Manin, "Checks, Balances and Boundaries: The Separation of Powers in the Constitutional Debate of 1787," in *The Invention of the Modern Republic*, ed. Biancamaria Fontana (Cambridge: Cambridge University Press, 1994), 59–61.

defects of a popular assembly," and that power must therefore not only be dispersed to other branches but those branches must also have the power to intervene in its operation.[232] Presidential veto power, judicial review by the Supreme Court, and the balancing power of the aristocratic Senate were thus all incorporated into the Constitution in order to limit the power of what was taken to be the more democratic element of the Constitution: the House of Representatives. Alexander Hamilton boasted that this system "is so complex, so skilfully contrived, that it is next to impossible that an impolitic or wicked measure should pass the scrutiny with success."[233]

The Anti-Federalists rejected these aristocratic and antimajoritarian checks on the legislature, and instead favored a clearly delineated and transparent constitution, where (similarly to Marx) the legislature was superior to the other branches, since they believed it to be "more representative of the people in their diversity than the President, and more accountable to them than the judges."[234] One of the many anonymous Anti-Federalists compared the virtue of transparent and simple forms of government to the "mechanic" who "understands the machinery" he works with because he can see through its entire operation, and he concluded that the "constitution of a wise and free people, ought to be as evident to simple reason, as the letters of our alphabet."[235] Marx's own characterization of "complicated and mysterious" government as the "craft of knaves" can be seen as an echo of this older radical republican constitutionalism.

A final aspect of Marx's constitutional critique of the bourgeois republic, at least in its particular instantiation in the 1848 French Constitution, deserves comment: his argument that it failed to properly extend its own vaunted rights to the working class. Paying close attention to the wording of each of the Constitution's articles that guaranteed rights to the French people, Marx highlighted how each of them allowed for the right to be limited either by the requirements of "public order" or by subsequent laws to regulate their exercise. The effect of this loophole, Marx argued, was to deny the working class the actual enjoyment of those rights. The promised freedom of the press was, for instance, Marx

---

232. David Wootton, "Liberty, Metaphor, and Mechanism: 'Checks and Balances' and the Origins of Modern Constitutionalism," in *Liberty and American Experience in the Eighteenth Century*, ed. David Womersley (Indianapolis: Liberty Fund, 2006), 264.

233. Cited in Storing, *What the Anti-Federalists Were For*, 54.

234. Manin, "Checks, Balances and Boundaries," 40–41. Where Marx's thought does differ from the Anti-Federalist position (but not most French radical republican thought) is his preference for the legislature to exercise both legislative and executive functions, which the Anti-Federalists would have opposed because of their "one branch, one function" doctrine.

235. [Anon], "Address by Denatus," in *The Complete Anti-Federalist*, vol. 5 (Chicago: University of Chicago Press, 1981), 262.

argued, subsequently limited by the requirement for onerous securities and stamp taxes with exorbitant fines for noncompliance, and since the "middle-class sat in the jury-box" to adjudicate these breaches "they crushed the working man's press." The guarantee of freedom of association was undermined by a decree subjecting meetings to police regulations, which meant associations were denied "almost every liberty" and subjected to the "caprice of the police." A further law banned workers from unionizing to raise wages; Marx thus concluded, "So much for the right of association and of public meeting."[236] The Constitution's protection of the right to male suffrage was undermined by the infamous electoral law of 31 May 1850 that further tightened residency requirements, with the result that "TWO-THIRDS of the French people are [rendered] incapable of voting!"[237] The right to trial by jury was similarly undermined by a literacy requirement for jurors "thus disqualifying two-thirds of the adult population!"[238] Finally, full freedom of movement and occupation was denied to workers by a law making it necessary for workers to show a pass with their details to their employer, which was then deposited with the police. The police controlled access to this pass—if a worker wanted to change their employer, and the police found the worker "obnoxious," they could send the worker back to their home district, leaving workers "utterly dependent on the police."[239] The sum total of these exclusions was that the bourgeoisie dominated the working class through their parliament, courts, and police, in what Marx calls a "dreadful despotism" where their "liberty has been trafficked away."[240]

Thus, in Marx's assessment, France's 1848 Constitution had pulled off the "trick of granting full liberty" on paper but was denying the working class those liberties in practice.[241] In Hauke Brunkhorst's neat summary, Marx's analysis

236. Marx, "The Constitution of the French Republic adopted November 4, 1848," *MEGA* I.10: 539 / *MECW* 10: 569.

237. Ibid., 541 / 571. The electoral law reduced the voting population by one-third, from roughly 9,600,000 to 6,800,000 men; see Agulhon, *The Republican Experiment*, 126. Marx's claim that it left "TWO-THIRDS of the French people" disenfranchised only makes sense if he is comparing it to the total adult population of France, which was around 20 million people at the time (as 6,800,000 is roughly one-third of this total). Assuming that Marx was not confused about the actual underlying figures, he would thus seem to be displaying a rare awareness of the fact that the female half of the "French people" was also excluded from the supposedly "universal" franchise.

238. Marx, "The Constitution of the French Republic adopted November 4, 1848," *MEGA* I.10: 544 / *MECW* 10: 576.

239. Ibid., 546 / 578.

240. Ibid., 546 / 579.

241. Ibid., 545 / 577.

shows how "politically inclusive constitutional law becomes a socially exclusive instrument of bourgeois class rule."[242] For Marx, this was one more way in which the constitution of the bourgeois republic could entrench the bourgeoisie's political and economic rule, in this case by doing its utmost to restrict the working class's access to the political and civic rights that would contest bourgeois power. In this, Marx saw a more general lesson for the democratic pretensions of the bourgeoisie and their bourgeois republic (or, as he referred to it for his English readers, "the REPUBLIC of the MIDDLE-CLASS"):

> The eternal contradictions of this Constitution of Humbug, show plainly enough, that the middle-class can be democratic in *words*, but will not be so in deeds—they will recognise the truth of a principle, but never carry it into practice . . . The *principles* were there—the *details* were left to the future, and in those details a shameless tyranny was reenacted![243]

The Necessity of the Bourgeois Republic

Marx's condemnation of the republic as a bourgeois republic was a staple of socialist arguments. Otto Lüning spoke for many when he claimed that a "republic . . . leads to the rule of money, of the selfish bourgeoisie."[244] As we showed in the opening section of this chapter, what distinguished Marx from so many other schools of early socialism was his insistence that though the bourgeois republic was insufficient for emancipation, it was a necessary step toward it. Marx was consequently always careful that even his harshest condemnation of the bourgeois republic was not misread as an argument that "the struggle over the form of the state is meaningless, illusory and futile" and to stress that the republic remained the "best form of state" in which to carry out the struggle for communism.[245]

Gareth Stedman Jones has maintained, however, that Marx's attacks on the republic exposed republicans to the same antipolitical arguments made by Karl Grün and true socialists, while at the same time never providing a "satisfactory" answer to the questions: "If the workers were crushed by a democratic republic based on manhood suffrage, if democracy did not provide a solution to the social question, then why fight for the attainment of a republic?" He

242. Hauke Brunkhorst, "Kommentar," in *Der achtzehnte Brumaire des Louis Bonaparte*, by Karl Marx (Frankfurt: Suhrkamp, 2007), 252n92.

243. Marx, "The Constitution of the French Republic adopted November 4, 1848," *MEGA* I.10: 546 / *MECW* 10: 578.

244. Lüning, "Politik und Sozialismus," 7.

245. Marx, "Die Junirevolution," *MEGA* I.7: 211 / *MECW* 7: 149.

judges Marx's attempt to do so "contradictory" and marked by "bluster" and "incoherence."[246] Stedman Jones provides little supporting argument or evidence for this judgment, but traces the tensions in Marx's account to his supposed general "hostility towards the modern representative state" and "consequent belittlement of the significance of manhood suffrage and the democratic republic."[247] In light of this criticism, this section will provide a detailed reconstruction of Marx's account of the necessity of the bourgeois republic, dividing it into (1) economic, (2) ideological, and (3) political considerations. Marx's account was certainly not free from tension but deserves proper study for what it reveals about the complicated relationship between socialism and politics. Contrary to Stedman Jones's position, I suggest that Marx's account in fact placed too much faith in the transformative potential of representative government and universal (manhood) suffrage.

Perhaps the most familiar argument Marx makes for the necessity of the bourgeois republic is the tight connection he drew between its institution and the completion of the *economic* rule of the bourgeoisie. He maintained that the bourgeoisie would use their newfound hold over the state to drive forward the development of capitalism by sweeping away the last feudal fetters on the economy. That in turn would have the unintended consequence of also driving forward the development of the proletariat. Since the development of the proletariat is an essential condition for the institution of communism, the bourgeois republic becomes a necessary condition in that larger process. As Marx argued in 1847, workers should "prefer" the "*direct bourgeois rule*" to that of the "*absolute monarchy*," because the bourgeoisie "in the service of their trade and industry, will call forth, against their will, the conditions for the uniting of the working class, and the uniting of the workers is the first requirement for their victory." Assisting the bourgeoisie in the creation of a bourgeois republic against the feudal forces of the absolute monarchy thus "accelerates" the eventual achievement of the workers' "own revolutionary movement."[248] The argument was closely tied to the conclusions Marx and Engels had drawn from the development of their materialist conception of history in the years before 1848. Communism could only come about through the prior development of capitalism, and since the bourgeois republic was a key component in the development of capitalism, communists had a historical materialist reason to support a bourgeois republic.

This short sketch does not, of course, do justice to a sophisticated philosophy of historical and social change. But an immediate problem that Marx faced

---

246. Gareth Stedman Jones, *Karl Marx: Greatness and Illusion* (London: Allen Lane, 2016), 271.

247. Ibid., 307.

248. Marx, "Die moralisierende Kritik und die kritisierende Moral: Beitrag zur deutschen Kulturgeschichte gegen Karl Heinzen," *MEW* 4: 352 / *MECW* 6: 332.

when making this argument in the heat of the revolutionary moment was precisely that it had little appeal for those who were unfamiliar with or denied the
underlying theory. The idea of fighting for a republic that would necessarily
involve a period of subordination to capitalist rule was a hard pill for workers
to swallow. Marx discovered this when he restated the argument in January 1849 in the pages of the *Neue Rheinische Zeitung*:

> But we say to the workers and the petty bourgeois: it is better to suffer in
> modern bourgeois society, which through its industry creates the material
> means for the foundation of a new society that will liberate you all, than to
> revert to a bygone form of society, which, on the pretext of saving your
> classes, thrusts the entire nation back into medieval barbarism![249]

That led to a swift and vicious intervention from his old foe Andreas Gottschalk in the workers' newspaper, *Freiheit, Arbeit* (*Freedom, Labor*):

> Why a revolution? Why should we, men of the proletariat, spill our blood?
> Must we really, as you, Mr Preacher, proclaim to us, escape the hell of the
> Middle Ages by throwing ourselves into the purgatory of a decrepit capitalist
> rule, in order to from there reach the cloudy heaven of your "communist
> credo"?[250]

Gottschalk thereby encapsulated the widespread skepticism toward the need
for a "purgatory of decrepit capitalist rule" and the political difficulties of making the economic argument for the necessity of a republic.

But Marx did not think that economic reasons exhausted the case for a
bourgeois republic. He also thought that the bourgeois republic would have
the *ideological* advantage of laying bare the class struggle between capitalists
and proletarians. Marx thought that the political inequality of nonrepublican
regimes masked their society's class differences and struggles. He argued that
the expansion of political equality had shown that social questions come to
the fore in a "constitutional monarchy more glaringly than in an absolute
monarchy, in a republic more glaringly than in a constitutional monarchy,"
and nowhere "does *social* inequality obtrude itself more harshly than in the
eastern states of North America, because nowhere is it less disguised by
political inequality."[251] Marx thought that monarchies were better at hiding
the underlying social oppression of capitalism, whereas "the republic has
bared the head of the monster by knocking off the crown which shielded and

249. Marx, "Montesquieu, LXI," *MEGA* I.8: 323–24 / *MECW* 8: 266.

250. [Andreas Gottschalk], "An Herrn Karl Marx, Redakteur der Neuen Rheinischen Zeitung," *Freiheit, Arbeit*, no. 13 (25 February 1849): 2.

251. Marx, "Die moralisierende Kritik," *MEW* 4: 342 / *MECW* 6: 323.

concealed it."[252] Monarchs were "the last feudal halo that hid the rule of the bourgeois class," and had the useful feature of providing the bourgeoisie with a "crowned scapegoat" for their own failings and a "lightning rod" for the people's anger.[253] A monarchy thus, through its protective smokescreen of feudal hangovers, shielded the bourgeoisie from direct criticism, but in a "republic . . . they must now confront the subjugated classes and contend without mediation, without the concealment afforded by the crown."[254]

Marx thought that the relative ideological transparency of the bourgeois republic was complemented by a broader ideological shift in society that challenged traditional justifications of authority. In a perhaps surprising passage celebrating democratic deliberation in a republic, Marx argues that the "debating club in parliament is necessarily supplemented by debating clubs in the salons and alehouses," and since parliament "leaves everything to the decision of majorities; how shall the great majorities outside parliament not want to decide?" In this new liberating democratic atmosphere, "Every interest, every social institution is here transformed into general ideas, debated as ideas," and once every aspect of political and social life is open to critique and must justify itself, Marx asks, "how shall any interest, any institution, sustain itself above thought and impose itself as an article of faith?"[255] (This was a justification Marx and Engels continued to emphasize, arguing twenty years later that the "republic means breaking with the entire political tradition; because in it every political institution is faced with the demand to prove its right to existence, because therefore all the traditional influences that support the powers that be under the monarchy fall away.")[256]

Marx thought that this ideological opening was made possible by the *political* changes in a republic, particularly the introduction of civic freedoms for all. As we saw in the previous section, Marx was critical of the way in which the French Republic's 1848 Constitution had surreptitiously undermined the actual exercise of these rights by the working class. But he remained convinced that these rights were in general worth fighting for. Marx emphasized that freedom of the press and freedom of association would mean that communists

---

252. Marx, "Die Junirevolution," *MEGA* I.7: 209 / *MECW* 7: 147. He similarly writes, "Under Louis Philippe the privileged part of the crown concealed its rule under the crown; in the parliamentary republic the rule of the bourgeoisie showed . . . its naked head." Marx, *Der achtzehnte Brumaire, MEGA* I.11: 176 / *MECW* 11: 183.

253. Marx, "Die Pariser 'Reforme' über die französischen Züstande," *MEGA* I.8: 56 / *MECW* 7: 494.

254. Marx, *Der achtzehnte Brumaire, MEGA* I.11: 123 / *MECW* 11: 129.

255. Ibid., 135 / 142.

256. Marx and Engels, "Die Republik in Spanien," *MEGA* I.24: 131-32 / *MECW* 23: 419.

would no longer have to organize in clandestine conspiratorial societies and publish in underground presses or dance around government censorship but could instead openly form parties and trade unions and publish their own newspapers. Marx positively compared the situation in America, England, and France to that in the German states, arguing that in the former the proletariat was able to reach "the status of a recognized party" by "utilizing the freedom of the press and the freedom of association," and he picked out the "English and French working men's newspapers" and "Chartist meeting[s]" for particular praise.[257] Marx observed that since these civic rights had originally been championed by the bourgeoisie in their fight against feudalism and absolutism, there was a certain pleasing irony that they would eventually be used by the proletariat against the bourgeoisie. He wrote that the bourgeoisie finds "that all the weapons which it had forged against feudalism turned their points against itself ... [as] the so-called bourgeois freedoms (*bürgerlichen Freiheiten*) and organs of progress attacked and menaced its *class rule*."[258]

In addition to civic freedoms, the other key political institution of the bourgeois republic that Marx saw as a critical weapon in the struggle for communism was manhood suffrage (which he refers to as "universal" suffrage). Though universal (manhood) suffrage might initially lead to the rule of the bourgeoisie (as it had in the Second Republic), Marx was confident that its introduction would eventually lead to the working class coming to political power, especially once it had become the majority of the population and properly organized itself. That was particularly pronounced in his and Engels's lavish praise of Chartism. We saw in chapter 3 that in 1846 they had already aligned themselves with its goal of "a democratic reconstruction of the Constitution upon the basis of the People's Charter," by which the working class "will become the ruling class of England" (here as elsewhere they use "England" as equivalent with "Britain").[259] That enthusiasm continued once they were both exiled to Britain. Marx argued that since "the proletariat forms the large majority of the population ... Universal Suffrage is the equivalent for political power for

257. Marx, "Der Kommunismus des 'Rheinischen Beobachters,'" *MEW* 4: 193–94 / *MECW* 6: 222–25.

258. Marx, *Der achtzehnte Brumaire*, *MEGA* I.11: 135 / *MECW* 11: 142. This echoes the more famous economic irony highlighted in the *Manifest*, where Marx and Engels argue that the restless internal drive of capital results in crises that will eventually destroy it, so that the "weapons with which the bourgeoisie felled feudalism to the ground are now turned against the bourgeoisie itself"; Marx and Engels, *Manifest der Kommunistischen Partei*, *MEW* 4: 468 / *MECW* 6: 490.

259. Marx and Engels, "Address of the German Democratic Communists of Brussels to Mr. Feargus O'Connor," *MEW* 4: 24 / *MECW* 6: 58.

the working class of England."[260] Marx is so sure of this consequence that he asserts that universal suffrage's "inevitable result, here is *the political supremacy of the working class*." He places such importance on this political goal that he even holds that achieving universal suffrage would "be a far more socialistic measure than anything which has been honoured with that name on the Continent."[261] Engels similarly proclaimed that the English working class had no "*guarantee for bettering their social position unless by Universal Suffrage*, which would enable them to seat a *Majority of Working Men* in the House of Commons."[262]

Marx and Engels's confidence in universal (manhood) suffrage similarly extended to France (though its less advanced class composition meant they thought that universal suffrage would initially bring a broader popular coalition of proletarians, peasants, and petty bourgeoisie to power). Particularly emblematic for them were the important by-elections of 10 March 1850, in which left-wing Montagnard candidates won several important victories despite repressive measures against them. Marx and Engels saw the elections as a prime example of how universal (manhood) suffrage would necessarily lead to a continual expansion of political power for the left. Engels argued that it showed "the vast mass of the people every day organising themselves stronger and stronger into an invincible phalanx."[263] For Marx, it was concrete evidence of universal suffrage's power to disrupt and threaten bourgeois interests:

> Universal suffrage, by constantly putting an end to the existing state power and creating it anew out of itself, does it not put an end to all stability, does it not at every moment question all the powers that be, does it not annihilate authority, does it not threaten to elevate anarchy itself to the position of authority? After 10 March 1850, who would still doubt it?[264]

The 10 March elections were indeed a severe political shock to the party of order, who concluded that the Second Republic's brief experiment with universal (manhood) suffrage was too dangerous to continue. They introduced a number of technical measures on 31 May 1850 that effectively excluded much of the working class and limited the franchise to two-thirds of its previous size.[265] Marx saw in this further confirmation of the threat universal (manhood) suffrage posed to the bourgeoisie, commenting that on "March 10 universal

---

260. Marx, "The Chartists," *MEGA* I:11: 327 / *MECW* 11: 335–36. Marx includes rural "hired laborers" in the proletariat, making the claim about the majority of the population more plausible.
261. Ibid.
262. Engels, "The Ten Hours' Question," *MEGA* I.10: 229 / *MECW* 10: 275.
263. Engels, "Letter from France IV," *MEGA* I.10: 252 / *MECW* 10: 28.
264. Marx, *Die Klassenkämpfe in Frankreich*, *MEGA* I.10: 195 / *MECW* I.10: 131.
265. Agulhon, *The Republican Experiment*, 125–26.

suffrage declared itself directly against the rule of the bourgeoisie; the bourgeoisie answered by outlawing universal suffrage."[266] The experience had shown that though "[b]ourgeois rule as the outcome and result of universal suffrage . . . is the meaning of the bourgeois constitution," their democratic commitment crumbles the "moment that the content of this suffrage, of this sovereign will, is no longer bourgeois rule."[267]

For Marx, the bourgeoisie's retreat from universal (manhood) suffrage captured the central tension of the bourgeois republic—that it tried to reconcile political equality with social inequality, i.e., representative democracy in the political sphere and capitalism in the economic. In a striking and underappreciated passage in *Die Klassenkämpfe in Frankreich*, he argued that,

> The fundamental contradiction of this constitution [the bourgeois republic], however, consists in the following: the classes whose social slavery the constitution is to perpetuate, proletariat, peasantry, petty bourgeoisie, it puts in possession of the political power through universal suffrage. And from the class whose old social power it sanctions, the bourgeoisie, it withdraws the political guarantees of this power. It forces the political rule of the bourgeoisie into democratic conditions, which at every moment help the hostile classes to victory and jeopardize the very foundations of bourgeois society. From the ones it demands that they should not go forward from political to social emancipation; from the others that they should not go back from social to political restoration.[268]

Marx believed that this political tension, combined with the ideological factors outlined above, explained a curious fact about the bourgeoisie and the bourgeois republic. Though "the republican form makes their political rule complete" and is even the "the most powerful and most complete form of their *class rule*," the bourgeoisie is reluctant to embrace it and actually "yearns for the former more incomplete, more undeveloped and precisely on that account less dangerous forms of rule" embodied in monarchical regimes.[269] On Marx's account, the bourgeoisie correctly sense that the bourgeois republic places

266. Marx, *Der achtzehnte Brumaire*, MEGA I.11: 139 / *MECW* 11: 146.

267. Marx, *Die Klassenkämpfe in Frankreich*, MEGA I.10: 195 / *MECW* 10: 130-31.

268. Ibid., 148 / 79. For the wider history of this relationship and Marx's place in it, see Maximilian Krahé, "Changing Accounts of the Relationship between Capitalism and Democracy: From Incompatibility to Partnership, and Back?," *History of Political Thought* 43, no. 1 (2022): 161-98.

269. Marx, *Die Klassenkämpfe in Frankreich*, MEGA I.10: 196 / *MECW* 10: 131; Marx, *Der achtzehnte Brumaire*, MEGA I.11: 123 / *MECW* 11: 129.

them in dangerous ideological and democratic terrain, where they will continually have to justify and defend their power.

Marx's account of the ideological and political advantages to the working class of the bourgeois republic's civic freedoms and democratic suffrage is an important counter to some of the tired antidemocratic stereotypes of Marx's thought. Marx was evidently supportive of their introduction and very optimistic about their eventual consequences. The irony is that Marx may in fact have been too optimistic. More extensive experience with bourgeois republics than Marx had access to produces a less encouraging picture. On the ideological front, Marx certainly makes a plausible case that a republic would sweep away some of the ideological protection provided by a monarchy. But he also underestimates the degree to which bourgeois republics could and would develop their own ideological safeguards. The removal of formal political and legal inequalities might help focus struggle on continuing social inequalities, but it can also make those social inequalities appear to be the result of individual talent and effort. Generations of twentieth-century Marxists have, of course, traced the myriad ways in which ideological legitimation and pacification in bourgeois republics is maintained through the cultural sphere. Moreover, the political structures of a republic can themselves provide a useful ideological shield, particularly the status that comes from being a regime elected by the people. As Maurice Agulhon has argued, Marx's belief that a republic would avoid the mystification of a monarchy by being a "depersonalised system of political relations . . . [and so] perfectly transparent in the matter of class relations," failed to see that "the Republic was not nearly as drily abstract as it appeared . . . but, on the contrary, was well and truly an idealism itself."[270]

The ideological sanction that universal suffrage provides to bourgeois republican regimes is one part of the explanation for their longevity and the failure of Marx and Engels's repeated prediction that, as Engels put it, "democracy has as its necessary consequence the political rule of the proletariat."[271] The sheer confidence of these predictions is striking. While Marx may have thought himself free from the supposed delusions of "republicans of the old school" who thought "universal suffrage . . . was a miracle-working divining rod," his own account undeniably carried a heavy dose of optimism.[272] To repeat just some of the descriptions given above, Marx claims that universal (manhood) suffrage's "inevitable result . . . is the political supremacy of the working class," that it "put[s] an end to all stability . . . question[s] all the powers that be . . . [and] annihilate[s]

270. Agulhon, *The Republican Experiment*, 191.

271. Engels, "Die Kommunisten und Karl Heinzen," *MEW* 4: 317 / *MECW* 6: 299.

272. Marx, *Die Klassenkämpfe in Frankreich, MEGA* I.10: 135 / *MECW* 10: 65.

authority," and "at every moment help[s] the hostile classes to victory and jeopardize[s] the very foundations of bourgeois society." At most, Marx thought there might be "various fluctuations" before the "compass needle" of universal suffrage "finally points to the class that is called to rule."[273] The record of universal suffrage in bourgeois republics has not been kind to these characterizations. Some elections have certainly had the kind of disruptive power Marx attributed to them, but these have been the exception compared to the overwhelming tendency of being peaceful endorsements of the existing order. Nor has the expectation aged well that a growing proletarian population would have an almost geometric relationship to the growth of a proletarian party in parliament.

The potential causes of this disappointment are too numerous to satisfactorily engage with here. But one of particular relevance to the overall trajectory of Marx's political thought is his largely uncritical view of representative institutions in this period. As we saw in chapters 1 and 2, in his early journalism and critique of Hegel, he had specified that if representatives were actually to represent the general interest they had to be tightly controlled by instructions and supplemented by participatory mechanisms in the wider administrative structure of the polity. As we will see in chapter 7, he returned to those views once confronted by the Paris Commune. But at the time of the 1848 Revolution, he held a much more sanguine view of representation once it was underpinned by universal (manhood) suffrage. Marx's statement that the bourgeois republic "puts [the popular classes] in possession of the political power through universal suffrage" is typical in assuming that universal (manhood) suffrage was tantamount to political rule.[274] Hardly anywhere does he consider the possibility that merely extending the franchise might not be sufficient to ensure this goal or that unconstrained representation could inhibit the growth and exercise of popular power.

The lone exception to this view is an interesting but brief aside from Marx that universal suffrage must be accompanied by "the conditions without which Universal Suffrage would be illusory for the working class; such as the [secret] ballot, payment of members, annual general elections."[275] This passing endorsement of the Chartist demand for annual parliaments (still the only one of the movements' six demands not to be instituted in Britain today) is the sole example in this period when Marx suggests further political safeguards to ensure that universal (manhood) suffrage actually represents the people. That was not for lack of opportunity. In Marx's detailed commentary on the 1848 French Constitution, he noted that Article 35 specified that representatives "are not to be

273. Marx, "Die Berliner 'National-Zeitung' und die Urwähler," *MEGA* I.8: 332 / *MECW* 8: 272.
274. Marx, *Die Klassenkämpfe in Frankreich*, *MEGA* I.10: 148 / *MECW* 10: 79.
275. Marx, "The Chartists," *MEGA* I.11: 327 / *MECW* 11: 335.

bound by any fixed instruction," but, unlike his very critical remarks on other constitutional provisions, this one goes entirely uncommented upon.[276] That essay is also noteworthy for a piece of somewhat uncharacteristic advice (given Marx's opposition to what he thinks of as utopian planning). Following his discussion of the importance of paying attention to constitutional details, he urged: "People! Make up your minds as to DETAILS, as well as to principles, before you come to power."[277] That is a piece of advice that Marx might himself have done more to integrate into his account—at this point—of what representative and administrative structures were necessary to reach socialism.

Coda

Marx's view that the bourgeois republic was an insufficient but necessary step for the emancipation of the proletariat was a significant departure from the antipolitical and antidemocratic threads that dominated early socialism. The contempt with which most early socialists held politics, democracy, and majority rule is hard to grasp without a detailed engagement with their thought. The extensive discussion of antipolitical socialisms (and the nuances within them) in this chapter was intended to show the extent of the challenge faced by Marx and Engels when they tried to displace them. By integrating the same criticisms that republicans had made of antipolitical socialism, they helped forge a merged republican communism committed to a democratic republic and political struggle. Contemporary academic critics who try to paint Marx as insufficiently political (explored in the introduction to this book) rarely pay sufficient attention to this background context and the extent to which Marx labored to distinguish his republican communism from it.

Yet, in Marx's eagerness to distinguish himself from the various antipolitical socialisms, he overlooked some of the more radical insights on representation and political participation from his own early republicanism. In taking much of the political structure of the bourgeois republic as given and advocating for the working class to take power within its strictures, Marx might also be seen to have insufficiently developed a key aspect of his own 1848 constitutional analysis—that the bourgeois republic was constitutionally set up to ensure bourgeois rule. That insight might have led to the conclusion (explored further in chapter 7) that if the working class was to emancipate itself socially, it would require its own republic, with a more radically democratic constitution.

276. Marx, "The Constitution of the French Republic adopted November 4, 1848," *MEGA* I.10: 541 / *MECW* 10: 571.

277. Ibid., 545–46 / 578.

5

People, Property, Proletariat

MARXIAN COMMUNISM AND RADICAL REPUBLICANISM, 1848–52

[P]roperty is declared *holy* from the outset. On this cornerstone has the whole political democracy rested for sixty years; on this boundary is politics divided from socialism.

—KARL GRÜN[1]

To assure the life, and, at the same time, the freedom of each, we must not abolish property, but, on the contrary, multiply it and render it accessible to all.

—FÉLICITÉ DE LAMENNAIS[2]

REPUBLICANS AND SOCIALISTS wrestled for leadership of the radical movement throughout the middle decades of the nineteenth century. Sometimes that took literal form. The republican Karl Heinzen recalled that when he ran into Karl Marx in a Brussels café in 1845, Marx jumped at the opportunity to prove "that he could throw me to the ground, and immediately began to grapple with me." Heinzen, known for his impressive physical stature, reported the inevitable result: "Through a clumsy attempt to resist this childish attempt with my elbow, he [Marx] was thrown into the glass door of the café." According to Heinzen, Marx then "gathered himself together and shouted, 'that is no

1. Karl Grün, *Die soziale Bewegung in Frankreich und Belgien* (Darmstadt: Carl Wilhelm Leske, 1845), 21.

2. [Félicité de] Lamennais, *Question du travail* (Paris: Au Bureau du Peuple Constituant, 1848), 13 / "Of Labour," *English Republic* (1853), 2: 286.

skill when one has elephant bones.'" To which Heinzen replied, "Of course . . . but it took skill to be so stupid as not to have realized that beforehand."[3]

Personal jealousies and wrestling aside, republicans and socialists in fact offered a principled program of distinct social ideals. While republicans associated socialism, and especially communism, with the idea of abolishing private property, republicans instead stressed that property should be universalized. To achieve that goal, they proposed a comprehensive social reform program that stretched from free education and free state credit to progressive income taxes and the abolition of inheritance, and even to minimum and maximum property limits. The underlying ideal of these policies was to defend and restore the independence of artisan workers and peasants that was being eroded by the advance of capitalist industry and its mass of propertyless proletarians. The republican response was thus not to abolish private property by collectivizing this capitalist industry, but to extend property ownership to the whole population. Republicans thus offered an anticapitalist but nonsocialist alternative to capitalism.

From a twentieth- and twenty-first-century perspective, that social program is difficult to categorize, overlapping with but not easily corresponding to socialism or the welfare-state capitalism associated with social democracy and left-liberalism.[4] The republican social program largely disappeared alongside republicanism itself as a distinct political formation. But while these ideas might be obscure today, in Marx and Engels's time they were the preeminent competitor for working-class and popular support. The republican exiles who gathered in London after the failure of the 1848 Revolutions, for instance, were far better known and influential than Marx, Engels, and their fellow communists.[5] Marx and Engels consequently devoted significant critical attention to displacing them. Some of this effort took the form of character assassination, as in Marx and Engels's 1852 eighty-page manuscript *Die großen Männer des Exils* (*The Great Men of the Exile*). This fortunately remained unpublished, since it was

3. Karl Heinzen, *Erlebtes. Zweiter Theil: Nach Meiner Exilierung*, vol. 4 of *Gesammelte Schriften* (Boston: Selbstverlag, 1874), 433–34. For Heinzen's size, see Carl Wittke, *Against the Current: The Life of Karl Heinzen (1809–80)* (Chicago: University of Chicago Press, 1945), 2–3, 111.

4. Their social program, however, has several features in common with the ideas of predistribution and a property-owning democracy that have been the subject of renewed acdemic and political interest. See John Rawls, *Justice as Fairness: A Restatement*, ed. Erin Kelly (Cambridge: Belknap Press, 2001), §41–§49; Martin O'Neill and Thad Williamson, *Property-Owning Democracy: Rawls and Beyond* (Chichester: Wiley-Blackwell, 2012); Alan Thomas, *Republic of Equals: Predistribution and Property-Owning Democracy* (Oxford: Oxford University Press, 2017).

5. Christine Lattek, *Revolutionary Refugees: German Socialism in Britain, 1840–1860* (London: Routledge, 2006), 83–84.

little more than a compendium of personal insults directed at popular German republicans, the intellectual level of which can be gauged by the descriptions of Arnold Ruge's "ferret-face" and Heinzen's "huge masses of flesh."[6]

But Marx and Engels also engaged in substantive critique of the republican program. As this chapter will show, they in fact agreed with large parts of it, but parted ways when it came to the question of private property. They insisted that though the general communist position might be roughly captured by the slogan "abolition of private property," communism's specific goal (at least in their formulation) was actually the abolition of *capitalist* private property and its replacement with common property. They maintained that the republican defense of private property was in fact a defense of *petty bourgeois* private property, essentially an attempt to defend a political economy of small-scale independent producers. Marx and Engels argued that this ideal was being irreversibly destroyed by the advance of capitalism. The only hope for social emancipation was to embrace this capitalist transformation and collectivize the large-scale industrial production it had wrought. Marx and Engels's central case against the republican defense of "private property" thus did not rest on a moral argument about its vices and virtues but on the historical constraints on social change.

The republican social ideal was not embraced by all forms of republicanism. In France, at least, there was a discernible faction of moderate republicans who rejected the social ideas of the more radical republicans. These moderate republicans clustered around the newspaper *Le National*, while the more radical were associated with *La Réforme*.[7] The provisional government of the Second Republic set up in February 1848 was a blend of these two republican factions, intermediary figures like Alphonse de Lamartine, as well as declared socialists like Louis Blanc.[8] Marx recognized the difference between the radical and moderate republican factions, distinguishing between what he labeled "*petty bourgeois* or *democratic republicans* ... [and] the *bourgeois republicans*." His criticism of the bourgeois republicans was that they were merely "pure republicans, political republicans, formalistic republicans" because their republicanism extended solely to the political sphere, while their social ideas remained indistinguishable from the royalist bourgeoisie.[9] For the "bourgeois

6. Marx and Engels, *Die großen Männer des Exils*, MEGA I.11: 256, 268 / MECW 11: 265, 275.

7. Christopher Guyver, *The Second French Republic 1848–1852: A Political Reinterpretation* (London: Palgrave Macmillan, 2016), 27–28; Peter McPhee, "The Crisis of Radical Republicanism in the French Revolution of 1848," *Historical Studies* 16, no. 62 (1974): 71–72.

8. Maurice Agulhon, *The Republican Experiment, 1848–1850*, trans. Janet Lloyd (Cambridge: Cambridge University Press, 1983), 17, 26, 32–33.

9. Marx, *Der achtzehnte Brumaire*, MEGA I.11: 107–8 / MECW 11: 112–14.

republicans of the *National*," Marx maintained, "the republic was only a new ball dress for the old bourgeois society."[10] Examinations of voting records in the Second Republic indeed shows that there was little to distinguish bourgeois republicans from liberal monarchists.[11] This chapter consequently focuses on the radical republicans because they provided a clear alternative to bourgeois liberalism and represented a threat to popular and working class support for socialism—and hence necessitated a distinct response from Marx and Engels.[12]

In order to reconstruct the social ideal of radical republicanism, I begin this chapter with a portrait of the life and social and political thought of two representative figures, Karl Heinzen and William James Linton. I then contrast their thought and that of the broader movement of radical republicanism with the communism of Marx and Engels. I turn first to Heinzen's political critique of Marx and Engels's materialist conception of history and how that undergirds their assessment of the possibilities for social change. This is followed by a discussion of which revolutionary actors were supposed to carry out this change, with Marx and Engels focusing on the proletariat and the republicans committed to the people. I then set out at some length what measures were supposed to achieve their respective social ideals, emphasizing their initial similarity. Finally, I show how the dividing line came down to the question of whether bourgeois private property should be replaced with the universalization of petty bourgeois private property or the institution of common property, and the contrasting visions of political economy and history embodied in those positions.

The Republicanism of Karl Heinzen and William James Linton

Karl Heinzen was born Charles Pierre Heinzen in 1809 in Grevenbroich, a town outside Düsseldorf, when the Rhineland was still under the temporary control of France, and it was only when it became part of Prussia that his name was Germanized.[13] A rebellious child, Heinzen joined the University of

---

10. Marx, *Die Klassenkämpfe in Frankreich*, MEGA I.10: 128 / MECW 10: 58.

11. George W. Fasel, "The French Election of April 23, 1848: Suggestions for a Revision," *French Historical Studies* 5, no. 3 (1968): 289.

12. Heinzen, for instance, blamed his rivalry with Marx on the fact that "the workers . . . this 'class' on which he [Marx] hoped to build his future" showed greater interest in his ideas than in Marx's; see Heinzen, *Erlebtes*, 435.

13. This biographical overview is taken from Paul Otto Schinnerer, "Karl Heinzen, Reformer, Poet and Literary Critic," *Deutsch-Amerikanische Geschichtsblätter* 15 (1915): 84–144; Hans Huber, *Karl Heinzen (1809–1880): Seine politische Entwicklung und publizistische Wirksamkeit*

Bonn to study medicine in 1827, only to be expelled two years later for his rowdy student lifestyle and failure to work.[14] The financial necessity of taking care of a young family meant that he spent an unhappy seven and a half years as a career Prussian tax official. Eventually, overcome with bureaucratic frustration, he resigned in anger and in 1844 published *Die preusische Bureaukratie* (*The Prussian Bureacracy*). The book was a provocative broadside against the Prussian administration and the absolutist regime, and it was immediately confiscated on publication, resulting in a charge of lèse-majesté for Heinzen, for which he went into exile, first in Brussels and then Zurich. In Zurich, he encountered Ruge, who was to play an important role in shaping his thought, and the two collaborated on a republican quarterly, *Die Opposition*.

During the revolution, he ran unsuccessfully for a Hamburg seat in the Frankfurt National Assembly, joined Friedrich Hecker's uprising in Baden, and propagandized tirelessly for a revolutionary dictatorship and a German republic. He collaborated, for instance, with the revolutionary leader Gustav Struve on two programmatic and strategic 1848 pamphlets, *Die Schilderhebung der deutschen Republikaner im April 1848* (*The Insurrection of German Republicans in April 1848*) and *Plan zur Revolutionierung und Republikanisierung Deutschlands* (*Plan for the Revolutionizing and Republicanization of Germany*), which argued that parliamentary methods had failed and instead called on the German people to rise up and "through the means of violence create a German republic."[15] Also of note in this period are the articles on "Der Mord," which he wrote in early 1849 and republished as *Mord und Freiheit* the following year, where he defended the right of tyrannicide through new explosive technologies (which has recently resulted in some scholarly interest in Heinzen as an early theorist of terrorism).[16]

After the failure of the revolutions, Heinzen found refuge in London. He joined the revolutionary exile circles there, and spent time with Mazzini, Ruge,

---

(Bern: Paul Haupt, 1932); and Wittke, *Against the Current*. A useful bibliography of Heinzen's writings can be found in Karl Schmemann, ed., *Gedenkbuch: Erinnerung an Karl Heinzen und an die Enthüllungsfeier des Heinzen-Denkmals am 12. Juni 1886 in Boston, Mass.* (Milwaukee: Freidenker, 1887), 101–5.

14. Heinzen's claim that he was actually expelled in response to a speech about academic freedom is, his biographer notes, "unconvincing"; Wittke, *Against the Current*, 9–10.

15. G. Struve and K. Heinzen, *Plan zur Revolutionierung und Republikanisierung Deutschlands* (Birsfelden: J. U. Walser, 1848), 1.

16. See, for example, Benjamin Grob-Fitzgibbon, "From the Dagger to the Bomb: Karl Heinzen and the Evolution of Political Terror," *Terrorism and Political Violence* 16, no. 1 (2004): 97–115, and Daniel Bessner and Michael Stauch, "Karl Heinzen and the Intellectual Origins of Modern Terror," *Terrorism and Political Violence* 22, no. 2 (2010): 143–76.

and others. But he found the city miserable, and he did not help his public reputation by publishing "Die Lehren der Revolution" ("The Lessons of the Revolution"), which made bloody predictions about how many millions of heads might roll in the next revolution. The bloodthirsty piece alienated him from other radicals and even resulted in the *Times* calling for his expulsion.[17] Struggling to support himself and his family, he moved to America in late 1850. He spent the rest of his remaining thirty years there, becoming one of the many radical German-American "forty-eighters." He engaged in a number of journalistic ventures—most importantly *Der Pionier*, which ran for a quarter century—and he threw himself into American radical political struggles, from abolitionism to women's emancipation.[18] He died on 1880 in Boston, and for several years afterward memorial events were held on his birthday by supporters in several cities, culminating in a monument erected in 1882, which still stands in Forest Hills Cemetery in Boston.

Though he is a nearly forgotten figure today, Heinzen was a tenacious and committed revolutionary. Veit Valentin, in his classic study of the 1848 Revolutions, called Heinzen "the most determined and most active German republican of the forties."[19] His biographer, Carl Wittke, summarized him as "an uncompromising, unbending, militant, radical republican, a crusader against censorship, bureaucracy, militarism, and reaction in his native Germany, and a champion of equal rights for women and many other political, economic and social reforms in the United States."[20] But alongside his ardent and committed republicanism, his "rabid anti-communism was notorious."[21] When Wilhelm Weitling, for instance, made an ill-advised attempt to recruit him to the communist cause, Heinzen raged that a "communist is as distant from me as the Czar of Russia. Communism is as hostile to freedom . . . and as barbaric as despotism" and insisted that his guiding principles were formed by "true

---

17. Wittke, *Against the Current*, 79.

18. For Heinzen's defense of women's emancipation, see his *Ueber die Rechte und Stellung der Weiber* (New York: Selbstverlag des Autors, 1852) / *The Rights of Women and the Sexual Relations*, trans. Emma Heller Schumm (Boston: Benjamin R. Tucker, 1891), and his *Programm der teutschen Revolutionspartei* (February 1850), International Institute of Social History, Karl Marx / Friedrich Engels Papers, S_1a, section II, articles 4 and 5. Marx and Engels responded to the latter with a lewd joke; see Marx and Engels, *Die großen Männer des Exils*, MEGA I.11: 271 / *MECW* 11: 279; Lattek, *Revolutionary Refugees*, 221n16.

19. Veit Valentin, *Geschichte der deutschen Revolution von 1849–49*, vol. 1 (Berlin: Ullstein, 1930), 286. Cited in Wittke, *Against the Current*, 77.

20. Wittke, *Against the Current*, v.

21. Lattek, *Revolutionary Refugees*, 84.

republicanism and not true communism."[22] But nowhere was his antipathy to communism demonstrated more clearly than in his attitude to Marx.

The Heinzen-Marx connection has received surprisingly little attention in Marx scholarship. Surprising, because Heinzen and Marx's life intersected several times, they penned angry polemics against each other, and they continued to mention each other in their work and correspondence late into their lives (each of them seems to have taken great enjoyment—bordering on obsession—with insulting the other).[23] Though Heinzen was nearly ten years older than Marx, they shared a certain biographical similarity in that both were Rhinelanders and attended the University of Bonn for a brief stint marked by their *unstudiousness*. Heinzen first got to know Marx through the latter's editorship of the *Rheinische Zeitung*, to which Heinzen contributed several articles, and they knew each other well enough to go out drinking together in Cologne. (Heinzen recalled one evening where Marx and he went to the pub for "several bottles of wine," after which Heinzen had to help Marx home, as he "could not stand much [alcohol]" and was in a "disheveled state." Once there, Marx suddenly "locked the door, hid the key, and comically mocked me that I was now his prisoner" and "began to attack me with threats and cuffs." Heinzen only escaped by tearing open the front door.)[24] In the ensuing years, Heinzen offered Marx a piece for inclusion in the *Deutsch-Französische Jahrbücher* in 1844, which came to nothing when the journal failed after the first issue.[25] They overlapped again in Brussels in 1845, but by this point they were on opposing sides of the republican-communist fence. Despite their diverging politics, they met and debated with each other, and Heinzen noted that even with their wrestling match, their parting was "not hostile."[26] Their relationship became irreconcilable, however, after a series of exchanges in late 1847 in the *Deutsche-Brüsseler-Zeitung*.[27]

The row began when Heinzen objected to an editorial note in the paper's 12 September issue, which reported that Heinzen had declared "war on the communists." Heinzen rejected the charge, but his reply in the paper did just that, managing in the space of a single paragraph to launch eight separate accusations against the communists, including that they had played into the

---

22. Karl Heinzen to Wilhelm Weitling [first draft], 16 February 1848, in Karl Heinzen Papers, University of Michigan Library (Special Collections Research Center), Box 2, Folder 7.

23. Wittke notes that "there was also something peculiarly personal about Heinzen's quarrel with communism. He had come to hate the founder of communism [Marx] as he hated few other men"; Wittke, *Against the Current*, 236.

24. Heinzen, *Erlebtes*, 426–27.

25. Heinzen to Marx, 16 February 1844, *MEGA* III.1: 424–25.

26. Heinzen, *Erlebtes*, 434.

27. The conflict is dealt with in Huber, *Karl Heinzen*, 54–65.

hands of reactionary forces by "paralyz[ing] the political struggle."[28] Engels saw an opportunity here to both trash Heinzen and show why his and Marx's form of communism was not susceptible to the typical republican criticisms of communism. Engels's scathing two-part response from 3 and 7 October declared that Heinzen was "one of the most ignorant men of this century" and should henceforth "maintain absolute silence and wait quietly" for the revolution.[29] Unsurprisingly incensed, Heinzen wrote an equally aggressive response that took up most of the 21 October issue and claimed that Engels had "never had an original thought" and his ideas consisted only of what he had "snapped up and pocketed from the French or English table."[30] The editors of the *Deutsche-Brüsseler-Zeitung* tried in vain to warn both sides that they should not split the radical movement and that the newspaper could not sustain such long polemics.

Engels could not bring himself to respond to Heinzen's reply—"save perhaps with a box on the ear"—and instead left the task to Marx. He rather forlornly hoped that Marx would restrict himself to "replying very *briefly*."[31] Marx (characteristically) did not stick to this plan, and the *Deutsche-Brüsseler-Zeitung* editors had to spread out his answer over five issues from 28 October to 25 November. The resulting article, "Die moralisierende Kritik und die Kritische Moral. Beitrag zur deutschen Kulturgeschichte. Gegen Karl Heinzen" ("Moralizing Criticism and Critical Morality: A Contribution to German Cultural History; Contra Karl Heinzen"), took the unusual step of mockingly framing Heinzen's polemics as a nineteenth-century version of German Reformation-era "*grobianische*" ("booby" or "boor") literature. Marx characterized this as "Flat, bombastic, bragging, thrasonical, putting on a great show of rude vigor in attack, yet hysterically sensitive to the same quality in others."[32] The editors, finally exasperated by the participants, denied Heinzen the space for a reply, so that he resorted to publishing (after some delay) a hundred-page pamphlet, *Die Helden des teutschen Kommunismus: Denn Herrn Karl Marx*

---

28. Karl Heinzen, "Polemik. Karl Heinzen und die Kommunisten," *Deutsche-Brüsseler-Zeitung*, no. 77 (26 September 1847): 4.

29. Engels, "Die Kommunisten und Karl Heinzen," *MEW* 4: 314, 316 / *MECW* 6: 296, 298.

30. K. Heinzen, "Ein 'Repräsentant' der Kommunisten," *Deutsche-Brüsseler-Zeitung*, no. 84 (21 October 1847): 3.

31. Engels to Marx, 25 / 26 October 1847, *MEGA* III.2: 115 / *MECW* 38: 139.

32. Marx, "Die moralisierende Kritik," *MEW* 4: 331 / *MECW* 6: 312. Marx was so pleased with this comparison that he continued to refer to Heinzen as "Heineke"—a character from a parody of grobian literature—in his personal correspondence into the 1870s, see Marx to Engels, 18 May 1870, *MEW* 32: 516; *MECW* 43: 522. For a literary discussion of Marx's grobian comparison, see S. S. Prawer, *Karl Marx and World Literature* (Oxford: Clarendon Press, 1976), 126–30.

gewidmet (*The Heroes of German Communism: Dedicated to Mr. Karl Marx*), in the summer of 1848, a work that has a claim to being the earliest book-length response to Marx's views.[33]

The entire exchange is characterized by personal mud-slinging, childish insults, and slanderous accusations and counteraccusations. But behind these often tiresome ad hominem attacks, the articles also contain serious and important engagements with each other's ideas. Heinzen developed his critique of the communist neglect of politics, Engels clarified the strategic imperatives of communists working with republicans, and Marx explored the economic (as opposed to political) foundations of revolution. "Die moralisierende Kritik" also represents perhaps Marx's most sustained theoretical engagement with radical republicanism. The exchange, written less than six months before the outbreak of the 1848 Revolutions, should be seen as part of a wider process of differentiation between republicans and communists in the prerevolutionary years. It also foreshadowed the uneasy alliances and occasional hostility that haunted the subsequent effectiveness of the party of movement. Finally, the articles are also noteworthy because they were written in the immediate buildup to Marx and Engels's composition of the *Manifest der Kommunistischen Partei* (a task they were assigned by the Bund der Kommunisten [Communist League] at its congress in late November/early December 1847 and which appeared in February 1848). Though republicans are only occasionally mentioned in the text, the arguments Marx and Engels honed against Heinzen do appear, as I show later in the chapter.[34]

In comparison to Heinzen, William James Linton played only a peripheral role in Marx's life. His inclusion in this study is instead justified by his contemporaneous attempt to set out a comprehensive republican political theory. Gregory Claeys notes that Linton "almost single-handedly . . . set about constructing a secure individualist philosophical foundation for radical political thought."[35] As we saw in the introduction, the contrast between Marx's communism and Linton's republicanism was notably on show in the side-by-side

33. Marx and Engels, busy with their participation in the 1848 revolution, declined to respond to Heinzen's final "old trashy piece (*Schund*)"; Marx to Engels, 29 November 1848, *MEGA* III.2: 171 / *MECW* 38: 181.

34. The opening lines of the *Manifest* mention "French Radicals," and the closing section urges communists to work together with the "social-democratic party" in France and the "Radicals" in Switzerland; see Marx and Engels, *Manifest der Kommunistischen Partei*, *MEW* 4: 461, 492 / *MECW* 6: 481, 518.

35. Gregory Claeys, *Citizens and Saints: Politics and Anti-Politics in Early British Socialism* (Cambridge: Cambridge University Press, 1989), 306.

publication of his "Republican Principles" and the *Manifest* in the pages of the *Red Republican* in September to November 1850.

Linton was born in Mile End, London, in 1812 to lower-middle-class parents.[36] He showed an early artistic talent and later began a successful career as an engraver. He became increasingly interested in politics, and set up his first weekly paper, the *National*, in 1839, which ran for just a few short months but gave him a lifelong taste for journalism. Around this time he encountered Lamennais's work and was entranced by his mix of republicanism and spiritualism. Linton translated Lamennais's hugely popular attack on wage-labor in *De l'esclavage Moderne* (1839) as *Modern Slavery* (1840), adding in an appendix that "ancient slavery subsists" not just in the modern wage-slave, but in the "woman-slave" who is denied "natural liberty and self-sovereignty."[37] Women's emancipation was a continuing concern for Linton: he analyzed at some length why the "equality of man and woman in a society is but a logical deduction from our republican principles," and while Marx and contemporaries blithely referred to the manhood suffrage of the Second Republic as "universal suffrage," Linton argued that it had never been a real republic because the "woman half of the population was left unenfranchised."[38]

Linton met Giuseppe Mazzini soon after his encounter with Lamennais, in 1841; the Italian patriot made a similarly powerful impression on Linton, and he became a devoted follower.[39] The association with Mazzini gave Linton his first taste of national politics when he played a significant role in assisting Mazzini in the letter-opening scandal of 1844 (Linton helped uncover the fact that Mazzini's mail was being intercepted on the order of the Home Secretary and the contents passed on to Metternich). The scandal "promoted Linton into a leading English contact-man for the exiles," and he became increasingly

36. Scholars of Linton are fortunate in that there is an excellent biography by F. B. Smith, *Radical Artisan: William James Linton 1812–97* (Manchester: Manchester University Press, 1973), from which the following overview is drawn.

37. W. J. L[inton], "Appendix," in F. Lamennais, *Modern Slavery* (London: J. Watson, 1840), 28, 32. For Linton's role in disseminating Lamennais's ideas in England, see W. G. Roe, *Lamennais and England: The Reception of Lamennais's Religious Ideas in England in the Nineteenth Century* (Oxford: Oxford University Press, 1966), 166–71.

38. [W. J. Linton], "Woman," *English Republic* (1853), 2: 311; [W. J. Linton], "Democracy and Republicanism," *English Republic* (1855), 4: 65. See also W. J. Linton, "Universal Suffrage: The Principle of the People's Charter," *The Republican: A Magazine Advocating the Sovereignty of the People* (London: J. Watson, 1848), 165–68.

39. For an extended discussion of their relationship, see Salvo Mastellone, *Mazzini e Linton: Una Democrazia Europea (1845–1855)* (Florence: L.S. Olschki, 2007).

involved in radical exile organizations.[40] This meant that when the revolution broke out in France, Linton was part of the delegation of the People's International League (one of Mazzini's many organizations) that was sent to Paris to congratulate the new republican Provisional Government.

But Linton became increasingly tired of life in London and, having fallen in love with the Lake District, moved his family there in April 1849. This isolated him from London's refugee politics, but he continued to contribute articles to radical papers and began editing his most important contribution to republican thought, *The English Republic*. This journal appeared variously weekly and monthly from January 1851 to April 1855; together with a few disciples he personally printed for its final two years. The final chapter in his life came when he decided to move to America in 1866. His American life was marked by growing success in the literary and cultural scene and widespread recognition for his engraving work. Though his artistic pursuits became the focus of his later life, he never abandoned his political beliefs. He attended meetings of the Anti-Slavery Society and the Reform League and, as we will see in chapter 7, was one of the few public supporters of the Paris Commune in America.[41] He died in 1897 at the age of eighty-five, leaving his papers to Yale University.

In his biography, F. B. Smith notes that Linton "stands at the edge of the remembered nineteenth-century world" and "deserves better."[42] While Linton's poetry, engraving, and literary output have received some attention in recent years, his political contribution to republicanism has been relatively overlooked.[43] That neglect deserves to be rectified because Linton was one of the clearest examples of a self-conscious attempt to apply the ideas and language of a premodern republican tradition to the political and social condition of the nineteenth century. Nowhere is this in greater evidence than in his *English Republic*, an enormous project that deserves a more prominent place in the history of republicanism.

Linton's reverence for his English republican inheritance was proudly proclaimed in the *English Republic*'s opening editorial. He addressed the "men in

40. Smith, *Radical Artisan*, 59.

41. Ibid., 174–76.

42. Ibid., ix.

43. Alastair Philip Lovett, *Creative Aspiration and Public Discourse: The Prose, Verse and Graphic Images of William James Linton (1812–1897)* (PhD thesis, Durham University, 2003), and Stephanie Weiner, *Republican Politics and English Poetry, 1789–1874* (Palgrave Macmillan, 2005), chapter 3. See, however, the discussion of Linton's politics in Gregory Claeys, "Mazzini, Kossuth, and British Radicalism, 1848–1854," *The Journal of British Studies* 28, no. 3 (1989): 238–44; and Stuart White, "The Republican Critique of Capitalism," *Critical Review of International Social and Political Philosophy* 14, no. 5 (2011): 566–67.

England . . . who respect the worth of Cromwell," "men who honour the memory of Milton" and those who held that neither "[Algernon] Sydney nor [Lord] Russell" (executed for treason in 1683) had given their lives simply to "procure the advent of a Dutch king or to establish the miserable finality of Whiggism." These men had fought and died trying to create, maintain, and then reestablish the Commonwealth—"the grandest period of English history." Linton argued that they were models for "we Republicans of the nineteenth century," even if modern republicans must now "advance beyond them."[44]

Alongside Linton's theoretical articles, the *English Republic* printed news from the Continent, political poems, and biographical sketches of prominent republican heroes and martyrs. Adding to an earlier glowing biography of the Haitian emancipator Toussaint Louverture, Linton covered a geographically and historically varied list of republicans including Robert Blum, Henry Ireton, Tadeusz Kościuszko, Jean-Paul Marat, John Milton, Algernon Sidney, and Mary Wollstonecraft.[45] The *English Republic* also carried translations of contemporary articles by Alexander Herzen, Victor Hugo, Mazzini, Ledru-Rollin, Lamennais, and Ruge, making the journal the "fullest and most venturesome transposition of European republicanism into English."[46] The cover of the *English Republic* was adorned with Linton's proposal for a blue, white, and green English tricolor (figure 10), the symbolism of which he explained in the poem "Our Tricolour":

44. W. J. Linton, "The English Republic," *English Republic* (1851), 1: 3–4. Linton's praise of Cromwell was unaffected by the latter's actions in Ireland, with Linton only commenting in passing that Cromwell had acted, "some say, with barbarous cruelty,—others say, with necessary severity"; see "Oliver Cromwell," *English Republic* (1854), 3: 110.

45. See *English Republic* I: 317–19, 339–45; III: 4–18, 242–47, 361–66, 418–24, and IV: 48–52 and [W. J. Linton], "Life of Toussaint L'Ouverture," in *The National: Library for the People*, ed. W. J. Linton (London: Watson, 1839), 158–59.

46. Smith, *Radical Artisan*, 105. Smith makes the intriguing claim that Alexander Herzen "tried, unsuccessfully, to persuade Arnold Ruge and Karl Marx to write on Germany" for the *English Republic*; see Smith, *Radical Artisan*, 106. But the letter he cites (Alexander Herzen to W. J. Linton, 6 December 1853, *Fondazione Giangiacomo Feltrinelli*, b.2, fasc. 63/2) contains no mention of Marx or Ruge. The confusion perhaps springs from an earlier letter (Alexander Herzen to W. J. Linton, 7 September 1853, *Fondazione Giangiacomo Feltrinelli*, b.2, fasc. 63/11), where Herzen does mention Ruge and Marx, but only in relation to a public spat they were involved in at the time regarding accusations that Bakunin was a czarist spy. Given the political orientation of the *English Republic*, it seems very unlikely that Marx would have had any interest in taking up such an offer. The letters are republished in Alexander Herzen, *Sobranie sochinenii v tridtsati tomakh*, vol. 25 (Moscow: Izdatel'stvo Akademii nauk SSSR, 1961), 112, 133–35.

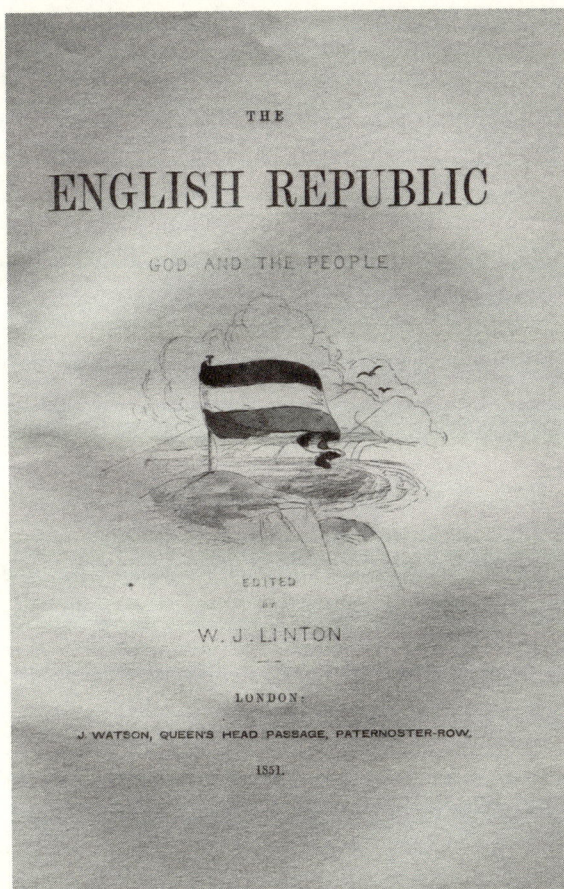

FIGURE 10. Frontispiece of W. J. Linton's *The English Republic* (1851). Courtesy of Melton Prior Institute. Linton proposed a blue-white-green English tricolor, representing the sky, the cliffs of Dover, and the ocean.

LET our Tricolour be wove, our true English Flag unfurl'd!—
Heirs of them who foremost strove when our Cromwell led the world,
Lift again in Freedom's van England's Flag republican!
Choose for *hope* the sky serene, *freedom* Albion's cliffs so white,
And the eternal ocean's green choose we for our native *right*:
Blue and *white* and *green* shall span England's Flag republican.[47]

47. Spartacus [W. J. Linton], "Our Tricolour," *English Republic* (1851), 1: 35.

Linton used three programmatic articles in the *English Republic* to set out the central elements of his political thought: "Republican Principles" (republished from the *Red Republican*), "Republican Organisation," and "Republican Measures." These respectively set out his political philosophy, the method of political organization, and the social and political measures that would bring about those principles. Linton covered everything from the administration of justice to tax reform and the organization of local government. Importantly, for our purposes, he also included an extensive attempt to work out a solution to the "Organization of labour" on land and industry, a program discussed in detail below. Linton thereby provided one of the most comprehensive attempts to apply republican ideas to the social and political problems of the nineteenth century.

The Political versus the Social

Marx's materialist conception of history (often shortened to "historical materialism"—though not by Marx himself) places great, sometimes even determinative, weight on productive forces and class relations in explaining the workings of society and historical events. Though there is considerable disagreement in the literature on how to characterize Marx's historical materialism, he broadly held that the way in which humans produced had a central role in explaining the shape and functioning of society's noneconomic institutions, such as its legal, political, and religious architecture. This understanding of society and history is frequently criticized for giving insufficient weight and independent space to politics. This criticism has a long history, ranging from Eduard Bernstein's revisionist criticisms of Marxism at the turn of the twentieth century,[48] to the debates around "post-Marxism" in the 1980s,[49] to some of the most recent biographical scholarship on Marx, where the "most prominent feature" of his conception of history is said to be "his refusal to accord independent space to the people's political concerns."[50] As we will see in this section, this criticism of Marx's historical materialism stretches back to the

48. Eduard Bernstein, *Die Voraussetzungen des Sozialismus und die Aufgaben der Sozialdemokratie* (Stuttgart: Dietz, 1899), 4–14 / *The Preconditions of Socialism*, ed. Henry Tudor (Cambridge: Cambridge University Press, 1993), 12–22.

49. For post-Marxism, see Ernesto Laclau and Chantal Mouffe, *Hegemony and Socialist Strategy: Towards a Radical Democratic Politics* (London: Verso, 1985). For responses, see Ellen Meiksins Wood, *The Retreat from Class: A New "True" Socialism* (London: Verso, 1986); and Norman Geras, "Post-Marxism?," *New Left Review*, no. 163 (1987): 40–82.

50. Gareth Stedman Jones, *Karl Marx: Greatness and Illusion* (London: Allen Lane, 2016), 341–42.

very beginnings of its formulation, when Marx's account was assailed by Heinzen.

The charge of vulgar materialism and economic determinism was a frequent one in republican criticisms of communism in the 1840s. In Mazzini's influential and controversial "Thoughts upon Democracy in Europe," he hammered socialists and communists for reducing everything to Benthamite utility, where "Man is there, as in the cold, dry, imperfect theory of the economists, nothing more than a producing machine."[51] When outraged readers disagreed, Mazzini doubled down, calling them "worshippers of *utility*, you have no other moral than that of interests, your religion is that of matter."[52] Similar sentiments were later expressed by Paul Harro-Harring in his anticommunist pamphlet *Historisches Fragment über die Entstehung der Arbeiter-Vereine und ihren Verfall in Communistische Speculationen* (1852), a text that Marx and Engels lampooned for its grandiloquence in *Die großen Männer des Exils*.[53] Harro-Harring argued that the communist "theory is: slavery under the yoke of matter; humanity a machine, which is only moved by material interest."[54]

This criticism of communism was thus well established in republican circles at the time, and, unsurprisingly, Heinzen repeated it in his general anticommunist attacks and honed it further in his critical exchange with Marx and Engels, arguing "that humanity is not always determined by 'class' or the size of their wallet."[55] He instead developed an extended critique of the idea that material interests were the driving forces in society and argued that politics has much greater weight than Marx and Engels's historical materialism allowed for. This critique can be broadly broken down into three claims: that political oppression is worse than social oppression, that the political sphere controls and has power over the social sphere, and that social concerns and development are insufficient to explain political revolution.

First, Heinzen claimed that the communist emphasis on the social oppression of the worker gave the impression that "the fight against Mammon was a

51. Joseph Mazzini, "Thoughts upon Democracy in Europe," *The People's Journal*, ed. John Saunders, vol. 3 (London: People's Journal Office, 1847), 221.

52. Joseph Mazzini, "A Last Word Upon Fourierism and Communism. In Reply to Messrs. Doherty and Barmby," *The People's Journal*, 3: 347. For this controversy, see Claeys, "Mazzini, Kossuth, and British Radicalism, 1848–1854," 231–33.

53. Marx and Engels, *Die großen Männer des Exils*, MEGA I.11: 275-80 / MECW 11: 284–90.

54. [Paul] Harro-Harring, *Historisches Fragment über die Entstehung der Arbeiter-Vereine und ihren Verfall in Communistische Speculationen* (London: C. Deutsch, 1852), 12. For Harro-Harring, see Peter Mathews, *Harro Harring—Rebell der Freiheit: Die Geschichte des Dichters, Malers und Revolutionärs 1798–1870* (Munich: Europa, 2017).

55. Heinzen, "Ein 'Repräsentant' der Kommunisten," 3.

higher task, than the fight against despotism."[56] This was unacceptable for Heinzen because he believed that the latter was clearly worse. He claimed that among the "men of the money-bags" there were at least some who recognized the rights of those without money, but there were no "men of power" who recognized the rights of those without power.[57] The man of money was prepared to interact with others without forcing them to "bow beneath his money," whereas the man of power was "only content" with forcing others to "subordinate" themselves to his power. Both kinds of men were "thirsty for power (*herrschsüchtig*)," but men of power also combined this with "jealousy," which made them "even thirstier for revenge."[58] Heinzen further argued that he "could not help being less outraged" by the "bourgeois" or "manufacturer" than by the "king" or "despot," because the former had "at least acquired his riches" justly, while the latter was a much "greater money wolf (*Geldwolf*)" because he "daily robbed" the people through the law. Moreover, the former could not be the "greater blackmailer" since he "at least does not use the worker for free," while the latter forces the people to "pay for their blackmailer."[59]

Second, according to Heinzen, communists had also placed so much emphasis on the social question that they had forgotten that power in fact lay with the political sphere. He accused Engels of having, "like all communists, become incapable of recognizing the connection between politics and social conditions" because he was "only engaged with enemies that possess money, rather than those that apart from money also possess power."[60] He argued that this was a problem because power actually lay with the forces of despotism rather than with the capitalists. It was the princes who had the "naked power" to "hold back all material development, economically ruin millions of people, rob millions of thalers for their extravagances, and [to appropriate] the enormous state property . . . as [their] private property."[61] Heinzen even claimed, with perhaps some exaggeration, that if King Louis-Philippe "suddenly became revolutionary and republican," he could "destroy the 'ruling bourgeoisie' in fourteen days."[62] He complained that when communists did recognize the importance of political power, it was only when it related to social concerns or when the bourgeoisie

56. K. Heinzen, "Gegen die Kommunisten," in *Die Opposition*, ed. Karl Heinzen (Mannheim: Heinrich Hoff, 1846), 58.

57. Ibid., 87–88. Here, as elsewhere, Heinzen uses "power (*Gewalt*)" by itself, to refer specifically to the political power of the forces of despotism.

58. Ibid., 88.

59. Heinzen, "Ein 'Repräsentant' der Kommunisten," 3.

60. Ibid.

61. K. Heinzen, *Die Helden des teutschen Kommunismus: Denn Herrn Karl Marx gewidmet* (Bern: Jenni, Sohn, 1848), 20–21.

62. Ibid., 25.

had obtained some political power as well. Thus, he accused Marx and Engels of "only recognising politics, where it reaches into the factory, or when it crawls out of the factory," and that the only kind of political power that interested them was that "power which the 'bourgeois' exercises though the mediation of the chamber of deputies."[63] According to Heinzen, Marx, Engels, and communists in general had thus failed to see that power emanated from the political sphere and controlled the social sphere. They were "too blind to see that power rules property" and not the other way around. Once this societal truth had been recognized, Heinzen believed it showed why "there was no important *social* question, than that of monarchy or republic."[64]

Marx and Engels hit back against Heinzen's account of the relative importance of the political sphere in comparison to the social. Engels argued that the German princes were in fact "impotent and feeble-minded puppets" and Heinzen was wrong to imbue them with a "fantastic, supernatural, demonic omnipotence." Not just wrong, but "exceedingly dangerous," because by trying to convince the people that their exploitation was the fault of the princes rather than the landowners and the capitalist, he was in effect "working in the interests" of those two classes.[65] Marx in turn decided to use his article in the *Deutsch-Brusseler-Zeitung* to give Heinzen, in the words of Hans Huber, a "small lesson in historical materialism."[66]

Marx first reminded Heinzen that social power was also "a kind of power"— namely, the "power over the labor of others." He then freely admitted that in Germany the bourgeoisie was indeed currently "harassed" by the state through arbitrary taxes, privileges, and bureaucratic intrusion. But this was not because of some "eternal truth" that the state had control over the bourgeoisie but because of the "transient" fact that the bourgeoisie had "not yet politically constituted itself as a class," and so the "state power was not yet their own power." The material forces that were driving the emergence of the bourgeoisie in Germany would eventually and necessarily have the concurrent consequence of handing them political power. Crucially, Marx argued, it is because of developments in the social sphere of production that there is a change in political power and not the other way around. As he put it, the bourgeois mode of production "by no means arises from the political rule of the bourgeois class, but vice versa, the political rule of the bourgeois class from these modern relations of production."[67]

Marx took this opportunity to explain to Heinzen and the readers of the *Deutsch-Brusseler-Zeitung* what this understanding of the relationship between

63. Ibid., 20.

64. Heinzen, "Ein 'Repräsentant' der Kommunisten," 3.

65. Engels, "Die Kommunisten und Karl Heinzen," *MEW* 4: 311-12 / *MECW* 6: 293–94.

66. Huber, *Karl Heinzen*, 60.

67. Marx, "Die moralisierende Kritik," *MEW* 4: 337-38 / *MECW* 6: 318–19.

politics and the social meant for revolution, setting out some of the ideas with which he is now so intimately associated with. Marx argued that since gaining political power was the consequence of developments in social production, then attempts to gain that political power when the "material conditions have not yet been created" were destined to fail.[68] Thus, if the bourgeoisie attempted to overthrow "absolute monarchy" before the economic preconditions for bourgeois rule had "become ripe," their rule would be "merely temporary." Similarly, if the proletariat tried to overthrow bourgeois rule before the conditions for its rule were in place, their "victory will be only temporary."[69] Marx insisted that the central point of this was that humanity "first" had to "*produce* the *material conditions* of a new society*" before it could liberate itself, and "no exertion (*Kraftanstrengung*) of mind or will can free them from this fate."[70]

The emancipation of the proletariat had to wait until the bourgeoisie had become sufficiently economically developed and conquered political power through a republic. Heinzen was therefore "accidentally" correct when he claimed that the social question meant settling the question of monarchy or republic, but only because the social question "increase[s] in importance in proportion as we leave behind us the realm of absolute monarchy."[71] In a rare acknowledgment by Marx of communism's republican inheritance, he credited the most radical elements of republicanism in previous bourgeois revolutions for also coming to this conclusion:

> The first manifestation of a truly active communist party is contained within the bourgeois revolution, at the moment when the constitutional monarchy is eliminated. The most consistent *republicans*, in England the *Levellers*, in France *Babeuf, Buanarroti*, etc., were the first to proclaim these "social questions" . . . [and] these republicans derived from the "movement" of history the realization that the disposal of the social question of *rule by princes* and *republic* did not mean that even a single "social question" has been solved in the interests of the proletariat.[72]

Heinzen was, unsurprisingly, not enamored of this account of revolution and replied with his third main criticism of Marx and Engels's historical materialism. In *Die Helden des teutschen Kommunismus* he quoted repeatedly from Marx's

---

68. Ibid., 338–39 / 319.

69. Ibid.

70. Ibid., 339 / 320.

71. Ibid., 340–41 / 321.

72. Ibid., 341 / 321–22. From the context, it seems likely that by "*Levellers*" Marx probably had in mind the Diggers or "True Levellers," since it was they who demanded not just manhood suffrage (as the Levellers did) but also a community of goods.

"Die moralisierende Kritik" to argue against its materialistic and what he took to be a deterministic account of revolution. He quite accurately summarized Marx's view as "no revolution is necessary or possible, where there is no bourgeoisie; the bourgeoisie must first rule and through its rule produce a factory proletariat, which [then] revolutionizes, to rule in turn." Heinzen thought that was a false and objectionable view of revolution. It was false because revolution was not simply the outcome of whether or not a "steam engine or some other factory instrument had been invented." He argued that Marx's dismissal of the "exertion (*Kraftanstrengung*) of mind or will" in producing a revolution failed to see the importance of "exertion" in the French Revolution and revealed, on Marx's part, a conception of the people who had "neither mind or will." It was objectionable because the consequence of Marx's view was that the proletariat had "neither reason nor right to revolution" until the material conditions were in place, and until then they "must patiently go hungry and starve, until an England has been made out of Germany." Heinzen was prepared to admit the "importance of industrial conditions" and the role of "material interests at the outbreak of revolution" to a certain degree, but he insisted that it was simply "narrow-mindedness" to think that revolution "only emerges from the *factory*."[73] Heinzen believed that doing so failed to see the importance of political ideals in motivating people's revolutionary participation. As he noted elsewhere, the revolution might "begin with the stomach," but the "proletarian has sacrificed himself for the idea and forgotten his stomach."[74]

Heinzen's criticisms of Marx's materialist conception of society and history did not end with their exchange in the *Deutsch-Brusseler-Zeitung*. Some twelve year later, when Marx published his *Zur Kritik der politischen Ökonomie* (*A Contribution to the Critique of Political Economy*) in June 1859, Heinzen swiftly reviewed it in his German-American paper *Der Pionier*.[75] Heinzen's review

---

73. Heinzen, *Die Helden des teutschen Kommunismus*, 21–23.

74. Heinzen, "Gegen die Kommunisten," 58. This was a common trope in republicanism. Linton, for example, argued that communists and socialists failed to see the importance of inspiring political ideals, arguing that in "one night the French Monarchy is overthrown by the very name of the Republic. And that charmed word Country, how men gave their blood for it in Hungary and Italy. Who follows to your [communist] shabby cry of personal gain?" [W. J. Linton], "Socialism and Communism," *English Republic* (1851), 1: 270.

75. The review does not name the author, but Heinzen's editorship of *Der Pionier* and the similarity of its tone and message to previous critiques make its ascription to Heinzen likely. Heinzen was probably made aware of Marx's book after *Das Volk* (the paper of the London German Workers' Educational Association) republished the preface on 4 June 1859, which was then circulated and republished in various German-American circles and papers; see *MEGA* II.2: 23* and 370–71.

zeroed in on what is often taken to be the most interesting section of Marx's book: a long passage in the preface in which Marx had described the "general conclusion" and "guiding principle of my studies."[76] It is one of the densest and richest passages of social and political thought, which contains some of the most central insights of his materialist conception of history. Marx wrote,

> In the social production of their life, men enter into definite relations that are indispensable and independent of their will, relations of production which correspond to a definite stage of development of their material productive forces. The totality of these relations of production constitutes the economic structure of society, the real foundation, on which arises a legal and political superstructure ... The mode of production of material life conditions the general process of social, political and intellectual life. It is not the consciousness of men that determines their existence, but their social existence that determines their consciousness. At a certain stage of development, the material productive forces of society come into conflict with the existing relations of production ... Then begins an era of social revolution.[77]

So important has this passage been in the subsequent understanding of Marx's conception of history and society that it is often referred to simply as the "1859 Preface" rather than by the title of the largely forgotten book that it precedes.[78] The passage is frequently seen as the clearest expression of what is sometimes called the technological determinist understanding of Marx's historical materialism, where the development of society's productive forces is given particular primacy. It played a foundational role in G. A. Cohen's analytic reconstruction of this version of historical materialism in his definitive *Karl Marx's Theory of History: A Defence* (1978), where Cohen used the passage as the epigraph to the book. The canonical status of the passage has, on the other hand, been questioned by those, such as Ellen Meiksins Wood, who prefer an interpretation of Marx's historical materialism that gives greater weight to class struggle.[79]

---

76. Marx, *Zur Kritik der politischen Ökonomie. Erstes Heft, MEGA* II.2: 100 / *MECW* 29: 262.

77. Ibid., 100–101 / 263.

78. William Clare Roberts, *Marx's Inferno: The Political Theory of Capital* (Princeton: Princeton University Press, 2017), 41.

79. Supporters of this interpretation point to the fact that the preface and the book were written under the threat of censorship, and that in order to get it published in Berlin, Marx had to be careful to avoid any mention of class struggle; see Arthur M. Prinz, "Background and Ulterior Motive of Marx's 'Preface' of 1859," *Journal of the History of Ideas* 30, no. 3 (1969): 437–50. Other proponents of the importance of class struggle do not deny the textual status of the 1859 Preface, but argue that we should be wary about putting an "enormous theoretical burden upon Marx's short-hand aphorisms" and should instead place greater weight on the analysis deployed

Heinzen's review reprinted the entire passage in full because he said this was where Marx "defines his standpoint."[80] The review began with Heinzen's customary Marx-denigration, noting that "the unbearable language in which this preface is written, will already form a great barrier to the propagandizing of Marxian theories."[81] He then argued that the whole theory of the preface was based on the "platitude" that people and their development are determined only by their "Hosentasche u. Maultasche"—a quite clever rhyming phrase not easily translated. Roughly, it refers to the "trouser-pocket" (i.e,. where people keep their money) and a type of German filled pasta that literally means "mouth-pocket" or "mouth-bag." In other words, the only determining factors in people's actions are money and food, or more broadly, the means of subsistence. Heinzen claims that Marx thereby reduces all history and society to the "doctrine of the two pockets (*Doktrin von den beiden Taschen*)," where all "other motives and motors" are unknown.[82] Consequently, even when,

> a woman's whim (*Weiberlaune*) overthrows a realm, a prince's whim (*Fürsten-laune*) devastates a continent, a Reformer's idea (*Reformator-Idee*) brings the whole world to its knees, and all "economy" and all "relations of production" are thrown aside—he will insist, that everything was brought about by the two pockets.[83]

The review annoyed Marx enough that eight years later he took the time to respond to it one of the longest footnotes in *Das Kapital*.[84] Here he (somewhat

---

across "his whole life's work"; Ellen Meiksins Wood, *Democracy against Capitalism: Renewing Historical Materialism* (Cambridge: Cambridge University Press, 1995), 129. See also G. E. M. de Ste. Croix, *The Class Struggle in the Ancient Greek World: From the Archaic Age to the Arab Conquests* (London: Duckworth, 1981), 46–47.

80. [Karl Heinzen], "Herr Karl Marx," *Der Pionier*, yr. 6, no. 26 (2 [12?] July 1859): 2. The review excludes the line "Then begins an era of social revolution," but this is most likely an editorial oversight.

81. Ibid., 3.

82. Ibid. Heinzen, probably aware of Marx's perennial money problems, adds here that Marx "could better look after both his pockets through other means, than by his critiques."

83. Ibid.

84. Marx does not precisely specify which review he has in mind. The *MEGA* and *MECW* editors identify Heinzen's "Herr Karl Marx" as the likely candidate (see MEGA II.8: 1005–6, II.9: 797–98, II.10: 823 and *MECW* 35: 772n78). Several considerations make this probable. Marx says in the footnote that he is responding to an "objection" to his *Zur Kritik der politischen Ökonomie* made in a "German-American paper," which would match Heinzen's *Der Pionier*. Marx then quotes several lines from the preface which he says the review had objected to, and these are the same ones that Heinzen had reproduced. Marx also makes a comparison with Don Quixote in the footnote, a character Marx had previously compared Heinzen to in "Die

schematically) took Heinzen to be saying that Marx's account might be true "for our own times, in which material interests predominate," but not for the "Middle Ages, dominated by Catholicism, nor for Athens and Rome, dominated by politics."[85] Marx responded to this argument by saying that the "Middle Ages could not live on Catholicism, nor could the ancient world on politics."[86] In other words, every society—no matter how much it might seem to be preoccupied by other concerns, such as religion and politics—still has to organize production. It is, in fact, the "manner in which they gained their livelihood," Marx continued, "which explains why in one case politics, in the other case Catholicism, played the chief part."[87] Thus Marx argued that in cases where it might seem that certain interests are driving history, proper investigation reveals that the actual driver is the underlying social requirement to organize production. How people gain "their livelihood" is thus the proper focus for historical explanation.

Marx gave the example of the Roman Republic to illustrate this point, arguing that the Republic's "secret history" is in fact the "history of landed property." Marx's reference seems to be to the conflicts between plebeians and patricians which dominated the final period of the republic. The conflict had several dimensions but centered on the control of the Roman public lands (*ager publicus*), which had over time increasingly fallen into the hands of the patricians. The attempts by the Gracchi brothers, Tiberius and Gaius, to restore a more equal distribution of the land are frequently blamed for the eventual downfall of the republic.[88] Thus Marx's point seems to be that while this conflict might appear to be a political dispute between different orders, actual investigation shows it to have been founded on one of the most basic social questions: control of land. Marx wryly notes that Heinzen was as misguided

---

moralisierende Kritik," *MEW* 4: 332 / *MECW* 6: 313. Finally, we know that Marx sometimes read *Der Pionier* in this period and referred to Heinzen's writings in them; see, for instance, Marx to Engels, 7 January 1858, *MEGA* III.9: 14, *MECW* 40: 243–44.

85. Marx, *Das Kapital*, vol. 1, *MEGA* II.6: 112n / *MECW* 35: 93n.

86. Ibid. Compare with Marx and Engels's earlier objection to historians who accept at face value how an "epoch imagines itself to be determined by purely 'political' or 'religious' motives," when in fact "'religion' and 'politics' are only forms of its true motives," "[Konvolut zu Feuerbach]," *MEGA* I.5: 48 / *MECW* 5: 55.

87. Marx, *Das Kapital*, vol. 1, *MEGA* II.6: 112n / *MECW* 35: 93n.

88. Marx discusses the *ager publicus* and its role in the Roman history and society at length in the section known as "Forms Preceding Capitalist Production" in *Grundrisse der Kritik der politischen Ökonomie*, *MEGA* II.1: 378–415 / *MECW* 28: 399–438.

about history as "Don Quixote who paid the price for mistakenly imagining that the knight errantry was compatible with all economic forms of society."[89]

Predictably, Marx and Heinzen's feud did not end there. Heinzen called *Das Kapital* "unreadable" and needled Marx for writing a book for workers that they could neither understand nor afford.[90] Marx in turn scoffed at Heinzen's seeming self-importance for believing he had "written 'Capital,' just so that *he* should not understand it."[91] The following years saw the two Karls continue to lob personal and public insults at each other.[92]

The People versus the Proletariat

Every revolution needs an agent, and republican and communist revolutionaries disagreed intensely about whether this should be the *people* or the *proletariat*. The manifesto of the European Central Democratic Committee (an organization for coordinating exiled republicans, set up in 1850 by Mazzini with Alexandre Ledru-Rollin, Albert Darasz, and Arnold Ruge), for instance, called on "the great realizer—the People" to come together in "one common accord."[93] Whereas the *Manifest* of the Bund der Kommunisten made it very clear that it was the *"proletarians of all countries"* that should *"unite."*[94] Republicans opposed this emerging socialist and communist rhetoric that prioritized the proletariat. They considered it a threat to their attempts to build a united front composed of several classes against the forces of reaction. Heinzen

89. Marx, *Das Kapital*, vol. 1, *MEGA* II.6: 112 / *MECW* 35: 93.

90. [Karl Heinzen], "Unser Redakteur," *Der Pionier*, yr. 16, no. 42 (13 October 1869): 4.

91. Marx to Engels, 6 November 1869, *MEW* 32: 384 / *MECW* 43: 367.

92. Heinzen devoted extensive space to Marx in his *Ueber Kommunismus und Sozialismus* (Indianapolis: Verein zur Verbreitung radikaler Prinzipien, 1872), vi–xii / *Communism and Socialism* (Indianapolis: Association for the Propagation of Radical Principles, 1881), 2–5, and *Erlebtes*, 414–44, while Marx called Heinzen a "democratic numbskull"; Marx to Friedrich Adolphe Sorge, 23 May 1872, *MEW* 33: 469 / *MECW* 44: 378.

93. "Aux Peuples! Organisation de le démocratie," *Le Proscrit: Journal de la république universelle*, no. 2 (August 1850), 8-9 / "To the Peoples, Organization of Democracy," *Red Republican* (7 September 1850): 95.

94. Marx and Engels, *Manifest der Kommunistischen Partei*, *MEW* 4: 493 / *MECW* 6: 519. It is a testament to the resilience of the rhetoric around the "people" that the first ever translation of the *Manifest*, into Swedish in December 1848, deleted the communist slogan and replaced it on the cover with the Swedish version of the Latin motto *Vox populi vox Dei* (*The voice of the people is the voice of God*). See Hans Haste, "Per Götrek och manifestet," in *Kommunismens röst. Förklaring af det Kommunistiska Partiet, offentliggjord i Februari 1848* (Stockholm: Pogo Press, 1976), xii; and Hal Draper, *The Adventures of the Communist Manifesto* (Alameda: Center for Socialist History, 2004), 25.

accused communists of "throwing themselves one-sidedly and exclusively on the proletariat" while at the same time "ignoring the rest of humanity."[95] Instead, they advocated, in Linton's words, "the regular association of all classes, the organized association of the people."[96]

But who were the *people* for the republicans and who did they think were fighting against? Broadly, the former meant not simply the entire citizen body, but the popular or non-elite subsection of it.[97] Thus Lamennais wrote that "The [few] compose, under different names, the superior—the upper classes;—of the [many] consists the PEOPLE."[98] The "few" included the old enemies: the king, his court, his bureaucrats and the aristocracy—all those who opposed popular sovereignty, universal suffrage, and the rights of the people. But republicans were also increasingly aware of a new emerging enemy. Take, for example, Julius Fröbel's list of the three "opponents of the republic": (1) the "birth-aristocracy (*Geburtsadel*)," (2) the "bureaucratic-aristocracy (*Beamtenadels*)," and (3) the "money-aristocracy (*Geldadels*)" or "competition-aristocracy (*Concurrenz-Adel*)." He argued that this last class were the "only opponents" worth discussing, because the other aristocracies were either without much power or quickly losing it, and because the "money-aristocracy" was only prepared to support a "constitutional monarchy" or at most a "capitalist's-republic (*Capitalisten-Republik*)."[99]

The extent to which the capitalist class (or its various early identifiers such as the "money-aristocracy") were seen as enemies of the people varied among republicans. We have already seen how Heinzen thought that the "men of power" were the primary enemies rather than the "men of the money-bags."[100] Linton on the one hand thought that "society ought not to depend upon the will of a few capitalists," but he also blamed socialists and communists for the

95. Heinzen noted that the communists seemed to think that one was only "entitled to human rights when one wears ripped trousers or goes hungry"; Heinzen, "Gegen die Kommunisten," 57.

96. W. J. Linton, "Republican Principles," *Red Republican*, vol. 1, no. 16 (5 October 1850): 125 / "Republican Principles," *English Republic* (1851), 1: 14.

97. For this difference, see Margaret Canovan, *The People* (Cambridge: Polity, 2005), 2–5; John P. McCormick, "People and Elites in Republican Constitutions, Traditional and Modern," in *The Paradox of Constitutionalism*, ed. Martin Loughlin and Neil Walker (Oxford: Oxford University Press, 2008), 107–25.

98. F. Lamennais, *Le livre du people* (Paris: H. Delloye et V. Lecou, 1838), 19 / *The Book of the People*, trans. J. H. Lorymer (London: H. Hetherington and J. H. Lorymer, 1838), 9.

99. Julius Fröbel, *Monarchie oder Republik? Ein Urtheil* (Mannheim: Heinrich Hoff, 1848), 10–11.

100. Heinzen, "Gegen die Kommunisten," 87.

failure of the Second Republic because of the "very hatred of the bourgeoisie directly fermented by them, by their incessant attacks upon competition and property."[101] Ruge wanted a society where there would be "neither a *bourgeois* nor a *proletarian*," but he also thought that getting to that society would require bourgeois allies.[102] Echoing Sieyès's famous slogan from the French Revolution, he argued that the workers were "not prepared in one stroke to become Everything, those who had until now been Nothing" and thus "property owners" had an "outstanding role" to play as the *"tribunus plebis sociali potestate (tribune of the people for the social power)."*[103] Republicans were thus conscious at times of the danger of the bourgeoisie to the people but also willing to ally with them against other enemies of the people.

The extent to which radicals should hope for support beyond the popular classes was a frequent source of division between republicans and communists. In a May 1852 article in George Julian Harney's paper the *Star of Freedom,* Linton criticized Chartism for having become a "Class Movement" when "we must have more than a Class Movement to obtain a national object." He advocated that Chartists should instead look to "what allies also we can obtain, from no matter what class," if they could be convinced to support Chartist aims. In general, he thought that the Chartists should avoid "confining the movement . . . to one class," because he was deeply "opposed to the people's movement being only a class movement."[104] Harney's advocacy of Chartist collaboration with the middle classes was one of the reasons why Marx and Engels distanced themselves from him, and Marx singled out his publishing of Linton's article as evidence that Harney was "rapidly getting into bad ways." In what seems to be Marx's only direct mention of Linton, he summarily dismissed Linton's views as "Genuine Mazzinian hot air (*Echtmazzinische Phrase*), etc., etc., etc."[105]

Marx's dismissive response to Linton was emblematic of his general antipathy to the republican rhetoric around the people. "The people" was a "broad and vague expression," and it was high time, he argued, to "replace" it with "a definite one, the proletariat."[106] Marx's objections to the people as a rhetorical appeal

101. W. J. Linton, "Republican Measures," *English Republic* (1851), 1: 155; [W. J. Linton], "Mazzini and his Socialist Opponents," *English Republic* (1852), 2: 123.

102. Arnold Ruge, *Die Gründung der Demokratie in Deutschland oder der Volkstaat und der Social-Demokratische Freistaat* (Leipzig: Verlagsbureau, 1849), 5.

103. Ibid., 65–66.

104. Spartacus [W. J. Linton], "The Sense of the Country," *The Star of Freedom,* vol. 1, no. 1 (8 May 1852): 4.

105. Marx to Adolf Cluß, between 10 and 14 May 1852, *MEGA* III.5: 121 / *MECW* 39: 107.

106. Marx, "Der Kommunismus des 'Rheinischen Beobachters,'" *MEW* 4: 193 / *MECW* 6: 222.

and as sociological category were that (1) the people actually consisted of several different classes with divergent and sometimes conflicting interests, (2) understanding these diverging and conflicting interests was central to political strategy, and (3) the language of the "people" and the associated idea of *fraternité* served the ideological function of obscuring these class differences.

Marx criticized what he saw as the republicans' simplistic sociological division of an elite versus the people. Marx acknowledged that "The democrat concedes that a privileged class confronts them," but at the same time criticized them for believing that "they, along with all the rest of the nation, form the *people*." Marx grumbled that republicans tended to brand those who "split the *indivisible* people into different hostile camps" as "pernicious sophists," but he emphasized that the republican position simply denied the sociological reality of a class-divided society.[107] He thus maintained that though the republicans' conception of the people rightly excluded a "privileged class," it failed to acknowledge that this subset of the population was further divided into different classes, such as proletarians, artisans, peasants, and petty bourgeoisie.

Marx argued that this denial allowed republicans to think that society consisted of a "majority . . . [of] *citoyens* with the same interests, the same understanding, etc." But this "*cult of the people (Volkskultus)*" resulted in an entirely skewed understanding of political realities. For Marx, this was exemplified by the first elections to the French Constituent National Assembly in April 1848, which, despite being held under manhood suffrage, returned an antirepublican majority. Marx argued that this upset rudely replaced the republicans' "*imaginary* people" with the "*real* people . . . that is, representatives of the different classes into which it falls." Republicans' failure to appreciate class differences and their differing class interests had left them unprepared for the possibility that the peasants and petty bourgeoisie could vote for the representatives of the bourgeoisie and landowners.[108] Furthermore, Marx maintained that the failure to "examine the interests and positions of the different classes" made them naïvely and dangerously overconfident in revolutionary situations. They thought that they "have merely to give the signal and the *people*, with all its inexhaustible resources, will fall upon the *oppressors*."[109]

Nothing captured the perniciousness of the republican emphasis of a united (rather than class-divided) people, for Marx, more than their invocation of *fraternité*. Marx repeatedly argued that this idea functioned as an ideological smokescreen, which disguised violently opposed class interests behind the

---

107. Marx, *Der achtzehnte Brumaire*, MEGA I.11: 127 / MECW 11: 133.

108. Marx, *Die Klassenkämpfe in Frankreich*, MEGA I.10: 135 / MECW 10: 65.

109. Marx, *Der achtzehnte Brumaire*, MEGA I.11: 127 / MECW 11: 133.

language of universal brotherhood. In February, right at the start of the revolution, it had perfectly captured the ecstatic and celebratory mood of the population. The "phrase" signified the "imaginary abolition of class relations," the "sentimental reconciliation of contradictory class interests" and the "visionary elevation above the class struggle."[110] But at that moment *fraternité* merely disguised the deeper class differences that were waiting to return to the surface. Marx maintained that the "brotherhood" it celebrated would last only "as long as there was a fraternity of interests between the bourgeoisie and the proletariat," and that came to a brutal halt in the June Days. There, *"fraternité . . .* found its true, unadulterated and prosaic expression in *civil war,* civil war in its most terrible aspect, the war of labor against capital."[111]

These criticisms were a perennial feature of Marx and Engels's polemical feuds with republicans. In their prerevolutionary clash with Heinzen they charged him with a class-blind conception of society, which they argued not only concealed his petty bourgeois (and even bourgeois) class bias but also hamstrung his calls for revolution. Engels accused Heinzen of having "never examined the position of the classes and parties" when it came to the possibility for revolution, and that he had only wildly and irresponsibly called to "Fight 'em, fight 'em, fight 'em!"[112] Marx in turn argued that though Heinzen *"differentiate[d]"* society into *"princes* and *subjects,"* he refused to recognize that there were "privileged and unprivileged subjects." In contrast, Marx insisted that as much as the "political *difference* between *prince* and *subject"* was a salient one, one also had to take into account the "social difference between *classes."*[113] (This was somewhat unfair to Heinzen, as his article had noted that there were bourgeois and proletarian subjects. However, his article had also called it a "communist narrow-mindedness to only address people class by class" and had mockingly suggested that Engels should set up a communist experiment "with 'small peasants,' 'petty bourgeoisie,' 'proletarians,' and miscellaneous classes in the primeval forests beyond the Mississippi."[114]) Marx further argued that Heinzen's refusal to engage in class analysis and his insistence instead that "all classes melt always before the solemn concept of 'humanity'" had an ideological function—namely, by invoking "humanity" as a "quality . . . which attaches to all men," he distracted from the brute fact that classes "are based on *economic*

110. Marx, *Die Klassenkämpfe in Frankreich, MEGA* I.10: 128 / *MECW* 10: 57–58.
111. Marx, "Die Junirevolution," *MEGA* I.7: 209 / *MECW* 7: 147.
112. Engels, "Die Kommunisten und Karl Heinzen," *MEW* 4: 313 / *MECW* 6: 295.
113. Marx, "Die moralisierende Kritik," *MEW* 4: 350 / *MECW* 6: 330–31.
114. Heinzen, "Ein 'Repräsentant' der Kommunisten," 3–4.

conditions independent of their own will," and that they cannot simply "shed their real relationships" in virtue of a supposed shared humanity.[115]

The same charges were repeated by Marx and Engels in their critique of the ECDC manifesto. They argued that the seemingly benign invocation of the "people," "fraternity," "association," and "common ground" on closer inspection revealed that the "authors of the manifesto deny the existence of the class struggles." The ECDC's strategy was in fact to "forbid the individual classes to formulate their interests and demands vis-à-vis the other classes" and "to forget their conflicting interests and to become reconciled under the flag of a vagueness as shallow as it is unblushing." Marx and Engels argued that "conceal[ed] beneath the apparent reconciliation" of different class interests lay the reality that they served the interests of "one party—the bourgeois party."[116]

Marx's attack on the category of the "people" and his advocacy of the proletariat did not mean that he wanted the proletariat to act entirely on its own, without the support of any other classes. The role that the proletariat was supposed to play in the revolution depended on: which revolution was being pursued (bourgeois or proletarian), the material and political circumstances of the country in question (especially the size and development of the different popular classes), and indeed at which point in Marx's intellectual evolution we are looking at (his pre- and postrevolutionary opinion on the matter). In general, we can say that Marx wanted the proletariat to lead the other popular classes that made up the "people" in a communist revolution. That meant primarily the peasants and elements of the petty bourgeoisie.[117] Marx thought that the peasants were, for various structural reasons, unable to lead the revolution, and thus it was up to the communists to show them that a "*constitutional republic* is the dictatorship of his united exploiters," whereas "*the social-democratic, the Red* republic, is the dictatorship of his allies."[118]

We should bear in mind that it is not surprising that republicans and communists would have different revolutionary agents since they were trying to achieve different revolutionary ends. Marx and Engels were aiming at a communist society in which wage-labor was abolished and replaced with the collectivization of the means of production. Republicans, on the other hand, were aiming for a society that would also radically alter social and economic conditions, but through the universalization of individual control of the means of

115. Marx, "Die moralisierende Kritik," *MEW* 4: 349-50 / *MECW* 6: 330.

116. Marx and Engels, "Revue. Mai bis Oktober 1850," *MEGA* I.10: 486 / *MECW* 10: 530.

117. Engels, for instance, notes, "the people, i.e., the proletarians, small peasants and petty bourgeoisie," and also that these classes "constitute . . . the 'people'"; "Die Kommunisten und Karl Heinzen," *MEW* 4: 312–13 / *MECW* 6: 294–95.

118. Marx, *Die Klassenkämpfe in Frankreich*, *MEGA* I.10: 187 / *MECW* 10: 122.

production. Given these diverging goals, it is not surprising that they would try to appeal to different constituencies. I turn now to the social measures that were supposed to bring about their alternative societies.

Republican versus Communist Social Measures

The social changes wrought by capitalism were not lost on republicans. Nor was the threat posed by the emerging communist movement. The social promises of communists threatened to undermine republicanism's traditional working-class support. They were accustomed to representing the advanced party of movement and were initially disconcerted by the emergence of communism. They responded by developing their own social program that would, they believed, fundamentally transform capitalism *without* instituting communism. Some of these social measures, such as progressive taxation and free education, may today strike us as hardly radical, but we should remember that they were nonexistent in the mid-nineteenth century, and advocating them put one on the far left of the political spectrum. Furthermore, many of the proposed social measures go beyond what has been achieved today and remain a radical alternative to contemporary capitalism. I will here outline the main institutional and policy ideas they proposed and defended. Not all republicans, even the more radical, defended every single one of these measures of course. But these measures show up again and again in disparate republican articles, pamphlets, and manifestos, to the extent that they amount to something close to a common social program. They were also united by an underlying concern to overcome the dependency of capitalist wage-labor by expanding property ownership.

The first social measure that republicans emphasized was to give the rural population free access to the land in order to restore their independence. The most radical republicans believed that the land was rightly the common property of the people. They argued that while people had a right to the proceeds from working the land, they had no right to own the land itself. Land was instead to be communally owned by the state.[119] These republicans thus held to the principle that "*the Nation is the sole proprietor of the of the Land and none hold rightfully except as tenants of the Nation.*"[120] Heinzen suggested that the state would become the sole landowner over time through a system of

---

119. K. Heinzen, "Kommunistisches," in *Teutsche Revolution: Gesammelte Flugschriften* (Bern: Jenni, Sohn, 1847), 372; Linton, "Republican Principles," 147 / 1: 20.

120. Linton, "Republican Measures," 1: 123.

compensated expropriation and abolition of inheritance.[121] Linton proposed a detailed plan for land reform where a uniform tax would be levied on every acre of land. Those with large landholdings would be forced by financial necessity to give up their excess lands (Linton added that if not enough land was made available in this way, a maximum limit on acres per person could also be instituted), and these lands would pass into state ownership. The state would then open these lands to settlement by agricultural laborers. These agricultural colonies would be supervised by a government officer and be provided with sufficient capital to farm the land. The proceeds would, after the deduction of the officer's salary, the per acre tax, and the (interest-free) repayment of the capital, be divided up between the laborers. Once they had paid back the capital, they would control the land in perpetual tenure.[122] Linton believed that these measures would remove the dependency of the landless rural population on the land-owning class. Agricultural laborers would no longer be at the "mercy of the farmer," because the option of working on state lands would give them the bargaining power to "force the master to terms." Those working on state lands would eventually control (but not own) their own land and thus be "their own masters, subject to no supervision." In this way, Linton hoped to create a "new race of independent peasant freeholders."[123]

However, these land reform measures would—as republicans recognized—only indirectly help the urban laboring population, by reducing the pressure on wages from rural migration to the cities. More direct measures were necessary if the republicans were to appeal to the urban working class. They thus proposed that the state had to provide every worker with access to free credit and free education. Linton once again provided a detailed plan of how the republican state should provide these benefits.

In order for the monopoly over capital exercised by the capitalist class to be broken, Linton argued that "the State must be the capitalist, the banker and the money-lender."[124] Expropriating the capitalist or forcing them to lend their capital was out of the question—"an infringement of individual right, a kind of spoliation"—but he thought that the state should set up a national bank with branches throughout the country that would give interest-free loans to laborers in order for them to buy tools and to cover them and their family's living costs if they had fallen ill or been thrown out of work because of market

---

121. Heinzen, "Gegen die Kommunisten," 81–82.

122. Linton, "Republican Principles," 147–48 / 1: 20; Linton, "Republican Measures," 1: 124–25.

123. Linton, "Republican Measures," 1: 124.

124. Linton, "Republican Principles," 156 / 1: 21.

fluctuations.[125] Importantly, these loans were interest free, but they were not grants; a laborer who refused or was unable to repay the credit would be put before a jury and potentially imprisoned.[126] The primary emphasis in this program was on individual laborers being able to apply for the means for them to work—a policy geared toward artisans. However, Linton did note in passing that worker associations should be allowed to apply for credit as well, arguing that they would only be able to successfully "contend or compete with the masters" if the state provided them with sufficient capital.[127] According to Linton, the provision of free credit was supposed to ensure the "independence of the workers," who would now "no longer be dependent upon the will of the monied classes."[128] Moreover, it would mean that "Capital will cease to be an engine in the hands of the few for the oppression of the many; and property, instead of being confined to the few, will be attainable by all."[129] Free credit also brought together the republican aim of securing independence for urban workers, with the emphasis on land reform. In the social republican program developed by Bronterre O'Brien's National Reform League, set up in 1850, it was held that "a sound system of National Credit" would give everyone the financial means "to rent and cultivate land on his own account instead of being subjected, as now, to the injustice and tyranny of wages-slavery."[130]

In republican plans, the provision of free credit was paired with free education. For adults, this meant that the state would "provide every citizen, without discrimination based on vocation or sex, the opportunity to learn their chosen vocation in an educational institution."[131] For children, this meant that the state would create public schools that were free and obligatory. Linton even advocated that all children—boys and girls—should attend state boarding schools so that they could be "subjected to that perfect equality which is the first lesson to be taught by the Republic." In Linton's proposal, boys and girls would start school at age seven (or nine if the parents wished) and board until they were fourteen. Girls would then have the option to live

125. Linton, "Republican Measures," 1: 155.

126. Ibid, 1: 155–56.

127. Ibid., 1: 156; [W. J. Linton], "Working-Men's Combinations. Strikes and Co-Operative Associations," *English Republic* (1852), 2: 18. Heinzen also made "working associations to be promoted with free credit from the state bank" one of the key social measures in his proposed republican program, *Programm der teutschen Revolutionspartei*, section II, article 3c.

128. Linton, "Republican Measures," 1: 156.

129. [W. J. Linton], "Republican Catechism," *English Republic* (1851), 1: 148.

130. *Propositions of the National Reform League: For the Peaceful Regeneration of Society* (London: Working Printers' Cooperative Association, 1850), 3.

131. Heinzen, *Programm der teutschen Revolutionspartei*, section II, article 3d.

at home again but would have to continue their studies in school until they were eighteen. Boys from age eighteen to twenty would carry out an apprenticeship, and then be sent to travel for a further year. On their return they would be "solemnly acknowledged a citizen, a free man, the uncontrouled [*sic*] master of his own actions, accountable only to the laws, and entitled to share in the common wealth." At eighteen both sexes would—like "the young Athenian [who] swore in the temple to make his Country greater and more glorious"—swear an oath that "henceforth their lives [were] to be devoted to their Country and to Humanity." Republican education was therefore not only a tool to address social inequality but also one used to inculcate the virtues necessary for republican citizenship. Giving each citizen the spiritual conditions for independence would mean that they would avoid becoming the "slave of the intelligent" and would also have the political advantage of protecting the republic from the dangers of demagogues and would-be despots.[132] As Ruge observed, "the democrat knows that an uneducated people always falls into the hands of charlatans, clerics and seducers."[133]

In industry and production, republicans advocated extensive state involvement, but deliberately stopped short of advocating complete state control of the economy. Linton opposed the state's setting up its own industrial workshops but proposed creating state-run public storehouses and bazaars where workers and peasants could at all times sell and buy produce at a *"fair price."*[134] For Heinzen, the state's proper role in the economy was as a "third person who represents the common interest." He thus advocated that for those industries which "can only be made profitable for the general public (*Allgemeinheit*) through the means of the general public," the state should take complete control of them. He singled out the railways as one such industry (roads and canals were also frequently included in republican proposals). For those industries where it was better that they were run by individuals and associations, Heinzen argued that the state should additionally set up competing state firms so that consumers are not cheated by firms making a higher than "normal profit."[135]

Ruge went perhaps the furthest in his recommendations, setting out a vision of production organized into a network of *Sozietäten* (partnerships).[136] Each *Sozietät* would generally be made of up of several families who would

132. Linton, "Republican Measures," 1: 180–83.

133. Ruge, *Gründung der Demokratie*, 38.

134. Linton, "Republican Measures," 1: 157.

135. Heinzen, "Kommunistisches," 374, 376.

136. Ruge, *Gründung der Demokratie*, 43–52. See the useful summary in Stephan Walter, *Demokratisches Denken zwischen Hegel und Marx: Die politische Philosophie Arnold Ruges; Eine Studie zur Geschichte der Demokratie in Deutschland* (Düsseldorf: Droste, 1995), 257–63.

produce together and as individuals. Instead of receiving a wage, each member of the *Sozietät* would receive a share of the total surplus according to their labor contribution. This would ensure that no surplus went to a distinct landlord or a capitalist. Members would have the option of leaving the *Societät* with their share of the partnership that they had earned, but when a member died all of their shares would be inherited by the united members to avoid shares becoming concentrated in a single individual. According to Ruge, the *Societät* system would mean the abolition of wage-labor, since the members would no longer rely on a master paying them wages. This was crucial to Ruge, as "*wage-labor* and *service* are incompatible with self-determination"; he adds that someone "who works for a foreign interest, is determined by a foreign will . . . [and] through wages a person becomes a tool of another person." In a democracy, however, the "highest principle is that everyone is their own master."[137]

Supplementing these large-scale social measures, republicans also endorsed a number of further measures to ensure the social basis of the republic. These included progressive taxation, state provision for the sick and elderly, centralization and regulation of the banking system, free access to justice, and—perhaps most radically—the restriction or even abolition of inheritance.[138] This last requirement was a "core demand of radical democrats during the Vormärz and Revolution."[139] As Heinzen argued, the "*right of inheritance* cannot be sustained in the face of reason," and in any case, inheritance would lose its common justification in a republic that provided its citizens with all of the social necessities listed above. He maintained that while a person could dispose of their property as they wished while they were alive, "what he leaves behind at his death, becomes property of the general public (the state)."[140]

Heinzen believed that the combination of progressive taxation and abolishing inheritance would indirectly set a "*maximum*" for how much property each person could own (which he noted could also be supplemented by a directly imposed maximum). The revenue collected through this maximum would in turn be used to fund a "*minimum*" for each citizen, which would consist in giving each "citizen who comes of age the basis and the means" for subsistence. This could mean a piece of land, free housing for a certain period, or the "material or certain sum" of money necessary to begin their chosen profession.[141] Heinzen does not explore this idea of a "*minimum*" further, but it has intriguing similarities

137. Ruge, *Gründung der Demokratie*, 47.

138. Linton, "Republican Measures," 1: 88; Heinzen, *Programm der teutschen Revolutionspartei*, section II, articles 3a, b, and e.

139. Walter, *Demokratisches Denken zwischen Hegel und Marx*, 258.

140. Heinzen, "Gegen die Kommunisten," 82–83.

141. Ibid.; Heinzen, "Kommunistisches," 372–73.

with the modern idea of basic stake holding or basic capital, where every citizen receives a lump sum from the state at age eighteen.[142] Perhaps surprisingly, the idea of basic income, where every citizen receives an unconditional and regular income, does not crop up in the list of common republican social measures.[143] This may be because giving each citizen an income regardless of whether or not they worked would have conflicted with the importance republicans placed on work and self-reliance (a value discussed in greater detail in the next section).[144]

Taken together, the various republican social measures represent a significant and far-reaching program of social reform. Republicans believed that they would ensure that the social relations of domination and servitude that marked their societies would be replaced by each citizen having the material and spiritual conditions for independence. The landless peasant would no longer be reliant on the landlord, but would be able to farm their own land. Access to credit would free the worker from the control of the capitalist and the indignities of wage-labor. Opportunities for worker cooperatives and economic partnerships would be greatly expanded. Universal education would create a new generation of self-reliant republican citizens. The state would take an active regulatory and interventionist role in the economy and the financial system. Concentrations of wealth would be severely restricted by the abolition of inheritance, the introduction of progressive taxes, and maximum limits placed on land and property ownership. The world they would have created would thus not only have been an enormous step forward by the standards of the mid-nineteenth century, but would, in several respects, go beyond what modern welfare states have achieved. It is a vision Ruge characterized as *"the solution of the social question"* by removing all relations of domination and

142. See Bruce Ackerman and Anne Alstott, *The Stakeholder Society* (New Haven: Yale University Press, 1999); Keith Dowding, Jurgen De Wispelaere, and Stuart White, eds., *The Ethics of Stakeholding* (Basingstoke: Palgrave Macmillan, 2003); and Stuart White, *The Civic Minimum: On the Rights and Obligations of Economic Citizenship* (Oxford: Oxford University Press, 2003), chapter 8.

143. An unconditional basic income was proposed by Joseph Charlier in 1848, but had little influence at the time; see John Cunliffe and Guido Erreygers, "The Enigmatic Legacy of Charles Fourier: Joseph Charlier and Basic Income," *History of Political Economy* 33, no. 3 (2001): 459–84, and John Cunliffe and Guido Erreygers, "The Archaeology of Stakeholding and Social Justice: The Foundations in Mid-19th-Century Belgium," *European Journal of Political Theory* 7, no. 2 (2008): 189–90.

144. Stuart White suggests that Rousseau would have been opposed to a basic income for similar reasons; see his "Rediscovering Republican Political Economy," *Imprints* 4, no. 3 (2000): 224.

dependency through the "implementation of the democratic principle to the economic, the political, and the free community."[145]

Republicans quite clearly saw this as offering an alternative to capitalism. Giving the state the responsibility to provide credit to the people would, in Linton's words, "rid us of all those mischievous middlemen called capitalists" and the "tyranny of capital would be at an end."[146] Heinzen declared that he would be "satisfied" if the end result of all these measures was that the "capitalists left their institutions to the state or that the workers became Associés."[147] Their vision was thus supposed to be and was self-consciously understood as a radical alternative to capitalism.

But, at the same time, republicans were always keen to stress that their social program did not amount to communism. Such denials were important because at first glance it was not always easy for an observer to tell the difference.

Take, for instance, the following extract from the ten communist demands listed by Marx and Engels in the *Manifest der Kommunistischen Partei*:

1. Abolition of property in land and application of all rents of land to public purposes.
2. A heavy progressive or graduated income tax.
3. Abolition of all right of inheritance ...
5. Centralization of credit in the hands of the State, by means of a national bank with State capital and an exclusive monopoly.
10. Free education for all children in public schools ... [148]

Or a similar selection from the seventeen-point program in the *Forderungen der Kommunistischen Parthei in Deutschland*, released a month later:

5. Legal services to be free of charge ...
10. A state bank, whose paper issues are legal tender, shall replace all private banks ...
14. The right of inheritance to be curtailed.
15. The introduction of steeply graduated taxes ...
17. Universal and free education of the people.[149]

The similarity of these social demands to republican ones was not lost on either side. Engels said of Heinzen's proposed reforms that "[t]hey are such as the

---

145. Ruge, *Gründung der Demokratie*, 35.

146. Linton, "Republican Principles," 156 / 1: 22; Linton, "Republican Measures," 1: 157.

147. Heinzen, *Programm der teutschen Revolutionspartei*, section II, footnote.

148. Marx and Engels, *Manifest der Kommunistischen Partei*, MEW 4: 481–82 / MECW 6: 505.

149. Marx, Schapper, H. Bauer, Engels, Moll, and Wolff, *Forderungen der Kommunistischen Parthei in Deutschland*, MEGA I.7: 25–26 / MECW 7: 3–4.

Communists themselves suggest"; while Heinzen responded to the *Forderungen* by arguing that "just like the demand for light and water, every reasonable person must share them, [but] without thereby belonging to the communist 'party.'"[150]

The line between the two camps thus cannot be drawn by these social reforms. Republicans could endorse them without becoming communists, and communists could advocate them without being straightforward republicans. The difference instead lies in whether these social measures were supposed to be a goal in and of themselves or as a step toward a further end. For republicans, the social measures were sufficient to ensure that the republic realized its social promise. But for communists, they formed only an initial package of revolutionary measures on the path to the final goal of communism. Karl Schapper thus argued that Heinzen "demands nearly the same thing as the communists demand. The only difference between us, is that Citizen Carl Heinzen sees his [program] as the basis of a new society; whereas we [see] it as the basis of a transition period, that will lead us to complete community."[151] Engels subsequently repeated Schapper's argument in his own response to Heinzen, arguing that for communists these social measures were "preparatory steps, temporary transitional stages, toward the abolition of private property . . . Herr Heinzen however wants all these measures as permanent, final measures. They are not to be a preparation for anything, they are to be definitive. They are for him not a means but an end."[152]

Abolition of (Bourgeois) Private Property versus Universalization of (Petty Bourgeois) Private Property

The key social difference between republicans and communism was the question of private property. Communism was, already before Marx and Engels, associated with the idea of *abolishing* private property. Republicans countered that the correct response to the problems of private property was not to abolish it but to *universalize* it. Typical formulations include Ruge's argument that in the republican social program "*property* is realized rather than abolished" and in place of "a community of goods . . . every person will come into possession [of

150. Engels, "Die Kommunisten und Karl Heinzen," *MEW* 4: 313 / *MECW* 6: 295; Heinzen, *Die Helden des teutschen Kommunismus*, 97.

151. [Karl Schapper], "Proletariar!," *Kommunistische Zeitschrift*, no. 1 (September 1847): 5; *BdK*, 1: 507.

152. Engels, "Die Kommunisten und Karl Heinzen," *MEW* 4: 313–14 / *MECW* 6: 295–96.

property]."[153] Similarly, Linton maintained that "Our complaint is not that there is too much individual property, but that there is too little; not that the few have, but that many have not."[154] This formed a central, perhaps even *the* central, difference between republicanism and communism. Thus, some republicans were occasionally willing to adopt the label "socialist" if this was, on Lamennais's account, loosely defined as being in support of social reform and the "principle of association"; but if socialism was taken to mean "the negation, explicit or implied, of property," then—Lamennais insisted—"no . . . we are not *Socialist*."[155] What republicans could never countenance was communism, which was always in their minds inherently associated with the abolition of private property.[156]

Marx and Engels were originally willing to associate their communism with the slogan "abolition of private property (*Aufhebung / Abschaffung des Privateigenthums*)."[157] But in the *Manifest der Kommunistischen Partei* they insisted that this slogan had to be refined. They claimed that the "abolition of existing property relations is not at all a distinctive feature of Communism," because this had been a continual feature of past social change (the French Revolution, for instance, had "abolished feudal property in favor of bourgeois property"). That meant that the "distinguishing feature of Communism is not the abolition of property generally, but the abolition of bourgeois property," that is, the kind of property based on the exploitation of wage-labor (i.e., capital). With that clarification in place, they continued, "In this sense, the theory of the Communists may be summed up in the single sentence: Abolition of private property."[158] Marx and Engels insisted on making this clarification because they were trying to sharpen the nature of their disagreement with republicans.[159] When republicans aimed to universalize private property, what they really meant (from Marx and Engels's perspective) was

153. Arnold Ruge, *Die Loge des Humanismus* (Bremen: Verlag des Herausgebers, 1852), 43.

154. Linton, "Republican Principles," 147 / 1: 18.

155. Lamennais, *Question du travail*, 8–9 / 2: 267–78.

156. Linton, "Socialism and Communism," 1: 267–68.

157. Marx and Engels, "[Konvolut zur Feuerbach]," *MEGA* I.5: 42 / *MECW* 5: 51; Engels, *Entwurf des Kommunistischen Glaubensbekenntnisses*, *BdK* 1: 470 / *MECW* 6: 96; Engels, *Grundsätze des Kommunismus*, *MEW* 4: 370–72 / *MECW* 6: 348–49; Engels, "Die Kommunisten und Karl Heinzen," *MEW* 4: 313, 322 / *MECW* 6: 295, 303–4.

158. Marx and Engels, *Manifest der Kommunistischen Partei*, *MEW* 4: 475 / *MECW* 6: 498. See also the clarification in Marx, *The Civil War in France (First Draft)*, *MEGA* I.22: 73 / *MECW* 22: 504; *The Civil War in France*, *MEGA* I.22: 142-43 / *MECW* 22: 335.

159. As is clear from Marx's insistence on the historical nature of the "question of property" in his reply to Heinzen a few months before; see Marx, "Die moralisierende Kritik," *MEW* 4: 341–42, 356–57 / *MECW* 6: 322–24, 337–38.

the universalization of "petty bourgeois . . . property," that is, the "self-acquired, self-earned property" based on one's own labor, the kind of property acquired by small artisans and peasants.[160] As we will see below, Marx and Engels thought there was no need to abolish this form of petty bourgeois private property because it was already being pushed aside by bourgeois private property and the efficiency associated with large-scale production. They thought the only realistic response was to collectivize this form of production so that bourgeois private property was "converted into common property, into the property of all members of society."[161] The question, for Marx and Engels, when given a chance to refine their views, was thus not simply about whether or not to abolish private property, but whether petty bourgeois property should be universalized or bourgeois private property abolished and replaced by collective property.[162]

Before looking at Marx and Engels's position in greater detail, it is worth exploring what arguments republicans made in favor of private property (that is, private property in the sense that they understood it). The three most prominent justifications for private property given by the republicans were that (1) people had the right to the fruits of their labor, (2) it was the basis of individuality, and (3) it was a condition for freedom and independence.[163] The centrality of work and its link to private property was enshrined in the ECDC's founding manifesto, which declared that "We believe in the holiness of work, in its inviolability, in the property which proceeds from it as its sign and its fruit."[164] Linton took it upon himself to flesh out and defend the ECDC's position. He gave the examples of clearing and working a piece of land, growing and tending to a rose-tree, raising a dog from a puppy, and decorating and improving your house. Linton argued that in all of these cases the property "is the result of the sign and the fruit of my toil" and is therefore "inviolable, sacred as individual right." Consequently, "No government, state, or commonweal has any right

160. Marx and Engels, *Manifest der Kommunistischen Partei, MEW* 4: 475 / *MECW* 6: 498.

161. Ibid., 476 / 499.

162. I am particularly grateful to William Clare Roberts for pushing me to clarify this point.

163. Republicans can be seen as concocting a mixture of Lockean and Hegelian arguments for private property; see Jeremy Waldron, *The Right to Private Property* (Oxford: Clarendon Press, 1988), chapters 6, 8.

164. "Aux Peuples! Organisation de le démocratie," 10 / 95. Marx and Engels, in their response to the ECDC manifesto, noted that the actual extent to which "bourgeois property is 'the fruit and sign of labour'" had already been shown by Adam Smith "eighty years" before these "revolutionary initiators"; "Revue. Mai bis Oktober 1850," *MEGA* I.10: 487 / *MECW* 10: 531. The implication is that modern bourgeois property was the result of the division of labor and modern production techniques and not the work of the property owner.

here, to trench upon my personal, private, individual right, to rob me for even the world's benefit."[165] Similar defenses were made by Heinzen, who argued that the "produce of my hands and my spirit, i.e., my work, is *mine* and *no one else's*."[166]

The second underlying justification given by republicans for the right to private property derived from work was that the property derived from it formed an essential element in the development and expression of a person's individuality. Linton stressed that each of the above examples created "a sacred thing to me," which were "a radiance from my own light of life, an emanation from myself," whereas for communists, he argued, the "denial of individualism is consistent with the denial of property."[167] Mazzini argued that property was the "representation of human individuality in the material world," and the "sentiments which naturally grow with its cultivation" meant that it deserved protection.[168] Heinzen similarly maintained that the "free unfolding of [a person's] natural abilities and instincts" required "the means, the possibility, to create his individual world."[169] Thus, in order to flourish as individuals, republicans believed that you had to have the ability to enjoy the property you create through labor without the interference of others.

The third republican justification for private property was that property formed an essential condition for freedom, understood as being free from the arbitrary power of others. Ruge, for instance, argued that property had to be made into "that which it is meant to be, the basis of freedom of every individual within the whole."[170] Republicans tended to make two kinds of argument linking property and freedom. On the one hand, republicans argued that one could not be free without property. A propertyless person was dependent on others for work and for the necessities of life, and this dependency made one unfree. As Lamennais summarized, "To be independent, master of one's-self, completely free,—one must have possession of that which is necessary for the life of the body. Property is the material condition of freedom."[171] Propertyless workers, Lamennais argued, needed "property, without which there is no liberty" in order to avoid the "harsh dependence" created by being "forced to

165. Linton, "Republican Principles," 147 / 1: 18.

166. Heinzen, "Gegen die Kommunisten," 80.

167. Respectively, Linton, "Republican Principles," 147 / 1: 18, and Linton, "Socialism and Communism," 1: 268.

168. Mazzini, "Thoughts upon Democracy in Europe," 3: 222.

169. Heinzen, "Gegen die Kommunisten," 74.

170. Arnold Ruge, "Drei Briefe über den Communismus," in *Gesammelte Schriften*, vol. 9 (Mannheim: J. P. Grohe, 1847), 402.

171. Lamennais, *Question du travail*, 12 / 2: 286.

obtain from the possessor of wealth and power the means of subsistence."[172]
On the other hand, republicans argued that if one tried to abolish property by
handing it over to the state (as they charged socialists and communists with
advocating), one would, similarly, be dependent on the state and hence also
unfree. Lamennais argued that the socialist and communist aim of "absolute
concentration of property in the hands of the state" meant that their attempt
to create the "conditions of universal liberty" actually resulted in the "basis of
a universal slavery." State ownership of property simply meant that it would
now be the "heads of the state" who decided on who worked, meaning that
they would be just like "the master in ancient times . . . with regard to those
placed under his orders, [who] are dependent on him for their labor and its
reward" (Lamennais claimed that this would be the case even if the state's
leaders were elected).[173] Lamennais was completely convinced that the "realization of the communist system" would be "forced labor, rewarded according
to the pleasure of the State."[174] For republicans the consequence of these two
arguments was that it was unacceptable—from the perspective of freedom—
for anyone to be without property and equally for property to be abolished,
and so they advocated the "extension of personal property [which] assures the
life of each in universal liberty."[175]

Insisting on the right to private property meant that republicans were willing to tolerate a greater degree of economic inequality than most communists,
for if people are allowed to keep the property earned through work, then
differing levels of talent and effort inevitably produce economic inequality
over time. Ruge was unembarrassed by this aspect of his system of *Sozietäten*.
He maintained that "economic equality is . . . impossible," for it could only be
upheld if the members were banned from having more than they consumed
or if the *Sozietät*'s surplus was shared communally.[176] The tolerance for economic inequality was exhibited in, and was a consequence of, how the republicans defined "equality" in the trinity of liberty and fraternity. Linton assured
his readers that "By *Equality* is not meant the equal of condition of all men—
as dreamed of by some socialists." Instead, the "equality we desire is at the
starting point."[177] Thus, rather than endorsing the stronger conception of

---

172. F. Lamennais, *Du passé et de l'avenir du people* (Paris: Pagnere, 1841), 130 / *Words of a
Believer and the Past and Future of the People*, trans. L. E. Martineau (London: Chapman and
Hall, 1891), 182.

173. Ibid., 152–53 / 194.

174. Lamennais, *Question du travail*, 11 / 2: 286.

175. Ibid., 13 / 2: 287.

176. Ruge, *Gründung der Demokratie*, 44–45.

177. Linton, "Republican Principles," 110 / 1: 10–11.

equality as equality of outcome, the democratic republicans defended "only the equality of opportunity."[178]

The commitment to private property also meant that republicans were more hesitant to implement social measures that involved the forced transfer of property. This is demonstrated by the processes they chose to implement some of the social measures discussed earlier. Linton preferred rich landlords to be indirectly forced to give up their land through a per acre tax, rather than its being forcefully expropriated, and Heinzen seems to have had a preference for having the "*maximum*" property level regulated by the removal of inheritance and introduction of progressive taxes, rather than a directly fixed upper level. Heinzen also emphasized that the state would become the "sole land- · owner . . . gradually," through the abolition of inheritance and compensated expropriation.[179] Linton provided a principled defense of this reticence. A "rich man" might be "dull, brutish, [and] selfish" for refusing to give up his property, but the correct response was to "educate me, enlighten me, better me" to share with others. Linton insisted that what no one had a right to do was "to cross my threshold, to touch the veriest trifle that I have honestly earned or obtained, to profane my household gods, to violate my individual right, which stands sovereignly, however savagely, defying the world."[180]

After the radicalism of the republican social measures, the unabashed defense of private property can come as a surprise—especially for modern readers used to radical politics being tied to opposing private property. Indeed, in the passages cited above, the republicans often sound more like reactionary opponents of communism than radical social critics. But an important qualifier must be added here: these republicans did not endorse the unlimited or even extensive right to accumulate private property. They made it very clear that the right to private property had to be limited by the state. For instance, Linton was keen to stress that the flipside of having a right to property fairly gained through work was that there was no automatic right to the property gained otherwise. A landlord had no right to land that their distant ancestor— "some duke (thieves' leader) of by-gone days"—had stolen. Or if an "usurer" or "*capitalist*" takes advantage of his "fellow's need to over-reach the common

---

178. Linton, "Republican Catechism," 1: 146.

179. Heinzen, "Gegen die Kommunisten," 81. In comparison, Marx and Engels urged that wherever republicans demanded the "purchase of the railways and factories," the communists should instead demand that they are "simply confiscated without compensation"; see "Ansprache der Zentralbehörde des Bundes der Kommunisten vom März 1850," *MEGA* I.10: 263 / *MECW* 10: 286.

180. Linton, "Republican Principles," 147 / 1: 19.

ground of human brotherhood," then his "profit is not his *property*."[181] (Linton thereby seemed in fact to allow for some forms of wage-labor and profit, those that do not "over-reach the common ground of human brotherhood.") He also specified that the accumulation of property had to be limited so that no one was "prevent[ed] [by] another from producing to the utmost of his capacity."[182] Heinzen's "*maximum*" was similarly intended to ensure that no "corrupting inequalities" between citizens could develop and that that "inequality . . . is not allowed to go so far, that one person through the other loses his means of subsistence and his existence."[183] He also emphasized that the social measures taken by the republic would ensure "the inequality of possession cannot lead to any other social or political differences which violate free humanity."[184] Broadly, republicans thus believed that no citizen should be allowed to accumulate so much property that it threatened the political equality of all citizens or meant that others were no longer able to provide for themselves and would thus fall into dependency.

While republicans provided an extensive set of normative arguments for why private property should be extended rather than abolished, Marx and Engels refused to meet them on this normative terrain. They explicitly refused to delve into a moral discussion of the underlying principle—whether, for instance, people have a right to property derived from work, when each person's ability to work might be seen as the consequence of morally arbitrary social backgrounds and natural talents.[185] Of course, arguments against the desirability of private property can be drawn from Marx and Engels's ethical writings and ideas. But this was not the kind of response that they were interested in providing in their direct political confrontation with republicans. Their response instead shifted the terrain to political economy and historical development. "The *property question*" was, as Marx explained, not about "simplistic questions of conscience and clichés about justice," but about the "the stage of development of industry." That meant dealing with the "conflicts which have arisen from large-scale industry, the development of the world market and free competition."[186]

181. Ibid.

182. Ibid., 148 / 1: 20.

183. Heinzen, "Kommunistisches," 372; "Gegen die Kommunisten," 81.

184. Heinzen, "Gegen die Kommunisten," 83.

185. The classic modern formulation of this idea is John Rawls, *A Theory of Justice*, rev. ed. (Cambridge: Belknap Press, 1999), 64.

186. Marx, "Die moralisierende Kritik," *MEW* 4: 341–42 / *MECW* 6: 322. That kind of answer differs sharply from the kind of answer Engels was forced to accede to in the June 1847 draft of the *Manifest der Kommunistischen Partei* that he hammered out with other leaders of the Bund

By this, Marx meant that republicans had failed to appreciate the transformative and destructive power of capitalist industry and market competition. This, Marx maintained, undermined all republican hope of widely dispersing property ownership because the associated political economy was an outdated vision of production based on artisanal and small-scale craft production. This "petty bourgeois" mode of production based on individual independent producers was being steadily swept aside by the relentless forward march of capitalist mass production. Republicans were thus, according to Marx and Engels, not so much morally misguided as mistaken on a historically epochal scale, because they were trying to defend a mode of production that was becoming increasingly and inevitably out of date. This was the response they gave in the *Manifest der Kommunistischen Partei* when discussing the right to acquire private property. While republicans (unlike various competing socialisms) were not explicitly targeted in the *Manifest*, they were the critics in question when Marx and Engels wrote, "We Communists have been reproached with the desire of abolishing the right of personally acquitting property as the fruit of a man's own labor, which property is alleged to be the groundwork of all personal freedom, activity and independence."[187] Heinzen had, for instance, argued just a few months before the *Manifest*'s publication that by "stripping away all private property . . . communism destroys individuality, it destroys independence, it destroys freedom."[188] Marx and Engels's mocking reply to this charge was to insist that "[h]ard-won, self-acquired, self-earned property!," was simply the property created by the "petty artisan" and the "small peasant." They argued that this kind of private property did not need to be abolished, since "the development of industry has to a great extent already

---

der Kommunisten. In response to the question "On what do you base your community of property?" the draft answered that it resulted not only from the "development of industry" but "on the fact that in the consciousness or feeling of every individual there exist certain irrefutable basic principles" including that "every individual strives to be happy"; see Engels, *Entwurf des Kommunistischen Glaubensbekenntnisses*, BdK, 1: 470 / MECW 6: 97. In Engels's own subsequent October draft these questions and answers were removed. See further Bert Andréas, "Einleitung," in *Gründungsdokumente des Bundes der Kommunisten (Juni bis September 1847)*, ed. Bert Andréas (Hamburg: Ernst Hauswedell, 1969), 22.

187. Marx and Engels, *Manifest der Kommunistischen Partei*, MEW 4: 475 / MECW 6: 498.

188. Heinzen, "Polemik. Karl Heinzen und die Kommunisten," 4. Salvo Mastellone maintains that this passage and others in the *Manifest* are "precise references" to Mazzini's "Thoughts upon Democracy in Europe"; see Salvo Mastellone, *Mazzini and Marx: Thoughts upon Democracy in Europe* (Westport: Praeger, 2003), 143–46. Marx and Engels may have been aware of Mazzini's article, but we have no evidence that they had read it (unlike Heinzen's articles).

destroyed it, and is still destroying it every day."[189] Those who attempted to maintain the form of production of the "lower middle class, the shopkeeper, the artisan, the peasant" were even, they claimed, reactionary because "they try to roll back the wheel of history."[190]

This was same argument they had already made in their dispute with Heinzen. Marx argued that Heinzen's proposal for a minimum and maximum level of property would fail because of "the 'economic laws' on whose cold-blooded inevitability all well-meaning 'measures' will necessarily founder."[191] Engels similarly argued that the "economists of the bourgeoisie are quite right in respect of Herr Heinzen when they present these measures as reactionary compared to free competition." They were reactionary because they tried to "restore more primitive stages in the development of property," and this would inevitably be "defeated once more by competition" with a result of a "restoration of the present situation."[192] Attempts to defend a republican political economy of independent producers was thus, by Engels's account, doomed to failure, because it would be outcompeted by the efficiency of large-scale capitalist industry.

Engels and Marx claimed that Heinzen's inability to appreciate this arose from his failure to understand the forces that drive history forward and the insights that could be gleaned by a proper study of political economy. Engels argued that Heinzen did not understand one of the foundational principles of their materialist conception of history, that the "property relations of any given era are the necessary result of the mode of production and exchange of the era." He argued that without an understanding of this central insight, Heinzen was unable to grasp that transforming "large-scale landownership" into "small-scale" (as his land reform measures intended) would affect the "whole pattern of agriculture" and its production. Proposals for social reform had to be based on a proper understanding of the underlying material forces and their historical progression; otherwise they were just *"Weltverbesserungsschwärmereien"* (roughly, "world-saving fantasies").[193] Engels consequently charged Heinzen with misunderstanding communism as if it were a *"doctrine . . . [that]* proceeds from a definite theoretical principle" (i.e., the principle of the abolition of private property) in order to then analyze and judge the world. Rather, communism, in Engels's presentation, begins with an analysis of the "course of previous

189. Marx and Engels, *Manifest der Kommunistischen Partei*, MEW 4: 475 / MECW 6: 498.

190. Ibid., 472 / 494.

191. Marx, "Die moralisierende Kritik," *MEW* 4: 356 / *MECW* 6: 336.

192. Engels, "Die Kommunisten und Karl Heinzen," *MEW* 4: 314 / *MECW* 6: 296.

193. Ibid., 314–15 / 296–97.

history" and the "actual results in the civilized countries at the present time," and from there makes predictions about the necessity of communism.[194]

Heinzen's reaction to this argument was a mixture of bafflement and outrage. He thought that Engels's reference to the necessary results of foundational principles of history was about as insightful as saying that an "apple is the 'necessary result' of an apple tree."[195] Heinzen thought that the refusal to defend the abolition of private property on the level of moral principle was a cowardly way to avoid spelling out what it would in fact entail. Arguing that private property would abolish itself "through the 'development,' 'the facts,' 'the movement,'" was just a 'childish ridiculousness.'"[196] Marx and Engels could attempt to deny that they proceeded from the principle of the abolition of private property all they wanted, but the "disowned principle will keep calling" and at some point they would have to think about what that society looked like. If Engels was really as "far-sighted" and "omniscient" about the "preconditions" for the abolition of private property as he claimed, then surely, Heinzen challenged, he could also "kindly cast his gaze at the conditions of things" once private property was in fact abolished and whether that society was desirable.[197]

Heinzen's bafflement is partly explicable by the fact that Marx and Engels's arguments relied on a conception of history that, at that moment at the end of 1847, barely existed in print. Marx's *Misère de la philosophie* (*The Poverty of Philosophy*) had appeared only a few months before (and Heinzen said he had not read it any case),[198] the manuscripts known today as *Die deutsche Ideologie* were and would remain unpublished in Marx and Engels's lifetime, and the programmatic statements in the *Manifest* and the preface to *Zur Kritik der politischen Ökonomie* had yet to be written. Heinzen and bystanders to the debate might thus be forgiven for thinking that Marx and Engels's dismissals relied more on assertion than on substantiated argument. Indeed, as is discussed in the next chapter, Marx's comprehensive case against the republican ideal of independent producers would not appear until *Das Kapital*, twenty years after the first skirmish with Heinzen.

For the moment we can say that even if Marx and Engels's initial case lacked some more substantial argumentation, they were not wrong to associate republicans with a petty bourgeois form of production. Even though republicans might not have used that language, it was clear that their ideal of widely

194. Ibid., 321–22 / 303.
195. Heinzen, "Ein 'Repräsentant' der Kommunisten," 3.
196. Heinzen, *Die Helden des teutschen Kommunismus*, 19.
197. Heinzen, "Ein 'Repräsentant' der Kommunisten," 4.
198. Ibid.

dispersed property corresponded to that vision of political economy.[199] Georg Wirth, for instance, explicitly argued that the republican measures of free credit would mean that every person could "open their own independent trade" and thereby "the enormously expanded gigantic factories and enterprises which excessively enrich just a few families and damn the mass of the people to disastrous dependence, are dissolved into many smaller but useful businesses, which secure true independence and civil dignity to the great mass of the population."[200]

Marx and Engels were also not wrong to charge republicans with having insufficiently grappled with the capitalist challenge to this ideal. Though republicans obviously recognized that the ideal was under threat (hence defenses like the one above), they left the factors behind that threat largely unexplored. The ever-intensifying division of labor, the development of the world market, the vast increase of the urban population, the restless drive for greater profits and unlimited accumulation—in short, the unrelenting forward drive of capitalism, which Marx and Engels so famously captured in the first chapter of the *Manifest der Kommunistischen Partei*—remained largely absent from republican writings.

This can be observed in their ideas on industrial organization, land reform, inheritance, and free credit. Ruge's system of *sozietäten*, for instance, reflected a largely "preindustrial social ideal" where each member of the *sozietät* produces nearly everything they need for themselves.[201] No consideration was given here to the interconnectedness of modern production methods or the efficiency gains of the division of labor. Nor was there any thought given to whether competitive pressures—both national and international—from capitalist firms and their lower prices would undermine and destroy this small-scale independent form of production. Stephan Walter further suggests that the proposal to abolish inheritance as a sufficient safeguard against corrupting levels of inequalities reflects the fact that republicans "could not yet imagine the dynamic of industrial capitalism," where huge fortunes could be amassed within one generation.[202]

The republican policy of free credit would certainly have been of special benefit to those petty bourgeois small-scale producers who lacked the capital

199. That distinguishes nineteenth-century republicans from contemporary defenses of property-owning democracy; see David Schweickhart, "Property-Owning Democracy or Economic Democracy?," in *Property-Owning Democracy: Rawls and Beyond*, ed. Martin O'Neill and Thad Williamson (Chichester: Wiley-Blackwell, 2012), 205–6.

200. J. G. A. Wirth, *Die Rechte des deutshen Volkes: Eine Vertheidigungsrede vor dem Assissen zu Landau* (Nancy, 1833), 37–38.

201. Walter, *Demokratisches Denken zwischen Hegel und Marx*, 261.

202. Ibid., 258n196.

to establish or expand their own business. But as a solution to the problems faced by industrial and urban laborers, it reveals the extent to which republicans understood this class as consisting primarily of skilled artisans.[203] While free credit might provide artisans with the necessary capital to set up their own workshops, fully proletarianized workers would, first of all, lack the necessary skills to do so. Republicans might have argued that free education (including vocational education) would solve that problem. But that raises the larger question of whether such small-scale artisan workshops once established would be able to compete with larger capitalist enterprises. The proposal that associations of workers should also be able to apply for credit, which as we saw also pops up in republican proposals, might go some way to addressing that concern. But that kind of proposal was largely an afterthought in republican accounts and secondary to their primary focus on independent individual production. More generally, republicans showed a striking confidence that free credit would simply "rid us of all those mischievous middlemen called capitalists."[204] Linton's assurance that the people should "Let the capitalist pass! At worst they will tease you with a financial crisis," displays a remarkable (one might even say dangerous) sanguinity about economic crises and ignorance of the power of capitalists to wreck attempts at social transformation.[205] Nor is much consideration given to financial concerns over the state's ability to fund a program of free credit for everyone, or at least one sufficient to make every worker independent.

The emphasis and importance placed on land reform (Linton calls it the "necessary preliminary to any real Organization of Labour")[206] might also strike us an example of the republicans' failure to grasp the nature of the emerging industrial society. But we should remember that the Europe of the 1840s was still a "continent of peasants," where even the most industrialized and urbanized regions still had roughly half their workforce employed in agriculture.[207] No serious social reformer could consequently neglect the plight of the rural population. But the republican hope that land reform could

---

203. Here, the class background of some republicans probably played a role in the formulation of their ideas. For instance, as a skilled engraver, Linton was often aloof from the concerns of less-skilled workers, and shared the concerns and ideas "typical of . . . the uneasy class of artisan and *petit bourgeois* reformers"; Smith, *Radical Artisan*, 34–35.

204. Linton, "Republican Principles," 156 / 1: 22.

205. W. J. Linton, "The French Republic," *The Republican: A Magazine Advocating the Sovereignty of the People*, ed. C. G. Harding (London: J. Watson, 1848), 103.

206. Linton, "Republican Measures," 1: 123.

207. Jonathan Sperber, *The European Revolutions, 1848–1851*, 2nd ed. (Cambridge: Cambridge University Press, 2005), 5.

create a "new race of independent peasant freeholders" failed to engage with any of structural forces that were driving land consolidation and rural population flight.[208]

Republicans thus largely failed to provide an adequate and economically convincing defense of their normative ideal. Subsequent experience would seem to confirm Marx and Engels's prediction that their vision of independent producers was bound to be destroyed. Capitalist mass production has to a great degree swept aside much of the productive world that the republican democrats idealized. Local variations and nuances aside, the last two hundred years have seen a tectonic shift in industrialized countries from populations that are largely self-employed to being overwhelmingly characterized by wage-labor. Though we might dispute Marx's prediction that communism would follow that transformation, the shift from self-employment to wage-labor remains "one of the most robust of Marx's predictions."[209]

But although this is the course that history did take, there is some question if history *had* to take this path. While the inevitable rise of mass production has long been a standard assumption in economic history—shared by both Marxists and capitalist enthusiasts—there have been critics of this position. A number of political economists, labor historians, and social theorists have argued that the victory of mass production (where unskilled workers and automated processes carry out fixed and simple tasks, producing uniform products) over craft production (where skilled workers engage in flexible production of varied goods) was not a historical inevitability but the outcome of specific social struggles and political choices.[210] They have argued that craft production was not the regressive and inefficient system so often assumed and pointed to examples that successfully operated much further into the twentieth century than standard assumptions would predict. More broadly they have argued for reconceptualizing technological progress from a "narrow track" to a "branching tree," where political and social struggle determines which technological branch is settled on.[211]

208. Linton, "Republican Measures," 1: 124.

209. Erik Olin Wright, *Class Counts: Comparative Studies in Class Analysis* (Cambridge: Cambridge University Press, 1997), 123–24.

210. Michael J. Piore and Charles F. Sabel, *The Second Industrial Divide: Possibilities for Prosperity* (New York: Basic Books, 1984); Charles Sabel and Jonathan Zeitlin, "Historical Alternatives to Mass Production: Politics, Markets and Technology in Nineteenth-Century Industrialization," *Past & Present*, no. 108 (1985): 133–76; Roberto Mangabeira Unger, *False Necessity: Anti-Necessitarian Social Theory in the Service of Radical Democracy* (Cambridge: Cambridge University Press, 1987), 28–30.

211. Piore and Sabel, *The Second Industrial Divide*, 15, 21–26, 38–43.

These arguments perhaps provide some basis for thinking that a republican political economy was a more feasible alternative to capitalism than the course of history might suggest. Whether that overturns Marx and Engels's criticisms is another question. That small-scale craft production could sometimes operate successfully within capitalist economies would seem to nuance rather than nullify the general argument that petty bourgeois production could not withstand the competitive pressures of capitalism. The actual course of history has to carry some weight in our calculations. We might say that the question is more open than Marx and Engels's polemical statements would allow, but not so open that a republican political economy was ever a very likely possibility—certainly not on a society-wide level. Ultimately, the question touches on deeper and more general questions about determinism and the relative role of technology and social struggles in historical change. While we might have good reason to accept an understanding of history that gives greater weight to class struggle in resolving different societal possibilities, such an understanding would still need to retain an appreciation for the fact that these possibilities lie within certain parameters.[212] To return to Heinzen's critique of Marx's theory of history, he was perhaps right that not everything comes down to whether a "steam engine or some other factory instrument had been invented," but neither can one simply rely on a voluntaristic "exertion" to bring about whatever social ideal one desires.[213]

Coda

Republicans and communists offered overlapping and yet distinct social visions in response to the dependency of capitalism and wage-labor. Both defended measures such as land nationalization, free education, progressive taxation, and abolition of inheritance. But republicans defended these measures in order to maintain and restore the kind of independence represented by self-employed artisans and peasants, thus *universalizing* private property. Republicans believed this followed from their moral commitments to property, work, and freedom. Marx and Engels's critique certainly had normative elements (as we will see in chapter 6's discussion of the unfreedom, domination, and exploitation they thought inherent to wage-labor), but in their response to republicans they insisted that the question of which social vision to pursue had to be based on an assessment of history and political economy.

212. Vivek Chibber, "What Is Living and What Is Dead in the Marxist Theory of History," *Historical Materialism* 19, no. 2 (2011): 88.

213. Heinzen, *Die Helden des teutschen Kommunismus*, 22.

They concluded that the efficiency of large-scale capitalist production was steadily and irreversibly destroying the world idealized by republicans. Social revolutionaries thus had to seize on these historical trends and build on capitalism's achievements by collectivizing the means of production, rather than try to restore a dying world of small independent producers. Marx and Engels believed this position was roughly but imperfectly captured by the communist slogan of *abolishing* private property, which they thought had to be more specifically understood as the abolition of bourgeois private property. Underlying Marx and Engels's assessment of the republican social alternative was their unique conception of historical and social change. In one of the earliest and until now neglected criticisms of this materialist conception of history, Karl Heinzen argued that it gave far too little space for political action to direct the course of history. Concerted political action would, Heinzen believed, make it possible to stave off capitalist development. Marx and Engels's response to Heinzen is a reminder that as important as normative and political arguments and possibilities might be, social and strategic analysis also has to be informed by the limits set by history and political economy.

6

Chains and Invisible Threads

LIBERTY AND DOMINATION IN MARX'S CRITIQUE OF CAPITALISM, 1867

That the emancipation of the workers must be the work of the workers themselves, that the efforts of the workers to conquer their emancipation must not be directed towards the creation of new privileges, but towards the establishment of equal rights and duties for all and the abolition of all class domination.

—PREAMBLE OF THE FOUNDING STATUTES OF THE IWMA[1]

It is not a question of making war against capital, but on the contrary, to put a stop to the war of all against all, which the arbitrary domination of capital and its corollary, unlimited competition, are blazing forth every day.

—CIRCULAR OF THE SWISS-GERMAN SECTION OF THE IWMA[2]

---

1. Marx, "Statuts de l'Association Internationale des Travailleurs votes à la séance du Congrès du 5 September 1866," *MEGA* I.20: 236. Marx wrote the original statutes in English in 1864 and took charge of the French translation. In the original the final line had read "the abolition of all class-rule"; see Marx, "Provisional Rules of the International Working-Men's Association," *MEGA* I.20: 13 / *MECW* 20: 14. Marx corrected a previous French translation, which misleadingly called for the "abolition of the domination of any class (*anéantir la domination de toute classe*)" rather than the "abolition of all class domination (*anéantir toute domination de classe*)"; see *MEGA* I.20: 623, 911, 1267. The reference to "equal rights and duties" was a concession to the Mazzinian currents in the IWMA.

2. [Johann Philipp Becker], "Rundschreiben der deutschen Abtheilung des Zentralcomités der Internationalen Arbeiterassociation für die Schweiz an die Arbeiter. Genf, den 1. November 1865," *Allgemeine deutsche Arbeiter-Zeitung*, no. 153 (3 December 1865): 856 / "The International Working Men's Association," *The Commonwealth*, no. 153 (10 February 1866), 6. Marx was responsible for publishing an earlier (less colorful) English translation of the circular in "The International Working Men's Association," *The Workman's Advocate*, no. 145 (16 December 1865): 4. See "Minutes of Central Council, 28 November 1865," *MEGA* I.20: 367, and Marx to Johann Philipp Becker, between 9 and 15 January 1866, *MEGA digital*: https://megadigital.bbaw.de /briefe/detail.xql?id=M0000007/*MECW* 42: 214.

ONE OF THE LASTING contributions of E. P. Thompson's *The Making of the English Working Class* is how powerfully it captured workers' experience of the industrial revolution as a "*catastrophic* change."[3] Thompson showed that the English working class's complaint during this period was not reducible to a decline in material well-being. What mattered to workers was how the conditions of their work had changed; that their working life was now characterized by overwork, monotony, discipline, and, most important, the loss of freedom and independence. Thompson thus observed that "People may consume more goods and become less happy or less free at the same time."[4] Thompson cited the example of a September 1818 address by a Manchester cotton spinner, which capped a long summer of militant strikes across Lancashire. The cotton spinner cataloged the changes wrought by the shift from independent hand-loom spinning to the new cotton mills powered by steam engines—the epitome of modern factory production. In emphatically republican language, the anonymous cotton spinner branded the new manufacturers "petty monarchs, absolute and despotic" who ruled over the "English Spinner slave." The cotton spinner argued that the formal freedom to sell their labor did not stop workers from still being "bondmen and bondwomen to their cruel taskmasters," insisting that "It is vain to insult our common understandings with the observation that such men are free; that the law protects the rich and poor alike, and that a spinner can leave his master if he does not like the wages. True; so he can; but where must he go? why to another to be sure."[5]

The anonymous cotton spinner's address, written in the year of Marx's birth, provides an early articulation of what would become a guiding thread of Marx's critique of capitalism: that the putatively free wage-labor contract disguised the actual domination that robbed workers of their freedom. Inside the workplace, Marx assessed the capitalist employer to be little more than the social equivalent of an absolute monarch, who subjected his workers to the "pettiest, most spiteful despotism."[6] But, like the cotton spinner before him, Marx insisted that it was not enough to look at the personal domination of the

---

3. E. P. Thompson, *The Making of the English Working Class* (London: Victor Gollancz, 1963), 191.

4. Ibid., 211.

5. Ibid., 199–201. See A Journeyman Cotton Spinner, "The Manchester Cotton Spinners to the Employers and the Public," *The Black Dwarf*, vol. 2 no. 39 (30 September 1818): 622–24. See further Robert G. Hall, "Tyranny, Work and Politics: The 1818 Strike Wave in the English Cotton District," *International Review of Social History* 34, no. 3 (1989): 433–80.

6. Marx, *Das Kapital*, vol. 1, *MEGA* II.6: 588 / *MECW* 35: 639.

individual capitalist master. The workers' formal freedom to sell their labor might allow them to leave any *particular* capitalist master, but because workers had no means of production of their own, they were forced to work for *a* master. Consequently, the worker *"belongs not to this or that bourgeois, but to the bourgeoisie, the bourgeois class."*[7] For Marx, the workers' domination by the individual capitalist and the capitalist class, because of their lack of means of production, played a central role in the reproduction of capitalist relations by enabling the exploitation of surplus labor. The separation of the worker from the means of production also meant that their labor-power became a commodity to be bought and sold on the market. That triggered what Marx took to be an even deeper level of capitalist domination, the subordination of all of society to the impersonal rule of the market. Marx thought that under capitalism everyone became the "plaything of alien forces."[8]

This chapter sets out Marx's account of the domination of capitalism: how the worker is dominated and exploited by the capitalist and the capitalist class, and how these are underpinned by the domination of everyone by markets. Central to this account were republican ideas of dependency, servitude, and unfreedom. Typical judgments include that "the relation of *wage-labor to capital*, [is] the slavery of the worker, the domination (*Herrschaft*) of the capitalist" and that for "the modern factory operative . . . freedom does not exist, they are slaves of capital."[9] But Marx also expanded and transformed those republican ideas from a focus on the arbitrary power of an individual to an analysis of how arbitrary power was exercised through and was constituted by a structure of property ownership and impersonal market forces. For Marx, this was necessary to account for the much less transparent domination of the proletarian in

---

7. Marx, "Lohnarbeit und Kapital," *MEW* 6: 401 / *MECW* 9: 203.

8. Marx, "Zur Judenfrage," *MEGA* I.2: 149 / *MECW* 3: 154. See Jonathan Wolff, "Playthings of Alien Forces: Karl Marx and the Rejection of the Market Economy," *Cogito* 6, no. 1 (1992): 35–41.

9. Marx, "Lohnarbeit und Kapital," *MEW* 6: 398 / *MECW* 9: 198; "Meeting of the General Council, July 28 1868," *MEGA* 21: 580–81. Quentin Skinner thus rightly observes that "The vocabulary of Roman legal and moral philosophy is strikingly prominent . . . in Marx's analysis of capitalism, especially in his discussions of wage-slavery, alienation and dictatorship"; Quentin Skinner, *Liberty before Liberalism* (Cambridge: Cambridge University Press, 1998), xn3. By comparison, Frank Lovett argues that though "[t]heories of domination are commonly attributed to Karl Marx," he does not use "the expression with much frequency"; Frank Lovett, *A General Theory of Domination and Justice* (Oxford: Oxford University Press, 2010), 11. The most charitable interpretation of this unlikely claim is that the frequency of Marx's use of *Herrschaft* is sometimes obscured in English translations through the use of more neutral equivalent terms like "rule," "power," or "sway."

comparison to previous forms of subordination. In his pregnant summary, "The Roman slave was held by chains; the wage-laborer is bound to his owner by invisible threads."[10]

The beginnings of this account were explored in the discussion of Marx's earliest economic writings in chapter 3. This chapter sets out Marx's mature critique of capitalism by focusing centrally (though not exclusively) on *Das Kapital* (*Capital*). After close to a decade of producing thousands of pages of unpublished manuscripts, Marx was finally able to publish the first volume in September 1867 (the only volume he was able to bring to publication in his lifetime).[11] As William Clare Roberts has artfully shown, the driving impetus behind Marx at long last bringing his studies to public view was the foundation of the International Working-Men's Association (IWMA) in 1864.[12] Having largely retreated from active political involvement since the dissolution of the Bund der Kommunisten (Communist League) in 1850, the IWMA represented for Marx a thrilling reemergence of working-class political activism, now combined with active trade union involvement. He placed great hopes in the IWMA as an internationalist working-class movement that would liberate itself from the rule of capital. As "Cit[izen] Marx proposed," in a meeting of IWMA's governing General Council two months before the publication of *Das Kapital*, he saw "its function . . . [as] a common centre of action for the working classes, female and male, in their struggle tending to their complete emancipation from the domination of capital."[13]

10. Marx, *Das Kapital*, vol. 1, *MEGA* II.6: 529–30 / *MECW* 35: 573.

11. Marx produced a second German edition in 1872–73, which primarily made improvements to its structure. Marx made more substantial changes to the text in the French translation that he closely supervised and which was serialized from 1872 to 1875, a format that he thought would make it "more accessible to the working class and that consideration is more important to me than any other"; Marx to Maurice La Châtre, 18 March 1872 (this letter to *Le Capital's* publisher was included as a facsimile in the original printed text; see *Le Capital*, *MEGA* II.7: 7, 9 / *MECW* 35: 23). Because of these changes Marx advised readers that the French translation "possesses a scientific value independent of the original and should be consulted even by readers familiar with the German language," in the closing "Notice to the Reader (*Avis au lecteur*)" in *Le Capital*, *MEGA* II.7: 690 / *MECW* 35: 24. I have consequently made frequent reference to the French text. For further discussion see the entries in Marcello Musto, ed., *Marx and* Le Capital: *Evaluation, History, Reception* (Abingdon: Routledge, 2022). Volumes 2 and 3 of *Das Kapital* were edited by Engels (out of the fragmentary and rough manuscripts Marx left behind) and published in 1885 and 1894, respectively.

12. William Clare Roberts, *Marx's Inferno: The Political Theory of Capital* (Princeton: Princeton University Press, 2017), 2.

13. "Minutes of the General Council of the IWMA, 9 July 1867," *MEGA* I.20: 570, 572 / *MECW* 20: 203.

From the start the IWMA was a colorful ideological mix, stretching from trade unionism and Comtean Positivism to the republican internationalism of Mazzini and the social republicanism of the followers of Bronterre O'Brien, to the better-known currents of Proudhonian mutualism and Bakunian anarchism.[14] From his influential (though far from dominant) position in the General Council, Marx cajoled, competed, and compromised with these divergent strands and factions.[15] His *Das Kapital* was an intervention into this crowded ideological field with the aim of winning over the IWMA and the broader working-class movement to his ideas. That included, as we will see, an attempt to wean workers from the still popular republican idea that the domination of capitalism could be overcome by individual property ownership.

Domination and the Workplace

The most tangible and direct aspect of the domination over workers is their subjection to the arbitrary rule of the individual capitalist and his managers and supervisors during working hours. Marx and Engels wrote that though workers were in general terms "slaves of the bourgeois class," inside the "despotism" of the modern factory they were "daily and hourly enslaved by the machine, the supervisor and, *above all,* by the individual bourgeois manufacturer."[16] Marx's earliest critique of the individual capitalist's domination inside the workplace was based on a philosophical account of how it led to the worker's alienation from the act of production. In his subsequent writings, Marx concretized this account through his long years of journalism, his own extensive sociological investigations, and the reports of workers' actual conditions that inundated the General Council of the IWMA from across Europe.

14. See, for instance, the entries by Anthony Taylor, "'Sectarian Secret Wisdom' and Nineteenth-Century Radicalism: The IWMA in London and New York"; Samuel Hayat, "The Construction of Proudhonism within the IWMA"; Gregory Claeys, "Professor Beesly, Positivism and the International: The Patriotism Question"; and Marianne Enckell, "Bakunin and the Jura Federation," in the invaluable collection *"Arise Ye Wretched of the Earth": The First International in a Global Perspective,* ed. Fabrice Bensimon, Quentin Deluermoz, and Jeanne Moisand (Leiden: Brill, 2018).

15. For Marx's involvement in the IWMA, see Jürgen Herres, "Karl Marx and the IWMA Revisited," in *"Arise Ye Wretched of the Earth,"* 299–312; Henry Collins and Chimen Abramsky, *Karl Marx and the British Labour Movement: Years of the First International* (London: Macmillan, 1965); and Gareth Stedman Jones, *Karl Marx: Greatness and Illusion* (London: Allen Lane, 2016), chapter 11.

16. Marx and Engels, *Manifest der Kommunistischen Partei, MEW* 4: 469 / *MECW* 6: 491 (emphasis added). They also note here that workers are "slaves . . . of the bourgeois state."

In an 1869 annual review, for instance, Marx reported on the IWMA's support for workers striking across the continent in response to "the despotism of the capitalist" and their treatment as "a modern wages-slave."[17] In Basel, ribbon weavers had been subjected to "a capricious and spiteful act of capitalist despotism," in which their employers had first tried to take away a traditional holiday and then summarily dismissed those who disobeyed and threw them out of their employee housing.[18] In Geneva, a strike by builders and compositors had been met with heavy police repression in order to break the strike and ensure that workers remained "subject . . . to a Decembrist regime."[19] In a Welsh coal mine, miners had assaulted a manager known for being a "most incorrigible petty oppressor"—an episode that ended with government soldiers shooting dead five miners who protested the imprisonment of the ringleaders of the assault.[20] Marx ended the report with a letter of solidarity sent by an American trade union expressing support for their common struggle against "capital . . . the same tyrant in all parts of the world."[21]

These descriptions of the relationship between workers and their capitalist employers in terms of despotism were entirely commonplace in Marx's writings. The power enjoyed by individual capitalists mirrored, Marx argued, the arbitrary power enjoyed by absolute rulers over their subjects. Just as a workers could have a "public despot" in the political sphere, they were also confronted by "private despots" in their workplace.[22] This criticism formed an important component of Marx's damning account of factory conditions in *Das Kapital*. Using the "extraordinary wealth of statistics, official reports and pieces of press reportage" he had gathered,[23] Marx documented how the workers' meager pay and long hours, their unsafe and unhealthy workplaces, their monotonous and intellectually unstimulating tasks, were compounded by the fact that the capitalist or "factory-autocrat" "subjects him [the worker] during the labor process to the pettiest, most spiteful despotism."[24]

17. Marx, "Report of the General Council to the Fourth Annual Congress of the International Working-Men's Association," *MEGA* I.21: 134 / *MECW* 21: 68.

18. Ibid., 135 / 70.

19. Ibid., 137 / 71, "Decembrist" being the despotic regime of Louis Napoleon, who had taken power in a coup in December 1851.

20. Ibid., 143–44 / 80.

21. Ibid., 145 / 81–82.

22. Ibid., 139 / 74.

23. Stedman Jones, *Karl Marx*, 428.

24. Marx, *Das Kapital*, vol. 1, *MEGA* II.6: 412n, 588 / *MECW* 35: 428n, 639, see also ibid., 351 / 362. In the French edition, Marx strengthened the description to read that the capitalist "subjects the worker . . . to a despotism as unlimited as it is petty"; see *Le Capital*, *MEGA* II.7: 568.

Marx presented the capitalist's autocratic rule in the factory as arising alongside the long process of the increasing social division of labor with a concurrent growth in the need for direction and supervision in the labor process. A modern factory required the complex cooperation of hundreds of people and thus also positions to direct and manage the process. But Marx was keen to emphasize that while such supervision partly reflected a legitimate need for coordination that arises when "many individuals cooperate" in an industrial enterprise, that had to be distinguished from the supervision that was made necessary by the "opposition (*Gegensatz*) between the laborer . . . and the owner of the means of production." To explain the difference, he compared it to the activities of "despotic states," which could be divided into the "performance of common activities that arise from the nature of any community" and those interferences made necessary by "the opposition between the government and the people."[25] Thus the real social need for the coordination of complex workplace interaction should not, Marx stressed, be confused with the specific supervision made necessary to uphold the capitalist's domination and exploitation of the worker. With a capitalist in control of the factory, the latter requirement means that the division of labor "confronts them [workers], in the realm of ideas, as a plan drawn up by the capitalist, and, in practice, as the authority of the capitalist, in the shape of the powerful will of another, who subjects their activity to his aims."[26] In contrast, Marx cited a report on a workers' cooperative experiment in the bourgeois English newspaper *The Spectator*, which was forced to admit that the experiment demonstrated that "associations of workmen could manage shops, mills and almost all forms of industry with success" but worried that this "did not leave a clear place for masters"—to which Marx replied, "Quelle horreur!"[27]

Marx argued that as capitalist production advanced and industrial enterprises expanded, the role of direct supervision was increasingly passed from the capitalist to his employed managers and overseers. These subjected the workers to what Marx described as a "barracks-like discipline," with the factory resembling the strict military hierarchy of soldiers and officers. Central to this military discipline, Marx argued, was a set of rules and regulations developed by the capitalist and enforced by the overseer. Marx bitterly observed that these rules were carefully designed through the "law-giving talent" of the "factory-Lycurgus" to ensure that any infraction was, wherever possible, more

25. Marx, *Das Kapital*, vol. 3, MEGA II.15: 374 / MECW 37: 382. See also Marx, *Das Kapital* (*Ökonomisches Manuskript 1863–1865*), *Drittes Buch*, MEGA II.4.2: 455.

26. Marx, *Das Kapital*, vol. 1, MEGA II.6: 328 / MECW 35: 337.

27. Ibid., 328n / 336n.

profitable to the capitalist than obeying them.[28] Moreover, these rules were drawn up entirely at the capitalist's discretion. Marx observed that, "In the factory code, capital formulates its autocracy over its workers, like a private legislator (*privatgesetzlich*) and as an emanation of its own will (*eigenherrlich*), unaccompanied by either the separation of powers otherwise so much approved of by the bourgeoisie, or the still more approved representative system . . ."[29] The passage is striking not only because of its comparison of the capitalist's arbitrary power to make their own rules with the power of an autocrat to dictate the law. (In a popularized edition of *Das Kapital*, checked and amended by Marx, this argument was summarized as "The capitalist *rules* like an absolute monarch.")[30] Marx also goes beyond this comparison to highlight the hypocrisy of the bourgeoisie, who insist that this kind of arbitrary power is unacceptable in the public realm (where political power has to be constrained by the separation of powers and representative government) but are entirely unconcerned when it occurs in the supposedly private realm of employment.[31]

In order to substantiate this picture of the capitalist's arbitrary rule, Marx cited (in full) a long passage from Engels's groundbreaking study of factory conditions in *Die Lage der arbeitenden Klasse in England* (*The Condition of the Working Class in England*), written some twenty years earlier. Here Engels had argued that,

> The slavery in which the bourgeoisie holds the proletariat chained, is nowhere more conspicuously brought into daylight than in the factory system. Here ends all freedom in law and in fact. The operative must be in the mill at half-past five in the morning; if he comes a couple of minutes too late, he is fined; if he comes ten minutes too late, he is not let in until breakfast is over and a quarter of the day's wages is withheld . . . He must eat, drink, and sleep at command . . . The despotic bell calls him from his bed, his breakfast, his dinner. And how goes it for him inside the factory? Here the employer is absolute lawgiver. He makes regulations at will, changes and adds to his codex at pleasure, and even if he inserts the craziest stuff, the courts say to the working-man: "You were your own master, no one forced

---

28. Lycurgus founded Sparta's oligarchical constitution.

29. Ibid., 411 / 427.

30. Joh[an] Most, *Kapital und Arbeit: Ein populärer Auszug aus "Das Kapital" von Karl Marx*, 2nd ed. (Chemnitz: Genossenschaftsbuchdruckerei Chemnitz G. Rübner u. Co., 1876), 33 / *Extracts from "The Capital" of Karl Marx*, trans. Otto Weydemeyer (Hoboken: F. A. Sorge, 1876), 21.

31. A theme recently explored in Elizabeth Anderson, *Private Government: How Employers Rule Our Lives (and Why We Don't Talk about It)* (Princeton: Princeton University Press, 2017).

you to agree to such a contract if you did not wish to; but now, when you have freely entered into it, you must be bound by it."[32]

As with Marx, Engels highlighted how factory rules were made entirely by the arbitrary will of the capitalist, just as in the case of an absolutist ruler. Engels further explicitly tied the worker's subjection to this arbitrary power to the end of "all freedom in law and in fact." He contrasted this with the official view that workers had no complaint of freedom because they had "freely entered" into a contract with the capitalist. Similarly, when Marx had earlier cited the same passage from Engels in his preparatory manuscripts for *Das Kapital,* he added it was the "*apologists for the factory system*" who defended "barracks-like factories, military discipline, subjugation to the machinery, regulation by the stroke of the clock, surveillance by overseers," who were also those who were loudest opponents to "the softest state interference" as an "infringement of individual freedom and the *free* movement of labour."[33] For both Marx and Engels, the supposedly free labor contract obscured the actual unfreedom experienced by workers once they entered the factory gates.

In both Marx and Engels's passage, attention is drawn to the arbitrary application of fines to control the worker. This was a repeated target of Marx's anger across his writings. He described how workers were penalized for the smallest infractions, from sitting down to take a rest to speaking or even laughing out of turn.[34] He depicted fines as a particularly modern form of control, arguing that in the factory, "In place of the slave-driver's whip steps the overseer's book of penalties."[35] What particularly upset Marx about this practice was that capitalists and their overseers were able to impose these fines without any method of contestation or redress by the workers. Marx argued that the capitalist was "a penal legislator within his own establishment" who could inflict "fines at will" as "the factory lord is subject to no controlling agency of any kind."[36] Since the factory fell under the capitalist's "*private jurisdiction,*" capitalists could judge workers based on "*a penal code of their own,*" despite being "gainers and parties to the disputes."[37] Moreover, Marx objected to how when it came to the decision to

32. Engels, *Die Lage der arbeitenden Klasse in England, MEGA* I.4: 397 / *MECW* 4: 467; cited in Marx, *Das Kapital,* vol. 1, *MEGA* II.6: 412n / *MECW* 35: 427n.

33. Marx, *Zur Kritik der politischen Ökonomie (Manuskript 1861–1863), MEGA* II.3: 2023-24 / *MECW* 33: 490–91.

34. Marx, *Discours sur la question du libre échange, MEW* 4: 448 / *MECW* 6: 456.

35. Marx, *Das Kapital,* vol. 1, *MEGA* I.6: 411–12 / *MECW* 35: 427.

36. "Minutes of the General Council of the IWMA, 28 July 1868," *MEGA* I.21: 581 / *MECW* 21: 383.

37. Marx, *Civil War in France (First Draft), MEGA* I.22: 45 / *MECW* 22: 472.

hand out fines the "employer combines in his own person the parts of legislator, judge and executor."[38] That is strongly reminiscent of Marx's early objection to how, in the Prussian government censor, "judge, accuser and defender are combined in a *single person*."[39] Marx's late complaint thus transferred his own early objection to arbitrary legal and political power to a criticism of how the bourgeois principles of the right to redress and impartiality do not extend past the factory gate. Once workers cross that threshold, they are denied the rights considered sacrosanct outside of it. (The arbitrariness of fines was indeed a cause of particular bitterness among workers. One English coal miner set out how the *"Coal Kings"* used fines to lower the worker's wages, "leaving him to the mercy, or caprice, or what is worse, the cupidity of the employer, who robs him of the rights of his industry whenever he thinks fit."[40])

A prominent dimension of an employer's domination in the workplace is how it facilitates sexual harassment and exploitation. Marx did not devote much attention in *Das Kapital* to what he rather primly called the "moral degradation (*moralische Verkümmrung*) caused by the capitalist exploitation of women and children." He instead directed readers to Engels's discussion of the issue in *Die Lage der arbeitenden Klasse in England*.[41] Engels had here set out how the "threat of discharge" made the employer the "master over the body and the charms of his female workers." Crucially, Engels argued that "If the master is mean . . . [then] his mill is also his harem; and the fact that not all manufacturers use their power, does not in the least change the position of the girls."[42] Engels thus drew on the classic republican insight to argue that the problem is not simply that "mean" manufacturers interfere with their female workers by demanding sexual favors, but that all manufacturers, good or bad, have this power to interfere.

While Marx's mature critique of workplace domination was more empirically grounded than his early philosophical account, there are important continuities. A consistent theme was Marx's insistence that the objectionable character of the capitalist workplace was not reducible to the effect on workers' material welfare, as laboring for a capitalist robbed workers of their freedom.

38. Marx, *Civil War in France, MEGA* I.22: 146 / *MECW* 22: 339.

39. Marx, "Bermerkungen über die neueste preußische Censurinstruction," *MEGA* I.1: 118 / *MECW* 1: 130.

40. One Who Suffered in the Mines, "A Voice from the Coal Mines. By a Sufferer," *Reynold's Political Instructor*, vol. 1, no. 21 (30 March 1850): 164. On the use of fines in early factories, see Sidney Pollard, "Factory Discipline in the Industrial Revolution," *The Economic History Review* 16, no. 2 (1963): 257, 261–62.

41. Marx, *Das Kapital*, vol. 1, *MEGA* II.6: 388 / *MECW* 35: 403.

42. Engels, *Die Lage der arbeitenden Klasse in England, MEGA* I.4: 372 / *MECW* 4: 441–42.

We saw how in his early writings he claimed that an *"increase in wages"* for the worker would "be nothing better than *payment for the slave.*"[43] Marx continued to express the same concern in *Das Kapital*, where he maintained that though an increase in wages might "extend the circle of [the workers'] enjoyments" by allowing them to buy and save more, it could not set the worker free; for "just as little as better clothing, food, treatment and a larger *peculium* abolish the relationship of dependence and the exploitation of the slave, so little do they abolish that of the wage-laborer."[44] Marx made this point again and again, arguing that a rise in wages "would not abolish, but only mitigate the slavery of the wage-laborer" and that wage-labor was "a system of slavery," regardless of "whether the worker receives better or worse payment."[45] This aspect of Marx's thought is missed by shallow interpreters who think that for Marx "wage slavery . . . meant being paid only" subsistence wages.[46] Marx in fact maintained that without fundamentally addressing the fact that the worker labored under the control and supervision of a master, the worker would remain unfree regardless of better or worse wages.

That did not mean, of course, that Marx was opposed to fighting for higher wages or incremental measures that reduced the workplace domination of the worker. He and Engels argued in 1869, for instance, that when it came to pensions and insurance against workplace accidents, workers should not rely on funds managed by their employers (as was the practice in some German coal mines). This would only result in "extending the despotism of capital (*Kapitaldespotismus*)" by making workers even more reliant on the capitalist who was *"minded to sack him"* at any moment and thus deny him his accrued benefits. Instead, they counseled that workers "must agitate for *this responsibility being regulated by the law*." Government regulation was thus one way in which workers could mitigate their workplace domination. Furthermore, Marx and Engels thought that an essential way to resist arbitrary interferences by the employer against the lone worker was for workers to build their collective counterpower. They thus urged the coal miners to build their own trade unions

---

43. Marx, *Ökonomisch-philosophische Manuskripte*, MEGA I.2: 373 / MECW 3: 280.

44. Marx, *Das Kapital*, vol. 1, MEGA I.6: 565 / MECW 35: 613. In Roman law, *peculium* was the property controlled by slaves, but still owned by their master.

45. Marx, [Draft for the Final Passage of "Value, Price and Profit"], MEGA I.20: 140 / MECW 20: 338; Marx, *Kritik des Gothaer Programms*, MEGA I.25: 19 / MECW 24: 92. See also "Value, Price and Profit," MEGA I.20: 169 / MECW 20: 129.

46. Niall Ferguson, "Capitalism, Socialism, and Nationalism: Lessons from History," in *The Human Prosperity Project: Essays on Socialism and Free-Market Capitalism from the Hoover Institution* (Stanford: Hoover Institution Press, 2022), 202.

that would help "protect individual workers from the arbitrariness of individual masters."[47]

Domination and the Means of Production

The subordination of the proletarian to the capitalist's arbitrary will inside the workplace is the most recognizable way in which they are dominated. But Marx insisted that this direct, personal relationship of domination was underpinned by a less visible form of domination. The background structure of property, with ownership of the means of production monopolized by capitalists, meant that proletarians were not only dominated by their individual capitalist but by the capitalist class. For Marx, this *structural domination* (to borrow a concept developed in the contemporary political theory literature),[48] was the background condition of all proletarians, which preceded and was independent of any individual relationship they had with a capitalist. As he put it, "The worker belongs in fact to the capitalist class before he has sold himself to the individual capitalist."[49]

Marx's account of the structural domination of proletarians arises from the two features that he argued distinguished proletarians from other subordinate producing classes: (a) they own their own labor power and thus have the freedom to sell it, and (b) they own no means of production and are thus forced to sell their labor power.[50] In comparison, slaves own *neither* their labor power nor means of production, while serfs own only *part* of their labor power and

---

47. Marx and Engels, "Bericht über die Knappschaftsvereine der Bergarbeiter in den Kohlenwerken Sachsens," *MEGA* I.21: 114–15 / *MECW* 21: 42–44. Engels wrote the original article in English (which has not survived) at Marx's request, who then translated it into German, possibly amending it in the process. While the *MEGA* attributes the essay to Marx and the *MECW* to Engels, a joint attribution seems fairest.

48. See, for instance, Lillian Cicerchia, "Structural Domination in the Labour Market," *European Journal of Political Theory* 21, no. 1 (2022): 4–24; Dorothea Gädeke, "Does a Mugger Dominate? Episodic Power and the Structural Dimension of Domination," *The Journal of Political Philosophy* 28, no. 2 (2020): 199–221; Alex Gourevitch, "Labor Republicanism and the Transformation of Work," *Political Theory* 41, no. 4 (2013): 591–617; Tom O'Shea, "Are Workers Dominated?," *Journal of Ethics and Social Philosophy* 16, no. 1 (2019): 1–24; Nicholas Vrousalis, "The Capitalist Cage: Structural Domination and Collective Agency in the Market," *Journal of Applied Philosophy* 38, no. 1 (2021): 40–54.

49. Marx, *Le Capital*, vol. 1, *MEGA* II.7: 502. In the German, Marx put it a little less precisely: "The worker belongs to capital before he has sold himself to the capitalist," *Das Kapital*, vol. 1, *MEGA* II.6: 533 / *MECW* 35: 577.

50. Marx, *Das Kapital*, vol. 1, *MEGA* II.6: 183–84, 645 / *MECW* 35: 178–79, 705.

means of production. Independent producers (such as peasants and artisans), on the other hand, own *both* their labor power and their own means of production.[51] Marx believed that the proletarians' formal freedom to sell their labor power was a significant improvement over the position of serfs and slaves. A proletarian could dispose of themselves and their wages as they wished and thus "a wide field of choice, caprice and therefore of formal freedom is left to him."[52] Proletarians were also not subjected to the same degree of interference and supervision over their labor, which Marx argued "reaches its maximum in the slave system."[53] Marx's critique of "wage-slavery" thus did not extend to arguing that wage-labor was worse than chattel slavery—as was frequently the case in reactionary and even radical critiques of capitalist wage-labor at the time.[54]

But though Marx believed the proletarian's formal freedom to be a significant historical advance over previous forms of unfree labor, he maintained that the proletarian's lack of means of production (in comparison to independent producers) undermined that freedom. Marx argued that when a serf or slave became a proletarian, their position *"becomes freer,"* since their relationship

51. These are, of course, ideal type categorizations, with some producers falling between these categories; see G. A. Cohen, *Karl Marx's Theory of History: A Defence* (Princeton: Princeton University Press, 1978), 65–68.

52. Marx, *Grundrisse der Kritik der politischen Ökonomie*, MEGA II.1: 372 / MECW 28: 392. See also Marx, *Arbeitslohn*, MEW 6: 555–56 / MECW 6: 436–37.

53. Marx, *Das Kapital*, vol. 3, MEGA II.15: 374 / MECW 37: 382.

54. A perspective missing in the critical account given in Iris Därmann, "'Schwarze' und 'weiße Sklaverei' in Karl Marx' Kritik des Amerikanischen Bürgerkrieges und der politischen Ökonomie," in *Undienlichkeit: Gewaltgeschichte und politische Philosophie* (Berlin: Matthes & Seitz, 2020), 170–71. For the wider history, see Marcus Cunliffe, *Chattel Slavery and Wage Slavery: The Anglo-American Context, 1830–1860* (Athens: University of Georgia Press, 1979). Bronterre O'Brien, in a judgment typifying the radical genre, argued that "wages-slavery . . . [is] immeasurably worse for white-slaves, than is chattel-slavery for the blacks"; see "The Rise, Progress, and Phases of Human Slavery," *Reynolds's Political Instructor*, vol. 15, no. 1 (16 February 1850): 118. Such judgments can also be found in Engels's early writings; see *Die Lage der arbeitenden Klasse in England*, MEGA I.4: 398 / MECW 4: 468–69. While Marx noted that slaves had one advantage over proletarians in that their masters provided them with their subsistence, he never took the position that this made wage slavery, all things considered, worse than chattel slavery; see Marx, "Value, Price and Profit," MEGA I.20: 181 / MECW 20: 143. Marx criticized Tory accounts of "white slavery" that tried to use the cruelty of wage-labor to defend slave labor. He considered slave labor in the American South to be one of most brutal known forms of subordination, since its integration into the pressures of global capitalist markets meant that the "civilized horrors of overwork are grafted on the barbaric horrors of slavery"; see *Das Kapital*, vol. 1, MEGA II.6: 242, 259, 259–60n / MECW 35: 244, 262, 262n.

with their master was now "formally voluntary." But when an independent producer became a proletarian, "a relationship of *supremacy and subordination* (*Ueber und Unterordnung*) replaces a previous *independence*."⁵⁵ That previous independence was grounded in ownership of the means of production, which Marx argued was critical because means of production provided the means of subsistence.⁵⁶ Independent producers could use their means of production to independently produce (or acquire) what they needed to survive. Proletarians had no such option and could only gain their means of subsistence by selling their labor-power to a capitalist, who did own means of production. That meant that though proletarians did not have to work for any specific capitalist (since they had the freedom to sell their labor power to whomever they wished), they did have to work for *a* capitalist from within the capitalist class. Marx thought that this distinguished the domination of proletarians from that of serfs and slaves, who were exclusively tied to a single individual lord or slave owner.⁵⁷ As Marx wrote, the "slave belongs to a particular *master*, the worker must sell himself to capital, but not to a particular capitalist and so, within a certain sphere, he has the choice to who he sells himself, and can change his master."⁵⁸ But what a proletarian could not do was have no master whatsoever. Their domination was (in this regard) not by any single capitalist, but by the capitalist class. Because the proletarian's "sole source of livelihood is the sale of his labor, [he] cannot leave the *whole class of purchasers, that is, the capitalist class*, without renouncing his existence. He belongs not to this or that bourgeois, but to the bourgeoisie, the bourgeois class."⁵⁹

Marx thought this made the unfreedom of wage-labor less transparent than previous forms of unfree labor. In slave labor and serf labor, the lack of freedom is patently observable in the serf's or slave's relationship with an identifiable individual lord or slave owner. But with wage-labor, the proletarian's formal

55. Marx, "Sechstes Kapitel. Resultate des unmittelbaren Produktionsprozesses," *MEGA* II.4.1: 99 / *MECW* 34: 432–33. Marx hence argued that "The capitalist relation appears as a step in the social scale [in comparison with slavery and serfdom]. It is the opposite when an independent peasant or artisan is transformed into a wage-laborer," ibid., 103 / 437.

56. Ibid., 77 / 411.

57. Alex Gourevitch, however, argues that slaves are structurally dominated by the third parties that uphold the legal and political structures that are necessary to maintain chattel slavery; see "Labor Republicanism and the Transformation of Work," 601.

58. Marx, *Zur Kritik der politischen Ökonomie (Manuskript 1861–1863), MEGA* II.3: 2135 / *MECW* 34: 100; "Sechstes Kapitel. Resultate des unmittelbaren Produktionsprozesses," *MEGA* II.4.1: 103 / *MECW* 34: 437.

59. Marx, "Lohnarbeit und Kapital," *MEW* 6: 401 / *MECW* 9: 203. See also Marx, *Grundrisse der Kritik der politischen Ökonomie, MEGA* II.1: 372 / *MECW* 28: 392; and Marx, *Zur Kritik der politischen Ökonomie (Manuskript 1861–1863), MEGA* II.3: 661 / *MECW* 31: 244.

freedom to sell their labor obscures the structural necessity of having to sell their labor to a master. Marx emphasized this point again and again in *Das Kapital*. He contrasted the "veiled slavery (*verhüllte Sklaverei*) of the wage-laborers in Europe" with the "unqualified slavery (*Sklaverei sans phrase*) of the New World" and argued that the proletarian is one who "cannot get free (*loskommen*) of capital and whose enslavement to capital is only concealed by the variety of individual capitalists to whom . . . [he] sells [himself]."[60] That is also the argument that lies behind the title of this chapter:

> The Roman slave was held by chains; the wage-laborer is bound to his owner by invisible threads (*unsichtbare Fäden*). The appearance of independence is maintained by a constant change in the person of the individual employer, and by the fictio juris [legal fiction] of a contract.[61]

(In the French edition, Marx modified this passage to bring the structural domination by a class even more to the fore, replacing the second line with "Only this owner is not the individual capitalist, but the capitalist class.")[62] Marx argued that the domination by "invisible threads" rather than clearly discernible "chains" served a useful ideological function. By giving workers "the consciousness (or better the *idea*) of free self-determination, of liberty," it spurred them to greater industriousness than formally unfree laborers.[63] Even more important, it allowed capitalism's bourgeois defenders to more easily obscure the unfreedom of the wage-labor relationship. Marx wrote that it enabled the "smug political economist . . . [to] transmogrify (*breimäulig umlügen*)" a "relationship of absolute dependency . . . into one of free contract between buyer and seller."[64]

There are two ways that we might understand the proletarian's structural domination as an inhibition of their freedom. According to one conception of freedom, proletarians are unfree because they have no choice but to sell their labor power to a capitalist because the alternative is starvation. In this regard, Engels called it a "Fine freedom, where the proletarian has no other choice than that of either accepting the conditions which the bourgeoisie offers him, or of starving, of freezing to death, of sleeping naked among the beasts of the forests!"[65] Bourgeois defenders of capitalism sometimes respond that even if

60. Marx, *Das Kapital*, vol. 1, *MEGA* II.6: 562, 680 / *MECW* 35: 609, 747.

61. Ibid., 529–30 / 573.

62. Marx, *Le Capital*, vol. 1, *MEGA* II.7: 498.

63. Marx, "Sechstes Kapitel. Resultate des unmittelbaren Produktionsprozesses," *MEGA* II.4.1: 98n, 101–2 / *MECW* 34: 432n, 435.

64. Marx, *Das Kapital*, vol. 1, *MEGA* II.6: 687 / *MECW* 35: 756.

65. Engels, *Die Lage der arbeitenden Klasse in England*, *MEGA* I.4: 309 / *MECW* 4: 376. But see also his argument that the proletarian only "*appears* to be free" because he has no individual master despite being a "slave . . . of the whole property-owning class," ibid., 312 / 379.

the alternative is starvation, this does not undermine freedom, since no one interferes with the proletarian to force them to work for a capitalist. But that fails to appreciate that we can be forced to do something even when we have an alternative option, if that option is an *unreasonable* or *unacceptable* alternative (as the case with starvation).[66] Even a view of freedom as noninterference can thus account for why proletarians' dispossession from the means of production means that they are forced to work for a capitalist and is therefore an unfree choice.[67]

But that view does not fully capture the force of the complaint of proletarian unfreedom or adequately distinguish the situation of proletarians from independent producers. Independent producers are also forced to work in order to avoid starvation.[68] But they can work and avoid starvation without giving themselves a master, whereas proletarians have no choice but to give themselves a master (even if not a particular master). The difference between the independent producer and the proletarian is thus that the former chooses between starvation and masterless work, while the latter chooses between starvation and working for a master. The proletarian's choice is thus unfree not only because starvation is an unacceptable alternative, but because the alternative to starvation is having to work for a master, which is also unacceptable because it makes them unfree.[69] That relies on a view of freedom as nondomination and the argument, explored above, that the capitalist is a master inside the workplace. It is that argument and view of freedom that lies behind Marx's contention that the proletarian's "economic bondage (*Hörigkeit*) is both brought about and concealed by, the periodic renewal of the act by which he sells himself, [and] his change of individual wage-masters (*Lohnherrn*)."[70]

66. As is powerfully argued in G. A. Cohen, "The Structure of Proletarian Unfreedom," *Philosophy & Public Affairs* 12, no. 1 (1983): 3–33. See also John Filling, "Liberty," in *Encyclopedia of Political Thought*, ed. Michael Gibbons (Oxford: Wiley-Blackwell, 2015), 8.

67. Jan Kandiyali, "Should Socialists Be Republicans?," *Critical Review of International Social and Political Philosophy*, forthcoming, 6–8, https://doi.org/10.1080/13698230.2022.2070834.

68. One could, however, argue that independent producers are not made unfree by this necessity, since it is imposed by nature and not other people. On the importance of the distinction, see David Miller, "Constraints on Freedom," *Ethics* 94, no. 1 (1983): 66–86.

69. Alex Gourevitch, *From Slavery to the Cooperative Commonwealth: Labor and Republican Liberty in the Nineteenth Century* (Cambridge: Cambridge University Press, 2015), 108–9. That view is also passingly suggested in Cohen, "The Structure of Proletarian Unfreedom," 28n.

70. Marx, *Das Kapital*, vol. 1, *MEGA* II.6: 533-34 / *MECW* 35: 577. Marx slightly amended the French edition to read "the periodic renewal of the act by which he sells himself, the fiction of a free contract, [and] the change in individual masters (*maîtres individuels*)," *Le Capital*, vol. 1, *MEGA* II.7: 502.

For Marx, the proletarian's structural unfreedom is thus constituted by the fact that they must always have a master, and that this unfreedom is disguised by their ability to change masters.

Marx was not the first to have made this argument, which was a relatively established feature of critiques of wage-labor. In addition to the aforementioned anonymous cotton spinner, Auguste Blanqui argued in 1834 that when a "privileged caste" had a "monopoly on property," while the great majority of citizens were "completely dispossessed of the instruments of labor," then the latter, "though not condemned to remain slaves of any given individual, nevertheless become absolutely dependent on that caste, since their only remaining freedom is the choice of which master will rule over them."[71] (In Blanqui's formulation the idea that the unfreedom of proletarians comes from always having to have a master is particularly clear.) Marx himself likely came into contact with the idea through Engels, whose *Die Lage der arbeitenden Klasse in England* was suffused with the vocabulary of wage slavery. Engels specifically argued that the novel feature of the proletarian's slavery, compared to the "old, frank and open (*offenherzige*) slavery," was that the worker was "not the slave of a particular individual, but of the whole property-holding class."[72] In Engels's catechistic drafts of the *Manifest der Kommunistischen Partei*, he answered the usefully titled section "*In what way does the proletarian differ from the slave?*" with the answer "The slave is the property of *one* master . . . [whereas] the proletarian is, so to speak, the slave of the entire bourgeois *class*, not of *one* master."[73]

Marx's account of the structural domination of the proletarian was thus an established feature of socialist discussions of wage slavery. Where Marx most extended this argument was to provide a methodical historical investigation into the origins of the proletarians' structural domination combined with a theoretical account of the centrality of this fact to the emergence of capitalism. In the celebrated concluding section of *Das Kapital*, on "So-Called Primitive Accumulation," Marx set out the long and brutal "historical process of

71. Auguste Blanqui, "La richesse sociale doit appartenir à ceux qui l'ont créée," in *Oeuvres*, vol. 1, *Des Origines à la Révolution de 1848*, ed. Dominique Le Nuz (Nancy: Presses Universitaires de Nancy, 1993), 285, 287 / "Social Wealth Must Belong to Those Who Created It," in *The Blanqui Reader: Political Writings, 1830–1880*, ed. and trans. Philippe Le Goff, Peter Hallward, and Mitchell Abidor (London: Verso, 2018), 50, 53.

72. Engels, *Die Lage der arbeitenden Klasse in England*, MEGA I.4: 312 / MECW 4: 379. See further Joseph Persky, "Wage Slavery," *History of Political Economy* 30, no. 4 (1998): 646–49.

73. Engels, *Entwurf des Kommunistischen Glaubensbekenntnisses*, BdK 1: 472 / MECW 6: 100. See also Engels, *Grundsätze des Kommunismus*, MEW 4: 366 / MECW 6: 343–44.

divorcing the producer from the means of production."[74] Marx charted the bloody history stretching from the end of the fifteenth century to the beginning of the nineteenth, whereby British peasants were forcibly driven from the land through clearances, evictions, and the enclosure of common land. That process meant that the peasants were divorced from their means of production and subsistence and thus "had to obtain their value in the form of wages from [their] new lord, the industrial capitalist."[75] Marx stressed that this separation from the land was critical, because while peasants controlled their own means of production, they had no need to sell themselves to a capitalist. The independence of the peasant consequently had to be broken, in order to create the "great masses of men . . . torn from their means of subsistence" that capitalist production requires to be freely available on the labor market.[76] Marx therefore concluded that capitalism required "a servile condition of the mass of the people" for its emergence.[77] Without that precondition, when the independent producer "remains possessor of his means of production—capitalist accumulation and the capitalist mode of production are impossible."[78] Marx made sure to emphasize that point one more time in the very final lines of Das Kapital: "the capitalist mode of production and accumulation, and therefore capitalist private property, requires the annihilation of self-earned private property, i.e, the expropriation of the laborer."[79]

A striking feature of Marx's historical and theoretical account of primitive accumulation is the extent to which it incorporates a republican idealization of independent producers. He portrayed the mode of production in which the "laborer is the private owner of his own means of labor . . . the peasant of the land which he cultivates, the artisan of the tool which he handles as a virtuoso" as one in which their small workplace was "the school in which the manual skill, the ingenious inventiveness (*l'adresse ingénieuse*), and the free individuality

74. Marx, *Das Kapital*, vol. 1, *MEGA* II.6: 645 / *MECW* 35: 705–6. In the first German edition, "So-Called Primitive Accumulation" was only a subsection of the final chapter. When Marx reorganized the text for the second German edition, he upgraded the importance of primitive accumulation to its own chapter. In the French edition he went even further and made "L'accumulation primitive" its own final section of the text. While nearly all subsequent German editions have followed the second edition (7 sections with 25 chapters), English translations have followed the French structure (8 sections with 33 chapters). See, however, the recent critical German edition that follows the French, Karl Marx, *Das Kapital: Kritik der politischen Ökonomie. Erster Band. Neue Textausgabe*, ed. Thomas Kuczynski (Hamburg: VSA Verlag, 2017), 778–79.

75. Marx, *Das Kapital*, vol. 1, *MEGA* II.6: 670 / *MECW* 35: 734.

76. Ibid., 646 / 707.

77. Ibid., 649 / 711.

78. Ibid., 685–86 / 754. Similarly, Marx claimed that "the expropriation of the mass of the people from the soil forms the basis of the capitalist mode of production"; ibid., 686 / 755.

79. Ibid., 692 / 761.

of the laborer are developed."[80] Marx decried the transformation of the artisan's tools "from means of independent existence . . . into means for commanding them and sucking out of them unpaid labor." In support of this statement, he cited Rousseau's bitter complaint that the rich say to the poor, "*I will allow you the honour of serving me, provided you give me the little you have left for the trouble I shall take to command you.*"[81] Marx then favorably cited Mirabeau (whom he called "the lion of the Revolution"), arguing that while large factories "wonderfully enrich one or two industrialists," in small workshops "no one becomes rich, but many laborers are prosperous," highlighting that Mirabeau calls the latter "the only *free* ones."[82]

In addition to these French-inspired tributes to the freedom and independence of the artisan, Marx celebrated England's independent yeoman farmers and favorably contrasted them with the dependent agricultural proletariat that replaced them. He wrote that the free peasant proprietorship of the fifteenth century was the basis of "popular wealth (*Volksreichthum*)," and he praised the yeomen for being the "backbone of Cromwell's strength" during the English Civil Wars.[83] Marx also slammed the greed of the "English oligarchy" who drove the process of dispossession that replaced the "independent yeoman . . . [with] a servile rabble dependent on the arbitrary will of the landlords."[84] He argued that England's laboring class thereby abruptly transitioned "from its golden age to its iron age," a process that Marx stresses was only interrupted by "Cromwell's time . . . [for] as long as the republic lasted the mass of the English people of all levels rose from the degradation into which they had sunk under the Tudors."[85] This popular English republican language was also conspicuous in his drafts of *Das Kapital*, in which he complained, "What difference there is between the proud yeomanry of England, of whom Shakespeare speaks, and the English agricultural day laborers!"[86] He made that same complaint public

80. Marx, *Le Capital*, vol. 1, *MEGA* II.7: 677–78. Compare with *Das Kapital*, vol. 1, *MEGA* II.6: 681 / *MECW* 35: 749.

81. Marx, *Das Kapital*, vol. 1, *MEGA* II.6: 670n / *MECW* 35: 735n; Jean-Jacques Rousseau, "Discours sur l'économie politique," in *Oeuvres complètes*, vol. 3: *Les écrits politiques*, (Paris: Gallimard, 1964), 273 / *Discourse on Political Economy* in *The Social Contract and Other Political Writings*, ed. and trans. Victor Gourevitch (Cambridge: Cambridge University Press, 1997), 32.

82. Marx, *Das Kapital*, vol. 1, *MEGA* II.6: 670–71 / *MECW* 35: 735. See the rephrasing in *Le Capital*, vol. 1, *MEGA* II.7: 664.

83. Marx, *Das Kapital*, vol. 1, *MEGA* II.6: 647, 651 / *MECW* 35: 708, 713.

84. Ibid., 652–53 / 714–15.

85. Ibid., 648, 672n / 709, 737n.

86. Marx, *Zur Kritik der politischen Ökonomie (Manuskript 1861–1863)*, *MEGA* II.3: 2135 / *MECW* 34: 101; "Sechstes Kapitel. Resultate des unmittelbaren Produktionsprozesses," *MEGA* II.4.1: 103 / *MECW* 34: 437.

in an important 1865 speech to the General Council of the IWMA (which showcased many of his developing arguments from his as yet unpublished *Das Kapital*), lamenting the historical conversion of "the wages labourer into a slave and Shakespeare's proud yeoman into a pauper."[87]

Marx's celebration of the independence of the artisan and the small yeoman farmer is a surprising and insufficiently appreciated feature of *Das Kapital*. It stands in stark contrast to a traditional (and not otherwise inaccurate) picture of Marx as an extoller of capitalism as a liberating advance over previous patriarchal, inefficient, and retrograde modes of production. It is certainly a marked shift from his earlier, nearly wholly dismissive attitude toward republican ideals of individual property ownership, which was explored in chapter 5. What accounts for this shift? William Clare Roberts has plausibly argued that the explanation for the appearance of this surprising "popular republican historiography that valorized the ancient constitution and the lost independence of the peasant producer" at the end of *Das Kapital* is rooted in the continued popularity of these ideas in the IWMA and the radical milieu in which its members moved.[88]

When, for instance, the General Council of IWMA began to search for an official press organ and settled on *The Workman's Advocate*, it promptly renamed it *The Commonwealth*, emphasizing continuity with the seventeenth-century radical tradition.[89] George Odger, shoemaker, leading trade unionist, and founding member of the IWMA, became the paper's editor and would later go on to defend plans for the government to rent out "small parcels" of land, reminiscing that the "battalions of our own Cromwell were mostly composed of men of a class of yeoman now almost unknown. They fought as men only fight who have something to fight for."[90] Marx's old associate Ernest Jones, having moved from his earlier socialism to a more diffuse radicalism, argued in a popular lecture first delivered a month after *Das Kapital*'s publication that the roots of "all the evils that exist in the relations of Labour and Capital, are the monopoly and consequent misuse of the land." The solution was to make available "two acres of good

87. Marx, "Value, Price and Profit," *MEGA* I.20: 183 / *MECW* 20: 145. The reference to "Shakespeare's proud yeoman" is probably to Henry V.

88. Roberts, *Marx's Inferno*, 197.

89. Margot C. Finn, *After Chartism: Class and Nation in English Radical Politics, 1848–1874* (Cambridge: Cambridge University Press, 1993), 242–43. For the history of the IWMA's takeover of the paper, see *MEGA* I.20: 1896–1901. Marx sat on the directorial board of the paper and was opposed to the name change but was too ill to stop it; see Marx to Engels, 10 February 1866, *MEGA digital:* https://megadigital.bbaw.de/briefe/detail.xql?id=M0000036/*MECW* 42: 224.

90. George Odger, "The Land Question," *The Contemporary Review*, vol. 17 (August 1871): 32–33.

land for the support of each individual man" and his family, since "If the injury is inflicted by driving the labourers from the soil, the cure is—just to lead them back again to whence they came." Jones ended his lecture with the slogan "Back to the land!" for land was the "only safeguard against the assaults of capital" and the "shield of freedom," rhetorically asking his audience,

> when was England truly powerful? When she had her yeomanry to win an Agincourt, her peasants to fight at Cressy and Poictiers. Give us a million peasant farmers, and you have a million patriot soldiers for old England, whose every cottage is a trusty fortress, with waving cornfields for its golden glacis, and stalwart yeoman for a gallant guard.[91]

Nostalgic dreams of returning to an ideal of agrarian independence through small landholdings (at the expense of social measures addressing factories and heavy industry) also played a central role in the social republican program of the artisan O'Brienites who joined the General Council of the IWMA after 1868, including Martin J. Boon, George Milner, George E. Harris, and William Townshend.[92] Boon argued that while "mills stand still, and furnaces are blown out," the country was the source of "our Hampdens, our Cromwells, and our Elliots," and insisted that the "safety of the state lies in the mass of the people having and holding the soil." For Boon, the "dispossessing of the petty yeoman" had led to a society with "only two classes . . . a few wealthy masters, and a huge population of unsecured wage-slaves." His answer was for the state to support the creation of small farms, which would free those "dependent for subsistence upon wages, and the caprice of employer," celebrating in contrast an image of the "industrious farmer . . . cultivating his little territory with his own hands, and enjoying the produce raised by his own labour and industry."[93]

91. Ernest Jones, *Labour and Capital: A Lecture delivered in the City Hall, Glasgow, October 10* . . . (London: Simpkin, Marshall & Co, 1867), 5, 16, 19. For the ideological shift in Jones's later life and Marx and Engels's view of it, see John Saville, *Ernest Jones: Chartist. Selections from the Writings and Speeches of Ernest Jones* (London: Lawrence & Wishart, 1952), 77–82, 241–47.

92. For the social program of the O'Brienites and their involvement in the IWMA, see the excellent neglected study, Watson Eugene Lincoln Jr., *Popular Radicalism and the Beginnings of the New Socialist Movement in Britain, 1870–1885* (PhD thesis, University College London, 1977), chapter 2. On British social republicanism in the 1860s–70s, see further Royden Harrison, *Before the Socialists: Studies in Labour and Politics, 1861–1881* (London: Routledge & Kegan Paul, 1965), chapter 5. For Marx's mixed view of the O'Brienites, see Marx to Friedrich Bolte, 23 November 1871, *MEW* 33: 327–28 / *MECW* 44: 251–52.

93. Martin J. Boon, *Home Colonization: Including a Plan Showing how All the Unemployed Might Have Profitable Work, and thus Prevent Want, Pauperism, and Crime* (London: National Reform League, 1869), 19, 22–23, 27.

This was the broad ideological field in which Marx's sympathetic portrait in *Das Kapital* of the "golden age" of English peasant independence should be understood. Marx's involvement in the IWMA had given him an appreciation for the continued and deeply held attractiveness of this ideal and the need to appeal to it rather than simply dismiss it.[94] As he wrote to Engels regarding his work in the IWMA, it was critical that "our view should appear in a form that would make it acceptable to the present outlook of the workers' movement."[95] Marx's discussion of the destruction of the artisan workshop and the dispossession of the peasants' land in the section on "So-Called Primitive Accumulation" was an effective rhetorical appeal to this lost world of independence. But unlike those who praised that world in the hope of its reincarnation, Marx's account was decidedly a eulogy meant to praise it *and* bury it.

At the close of his discussion of primitive accumulation Marx "pivots dramatically."[96] Having spent the previous forty pages praising independent production, Marx suddenly insists,

> This industrial regime of small independent producers, working for themselves, presupposes parceling of the soil, and scattering of the other means of production. As it excludes concentration of the means of production, it also excludes cooperation on a large scale; division of labor in the workshop and the fields; mechanization; the learned domination of man (*la domination savant de l'homme*) over nature; the free development of the productive forces of society; the concert and unity in the ends, means and efforts of collective activity. It is only compatible with a narrowly limited state of production and society. To perpetuate it would be, as Pecqueur rightly says, "to decree mediocrity in everything."[97]

The old world of independent production was just that, a bygone world that could make no use of the tremendous productive powers of society. Its small-scale individualized structure inhibited it from taking advantage of the gains from cooperation, division of labor, the application of scientific and technical

94. For an example of such debates within the General Council, see "Meeting of the General Council, 6 July 1869," *MEGA* I.21: 670–73.

95. Marx to Engels, 4 November 1864, *MEGA* III.13: 43 / *MECW* 42: 18.

96. Roberts, *Marx's Inferno*, 208.

97. Marx, *Le Capital*, vol. 1., *MEGA* II.7: 678. This pivot is particularly clear in the French edition, where Marx separated this passage into a new paragraph and reformulated it and the preceding discussion. Constantin Pecqueur (an early French socialist) had argued that "to perpetuate *agricultural, commercial and manufacturing fragmentation,* is the death of civilization, it is to decree mediocrity in everything"; see his *Théorie nouvelle d'économie sociale et politique, ou études sur l'organisation des sociétés* (Paris: Capelle, 1842), 435.

knowledge, and doomed it in the face of a mode of production that could. Marx insisted that independent production stood no chance when confronted by capitalist production: "It must be annihilated, it is annihilated." The "dwarf-like property of the many" is necessarily replaced by the "huge property of the few."[98] The whole structure of Marx's argument in the closing sections of *Das Kapital* thus serves to highlight that as attractive as the world of independent production might have been, it was an untenable ideal for the modern world.

That conclusion would make for grim reading for any supporter of individual property ownership. But Marx offered his readers a lifeline out of that dying world. He insisted that the same "immanent laws of capitalist production" that allowed large capitalists to destroy the small workshops of artisans and peasant farms also leads to the ever greater concentration of capitalist production, as "One capitalist always kills many." (Here Marx was relying on the arguments he had made in the huge historical survey in part 4 of *Das Kapital* of how the benefits to cooperation, division of labor, and the introduction of machinery had continually destroyed smaller enterprises.[99]) Hand in hand with that concentration would be the growth of a "disciplined, united" working class who, dispossessed of the means of production, would now in turn dispossess the capitalist class, and so "The expropriators are expropriated."[100] Thus the tragedy of the "first negation of individual private property" would eventually be avenged through a second negation of the capitalist's private property: "It is the negation of the negation. This does not reestablish private property for the producer, but individual property based on the acquisitions of the capitalist era, on cooperation of free workers and the common possession of all the means of production, including the soil."[101] While it was not possible to restore the individual property ownership of the independent artisan and the peasant, the dependency of capitalism could and would be overcome by socialized production in which everyone owned the means of production together.

The primarily critical nature of *Das Kapital* and Marx's own antiutopian theoretical commitments meant that he gave few hints in the book itself of

98. Marx, *Das Kapital*, vol. 1, *MEGA* II. 6: 681 / *MECW* 35: 749.

99. Marx here argued that the destruction of small workshops by large factories was "as sure as the result of an encounter of an army armed with breech-loading rifles and an army of archers"; *Das Kapital*, *MEGA* II.6: 434 / *MECW* 35: 453. Perhaps to appeal to the historical references of his French audience, "archers" was changed to "crossbowmen (*arbalétriers*)" in *Le Capital*, vol. 1, *MEGA* II.7: 388.

100. Marx, *Das Kapital*, *MEGA* II.6: 682 / *MECW* 35: 750.

101. This combines the versions in Marx, *Le Capital*, vol. 1, *MEGA* II.7: 679, and *Das Kapital*, *MEGA* II. 6: 683 / *MECW* 35: 751.

what he called an "association of free men," in which ownership of the means of production was "societal instead of individual," should look like.[102] But his work in the IWMA had led to an important shift in his thinking. In his earlier writings he had simply assumed common ownership would mean the concentration of the means of production in the "hands of the state"[103] (an assumption heavily criticized by republicans, as we saw in chapter 5). But through the IWMA, he became increasingly open to the idea of socializing the means of production through cooperatives. As he put it in the inaugural 1864 address to the IWMA, cooperatives had shown that "production on a large scale, and in accord with the behests of modern science" could be successfully carried out without "a class of masters" exercising "dominion over" their workers.[104] While he thought (as we will see below) that cooperatives were not by themselves sufficient to overcome the manifold aspects of capitalist domination, he did think that inside cooperative factories "the antithesis between capital and labour is overcome" and that they were a promising sign of how "a new mode of production naturally grows out of an old one."[105] Cooperatives showed, as Marx argued in the explicitly republican language of his instructions to the British delegates to the IWMA's Geneva Congress in 1866, that the "despotic system of the *subordination of labour* to capital can be superseded by the republican and beneficent system of *the association of free and equal producers*."[106]

Domination and Exploitation

Marx's account of the domination of the capitalist and capitalist class highlighted their many gross abuses of their power. But though Marx was outraged by the working class's unfreedom and dependency, his account of capitalist domination was not limited to normative condemnation. Marx thought that domination played a central role in a sociological understanding of the reproduction of capitalism, because of how it enabled the exploitation of the working class.[107] While the personal domination of the capitalist in the

102. Marx, *Das Kapital*, vol. 1, MEGA II.6: 109 / MECW 35: 89.

103. Marx and Engels, *Manifest der Kommunistischen Partei*, MEW 4: 481 / MECW 6: 504.

104. Marx, "Address of the International Working Men's Association (Inaugural Address)," *MEGA* I.20: 10 / *MECW* 20: 11.

105. Marx, *Das Kapital*, vol. 3, MEGA II.15: 431 / MECW 37: 438. See also *Das Kapital*, vol. 1, MEGA II.6: 328n / MECW 35: 336n.

106. Marx, "Instructions for the Delegates of the Provisional General Council. The Different Questions," *MEGA* I.20: 232 / *MECW* 20: 190.

107. For the useful suggestion that this can be understood as "extractive domination," see Michael J. Thompson, "The Two Faces of Domination in Republican Political Theory," *European*

workplace was necessary for the continual and ever greater extraction of surplus labor from the worker during their working hours; the structural domination of workers through their dispossession from the means of production meant that they were continually forced to enter the labor market to find a capitalist master who used their domination to set the terms of the labor contract in their exploitative favor. Marx argued that this underlying structural necessity was critical to

> reproduce and perpetuate the conditions for exploiting the worker. It incessantly forces the worker to sell their labor-power, in order to live, and enables the capitalist to purchase labor-power, in order to enrich himself. It is no longer an accident that capitalist and worker confront each other in the market as buyer and seller. It is the double mill (*Zwickmühle*) of the process itself that hurls the worker back onto the market again and again as a seller of his labor-power.[108]

Marx's account of domination and exploitation was developed in chapter 8 (chapter 10 in the French and English versions) of *Das Kapital* on "The Working Day (*Der Arbeitstag*)." Marx here elaborated on the specifically capitalist way in which the subordinated laboring class is forced to go beyond the necessary labor they need to survive and carry out "surplus labor" for a ruling class. Marx accorded central importance to the idea of surplus labor in his social theory, arguing that "What differentiates different economic forms of society, e.g., a society based on slavery and one based on wage-labor, is solely the form in which surplus labor is extracted from the immediate producer, the laborer."[109] Marx thought that the difference between necessary labor and surplus labor was most obvious in feudal societies, since the time spent by a serf

---

Journal of Political Theory 17, no. 1 (2018): 47–50; Michael J. Thompson, "The Radical Republican Structure of Marx's Critique of Capitalist Society," *Critique: Journal of Socialist Theory* 47, no. 3 (2019): 394–95.

108. Marx, *Das Kapital*, vol. 1, *MEGA* II.6: 533 / *MECW* 35: 577. There is no easy translation for *Zwickmühle*, which refers to both a grave dilemma and a particular situation in the game of mill, or Nine Men's Morris, that allows a player to continuously remove the other player's pieces, known as "double mill." In the French translation it is rendered "double mill (*double moulinet*)"; *Le Capital*, vol. 1, *MEGA* II.7: 502. The 1887 English translation (reproduced in *MECW*) skipped the term entirely, while the Penguin edition unsatisfyingly renders it as "alternating rhythm," *Capital*, vol. 1, trans. Ben Fowkes (London: Penguin, 1976), 723. Marx's original evokes an image of being trapped in a continuous cycle of dispossession and exploitation.

109. Marx, *Das Kapital*, *MEGA* II.6: 226 / *MECW* 35: 226–27. When introducing the term in the original German Marx wrote "Mehrarbeit (surplus labor)," emphasizing its origins in English political economy.

working on the lord's fields (the corvée system) was geographically and temporally distinct from when they worked on their own fields. By comparison, in capitalist production, where a worker spends all day working in the same workplace, this distinction "is not visible. Surplus labor and necessary labor blur into each other (*verschwimmen in einander*)."[110] Marx emphasized the ideological advantage of this feature of capitalism, since (unlike for the serf) the surplus labor carried out for a capitalist is obscured from the worker. This obfuscation of the fact that the worker carried out unpaid surplus labor for the capitalist was at the heart of the "mystifications of the capitalist mode of production, and all of its illusions of freedom."[111]

In order to cut through this ideological mist, Marx argued that we should imagine a working day divided into two parts: *necessary labor-time*, the period when the laborer works to sustain themselves; and *surplus labor-time*, the period when the laborer works beyond that minimum and creates a surplus. The worker thus works part of the day for themselves and part of the day for the capitalist. Marx, who was not usually given to diagrammatic presentations of his ideas, illustrated this two-part division of the working day as shown in figure 11.[112] In this example, the period of necessary labor-time (AB) and the period of surplus labor-time (BC) are both six hours, giving a total working day (AC) of twelve hours.

Marx stressed that the length of the working day was not a fixed quantity. It could fluctuate between a minimum, set by necessary labor-time (as the worker, or better, the working class a whole, could not work less than the time needed to sustain themselves), and a maximum, set by both social norms and the absolute physical limits of the working class.[113] Marx insisted that in capitalist production the working day could not stay at the minimum level set by necessary labor-time, because then no surplus would be created for the capitalist to appropriate. Moreover, capitalists have an interest in extending the total length of the working day as much as possible, in order to increase the period of surplus labor-time and hence the surplus value they extract from the workers.[114] Workers, on the other hand, have an interest in reducing the length of

110. Ibid., 243 / 245.

111. Ibid., 502 / 540. Marx interestingly noted that while unpaid surplus labor is hidden in capitalism, slave labor hides the fact that part of the slave's labor for their master is necessary labor to sustain themselves. See also Marx, "Value, Price and Profit," *MEGA* I.20: 171–72 / *MECW* 20: 132–33.

112. Marx, *Das Kapital*, vol. 1, *MEGA* II.6: 238 / *MECW* 35: 239. I have slightly adapted the diagram for clarity.

113. Ibid., 239–40 / 240–41.

114. As G. A. Cohen has shown, this argument does not, whatever Marx may have thought, rely on a labor theory of value. There is a subtle but enormous difference between saying that

A – – – – – B – – – – – C

Necessary labor-time
(6 hours)

Surplus labor-time
(6 hours)

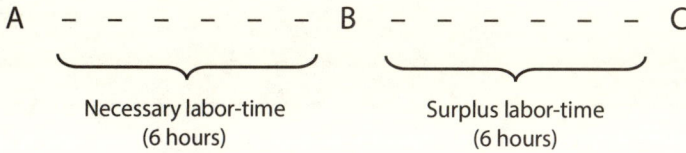

FIGURE 11. Working day of 12 hours

the working day in order to have more free time for themselves. Hence, when it comes to setting the length of the working day, Marx argued that there was a clash between these two conflicting drives, "an antimony, of right against right." In such cases, "Between equal rights, force decides."[115]

The working day is thus a site of class struggle, with workers and capitalists competing to drive it in opposite directions, with its ultimate length a function of their relative power. As Marx puts it, the working day "resolves itself into a question of the respective powers of the combatants."[116] The greater the power of capitalists over the worker, the more they are able to extend the length of the working day, and hence the greater the period of surplus labor-time, and the greater the surplus they extract from the workers. Marx referred to this kind of exploitation (simple extension of the working day) as an extraction of "absolute surplus value." In terms of our first example, a capitalist's increased power might enable them to increase the total working day (AC′) to fourteen hours, giving a new extended surplus labor-time (BC′) of eight hours (see figure 12). Capitalists' increase in relative power allows them to extend the working day, resulting in an increase in exploitation. Greater domination over the workers thus leads to greater exploitation.[117]

---

the worker's labor produces value and saying that the worker's labor produces a product that has value. Only the latter claim is required to ground an argument of exploitation, and it exists in what Cohen calls a state of a "mutual irrelevance" to the labor theory of value. See G. A. Cohen, "The Labor Theory of Value and the Concept of Exploitation," *Philosophy & Public Affairs* 8, no. 4 (1979): 338, 353–56.

115. Marx, *Das Kapital*, vol. 1, MEGA II.6: 241 / MECW 35: 243.

116. Marx, "Value, Price and Profit," MEGA I.20: 183 / MECW 20: 146.

117. This might seem to rely on a simple "imbalance of power" conception of domination rather than a republican view of domination as arbitrary power. But capitalists' ability to hire a worker is an entirely arbitrary power they hold (i.e., it is a decision at their own discretion), and their ability to set the terms of the labor contract (including the length of the working day) is a more or less arbitrary power contingent on their power relative to the workers. The greater their relative power, the greater their arbitrary ability to set the terms of the labor contract (and, conversely, the more their ability is restricted, e.g., by legal prohibitions, the less arbitrary that power is). The offer of a labor contract is also not just any potential relationship one could enter

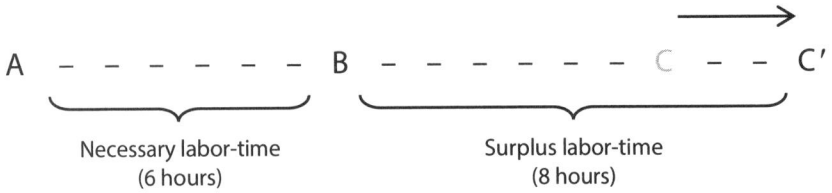

FIGURE 12. Working day of 14 hours (absolute surplus value)

Marx laid out several factors that could increase the power of the capitalist and the capitalist class over that of the worker and the working class, chief among them the extent of the division of labor and the size of the industrial reserve army of the unemployed. Marx argued that the progression of the division of labor in production results in workers becoming more and more specialized on a particular task, which means that they increasingly lose their ability to work independently or carry out alternative work. That in turn gives the capitalist who provides that specialized work greater negotiating power over the worker with few alternative options. Marx thus argued that the worker's "lifelong specialism" results in his "helpless dependence . . . upon the capitalist" and approvingly cited the words of the Scottish Enlightenment thinker Adam Ferguson, who claimed that the division of labor meant that "we make a nation of helots, and have no free citizens."[118] The reserve army of the unemployed, on the other hand, provides every capitalist with an easily accessible pool of alternative candidates should any worker consider rejecting the terms of the labor contract. The larger the reserve army, the greater the competition among workers and the more they are forced to "submit to overwork and to subjugation under the dictates of capital."[119] Marx thus argued that the industrial reserve army ensures the "absolute dependence of the working class upon the capitalist class," "completes the despotism of capital," and "rivets the worker to capital more firmly than the wedges of Hephaestus held Prometheus to the rock."[120]

But despite this bleak picture, Marx was also keen to stress that there were countermeasures available to the working class to check the power of the

---

into, but one on which the worker is dependent for survival. For further discussion of how domination must include all three conditions of an imbalance of power, dependency, and arbitrariness, see Lovett, *A General Theory of Domination and Justice*, chapters 3–4.

118. Adam Ferguson, *An Essay on the History of Civil Society*, ed. Fania Oz-Salzberger (Cambridge: Cambridge University Press. (1995 [1767]), 177. Cited in Marx, *Das Kapital*, vol. 1, *MEGA* II.6: 349 / *MECW* 35: 359.

119. Marx, *Das Kapital*, vol. 1, *MEGA* II.6: 579 / *MECW* 35: 630.

120. Ibid., 583, 588 / 634, 639–40.

capitalist to dictate the terms of the labor contract. One was the formation of trade unions, which Marx believed could counteract the effects of the reserve army of the unemployed by "removing or at least checking that competition [among the workers], in order to conquer such terms of contract as might raise them at least above the condition of mere slaves."[121] The other was the working class's power to collectively fight for state regulation of the labor contract. Marx set aside a significant chunk of the chapter on the working day to tell the history of the British working class's campaign for a legal limit on the working day, especially the "epoch-making" years that led to the 1847 Factory Act, limiting the working day to ten hours.[122] The history of the fight showed that "the isolated worker, the worker as a 'free' vendor of his labor power . . . succumbs without any power of resistance."[123] But if the working class "put their heads together" they could "as a class compel the passing of a law, an all-powerful social barrier that stops them from selling, by free contract with capital, themselves and their families into death and slavery." That law was a "modest Magna Charta of a legally limited working day" that protected the worker's free time from the capitalist.[124] We can express the result of that legal limitation by modifying Marx's initial presentation of the division of the working day so that the total working day (AC″) is reduced to ten hours, with a consequent shortening of surplus labor-time (BC″) to four hours (see figure 13).

The inclusion of this argument in *Das Kapital* mattered to Marx because he wanted to push back against antipolitical strains in socialisms that thought there was no point in struggling for state regulation. In his discussion of the working day, he specifically highlighted the passing of a resolution at the 1866 Geneva congress of the IWMA that pushed for a legally enforced eight-hour working day.[125] Marx saw this as an important victory against the French Proudhonist section of the IWMA who "spurn all *revolutionary* action, i.e., arising out of the class struggle itself, every concentrated social movement, and therefore also that which can be achieved by *political means* (such as limitation of the working day by *law*)."[126] Marx thus wanted to emphasize that legal inhibitions

121. Marx, "Instructions for the Delegates of the Provisional General Council. The Different Questions," *MEGA* I.20: 232 / *MECW* 20: 191.

122. Marx, *Das Kapital*, vol. 1, *MEGA* II.6: 285 / *MECW* 35: 288.

123. Ibid., 300 / 303.

124. Ibid., 302 / 306–7. For the importance Marx placed on protecting "free time" from "the tyrannical usurpations of capital," see Marx, "Value, Price and Profit," *MEGA* I.20: 180 / *MECW* 20: 142.

125. Marx, *Das Kapital*, *MEGA* II.6: 301–2 / *MECW* 35: 305–6.

126. Marx to Louis Kugelmann, 9 October 1866, *MEGA digital*: https://megadigital.bbaw.de /briefe/detail.xql?id=M0000183/ *MECW* 42: 326.

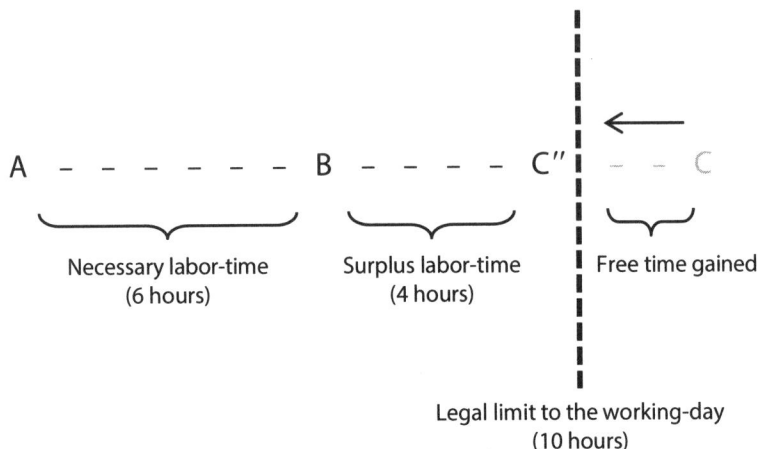

FIGURE 13. Working day of 10 hours (with legal limits)

on the capitalists' power, obtained through a campaign of organized class struggle, was an important way workers could combat their domination and resulting exploitation.

The battle over the length of the working day (Marx called it a "protracted, more or less hidden civil war")[127] is a particularly stark and crude way in which the capitalist tries to use their domination over the worker to expand their exploitation. But Marx also outlined a subtler form of how domination was linked to exploitation. He argued that while surplus labor-time could be directly increased by extending the length of the working day, it could also be indirectly increased by reducing necessary labor-time. This occurs through increases in the productivity of labor which reduce the time it takes for workers to produce the products with the value necessary to sustain themselves. This decrease in necessary labor-time (assuming the working day stays the same length) automatically increases the period of the working day dedicated to surplus labor-time. In comparison to the "absolute surplus value" created by extending the length of the working day, Marx called this form of exploitation the extraction of "relative surplus value."[128] He clarified the idea by modifying his depiction of the working day to show how an increase in productivity affects the ratio of surplus to necessary labor-time within the working day (see figure 14).[129] In this example, an increase in productivity reduces necessary

127. Marx, *Das Kapital*, vol. 1, *MEGA* II.6: 300 / *MECW* 35: 303.
128. Ibid., 313–14 / 320.
129. Ibid., 311 / 317.

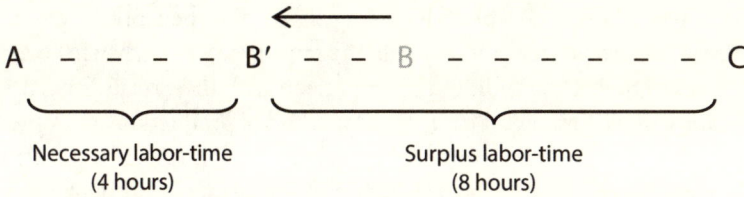

FIGURE 14. Working day of 12 hours (relative surplus value)

labor-time by two hours, giving a new necessary labor-time (AB´) of four hours. Assuming that the total working day (AC) stays constant at twelve hours, then the period of surplus labor-time (B´C) automatically increases to eight hours. Increasing productivity has thus achieved the same result (extending surplus labor-time by two hours) as the direct extension of the working day did in figure 12.

Marx set out two ways in which domination was important to the extraction of relative surplus value. First, he argued that some increases in productivity were due to the capitalist's increased personal domination over the worker in the workplace, arguing that greater supervision and discipline allowed the capitalist to intensify production. He described how the "*supervision* and *discipline* of the capitalist" was vital to ensuring that the production process was "not disturbed, nor interrupted" and to raise the "intensity of labor" so as to "extract as much work from him [the worker] as is possible in a given time."[130] But raising productivity, of course, does not necessarily have to involve capitalists extending their domination, since that can occur through the introduction of machinery and better technology or more efficient organization of the division of labor.

The other link Marx made to domination is the question of who decides how the gains of productivity are spent. Marx argued that gains in productivity "set free" a block of time (the two hours from B´-B in the example above). In theory this could be used to shorten the working day and hence convert the gains from productivity into more free time for the workers. But under the capitalist mode of production, the hours "set free" by gains to productivity are "annexed to the domain of surplus labor."[131] The reason this occurs is because the individual capitalist is (at least initially) in charge of deciding how

130. Marx, "Sechstes Kapitel. Resultate des unmittelbaren Produktionsprozesses," *MEGA* II.4.1: 61–62, 84 / *MECW* 34: 395–96, 418.

131. Marx, *Das Kapital*, vol. 1, *MEGA* II.6: 317–19 / *MECW* 35: 324–26. For Marx's criticism of capitalism for failing to convert rising productivity into more free time, see ibid., 493–94 / 530–31, and Cohen, *Karl Marx's Theory of History*, 302–7.

gains of productivity are spent. Rather than shorten the working day, they use those gains to produce more within the same time period, hence lowering the prices of their commodities in comparison with their rivals. In that way "the capitalist who applies the improved method of production, appropriates to surplus labor a greater portion of the working day, than the other capitalists in the same trade" and that "augmentation of surplus value [through productivity gains] is pocketed by him."[132] In order for this to occur, of course, the capitalist has to be the one in charge of the labor process, so that the decision on how to spend the time gained from increased productivity rests with them rather than the workers. Marx cited the words of English political economist John Cazenove: "A man's profit does not depend upon his command of the *produce* of other men's labor, but upon his command of *labor itself*."[133] The capitalist thus must control the labor process in order to appropriate the gains from productivity. They must, in other words, be in a position of domination over the workers in order to continuously exploit them.

But Marx immediately stressed that this was not the end of the story. As soon as one capitalist drives down the prices of their commodities, the "coercive law of competition forces his competitors to adopt the new method" of production, wiping out the individual capitalist's temporary increased extraction of surplus value.[134] As we will see below, this dynamic meant that though the individual capitalist had some initial power to decide on the gains of productivity, the decision was ultimately outside of their control.

For the moment, however, it is worth remarking on an important upshot of Marx's argument connecting domination with exploitation. His account shows how domination brings clear material benefits to the dominator. In some contemporary republican discussions of domination, the idea is too easily seen as merely the outcome of a master's sadistic or irrational desire for power over others.[135] The material underpinnings of domination are too easily lost in such accounts. By contrast, Marx provides an important explanatory account for why domination is such a persistent feature of social life—because of the exploitation that it enables. Capitalists have a permanent interest in expanding their personal and structural domination over the working class in

---

132. Marx, *Das Kapital*, vol. 1, MEGA II.6 316–17 / MECW 35: 322–24.

133. Cited in ibid., 316n / 323n. See John Cazenove, *Outlines of Political Economy* (London: Pelham Richardson, 1832), 49.

134. Marx, *Das Kapital*, vol. 1 MEGA II.6: 317 / MECW 35: 324.

135. A point aptly made in Gourevitch, *From Slavery to the Cooperative Commonwealth*, 114. For an account that emphasizes the connection, see Nicholas Vrousalis, "Exploitation, Vulnerability, and Social Domination," *Philosophy & Public Affairs* 41, no. 2 (2013): 131–57, and, more recently, Nicholas Vrousalis, *Exploitation as Domination: What Makes Capitalism Unjust* (Oxford: Oxford University Press, 2023).

order to extract more surplus labor. If we care about ending domination, then we should take that connection seriously.

Domination and the Market

In an early chapter of *The Grapes of Wrath*, Steinbeck depicted the eviction of Oklahoma tenant farmers and their families by the bank that owns the land. The bank has decided that large farms will be more profitable than sharecropping, and so the tenants and their homes have to go. The tenants try to reason with the bank's representatives, but they explain that there is nothing they can do,

"We're sorry. It's not us. It's the monster. The bank isn't like a man."

"Yes, but the bank is only made of men."

"No, you're wrong there—quite wrong there. The bank is something else than men. It happens that every man in a bank hates what the bank does, and yet the bank does it. The bank is something more than men, I tell you. It's the monster. Men made it, but they can't control it."

One of the tenants threatens to shoot the man hired by the bank to bulldoze their homes. The man protests that he has to make a living as well.

"That's so," the tenant said. "Who gave you orders? I'll go after him. He's the one to kill."

"You're wrong. He got his orders from the bank. The bank told him, 'Clear those people out or it's your job.'"

"Well, there's a president of the bank. There's a board of directors. I'll fill up the magazine of the rifle and go into the bank."

The driver said, "Fellow was telling me the bank gets orders from the East. The orders were, "'Make the land show profit or we'll close you up.'"

"But where does it stop? Who can we shoot? I don't aim to starve to death before I kill the man that's starving me."

"I don't know. Maybe there's nobody to shoot. Maybe the thing isn't men at all. Maybe like you said, the property's doing it."[136]

Steinbeck captures the frustration and hopeless desperation of being faced with forces far beyond one's control. The tenants' way of life, based on their intimate and personal relations with their land and with each other, comes into brutal contact with the abstract and impersonal imperatives of the market. The desperate tenant who vainly tries to find someone to shoot is forced to accept that there is no identifiable individual to blame for their predicament. Marx thought that this impersonal character of the market forces that control people's

---

136. John Steinbeck, *The Grapes of Wrath* (London: Penguin Classics, 2000[1939]), 35–41.

lives distinguished capitalism from previous modes of production. In an 1853 discussion of how English peasants were being driven from the land that could just as easily describe the plight of Oklahoma farmers some eighty years later, Marx argued that that in precapitalist societies, the "executioners are themselves tangible and hangable beings," but in capitalist ones it is an "invisible, intangible and silent despot" that drives, "in its noiseless, everyday working, whole races and whole classes of men from the soil of their forefathers."[137]

The invisible, intangible, silent despot of the market formed, for Marx, the final and most impersonal aspect of capitalist domination. We have already seen how Marx thought the personal domination inside the workplace by one master was underpinned by the structural domination by the many masters of the capitalist class. The impersonal domination of the market, by comparison, subjected all of society to a form of rule over which no one was master.[138] That rule was the subordination of society to the overriding market imperative of maximizing profits, or, in more Marxian terminology, the competitive drive for ever greater accumulation of capital through the extraction of surplus value. Marx considered this impersonal drive, along with the structural separation of workers from the means of production, to be a defining feature of capitalism and distinguished as such from earlier predominantly personal forms of domination.[139] Marx, for instance, argued that the "capital relationship as a *relationship of compulsion* to force out surplus labor" could not only be understood in terms of "relationships of personal domination and dependency."[140] Similarly, in *Das Kapital* he noted that,

> The contrast between the power of landed property, based on personal relations of domination and servitude, and the impersonal power of money, is clearly expressed by the two French proverbs, 'Nulle terre sans seigneur [No land without a lord],' and 'L'argent n'a pas de maître [Money has no master]."[141]

137. Marx, "Parliamentary Debates—The Clergy against Socialism—Starvation," *MEGA* I.12: 54 / *MECW* 11: 527.

138. I take the term "impersonal domination" from the analysis in Roberts, *Marx's Inferno*, chapter 3.

139. As has been recently explored in Søren Mau, *Mute Compulsion: A Marxist Theory of the Economic Power of Capital* (London: Verso, 2023), which I have unfortunately not been able to integrate into this book's discussion.

140. Marx, "Sechstes Kapitel. Resultate des unmittelbaren Produktionsprozesses," *MEGA* II.4.1: 93 / *MECW* 34: 426.

141. Marx, *Das Kapital*, vol. 1, *MEGA* II.6: 165n / *MECW* 35: 157n. Marx elsewhere argued that the phrase "Money has no master ... translated into political language" was that "[t]he bourgeoisie has no king, the true form of its rule is the republic," suggesting that the impersonal domination

Readers might remember that Marx had cited the same two proverbs in his 1844 economic writings to illustrate the idea that "competition . . . manifests its domination over both the working class and the proprietors themselves who are ruined or raised by the laws of movement of capital."[142] The domination of the market (which operated over *both* workers and capitalist) was thus for Marx in an important sense impersonal—because it was not an identifiable *maître*, a master, who dominated but the market imperative itself.[143]

Marx thought that this impersonal domination of the market manifested itself for workers in terms of their unique dependence on the labor market. Their separation from the means of production meant that they had to sell their labor power on a market, and their livelihood was thus dependent on the shifting prices they could sell themselves for and, more brutally, whether there was a market at all for their labor power. This dependency was powerfully sketched by Marx and Engels in the *Manifest der Kommunistischen Partei*, where they argued that proletarians "are a commodity, like every other article of commerce, and are consequently exposed to all the vicissitudes of competition, to all the fluctuations of the market," and that "[t]he growing competition among the bourgeois, and the resulting crises, make the wages of the workers ever more fluctuating."[144] That view had been developed by Engels in his drafts of the manifesto, in which he had argued that proletarians were defined by the necessity of living from the "sale of their labor" and, consequently, "whose life and death, whose whole existence depends on the demand for labor, hence, on the alternation of times of good and bad business, on the fluctuations from unbridled competition."[145] Engels argued that the proletarians' exposure

---

that characterizes the modern economy is mirrored in the impersonal rule that characterizes modern states; see *Die Klassenkämpfe in Frankreich*, MEGA I.10: 146 / *MECW* 10: 76.

142. Marx, *Ökonomisch-philosophische Manuskripte*, MEGA I.2: 360 / *MECW* 3: 267.

143. That idea goes against definitions of domination that insist only identifiable agents can be dominators; see Philip Pettit, *Republicanism: A Theory of Freedom and Government* (Oxford: Oxford University Press, 1997), 52. There are ways to reformulate the idea of market domination so that it is not the market imperatives that do the dominating, but they confer on agents the power to dominate; see Nicholas Vrousalis, "Freedom and Republicanism in Roberts' Marx," *Capital & Class* 41, no. 2 (2017): 378–83. While that may be an important conceptual nuance, I do not think it captures Marx's view. For differing views of whether markets contravene republican freedom as nondomination, see Philip Pettit, "Freedom in the Market," *Politics, Philosophy & Economics* 5, no. 2 (2006): 131–49; and Steven Klein, "Fictitious Freedom: A Polanyian Critique of the Republican Revival," *American Journal of Political Science* 61, no. 4 (2017): 852–63.

144. Marx and Engels, *Manifest der Kommunistischen Partei*, MEW 4: 468, 470 / *MECW* 6: 490, 492.

145. Engels, *Grundsätze des Kommunismus*, MEW 4: 363 / *MECW* 6: 341.

to the periodic crises inherent to capitalist competition distinguished them from other producing classes. Peasants and serfs were relatively insulated from market competition because of their direct access to the land (and hence an independent ability to sustain themselves), while slaves were dependent on their master for their livelihood rather than the labor market, and thus the "slave stands outside competition, the proletarian stands within it and feels all its fluctuations."[146]

For Marx, the dependency of the worker on the labor market was most brutally expressed in the crises to which capitalist production was prone, and which resulted in workers being thrown out of employment. He observed that "capital not only *lives* from labor" (through its exploitation of the worker) but is "at the same time [a] noble and barbaric lord . . . [that] drags with it into the grave the corpses of its slaves, whole hecatombs of workers who perish in the crises."[147] In *Das Kapital*, Marx expanded that analysis to argue that the ability to hire and fire workers according to fluctuating needs set by the market was an essential feature of capitalist production. The nature of capitalist production, with its "varying phases of the industrial cycle," meant that there were moments when the "market suddenly expands" as well as "periods of average activity, production at high pressure, crisis and stagnation." In order to adequately track these "changing needs of the self-expansion of capital," capitalist employers needed the "possibility of throwing great masses of men" from their employment during a crisis, and correspondingly for those same masses to form a readily available pool when business improved. The "disposable industrial reserve army" was thus a "condition of existence of the capitalist mode of production."[148] The dependency of the workers on the fluctuating needs of the labor market was thus not just coincidental but a necessary feature of capitalist production. Marx thus argued that "The movement of the law of supply and demand of labor on this basis completes the despotism of capital."[149]

---

146. Ibid., 366 / 343–44. Peasants and serfs may engage in some market activity, but with their direct access to the means of sustenance, they do not have the same imperative to do so. On the difference between market opportunities and market imperatives, and the centrality of the latter to capitalism, see Ellen Meiksins Wood, *The Origins of Capitalism: A Longer View* (London and New York: Verso, 2002), 6–8. Independent artisans might also be thought to be dependent on market fluctuations, though more indirectly, because they rely on a market for their goods rather than on a labor market.

147. Marx, "Lohnarbeit und Kapital," *MEW* 4: 423 / *MECW* 9: 228.

148. Marx, *Das Kapital*, vol. 1, *MEGA* II.6: 576–77 / *MECW* 35: 626–27.

149. Ibid., 583 / 634. For a discussion of how economic crises relates to domination, see Alexander Bryan, "The Dominating Effects of Economic Crises," *Critical Review of International Social and Political Philosophy* 24, no. 6 (2021): 884–908.

As terrible as the worker's domination by the market was, Marx thought one could not fully grasp the impersonal domination of capitalism if one did not understand that the capitalist was also dominated by the same forces. As he frequently put it, "the law of capitalist production—the creation of surplus value, etc . . . appears as coercion that alternatively coerces the capitalist and the worker, thus in fact as a law of capital against them both."[150] To see what Marx meant by this, we return to our preceding discussion of the extraction of relative surplus value, where we saw how Marx portrayed the decision over what to do with productivity gains as one resting initially with the individual capitalist. Marx stressed that this was only an initial appearance. The "coercive law of competition (*Zwangsgesetz der Konkurrenz*)" meant that each individual capitalist was in a continual race with other capitalists to convert productivity gains into cheaper commodities.[151] Individual capitalists who failed to do so would be driven out of business by those who did. If they wanted to keep their capitalist enterprise afloat, they thus had to ensure they extracted as much surplus labor-time from their workers as possible. That meant that the decision over whether productivity gains were spent on cheaper commodities or on shortening the working day (and hence expanding the period of free time) was not in the hands of the capitalist but determined by the impersonal imperatives of the market. Marx observed, "But looking at these things as a whole, it is evident that this [the length of the working day] does not depend on the good or bad will of the individual capitalist. Free competition makes the immanent laws of capitalist production confront the individual capitalist as a coercive force external to him."[152] It was, according to Marx, a mistake to focus on the individual character of the capitalist, whether they were a sympathetic boss hoping to lighten their workers' toil or a rapacious tyrant—all individual capitalists were dominated by the market and required by its demands to exploit their workers. As we saw in the above discussion of sexual exploitation in the workplace, it is a classic and important republican insight that it does not matter whether a master is good or bad, because regardless of their personal dispositions, they remain a master who has the arbitrary power

150. Marx, "Sechstes Kapitel. Resultate des unmittelbaren Produktionsprozesses," *MEGA* II.4.1: 123 / *MECW* 34: 459–60.

151. Marx, *Das Kapital*, vol. 1, *MEGA* II.6: 317 / *MECW* 35: 324. See also ibid., 315 / 321, and Engels, *Anti-Dühring*, I.27: 441 / *MECW* 25: 262.

152. Marx, *Das Kapital*, vol. 1, *MEGA* II.6: 273 / *MECW* 35: 276. See, similarly, Samuel Arnold, "Capitalism, Class Conflict, and Domination," *Socialism and Democracy* 31, no. 1 (2017): 115; Michael J. Thompson, "Reconstructing Republican Freedom: A Critique of the Neo-Republican Concept of Freedom as Non-Domination," *Philosophy & Social Criticism* 39, no. 3 (2013): 287–88.

to interfere. But Marx's point when it comes to markets is subtly different. His argument is that the capitalist's individual character is besides the point, not because they remain a master regardless, but because they are not in fact the master. The master, if there is one, is the impersonal market.

It was for this reason that Marx thought it in general a mistake in political economy to focus too much "on the *mere will* of the capitalist." While he thought it was normally the case that the "*will* of the capitalist is certainly to take as much as possible," what was required was "not [to] talk about his *will*, but to inquire into his *power*, the *limits of that power*, and the *character of those limits*."[153] An understanding of those limits, Marx insisted, showed that the arbitrary will of the capitalist in their workplace was in fact circumscribed by the market imperatives in which they operated. Marx did not think those imperatives completely obviated the individual capitalist's arbitrary will. Certainly, in a capitalist's dealings with any individual worker, Marx thought the capitalist enjoyed a quite extensive degree of discretionary power. He highlighted, for instance, that in cases where there was no regular daily labor contract between the worker and capitalist, the capitalist could "entirely in accordance with his own convenience, caprice (*Willkühr*) and momentary interest" decide how many hours, if at all, the worker was to work that day.[154]

Even more importantly, Marx thought that we had to understand that it was only the capitalist's will, *as a capitalist*, that was dominated by the market. Marx reminded readers of *Das Kapital* that every individual capitalist had the choice simply to consume their existing capital (say, by living a life of luxury) rather than accumulate more capital by continuing and extending their exploitation. That choice was "an act of his will (*acte de sa volonté*)." Insofar as he chose to continuously reinvest his capital, he carried out "the function of a capitalist, which is to enrich himself." It was "in this role (*dans ce rôle*) [that] he is . . . dominated by his blind passion for abstract wealth." The combination of each capitalist performing this role was that "competition imposes the immanent laws of capitalist production on each individual capitalist as external coercive laws." And so each individual capitalist performing their function of capitalist is led by the impersonal domination of the market to extend their exploitation by "extending their personal domination (*domination personnelle*)" over their workers.[155]

153. Marx, "Value, Price and Profit," *MEGA* I.20: 147 / *MECW* 20: 105.

154. Marx, *Das Kapital*, vol. 1, *MEGA* II.6: 507 / *MECW* 35: 545.

155. Marx, *Le Capital*, vol. 1, *MEGA* II.7: 514 / *MECW* 35: 587. Marx made several changes to these passages in the French edition, some (but not all) of which were incorporated into subsequent German editions. Compare *Das Kapital*, vol. 1, *MEGA* II.6: 542–43 with *MEGA* II.8: 555–56. Marx similarly argued in his drafts that it was in the capitalist's role as a "mere

But it follows, of course, that a capitalist is only dominated in this way if they wish to continue their social role as a capitalist. As an individual they have the choice (at least in this regard) to escape their market domination, exiting their role as capitalist by simply consuming their capital. Workers by comparison have no such choice; they also experience market domination in their social role as workers, but that is a role they cannot so easily shrug off. Marx consequently qualified that the market domination over both worker and capitalist should not be entirely equated. Thus, when he argued that "the creation of surplus value is therefore the determining, dominating and over-riding purpose of a capitalist," he specified that this made it "appear as if the capitalist is just as much under the servitude of the capital-relation as at the opposite pole is the worker, even if from a different angle."[156]

The market domination of the worker and the capitalist was the final ele-ment in Marx's account of how capitalism's surface appearance of freedom obscured its underlying domination. As he and Engels had put it in their earli-est joint work, *Die Heilige Familie* (*The Holy Family*), "The size of wages is de-termined at the beginning by *free* agreement between the free worker and the free capitalist. Later it turns out that the worker is compelled to allow the cap-italist to determine it, just as the capitalist is compelled to fix it as low as pos-sible. *Freedom* of the contracting parties has been supplanted by *compulsion*."[157] While the worker is forced by the capitalist's personal and structural domina-tion to accept what they can get, the impersonal domination of the market forces the capitalist (in their role as capitalist) to dominate the worker. The worker is dominated by the capitalist, and both worker and capitalist are domi-nated by the market. The consequence might easily be quietism in the face of these overwhelming forces. The domination of the market over our collective lives can appear as if "a society that has conjured up such gigantic means of production and exchange, is like a sorcerer who is no longer able to control the powers of the nether world whom he has called up his spells."[158] But the point of such metaphors was not to counsel acquiescence. If the market had been conjured into being by humans, then it could also overcome by humans.

Marx believed that through the conscious and democratic planning of the economy, society could escape its subjection to the market imperative. He

---

functionary of capital" that the capitalist "is dominated (*beherrscht*) by the same absolute drive to enrich himself"; *Zur Kritik der politischen Ökonomie (Manuskript von 1861–63)*, MEGA II.3: 601 / MECW 31: 179.

156. Marx, "Sechstes Kapitel. Resultate des unmittelbaren Produktionsprozesses," *MEGA* II.4.1: 65 / *MECW* 34: 399.

157. Marx and Engels, *Die Heilige Familie*, MEGA I.4: 34 / MECW 4: 32–33.

158. Marx and Engels, *Manifest der Kommunistischen Partei*, MEW 4: 467 / MECW 6: 489.

contrasted the "blind rule of the supply and demand laws which form the political economy of the middle class" with "social production controlled by social foresight, which forms the political economy of the working class."[159] Establishing real control over societal production through democratic planning was, for Marx, an important element in establishing a free society: "Freedom in this sphere [of production] can only consist in socialized man, the associated producers, rationally regulating their interchange with nature, bringing it under their common control, instead of being dominated by it as a blind power."[160]

Marx, as ever, did not give much detail to what this planning would look like. What hints he gave suggest he did not have in mind the centralized and technocratic schemes imputed to him and carried out in his name, but that planning would have to be democratically controlled.[161] He thought that this democratic planning of the economy was an essential complement to the democratizing of the workplace through cooperatives, and that these, as we saw above, would help overcome the personal and structural domination of the worker. But, Marx insisted, cooperatives would not, by themselves, be enough to end capitalist domination, as they would still be dominated by the impersonal imperatives of the market. Cooperatives would be driven by the same "coercive laws" of capitalist production to self-exploit and thus be unable to provide their workers, and society, with a choice over how to spend the enormous gains of human productive power, including the expansion of free time. He thus argued that "[i]f co-operative production is not to remain a sham and snare," then "united co-operative societies" must "regulate national production upon a common plan, thus taking it under their own control."[162] Through these two mechanisms—giving workers control over their workplace through cooperative production, and the democratic planning of the economy overall—Marx thought that the capitalist domination of the worker and society—the "invisible threads" that undermined their freedom—would be severed.

159. Marx, "Address of the International Working Men's Association (Inaugural Address)," *MEGA* I.20: 10 / *MECW* 20: 11.

160. Marx, *Das Kapital*, vol. 3, *MEGA* II.15: 795 / *MECW* 37: 807. Note that here Marx adds that while this is what freedom in "the realm of necessity" looks like, the "true realm of freedom" lies beyond it, in the time and activities outside of necessary labor focused on the "development of human energy which is an end in itself." His overall understanding of freedom includes a conception of freedom focused on individual self-realization—a reminder that Marx's view of freedom cannot be reduced to any single conception. On this passage, see further Jan Kandiyali, "Freedom and Necessity in Marx's Account of Communism," *British Journal for the History of Philosophy* 22, no. 1 (2014): 104–23; William Clare Roberts, "Marx's Social Republic: Political Not Metaphysical," *Historical Materialism* 27, no. 2 (2019): 41–58.

161. Roberts, *Marx's Inferno*, 78n94, 251–55.

162. Marx, *The Civil War in France, MEGA* I.22: 143 / *MECW* 22: 335.

Coda

It is not sufficiently appreciated that freedom and domination lay at the heart of Marx's critique of capitalism. Within the workplace, capitalists and their supervisors subjected workers to their arbitrary personal rule. Like public despots, capitalists had free rein to interfere with and command their subjects, though Marx emphasized workers' ability to check this uncontrolled power through trade unions and state legislation. Outside the workplace, workers were subjected to the structural domination of the capitalist class, whose ownership of the means of production meant workers had no choice but to work for a capitalist master. Marx believed that the formally free labor contract disguised these forms of domination and the workers' actual unfreedom. The workers' separation from the means of production also played a central role in Marx's historical and theoretical account of the rise of capitalism and how it relied on the destruction of the republican ideal of independent producers. In *Das Kapital* he provided a much more sympathetic portrait of this ideal than in his earlier engagements with republicanism, but he did so in order to show more effectively the irreversibility of its defeat and the necessity of overcoming capitalism through the collective ownership of the means of production. Marx came to believe that cooperatives, in which workers owned and managed their own workplaces, would play an important role in achieving that collective ownership and ensuring that workers were no longer subject to the domination of the individual capitalist and the capitalist class. Domination was furthermore a crucial component in Marx's account of exploitation. He set out to show how the capitalist's and capitalist class's arbitrary power was necessary in order to extract surplus labor from their workers. It allowed them to maintain or extend the working day beyond the minimum required for workers to sustain themselves and (initially) to decide on the gains of productivity that could have been used to expand the workers' free time. Marx thereby provided an important sociological account of the function of domination in capitalist society (too often missed in some contemporary conceptual accounts of domination). Yet Marx always emphasized that exploitation was driven by the impersonal domination of the market, which subjected all of society to its imperatives. Benevolent capitalists and even cooperatives could not escape the market demands of efficiency and ever greater accumulation, the impersonal tyranny of which Marx believed could be ended only through democratic control of the economy. Marx's account reminds us that these market imperatives can also be a considered a form of domination that rob society of the freedom to decide its future.

PART III

The Social Republic

7

A Communal Constitution

THE SOCIAL REPUBLIC AND THE POLITICAL INSTITUTIONS OF SOCIALISM, 1871

Honored citizen, I request that in the name of our great cause that you send me an answer as soon as possible. Excuse my urgency, but haste is necessary, for we must before all else lay the foundation stone of the social republic.

—LEÓ FRANKEL TO KARL MARX, 30 MARCH 1871[1]

Citizen Marx . . . said, "He was afraid the end was near, but if the Commune was beaten, the struggle would only be deferred. The principles of the Commune were eternal and could not be crushed; they would assert themselves again and again until the working classes were emancipated."

—MINUTES OF THE GENERAL COUNCIL OF THE INTERNATIONAL WORKING-MEN'S ASSOCIATION, 23 MAY 1871[2]

Long live the universal and social republic! Down with the cowards!

—LAST WORDS OF THREE EXECUTED COMMUNARDS, 18 SEPTEMBER 1871[3]

1. Letter reprinted in Magda Aranyossi, *Leo Frankel* (Berlin: Dietz, 1957), 260–61. Extracts translated in Eugene Schulkind, ed., *The Paris Commune of 1871: The View from the Left* (London: Jonathan Cape, 1972), 117–18. See further Julien Chuzeville, *Léo Frankel: Communard sans frontières* (Montreuil: Libertalia, 2021), chapter 2.

2. "Meeting of the General Council May 23, 1871," *MEGA* I.22: 555 / *MECW* 22: 595.

3. Cited in [Prosper-Olivier] Lissagaray, *Histoire de la Commune de 1871* (Brussels: Henri Kistemaeckers, 1876), 491 / *History of the Commune of 1871*, trans. Eleanor Marx Aveling (London: Reeves and Turner, 1886), 439.

WILLIAM MORRIS'S EPIC poem cycle *The Pilgrims of Hope* tells the story of three English communists who travel to Paris to fight for the Commune, the working-class insurrection that held the city for seventy-two days from 18 March to 28 May 1871. Two of them die fighting on the barricades, and the third only narrowly escapes back to England, after the Versailles government brutally crushes the Commune. But in a moving stanza from "A Glimpse of the Coming Day," the hero describes what it was like to see the city in that fleeting moment when "Paris was free":

> And that day at last of all days I knew what life was worth;
> For I saw what few have beheld, a folk with all hearts gay.
> Then at last I knew indeed that our word of the coming day,
> That so oft in grief and in sorrow I had preached, and scarcely knew
> If it was but despair of the present or the hope of the day that was due,
> I say that I saw it now, real, solid and at hand.[4]

That experience was comparable to the effect that the Commune had on Karl Marx. He heaped praise on the Parisian workers for "storming the heavens" and ensuring that a "new point of departure of world-historical importance has been gained."[5] His enthusiasm was based partly on firsthand reports that reached him from across the Channel, including that of Leó Frankel, an Austro-Hungarian member of the International Working-Men's Association who had been elected to the Commune Council and headed its Commission of Labor and Exchange. He had written to Marx soliciting his urgent advice for what social reforms the Commune should undertake to establish the "social republic." We do not know whether Marx responded to Frankel's request (Marx's extant correspondence to Frankel dates from the latter period of the Commune). But we do know that it was not the modest social measures the Commune managed to implement in its short existence that so excited Marx.

What electrified Marx were the political institutions of the Commune, which he believed were "the political form at last discovered under which to work out the economical emancipation of Labour."[6] The radical democratic experiment, "real, solid and at hand," in Morris's words, roused Marx into reconsidering and clarifying what political structures were necessary for

---

4. William Morris, *The Pilgrims of Hope*, *The Commonweal*, 2, no. 17 (8 May 1886): 45.

5. Marx to Ludwig Kugelmann, 12 April and 17 April 1871, *MEW* 33: 205–6, 209 / *MECW* 44: 131–32, 137.

6. Marx, *The Civil War in France*, *MEGA* I.22: 142 / *MECW* 22: 334.

communism. He now recognized that the political form of bourgeois society, the bourgeois republic, was an inappropriate political form for bringing about communism. He warned that the "working class cannot simply lay hold of the ready-made State machinery, and wield it for its own purposes."[7] If the working class was going to emancipate itself it would require its own political form that transformed the existing state machinery. In place of a bourgeois republic it needed "a 'Social Republic,' that is a Republic which . . . guarantees . . . social transformation by the Communal organisation."[8]

This chapter sets out the nature of Marx's social republic and how it represents a return to Marx's own early republican thought. I discuss two aspects of this republican resurgence in his thought: (1) Marx's critique of representation and advocacy of popular delegacy and (2) his account of the transformation of state administration by subordinating it to popular control and widespread citizen participation. This discussion is preceded by a contextualizing outline of the Paris Commune and the divergent republican responses to it. The chapter closes by considering the question of whether Marx believed that the political institutions of the social republic—and "politics" more broadly—would eventually disappear once communism had established itself. I argue that, contrary to widespread assumptions, Marx did not definitely commit himself to the end of politics and political institutions. But Marx was opposed to detailed reflection on the matter, and I end the chapter by suggesting some republican reasons for thinking there is a continued need for political institutions.

Republicanism and the Commune

The background context for the Commune was the Franco-Prussian War, which had led to the downfall of Napoleon III, the establishment of the Third Republic in September 1870, and the subsequent siege of Paris by Prussian troops. During the siege, ordinary Parisians were increasingly radicalized and came into possession of their own arms through the expansion of the National Guard (the city's civic militia). After a ceasefire had been brokered with Prussia, the provisional government of the Republic, led by Adolphe Thiers, decided that Paris needed to brought under control. An attempt to take back the National Guard's cannons on 18 March backfired, and Thiers responded by evacuating the city's government and administration to Versailles. Finding itself almost accidentally in charge of Paris, the Central Committee of the National Guard called for elections to an assembly, the Commune (or Commune

7. Ibid., 137 / 328.
8. Marx, *The Civil War in France (First Draft)*, MEGA I.22: 64 / MECW 22: 497.

Council, to distinguish it from the wider uprising). This was a ninety-seat body, elected from the arrondissements of Paris, of which eighty or so members actually took up their seats. Party affiliations did not exist in the modern sense, but the Commune included some thirty-seven members who had connections to socialist groups (eleven Blanquists and twenty-six affiliates of the French section of the International Working-Men's Association, including Frankel), and thirty-four who can be classified as radical republicans, sometimes referred to in this period as neo-Jacobins.[9] Though none of the Commune members were unskilled laborers, nearly half of them were skilled workers or artisans, an "unprecedented share of the political leadership" that has "probably never been equalled in any European revolutionary government."[10] The ordinary Communards who fought in the National Guard were themselves overwhelmingly working class, though (given the structure of Parisian economy) primarily made up of skilled artisans rather than proletarian factory workers.[11]

The Commune lasted for just over two months and during that time Paris witnessed a flowering of democratic engagement and cultural and social liberation for the city's population. Parisian women, for instance, set up the Union des femmes pour la défense de Paris et les soins aux blessés (The Women's Union for the Defense of Paris and Aid to the Wounded), which pushed for working-class women's social emancipation in the home and the workplace as well as assisting in the defense of the Commune.[12] But this "working laboratory of political institutions"[13] was forcibly put down before it had the opportunity to properly establish itself. Thiers and the provisional government of the Third Republic opted for war over conciliation and sent the regular army to take Paris. Heavy fighting ensued, with the last barricade falling on 28 May. From the day the army troops entered Paris they began a campaign of summary executions of Communard prisoners and suspected

9. Roger L. Williams, *The French Revolution of 1870–1871* (London: Weidenfeld and Nicolson, 1969), 132.

10. Robert Tombs, *The Paris Commune* (London and New York: Longman, 1999), 111–16.

11. Ibid.; David A. Shafer, *The Paris Commune: French Politics, Culture, and Society at the Crossroads of the Revolutionary Tradition and Revolutionary Socialism* (Basingstoke: Palgrave Macmillan, 2005), 115.

12. See further Carolyn J. Eichner, *Surmounting the Barricades: Women in the Paris Commune* (Bloomington and Indianapolis: Indiana University Press, 2004); James Muldoon, Mirjam Müller, and Bruno Leipold, "'Aux Ouvrières!': Socialist Feminism in the Paris Commune," *Intellectual History Review* 33, no. 2 (2023): 331–51; Eugene Schulkind, "Socialist Women during the 1871 Paris Commune," *Past & Present*, no. 106 (1985): 124–63.

13. Kristin Ross, *Communal Luxury: The Political Imaginary of the Paris Commune* (London and New York: Verso, 2015), 11.

sympathizers. Much like the 1848 June Days, exact figures for how many died in what came to be known as *la semaine sanglante* (the Bloody Week) is hard to establish. The traditional figure (which is probably overstated) is some 20,000 deaths.[14] It was largely because of this bloody and cruel end—this "extraordinary attempt to eliminate, one by one and en bloc, one's class enemy"— that the Commune came to play such a central role in subsequent left-wing thought and popular memory.[15]

Republican responses to the Commune ran the full spectrum from enthusiastic participation to outright hostility. The first category includes the radical republican members of the Commune Council and prominent leaders such as Louis Charles Delescluze, who famously gave his life on the barricades, as well as Félix Pyat, whom we encountered in chapter 4.[16] Recent historiography has also tended to emphasize that the Communards, from the ordinary National Guard members upward, were "first and foremost republicans."[17] Many of them believed that they were the legitimate heirs of France's republican tradition, carrying out the promise of 1789. On the other side, the moderate or bourgeois wing of republicanism sided with the Versailles government. Reminiscent of the response to the June Days, they believed that the Commune was an illegitimate uprising against the legally constituted Assembly.[18] This moderate republican faction, including Assembly representatives like Edgar Quinet and Jules Ferry, aligned themselves with the Versailles leader Adolphe Thiers and supported his attack on the Commune. Finally, a third faction can be identified that unsuccessfully tried to conciliate between the two groups.[19] The Paris Commune was thus just as much a conflict *within* republicanism as one *between* republicanism and other competing ideologies, such as anarchism and communism.

These divisions extend to the international republican response to the Commune, exemplified by the starkly opposed reactions of William James Linton and Giuseppe Mazzini, who had been close collaborators in the 1848

---

14. One recent investigation has suggested that this figure should be revised significantly downward, to between 5,700 and 7,400; see Robert Tombs, "How Bloody Was *La Semaine Sanglante* of 1871? A Revision," *The Historical Journal* 55, no. 3 (2012): 691.

15. Ross, *Communal Luxury*, 36.

16. For Pyat's less than stellar record during the Commune, see Lowell L. Blaisdell, "Félix Pyat, the 'Evil Genius' of the Commune of Paris," *Proceedings of the American Philosophical Society* 132, no. 4 (1988): 330–70.

17. Tombs, *The Paris Commune*, 116.

18. Shafer, *The Paris Commune*, 80.

19. Philip G. Nord, "The Party of Conciliation and the Paris Commune," *French Historical Studies* 15, no. 1 (1987): 1–35.

Revolutions. Linton was one of the few in America who publicly rallied to the Commune's defense.[20] He wrote supportive articles for the influential anti-slavery *National Standard* and the *Radical,* and he reprinted the latter in a separate pamphlet, which tried to counter the slanders, inaccuracies, and panicked exaggerations of Communard violence that dominated the American press. He took special aim at the coverage of the *New York Tribune,* a traditionally progressive paper that emerged as a fervent critic of the Commune (Marx was the paper's European correspondent from 1852 to 1862).[21] In his pamphlet, Linton carefully dissected the *Tribune's* reports, exposing where its observations reflected its underlying bias or were simply inaccurate.

To the charge that the Commune was communist, Linton replied that communism, defined as "having all things in common, abolition of property and family," was not to be found in "either in the words or acts, of *Communal (not Communistic)* Paris." Despite his personal objections to communism, he struck a conciliatory tone, arguing that even if communism was misguided, a "communist has the right to put his belief into action." He also played down the communist danger, presenting it as a passing fad of an older revolutionary generation that had had its day. He argued that these "old Communist theories, though still perhaps held by a few individuals, have never moved the masses" and claimed that it was only "elder politicians, like Blanqui" with whom "dreams of the old Communist utopias might yet linger."[22] Linton's account thus combined a largely accurate judgment of the composition of the Commune with a considerable misdiagnosis of the future trends of support for communism and republicanism.

Linton did offer some measured criticism of the Commune. He interpreted the demand for a "commune" as a backward-looking longing for the medieval system of independent communes, which he thought failed to appreciate the interconnections of the modern world.[23] Linton instead articulated a vision of what has been called "republican patriotism," a view that combines a commitment to one's particular national republic with a universal solidarity with

20. F. B. Smith, *Radical Artisan: William James Linton 1812–97* (Manchester: Manchester University Press, 1973), 174–76.

21. Adam Tuchinsky, *Horace Greeley's New-York Tribune: Civil War-Era Socialism and the Crisis of Free Labor* (Ithaca: Cornell University Press, 2009), 196–204.

22. W. J. Linton, *The Paris Commune: In Answer to the Calumnies of the New York Tribune* (Boston, 1871), 19, 22.

23. Ibid., 22–24. Marx countered the view that the Commune "was a reproduction of mediæval Communes," noting that it was "generally the fate of completely new historical creations to be mistaken for the counterpart of older and even defunct form of social life"; *The Civil War in France, MEGA* I.22: 141 / *MECW* 22: 333.

other peoples.[24] He argued that the "hermit must quit his cell for active citizenship, the Commune labour *for and with and under order of* the nation, the nation own itself a citizen of the world." In this multitiered patriotism every citizen was a "sworn soldier, or, if need be, martyr, of universal republicanism."[25] This criticism aside, the overwhelming message of Linton's intervention was that the Communards had put up a brave and commendable fight in the service of republicanism, which deserved respect and even reverence. He thus ended his pamphlet with a rousing defense of what the Communards had achieved: "these men of Paris have given to the world the ever-needed example of heroic daring and devotedness, [they] have laid one more broad stone (though it to be their own grave-stone) of that glorious causeway over which Humanity, defeated or triumphant, marches firmly to the Republic."[26]

Linton's response differed markedly from the far more consequential reaction of his old associate, Mazzini. For forty years, Mazzini had been one of the most prominent republicans on the international stage, respected and admired across Europe and the Americas for his lifelong commitment to popular struggles, from founding the Young Europe societies in the 1830s to his leading role in the Roman Republic of 1849 and his subsequent part in the Italian Risorgimento.[27] His response to the Commune therefore mattered a great deal. His decision to harshly and repeatedly condemn the Commune dismayed and alienated a younger generation of Italian radicals who had enthusiastically followed the events in Paris. Less familiar with Mazzini's radical past, his attacks appeared to them out of touch, bordering on reactionary. His failure to take the side of the Commune thereby played an inadvertent role in pushing them away from republicanism and toward socialism and anarchism.[28]

---

24. For an explication of this view, see Stuart White, "Republicanism, Patriotism, and Global Justice," in *Forms of Justice: Critical Perspectives on David Miller's Political Philosophy*, ed. Daniel A. Bell and Avner de-Shalit (Oxford: Rowman & Littlefield, 2003), 251–68.

25. Linton, *The Paris Commune*, 25. For a recent critical account of the extent of the Commune's republican universalism, see Niklas Plaetzer, "Decolonizing the 'Universal Republic': The Paris Commune and French Empire," *Nineteenth-Century French Studies* 49, no. 3–4 (2021): 585–603.

26. Linton, *The Paris Commune*, 26.

27. For this influence and legacy, see C. A. Bayly and E. F. Biagini, eds., *Giuseppe Mazzini and the Globalization of Democratic Nationalism, 1830–1920* (Oxford: Oxford University Press, 2008), and Nadia Urbinati and Stefano Recchia, "Giuseppe Mazzini's International Political Thought," in *A Cosmopolitanism of Nations: Giuseppe Mazzini's Writings on Democracy, Nation Building, and International Relations*, ed. Stefano Recchia and Nadia Urbinati (Princeton: Princeton University Press, 2009), 1–30.

28. Nunzio Pernicone, *Italian Anarchism, 1864–1892* (Princeton: Princeton University Press, 1993), 36–37; T. R. Ravindranathan, "The Paris Commune and the First International in Italy:

In a series of articles in his paper *La Roma del Popolo*, Mazzini set out the case for why "the Republic, as it is understood by the Commune, is not ours."[29] He condemned the Commune as a violent class struggle, which ruined the possibility of national unity. He argued that the Commune "sprang forth not from a superior *principle* of Country or Humanity, but from a narrow Parisian *interest*" and that the "*social* question . . . weakened the worker's love and worship of country." The Commune was thus an "absurd, backward, politically immoral notion of the republic." The condemnation of the Commune did not, however, mean that Mazzini sided with the Versailles government. He equally condemned the violence against the Communards and argued that republicans should endorse neither party. The tone of his articles suggests that Mazzini was genuinely aggrieved by the episode. He interpreted it as an outcome of a growing trend in society toward egoistic material interests over a proper attitude of duty toward others. He tried to reach out to the workers by arguing that republicans also had answers to their social despair. He noted, rather vaguely, that republicans "want to peacefully and gradually substitute *associated* labor for the current system of *wage* labor."[30] Instead of socialism, Mazzini still clung to the old independent republican ideal where workers would be able "to acquire capital and change from being wage-earners into workers who are free and independent of the arbitrary power of others."[31] Mazzini's articles denouncing the Commune were swiftly translated in the British press, prompting Marx to reply that "Mazzini had always been opposed to the Workmen's movements . . . The fact was, Mazzini with his old fashioned Republicanism knew nothing and accomplished nothing."[32]

Having dealt with the Commune, Mazzini turned in the late summer of 1871 to criticizing the International Working-Men's Association. That involved a

---

Republicanism versus Socialism, 1871–1872," *The International History Review* 3, no. 4 (1981): 482–516.

29. G. Mazzini, "Sul Manifesto del Comune Parigino," *La Roma del Popolo*, no. 10 (3 May 1871): 75; *Scritti editi ed inediti di Guissepe Mazzini*, vol. 92 (Imola: Galeati, 1941), 208 / "The Commune in Paris," *The Contemporary Review*, vol. 17 (June 1871), 315.

30. G. Mazzini, "Il Comune e l'Assemblea," *La Roma del Popolo*, no. 15 (7 June 1871): 118; no. 17 (21 June 1871): 129, 131; no. 18 (28 June 1871): 139; *Scritti editi ed inedita*, 92: 268, 275, 282, 295 / "Neither Pacifism nor Terror: Considerations on the Paris Commune and the French National Assembly," in *A Cosmopolitanism of Nations: Giuseppe Mazzini's Writings on Democracy, Nation Building, and International Relations*, ed. and trans. Stefano Recchia and Nadia Urbinati (Princeton: Princeton University Press: 2009), 153, 158–59, 164.

31. G. Mazzini, "Ai rappresentanti gli Artigiani nel Congresso di Roma," *La Roma del Popolo*, no. 33 (12 October 1871): 44; *Scritti editi ed inediti*, 93: 65. Cited in Nadia Urbinati, "Mazzini and the Making of the Republican Ideology," *Journal of Modern Italian Studies* 17, no. 2 (2012): 191–94.

32. "Meeting of the General Council June 6, 1871," *MEGA* I.22: 560 / *MECW* 22: 598.

direct critique of Marx, whom he called "a man of acute intellect, but ... of a dissolving character, and of domineering temper, who is jealous of others' influence, [has] no strong philosophical nor religious beliefs, and [is] moved, I am afraid, more by—however legitimate—rage rather than love." Mazzini accused Marx and the International of promoting three "negations": the "negation of God," the "negation of country," and the "negation of all individual property."[33] As part of that critique Mazzini analyzed the International's founding documents from 1864 (written by Marx). These had opened with the declaration that the economic subjection of the worker by the capitalist "lies at the bottom of servitude in all its forms."[34] Mazzini responded that while this was "true in part, [it] is certainly exaggerated" and showed that the association "concentrate[d] ... exclusively upon the economic problem," to the exclusion of politics. Mazzini maintained that focusing only on economics and on the working class, rather than also appealing to the middle class, meant it was an "utter delusion" to think that "republican institutions can ever be laid, or any great work of political emancipation achieved, by the *International*."[35]

Given this intense hostility to the Commune and the International, it is not surprising that Marx took a similarly dismissive view of Mazzini. In a July 1871 interview for a New York newspaper, Marx was questioned on Mazzini's supposed involvement in the International:

R [interviewer]—And Mazzini, is he a member of your body?

DR. MARX (laughing)—Ah, no. We should have made but little progress if we had not got beyond the range of his ideas.

R.—You surprise me. I should certainly have thought that he represented the most advanced views.

DR. M.—He represents nothing better than the old idea of a middle-class republic.[36]

33. G. Mazzini, "Agli operai italiani," *La Roma del Popolo*, no. 20 (13 July 1871): 153–54; *Scritti editi ed inedita*, 92: 306, 308–12 / "The International: Addressed to the Working Class. Part I," *The Contemporary Review*, vol. 20 (July 1872): 155, 157–60. Engels replied to Mazzini's criticism in "L'intervento di Giuseppe Mazzini contro l'Associazione Internazionale degli Operai," *MEGA* I.22: 256–59 / *MECW* 22: 385–87.

34. Marx, "Provisional Rules of the International Working Men's Association," *MEGA* I.20: 13 / *MECW* 20: 14.

35. G. Mazzini, "L'Internazionale—Cenno storico," *La Roma del Popolo*, no. 30 (21 September 1871): 18–19; *Scritti editi ed inedita*, 93: 26, 30/ "The International: Addressed to the Working Class. Part II," *The Contemporary Review*, vol. 20 (September 1852): 567, 570.

36. R. Laynor, "The Curtain Raised: Interview with Karl Marx, the Head of L'Internationale ...," *The World*, vol. 11, no. 3622 (18 July 1871): 1. Facsimile reprint in *The Massachusetts Review* 12, no. 3 (1971): 445f, see also *MEGA* I.22: 456–57 / *MECW* 22: 605.

Marx and the Commune

Marx's primary account of the events and ideas of the Paris Commune was *The Civil War in France*. The pamphlet was published in London on 13 June 1871—just two weeks after the final barricade had fallen in Paris. It appeared as an "Address" of the General Council of the International Working-Men's Association, which had taken up Marx's proposal that it issue a defense of the uprising. It was thus, much like the *Manifest der Kommunistischen Partei*, a party document issued in the name of an organization (though Marx's authorship was made public much more rapidly than in the former).[37] The pamphlet proved to be a spectacular success, selling thousands of copies, with a third edition required by August 1871. By the end of 1872, translations of the English text had appeared in Danish, German (by Engels), Flemish, French (supervised by Marx), Dutch, Italian, Polish, Russian, Serbo-Croat, and Spanish.[38] *The Civil War in France* was one of Marx's most widely read texts in his lifetime, catapulting him into public notoriety and, along with the International's widely presumed (but exaggerated) role in the uprising, playing a significant role in raising his political and personal profile (leading to interviews like the one cited above).[39]

Marx began writing the address while the Commune was in full swing, when the address might still have been a celebration of an ongoing revolution. But several delays (including an illness apparently brought on by Marx's personal despair at the Commune's worsening prospects) meant that he "found himself finally writing the Commune's obituary."[40] He read the final version of the address to the General Council on 30 May. In writing the text, Marx relied on the direct reports he'd received from associates as well as a notebook he had kept from the very beginning of the uprising, in which he copied out copious press reports on the Commune and updated it daily with news in the London papers and Communard papers that he managed to get hold of from across the

---

37. Engels, "To the Editor of the Daily News [20 June 1871]," *MEGA* I.22: 229 / *MECW* 22: 367.

38. For the publishing history of *The Civil War in France*, see *MEGA* I.22: 798–804. The German and French translations are reproduced in *MEGA* I.22: 179–226, 481–515.

39. "I have the honor to be at this moment the best calumniated and the most menaced man of London," Marx gleefully reported to Ludwig Kugelmann, 18 June 1871, *MEW* 33: 238 / *MECW* 44: 158.

40. Roger Thomas, "Enigmatic Writings: Karl Marx's *The Civil War in France* and the Paris Commune of 1871," *History of Political Thought* 18, no. 3 (1997): 483–84. For Marx's illness, see Jenny Marx (daughter) to Ludwig Kugelmann, 18 April 1871, in Bert Andréas, "Briefe und Dokumente der Familie Marx aus den Jahren 1862–1873," *Archiv für Sozialgeschichte*, 2 (1962): 242.

Channel.[41] Marx also wrote two lengthy rough drafts of *The Civil War in France*, which fortunately survive and were eventually published in 1934. The two drafts (together with the press notebook) form an important interpretive complement to the main text.[42] The drafts not only provide valuable illumination of what material Marx chose to publish but also help clarify ideas that had to be compressed from the drafts to create a shorter, accessible pamphlet.[43]

Much of *The Civil War in France* is taken up with a moving defense of the Commune's actions and corresponding condemnation of the atrocities committed by the Versailles government. But its theoretical appeal comes from its third section, where Marx gave a glowing endorsement of the Commune's political institutions and identified them as the appropriate political form to bring about a socialist society. In one of many statements of this core idea, Marx argued that "the Communal Constitution would . . . serve as a lever for uprooting the economical foundations upon which rests the existence of classes, and therefore of class rule."[44] It was this political breakthrough that Marx thought was the signal contribution of the Commune rather than any of its social reforms. He maintained that "[t]he great social measure of the commune was its own working existence" and what few "special measures" it had introduced (such as the abolition of night work and workplace fines) flowed

41. This is reproduced in Karl Marx, *Notebook on the Paris Commune: Press Excerpts and Notes*, ed. Hal Draper (Berkeley: Independent Socialist Press, 1971), and Karl Marx, *La Guerre Civil en France, 1871: Édition nouvelle accompagnée des travaux préparatoires de Marx* (Paris: Éditions sociales, 1972), 67–165.

42. It has recently been suggested that an additional source of Marx's views on the Commune are the extensive additions to the 1877 German translation of Prosper-Olivier Lissagaray's *Histoire de la Commune de 1871*, which Daniel Gaido argues were added by Marx when he oversaw the translation; see "The First Workers' Government in History: Karl Marx's Addenda to Lissagaray's *History of the Commune of 1871*," *Historical Materialism* 29, no. 1 (2021): 49–112. Though I think this usefully highlights Marx's extensive role in the translation, I am not convinced that all the additions can be attributed to Marx, not least because Marx himself said that the changes from the French original were made by Lissagaray; see Marx to Wilhelm Bracke, 14 February 1877 (as well as the letters of 21 April, 26 May, and 1 August 1877), *MEW* 34: 251, 267, 277, 287 / *MECW* 45: 196, 222, 230, 262.

43. Marx noted that "[m]aterial for four to five sheets has been compressed into two"; Marx to Edward Spencer Beesly, 12 June 1871, *MEW* 33: 229–30 / *MECW* 44: 151. For an attempt to drive a wedge between the main text and the drafts (as well a generally deflationary account of the text's importance), see Shlomo Avineri, *The Social and Political Thought of Karl Marx* (Cambridge: Cambridge University Press, 1968), 247. For criticism, see Monty Johnstone, "The Paris Commune and Marx's Conception of the Dictatorship of the Proletariat," *The Massachusetts Review* 12, no. 3 (1971): 448.

44. Marx, *The Civil War in France*, MEGA I.22: 142 / *MECW* 22: 334.

precisely from it being "a government of the people by the people."[45] Or, as he otherwise summarized it, "the actual 'social' character of their Republic consists only in this, that workmen govern the Paris Commune!"[46] (Marx seems to have been unaware of, or deliberately omitted, the radical social work of the Union des femmes, which tried to set up cooperative workshops for women).[47]

For Marx, the social republic of the Commune was "social" not because it was a socialist economy but because it had the right political and constitutional features to reach it. That is particularly evident in the first draft of *The Civil War in France*, where in a section entitled "Republic only possible as avowedly Social Republic," Marx argued that,

> a Republic is only in France and Europe possible as a "Social Republic," that is a Republic which disowns the capital and landowner class of the State machinery to supersede it by the Commune, that frankly avows "social emancipation" as the great goal of the Republic and guarantees thus that social transformation by the Communal organisation.[48]

This represents an important shift from Marx's usage of "social republic" in his 1848 writings. To return to the three aspects of a republic we outlined in chapter 4,[49] Marx there understood a "social republic" to mean either (i) workers forming the *governing class* in a republic or (ii) that the *economy* of the republic was a socialist one. There was no sense in his 1848 writings that a social republic referred to (iii) a republic with a *constitution* that was particularly suited to maintaining or bringing about those first two aspects. By comparison, in his 1871 writings on the Commune, Marx explicitly dropped the economic meaning

---

45. Ibid., 146 / 339.

46. Marx, *The Civil War in France (First Draft)*, MEGA I.22: 66 / MECW 22: 499. Marx later commented that "the majority of the Commune was in no sense socialist, nor could it have been"; see Marx to Ferdinand Domela Nieuwenhuis, 22 February 1881, MEW 35: 160 / MECW 46: 66. This is sometimes taken to represent a more critical stance on Marx's part toward the Commune. While some of his enthusiasms may have been tempered, his later point is compatible with his earlier description (cited above), in which the Commune's "social" achievement was not its socialist measures but that it was ruled by workers (not necessarily socialists) and that it had revealed the political structures required for socialist reform. Marx's initial account of Commune was also not free of criticism; see *The Civil War in France*, MEGA I.22: 134 / MECW 22: 324, and Marx to Ludwig Kugelmann, 12 April 1871, MEW 33: 205 / MECW 44: 132.

47. Thomas, "Karl Marx's *The Civil War in France* and the Paris Commune of 1871," 487, 502–3. Much of the Union des femmes' plan remained unrealized, but a few workshops were opened; see Schulkind, "Socialist Women during the 1871 Paris Commune," 152.

48. Marx, *The Civil War in France (First Draft)*, MEGA I.22: 64 / MECW 22: 497.

49. See chapter 4, section "The Many Republics of 1848".

he attached to a social republic, while continuing to use it to refer to the working class being the governing class (e.g., "the actual 'social' character of their Republic consists only in this, that workmen govern the Paris Commune" and "a 'social republic' . . . disown[s] the capital and landowner class of the State machinery"). Moreover, Marx now also defined the social republic in the constitutional sense: that it has a specific form suited to maintaining and bringing about working-class social and political rule (e.g., "a 'social republic' . . . guarantees thus that social transformation by the Communal organisation"). That changed usage can also be seen in the second draft of *The Civil War in France*, where Marx argued that "hoist[ing] the colours of the 'social Republic' . . . [shows that] the workmen do want the republic, no longer as a political modification of the old system of class rule, but as the revolutionary means of breaking down class rule itself."[50] In the final text of the address the shift in meaning is less immediately obvious, but Marx similarly argued there that,

> The cry of "Social Republic," with which the revolution of February [1848] was ushered in by the Paris proletariat did but express a vague aspiration after a Republic that was not only to supersede the monarchical form of class rule, but class rule itself. The Commune was the positive form of that Republic.[51]

While previous calls for a "social republic" had provided only a "vague" idea of the kind of republic needed to overcome capitalism, the Commune provided a "positive" demonstration of it.

Marx's changed understanding of the social republic went hand in hand with a new attitude to the bourgeois republic. While his Commune writings contain similar condemnations of the emancipatory limits of the bourgeois republic that we find in his 1848 writings,[52] we find no corresponding statements that the bourgeois republic still remains the terrain on which this emancipation is to be fought for. Marx insisted that the "Social Republic" had replaced the "other Republic," and it is now this republic that he identifies as the political structure, which, though it itself "does not [immediately do] away with the class struggles" is the structure in which to "strive to the abolition of all classes and, therefore, of all class rule . . . [and which] affords the rational medium in

50. Marx, *The Civil War in France (Second Draft)*, MEGA I.22: 115 / MECW 22: 549.

51. Marx, *The Civil War in France*, MEGA I.22: 139 / MECW 22: 330–31.

52. "[T]his Bourgeois Republic, this Republic of the *Party of Order* is the most *odious* of all political regimes. Its direct business, its only *raison d'être* is to crush down the people"; Marx, *The Civil War in France (First Draft)*, MEGA I.22: 36 / MECW 22: 461.

which class struggle can run through its different phases in the most rational and human way."[53]

Marx's changed understanding of the social republic, and attitude to the bourgeois republic, reflects a genuine and important shift in his political thought. He now recognized that the governmental and administrative structures of existing states, even in the form of a bourgeois republic, were an inappropriate vehicle for socialist transformation. In *The Civil War in France*'s perhaps most cited line, Marx argued that the "working class cannot simply lay hold of the ready-made State machinery, and wield it for its own purposes."[54] Marx took some care in crafting this, redrafting it several times, with the manuscript pages thick with crossings-out and reformulations.[55] In one variation it was accompanied by the claim that "The first condition for the holding of political power, is to transform the traditional working machinery [of the state] and destroy it as instrument of class rule" and in another by the pregnant observation that the "political instrument of their [the working class's] enslavement cannot serve as the political instrument of their emancipation."[56] Simply taking hold of the existing state machinery and using it to bring about communism was thus ruled out. The working class would need first to radically reshape the state. (Such ideas were not unique to Marx; Commune Council member Auguste Vermorel argued that "[t]he error of preceding governments must not be continued, that is to say there must not be a simple substitution of workers in the places occupied previously by the bourgeoisie . . . It is necessary to overthrow the old governmental edifice completely.")[57]

Marx himself recognized that this insight—that the state needed to be fundamentally transformed—represented a shift in his own thinking. When the *Manifest der Kommunistischen Partei* was republished in 1872, Marx and Engels made sure that this insight was reflected in a new preface:

in view of the practical experience gained, first in the February Revolution, and then, even more so, in the Paris Commune, where the proletariat for

53. Ibid., 58–59 / 491. Though the change in attitude does not entail that Marx thought the bourgeois republic was not worth fighting for in comparison to even more authoritarian political forms.

54. Marx, *The Civil War in France*, MEGA I.22: 137 / MECW 22: 328.

55. Marx, *The Civil War in France (Second Draft)*, MEGA I.22: 100, 114 / MECW 22: 533, 548. A facsimile of the relevant manuscript page, as well as an edited version, is reproduced in *MEGA* I.22: 101, 944.

56. Ibid., 100 / 533.

57. [Auguste Vermorel], *L'ami du peuple*, no. 2 (24 April 1871): 3, cited in Thomas, "Karl Marx's *The Civil War in France* and the Paris Commune of 1871," 492.

the first time held political power for two whole months, this program has in places become antiquated. Particularly, the Commune delivered the proof that "the working class cannot simply lay hold of the ready-made State machinery, and wield it for its own purposes." (See *The Civil War in France* ... where this point is further developed.)[58]

Marx and Engels's public admission that they had been mistaken in their earlier political program is a rare example of explicit self-criticism and self-correction (especially in the case of Marx, who was not usually given to such reflective displays). Marx clearly thought the Commune was a historical breakthrough important enough for him to publicly revise his views. Indeed, the idea that the Commune represented something unprecedented in revolutionary history is found throughout his writings on the uprising. He argued that the Parisian workers' "displacing of the government of the ruling class by a governmental machinery of their own" was a "new feature" that distinguished the Commune from previous French revolutions.[59] Most notably, he presented the Commune as "the political form *at last discovered* under which to work out the economical emancipation of Labor."[60]

Without downplaying the Commune's genuine role in providing a practical example of many radical democratic ideas, Marx's presentation of the Commune's novelty does not do justice to their long pedigree in republican thought, and indeed to Marx's own intellectual biography. As the following sections discuss at greater length, key features that Marx identifies with the Commune's novelty are ones that he had already defended in his own early republican writings.[61] Marx's youthful enthusiasm for a polity in which representatives are subordinated to popular control and citizens carry out public administration themselves makes a quite sudden reappearance in his mature defense of the Commune. Those ideas had, by comparison, largely lain relatively dormant in the intervening thirty years, when Marx had assumed that the political institutions of the bourgeois republic, for the most part, would be sufficient for achieving social transformation.

---

58. Marx and Engels, "Vorwort," in *Manifest der Kommunistischen Partei*, German ed. (1872), *MEW* 18: 96 / *MECW* 23: 175. Engels also made sure to include this statement in his preface to the 1888 English edition; see Engels, "Preface," in *Manifesto of the Communist Party*, English ed. (1888), *MEGA* I.31: 120-21 / *MECW* 26: 517–18.

59. Marx, *The Civil War in France (First Draft)*, *MEGA*, I.22: 66 / *MECW* 22: 498.

60. Marx, *The Civil War in France*, *MEGA*, I.22: 142 / *MECW* 22: 334 (emphasis added).

61. Miguel Abensour, *Democracy against the State: Marx and the Machiavellian Moment*, trans. Max Blechman and Martin Breaugh (Cambridge: Polity, 2011), 84–88; and Lucio Colletti, "Introduction," in *Early Writings*, by Karl Marx (London: Penguin, 1975), 42–44.

That is not to say that Marx had previously been wholly uncritical of the state and the bourgeois republic's political institutions. Marx had long endorsed replacing the state's standing army with a civic militia, and, as we saw in chapter 4, he had made extensive criticisms of the centralization of power in the hands of the executive at the expense of the legislature. (Marx was consequently very positive toward the Commune Council for having been a "working, not a parliamentary, body, executive and legislative at the same time").[62] Nor would it be accurate to say that there are *no* traces of a more critical attitude toward representation and the state bureaucracy in Marx's intervening writings. We saw in chapter 4, how in 1852 Marx made a passing reference to how annual elections was one of the conditions without which "Universal Suffrage would be illusory for the working class."[63] That brief aside has, however, no other equivalent in the writings from the period. Marx devoted more attention in that period to a critique of bureaucracy, which was an important theme of his *Der achtzehnte Brumaire*. There he made the criticism that the state bureaucracy idealizes itself as defending general interests when in fact it defends its own internal, particular interests. That criticism had been one of Marx's main objections to Hegel's civil service and is one that reappears in his discussion of the Commune.[64] Marx's deeply hostile attitude to the bureaucracy is thus a consistent (and underappreciated) theme of all of Marx's main political writings, from the *Kritik der Hegelschen Rechtsphilosophie* in 1843, to *Der achtzehnte Brumaire* in 1852 and *The Civil War in France* in 1871.

What is missing from *Der achtzehnte Brumaire* is a positive account of the desirability of the people taking over public administration, and there is only a limited sense of the necessity of fundamentally transforming it. In a letter written during the Commune, Marx tried to claim that "If you look at the last chapter of my *achtzehnte Brumaire* you will find that I say that the next attempt

---

62. Marx, *The Civil War in France*, *MEGA* I.22: 139 / *MECW* 22: 331. The Commune Council set up ten commissions to cover various aspects of public administration (such as War, Finance, Education, and Labor), each of which was headed by a member of the Commune (such as Leó Frankel), who was elected by the body as a whole, and was joined by another five to eight other members. In this way, some two-thirds of the members had some kind of administrative role in additional to their legislative one. See Richard N. Hunt, *The Political Ideas of Marx and Engels*, vol. 2 (Pittsburgh: University of Pittsburgh Press, 1984), 145–46; and Tombs, *The Paris Commune*, 80–81.

63. Marx, "The Chartists," *MEGA* I.11: 327 / *MECW* 11: 335.

64. Marx argued that the bureaucracy takes "Every minor solitary interest" in society, "separate[s] [it] from society itself," and then makes it "independent of it and opposed to it in the form of state interest." The state bureaucracy thereby "pretend[s] to be its [society's] ideal counterpart"; Marx, *The Civil War in France (First Draft)*, *MEGA* I.22: 53 / *MECW* 22: 484.

of the French revolution will be no longer, as before, to transfer the bureaucratic military machine from one hand to another, but to *break* it."[65] Yet a reader taking up that suggestion is likely to be disappointed. The text simply observes that "All revolutions perfected this [state] machine instead of breaking it."[66] Marx gives no indication what a break might concretely look like, whereas in *The Civil War in France* he specified how the bureaucracy is to be transformed by making public officials either appointed by the legislature or directly elected and subjected to recall. *The Civil War in France* also makes the necessity of transforming the state bureaucracy (and its representational structures) a central component of its political intervention—as Marx and Engels highlighted in their 1872 preface to the *Manifest der Kommunistischen Partei*.

Marx's more detailed account of the transformation of the state's governmental and administrative institutions did not amount to a political blueprint for a future socialist society. While Marx certainly showed great interest in the institutional innovations of the Commune (more so than its explosion of popular street-level politics),[67] he did not abandon his long-standing opposition to what he saw as utopian system-building. He claimed that the Communards had "no ready-made Utopias to introduce *par décret du peuple*" (by order of the people).[68] Marx's description of the political institutions of the social republic was consequently suggestive rather than comprehensive, enough for a rough picture to emerge rather than a fully detailed constitutional setup (figure 15 is an attempt at summarizing Marx's inchoate account).[69] Consequently, several questions of how the institutions would practically function are left unaddressed.

Marx's account of these political institutions—supposedly based on the Commune—did not always correspond to what the Commune had in fact implemented. The discrepancy might partly be explained by his imperfect access to information from Paris. But the more pertinent explanation lies in that Marx was not trying to provide "an account of what the *Commune* was, but of what it

65. Marx to Ludwig Kugelmann, 12 April 1871, *MEW* 33: 205 / *MECW* 44: 131.

66. Marx, *Der achtzehnte Brumaire*, *MEGA* I.11: 179 / *MECW* 11: 186. See also the similar passing statement in Marx, "Verteidigungsrede im ersten Presseprozess gegen die 'Neue Rheinische Zeitung,'" *MEGA* I.8: 420 / *MECW* 8: 317.

67. As is shrewdly observed in Thomas, "Karl Marx's *The Civil War in France* and the Paris Commune of 1871," 500–502.

68. Marx, *The Civil War in France*, *MEGA* I.22: 143 / *MECW* 22: 335.

69. For similar, less detailed lists, see Hal Draper, *Karl Marx's Theory of Revolution*, vol. 3 (New York: Monthly Review Press, 1986), 273; and Richard J. Arneson, "Democratic Rights at the National and Workplace Levels," in *The Idea of Democracy*, ed. David Copp, Jean Hampton, and John E. Roemer (Cambridge: Cambridge University Press, 1993), 130.

Commune Council
- Combined executive and legislative body
- Members elected by universal (manhood) suffrage, subject to recall and for short terms
- Members paid workmen's wages
- Council's workings publicly available

Public administration
- Subordinate to the Commune Council
- Public officials elected or appointed by Commune Council and subject to recall
- Public officials paid workmen's wages
- High dignitaries of state, and their privileges, removed

Established Church
- Separation of church and state
- Clergy removed from public roles
- Education made free and independent of the church

National structure
- Every city, town, and village to have its own commune
- Rural communes send delegates to a district assembly in a central town
- District assemblies send delegates to a National Delegation in Paris
- Every delegate bound by imperative mandates and subject to recall
- Central government exercises remaining functions not carried out by local and regional communes

Forces of physical repression
- Standing army replaced by a people's militia
- Police placed under control of the Commune Council and subject to recall

Judiciary
- Judges elected and subject to recall

FIGURE 15. The political institutions of Marx's social republic

might have become."[70] With *The Civil War in France*, Marx was making a political intervention into how the Commune should be interpreted. With anarchists, Blanquists, radical republicans, and even Comtean Positivists vying to appropriate the Commune, Marx wanted to stamp his own account on what it implied for radical politics. That meant highlighting those aspects that he endorsed and seizing on tendencies that he believed should be developed in future revolutionary iterations.[71] Consequently, as will be shown later in the chapter, by comparing Marx's writings with the actual institutions of the Commune, we can gain even greater insight into the political institutions Marx supported.

70. Gareth Stedman Jones, *Karl Marx: Greatness and Illusion* (London: Allen Lane, 2016), 502.

71. Maximilien Rubel writes of this dimension of Marx's interventions, "Of course, Marx is exaggerating: he is creating in literary imagination those events which he expects and hopes for as consequences of a creative revolutionary act," in "Socialism and the Commune," in *Paradigm for Revolution? The Paris Commune 1871–1971*, ed. Eugene Kamenka (Canberra: Australian National University Press, 1972), 46.

Before delving into the discussion of these political institutions, it is unfortunately unavoidable to pause for a discussion of the nomenclatorial issue of how to refer to them. The most widely known term Marx uses for the political form that is supposed to accomplish the transition from capitalism to communism, is, of course, the "dictatorship of the proletariat." No other concept in the Marxian corpus has been as "scorned, misunderstood, celebrated or feared."[72] But thanks to the exhaustive research of Hal Draper, we have a much better sense of the actual, quite limited role the term played in Marx's writings in comparison to its dramatic subsequent trajectory. Draper identifies half a dozen instances or so across Marx's works clustered in two periods (1850–52 and 1871–75) in which Marx and Engels were especially engaged with Blanquism. Draper argues that Marx (and Engels's) use of the term in these periods served to differentiate their position (the dictatorship of the *class* of proletarians) from the Blanquist idea of a dictatorship *over* the proletariat by a small number of revolutionaries.[73] Draper further cautions that the term "dictatorship" in the nineteenth century had not yet taken on its modern meaning of an authoritarian regime inherently opposed to democracy and still retained echoes of the original Roman institution (a temporary, limited, and constitutional response to state emergencies). Finally, Draper emphasizes that the term played no special role in Marx's thought, but functions interchangeably with phrases like the "political rule of the proletariat" or "conquest of political power by the proletariat."[74]

To this we can add the various terms that Marx uses in his Commune writings, including "Communal Constitution," "Communal Republic," "Republic of Labour," and indeed "Social Republic."[75] Marx did not directly use "dictatorship of the proletariat" in *The Civil War in France* and its drafts, but in a speech a few months later he identified the Commune with a "proletarian dictature."[76] (Many years later Engels insisted that those worried about what the "dictatorship of the proletariat" meant should "Look at the Paris Commune. That was

72. Lea Ypi, "Democratic Dictatorship: Political Legitimacy in Marxist Perspective," *European Journal of Philosophy* 28, no. 2 (2020): 277.

73. As is particularly clear in Engels's criticism of the Blanquist belief in "dictatorship, not it should be understood, of the whole revolutionary class of the proletariat, but the small number who carried out the coup'; Engels, "Flüchtlings-Literatur. II," *MEGA* I.24: 373 / *MECW* 24: 13.

74. Hal Draper, *Karl Marx's Theory of Revolution*, vol. 3, *The "Dictatorship of the Proletariat"* (New York: Monthly Review Press, 1986), esp. 1, 111, 212, 264, 302, 385–86.

75. Marx, *The Civil War in France (First Draft)*, *MEGA* I.22: 60, 62, 64 / *MECW* 22: 492, 495–97; *The Civil War in France (Second Draft)*, *MEGA* I.22: 115 / *MECW* 22: 549; *The Civil War in France*, *MEGA* I.22: 139-43 / *MECW* 22: 330, 332–34, 336.

76. "The Reds in Session. Authentic Account of the Seventh Anniversary of the International in London," *The World*, no. 3711 (15 October 1871), reproduced in *MEGA* I.22: 479 / *MECW* 22: 634.

the dictatorship of the proletariat."[77]) There seems little basis for making a distinction between the various terms Marx used for the political form that guides the transition from capitalism to communism.[78] The shadow of the twentieth century, of course, falls heavily and perhaps inescapably on the "dictatorship of the proletariat." Some of that baggage might be avoided by the use of "Communal Constitution" or "Social Republic" instead. That may help us get closer to what Marx actually thought these political institutions should look like—how he thought that the social republic of the Commune "supplied the Republic with the basis of really democratic institutions."[79]

Real Democracy and the "Vile Multitude"

Underlying Marx's defense of the Commune's "really democratic institutions" was a sustained confidence in the capacity of the people to rule and administer themselves. Marx was scornful: "The Delusion as if administration and political governing were mysteries, transcendent functions only to be trusted to the hands of a trained caste, state parasites, richly paid sycophants and sinecurists, absorbing the intelligences of the masses and turning them against themselves in the lower places of the hierarchy."[80] Marx explained the "rage" that the Commune had provoked by the fact that not only had "plain working men for the first time dared to infringe upon the Governmental privilege of their 'natural superiors,'" but they had shown that they could carry out this work "modestly, conscientiously, and efficiently."[81] In terms of elections, Marx further expressed confidence in how "individuals . . . generally know how to put the right man in the right place" and in their ability to "promptly" correct themselves if necessary through recall.[82] Marx was thus convinced that the ability to carry out political decision-making and public administration were not capacities reserved for a select elitist few—the "trained caste"—but were shared by the people as a whole.

This confidence can also be gleaned by Marx's repeated contrast in *The Civil War in France* between the "Paris of M. Thiers" (the leader of the republican

77. Engels, "Einleitung [in *Der Bürgerkrieg in Frankreich*, 3rd German Edition (1891)]," *MEGA* I.32: 16 / *MECW* 27: 191.

78. That was certainly the case for Marx's opponents. Karl Vogt attacked Marx and his associates for adhering to the "watchword 'social republic; workers' dictatorship'"; see *Mein Prozess gegen die Allgemeine Zeitung* (Geneva: Selbst-Verlag des Verfassers, 1859), part 3, p. 31, and part 1, p. 30. Marx copied out this charge in his response to Vogt and did not dispute it; see *Herr Vogt*, *MEGA* I.18: 58 / *MECW* 17: 29.

79. Marx, *The Civil War in France*, *MEGA* I.22: 142 / *MECW* 22: 334.

80. Marx, *The Civil War in France (First Draft)*, *MEGA* I.22: 57 / *MECW* 22: 488.

81. Marx, *The Civil War in France*, *MEGA* I.22: 143 / *MECW* 22: 336.

82. Ibid., 141 / 333.

provisional government that fled to Versailles) and the "real Paris of the 'vile multitude.'"[83] While Marx's reference to the "vile multitude" might be obscure today, its meaning would have been immediately clear to his contemporary readers. The phrase has its modern origins in an infamous speech Thiers had delivered twenty years earlier in the National Assembly debate that led to the abolition of universal (manhood) suffrage on 31 May 1850. Thiers was one of the law's foremost backers, and in his speech he made the provocative statement that "the vile multitude has been the downfall of all republics." (This was a rather cynical profession of republican sympathies, since Thiers had been a staunch liberal monarchist, who only grudgingly supported the republic when it became clear that no monarchy could unite the sparring dynastic factions.) Making his way through some of the most famous episodes in the history of republics, Thiers claimed that "it is this multitude that gave Caesar the liberty of Rome [in exchange] for bread and circuses," "this vile multitude that gave the Medici the liberty of Florence; that has in Holland, in the wise Holland, cut the throat of the de Witts"; and finally, "this vile multitude that . . . applauded the execution, which was nothing but an abominable assassination, of the Girondins, [and] that then applauded the deserved execution of Robespierre."[84] Thiers's historical overview touched on most of the standard tropes in antidemocratic thought seeking to explain why the people is supposedly incapable of self-rule, from their penchant for despots to their inconsistent and violent judgments and, especially, that they are "prone to arbitrary displays of aggression towards prominent citizens."[85] Thiers's view of the lower classes' incapacity for self-rule is succinctly summarized in his statement that "it is necessary to do everything for them [the poor], except to let them decide the great questions upon which depends the future of the country. Yes, to everything for the poor, but not government!"[86] Thiers's "vile multitude" subsequently came to symbolize for radicals the unabashedly elitist view of the people held by their enemies. By contrasting "the Paris of M. Thiers . . . [with] The real Paris, working, thinking, fighting Paris, the Paris of the people, the

83. Marx, *The Civil War in France*, *MEGA* I.22: 149 / *MECW* 22: 342; See also ibid., 138 / 329; *The Civil War in France (First Draft)*, *MEGA* I.22: 30, 33 / *MECW* 22: 453, 457; *The Civil War in France (Second Draft)*, *MEGA* I.22: 110, 115 / *MECW* 22: 543, 549. Marx also objected to the phrase in *Der achtzehnte Brumaire*, *MEGA* I.11: 181 / *MECW* 11: 189.

84. Thiers, "Speech to the National Assembly, 24 May 1850," *Compte rendu des séances de l'Assemblée Nationale Législative*, vol. 8 (Paris: Imprimerie de l'Assemblée Nationale, 1850), 156. Johan and Cornelius de Witt were leading Dutch republican politicians who were brutally lynched by a mob in the prelude to the establishment of the monarchy.

85. John P. McCormick, *Machiavellian Democracy* (Cambridge: Cambridge University Press, 2011), 66.

86. Thiers, "Speech to the National Assembly, 24 May 1850," 156.

Paris of the Commune is a 'vile multitude,'"[87] Marx was ironically reclaiming Thiers's epithet to emphasize how the Commune had itself disproved Thiers's elitist predictions.

The contrast Marx draws between the Paris envisaged by Thier's Versailles government and that of Paris under the Commune is found throughout *The Civil War in France* and its drafts. Marx maintained that "fighting, working, thinking, Paris" is the "new society in its throes," while "opposed at Versailles [is] the old society, a world of antiquated shams and accumulated lies."[88] Perhaps the most vital contrast that Marx made was between what he argued was *real* democracy of the Commune compared with *sham* democracy of the Versailles government. Marx dismissed the Versailles government's "pretentions of selfgovernment" in comparison to the "real selfgovernment" achieved by the Commune.[89] Marx furthermore parodied the horrified reaction of the British press to the Commune's understanding of self-government for not being "what *we* [the British] use to understand by selfgovernment."[90] In an amusing passage sadly only included in the first draft, Marx argued that the British conception of self-government amounted to being locally administered by "turtle-soup guttling aldermen, jobbing vestries, and ferocious workhouse guardians" and at the national level ruled by "an oligarchic club and the reading of the *Times* newspaper."[91] In contrast, Marx maintained that the Commune's conception of self-government meant "the people acting for itself by itself."[92]

Marx repeated variations of this slogan several times, arguing that the Commune was "a government of the people by the people" and the "resumption by the people for the people, of its own social life."[93] To modern ears, these naturally sound like deliberate echoes of Lincoln's famous speech delivered in Gettysburg eight years earlier in 1863, in which he expressed his resolve that "government of the people, by the people, for the people, shall not perish from the earth." That is certainly possible, as Marx held Lincoln in very high regard (he authored the International's address to Lincoln congratulating him on his reelection in November 1864). Both drafts of *The Civil War in France* ridicule Thiers's attempt to associate himself with Lincoln by arguing that he was defending France from Parisian secessionists, akin to the southern secessionists from

87. Marx, *The Civil War in France (First Draft)*, MEGA I.22: 33 / MECW 22: 457.

88. Marx, *The Civil War in France (Second Draft)*, MEGA I.22: 106 / MECW 22: 538.

89. Marx, *The Civil War in France (First Draft)*, MEGA I.22: 56 / MECW 22: 486; *The Civil War in France (Second Draft)*, MEGA I.22: 105 / MECW 22: 536.

90. Marx, *The Civil War in France (First Draft)*, MEGA I.22: 39 / MECW 22: 463–64.

91. Ibid., 39 / 464.

92. Ibid.

93. Marx, *The Civil War in France*, MEGA I.22: 146 / MECW 22: 339; *The Civil War in France (First Draft)*, MEGA I.22: 55 / MECW 22: 486.

the Union.[94] Indeed, the title of Marx's pamphlet is itself likely a partial reference to the recently concluded American Civil War, with Marx repeatedly denouncing the Versailles government's march on Paris as a "slaveholder's rebellion," implying that they were trying to maintain wage slavery in the same way that the slaveholders' rebellion of the Confederacy had fought to maintain chattel slavery.[95] These factors give us some reason to think Marx may have wanted to invoke the authority of Lincoln for his defense of the Commune.

But we need to bear in mind that the phrase (in its various forms) was actually in common usage in republican discourse for much of the nineteenth century. As early as 1833, Mazzini had noted that his Young Italy organization wanted revolution "in the name of the people, for the people, and by the people."[96] Under his influence, the ECDC had declared itself in favor of a "republic of the people, by the people, and for the people."[97] Similarly, among the figures explored in this book, we find George Julian Harney writing that "DEMOCRACY, or, in other words a government of the people, for, and by, the people" as well as Linton arguing that "government of all, by all, for the good of all—is the Republic."[98] The phrase was thus not exclusive to Lincoln, but one that "permeated the international republican discourse."[99] Marx can thus be seen as claiming one of republicanism's most popular slogans and

94. Marx, *The Civil War in France (First Draft, MEGA* I.22: 34 / *MECW* 22: 458; *The Civil War in France (Second Draft) MEGA* I.22: 109 / *MECW* 22: 542. Thiers had declared that "any attempted secession . . . will be energetically repressed in France as in America," cited in Tombs, *The Paris Commune,* 2.

95. For instance in Marx, *The Civil War in France, MEGA* I.22: 130, 136, 148 / *MECW* 22: 319, 328, 341; *The Civil War in France (Second Draft), MEGA* I.22: 98 / *MECW* 22: 531. For further discussion, see Robin Blackburn, *Marx and Lincoln: An Unfinished Revolution* (London: Verso, 2011).

96. Mazzini, "Lettera al Redatorre del *Précurseur,*" *Scritti editi ed inedita,* 3: 341. This has led to some speculation over whether Lincoln might have been influenced by Mazzini; see Timothy Roberts, "The Relevance of Giuseppe Mazzini's Ideas of Insurgency to the American Slavery Crisis of the 1850s," in *Giuseppe Mazzini and the Globalization of Democratic Nationalism, 1830–1920,* ed. C. A. Bayly and E. F. Biagini (Oxford: Oxford University Press, 2008), 322. See however the alternative source given in Jared Peatman, *The Long Shadow of Lincoln's Gettysburg Address* (Carbondale: Southern Illinois University Press, 2013), 28.

97. ECDC, "Aux Italiens," *Scritti editi ed inediti,* 46: 104. Cited in Denis Mack Smith, *Mazzini* (New Haven: Yale University Press, 1994), 84.

98. [George Julian Harney], "Monarchy," *The Democratic Review,* no. 2 (July 1849), 70; [W. J. Linton], "Democracy and Republicanism," *English Republic* (1854), 4: 66. Linton elsewhere cites Charles Delescluze as having said "the Republic, we cannot too often repeat, is the government of all by all and for all," in "Republican Measures," *English Republic* (1851), 1: 154.

99. Don H. Doyle, "Widely Noted and Long Remembered: The Gettysburg Address around the World," in *The Gettysburg Address: Perspectives on Lincoln's Greatest Speech,* ed. Sean Conant (New York: Oxford University Press, 2015), 277.

reserving it for the social republic of the Commune rather than the bourgeois republic in Versailles.

Popular Delegacy and Representative Government

At the outbreak of the Commune, authority over Paris first passed into the hands of the Central Committee of the National Guard. Marx enthusiastically described the National Guard's democratic organization through "a political federation according to a very simple plan" in which delegates sent from companies appointed the delegates of battalions who in turn sent delegates to the Central Committee. Marx claimed that in this system "Never were elections more sifted, never delegates fuller representing the masses from which they had sprung."[100] Marx extended this praise to the federative ideas and electoral mechanisms of the Commune Council which assumed control from the Central Committee after elections on 26 March 1871. Marx argued that these electoral mechanisms transformed an unaccountable system where elected representatives ruled over the people to one where delegates were subordinated to their oversight and control. As he summarized in *The Civil War in France*, "[i]nstead of deciding once in three or six years which member of the ruling class was to misrepresent the people in Parliament, universal suffrage was to serve the people."[101] Or, as he put it even more vividly in the first draft,

> The general suffrage, till now abused either for the parliamentary sanction of the Holy State Power, or a play in the hands of the ruling classes, only employed by the people to choose the instruments of parliamentary class rule once in many years, adapted to its real purposes, to choose by the communes their own functionaries of administration and initiation.[102]

Marx highlighted three institutions introduced by the Commune that ensured that universal (manhood) suffrage would properly serve the interests of the people rather than the ruling class: imperative mandates (where delegates are given binding instructions), the power to recall representatives, and short terms of office. He praised the Commune Council for having its members "chosen by universal suffrage . . . responsible and revocable at short terms," as well as the Commune's plans for a national assembly in which "each delegate to be at any time revocable and bound by the *mandat impératif* (formal

---

100. Marx, *The Civil War in France (First Draft)*, MEGA I.22: 52–53 / MECW 22: 483.

101. Marx, *The Civil War in France*, MEGA I.22: 141 / MECW 22: 333.

102. Marx, *The Civil War in France (First Draft)*, MEGA I.22: 57 / MECW 22: 488.

instructions) of his constituents."[103] Marx's preference for short periods of office is suggested by his reference to "short terms" and his opposition to representatives having "three or six years . . . to misrepresent the people" and constituents only being able to replace them "once in many years."[104] Marx thus aimed to force representatives to act in the interests of the people through frequent elections and giving constituents the power to instruct representatives and recall them from office.

Marx does not dedicate much space to considering how these electoral institutions would have this effect. One suggestion Marx makes is that they would change the class composition of representatives and hence the interests they defend. He observed that in an assembly chosen by "the suffrage of all citizens, responsible, and revocable in short terms . . . [t]he majority of that body would naturally consist of workmen or acknowledged representatives of the working class."[105] Marx would thus seem to be subtly amending his earlier 1848 position by insisting that universal (manhood) suffrage would need further constraints in order to have the expected outcome of majority working-class representation in the legislature. Marx suggests a further mechanism by which these electoral institutions would enhance accountability in a passage comparing voters choosing representatives to employers hiring workers:

> universal suffrage was to serve the people . . . [just] as individual suffrage serves every other employer in the search for the workmen and managers of his business. And it is well known that companies, like individuals, in matters of real business generally know how to put the right man in the right place, and, if they for once make a mistake, to redress it promptly.[106]

With heavy irony, Marx thus equated the voters' right to instantly recall a representative with an employer's right to fire their workers at will. Just as workers can thereby be expected to tailor their behavior to the wishes of the employer on pain of being "promptly" dismissed, so representatives can be expected to closely follow their constituents' wishes if they are at risk of being recalled immediately rather than at the end of their lengthy mandate. The passage can also be seen as subtly needling bourgeois ideologues for insisting on an

---

103. Marx, *The Civil War in France*, MEGA I.22: 139-40 / MECW 22: 331–32.

104. Though Engels's slightly differing German translation of "revocable at short terms" as "immediately revocable *(jederzeit absetzbar)*" suggests this is may be a reference to how quickly delegates can be recalled and not the length of the mandate; see Marx, *Der Bürgerkrieg in Frankreich*, MEGA I.22: 201.

105. Marx, *The Civil War in France (Second Draft)*, MEGA I.22: 105 / MECW 22: 537; see also *The Civil War in France*, MEGA I.22: 139 / MECW 22: 331.

106. Marx, *The Civil War in France*, MEGA I.22: 141 / MECW 22: 333.

employer's right to dismiss workers while denying voters that power when it comes to their representatives.

Marx thought that the Commune's electoral accountability mechanisms would finally allow universal suffrage to live up to its emancipatory promise, contrasting it with the "delusion of unorganized 'universal suffrage'" that had existed under the French Empire.[107] But Marx was also eager to ensure that his criticism of unconstrained forms of universal suffrage was not misunderstood as opposition to universal suffrage itself. Directly following his critique that unconstrained universal suffrage allows representatives of the "ruling class . . . to misrepresent the people," Marx cautioned, "On the other hand, nothing could be more foreign to the spirit of the Commune than to supersede universal suffrage by hierarchic investiture."[108] This oblique aside was likely meant as a subtle rebuke of Comtist (or Positivist) responses to the Commune. English Comtists had idiosyncratically combined defending the Commune with a principled opposition to universal suffrage. The leading Comtist, E. S. Beesly, argued (in an article that Marx kept a clipping of) that the Commune had shown that the "majority" had no right to rule and "political power belongs of right to the energetic and intelligent."[109] Beesly congratulated "[t]he Paris Republicans [for] hav[ing] at length discovered that the dogma of universal suffrage cannot be applied in France without subordinating the intelligent and energetic populations of the large towns to an ignorant and narrow peasantry."[110] His associate Frederic Harrison similarly claimed that "the principle which the Commune involves in [sic] the repudiating of the dogma of universal suffrage," since the revolt revealed a Parisian refusal to be ruled by a government elected by the suffrage of the ignorant rural peasantry. This refusal, Harrison asserted, was in line with the "cardinal doctrine of the Positivist system that government by the suffrage—the election of the superior by the inferior—the basing of authority on the nomination of a majority—is inherently vicious."[111]

107. Marx, *The Civil War in France (Second Draft)*, MEGA I.22: 64 / MECW 22: 497. Napoleon III's regime formally maintained the universal (manhood) suffrage inherited from the Second Republic but subjected elections to heavy government interference and none of the Commune's accountability mechanisms.

108. Marx, *The Civil War in France*, MEGA I.22: 141 / MECW 22: 333.

109. E. S. Beesly, "Professor Beesly on the Paris Commune," *The Bee-Hive: The People's Paper*, no. 493 (25 March 1871): 1. The clipping is among Marx's papers in *Russian State Archive of Socio-Political History (RGASPI)*, f. 1, op. 1, d. 2784.

110. E. S. Beesly, "Professor Beesly on the Paris Commune," *The Bee-Hive: The People's Paper*, no. 494 (1 April 1871): 1.

111. Frederic Harrison, "The Revolution of the Commune," *The Fortnightly Review*, vol. 9, no. 53 (May 1871): 570–71. Other aspects of Harrison's praise of the Commune come closer to

This was a rather tendentious reading of the Communards' actions and anathema to Marx's politics, and he was keen to distance the Commune from the Comtist interpretation but without directly airing their differences. The Comtists had been some of the few public defenders of the Commune as well as long-standing allies of English trade union struggles (Beesly, who was friendly with Marx, had chaired the first meeting of the IWMA). Marx consequently seems to have decided that it would be undiplomatic to openly criticize them in *The Civil War in France* (which was, after all, published in the name of the International).[112] While the first draft of the pamphlet had two sections reserved for Comtism, in which Marx noted their "personal valour" but criticized their support for "personal *Dictatorship*" and "hierarchy in all spheres of human action," these were cut from the final text, leaving only the oblique comment cited above.[113] (When speaking in a more personal capacity, in an interview a few months after the Commune, Marx made it very clear that the Comtist participation in the International did not entail influence over its program, as they "will have nothing do with popular government as we understand it, and which seeks only to put a new hierarchy in place of the old one.")[114] Marx's indirect critique of Comtism in *The Civil War in France* served to clarify that the electoral accountability mechanisms introduced by the Commune

Marx. In spite of his rejection of universal suffrage, Harrison argued that the Commune had shown that "[t]he idea . . . that the whole system of administration from top to bottom is a peculiar mystery, in which they [the wealthy] alone have been initiated, is a dogma" and that "[p]laced in a position of unparalleled difficulty . . . the work men who, for the first time in the history of modern Europe, assumed the functions of government, have shown extraordinary energy and singular skill"; ibid., 573. Those descriptions bear a strong resemblance (potentially suggesting influence) to Marx's claim that the Commune had revealed "[t]he Delusion as if administration and political governing were mysteries, transcendent functions only to be trusted to the hands of a trained caste," and his description of "[w]hen the Paris Commune took the management of the revolution in its own hands; when plain working men for the first time dared to infringe upon the Governmental privilege of their 'natural superiors,' and, under circumstances of unexampled difficulty, performed their work modestly, conscientiously, and efficiently"; see Marx, *The Civil War in France (First Draft)*, MEGA I.22: 57 / MECW 22: 488; *The Civil War in France*, MEGA I.22: 143 / MECW 22: 336.

112. Hal Draper, *Karl Marx's Theory of Revolution*, vol. 4 (New York: Monthly Review Press, 1990), 195–96; Royden Harrison, "Introduction," in *The English Defence of the Paris Commune (1871)* (London: Merlin Press, 1971), 14–18. See also F. B. Smith, "Some British Reactions to the Commune," in *Paradigm for Revolution? The Paris Commune 1871–1971*, ed. Eugene Kamenka (Canberra: Australian National University Press, 1972), 81–83.

113. Marx, *The Civil War in France (First Draft)*, MEGA I.22: 65, 73 / MECW 22: 498, 504–5.

114. Laynor, "The Curtain Raised. Interview with Karl Marx, the Head of L'Internationale . . . ," MEGA I.22: 457 / MECW 22: 605.

would not be misconstrued as entailing a breach with the established practice of universal (manhood) suffrage in France. Marx still believed this to be an essential (if not sufficient) political element in socialist transformation.

The institutional mechanisms that Marx embraced to constrain representatives (or delegates) conflict with one of the core principles of representative government. This holds, as Bernard Manin identifies in his authoritative account of the topic, that representatives retain partial independence from the will of the people who elected them.[115] That is, once representatives are elected, they are not required to act in accordance with the preferences of their constituents and can instead decide on legislation based on their own judgment. Manin stresses that representatives are not entirely independent of their constituents either, as they are subject to both citizen pressure during their mandate and the threat of not being reelected at the end of their mandate. This means that representatives have an incentive to act in accordance with their constituents' preferences, yet are not legally required to do so, giving them a certain degree of discretion. Manin outlines several constitutional mechanisms that can reduce the degree of this discretion, focusing particularly on imperative mandates and the right to recall representatives. These have, however, been almost universally absent from or even explicitly banned by the constitutions of representative governments. Manin writes, "None of the representative governments established since the end of the eighteenth century has authorized imperative mandates . . . Neither has any of them durably applied permanent revocability of representatives."[116] Constitutional provisions banning the imperative mandate can be found in constitutions of countries as diverse as France, Germany, Korea, Senegal, and Spain.[117]

However, there was a long radical republican tradition, from the French Revolution to the Paris Commune, which, inspired by Rousseau, contested this ultimately victorious model of largely unconstrained representation.[118] Across various republican constitutional moments we find the more radical elements of the tradition voicing a more accountable and delegative understanding of representation. One of the French Revolution's key radical participants,

115. Bernard Manin, *The Principles of Representative Government* (Cambridge: Cambridge University Press, 1997), 6, 163–67.

116. Ibid., 163.

117. Christoph Müller, *Das imperative und freie Mandat: Überlegungen zur Lehre von der Repräsentation des Volkes* (Leiden: A. W. Sijthoff, 1966), 50–53; Marc Van der Hulst, *The Parliamentary Mandate: A Global Comparative Study* (Geneva: Inter-Parliamentary Union, 2000), 8.

118. Pierre-Henri Zaidman, *Le mandat impératif: De la Révolution française à la Commune de Paris* (Paris: Les Editions Libertaires, 2008); Marco Goldoni, "Rousseau's Radical Constitutionalism and Its Legacy," in *Constitutionalism beyond Liberalism*, ed. Michael W. Dowdle and Michael A. Wilkinson (Cambridge: Cambridge University Press, 2017), 227–53.

Jean-Paul Marat, had already advised the English people in 1774 that "representatives of the people ought ever to act according to the instructions of their constituents," otherwise "What then are our representatives, but our masters?"[119] When deputies assembled in the Estates General in 1789 they carried instructions (*Cahiers*) from their constituencies, which were almost immediately declared void in response to the aristocratic Second Estate's cynical attempt to use them to block the early constitutional process of the Revolution, and the imperative mandate was subsequently banned in the 1791 Constitution. However, as the Revolution progressed various radical groupings, including the sans-culottes, concluded that this had resulted in the "establishment of an unrestrained power" that had replaced the king's despotism with "legislative tyranny."[120] They waged a campaign to legalize the imperative mandate, having some success with the Jacobin Constitution of 1793, which also included a provision for representative recall.[121] More radical constrained forms of representation continued to be defended throughout the nineteenth century, with French radical republicans declaring in 1845 that representatives were (in phraseology very similar to that which Marx would later use) only "mandatories of the people: they must therefore be responsible and revocable."[122] Those sentiments were also repeated in the 1848 Revolution, with radicals pushing the idea that "*sovereignty of the people*" implied that "the National Assembly has an imperative mandate from the people" and that "The mandate of the representative is imperative; if he violates it, his constituents have the right, the duty to reprimand him first, then to strip him of his mandate."[123] The Paris Commune itself corresponded with a revival

119. Jean-Paul Marat, *The Chains of Slavery: A Work Wherein the Clandestine and Villainous Attempts of Princes to Ruin Liberty Are Pointed Out, and the Dreadful Scenes of Despotism Disclosed* ... (London: 1774), 203. See further discussion in Rachel Hammersley, *The English Republican Tradition and Eighteenth-Century France: Between the Ancients and the Moderns* (Manchester: Manchester University Press, 2010), 142.

120. Jean-François Varlet, *Projet d'un mandat spécial et impératif, aux mandataires du peuple à la Convention nationale* (Paris: Imprimerie du Cercle social, 1792), 6–7 / "Proposal for a Special and Imperative Mandate," in *Social and Political Thought of the French Revolution 1788–1797: An Anthology of Original Texts (Abridged Edition)*, ed. and trans. Marc Allan Goldstein (New York: Peter Lang, 2001), 154–55.

121. For an overview of this episode, see Nicolai von Eggers, "When the People Assemble, the Laws Go Silent: Radical Democracy and the French Revolution," *Constellations* 23, no. 2 (2016): 256–58.

122. "Aux démocrates," *La Réforme* (15 July 1845): 1.

123. "Le droit de Pétition," *La Republique Rouge*, no. 2 (11–13 June 1848): 1; "De la Constitution," *La Republique Rouge*, no. 4 (16–18 June 1848): 1. See the discussion in Samuel Hayat, *Quand la République était révolutionnaire: Citoyenneté et représentation en 1848* (Paris: Seuil, 2014), 303–8.

of interest in the imperative mandate, with Commune members citing the *mandat impératif* given to them by their constituents in the justification of their votes.[124] Even after the Commune's demise, radical republicans waged an unsuccessful campaign for imperative mandates to be included in the constitution of the Third Republic.[125] They argued that the choice for the French people lay between the *"imperative mandate or carte blanche to our mandatories, masters or slaves, this is the alternative."*[126]

These ideas were also, as we saw in chapters 1 and 2, a feature of Marx's early republican writings in 1842–42. In his journalism, Marx argued that "A representation which is divorced from the consciousness of those whom it represents is no representation."[127] He consequently criticized Hegel for his opposition to binding instructions for representatives, arguing that, without them, representatives "form a society which is not linked with those who commission them." Marx held that representatives without instructions "are are *no* longer *mandatories. They* are supposed to *be delegates*, and they are *not.*"[128] Channeling the influence of his contemporaneous reading of Rousseau, the early Marx also objected to reducing the people's political participation to "a *single and temporary*" act of taking part in elections, reducing participation to simply "a *sensational* act . . . a moment of *ecstasy*" rather than an ongoing intervention in public life.[129] Marx's endorsement of the Communal institutions that ensure that representatives do not "misrepresent the people in Parliament" marks a return to these earlier concerns, linking the "true democracy" of his early writings with the "social republic" of 1871. The return of this early commitment after the experience of the Commune can also be seen in a small but not insignificant addition he made to the French edition of *Le Capital* (1872–75) that was not in the original German edition of *Das Kapital* (1867). Here Marx introduced a discussion of how the development of capitalism is associated with the growth of various kinds of mediating middlemen who exploit their position, of which one example, he argued, was that "in politics, the representative is more important than his voter."[130]

124. See particularly the minutes of the session on May 1, 1871, in *Les 31 séances officielles de Commune de Paris* (Paris: Revue de France, 1871), 140–42.

125. Daniel Mollenhauer, *Auf der Suche nach der "wahren Republik": Die französischen "radicaux" in der frühen Dritten Republik (1870–1890)* (Bonn: Bouvier Verlag, 1997), chapter 4.

126. Anon. [Charles Ferdinand Gambon], *Le mandat impératif par un paysan et lettre du citoyen Félix Pyat* (Genève: L'imprimerie Coopérative, 1873), 21.

127. Marx, "Debatten über Preßfreiheit," *MEGA* I.1: 136 / *MECW* 1: 148.

128. Marx, *Kritik, MEGA* I.2: 133 / *MECW* 3: 122.

129. Ibid., 121 / 112.

130. Marx, *Le Capital, MEGA* II.7: 662n / *MECW* 35: 733n. Compare with *Das Kapital*, 1st ed., *MEGA* II.5: 596. This addition did not make it into the 1872–73 second German edition; see *Das Kapital*, 2nd ed., *MEGA* II.6: 669n. But Marx noted that he had not had the time to include all

Marx's defense of imperative mandates, representative recall, and short terms of office positions him within a tradition that rejects the standard form of representative government and instead endorses what we might call (for lack of an established term) a system of popular delegacy. In the former, representation is understood as the ceding of decision-making power by the people to representatives, and the people's role is reduced to deciding whether or not to renew or decline their mandate at the next election. In representative government, representatives exercise their mandate with a large degree of discretion and without the formal involvement of the people. In a system of popular delegacy, representation is instead understood as a form of commission, where representatives (or perhaps better delegates) enact the wishes of their constituents. The people also retain the continuous power to intervene in the decision-making of their representatives by giving them formal instructions or recalling them entirely. One of the key insights that Marx took from the Paris Commune was that representative government could not serve as an adequate realization of the idea of democracy; the more radical form of popular delegacy would be required to effect a transition to socialism.

Popular Administration and Transformation of the State

Marx's account in *The Civil War in France* of the transformation of the state administration by subjecting it to popular control begins with a critique of the existing French state. In a vivid metaphor, he depicts the state as a "huge governmental parasite," "entoiling like a boa constrictor the real social body in the ubiquitous meshes of a standing army, a hierarchical bureaucracy, an obedient police, clergy and a servile magistrature."[131] Marx condemned the state as a professionalized, hierarchical, and centralized body that has escaped the control of its citizens. He criticized the state's "systematic and hierarchic division of labour," its "trained caste" of bureaucrats, its "centralized state machinery," and attacked it for being "separate . . . and independent from society" and a "usurpatory dictatorship of the governmental body over society itself."[132] Marx argued

---

the changes he had wanted to make and was able to include in the French edition; see Marx, "Nachwort," in *Das Kapital*, 2nd ed., *MEGA* II.6: 700–701 / *MECW* 35: 13. Engels incorporated the change in *Das Kapital*, 3rd ed.. *MEGA* II.8: 696n.

131. Marx, *The Civil War in France (Second Draft)*, *MEGA* I.22: 100-103 / *MECW* 22: 533–34. The evocative comparison of the state to a boa constrictor appears in both drafts but, sadly, not in the final version. Perhaps Marx realized that it was an imperfect metaphor, as boa constrictors are not parasites but predators that kill (rather than live off) their prey.

132. Marx, *The Civil War in France*, *MEGA* I.22: 137 / *MECW* 22: 328; *The Civil War in France (First Draft)*, *MEGA* I.22: 53, 56, 57 / *MECW* 22: 483, 486, 488; *The Civil War in France (Second Draft)*, *MEGA* I.22: 100 / *MECW* 22: 534.

that these characteristics had become increasingly pronounced as the state developed. He noted that the state tends to "expand the circumference and the attributes of state power, the number of its tools, its independence of, and its supernaturalist sway of real society."[133] Consequently, the existing state was the "master instead of the servant of society."[134]

Given these characteristics (hierarchical, centralized, professionalized, and unaccountable), Marx argued that the existing state was an inappropriate vehicle for a working-class revolution. Instead, Marx argued that the working class had to "transform the traditional working machinery" of the state into a polity that lacked the objectionable features of the existing state.[135] Marx argued that this entailed fundamentally transforming each of the existing state's five main organs: the bureaucracy or civil service, the standing army, the established church, the police, and the judiciary.[136]

For the judiciary, Marx advocated for their "sham independence . . . [and] abject subserviency to all succeeding governments" to be broken, by making "magistrates and judges . . . elective, responsible, and revocable." For the police, Marx similarly endorsed "turn[ing] [them] into the responsible and at all times revocable agent of the Commune."[137] Making the police subject to properly democratic oversight and control entailed, Marx believed, that "its ruffians [would be] supplanted by servants of the Commune," marking an end to the "arbitrary rule of the police." (Marx also suggestively cited one of manifestos released during the Commune, which described how "citizens do their police business themselves."[138]) For the church, Marx advocated its separation from the state, including by freeing education from religious control. Along with the abolition of the police, this meant the Commune had tackled both the "physical . . . [and] spiritual force of repression."[139]

Turning to the standing army (to which Marx devoted more attention than the above institutions), Marx argued that it should be turned into a civic

---

133. Marx, *The Civil War in France (First Draft)*, *MEGA* I.22: 53 / *MECW* 22: 484.

134. Ibid., 56 / 487.

135. Marx, *The Civil War in France (Second Draft)*, *MEGA* I.22: 100 / *MECW* 22: 533. I use the less loaded term "polity," as Marx at several points implies that the Commune was no longer a "state."

136. For reasons of space, I do not discuss how the new polity is to be both decentralized in comparison to the existing state, and at the same time (Marx insisted) maintain some kind of central structure. For a clarifying discussion of the latter and how it relates to Marx's earlier centralizing impulses, see Hunt, *Political Ideas of Marx and Engels*, 2:147–61.

137. Marx, *The Civil War in France*, *MEGA* I.22: 139–40 / *MECW* 22: 331–32.

138. Marx, *The Civil War in France (First Draft)*, *MEGA* I.22: 45, 57, 74 / *MECW* 22: 473, 488, 505.

139. Marx, *The Civil War in France*, *MEGA* I.22: 139–40 / *MECW* 22: 331.

militia, and he praised the Commune for having made its first act the "suppression of the standing army, and the substitution for it of the armed people."[140] (Broadly, a civic militia differs from a standing army in that it consists of part-time citizen-soldiers rather than full-time professional soldiers.) Marx credited the National Guard, Paris's civic militia, with making the Commune possible in the first place. He argued that it was only because the working class was armed and organized in a militia that it could resist the Versailles government's troops and set up its own administration. The National Guard was indeed a quite unique institution that played a central role in the events leading up to and during the Commune. While it had traditionally been a bourgeois militia, its ranks had become increasingly composed of the working classes, and by 1871 it was "widely understood to be a democratic body of citizen soldiers" far removed from the "army's authoritarian and militaristic traditions."[141] In contrast to the army, it elected its own noncommissioned officers and junior officers, and units were recruited and organized locally. The siege of Paris had meant that the National Guard had grown spectacularly to 340,000 men and became the epicenter of local social and political life, providing working-class neighborhoods with everything from a "substitute workplace" to a "provider of family income," a "political club," and a "recreation organization."[142] The immediate context for the outbreak of the Commune was thus a situation of "local, democratic, armed organizations on an unprecedented scale."[143]

Marx's comments on the National Guard suggest four advantages that he saw in a civic militia rather than a standing army. First, it is cheaper. Marx maintained that removing the standing army discards "the most fertile source of all state taxation and state debts" and is the "first economical *condition sine qua* [*non*] for all social improvements."[144] Second, a civic militia makes for a better army. Marx argued that the National Guard was the "safest guarantee against Foreign aggression."[145] He thought that had the Commune been formed at the start of the Franco-Prussian War, it would have "taken the defence [of Paris]

---

140. Ibid.

141. Shafer, *The Paris Commune*, 137.

142. Tombs, *The Paris Commune*, 50.

143. Ibid., 46.

144. Marx, *The Civil War in France (First Draft)*, MEGA I.22: 57 / MECW 22: 488. We should remember that military spending comprised a much larger proportion of public spending in nineteenth-century European states.

145. Ibid. There is a possibility that by "Foreign aggression" Marx is referring to the obverse characteristic of a civic militia: that it less likely to engage in foreign wars. However, the context of the Prussian siege suggests that, here at least, he means that the civic militia is better at defending the nation from foreign attack.

out of the hands of traitors" and "imprinted its enthusiasm" on the armed forces and turned the struggle into a real "war of republican France."[146] Third, a civic militia improves the character of its soldiers relative to professional solders. Marx argued that professional soldiers acquire "inveterate habits . . . under the training of the enemies of the working class" (such as shooting prisoners without trial), which would over time be remedied when those soldiers joined the workers in the civic militia.[147] Fourth (and most importantly for Marx), a civic militia is less prone to siding with reactionary forces against popular movements. Marx branded the standing army a "constant danger to government usurpation of class rule."[148] He believed that a standing army was a continual source of potential reaction, providing the ruling class, or a leader with Caesarist ambitions, with the means by which they can put an end to the turmoil of a revolution. Marx believed that a civic militia was less likely to be used in this manner because of its closer ties to the people. His specification that the civic militia should have an "extremely short term of service" suggests a concern with ensuring that they do not develop a separate existence from the people.[149] His description of army troops as "French soldatesca," as "mercenary vindicators" of bourgeois society, and as the "iron hand of mercenary soldiery" further presents them as a force external to society, paid by the government to crush the people.[150] In summary, Marx believed that the standing army "defend[s] the government against the people," while a civic militia is "the people armed against governmental usurpation."[151]

In this defense of the civic militia we can detect traces in Marx's thought of what R. Claire Snyder calls the republican "citizen-soldier" tradition.[152] She argues that republican thinkers in this tradition, from Machiavelli to Rousseau,

146. Ibid., 51 / 481.

147. Marx, *The Civil War in France*, MEGA I.22: 133 / MECW 22: 323; *The Civil War in France (Second Draft)*, MEGA I.22: 95 / MECW 22: 526–27.

148. Marx, *The Civil War in France (First Draft)*, MEGA I.22: 57 / MECW 22: 488.

149. Marx, *The Civil War in France*, MEGA I.22: 140 / MECW 22: 332.

150. Marx *The Civil War in France (Second Draft)*, MEGA I.22: 95 / MECW 22: 526; *The Civil War in France*, MEGA I.22: 153, 158 / MECW 22: 348, 354.

151. Marx, *The Civil War in France (Second Draft)*, MEGA I.22: 105 / MECW 22: 537. This may have been inspired by the Central Committee of the National Guard's declaration that a civic militia "defends the citizens against the [governmental] power, instead of a standing army which defends the [governmental] power against the citizens"; see "Journal Officiel de Paris (Numéro du 25). Comité central," *Le Rappel*, no. 650 (25 March 1871): 2, col. 1. Marx copied out parts of this press report and underlined this statement; see Marx, *Notebook on the Paris Commune*, 24, 89.

152. R. Claire Snyder, "The Citizen-Soldier and the Tragedy of *The Eighteenth Brumaire*," *Strategies: Journal of Theory, Culture & Politics* 16, no. 1 (2003): 23–37.

warned of the danger of professional soldiers to the republic, either as merce-naries or as a standing army.[153] They argued that professional armies stand apart from the people and can hence be used by the elites to crush them. They emphasized that arming the people allowed them to defend themselves against this threat to their domestic liberty, as well as acting as a bulwark against for-eign domination. Rousseau, for instance, argued that a standing army is "good for only two purposes: to attack and conquer neighbors, or to shackle and enslave citizens." Instead, he proposed that "Each citizen ought to be a soldier by duty, none by profession." He argued that a militia "costs the Republic little," fights better than a professional army (since "one always defends one's goods better than another's"), and does not harass the local population as professional soldiers are wont to do.[154]

Marx's arguments in favor of a civic militia bear a strong resemblance to these positions.[155] His concern with ensuring that the armed forces do not form a separate body from society reflects, as Snyder argues, "one of the main principles of the citizen-soldier tradition: a military staffed by the people is less likely to fire on their own neighbors and comrades."[156] Furthermore, Marx's defense of the National Guard as the best protection against foreign invasion and his criti-cism of the army generals who had failed to properly use them against the Prus-sian forces were in line with the widely held opinion among contemporary radi-cals (republican and communist) that Paris could have beaten the Prussians if they had unleashed popular enthusiasm by reenacting the legendary republican *levée en masse* from the French Revolution.[157]

---

153. R. Claire Snyder, *Citizen-Soldiers and Manly Warriors: Military Service and Gender in the Civic Republican Tradition* (Lanham: Rowman & Littlefield, 1999). See also J. G. A. Pocock, *The Machiavellian Moment: Florentine Political Thought and the Atlantic Republican Tradition* (Prince-ton: Princeton University Press, 1975), 199–211.

154. Rousseau, *Considérations sur le gouvernement de Pologne*, in *Oeuvres complètes*, vol. 3 (Paris: Gallimard, 1964), 1013-14 / *Considerations on the Government of Poland* in in *The Social Contract and Other Later Political Writings*, ed. Victor Gourevitch (Cambridge: Cambridge Uni-versity Press, 1997), 233–34.

155. Additionally, Marx at one point refers to the National Guard as the "armed manhood" of Paris; see *The Civil War in France (First Draft)*, MEGA I.22: 52 / MECW 22: 482. We can detect here a faint echo of an objectionable element of the citizen-soldier tradition that associ-ates the civic militia with the promotion of manly virtue or "*armed masculinity*"; see Snyder, *Citizen-Soldiers and Manly Warriors*, 24–31, 55–59. Marx does, however, also defend the role women played in fighting on the barricades; see *The Civil War in France*, MEGA I.22: 154 / MECW 22: 350.

156. Snyder, "The Citizen-Soldier and the Tragedy of *The Eighteenth Brumaire*," 33.

157. Tombs, *The Paris Commune*, 47–48.

Marx's discussion of the civic militia in *The Civil War in France* is primarily concerned with the role it plays in defending the revolution from reactionary forces, and not with the connection republicanism often makes between service in the militia and developing the virtues necessary for citizenship.[158] However, that link is displayed in an 1848 article discussing the Prussian government's attempt to create a watered-down civic militia. Marx condemned the government's stipulation that a serving militia member "may neither think nor speak of public affairs" and must "relinquish his primary political rights," arguing that this would produce citizens that mirrored the "passive, will-less and disinterested obedience of the soldier." Marx bitterly commented that the proposed civic militia was thus incapable of fulfilling its function as a "school . . . to bring up the republicans of the future!"[159]

Turning to the final state organ, the bureaucracy, its transformation was perhaps closest to Marx's heart. At its core, Marx envisaged its conversion from a professional, unaccountable, elite body into one subordinated to the control of both the legislature and the people by making public officials either appointable and recallable by the legislature or popularly elected and subject to recall. A repeated refrain in *The Civil War in France* and its drafts is the specification that "public servants . . . were to be elective, responsible, and revocable."[160] Marx thereby transferred the same system of accountability that he applied to political representation to public administration as a whole. Just how many of the total positions in the public administration Marx thought should be chosen by election is not entirely clear. We could imagine it being limited to just the most senior administrative posts or extending to most, or even all, public officials. Some of Marx's rhetoric certainly suggests that he thought elections should be quite extensive. Marx noted that, in addition to judges and magistrates, the "rest of public servants" were to be elected, and he argued that even rural public officials, such as the "notary, advocate, [and] executor" (who were currently "judicial vampires" and "blood-suckers" of the peasants), would be transformed "into salaried communal agents, elected by, and responsible to, himself [the peasant]."[161] At other points, he suggested that it would be sufficient for some public officials to be appointed by the legislative body (the Commune). He argued that in addition to turning the police into

158. For the link, see Snyder, *Citizen-Soldiers and Manly Warriors*, 22–24, 54–55.

159. Marx, "Der Bürgerwehrgesetzentwurf," *MEGA* I.7: 371–72; *MECW* 7: 256–57. Marx's explicit appeal to republicanism was (as discussed in chapter 4) the result of Marx and Engels's strategy of situating the *Neue Rheinische Zeitung* within the broader radical democratic movement.

160. Marx, *The Civil War in France*, *MEGA* I.22: 140 / *MECW* 22: 332.

161. Ibid., 140, 144 / 332, 337.

the "responsible and at all times revocable agent of the Commune," the same would also occur with "the officials of all other branches of the Administration," and in the drafts he argued that the "functionaries in all the other departments of administration, [were] to be appointed and always revocable by the Commune."[162] Marx thus seems to have envisaged a combination of some public officials being directly elected by the people and some appointed by the legislature (and both subject to recall).[163]

The outcome of making the bureaucracy elected and legislatively appointed would be a considerable deprofessionalization of public administration. Marx thought it would remove the "army of state parasites" and make "public functions—military, administrative, political—*real workmen's functions*, instead of the hidden attributes of a trained caste." He further believed that making those officials subject to recall would make public administration properly accountable. He said that it would mean "doing away with the state hierarchy altogether and replacing the haughteous masters of the people into [*sic*] its always removable servants, a mock responsibility by a real responsibility, as they act continuously under public supervision."[164] Marx likely drew these ideas from the Commune's 19 April *Déclaration au peuple français* (*Declaration to the French People*), which was one of the most prominent statements of its program.[165] The declaration called for the "permanent intervention of the citizens in communal affairs," and gave a glimpse of its administrative ideal, by proclaiming "The choice by election or competitive examination, with accountability (*responsibilité*) and permanent right of supervision (*contrôle*) and dismissal (*révocation*), of magistrates and communal officials of every grade."[166] Marx's repeated call for all public officials to be "elective, responsible, and revocable" can be seen as a pithy formulation of this demand. But Marx's account also subtly departs (perhaps deliberately so) from the Commune's declaration by omitting its specification that public officials could be appointed "by election or competitive examination." Marx may have thought that examinations would maintain an objectionably elitist and

162. Ibid, 139–40 / 331–32; *The Civil War in France (Second Draft)*, MEGA I.22: 105 / MECW 22: 537.

163. I overlooked this combined view in an earlier version of this chapter; see Bruno Leipold, "Marx's Social Republic: Radical Republicanism and the Political Institutions of Socialism," in *Radical Republicanism: Recovering the Tradition's Popular Heritage* (Oxford: Oxford University Press, 2020), 190.

164. Marx, *The Civil War in France (First Draft)*, MEGA I.22: 57–58 / MECW 22: 488–90.

165. Marx references the declaration in *The Civil War in France*, MEGA I.22: 140 / MECW 22: 332 and *The Civil War in France (First Draft)*, MEGA I.22: 70 / MECW 22: 503, and he copied it out in full from a press report in Marx, *Notebook on the Paris Commune*, 63–64.

166. See the translation of the declaration in Tombs, *The Paris Commune*, 217–19.

exclusive element of the old bureaucracy. If we remember the discussion in chapter 2, one of the young Marx's most biting criticisms of Hegel's civil service was its Prussian-inspired faith in examinations.

A tangible financial dimension of Marx's deprofessionalization of the bureaucracy was his praise for how, "[f]rom the members of the Commune downwards," all public officials were to be paid *"workmen's wages."*[167] In the context of the pay structure of nineteenth-century France's civil service, that was an especially revolutionary demand. From the time of Napoleon I to World War I, the French state had a small number of extremely well-paid civil servants, who received fifty to one hundred times the average income (so that they could lead a similarly "dignified" life to those living off inherited capital).[168] In Balzac's *La Cousine Bette* (1846), for example, the irresponsible and philandering Baron Hulot d'Ervy earns 25,000 francs per year from his high-ranking post in the War Ministry, when day wages for workmen were, at the time, just 1 to 1.5 francs, giving them in the region of 300 to 450 francs a year.[169] Radically cutting the salaries for these top posts would have been a powerful symbol of how public administration had been taken out of the hands of aristocratic dignitaries and placed in the hands of ordinary workers. Elite functionaries like Baron Hulot (the "state parasites" Marx referred to) would no longer suck the financial resources out of the country for their own personal gain.[170] Limiting wages to the level of workers would thus be an important part of the process whereby "the high dignitaries of State disappeared."[171] But, similarly to the case of examinations, Marx's praise of the Commune's supposed egalitarian wage structure departed from what the Commune had actually done. The Commune had in fact only limited the salaries of public officials to a maximum of 6,000 francs a year when workers (in 1871) earned about 5 francs a day, giving them roughly 1,500 a year.[172] Marx was

167. Marx, *The Civil War in France, MEGA* I.22: 139 / *MECW* 22: 331.

168. Thomas Picketty, *Capital in the Twenty-First Century,* trans. Arthur Goldhammer (Cambridge: Harvard University Press, 2014), 416–17.

169. See the financial appendix in Honoré de Balzac, *Cousin Bette,* ed. David Bellos, trans. Sylvia Raphael (Oxford: Oxford University Press, 2008), 463–65. Balzac was one of Marx's favorite contemporary authors, and he references *Cousine Bette* in *Der achtzehnte Brumaire, MEGA* I.11: 188 / *MECW* 11: 196.

170. Marx discusses how the bourgeois state combines the "direct economic exploitation" of the worker by the capitalist, with a "second exploitation of the people" by the families of capitalists taking all the "rich places of the State household"; *The Civil War in France (First Draft), MEGA* I.22: 54 / *MECW* 22: 484.

171. Marx, *The Civil War in France, MEGA* I.22: 139 / *MECW* 22: 331.

172. Tombs, *The Paris Commune,* 86; Shafer, *The Paris Commune,* 138. The pay figures for workers (1–1.5 francs and later 5 francs) are taken from the respective sources and may reflect different methods of accounting rather than rising wages or inflation.

aware of the actual figures, so his bending of the facts was a deliberate exaggeration of what the Commune had in fact achieved (an already radical step), in the direction of what he hoped future communist regimes would do.[173]

Marx's specification that public posts were to be either elected or legislatively appointed, as well as being paid the same workmen's wages, presents what Richard Hunt calls a "tantalising vision of a democracy without professionals."[174] In Marx's conception of the social republic, public functions are no longer reserved for a "trained caste" but carried out by the people as a whole. This deprofessionalization of the state's administrative and repressive functions is one of Marx's much less appreciated political ideas. It is a vision that stands in stark contrast to the massive expansion of the state and its professional personnel since Marx's writings. The prospect of replacing it with a democratically appointed and elected citizen-administrators might seem riddled with insurmountable hurdles (from insufficient technical expertise and the corporate capture of inexperienced administrators to the sheer time needed for so many elections). Marx does not engage further with how such concerns might be overcome (and might have considered doing so an example of objectionable utopian planning).

Marx was hardly alone in his vision of a deprofessionalized citizen public administration. In addition to the radicals of the Paris Commune, such hopes were periodically raised by republicans across the nineteenth century—as has been highlighted at several points in this book. Johann Georg Wirth had already set out an account in 1833 whereby the "very great number of state officials becomes superfluous, through the passing of their functions to citizens, who perform this service alternating in turns," and in which "all public officials elected *by all and from all the citizens of the state*, directly accountable to the people and dismissible by the same."[175] Arnold Ruge, Marx's onetime collaborator and subsequent adversary, made the first plank of his 1848 election manifesto a call for the "[a]bolition of the standing army of soldiers" and its replacement by a civic militia, and immediately followed it with the parallel demand for the "[a]bolition of the standing army of officials and its replacement with a cheap government consisting of freely elected men of the people."[176]

---

173. We know that it was deliberate since Marx copied out a press report of the maximum salary announcement; see Marx, *Notebook on the Paris Commune*, 36. He also cited the maximum in the drafts and described it there, more accurately, as the wage of "skilled workmen"; *The Civil War in France (First Draft)*, MEGA I.22: 57 / MECW 22: 488.

174. Hunt, *Political Ideas of Marx and Engels*, 2: 367, see also 132–34.

175. J. G. A. Wirth, *Die Rechte des deutschen Volkes: Eine Vertheidigungsrede vor den Assisen zu Landau* (Nancy, 1833), 47, 57–58.

176. Arnold Ruge, "Wahl-Manifest der radicalen Reformpartei für Deutschland," *Die Reform*, no. 16 (16 April 1848): 124.

The inspiration behind these ideas was often an interpretation of ancient Athenian democracy where nearly all public administrative officials (magistracies) were selected from the citizen body as a whole. That system was based on the principle of rotation, which held that a citizen was not simply someone with the right to choose their rulers but someone who rules and is ruled in turn, an idea founded on a "deep distrust of professionalism" and the belief that "every political function was performable by non-specialists unless there were compelling reasons to think otherwise."[177] That ancient ideal had, as we explored in chapter 2, inspired the young Marx. He had admiringly written of how, "in Greece, the *res publica* is the real private affair of the citizens" and how they had achieved a praiseworthy "substantial unity between the state and people."[178] Marx similarly applauded the Commune for having achieved the "reabsorption of the State power by society, as its own living forces instead of as forces controlling and subduing it, by the popular masses themselves," and that "[t]he Communal Constitution would have restored to the social body all the forces hitherto absorbed by the state parasite."[179] The Commune can thus be seen as a concrete realization of the "reabsorption" of the separated political sphere and thus the unification between civil society and the political sphere that Marx envisioned in the *Kritik*.

An important difference, however, between Marx's social republic and democratic Athens is that Marx only discusses selecting officials via elections or legislative appointment, whereas Athens made extensive use of sortition. The overwhelming majority of Athens's public officials were selected by random selection by lot rather than elections. This was regarded by Athenians as a defining component of democracy, with Aristotle commenting that "the appointment of magistrates by lot is thought to be democratic, and the election of them oligarchical."[180] As Bernard Manin has brilliantly charted, this was a long-prevailing view about democracy. It was only from the foundation of representative governments at the end of the eighteenth century onward that democracy came to be associated with elections, while the idea of lotteries slipped nearly entirely from political practice and constitutional thought.[181] It is thus unsurprising that Marx makes no reference to sortition and instead focuses upon elections (indeed, it was not until sometime after Marx's death, at the end of nineteenth century, that the political importance of lotteries to

177. Manin, *Principles of Representative Government*, 28–32.

178. Marx, *Kritik, MEGA* I.2: 34 / *MECW* 3: 32.

179. Marx, *The Civil War in France (First Draft)*, *MEGA* I.22: 56 / *MECW* 22: 487; *The Civil War in France, MEGA* I.22: 141 / *MECW* 22: 333.

180. Aristotle, *Politics*, in *The Politics and the Constitution of Athens*, ed. Stephen Everson (Cambridge: Cambridge University Press, 1996), bk. IV, ch. 9, 1294b 7–9.

181. Manin, *Principles of Representative Government*, 79–93.

the Athenian system began to be understood).[182] In contrast to this long historical neglect, sortition has in recent years increasingly come to be seen as a promising way to counteract the oligarchic tendencies of representative government.[183] Much of that interest has focused on the use of lotteries in legislative settings, but there have been some suggestive attempts to consider how they might be used to expand democratic participation and oversight in public administration.[184] Given some of the practical concerns associated with electing so many public officials, selecting at least some of them by lot may be one way of realizing Marx's underlying vision of public administration carried out by all citizens rather than elite bureaucrats.

An End to Politics?

There is an old expectation and hope in socialist thought that the grueling political struggles required to overthrow capitalism will one day give way to a society that has no need for politics and political institutions. In his 1890 utopian novel, *News from Nowhere*, William Morris depicted the journey of the protagonist William Guest, who was transported to the future socialist society of the twenty-second century. Guest is taken on a tour of London to see the myriad ways that society has been transformed. Private property has of course been abolished, and the police, prisons, and law courts have all disappeared along with it. The harsh divide between town and countryside has been overcome, with London's urban spaces now interspersed with woods and gardens. Children are not forced into schools but are left to play and learn as they see fit. People are no longer tied to repetitive and unfulfilling work, but instead engage in a flourishing variety of productive and artistic activities. The goods and services they produce are rendered freely, so that the socialist citizens of the future are left repeatedly puzzled when Guest tries to pay for them. In the chapter "Concerning Government," Guest learns from his guide Old Hammond that "we have no longer anything which you, a native of another planet, would call a government" and that the Parliament building has been converted to a more useful function

182. Ibid., 24–27.

183. For instance, McCormick, *Machiavellian Democracy*, chapter 7; John Gastil and Erik Olin Wright, eds., *Legislature by Lot: Transformative Designs for Deliberative Governance* (London: Verso, 2019).

184. See Chiara Cordelli, *The Privatized State* (Princeton: Princeton University Press, 2020), 111–12; and the helpful critique in Anna Stilz, "Kantian Democracy and Public Administration," *Critical Review of International Social and Political Philosophy* 26, no. 2 (2022): 240–42. See also Jerry Frug, "Administrative Democracy," *The University of Toronto Law Journal* 40, no. 3 (1990): 572–73, 580–81; Samuel Bagg, "Sortition as Anti-Corruption: Popular Oversight against Elite Capture," *American Journal of Political Science* 68, no. 1 (2024): 100–102.

as a "dung-market." Indeed, a subsequent chapter "Concerning Politics," consists solely of the following exchange:

Said I: "How do you manage with politics?"

Said Hammond, smiling: "I am glad that it is of *me* that you ask that question; I do believe that anybody else would make you explain yourself, or try to do so, till you were sickened of asking questions. Indeed, I believe I am the only man in England who would know what you mean; and since I know, I will answer your question briefly by saying that we are very well off as to politics,—because we have none. If ever you make a book out of this conversation, put this in a chapter by itself, of the model of old Horrebow's Snakes in Iceland."[185]

Hammond's reference is to an eccentric feature of Niels Horrebow's *The Natural History of Iceland* (1758), where the chapter "Concerning Snakes" notably consists of a single sentence: "No snakes of any kind are to be met with throughout the whole island."[186] Thus, according to Hammond, just as *Iceland* has *no snakes*, socialism has *no politics*.

The question I want to end this chapter with is to what extent did Marx share this conception of the end of politics in a future communist society? Or, to put the question differently, do the political institutions of the social republic that Marx endorsed for the *transition* to communism continue to exist in the *future*—at some point, in other words, does the social republic end? Marx himself gestured toward the possibility of some kind of difference between the "future body politic (*Staatswesen*) of the communist society" and the "political transition period in which the state can be nothing but *the revolutionary dictatorship of the proletariat.*" As he put it,

The question then arises: what transformation will the body politic (*Staatswesen*) undergo in communist society? In other words, what social functions will remain in existence there that are analogous to present state functions (*Staatsfunktionen*)? This question can only be answered scientifically ...[187]

185. William Morris, *News from Nowhere or an Epoch of Rest: Being Some Chapters from a Utopian Romance*, ed. David Leopold (Oxford: Oxford University Press, 2003[1890]), 64–65, 73.

186. N. Horrebow, *The Natural History of Iceland* (London, 1758), 91. This well-known chapter is, however, the result of the English translation cutting short the paragraph-long entry in the original Danish edition; see Edwards Charlton, "Snakes Conspicuous by Their Absence," *Notes and Queries* 4, no. 3 (1870): 186–87.

187. Marx, "Kritik des Gothaer Programms," *MEGA* I.25: 21-22 / *MECW* 24: 95. As Guy Mor has perceptively noted, when Marx discusses the future polity he uses *Staatswesen* rather than *Staat*, which is missed in the *MECW* translation. See Guy Mor, "Whither the State? The

But rather than attempt to answer the question "scientifically" (by which Marx means through rigorous study), Marx immediately changed the topic and failed to engage in further speculation.

The question is of importance to our study because though Marx's writings on the Commune reintegrated core ideas from his early republicanism (most importantly popular delegacy and deprofessionalized public administration), it might be thought that a continuing source of divergence is Marx's supposed belief that these (and indeed all other) political institutions eventually disappear once communism is fully developed. Indeed, few things might be thought more alien to a republican sensibility than an endorsement of a society without politics. To return to the tripartite temporal conception of antipolitics we introduced in chapter 4, it might be thought that while Marx challenged socialism's traditional antipolitics when it came to contemporary analysis and transitional strategies, he simply transplanted that antipolitical commitment into the future. In Alan Megill's presentation, Marx was an "antipolitical political activist," who was committed to politics *"for now* . . . But Marx held that politics and the political state will not exist once socialism has been achieved." Megill maintains that "since republicanism involves seeing politics as an essential part of human existence" and as there is no evidence that Marx ever believed in a "politics that would persist" then "any claim for a 'republican' commitment on Marx's part at any point in his career is highly questionable."[188]

That Marx believed in the end of politics is certainly one of the standard elements in textbook presentations of his ideas. Jon Elster argues that in Marx's "final stage of communism, all political institutions disappear" and that communist society becomes so "transparent that the need for politics itself withers away."[189] Alan Gilbert similarly presents Marx as having "projected a communist 'withering away of politics.'"[190] Alan Ryan goes so far as to assert that Marx's "most striking claim about politics was that in a fully socialized economy there

---

Abolition of the State in Marx and Engels," unpublished manuscript, 33; available at: https://politics.huji.ac.il/sites/default/files/politics/files/whither_the_state.pdf.

188. Allan Megill, *Karl Marx: The Burden of Reason (Why Marx Rejected Politics and the Market)* (Lanham: Rowman & Littlefield, 2002), 57, 99–100, 120.

189. Jon Elster, *An Introduction to Karl Marx* (Cambridge: Cambridge University Press, 1986), 165, 179.

190. Alan Gilbert, "Political Philosophy: Marx and Radical Democracy," in *The Cambridge Companion to Marx*, ed. Terrell Carver (Cambridge: Cambridge University Press, 1991), 169. Gilbert's use of quotation marks here is misleading; the phrase "withering away of politics" is found nowhere in Marx's writings.

would be no politics."[191] Such claims are usually presented (as in the case with Elster, Megill, and Ryan) as points of serious weakness in Marx's thought. In her important defense of law in a socialist society, Christine Sypnowich contrasts her approach with Marx, who, she argues, believed in the "dissolution of the legal and political spheres."[192] Versions of the criticism also feature in modern republican responses to Marx. Hannah Arendt condemned Marx for having "predict[ed] and hope[d] for the 'withering away' of the whole public realm."[193] Richard Bellamy, otherwise sympathetic to what Marx has to offer republican theory, argues that Marx "notoriously made the incorrect inference that collective ownership of the means of production would remove the need for politics."[194]

In order to engage with this critical consensus, it is crucial to first make a distinction (too often elided in the literature) between the *end of the state* and the *end of politics and political institutions*. That Marx believed in the former is not in question (though what he meant by that requires specification). What is, as I will try to show, much more questionable is whether he also believed in the end of politics.[195] Politics is a thorny subject to define, but for our purposes we can take the question of the end of politics to mean whether a communist society has a need for and consequently has institutions in place for "interpersonal deliberation, negotiation and authoritative decision-making in matters of public scope or concern" (the apt summation given by Norman Geras).[196] The potential differences between this and the end of the state might already suggest itself. But to come to a firmer grasp of the issue, we need to make a further distinction between two conceptions of the state in Marx and Engels's writings: first, as a hierarchical, professionalized political structure; and second, as a political structure of organized coercion.[197]

191. Alan Ryan, *On Marx: Revolutionary and Utopian* (New York: Liveright, 2014), 43. Megill similarly argues that "the most striking thing about Marx's attitude toward politics remains his wish to get beyond it"; Megill, *Karl Marx: The Burden of Reason*, 120.

192. Christine Sypnowich, *The Concept of Socialist Law* (Oxford: Clarendon Press, 1990), 1.

193. Hannah Arendt, *The Human Condition*, 2nd ed. (Chicago: University of Chicago Press, 1998 [1958]), 60.

194. Richard Bellamy, "Being Liberal with Republicanism's Radical Heritage: Review of Philip Pettit's Republicanism," *Res Publica* 8, no. 3 (2002): 272.

195. For an idiosyncratic attempt to show that Marx believed in the end of politics but not the end of the state, see Richard Adamiak, "The 'Withering Away' of the State: A Reconsideration," *The Journal of Politics* 32, no. 1 (1970): 3–18.

196. Norman Geras, "Seven Types of Obloquy: Travesties of Marxism," *Socialist Register* 26 (1990): 27. I will assume that the end of politics is closely tied to the end of political institutions, in that the former justifies the latter.

197. See the illuminating discussion in Hunt, *The Political Ideas of Marx and Engels*, 2: 231–46.

While each of them seems to have understood the end of the state as the overcoming of both of these features, Marx and Engels placed different degrees of emphasis on them. For Marx, the end of the state was primarily connected with the replacement of the state as a professional body with public administration instead carried out by the citizens themselves. It was this feature of the Commune that led Marx to praise it for "break[ing] the modern State power" and for being "a Revolution against the *State* itself . . . a resumption by the people for the people, of its own social life."[198] The Commune was, however, still a state in the sense of being a body of organized coercion (it continued to have a civic militia, police and judiciary—albeit deprofessionalized). Marx was much less animated by this aspect of the state disappearing, and it is absent from his own discussions of the end of the state.[199]

Engels undoubtedly shared Marx's view that the end of the state was partly constituted by the end of its professional character. He similarly assessed the Paris Commune as having "ceased to be a state in the true sense of the term (*im eigentlichen Sinne*)" because of this feature. (He consequently thought it better to "replace [talk of the] *State* with 'Gemeinwesen,' a good old German word that can very well stand in for the French 'Commune.'"[200]) Furthermore, Engels endorsed "the shattering of the existing state power and its replacement with a new, truly democratic [body]," arguing that it was this professionalized feature of the state that must be "lopped off at once." After this initial stage, "the state . . . as a machine for the suppression of one class by another" eventually disappears, as "a generation reared in new free societal conditions is able to dismiss the whole state rubbish (*Staatsplunder*)."[201] Engels thus suggested

198. Marx, *The Civil War in France*, MEGA I.22: 141 / MECW 22: 333; *The Civil War in France (First Draft)*, MEGA I.22: 55 / MECW 22: 486.

199. A partial exception may be an unsigned review for which the single or joint authorship of Marx and Engels remains unclear, where the end of the state is associated with how "the organised power of one class to hold down another falls away by itself"; Marx and Engels, "[Review:] Emile de Girardin, *Le Socialisme et l'impôt* (Paris, 1850)," MEGA I.10: 297 / MECW 10: 333. The MEGA editors refrain from a definitive judgment but suggest there is some basis for thinking that Marx may have been the sole author; see MEGA I.10: 876. But even if we assign the review to Marx, it is not clear that the end of the "organized power of one class to hold down another" is necessarily a claim about the end of coercion, as a polity could have coercive laws that are not based on class domination. I am grateful to William Clare Roberts for suggesting this.

200. Engels to August Bebel, 18–28 March 1875, MEW 34: 128–29; MECW 45: 63–64. As we previously discussed, *Gemeinwesen* can be variously translated as "community," "commonwealth," or "polity."

201. Engels, "Einleitung," in *Der Bürgerkrieg in Frankreich*, 3rd German edition (1891), MEGA I.32: 15-16 / MECW 27: 190. Note that Engels's description of the end of the state as a "machine for the suppression of one class by another" could also be read as a claim about the end of

a two-stage revolutionary process whereby the state as professional body is removed immediately, followed by a longer process of its coercive aspects disappearing.[202]

It was this second aspect that formed the crux of Engels's most famous discussion of the end of the state, which he first introduced in his immensely influential 1877–78 *Herrn Eugen Dührings Umwälzung der Wissenschaft* (*Mr. Eugen Dühring's Revolution of Science*), commonly known as *Anti-Dühring*. Engels here argued that the state was in all historical modes of production "an organization of the respective exploiting class . . . for the coercive subjection (*Niederhaltung*) of the exploited class." Since a communist society, however, is a classless society, this coercive function is no longer required: "as soon as there is no societal class being kept in suppression . . . there is nothing to be repressed, nothing that makes a special repressive force, a state, necessary." And so, Engels concluded, the state comes to an end and "The government of persons is replaced by the government of things and the conduct of production processes. The free society does not need and cannot tolerate a 'state' between itself and its members."[203] Here, in this less familiar version of the passage, we can still detect, in the phrasing of the second sentence, a trace of a conception of the state as an elite, professional body separated from society. That meaning disappears, however, in the much more famous version of the passage found in Engels's reformulation of it in *Die Entwicklung des Sozialismus von der Utopie zur Wissenschaft* (*The Development of Socialism from Utopia to Science*) (1883), a popular pamphlet formed out of three chapters from *Anti-Dühring*.[204] Here Engels argued that:

The interference of the state power (*Staatsgewalt*) in social relations becomes, in one domain after another, superfluous and falls asleep by itself (*schläft dann von selbst ein*). The government of persons is replaced by the administration of things and the conduct of production processes. The state is not "abolished," *it dies out* (*es stirbt ab*).[205]

---

coercion based on class domination and not coercion as such (see the discussion in n199, above). But Engels's other remarks on the end of the state (cited in the following discussion) do suggest that he means the end of all coercive institutions.

202. Hunt, *Political Ideas of Marx and Engels*, 2: 235, 246.

203. Engels, *Anti-Dühring*, 1st ed., *MEGA* I.27: 444–45. The *MECW* translates the altered 3rd German edition from 1894; see *MECW* 25: 268.

204. The pamphlet was first produced in an 1880 French edition, but here Engels kept the original formulation from the first edition of *Anti-Dühring*; see Engels, *Socialisme, utopique et socialisme scientifique*, *MEGA* I.27: 576. The reformulated version was integrated into subsequent editions of *Anti-Dühring*; see *MEGA* I.27: 535.

205. Engels, *Die Entwicklung des Sozialismus von der Utopia zur Wissenschaft*, *MEGA* I.27: 620. The *MECW* reproduces the 1892 translation of the text by Edward Aveling, which (though

(In subsequent English-language discussion, the idea that the state "dies out" has usually, but less accurately, been translated as the state "withers away" or the "withering away" of the state.)[206] In this reformulated version of the passage, the state that dies out (or withers away) is understood only in terms of the state as a body of organized coercion. That meaning is also paramount in a contemporaneous letter by Engels, in which he addresses the "gradual dissolution and ultimate disappearance of that political organization called *the State*" and argues that "With the disappearance of a wealthy minority the necessity for an armed repressive or state-force disappears also."[207]

The difference in emphasis between Marx and Engels is also evident in their discussion of how the end of the state relates to freedom. That can be seen in their subtly differing reactions to the 1875 Gotha Program, which united two competing German workers' parties to create the forerunner of the Sozialdemokratische Partei Deutschlands (Social Democratic Party of Germany). Both Marx and Engels were heavily critical of the program's lack of more ambitious democratic demands and its endorsement of a "free state (*freien Staat*)." Engels first argued that the Gotha Program included no reference to "[a]dministration through the people" or even what he argued was "the first condition of all freedom"—that state officials are subordinated to the law and the courts. Engels thus made some connection between freedom and transforming the state's institutions through popular control. But Engels continued that the "free state" was a socialist demand that made no sense, since the "state is only a transitional institution . . . to suppress one's enemies by force," and "as soon as there can be any question of freedom, the state as such ceases to exist."[208] Here Engels equated the full realization of (political) freedom with the end of

---

authorized by Engels) does not include the suggestive phrase in the German that the "state falls asleep by itself," and instead translates it as "the state dies out of itself"; see *MECW* 24: 321. The idea that the state falls asleep has the interesting (but likely unintended) implication that it could awaken once again.

206. The authorized English translation included the correct translation that the state "*dies out*"; see Engels, *Socialism: Utopian and Scientific*, trans. Edward Aveling (London: Swan Sonnenschein, 1892), 76–77; as did the pirated American edition, *The Development of Socialism from Science to Utopia*, trans. [Daniel De Long & H. Vogt] (New York: The People, 1892), 24. The phrase "withers away" seems to have entered English language discussions via a retranslation of the (accurate) Russian translation of Engels's passage that appears in Lenin's *Gosudarstvo i revolutsia* (*State and Revolution*) (1917); see V. I. Ulianov (N. Lenin), *The State and Revolution: Marxist Teaching on the State and the Task of the Proletariat in the Revolution* (London: British Socialist Party and the Socialist Labour Press, 1919), 19–21.

207. Engels to Philipp von Patten, 18 April 1883, *MEW* 36: 11 / *MECW* 47: 10.

208. Engels to August Bebel, 18–28 March 1875, *MEW* 34: 128–29 / *MECW* 45: 63–64.

the state as a coercive force. The conception of freedom appealed to by Engels here simply amounts to the absence of coercive interference. By comparison, in Marx's response to the Gotha Program, he too objected to the demand for a "free state." But Marx justified this by arguing that "freedom consists in transforming the state from an organ superimposed upon society into one completely subordinate to it."[209] The realization of (political) freedom is thus, for Marx, about establishing the right kind of control over the state (or the polity that replaces it). Freedom here amounts not necessarily to the absence of coercive interference, but potentially (without stretching Marx's remarks too far) to the absence of interference uncontrolled by the people.

The differences between Marx and Engels on this question are important and ones (as we touched on in chapter 3) that can be traced right back to their early writings on the state. But they are also differences of degree. Marx may not have focused on the end of the state as a coercive body in his own writings, but he also does not seem to have opposed Engels's views on the matter. Marx extensively assisted Engels in his writing of *Anti-Dühring*, wrote the foreword to the (French edition) of *Die Entwicklung des Sozialismus von der Utopie zur Wissenschaft*, and was willing to associate himself with the idea in some of their joint publications. There is thus some basis for thinking that Marx was open to the idea that the repressive aspects of the state might gradually disappear in a future socialist society, and, consequently, he may have been willing to entertain the idea that among the political institutions of the Commune that he had endorsed, those with repressive functions (the civic militia, the reformed police, and perhaps the elected judiciary) would one day become unnecessary and disappear. But that still leaves other key political institutions of the social republic, including that government and administration are carried out by delegates and public officials who are elected and subject to recall. Is there any basis for thinking that Marx thought that these political institutions would also disappear?

A case could be built from textual passages where Marx seems to endorse the end of all political institutions. In the final pages of *Misère de la philosophie* (*The Poverty of Philosophy*), Marx had argued that,

> The working class, in the course of its development, will substitute for the old civil society an association which will exclude classes and their antagonism, and there will be no more political power properly so called (*proprement dit*), since political power is precisely the official expression of antagonism in civil society.[210]

---

209. Marx, "Kritik des Gothaer Programms," *MEGA* I.25: 21 / *MECW* 24: 94.
210. Marx, *Misère de la philosophie*, *MEW* 4: 182 / *MECW* 6: 212.

Similarly, in the *Manifest der Kommunistischen Partei*, Marx and Engels wrote,

> When, in the course of development, class distinctions have disappeared, and all production has been concentrated in the hands of a vast association of the whole nation, the public power will lose its political character. Political power, properly so called (*im eigentlichen Sinne*), is merely the organized power of one class for oppressing another.[211]

Both of these statements might seem like unambiguous endorsements of the end of politics and political institutions and have been frequently read as such. But closer inspection reveals that the matter is not quite so straightforward. As Norman Geras has perceptively identified, these passages do not say that politics comes to an end, but that "political power properly so called" comes to an end.[212] That indicates that Marx and Engels are using "political power" in a stipulative sense—namely, as the "expression of antagonism in civil society" and "the organized power of one class for oppressing another." That suggests that what they mean by the disappearance of politics, in these locutions, is the disappearance of politics based on class. Geras argues that commentators, however, frequently engage in "conceptual elision" between Marx and Engels's use of politics in this stipulative class sense and "politics *tout court*," in the broader sense of deliberation and authoritative decision-making about issues of public concern.[213] Though we might regret Marx and Engels's narrow definition of "politics," that does not mean that they were opposed to the continuation of politics in the broader sense.

A case might instead be built on the presentation of decision-making in communism in the depoliticized language of administration. As we saw in the influential passage from *Anti-Dühring* and *Die Entwicklung des Sozialismus*, Engels predicted that the disappearance of the state would entail that the "government of persons is replaced by the administration of things." Engels was fond of this administrative language. In 1873 he wrote that "public functions will lose their political character and be transformed into the simple administrative

---

211. Marx and Engels, *Manifest der Kommunistischen Partei*, MEW 4: 482 / MECW 6: 505. The 1850 MacFarlane translation interestingly gives this key quote as "Political power in the exact sense of the word," *Red Republican*, no. 23 (23 November 1850): 183.

212. Geras, "Seven Types of Obloquy," 27. Geras also points to several further examples where Marx and Engels qualify the end of the state and politics in similar terms. For a useful collection of the relevant textual locutions, see Hal Draper, "The Death of the State in Marx and Engels," *Socialist Register* 7 (1970): 281–307. For discussion of what might seem to be an exception, see Hunt, *Political Ideas of Marx and Engels*, 2: 234.

213. Geras, "Seven Types of Obloquy," 25, 27. See also William Clare Roberts, *Marx's Inferno: The Political Theory of Capital* (Princeton: Princeton University Press, 2017), 251–55.

functions of watching over the true interests of society."[214] By comparison, Marx showed little enthusiasm for such administrative rhetoric, and it is absent from his own writings. We do, however, find it in work on which they collaborated. In a jointly authored 1872 pamphlet, published in the name of the General Council of the International, they wrote that once the "abolition of classes, is attained, the power of the State . . . disappears, and the functions of government become simple administrative functions."[215] Similarly, in the *Manifest der Kommunistischen Partei*, Marx and Engels expressed support for the utopian socialist proposals for "the conversion of the State into the mere superintendence of production."[216] Thus, similarly to the question of the end of organized coercion, though Marx may himself not have expressed much interest in the idea of administration replacing government, he was happy to go along with Engels's enthusiasms on the matter.

The notoriety of Engels's phrase that the "government of persons is replaced by the administration of things" competes with that of the "dictatorship of the proletariat." The "administration of things" has driven the impression, shared by both opponents and supporters, of communism as a thoroughly depoliticized society, one in which there are no longer any serious matters for debate and deliberation but only straightforward tasks requiring technocratic direction. Isaiah Berlin held that "the meaning of Engels' famous phrase" was that "[w]here ends are agreed, the only questions left are those of means, and these are not political but technical, that is to say, capable of being settled by experts or machines."[217] In *Azbuka Kommunizma (The ABC of Communism)* (1919), one of the most influential statements of pre-Stalinist Bolshevik thought, Nikolai Bukharin portrayed the administration of things in a future communist society in the following celebratory account:

> The main direction will be entrusted to various kinds of book-keeping offices or statistical bureaux. There, from day to day, account will be kept of production and all its needs; there also it will be decided whither workers must be sent, whence they must be taken, and how much work there is to be done . . . [A]ll will work in accordance with the indications of these statistical bureaux. There will be no need for special ministers of State, for

214. Engels, "Dell'Autorità," *MEGA* I.24: 86 / *MECW* 23: 425.

215. Marx and Engels, *Les Prétendues Scissons dans L'Internationale, MEW* 18: 50 / *MECW* 23: 121.

216. Marx and Engels, *Manifest der Kommunistischen Partei, MEW* 4: 491 / *MECW* 6: 516.

217. Isiah Berlin, "Two Concepts of Liberty," in *Liberty*, ed. Henry Hardy (Oxford: Oxford University Press, 2002), 166 (earlier versions of Berlin's essay attributed the "famous phrase" to Saint-Simon).

police and prisons, for laws and decrees—nothing of the sort. Just as in an orchestra all the performers watch the conductor's baton and act accordingly, so here all will consult the statistical reports and will direct their work accordingly.[218]

How much of Berlin's condemnation and Bukharin's celebratory elaboration can actually be found in Engels's original formulation of the "administration of things" replacing the "government of persons"? We can gain some purchase on what Engels meant by looking at the source that Engels himself credited with the initial formulation of the idea: Henri Saint-Simon.[219] Saint-Simon certainly frequently celebrated "superimposing administrative power on government power" and looked forward to a time when "governments will no longer command over men."[220] (The exact formulation used by Engels, however, does not appear in Saint-Simon's writings. As Ben Kafka has interestingly shown, the closest contender seems to be a statement by Auguste Comte, in a text sometimes attributed to Saint-Simon, in which Comte argued that "The government of things replaces that of men (*Le gouvernement des choses remplace celui des hommes*).")[221] But, despite Engels's attribution of the idea to Saint-Simon, there is in fact a crucial difference between them, insufficiently stressed by Engels himself, that is brought to the fore by returning to Engels's earliest writings on government and administration.

As was shown in chapter 3, Engels's initial conversion to socialism was strongly marked by the antipolitical and antidemocratic threads that dominated early socialism. In 1844, aged twenty-three, Engels had enthusiastically

218. Nikolai Bukharin and Evgenii Preobrazhensky, *The ABC of Communism*, ed. E. H. Carr, trans. Eden Paul and Cedar Paul (Harmondsworth: Penguin, 1969), 118, 240 (these sections are those written solely by Bukharin).

219. Engels, *Anti-Dühring*, MEGA I.27: 428 / MECW 25: 246–47; *Die Entwicklung des Sozialismus*, MEGA I.27: 593–94 / MECW 24: 291–92.

220. Henri Saint-Simon, "Lettres de Henri Saint-Simon à un Américain' (1817), in *Henri Saint-Simon, Oeuvres complètes* (hereafter *OCSS*), vol. 2 (Paris: Presses Universitaires de France, 2012), 1488 / *Selected Writings on Science Industry and Social Organisation* (hereafter *Selected Writings*), trans. and ed. Keith Taylor (London: Croom Helm, 1975), 165; Henri Saint-Simon, "De l'organisation sociale: Fragments d'un ouvrage inédit' (1825), *OCSS*, 4: 3084 / *Selected Writings*, 267.

221. Auguste Comte, "Plan des travaux scientifiques nécessaires pour réorganiser la société," in *Système de politique positive*, vol. 1, pt. 1 (Paris: Principaux Libraires, 1824), 117 / "Plan of the Scientific Work Necessary for the Reorganization of Society," in *Early Political Writings*, ed. and trans. H. S. Jones (Cambridge: Cambridge University Press, 1998), 108. See further Ben Kafka, "The Administration of Things: A Genealogy," *West 86th*, 21 May 2012, https://www.west86th .bgc.bard.edu/articles/the-administration-of-things-a-genealogy/.

endorsed "the abolition of all government by force and by majority, and the establishment in its stead of a mere administration," in which "officers of this administration" were chosen "not by a majority of the community at large, but only by those who have a knowledge of the particular kind of work the future officer has to perform."[222] This openly antidemocratic interpretation of a future socialist administration was in keeping with Saint-Simon's ideas that production should not be directed by the people, but by the most capable and knowledgeable, which Saint-Simon confidently believed would reduce the need for government coercion.

When it comes to Engels's later writings on administration, we find that while he continues to foresee an end to government coercion, the antidemocratic references he made in his earlier writings ("government by force and by majority") completely disappear. The later Engels makes no direct statement on *who* is to carry out the "administration of things," but there is little basis for thinking he still agrees with his younger self that it would be carried out by elite administrators. For one, it would be odd if he thought "[a]dministration through the people" was a necessary feature for the transition to communism but not for its final form.[223] The idea of popular administration is also implicit in Engels's original formulation of the famous phrase in *Anti-Dühring*, where the "government of persons is replaced by the government of things" is justified in terms of the idea that a "free society does not need and cannot tolerate a 'state' between itself and its members."[224] Moreover, in the essay where Engels welcomes the transformation of government into "simple administrative functions," he simultaneously stresses that authoritative decisions over production will still be necessary and carried out inside factories by "a delegate in charge of each branch of labor or, if possible, by a majority vote."[225] We could also point to Marx and Engels's statement making fun of socialists who propose "in place of the state, a committee of administrators."[226] There is thus little reason to think that the "administration of things" in the future communist society would be the preserve of elite administrators rather than the people as a whole.[227] Berlin's suggestion that the "administration of things" amounted to rule by "experts or machines" is thus misleading. In comparison, Bukharin

222. Engels, "'The 'Times' on German Communism," *MEGA* I.3: 560–61 / *MECW* 3: 413.

223. Engels to August Bebel, 18–28 March 1875, *MEW* 34: 128 / *MECW* 45: 63.

224. Engels, *Anti-Dühring*, 1st ed., *MEGA* I.27: 445.

225. Engels, "Dell'Autorità," *MEGA* I.24: 85 / *MECW* 23: 423.

226. Marx and Engels, "[Review:] *Le Socialisme et l'impôt*," *MEGA* I.10: 295 / *MECW* 10: 332.

227. That is certainly how Engels was understood by contemporaries. William Morris argued that it was necessary "to give all men a share in the responsibility of the administration of things which I hope will take the place of the government of persons"; see "How Shall We Live Then?'

recognized that the "administration of things" had to involve the "participation of the masses" in "continuous rotation." But his extravagant elaboration of "book-keeping offices" and "statistical bureaux" is just that—*his* elaboration.[228] What Engels meant to indicate by the idea that the "government of persons is replaced by the administration of things," beyond that organized coercion would disappear and that administration would be carried out by the people, remains largely unspecified.

The unspecified nature of the politics and political institutions of a communist society was not because Marx and Engels "simply forgot to portray future developments in any detail," but is rather the deliberate consequence of their objection to providing detailed blueprints and plans for a socialist society.[229] In just one of many injunctions, Marx famously claimed that he was concerned with the "critical analysis of existing circumstances" and not "writing recipes . . . for the cook-shops (*Garküche*) of the future."[230] This "Marxian utopophobia," as David Leopold argues, was founded on a (questionable) set of beliefs that such plans were normatively undemocratic (because they limit the choices of future people), epistemologically impossible (because we do not know what the future will look like), and, especially, that they were empirically unnecessary (because the future society will emerge out of an unfolding historical process rather than a prescriptive design).[231] Marx and Engels believed that their avoidance of detailed institutional plans and focus on a critique of existing circumstances and trends was an important element in what distinguished their *scientific* socialism from what they identified as the *utopian* socialism of Saint-Simon, Fourier, Owen, and their followers.[232] Marx

(1889), in Paul Meier, "An Unpublished Lecture of William Morris," *International Review of Social History* 16, no. 2 (1971): 233.

228. A further difference from Engels and Marx is Bukharin's position that a key hindrance to popular administration was the people's current "imperfect development, the lack of enlightenment . . . [the] half-savage condition," which made it necessary for the party to "raise the general cultural level of the workers and peasants"; Bukharin and Preobrazhensky, *The ABC of Communism*, 237–40, see also 439. That begins to reproduce the Blanquist idea that a dictatorship is justified because it educates the people to be ready for political rule. That idea is absent from Marx and Engels, who emphasize the people's already existing administrative capacity.

229. David Leopold, *The Young Karl Marx: German Philosophy, Modern Politics, and Human Flourishing* (Cambridge: Cambridge University Press, 2007), 279–80.

230. Marx, "Nachwort," in *Das Kapital*, 2nd ed., *MEGA* II.6: 704 / *MECW* 35: 17.

231. David Leopold, "On Marxian Utopophobia," *Journal of the History of Philosophy* 54, no. 1 (2016): 111–34.

232. David Leopold, "The Structure of Marx and Engels' Considered Account of Utopian Socialism," *History of Political Thought* 26, no. 3 (2005): 454–56, 461–66.

and perhaps especially Engels occasionally breached their own injunction against future institutional speculation (as is discussed below). But on the whole they kept to their commitment and deliberately provided scant details about the future society. It is thus unsurprising—to go back to our opening discussion— that Marx failed to engage further with the question of "what transformation will the body politic (*Staatswesen*) undergo in communist society?"[233]

This has not stopped various commentators from providing confident accounts of what the Marxian future society looks like in terms of politics and political institutions. Bertell Ollman claims that though Marx "never gives a full answer, it is clear what his answer would be" to the question of political institutions, arguing that Marx envisaged there being *no legislature* (because "the people of communism are agreed on all the subjects which could possibly come before a parliament"), *no judiciary* (because the "judicial arm of government, too, is based on an assumption of necessary conflict between people"), *no laws* (because "where social norms are accepted and heeded by all, this function no longer exists") and that *elections* are "probably uncontested" (because "everyone agrees on matters of policy"), leaving only the administration of production.[234] Allan Megill is similarly confident that Marx saw no need for "processes of political deliberation, negotiation, and compromise" for future socialist citizens to "decide what arrangements they are going to support and what actions they are going to undertake in their lives together as human beings." Marx supposedly believed that "science (natural and social) will tell us, unequivocally and without room for doubt or disagreement, what needs to be done. In other words, matters of state and administration can be so scientifically structured that deliberation will be unnecessary . . . Thus Marx concluded that politics is *unneeded*."[235]

If Marx (and Engels) had provided sufficient reflection for these confident conclusions, then their own antiutopian commitments would be in doubt. Nor are these conclusions particularly plausible (let alone charitable) extrapolations from what Marx does say. The idea that there would be no need for institutions to handle deliberation and disagreement because socialism would involve a nearly complete identity of interests and opinions, conflicts, as Geras argues, with Marx's repeated suggestion that communism would involve an "unprecedented flourishing of human individuality."[236] The idea that Marx thought that science would provide decisive answers to all societal questions

233. Marx, "Kritik des Gothaer Programms," *MEGA* I.25: 21-22 / *MECW* 24: 95.

234. Bertell Ollman, "Marx's Vision of Communism: A Reconstruction," *Critique* 8, no. 1 (1977): 32–33. See also the list in David Held, *Models of Democracy*, 3rd ed. (Cambridge: Polity, 2006), 112.

235. Megill, *Karl Marx: The Burden of Reason*, 58.

236. Geras, "Seven Types of Obloquy," 26.

is unsupported by any of the suggestive remarks Marx makes about science in the future society. When Marx, for instance, wrote that "Science can only play its genuine part in the Republic of Labour," he did not mean that science will determine all decisions in communism, he meant that it will no longer be perverted as an "instrument of class rule" by having to serve the interests and whims of the state and capital.[237] Insofar as Marx addressed the question of deliberative forums and elections in a future society, we have only a few cryptic remarks from his (unpublished) notes on Bakunin's *Gosudarstvennost' i anarkhiia* (*Statism and Anarchy*) (1873). There he said that there would be elections, but they would lose their "present political character," which, given the specific meaning he attached to "political" (explored above), implies that they would no longer be contested on the basis of class, not that they would be uncontested. It may also be a reference to elections losing their present character of establishing a body of representatives uncontrolled by the people who elected them (perhaps because in the future polity they are subjected to the mechanisms of imperative mandates, recall, and short terms of office). Marx further suggests that all members of society will "administer the common interests" through what he calls "the self-government of the communities," perhaps (though we cannot know for sure) a reference to the federal electoral structures and popular administration he defended with the Commune.[238]

Thus, what little Marx has to say suggests he did not think a future communist society would have no institutions (or need) for deliberation and authoritative decision-making about matters of public concern. In the pointed summary of Richard Hunt, there is scant evidence for thinking that Marx thought it possible or even desirable for humans to "live together like herds of animals without any conscious organization at all."[239] Engels's repeated refrain (supported by Marx) that organized coercion comes to an end does, however, imply that some institutions—those with repressive functions—disappear. It might be hard to imagine a society where politics is not accompanied by coercion, but it is not impossible to do so. It might involve something like people voluntarily submitting themselves to authoritative decision-making processes that they have democratically participated in. That is perhaps a "a highly utopian expectation," but it is "nonetheless a different expectation from that of an end of politics, in the broad sense."[240] (William Morris, after comparing politics in socialism to snakes in Iceland, in fact outlines an iterative deliberative process whereby

237. Marx, *The Civil War in France (First Draft)*, MEGA I.22: 64 / MECW 22: 496.

238. Marx, "Exzerpte aus Bakunin," *MEW* 18: 635 / *MECW* 24: 519.

239. Hunt, *The Political Ideas of Marx and Engels*, 2: 246.

240. Geras, "Seven Types of Obloquy," 28. See also Hunt, *Political Ideas of Marx and Engels*, 2: 248.

members of the future socialist community first try to come to consensual decisions and then turn to majority vote if consensus cannot be reached, with the minority then voluntarily giving way.[241])

The overwhelming portrayal of Marx as definitively committed to the end of all politics and political institutions is unsustainable in the face of a proper investigation of what Marx had to say and consideration of what we mean by the end of the state, politics, and political institutions. The related claim that Marx diverges from republicanism in the long run (despite his commitment to republican political institutions in what we might call the short and medium term) is also untenable. Marx seems to have believed that at least some of the political institutions of the social republic would continue to be a feature of a future socialist society. A claim about Marx's divergence from republicanism cannot be made on this basis.

A more plausible position is that Marx's distance from republicanism (in this regard) is not that he thought politics and political institutions would end but that he was opposed to sustained reflection of the question. Marx's anti-utopian commitments mean that there is very little evidence on the nature of future political institutions or discussion of why politics would continue to feature in a socialist society. We are stuck with sifting through ambiguous private notes on other authors for potential clues, rather than an even halfway systematic discussion of the necessity, let alone desirability, of politics and political institutions. This opposition to sustained and detailed reflection about the nature of political institutions of a future communist society, or whether politics will be a permanent feature of that society, is the more accurate position to consider as the point at which Marx diverges from republicanism.

What republican reasons might there be for thinking politics is a permanent feature of human society, even a classless one? Such a discussion is complicated by the fact that republicanism has not, in general, accepted the communist premise of a classless society.[242] But that does not foreclose the possibility that republicanism could provide some resources for thinking through the question. One republican consideration, not very popular today, might be that there is inherent value to political participation.[243] The early republican Marx certainly thought that a desire for participation in public decision-making was an important part of our human nature and that its denial was one cause of our alienation

241. Morris, *News from Nowhere*, 76–77.

242. Vincent Harting, "An Egalitarian Case for Class-Specific Political Institutions," *Political Theory* 51, no. 5 (2023): 853–54; Camila Vergara, *Systemic Corruption: Constitutional Ideas for an Anti-Oligarchic Republic* (Princeton: Princeton University Press, 2020), 113–14.

243. For typical criticisms, see John Rawls, *Justice as Fairness: A Restatement*, ed. Erin Kelly (Cambridge: Belknap Press, 2001), 142–45.

from the modern state. That idea never reemerged in Max's thought, even with his democratic enthusiasms about the Commune. He held that though the Commune had rightly "supplied the Republic with the basis of really democratic institutions . . . neither cheap government nor the 'true Republic' was its ultimate aim; they were its mere concomitants" of the ultimate aim of the "economical emancipation of Labour."[244] We do not need to return to a full-blown Aristotelian view about the centrality of politics to the good life to think that democratic institutions are more than "mere concomitants" of economic emancipation. The commitment to political democracy springs from the same source as the commitment to economic democracy: that people should have control over the structures and forces that shape their lives.

A second consideration is a republican resistance to the idea that political conflict can be reduced to class. Karl Heinzen took communists to task for believing the "chimera, that man, when he is no longer spellbound by the addiction to property, completely puts aside all hostile passions."[245] He thought that this misconception led to the communist belief that once class was removed, there would be "nothing left but a so-called *administration* (*Verwaltung*), an accounting system, a book-keeping system, etc." Because communists started "exclusively from material interests," they could only conceive of a "state form" in terms of the administration of material interests.[246] Heinzen did not elaborate on what nonclass sources of "hostile passions" there might be, but a familiar list might include religious and philosophical differences; ethnic and racial discrimination; oppression based on gender and sexuality; discrimination against those with differing mental and physical abilities; conflicting national, regional, and local loyalties; and attitudes to the natural environment. Less familiar ones might also include the moral and political status of nonhuman animals and artificial intelligence, and beyond that, forms of social antagonism that we are not even aware of today. All of these (as well as simple individual divergent preferences) could be expected to lead to sustained differences on what actions and projects a socialist society should undertake and how it should prioritize competing considerations and restricted resources (even if the latter are assumed to be abundant, it does not seem feasible that they are unlimited).[247] We might expect that taking class out of the equation might take the sting out of some of these social

244. Marx, *The Civil War in France*, MEGA I.22: 142 / *MECW* 22: 334.

245. K. Heinzen, "Gegen die Kommunisten," in *Die Opposition*, ed. Karl Heinzen (Mannheim: Heinrich Hoff, 1846), 66.

246. Ibid., 69.

247. Though Marx believed that communism required a degree of abundance, the kind of unlimited "superabundance" view often attributed to him is an exaggeration of the textual evidence; see Jan Kandiyali, "What Makes Communism Possible? The Self-Realisation

cleavages and antagonisms (if it is even possible or desirable to disentangle overcoming class from the overcoming of these other oppressions, which I doubt). But the broader point is that even without class, the plurality of conceptions of the good life means that there will always be societal disagreement over the nature of communal life. That need not be regretted but instead should be embraced as one reason for why we need political institutions.

Finally, there is a republican skepticism toward the idea that it is possible, even in a classless or broadly classless society, to completely remove the drive to reintroduce class hierarchies. Here it might be instructive to delve further back in the history of republicanism, to the thought Machiavelli. Machiavelli did not of course believe in a classless society, but he did believe that large degrees of material inequality were corrosive to a republic and that drastic measures were required to cow its oligarchic enemies. What is alien to Machiavelli's political theory is the idea that greater material equality might result in the republic no longer having to guard itself against its enemies who want to reestablish inequality. That is partly because of Machiavelli's pessimistic account of human nature. Machiavelli believed we had an insatiable, corruptible, and ambitious desire for greater property, status, and honours. At the same time, Machiavelli argued that our ability to acquire these goods was limited by scarce resources and the fickleness of fortune. The tension between these facts means that conflict is the inevitable result:

> whenever the necessity for fighting is taken away from them [men], they fight for the sake of ambition, which is so powerful a passion in the human breast that, no matter the rank to which a man may rise, he never abandons it. The reason is that nature has created men in such a way that they can desire everything but are unable to obtain everything, so that their desire is always greater than their power of acquisition, and discontent with what they possess and lack of satisfaction are the result.[248]

Machiavelli's point was that the absolute scarcity of resources is not the only cause of this conflict. His argument was that human ambition is relational and positional—that humans desire to have *greater* property, status, and honors than others.

The implication for a classless society, even one with greater material abundance that allows enough for all, is that there would be a lingering motivation

Interpretation," *Politics, Philosophy & Economics* (2023), https://journals.sagepub.com/doi/10 .1177/1470594X231219764.

248. Machiavelli, *Discorsi sopra la prima deca di Tito Livio*, in *Opere I: Primi Scritti Politici*, ed. Corrado Vivanti (Torino: Einaudi-Gallimard, 1997) / *Discourses on Livy*, ed. and trans Julia Conaway Bondanella and Peter Bondanella (Oxford: Oxford University Press, 1997), book I, chapter 37.

to have even more than others. Marx believed (plausibly, we might think) that human nature was not immutable and that communist society would have a significant effect on the motivations and desires of its citizens.[249] But even if this ambitious and corruptible aspect of human nature can be significantly ameliorated, one insight we can take from Machiavelli is that it might not be possible to remove it entirely. If that is indeed the case, then it would mean that the danger posed by the human drive to reestablish inequalities in property and status is a permanent feature of human society. It was because Machiavelli thought this was such an ingrained feature of human nature that he believed that if a republic wanted to maintain its liberty it had to design its political institutions to constantly guard against this threat. He thus advised that "it is necessary for anyone who organizes a republic and establishes laws in it to take for granted that all men are evil and that they will always act according to the wickedness of their nature whenever they have the opportunity."[250] We do not need to take quite such a strong view to recognize the underlying importance of designing the political institutions of socialism so that they guard against corruption and the reestablishment of a class society.

Taking that thought seriously might lead to the conclusion that the political institutions of the social republic that Marx believed were necessary to reach communism might also be vital to staying there. As Marx repeatedly insisted, the grand contribution of the Communards was to have "taken the actual management of their Revolution into their own hands and found at the same time . . . the means to hold it in the hands of the People itself," by displacing "the governmental machinery of the ruling classes by a governmental machinery of their own."[251] Maintaining the governmental machinery of the people might thus be necessary to maintaining a classless society.

Coda

Marx's social republic integrated some of his earliest republican ideas into his late account of the political institutions necessary to bring about socialism. The example of the Paris Commune pushed Marx to rethink his assumption that the limited conception of democracy associated with a bourgeois republic

---

249. For an invaluable account of Marx's (often misunderstood) views of human nature, see Norman Geras, *Marx and Human Nature: Refutation of a Legend* (London: Verso, 1983).

250. Machiavelli, *Discorsi*, book I, chapter 3. I am here particularly guided by the interpretation of Machiavelli advanced by John McCormick in his *Machiavellian Democracy*, and in John McCormick, *Reading Machiavelli: Scandalous Books, Suspect Engagements, and the Virtue of Populist Politics* (Princeton: Princeton University Press, 2018).

251. Marx, *The Civil War in France (First Draft)*, MEGA I.22: 66 / MECW 22: 498.

would be adequate for the struggle for socialism. Returning to ideas he had defended as a young republican (and which were standard among nineteenth-century republicans), he now emphasized the need for a much more encompassing democratic transformation of government and administration. Delegates would need to be elected not only by universal (manhood) suffrage, which Marx continued to defend against its elitist critics, but would also need to be subjected to continuous popular scrutiny and control through the right to recall, the use of imperative mandates, and frequent elections. Public administration by elite, unaccountable bureaucrats would be overturned through legislative oversight and direct elections of public officials by the people, who (like delegates) would be recallable and paid workers' wages. In contrast to the commonplace depiction of Marx as uninterested in constitutional questions, his writings on the Commune show how seriously he took the question of which political institutions were necessary to bring about socialism. Contrary to the similarly widespread assumption that Marx thought all such political institutions, and politics itself, would eventually disappear in a future socialist society, we saw that Marx held a much more nuanced position. What little he had to say (deliberately so, because of his anti-utopianism) does not suggest that he thought that socialism would be a society without politics or any political institutions. The chapter ended with some republican reasons for more firmly committing to the idea that politics and political institutions would be a permanent feature of socialism.

Postface

A socialist republic is the application to agriculture and industry; to the farm, the field, the workshop, of the democratic principle of the republican ideal.

—JAMES CONNOLLY[1]

THE LASTING POTENCY of republicanism as an alternative to socialism can be gleaned from a preamble that Marx wrote for the 1880 electoral program of what would become the *Parti ouvrier français* (French Workers' Party), at the request of Jules Guesde and Paul Lafargue (Marx's son-in-law). It began,

Considering that the emancipation of the producing class is that of all human beings without distinction of sex or race;

That the producers can be free only when they are in possession of the means of production;

That there are only two forms under which the means of production can belong to them; 1) the individual form which has never existed in a general state and which is increasingly eliminated by industrial progress; 2) the collective form, the material and intellectual elements of which are constituted by the very development of capitalist society.[2]

---

1. [James Connolly], "Labour Representation," *The Workers' Republic*, vol. 1, no. 3 (27 August 1898): 4.

2. Marx, "Considérants du Programme socialiste," *MEGA* I.25: 208 / *MECW* 24: 340. See further, Marx to Friedrich Adolph Sorge, 5 November 1880, *MEW* 34: 475–76 / *MECW* 46: 43–44; Engels to Eduard Bernstein, 25 October 1881, *MEW* 35: 232 / *MECW* 46: 148–49. For the reception of Marx, and his involvement in French socialism in the 1870s and 1880s, see Julia Nicholls, *Revolutionary Thought after the Paris Commune, 1871–1885* (Cambridge: Cambridge University Press, 2019), chapters 5–6.

The preamble concisely summarized much of the argument that Marx had been making against the republican social ideal for more than thirty years. The only realistic path to freedom for the working class lay in collectivizing the means of production and not universalizing individual property. That Marx thought it was still necessary to critique this alternative, as late as 1880, reflected its continuing working-class appeal and the surprisingly protracted process of the proletarianization of the artisan working class.[3]

The preamble also called for using "all the means at the disposal of the proletariat, including and above all universal suffrage." That in turn reflected the need to counter the continued strength of antipolitical socialisms. For, as long as Marx had been combating the social ideal of republicanism, he had also been struggling against socialists who rejected the republican insistence on the need for politics. Marx thus continued to fight a struggle on two fronts: using his republican communism to critique both anticommunist republican-isms and antipolitical socialisms. The 1880 preamble is one more example of the way in which republicanism repeatedly intersected with Marx's thought and politics. Without simply assimilating Marx to the republican tradition, this book has tried to set out the ways in which his communism cannot be understood without understanding how it developed both in opposition to and in debt to the republican tradition.

The preamble is also noteworthy because it called for the use of not just universal suffrage but "universal suffrage . . . transformed from the instrument of deception which it has hitherto been into an instrument of emancipation." That language was reminiscent of Marx's call in *The Civil War in France* and its drafts for the use of imperative mandates, frequent elections, and the power to recall representatives to ensure that universal suffrage did not serve "to choose the instruments of parliamentary class rule" and "misrepresent the people in Parliament," but was "adapted to its real purposes" "to serve the people."[4] But in this 1880 program the mechanism that Marx claimed would turn universal suffrage into "an instrument of emancipation" was not a set of constitutional changes but the "proletariat organised into an independent

3. William H. Sewell notes that "Even as late as 1876, the [French] industrial population employed in small-scale industry was twice that in large-scale industry. Even in Britain, artisans outnumbered factory workers until past the middle of the century," see "Artisans, Factory Work-ers, and the Formation of the French Working Class, 1789–1848," in *Working-Class Formation: Nineteenth-Century Patterns in Western Europe and the United States*, ed. Ira Katznelson and Aris-tide R. Zolberg (Princeton: Princeton University Press, 1986), 49.

4. Marx, *The Civil War in France, MEGA* I.22: 141 / *MECW* 22: 333; *The Civil War in France (First Draft), MEGA* I.22: 57 / *MECW* 22: 488.

party."[5] That reflected the beginnings of an important shift in socialist and social-democratic politics (and indeed democratic thought and practice more broadly).[6] Rather than the state requiring fundamental constitutional changes in order to realize popular control and social transformation, the party acting within the state's institutions provides the necessary democratic link between workers and their party representatives. The former idea never entirely disappeared from socialist thought, and at moments made an explosive reappearance,[7] but it was increasingly eclipsed by the latter.

The formation of a political party under real popular control remains an important socialist goal (one much neglected in the modern decline of mass parties). But that should not overshadow the importance of radical constitutional change to social transformation. One resource we might draw out from Marx's republican inheritance is the importance of popular control and participation in representation and public administration. As Engels aptly summarized in his later introduction to *The Civil War in France*: "the working class, once come to power ... must protect itself against its own deputies and officials, by declaring them, without exception, subject to recall at any moment."[8] The republican institutions that Marx and Engels defended should be part of the arsenal of socialist constitutionalism.[9] But almost more important than the particular constellation of institutions they endorsed is the insight that motivated them. Marx came to believe that the standard institutions of a bourgeois republic (and which are today conflated with "democracy") were insufficient

5. Marx, "Considérants du Programme socialiste," *MEGA* I.25: 208 / *MECW* 24: 340. The subsequent program did, however, also call for the universal arming of the people and for public administration and the police to be subordinated to the Commune.

6. For the rise of "party democracy" at the end of the nineteenth century, see Bernard Manin, *The Principles of Representative Government* (Cambridge: Cambridge University Press, 1997), 206–18.

7. See, for instance, the entries in Gaard Kets and James Muldoon, eds., *The German Revolution and Political Theory* (Cham: Palgrave Macmillan, 2019).

8. Engels, "Einleitung," in *Der Bürgerkrieg in Frankreich*, 3rd German edition (1891), *MEGA* I.32: 14 / *MECW* 27: 189.

9. For further accounts of how republicanism constitutionalism might contribute to an antioligarchical egalitarian politics, see, for instance, John P. McCormick, "People and Elites in Republican Constitutions, Traditional and Modern," in *The Paradox of Constitutionalism*, ed. Martin Loughlin and Neil Walker (Oxford: Oxford University Press, 2008), 107–25; Camila Vergara, "Republican Constitutionalism: Plebeian Institutions and Anti-Oligarchic Rules," *Theoria* 69, no. 171 (2022): 25–48; and Stuart White, "Citizens' Assemblies and Republican Democracy," in *Radical Republicanism: Recovering the Tradition's Popular Heritage*, ed. Bruno Leipold, Karma Nabulsi, and Stuart White (Oxford: Oxford University Press, 2020), 81–99.

for the task of social transformation. Marx rightly insisted that "the working class cannot simply lay hold on the ready made state-machinery and wield it for their own purpose. The political instrument of their enslavement cannot serve as the political instrument of their emancipation."[10] Social transformation consequently requires a constitutional setup that provides "the Republic with the basis of really democratic institutions."[11] We need, in other words, a social republic that is a *social* republic not only because it is a republic committed to social emancipation but a republic that is constitutionally structured to carry out that social emancipation.

If one contribution of republicanism to socialist politics is the importance of formulating alternative constitutional configurations, another is a reminder that the socialist complaint against capitalism is also rooted in the value of freedom. At the heart of Marx's critique of capitalism was a republican objection to arbitrary and uncontrolled power, whether of individual despotic employers, the rule of the capitalist class, or the tyranny of the market. Freedom, Marx insisted, required liberation from all these forms of domination. The struggles to overcome this domination have managed to constrain many of its dimensions (though they have also been continually eroded by the ceaseless reactionary drive to reestablish domination). Yet the picture some might want to paint of the unfreedom and dependency of nineteenth-century workers being a thing of the past depicts an altogether too rosy and ideological picture of our world today. Workers are still subject to arbitrary and degrading treatment by their employers, only further exacerbated by the rise of more precarious forms of labor and the decline of the bulwarks of trade unions. Workers are also still denied their rightful democratic ownership and control of their workplace. And society continues to be governed by the imperatives of the market and its headlong rush to ever greater and destructive accumulation. There is, in other words, still a need for the "despotic system of the *subordination of labor* to capital" to be "superseded by the republican and beneficent system of *the association of free and equal producers*."[12] The republican opposition to domination offers socialists a language in which they might formulate their critique of capitalism in terms of freedom.[13] The terrain of freedom has too easily been abandoned to

---

10. Marx, *The Civil War in France (Second Draft)*, MEGA I.22: 100 / MECW 22: 533.

11. Marx, *The Civil War in France*, MEGA I.22: 142 / MECW 22: 334.

12. Marx, "Instructions for the Delegates of the Provisional General Council. The Different Questions," MEGA I.20: 232 / MECW 20: 190.

13. For elaboration of this idea, see Corey Robin, "Reclaiming the Politics of Freedom," *The Nation*, 6 April 2011, https://www.thenation.com/article/archive/reclaiming-politics-freedom/; Corey Robin, "The New Socialists," *New York Times*, 24 August 2018, https://nytimes.co/2018/08/24/opinion/sunday/what-socialism-looks-like-in-2018.html; Alex Gourevitch,

conservatives and liberals. Marx's critique reminds us that socialists have a legacy of freedom waiting to be reclaimed. Along with the importance of popular constitutionalism, this might be one way in which a study of Marx and republicanism in the nineteenth century could help with the formulation of a socialism for the twenty-first.

The epigraph to this concluding discussion was taken from James Connolly, the person most responsible for the introduction of Marxist socialism into Ireland.[14] He was the driving force behind the foundation of the Irish Socialist Republican Party (ISRP) in 1896, which combined the radical demand for Irish independence with an explicitly socialist platform. His execution by the British state for his role in the Easter Rising (1916) robbed the Irish people of a courageous leader and socialists everywhere of an original and passionate thinker. This is not the place to look at the role of republican ideas in socialist movements after Marx's death in 1883 (see figures 16 and 17 for an iconographic glimpse). That task is being admirably taken up by a bourgeoning literature uncovering the history of socialist republicanism and its potential for emancipatory politics.[15] In Connolly's case, I am struck by the ease and fluency with which he managed to weave together his republican and socialist principles. It is a characteristic that is aptly demonstrated by his choice of title for the ISRP's newspaper, *The Workers' Republic*, and in the language of the party's founding manifesto, which held "That the agricultural and industrial system of a free people, like the political system, ought to be an accurate reflex of the democratic principle, by the people, for the people, solely in the interests of the people."[16]

"Wage-Slavery and Republican Liberty," *Jacobin*, 28 February 2013, https://jacobinmag.com/2013/02/wage-slavery-and-republican-liberty/; Tom O'Shea, "Freedom Yet to Come," *New Socialist*, 7 June 2018, https://newsocialist.org.uk/labor-republicans-freedom/.

14. Fintan Lane, *The Origins of Modern Irish Socialism, 1881–1896* (Cork: Cork University Press, 1997), 214–23.

15. Ben Lewis, "Karl Kautsky's Democratic Republicanism," in *Karl Kautsky on Democracy and Republicanism* (Leiden: Brill, 2020), 1–40; Andreas Møller Mulvad and Benjamin Ask Popp-Madsen, "From Neo-Republicanism to Socialist Republicanism: Antonio Gramsci, the European Council Movements and the 'Second Republican Revival,'" *Theoria* 69, no. 171 (2022): 97–118; James Muldoon, *Building Power to Change the World: The Political Thought of the German Council Movements* (Oxford: Oxford University Press, 2020), chapter 4, "Socialist Republicanism"; Tom O'Shea, "Eugene Debs and the Socialist Republic," *Political Theory* 50, no. 6 (2022): 861–88; Camila Vergara, *Systemic Corruption: Constitutional Ideas for an Anti-Oligarchic Republic* (Princeton: Princeton University Press, 2020), chapter 6, "Luxemburg on Popular Emancipation."

16. "Programme of the Irish Socialist Republican Party," *The Workers' Republic*, vol. 1, no. 1 (13 August 1898): 8.

FIGURE 16. *La Terre promise* (*The Promised Land*), *Le Figaro-Graphic* (1 May 1892), supplement. Courtesy of Bibliothèque nationale de France. Translation of a German original by F. Kaskeline in *Glühlichter*, no. 38 (1 May 1891): 4–5.

FIGURE 17. [Walter Heubach?], *Huldigung der Freiheit. Zur Erinnerung an die Reichstagswahl 1893* (*Tribute to Freedom. In memory of the 1893 Reichstag Election*), *Der Wahre Jakob*, no. 183 (1893): 1516–17. The goddess Liberty, wearing a Phrygian cap and with Marx seated beside her, congratulates workers on using "universal suffrage (*Allgemeines Wahlrecht*)" to crush the dragon of reaction. To Marx's left stands Ferdinand Lassalle, while the background depicts an eclectic group of historical influences from Florian von Geyer to Gotthold Ephraim Lessing and Charles Darwin, as well as several republican martyrs (from left to right): Camille Desmoulins (French Revolution), Louis Charles Delescluze (Paris Commune), Robert Blum (1848 Revolutions), and the Gracchi brothers (Roman Republic). Note the exclusion of (nonallegorical) women from both the historical figures and the workers. For attribution and further discussion, see Klaus-Dieter Pohl, *Allegorie und Arbeiter: Bildagitorische Didaktik und Repräsentation der SPD, 1890-1914* (Osnabrück: PhD Thesis, 1986), 193-98.

INDEX

A NOTE ON THE TYPE

This book has been composed in Arno, an Old-style serif typeface in the classic Venetian tradition, designed by Robert Slimbach at Adobe.